S0-BBF-786

ROMANESQUE

Architecture Sculpture Painting

ROMANESQUE

Architecture Sculpture Painting

Edited by Rolf Toman

Photos by Achim Bednorz

ULLMANN & KÖNEMANN

FRONT COVER:
San Vicenç, Cardona
Nave with chancel
1029-ca. 1040
Photo: Achim Bednorz

BACK COVER:
St. Michael, Hildesheim
Wooden ceiling (detail)
Second quarter of the thirteenth century
Photo: Achim Bednorz

FRONTISPIECE:
Silos, monastery of Santo Domingo
Doubting Thomas
Cloister, relief on corner pillar (detail)
Mid twelfth century

© 2004 Tandem Verlag GmbH
KÖNEMANN is a trademark and an imprint of Tandem Verlag GmbH
Original title: Romanik
ISBN-10: 3-8331-1039-2
ISBN-13: 978-3-8331-1039-9

Editing and production: Rolf Toman, Espéraza, Birgit Beyer, Angelika Gundermann, Cologne
Photographs: Achim Bednorz, Cologne, Klaus Frahm, Börnsen
Picture research: Sally Bald, Cologne
Graphics: Ehrenfried Kluckert, Bierlingen
Cover design: Werkstatt München

Translation from German: Fiona Hulse, Ian Macmillan
Copy-editing of the English edition: Con Coroneos for Hart Mcleod, Cambridge
Typesetting: Goodfellow & Egan, Cambridge

© 2007 for this edition: Tandem Verlag GmbH
ULLMANN & KÖNEMANN is an imprint of Tandem Verlag GmbH
Special edition
ISBN 978-3-8331-3600-9

Printed in China

10 9 8 7 6 5 4 3 2 1
X IX VIII VII VI V IV III II I

Contents

Malay (Saône-et-Loire), former priory
church of Notre-Dame, eleventh century,
view from the south-west

Rolf Toman

Introduction

A Romanesque church in a cemetery surrounded by countryside – such peaceful places give us a feeling of historical continuity. This, or something like it, one thinks, is what it looked like in the Middle Ages, when the church was built. Occasionally one is able to find a vantage point where there is nothing to remind one of the present. The attraction of these Romanesque country churches has something to do with their human proportions; they do not compel admiration by means of their imposing size, as city cathedrals do. And in addition, they are well away from the hurly-burly of everyday existence, and this sense of seclusion is reassuring.

Many of these Romanesque churches used to be monastery churches, and some still are. The reason so many Romanesque monasteries are surrounded by beautiful countryside is that monasteries in the eleventh and twelfth centuries devoted themselves to their rural surroundings. This coincided with the interests of the feudal lords under whose protection monasteries were often placed. Preferred sites for new monasteries were quiet valleys – still in plentiful supply at that time, as European countries were only sparsely populated. Around 1200 (following a huge leap in the population after 1150), it is thought that 12 million people lived in France, 2.2 million in England, and 7 to 8 million people in the enormous (450,000 square miles) area that was the Holy Roman Empire.

Monasticism in the high Middle Ages

The importance of monastic life, both in terms of the culture and the politics of the high Middle Ages, cannot be overestimated. The cultural philosopher Hugo Fischer even subtitled one of his books the "Birth of Western civilization out of the spirit of Romanesque monasticism." The importance of monasticism in the Middle Ages can be seen in the large number of monks and monasteries that existed: at the height of its development, Cluny controlled well over 1,000 monasteries; it played an outstanding role amongst the reformed monasteries of the High Middle Ages. The Cistercian order extended throughout Europe, and the momentous work of its most important figure, Bernard of Clairvaux, has been decisive in provoking judgements of the twelfth century as the "Age of the Cistercians."

How did the monasteries of this age achieve their cultural influence? To answer this question, it is useful to examine more closely the three levels of social rank that were so important to the way people saw themselves in the Middle Ages. This sense of social order was summed up neatly in the 1020s by Adalbero, the Bishop of Laon: "The House of the Lord is in three parts, which some wrongly believe to be one: here on Earth one part prays (*orant*), another fights (*pugnant*), and yet another works (*laborant*); these three belong together and will not tolerate being set at variance with each other; to such a degree, that the functioning (*officium*) of one is necessary to the work (*opera*) of the other two, and each will bestow its aid on the others."

Other terms used for this three-part concept are teaching, defending and nurturing; they refer to clergymen, knights and farmers respectively. This trinity of order, which was considered to be God-given, superseded the division into two of Church and World, clergy and laity, that had characterized life until the ninth century. The new tripartite order was to hold its own to the end of the Middle Ages, despite the fact that it did not take actual variations within each rank into account, nor allow for the merchants and middle-class citizens that appeared on the social stage during the late Middle Ages as a result of the forced development of cities. Therefore, the trinity of order largely reflects the agrarian world of the high Middle Ages, or for the purposes of this volume the Romanesque period from 1000 to 1250.

Monks played a special role within the rank of the *oratores*, the men of prayer. The medieval historian Hans-Werner Goetz has the following to say: "While originally quite deliberately separated from the official Church, monasticism soon became an integral part of the Church, which in any case played a quite different, influential role in the Middle Ages compared to its role today. To an extent, the monks formed a third rank between the clerics and laymen; their way of life was also an example for communities of clerics and laymen to follow." In the early Middle Ages, monasteries were still largely communities composed of laymen. It was not until the ninth century that being ordained as a priest was generally considered to be the culmination and fulfilment of religious life. From that time, monasteries increasingly developed into communities of clerics, and scarcely a monk was not ordained.

Monasticism and worldly rule were not completely separate worlds, least of all where the recruitment of the next generation of monks was concerned. It should be borne in mind that being accepted into a medieval monastery was dependent on two conditions being met: proof of a spiritual suitability for life as a monk (normally demonstrated during the novitiate), and a gift. These gifts, made to gain admission, and originally described as "alms" in the relevant Benedictine Rule, were later increasingly large pieces of land. Monasticism almost took the ownership of land for granted, and many monasteries gradually filled up with members of the nobility. In turn, of course, this affected their position of power, and strengthened their independence. Cluny springs to mind in this respect as well; it was founded by William of Aquitaine as his family monastery in 910, and was answerable directly to the Papal See. In its foundation charter, William not only gave up his right to all the monastery's income and investitures, but even laid down that no one, whether a bishop or even the pope, should be allowed to seize the property belonging to the monastery. Following the death of Berno, the abbot William had appointed, the monks were supposed to elect a successor from amongst their own ranks. As early as 932, Abbot Odo received permission from Rome to spread the Cluniac reforms by founding daughter-houses, and – even more importantly – to reform existing monasteries and make them subordinate to Cluny. The daughter-houses were not governed by their own abbots, but by priors answerable to the abbot of Cluny. This created a tightly knit community of monasteries, and Cluny became a sort of secular

The Dream of Henry I.
Chronicle of Florence and John of
Worcester, *c.* 1130.
Oxford, Corpus Christi College
Ms. 157, fol. 382

"Pronosticatio in latino," astrological
work by Johannes Lichtenberger, 1488
(woodcut from the Jacob Meydenbach
edition).
Mainz 1492, no. 10082, fol. 6r

feudal lord itself, responsible for the investitures and incomes of its own enfeoffed monasteries. Cluny's power was almost unlimited, and it was inevitable that it should have to take political sides – as in the Investiture Contest between Pope Gregory VII and Emperor Henry IV. So, for many, monasticism was, as Goetz commented, the religious equivalent of living like a lord. Its ennoblement is an important factor behind its success and huge historical significance.

The cultural creative achievements of the monasteries are not something that could be expected of poor, untutored *oratores*. Even during the reign of Charlemagne, monks were pioneering techniques in the crafts and trades, and many monasteries were even agricultural trade centers. In addition, Charlemagne, and his son Louis after him, assigned the modest but nevertheless important cultural tasks of his empire to the monasteries: they were responsible for the Latin liturgy and books, the Classical and Christian traditions and higher education. Scholars were gathered from all over Europe and brought to Charlemagne's palace school; it was their task to revise traditional works and create reliable models which Charlemagne could then make compulsory throughout his empire. The churches and monasteries were instructed to build schools and choose suitable teachers. In addition, monks were ordered not just to pray, but also carefully to copy whatever books were necessary for teaching. Europe has their diligence to thank for the foundations of its libraries and the preservation of the spiritual and secular knowledge of the Ancient World. Carolingian

reforms to education were the basis upon which the cultural flowering of the "Carolingian Renaissance" was able to take place; the poetry of Theodulf, and Einhard's *Vita Karoli Magni* are two outstanding examples of this process.

As Albert Mirgeler explains, Cluny was connected to the Carolingian spiritual world by a number of direct affiliations: through its first abbot Berno, who was previously abbot of Baume; with the model monastery of Inda via the monastery of St. Martin in Autun; and, through Alger and Gerhard, with the cathedral schools in Liège and Regensburg. Finally, Cluny was connected to Charlemagne by the common goals of the *civitas dei* in the sense of earthly and social fulfilment, a misunderstanding of St. Augustine's original work. In the case of the Cluniacensians, the change-over from empire to the monastic community went hand in hand with a correspondingly higher emphasis on the monks themselves. The almost autocratic position of the abbots of Cluny, and their exceptionally long life spans – only three ruled in the period from 958 to 1109! – facilitated a radical planning of both spiritually cultural and social art.

In Cluny, the celebration of the liturgy was moved into the center of monastic life, indeed existence in general, in a way unknown until then. Along with the extension of the convent mass (the standard monastic celebration of the mass with chant) by a procession and a litany of all the saints, a mass was added in the mornings, which on days which were not feast days was celebrated as a requiem mass. In addition, every monk who

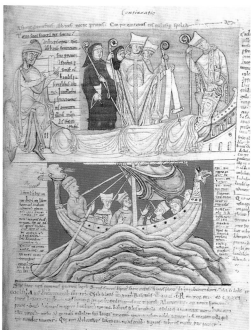

The three social classes as they appeared to King Henry I in a dream: they are the clergy, knights and farmers (left). Despite its shortcomings, this interpretational plan, which was linked to ideas about the Holy Trinity, held sway until the end of the Middle Ages. On a wood carving from the end of the 15th century, each class is expressly allocated its task in life: "You say prayers, you protect and you till the fields."

Eadwinus the monk writing
Eadwinus Psalter, c. 1170.
Cambridge, Trinity College Library
Ms.R.17.1, fol. 283v

Santo Domingo de Silos (Burgos)
Capitals in the cloister. Twelfth century

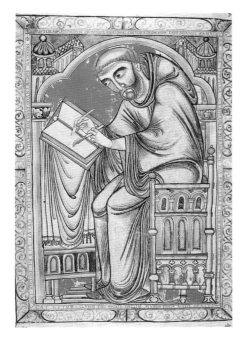

had been ordained was required to read a private mass and to sing the entire psalter every day. The convent masses were attended by 200 monks dressed in white albs, and on feast days in choir robes, and they were celebrated with an incredible display of splendor. This developing splendor extended to the equipment used in the ceremonies, and even to the churches themselves, which were lavishly decorated to the greater glory of God. The celebration of mass, which took up most of the day, became increasingly extravagant; it required special rooms and spaces in order to create and maintain a proper feeling of reverence. The second church in Cluny, and certainly the third, must have complied perfectly with these requirements. As Georges Duby puts it, "the flowering of sacred art in the eleventh century was a product of the liturgical functions which the monks fulfilled for the population in general."

Cluny also adopted the new mass movement of pilgrimages to faraway Santiago. Two of the four great pilgrimage routes to Santiago, Vézelay and St. Gilles, started at Cluniac abbeys. In addition, the routes were lined with numerous hostels belonging to Cluniac monasteries; the church façades of the latter appealed to pilgrims much more strongly than liturgy was able to. Pilgrims were carrying out *in concreto* man's business on earth, namely arduous pilgrimages to the distant Christian Promised Land, with all the temptations to err from the straight and narrow that a devout pilgrim could expect to be exposed to on his adventurous and sometimes dangerous journey; in order to appeal to these pilgrims, Romanesque art developed its characteristic iconographic program.

Some of the most remarkable evidence exists in the shape of the tympana over church portals. Together with capitals, they were favorite places for attaching the wealth of Romanesque architectural sculpture along the pilgrimage routes. If one looks more closely at pictures on these tympana, the historical distance separating us from the medieval imagination becomes all the more apparent. Many of them include scenes from the Last Judgement – with God the Father in his role as stern judge of the world and frightful representations of hell (see pp. 328 ff.). Today, we can only guess from the graphic quality of these images what fears must have tormented people at that time, given the punishments which, according to their Christian faith, they would have to face for their sinful existence on earth. Behind these images of fear – and the opposite image (though rarely depicted in such diverse and concrete terms) of hope that one might be counted amongst the just – are ideas regarding death and dying which diverge radically from modern notions.

Death and mortal agony

Historical differences in the way death is understood should perhaps be clarified a little, given that they can help us approach other medieval phenomena which may seem alien to us, such as the cult of relics or the apparently fantastic willingness to take part in crusades that were little more than campaigns of pillage and murder which led to the deaths of hundreds of thousands of people. It is with a sense of astonishment and disquiet that we encounter many aspects of medieval life, which were

Semur-en-Brionnais (Saône-et-Loire),
Saint Hilaire, detail from the tympanum
of the west portal. Twelfth century

BOTTOM RIGHT
Elne (Western Pyrenees), tombstone in
the cathedral of Sainte-Eulalie

BOTTOM LEFT
Fenioux (Charente-Maritime), burial
lantern in the former cemetery. Twelfth
century

rooted in Christian fundamentalism and a corresponding idea of death. Nearly everyone assumed that the earth was only a transitional stage to another, eternal life. And everyone hoped that his earthly life would be continued in Heaven, the image of Paradise Lost in the hereafter. But anyone who did not live on earth in accordance with the commandments of God, and thus God's approval, was certain to suffer eternal torment in Hell. Death marked the transition from existence in this world to life after death, and one had to prepare for this while still living on earth. No other era in Western art has such a wealth of artistic representations of death, and the associated central theme of crossing into the hereafter, as the Romanesque period.

Mankind was filled with great fear at the prospect of death coming unexpectedly, without time for prayer and practical repentance for the forgiveness of sins. Even a pope could be visited with such a terrible death, as was shown on the tympanum of the west portal of St. Hilaire in Semur-en-Brionnais (photo, top). The pope is shown sitting on the toilet, a humiliating place to die; his soul escapes his mouth in the form of a small child, which is immediately seized by three horned devils. To the left is the abandoned Papal See. A quite different, more merciful death is depicted on a tombstone in Elne, Roussillon (photo, bottom right). The *gisant*, recumbent figure – which, according to Philippe Ariès, is actually "not a corpse lying down, but an unreal, standing figure … which has been placed into a lying position with its eyes opened and its head resting on a cushion – is being accompanied by two angels to Heaven, which in this case is symbolized by the hand of God resting on his head." This explains the meaning of this type of representation of death: the *gisant* "represents neither a dead nor living person, but one of the fortunate few."

Between distant Heaven and the much closer Hell, whose terrible gates could be opened by heavenly messengers (photo, opposite), lay the place every sinning believer had to reckon with: Purgatory. That was the third place one might end up after death, and was seen as a stage of suffering which gave one time to repent one's transgressions on earth.

The theological concept of Purgatory, which had long been current in popular beliefs, was not developed until the twelfth and thirteenth centuries. It modified the polarity of Heaven and Hell, thereby providing a solution to some contemporary theological problems involving the mixture of good and evil in man's deeds and the Grace of God – a concept which was difficult to comprehend. It is possible that the belief in the existence of Purgatory resulted from a particular uncertainty: the Gospels speak of both a judgement "at the end of time," upon the return of Christ, and also of the punishments and rewards that sinners and the just should expect immediately after death. The theological conception of death as a type of sleep which the dead person experiences while waiting for Judgement Day does not appear to have satisfied people in general. The idea of Purgatory, a place in which – like earth – one could endure suffering with a degree of hope, in which something was happening for one's salvation, was altogether more bearable. Indeed, the construction of such a stage between Heaven and Hell fitted in much better with the view of the function of the saints by the Throne of Judgement. They had already

An angel locking the gates of Hell.
Psalter of Henry of Blois, Winchester.
Mid twelfth century.
London, British Library, Cotton Ms.
Nero C.IV, fol. 39

been redeemed and received in Heaven, and were viewed as mediators between God and mankind, who could defend those souls awaiting judgement or who had been temporarily punished, but not damned for all time.

The cult of relics

Due to their proximity to God and ability to plead for mercy on behalf of anyone who called on them, saints had become mediatory figures who fired everyone's fantasies and hopes. Most people sought to have their illnesses healed, and if this happened, it was considered to be a miracle which that particular saint had brought about by obtaining mercy. The processes which led to this happening, and which are recounted in numerous reports about miracles, are some of the most impressive witnesses to the medieval search for identity.

Spontaneous cults, such as the pilgrimage to St. Elisabeth, were powerful manifestations of popular religion, and something to which the Church had to react. Uncontrolled veneration of a saint undermined the Church's authority as the worldly agent of God's salvation. In order to deal with this, the Church adopted whoever was being venerated by incorporating them into the canon of saints. This gave the Church much greater control over the cult. The greater the number of people going on pilgrimages, the more important became the cult site, the grave and church dedicated to the saint – not only theologically but on a political level, too. It is therefore no surprise that even secular princes sought to involve the relics of (usually important) saints in their dealings; an example is the one discussed in Uwe Geese's dissertation, about the visit of the excommunicated Hohenstaufen emperor Frederick II to the grave of St. Elisabeth in Marburg, in 1236. The emperor used the occasion of the translation or moving of the remains of the landgravine, who had been canonized the previous year, to demonstrate to the Pope his independence from the Church: he was suggesting that she was the more authentic intercessor between himself and God.

The huge increase in the number of sacred buildings during the Romanesque period created a rapid rise in the demand for relics. Every church, indeed every altar, needed the relics of a saint to act as its sacred guarantor of consecration. Due to the large demand for relics, the teaching that the body had to remain completely intact, which had been adhered to until the tenth century, was largely abandoned. This teaching had forbidden the removal of individual parts of the body as relics, with the exception of things that regrew, such as hair, teeth, and finger and toe nails. Another idea, equally old, now gained greater prominence – namely, that the saint was actually present in every part of his body. A small bone was all that was required to have the entire saint at hand. This conception was to assert itself over the course of the Middle Ages. By the high and late Middle Ages, all misgivings had long been forgotten. There are reports that people who were dying or had just died, and were likely to be canonized, were put under pressure or even robbed because of their relics. Well-known examples are St. Francis and St. Elisabeth. The version involving Elisabeth's corpse reads as follows: "While this holy corpse, wrapped in a grey shirt with cloths around the face, was laying on the bier,

many of those present, who well-knew the holiness of the body and were inflamed by their worship, came and cut, even tore, parts of her robes off; some cut the nails off her hands and feet; others cut off the tips of her breasts and a finger off her hand, in order to keep them as relics." In addition, many relics were stolen or forged in large quantities. The Church was quite helpless in the face of this, and dealt with these activities by saying that anything was permissible as long as it promoted faith.

Many of these reports, which today would be considered odd to say the least, can be found in a work by Guibert Nogent (d. 1124), entitled *Pignora Sanctorum* (The Relics of Saints). Nogent criticizes the obsession with getting hold, and disposing, of relics, and uses particularly laughable examples to show the foolishness of such a course of action and, above all, the mistake of equating the venerable relics of a saint with a favorite talisman, to which one ascribes magical powers of healing. Such critical

After Gregory VII had demoted Emperor Henry IV to "King of the Germans," starting the process which removed secular rule from the sacred sphere, there arose in the twelfth century the allegorical teaching of "Two Swords" intended to mediate between the Church and secular powers. It could not in the long term prevent a desire for pre-eminence emerging. The depiction of the imperial coronation of Henry VI in Rome in 1191 (opposite) shows Henry being anointed, given the scepter and ring and, finally, being crowned with a miter by the Pope (Celestine III). The miter is a religious sign of dignity and was intended to express the "vicarious position of the Emperor with respect to the Pope" (G. Ladner).

contemporary accounts are of special interest to any reader who is concerned with historical accuracy, as they are the best and earliest witnesses of the popular cult of relics. This is a subject about which many strange stories were later put about, many no doubt solely for the purposes of entertainment.

The magical practices of venerating relics were always connected to material items. The many wax votive offerings displayed at saints' graves during the Middle Ages were for the most part representations of afflicted parts of the body, or in some other way referred to the person who was appealing to the saint to be healed. These objects were considered to be magical because they forced the saint to become aware of the nature of the illness and the person praying to be healed. Even today, many churches in the Catholic parts of Europe have votive objects, expressing gratitude for recovery from illness, being rescued from drowning, etc. (photo, left). But these votive objects, placed there to give thanks, lack the magical urgency and power of the medieval petitioning votive offerings.

If one considers all Romanesque forms of art – churches, all the *ornamenta ecclesiae*, from the stone architectural sculpture complete with scenes of the Judgement and Hell, to the golden Madonnas holding the Child destined to die for our salvation, and from crucifixes to relics and the ceremonial equipment with which the death of Christ on the Cross is commemorated – the impression of a great cult of death is overpowering. And the clergy of the Middle Ages, in particular the monks who governed

large tracts of land, were the main agents of this cult in this period of European history. For monasteries had developed into the main places where relics were kept. As Duby puts it, "Most abbeys were built over the tomb of a martyr or preacher of the Gospels, one of the heroes of the battle against evil and Hell ... Being the guardians of order in the cult of relics, which was kept up near the sarcophagi, monks served as mediators between the subterranean world of the dead and life on earth. This was their second main function, a function which found solemn expression in artistic form." Duby makes the point that "Christians of the eleventh century paid very careful attention to death."

It is typical of these works of art that they should enable one to forget their prerequisites in the light of the entirely self-sufficient aesthetic perfection of their formal coherence. But if they are made subject to an ahistorical interpretation that entirely ignores these prerequisites of ritual and numinous power in Romanesque art, they will become mere objects with form and we relinquish the wealth of opportunities they offer us to help towards a more complete historical understanding of them.

Architecture and meaning

There are other points of view which are highly relevant to an understanding of Romanesque art, and in particular architecture. For example, it has frequently been stated that the churches in the Harz mountains, and the monumental cathedrals of the central Rhine region, belong to a special "imperial" Romanesque style. According to Schütz and Müller, "Romanesque architecture in Germany was supported by the powerful members of the empire, primarily by bishops and monasteries, and also by emperors and in many cases by territorial rulers. This meant that the German Romanesque style was associated with ideas of the greatness of the Holy Roman Empire, and of the glory and power of the emperor. This is shown above all by the imperial cathedrals. They went far beyond the purpose they were needed for, and were an architectural display of imperial power, the architectural embodiment of the idea of the Roman Empire for all those who had eyes to see. Churches were not just built to hold services, but were important on a political level, as they demonstrated the rank of their builders to the world at large."

Compared with France and England, Germany enjoyed relatively stable political conditions around the middle of the eleventh century due to a continuity of royal and imperial power. This did not change until the 1070s, when Pope Gregory VII intensified and clarified his demands that the Church should take precedence over the secular state – a process which was led by the reforms at Cluny. The central demand was that the investiture of bishops and abbots of imperial abbeys should no longer be under the control of the emperor, as it had been until then; this would clearly restrict the power of the state to a considerable degree. The result was the well-known contest between Henry IV, who challenged the pope's claims, and Gregory, who excommunicated and deposed the emperor. Henry was forced to make a penitential pilgrimage to Canossa in 1077, something that was a humiliation to his royal dignity. He managed to have his excommunication rescinded, but that was by no means the end of his

Imperial coronation of Henry VI in Rome.
Petrus de Ebulo, Liber ad honorem Augusti, 1195–1196.
Berne, Bürgerbibliothek
Cod. 120, fol. 105r

The outward form of Speyer Cathedral is still much as it was when rebuilt (the apse, blind arcades, dwarf gallery and towers were new) at the instigation of Henry IV in 1082.

differences with the pope. Within Germany, the empire had divided into parties loyal to the Church and to the emperor, a division that was to have long-term consequences.

Once Henry had got over this low ebb in his power, he soon started work on rebuilding Speyer Cathedral, the prestigious building of his Salian ancestors, making it even more magnificent. Clearly a demonstration of the power which he felt he had regained, or indeed never lost. Other German cities apart from Speyer also developed this imperial architecture (see pp. 46 ff.). In this context, Günter Bandmann states that "Especially after the struggle over investiture, when the Emperor had come into conflict with the Curia, and sovereign states to the west no longer recognized the universal status of the Empire, the emperors attempted to construct an imperial metaphysics in which the pope played a subordinate role … The widening of thoughts of empire in the Classical mould only occurred gradually under pressure from its rival party, the Church … This probably also explains the fact that after Henry IV's reign, and during the

Hohenstaufen dynasty, Classical and secular forms such as vaults and galleries became part of official architecture; the wealth of forms that were part of the Christian tradition were being extended to include heathen forms." By giving this example of royal architecture, and correlating it with many other meanings, Bandmann clearly shows that intellectual and symbolical and/or sociological aspects played a very important role in medieval sacred buildings.

The Divine and the bitter contest for the earthly Jerusalem

One motif that occurs time and again in Romanesque art is that of the City of God, Jerusalem. It plays a part in architecture, sculpture and painting (see pp. 434 ff.). Its relevance is probably most far-reaching in the field of architecture, especially if one considers that all the ecclesiastical structural forms – such as columns, apses, arches, towers, vaults – are references to the City of God, "a modification of ancient concepts of the House of the Lord." As Bandmann says, "church architecture is … the type and symbol

Collectar, St. Bertin (?), *c.* 1170/80.
Parchment, pen drawing, height
10 inches.
The Hague, Koninklijke Bibliotheek
Ms. 76 F5

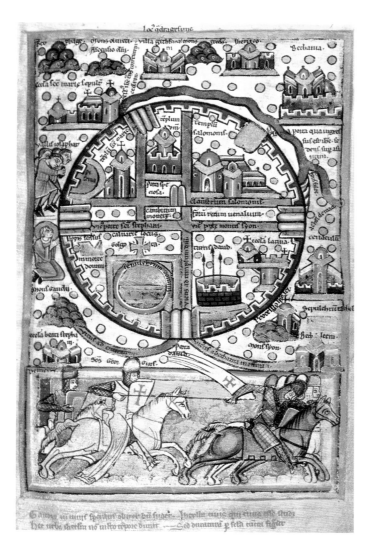

of the Heavenly City, the Kingdom of God, which believers were helping to fashion." One of the Fathers of the Church, St. Augustine himself, stressed this identification in his work *De Civitate Dei*. A generalized approach in ascribing meaning is of little help in understanding particular architectural characteristics. Their symbolic nature will remain abstract in the face of such generalizations. In contrast, the references to the City of God in a painted or sculpted urban shorthand are concrete and obvious: a castle or a wall connected to towers, or in sacred architecture, the façade with twin towers, which – probably for this reason – found increasing favor during the Middle Ages.

The depiction of the earthly Jerusalem is also done using a circle, which is a symbol of the Divine, and a reference to the life hereafter; it appeared on many plans of Palestine in the customary pattern of a circle divided into four quarters. On the map of Palestine on p. 14, this identification is emphasized by the text on the bottom edge of the page: "Anyone making efforts to be one of your citizens, O Jerusalem, and who is looking forward to your delights, must exert himself greatly. This City of Jerusalem will not last for long, but will be an image of permanence for all time." Immediately above the text, separated only by the picture frame, are Christian knights who are putting Muslim mounted warriors to flight. The knight on the white horse is St. George, who to some extent is viewed as sanctifying the crusades by taking part in them; his success makes plain that they are acting with God's support. This drawing, made nearly 100 years after the First Crusade at a time when it was hoped that Jerusalem could be re-conquered, is ideological in character. It casts an idealizing light on an event that in reality was rather unholy, as even some contemporaries felt at the time. (There was a desire to be able to view the Holy Land as God's country on earth but, in the view of Bishop Jacob of Vitry, it was lost because the scum of the earth had gathered there. And indeed, Palestine was temporarily used as a penal colony.)

The "armed pilgrimages to Jerusalem" are some of the most sinister aspects of medieval Christian fundamentalism. Their cruelty and blindness are frightening, and are a historical lesson for all, including the Church, given that by conservative estimates they cost upwards of 22 million lives.

Construction work

Anyone who reads the Bible carefully will notice that some of the images and phrases used are borrowed from the building trade. Architecture clearly played a very important role from an early stage, as well as the process of building. This changed little during the Middle Ages: sources, whether in pictures or writing, paint a vivid picture of the processes at large building sites. It is not just the manuscripts that were produced from about 1000 onwards that enable us to picture these construction sites; there are also scenes from the building trade in glass windows, tapestries, frescoes, and even relinquaries and altarpieces. Written sources are scarcely less powerful – letters, accounts of lives, descriptions of building processes, such as those concerning the reconstruction of Canterbury Cathedral from 1174 to 1185, or Abbot Suger's work *De consecratione ecclesiae Sancti Dionysii*, which was produced between 1144/45 and

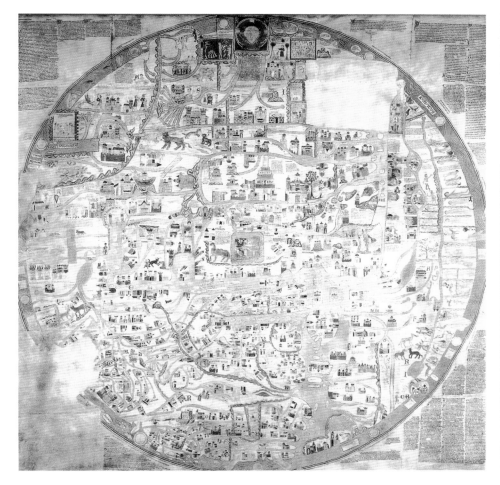

Ebstorf map of the world
Ebstorf (?), 1208/18 (?).
Copy of the destroyed original.
Height approx. 144 inches. Kulmbach,
Landschaftsmuseum Obermain
Plassenburg

Aquamanile of a knight, France,
thirteenth century.
Bronze, chased, height 11 inches.
Copenhagen, Danmarks Nationalmuseet
København

On the Ebstorf map of the world, with
Jerusalem in the center, and the top,
bottom and sides edged with the crucified
Christ, the earth appears as the Body of
Christ. Material to do with the story of
Christ's life and other sacred events are
interrelated in numerous detail pictures.
Included in the sequence of events are
Adam and Eve in Paradise, Alexander the
Great and the origins of the Saxons, and
the Crusades.

Two pairs of knights doing battle.
Sheet from a *speculum virginum*.
Middle Rhine or Trier, *c.* 1200.
Hanover, Kestner Museum

Archbishop Anno II of Cologne with the
five churches he founded. Miniature, at
the front of a *Vita Annos*, *c.* 1183
Darmstadt, Hessische Landes- und
Hochschulbibliothek, Hs. 945

Archbishop Anno II (1056–1175) was
the last great bishop-cum-builder in
Cologne. His death saw the end of the

first great building boom in the city,
which gave Cologne its high rank
amongst the principal European cities
during the Romanesque period. The
illustration at the bottom left shows
Anno II with the five churches he
founded, which ensured his fame after
death: they are St. Michael in Siegburg,
St. George and St. Mary ad Gradum in

Cologne, the monasteries of Saalfeld in
Thuringia and Grafschaft in the
Sauerland.

1151. Günther Binding has introduced and evaluated these sources
thoroughly.

First of all, with an expenditure of human labor that is scarcely
imaginable today, the foundations were laid – frequently on damp or
unstable ground. The description of the building of the monastery of
Wittewierum, around 1238, discusses problems such as poor foundation
soil – as well as more short-term problems such as cave-ins and heavy
rainfall.

Once the foundations were ready, the building materials had to be
acquired. It is reported that Louis the German had the walls of both
Frankfurt and Regensburg torn down in order to build his two churches.
In 1192, the marble and limestone to build Lyons cathedral were
transported to Lyons from Trajan's forum in nearby Fourvire. Indeed,
Classical buildings in general were popular sources of stone. Other
builders had to make even more costly arrangements: after 1026, Gauzlin,
the abbot of Fleury (Saint-Benoît-sur-Loire), obtained marble "a partibus
Romanie" and limestone from the Nivernais, which was brought to
Fleury by ship. The stones to build Battle Abbey were also transported by
ship across the Channel until, by a miracle, a quarry was discovered
nearby.

Then the stone masons, bricklayers and sculptors got to work, together
with the mortar stirrers, plasterers and whitewashers, carpenters and
roofers, labourers and handymen. Their activities and tools are depicted in
countless pictures. Wooden scaffolding, similar to that used at construction sites until the beginning of the twentieth century, when steel
scaffolding became more common, does not appear to have been used

north of the Alps until the middle of the fourteenth century. Before that,
work was done using cantilever scaffolding, and there are thorough
records of the various ways in which it was constructed. At each stage
of work, a level working area was created at the wall coping, and once
the wall had been built higher, the scaffolding was removed and attached
higher up. The construction materials were probably moved up the wall
using ramps, and transported using stretchers, skips and baskets. The
second half of the twelfth century saw the use of simple cranes which
at first were nothing more elaborate than a rope with a basket tied to it.
It was not until later that pulleys were introduced as the first technical aids. The various craftsmen got up to the higher sections of the
building by means of ladders or sloping walkways, which were normally
wickerwork.

Builders and founders – building as a form of Divine plan for salvation

It is now clear that the large-scale buildings of the Middle Ages were
produced with enormous effort and in the face of incalculable risks. And
everybody took part in the work because building a place of worship was
part of the plan for salvation. Whoever took part in the construction
work, either by giving building materials or physically working on the site,
was blessed with the Grace of God – long before indulgences started to be
sold for the same purpose. The very act of building a church included a
degree of worship.

This was especially significant for those who had churches founded
and built. In his second will Bishop Bernward of Hildesheim has this to
say: "I have given much thought to the question of what commendable

Architectural drawing by G. Binding,
from Bible, beginning of the thirteenth
century, Manchester, John Ryland's
Library, Ms. fr5, fol 6

Building of the Tower of Babel.
Hrabanus Maurus, "De originibus,"
1023.
Monte Cassino, monastery library, cod.
132

Saintes (Charente-Maritime), former abbey church of Sainte-Marie-des-Dames. Three-part crossing tower with columns and capitals

The sculptural decoration of buildings even extended onto the church tower, in detail scarcely visible from the ground. The churches in question, like this one in Saintes, were usually pilgrimage churches

building I could erect, what I would have to spend … in order to earn myself the Grace of God … I started … to found a new church which I could build to the praise and glory of the name of the Lord, thereby both fulfilling my own promise and providing for holy Christendom." Bishop Conrad of Constance, who was later made a saint, had the same goal in mind; one of the places he built was the Church of the Holy Sepulchre, which was attached to the minster and was intended to save the faithful from having to make the journey to Jerusalem, or alternatively to make it easier for them to do so. This addressed the idea of copies. In those days, it was unnecessary for copies to be duplicates as they tend to be today. All that was required was a particular form – round in the case of churches of the Holy Sepulchre – to serve as a reminder of the importance of the original, or even to replace it. In the end, it was no longer important whether one had visited the Holy Sepulchre in Jerusalem or in Constance. In any case, Bishop Conrad had much greater things in mind: apart from the existing minster, which was dedicated to the Mother of God, and the monastery of St. Peter in Petershausen, he founded three further churches in Constance, those of St. John, St. Lawrence and St. Paul. By doing so, he had recreated the five main churches of Rome (San Giovanni in Laterano, San Lorenzo, San Paolo fuori le mura, Old St. Peter's and Santa Maria Maggiore), and with them the Holy City itself, in Constance, the "felix mater Constantia."

This is also quite revealing as to the relationship of the founder or builder to the work itself. The builder as both *autor* and *auctor*, decided on the type of building and in many cases also prescribed a model. To quote Günter Bandmann once again, "yes, we are quite justified in stating that only a few, unimportant building contractors in the Middle Ages relinquished the opportunity to make deliberate links with outstanding models in order to keep to simple customs and traditional crafts. The architects of larger contractors had to focus their ingenuity on the copy, not on creating original forms."

The clients quite frequently took care of obtaining the building materials. Thus, Einhard's *Vita Karoli Magni*, about the life of Charlemagne, recounts that the emperor personally brought columns and marble slabs from Rome and Ravenna to be used in his palatine chapel in Aachen. Notker Balbulus, a monk at St Gallen, relates in his *Gesta Karoli*, written in 885, that the emperor brought together "masters and craftsmen of all such arts from all regions this side of the ocean." But despite this, the names of the artists have been forgotten almost everywhere. Bandmann attempts to explain away this fact in terms of it being part of "the character of serving an all-embracing idea." Meanwhile, the example of Bernward of Hildesheim clearly shows that the bishop was concerned about safeguarding his soul's salvation. Both Bishop Conrad of Constance and Abbot Suger of Saint-Denis were buried at the entrances of the churches they founded. This is not so much an expression of devotion as of the hope that they would benefit from the innumerable prayers of gratitude of those visiting the churches. For the churches they founded were not just the price of God's mercy, but also guarantors that they would never be forgotten.

Besalú, Catalonia
Romanesque bridge, twelfth century

Bridges played an important role amongst the secular functional buildings of the Middle Ages. Without them, it would scarcely have been possible to proceed along the roads and paths in many places. Travelers in the Middle Ages were a rather mixed bunch. On the great long-distance routes one would encounter the *peregrinus*, the stranger who had left his homeland, together with pilgrims, poor homeless people, travelers (minstrels and players), traders, mercenaries and craftsmen. Monks would be journeying to fellow monasteries of their order, and messengers would be on their way to other towns.

OPPOSITE
"We are the first, having learned how to build with concrete, glass and steel, to have become aware of the special rank and power of stone, something which our ancestors had lost; to them, building in stone seemed to be the only possible, as well as the customary, method of construction."
"There is a fundamental difference between living in a cave and piling erratic boulders on top of each other, and actually working stone ... Working stones elevates them to a position of symbolism and meaning."
(Bandmann)

Religious buildings

Types of building

Linear planform ———— basilica
———— aisle-less church
———— hall church
———— church with raised nave
and lower side aisles

Central planform
———— circular layout
———— four-sided layout
(Greek cross)
———— polygonal layout

Romanesque churches are characterized by the clarity of their conception in their ground plan, elevation, and clear arrangement of space. If we leave aside for the moment any individual architectural elements that allowed for diversity (please refer to the

table opposite), several fundamental building types can be distinguished. The first main group of buildings are those based on the linear planform. The second main group are centrally planned buildings, a style frequently found in eastern Europe.

octagon (Aachen, Palatine Chapel)

polygonal rotunda dodecagonal (chapel, Drüggelte)

domed rotunda (Mantua, San Lorenzo)

Greek cross (Montmajour, Saint Croix)

Long aisled/centrally planned (Gravedona, S. Maria del Tiglio)

baptistery (Milan, San Lorenzo Maggiore)

The **Byzantine basilica** (best translated as "hall of the king") with its high central nave and low side aisles served as the model for medieval religious architecture.
1 Nave. 2 Side aisles (in some cases there may be four side aisles). 3 Transept. 4 Choir/apse. 5 Clerestory (upper section of the nave walls providing lighting for the interior). 6 Crossing (intersection of the nave and transept).

The interior (top) St. Aegidius, Kleinkomburg (twelfth century), and exterior (below), St. Godehard, Hildesheim (twelfth century), both based on the **linear planform of the basilica.** The central nave of a basilica is usually wider than and projects far above the side aisles. The windows in the top section of the wall of the nave (the clerestory), provide for direct light to enter the church interior. The basilica is the most common type of Romanesque religious building.

The church in Schortens – Sillenstede (formerly St. Florian, above) dates from the twelfth century and is a good example of an **aisle-less church.** This type of church with integrated apse developed from the early medieval house church. Its homogeneous interior space is not articulated by supports. The walls are broken up by large lancet windows which allow plenty of light into the church, emphasizing the celebratory character of the sacred interior.

In **centrally planned buildings** all elements relate to one central point. The ground plan is often based on a circle or a square or variants of the two. At best, this central plan integrates any apses, chapels and portals, although these are often added to the detriment of the symmetrical design.

The cemetery chapel of St. Michel – d'Entraygues (below) is circular in design with eight radiating apses.

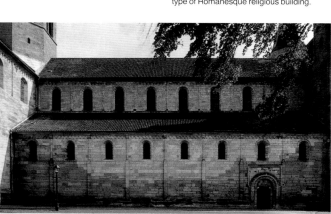

Hall church Lohne/Soest (left).
Hall church with raised nave and lower side aisles Poitiers, Notre Dame (right)

In south-western Europe, particularly in the Poitou region (Poitiers, St. Pierre), one often comes across **hall churches** and a variant of the same, the **church with raised nave and lower side aisles.**
In contrast to the the latter type of church, the side aisles of the hall church are of the same height as the central nave.

Building components of Romanesque religious architecture

1. Narthex or atrium (forecourt), already present in early Christian church buildings.
2. The interior western section of the forecourt has often been developed as the "galilee."
3. The narthex together with the
4. west towers forms a twin-towered façade.
5. The central nave of the basilica is flanked by
6. the two side aisles. In our example we see a simple aisled basilica.
7. The crossing is surmounted by a central tower.
8. This is also the point from which the arms of the transept start.
9. Continuing from the central nave, the choir or presbytery extends eastwards.
10. To this is connected the apsidal-ended sanctuary and in some cases also an
11. ambulatory, often incorporating chapels.

In an aisled basilica, the nave and the transept intersect. This intersection forms the crossing which is surmounted by the central tower. Continuing the side aisles in an eastern direction and penetrating, as it

were, the arms of the transept, there may be an ambulatory furnished with chapels. Instead of such an ambulatory there may be a number of apses adjoining the choir on the eastern side as a continuation of the side aisles. The choir ambulatory is seen as an important preliminary stage to the ambulatories of the Gothic period.

Familiar features of Romanesque architecture are the twin-towered or the single-towered west fronts. Less commonly found are a distinctive forecourt (called the "paradise" in Maulbronn), the narthex and the atrium.

The narthex makes its first appearance in early Christendom as an outer hall placed horizontally to the main body of the Roman Lateran basilica. This type can be traced back to Constantine who built the first large Christian assembly hall in Rome, the basilica by the Lateran Palace (313 – 319). Another standard building type is the basilica without a transept: in the fourth century, Sta. Maria Maggiore in Rome was conceived as an aisled hall without a transept. The central nave, flanked by the side aisles with flat ceilings, continues into the semi-circular apse at its eastern end.

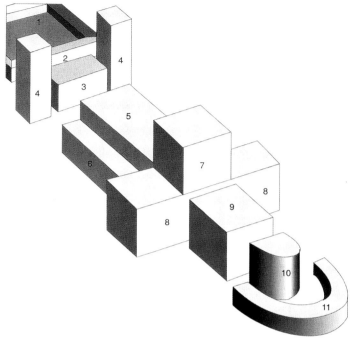

Hildesheim, St. Michael's Church, 1010 – 1033
View of the westwork with atrium and porch (drawing). View of the choir with side apses and transept turrets (photo).

1. atrium/narthex
2. porch/galilee
3. western façade
4. western central tower
5. western staircase turrets
6. central nave (clerestory)
7. side aisle
8. central tower
9. transept
10. transept towers
11. choir apses
12. apse

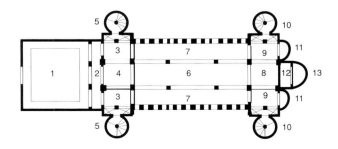

21

The exterior / west I

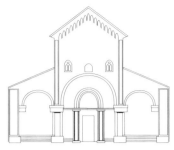

West front without a tower

The towerless west front is very common in Italy and in the south of France. It is marked by articulating and structural devices such as pilasters, attached pillars, lesenes, ornamental band courses or sculptures. In Italy, the bell-tower or campanile is often erected next to the west front, whereas in France this is not often the case.

West front with flanking towers

The west front with twin towers is the typical design employed for the Romanesque basilica and widespread in northern and western Europe. It is a symbolic reference to the gateway of the Heavenly Jerusalem.

West front with transept

and with central tower
There are two variations:
1 the tower is integrated into the western transept (see above).
2 the tower is placed within the axis of the central nave in front of the west front transept façade.

Romanesque churches are often distinguished by their decidedly fortified appearance, a feature that is further emphasized by massive porches with towers at the western end. A particularly striking development is the **westwork**, consisting of several components, often flanked by towers and furnished with a portico.
Both liturgically and architecturally, the westwork is an independent building component comprising several storeys and erected in front of the actual church. According to the symbolically meaningful polarity of east and west, the latter was regarded as the side threatened by evil powers. The fortified porches were meant to defend the church against these powers. The **west front** is the main view and at the

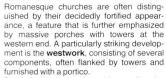

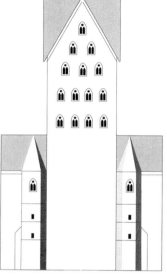

West front with central tower

Tower of the cathedral of Paderborn. Around 1075.
The massive tower has no windows in the lower section and possesses two circular stair turrets – all features relating to the original fortified character of the building.

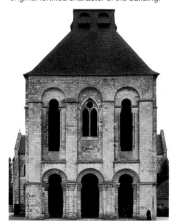

Central west tower above porch

St. Benoît-sur-Loire, mid eleventh century. An exceptional single-tower west front.

same time displays the image of a building. Here we generally find the entrances or the single main portal as well as a sophisticated system of articulation. The area of the portal itself can be emphasized by complex building sections. This is also the area where sculpture is situated.
The term **narthex area** is used if the west front is situated in front of the basilica-type nave like a cross-section. In most cases, the structure of the façade provides clues as to the articulation of the interior space. The use of pilasters or lesenes can indicate the distribution of the main nave and side aisles.
A **blind west front (screen west front)** is conceived independently of both the interior space and the shape of the roof.

Westwork with western choir and atrium/forecourt

1 atrium/forecourt
2 western choir
3 western transept
4 circular side towers
5 western central tower

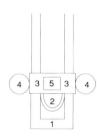

West front with three towers

The Benedictine Abbey church of Maria Laach (pictured) takes its place amongst the monumental Romanesque buildings and has remained virtually unaltered since the twelfth century. Boasting two transepts and two sets of triple towers, this church has to be seen in relation to the imperial cathedrals of Worms and Speyer.

The westwork makes its distinctive appearance in the Carolingian architecture of the late eighth century and comes to the fore in the first part of the ninth century. From about the year 1000, a modified version of the Carolingian westwork together with numerous architectural details were taken over or developed further and varied by Ottonian architecture. Examples of Ottonian buildings can be found all over northern and eastern France, in the southern part of modern Holland, in Belgium and throughout Germany. There is a wealth of variations which reflect the diversity between different countries and different cultural regions.
The westwork usually consists of a central part with an **atrium** (forecourt) and a multi-storey upper church, and may also be connected with transept-like side-wings, galleries and various flanking towers.
The characteristic exterior feature of the Carolingian westwork is the **west front with three towers** which remained in use

Typically rectangular and devoid of any pediments, it often lines the end of the basilica-type nave. Thus it serves to hide the latter's outlines while at the same time enjoying a structurally aesthetic life of its own. In many instances the west front is highly structured and richly decorated. (Examples of the structural and ornamental repertoire of Romanesque architecture can be found on the page opposite.)
A further criterion to distinguish between the various types of west front is provided by the number of the staircase turrets (and the presence or absence of a west choir and/or an antechurch, if applicable).

for centuries. The fact that all westworks are built in a similar fashion and their wide geographical distribution clearly suggest that this building type must have been based on the architectural style and program of the Carolingian Empire.

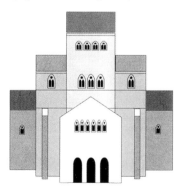

One variant of westwork takes the form of a transverse structure the width of the nave and aisles. The windows above the portal indicate galleries for the nobility.

The exterior / west II

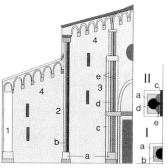

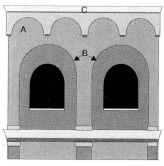

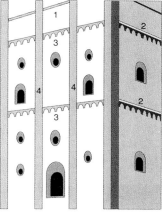

Blind west front

The blind west front of San Michele in Pavia is reminiscent of an imposing theatrical backdrop. One can frequently see such steep, high façades in the cities of Northern Italy. The west front is divided into three parts by powerful, vertical **clustered pilasters**.

The raking blind arcades along the edge of the gable reconcile the horizontal sweep of the pitched roof and the vertical lines of the pilaster strips. The west front is further accentuated by the symmetrical arrangement of the portals and the windows. There are also numerous reliefs distributed freely along the wall spaces.

West front with central tower

The west front of Santa Maria di Tiglio at Gravedone features a number of details which emphasize the ascending line and the height of the whole building. Set onto the lower rectangular base, the octagonal tower extends as far up as the ridge of the roof and is divided into several storeys.

The lower rectangular part of the integrated bell tower is traversed by a slender lesene – a simple and elegant solution to the problem of dividing the base into two zones.

Pilasters and columns

1. Engaged pilaster 2. engaged column, half-column 3. multi-shaft, compound or clustered pilaster (II) 4. blind arcades, raking.

I and II: ground-plans of engaged column and multi-shaft pilaster: a. plinth; b. engaged column; c. pilaster strip; d. engaged column/infill pilasters; e. attached column/three-quarter circle profile.

Arcades and arches

It is in the top belfry of church towers where one can often observe the interplay of blind arcades (A) and blind arches (B). The blind arcades take up and vary the arch motif. Together with the cornice (C) and the cupola, they form the completion of the tower.

Articulation of the west front

The west front of Notre-Dame-la-Grande in Poitiers (above) is regarded as the perfect example of a façade rich in sculptural decoration that has been worked out in great detail.

Emphasized by vertical friezes of round arcading, the structure can be understood to represent an all-encompassing iconographical program.

Structural elements

The horizontal cornice (1) often occurs in conjunction with a frieze of blind arcading (2). Horizontal blind arcades (3) and vertical lesenes (4) are elements frequently used to articulate towers and façades. The towers in question are usually massive west towers.

Romanesque friezes

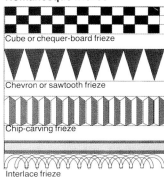

Cube or chequer-board frieze

Chevron or sawtooth frieze

Chip-carving frieze

Interlace frieze

West front with central apse and twin towers

Trier, St. Peter's Cathedral

The church with two choirs was first introduced in the Carolingian period. It finally produced its own distinctive west front, known as the **west front with central apse and towers** and included two or more towers. Trier's Salian cathedral is a pronounced variation of this type, with a central pediment and four towers. The west choir which defines it as a building with twin focus space (see ground plan) is usually found in the German-speaking areas of Europe. This type also occurs sporadically in Burgundy, Lorraine, Lombardy and Tuscany.

Ground plan (left):

A: east choir; B: west choir; C: nave; D: side aisles; E: staircase turrets of the west front.

The exterior / east I

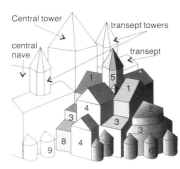

Central tower
central nave
transept towers
transept

1. Choir. 2. Sanctuary. 3. Ambulatory. 4. Choir transept. 5. Choir crossing tower. 6. Apsidal chapels (chevet). 7. Choir transept chapels. 8. Side chapel. 9. Transept chapels.

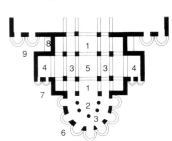

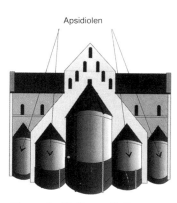

Apsidiolen

The choir, its spatial structure and its elements

Originally the choir was the place in the church where the clergy sang. This space was extended and later became the liturgical center containing the high altar. Later a sanctuary or apse was added at the eastern end. The whole complex was now generally referred to as the choir. The extension of the side aisles into the choir resulted in the ambulatory. From the ninth century onwards the latter is often accompanied by semi-circular chapels known as radiating chapels which are

organized into a chevet (St. Martin at Tours). The enlargement of the choir area began at Cluny III (1088): the erection of a choir transept created a crossing which was surmounted by the central choir tower. The eastern sides of the transept are furnished with side apses which together with the radiating chapels form a dense ring of apses. This development of the choir area made Cluny III the model for many Romanesque churches, not only its affiliated monasteries such as La Charité, but also for other buildings outside France which, however, tended to be executed on a more modest scale than Cluny III.

Central apse with side apses

The central apse with the smaller side apses (Rivolta d'Adda, Sta. Maria e San Sigismondo, twelfth century) point to the basilica form of a high nave and lower side aisles. The side apses with the friezes of round arcading below the roof-line form the end of the side choirs. The central apse is decorated with a high band of blind arcading.

Chancel with five radiating apsidal chapels

At St. Maria in Gengenbach we find a choir end with five radiating apsidal chapels. Two smaller apses are placed in the axis of the transepts, next to the central apse. A further apse is added to each of the transept arms. These strikingly small apses are also known as apsidioles.

Choir with chapels in echelon

The east end of the former abbey church of St. Sever (photo and ground plan) is a remarkable example of a choir with chapels in echelon. The transept seems to have disappeared, as the area broadens out towards the choir as a result of the 'flight' of apses. There are a total of seven chapels to the east of the crossing oriented towards the choir. The central transept chapels communicate with each other via arcades, thus enhancing the prominence of the choir.

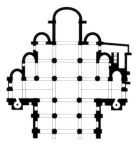

Klosterreichenbach

tower
choir
tower
Chorus maior

Choir with chapels in echelon
The stepped arrangement of lower chapels parallel to the choir – also called "Benedictine choir."

Alpirsbach

tower
choir
Chorus maior

Hirsau / St Aurelius

choir
Chorus maior

Hirsau / St. Peter and Paul

transept apses

choir
Chorus maior
Chorus minor

Hirsauer Bauschule (The Hirsau School)

Characteristic features of the so-called Hirsau School are the choir with chapels in echelon and the absence of a crypt. Another typical and novel development is the choir side aisles which communicate with the main choir via arcades. This Chorus Maior further underlines the already dominant position of the choir. Situated in front of it is the Chorus Minor (for the lay brothers not taking part in the singing).
The first church of Hirsau, St. Aurelius, probably served as the model for Klosterreichenbach in its conception of the choir. St. Aurelius was, however, built with

towers flanking the choir. It is very likely that these were also included in the plans for St. Peter and Paul but were never completed.
St. Peter and Paul provided the inspiration for the positioning of the choir and transept of the Allerheiligenmünster (All Saints Cathedral) of Schaffhausen. Alpirsbach, too, was probably influenced by St. Peter and Paul, since at Alpirsbach, too, the crossing was transformed into a Chorus Maior. Many factors indicate that a second choir-flanking tower was planned for Alpirsbach, similar to those at St. Aurelius and in Klosterreichenbach.

The exterior / east II

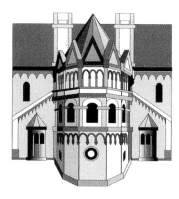

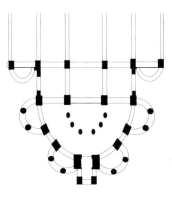

Polygonal choir

The semicircle of an apse is broken up into a number of facets. The basic models most frequently employed are the octagon or the dodecagon whose interior opens into the choir area. This method enables the construction of a polygonal termination like the one in the parish church of Neuengeseke (thirteenth century).
The simple design of the choir is articulated only by a frieze of round arcading, circular windows and a shallow plinth.

The **polygonal choir** of St. Peter in Sinzig (thirteenth century) boasts a wealth of details: the two-storey complex is articulated by a plinth and blind arcading and by lesenes made of masonry.
Interest is created by the alternation of semi-circular headed and barrel-vaulted windows. The second storey terminates in a blind arcade which is surmounted by pediments.
Small side turrets have been inserted between the apse and the choir, and there are apsidioles attached to the choir side aisles.

Ambulatory with three apsidal chapels

The eastern part of the Church of St. Godehard in Hildesheim consists of the ambulatory with three apsidal chapels or apsidioles, the apse, the choir and the choir side aisles. The shallow apses of the transept emphasize its close structural affinity with the choir complex. The eastern part of the church forms the central tower rising above the choir square. The architectural structuring results in a heightened symbolic significance of the choir.

Ambulatory and radiating chapels (Chevet)

Typical of the Romanesque architecture of the Auvergne are basilicas featuring an ambulatory surrounding the choir with a ring of radiating chapels (chevet). St. Austremoine in Issoire is further distinguished by a rectangular Lady Chapel placed between the innermost of the four ambulatory apsidally rounded chapels. This formation may be the result of a change in the building plans. One can also detect the beginnings of the design that was to evolve into the Gothic choir ambulatory.

Saint-Martin-de-Londres

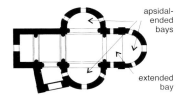

apsidal-ended bays

extended bay

Triple-apse (trefoil) plan

The little priory church of Saint-Martin-de-Londres (see ground plan above) was founded in 1088 and is a remarkable example of the early Romanesque style in the Bas-Languedoc region. The double-bayed nave leads over into a crossing from which apses extend in a way similar to a transept. The main apse is separated from the crossing by means of an extended bay. This "east formation" is referred to as trefoil or triple-apse plan.

Churches with towers above the choir area – variations

The little church of St. Candidus at Kentheim in the northern part of the Black Forest (eleventh century) exemplifies the southwest German Romanesque church of this type. There are numerous little Romanesque village churches nearby with similar towers above the choir area, forming a real landscape of choir towers in this region. One reason might be the fact that the dedications are dominated by the saints Stephanus, Remigius, Markus and Maria, and not by Martin and Michael, as is usually the case. This change of patron saint is one result of Frankish missionary work: using Frankish patron saints such as Remigius or Stephanus was a means of emphasizing that the Alemannian region was part of the Frankish Empire.
The choir, usually rectangular in shape, is surmounted by the tower, which thus provides a symbolic link between heaven and altar.

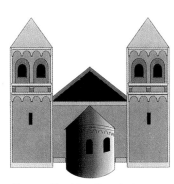

Kentheim, St. Candidus

Tournus
Abbey-church of St. Philibert (tenth – twelfth century)

choir ambulatory

radiating chapels

Ambulatory and radiating chapels

Following the basic basilica plan, the long central nave leads via the crossing into a choir which is surrounded by an ambulatory. Radiating out from this ambulatory are three rectangular chapels (apses) which are arranged concentrically but not connected with each other.
The choir, the ambulatory and the radiating chapels are constructed over a crypt built according to the same shape and design.

Tower above the choir area

Often this type of church also possesses an apse. If this is the case, the tower, as a kind of raised choir, is rounded off by an apse.

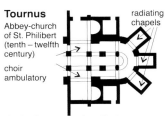

Towers flanking the choir

The choir bay is flanked by the east towers which are flush with the side aisles. They frame the choir with the apse and contain the choir side chapels.

The interior / west

In the basilica of the early Middle Ages, the western end had the character of an independent structure in front of the main church. It usually consisted of a two-storey central hall with three-storey side compartments. The galleries enabled the rulers to be present at the service and participate from an elevated position. Until the time of the Cluniac reform, the westwork was used for worldly matters, for example as a courtroom for the ruler. It was not until the twelfth and thirteenth centuries that alterations were made which integrated the western section into the main body of the church.

The westwork with its own choir is a reference to the liturgical autonomy of this section of the building, and to the place of the rulers. The latter often had a gallery built in the west choir from which they would take part in the services and beneath which they would later be laid to rest. Thus the western transepts with their galleries gradually emerged as a symbol of majestic dignity for the dignitaries of the realm, such as the archbishop or the emperor.

The galilee

The galilee is a variation of the atrium or the narthex in the western part of a church (see page 21). The galilee to the convent church of Maulbronn is also called the paradise (1210–15). It is regarded as a unique and perfect example of art from the time of the Hohenstaufen dynasty (left).

The influences from Burgundy are obvious and can be seen in the special finish of the capitals and in the high plinths.

Each of the three bays has been constructed above a square. The portal and the twin arcades open onto the forecourt. The monumental cross-ribs extend like transverse arches from the mighty responds which are placed on high plinths. Together with the transverse ribs, the ribs which diagonally cross the cross vault form semi-circles. The varying spans of the bay arches contribute to the dynamics of the interior. In spite of the massive elements used for its articulation, and despite the squat proportions, the interior has an atmosphere which is anything but heavy or dark – a quality that was emphasized as a specific characteristic of classical Hohenstaufen architecture.

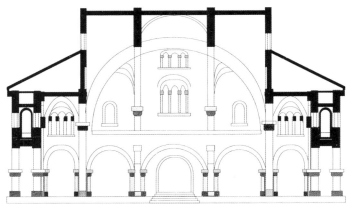

Basilica /hall church

Elevation of the galilee of the cathedral of Casale Monferrato (twelfth century)
The Piedmontese cathedral of San Evasio, built at the time of the Lombards, represents a blend of basilica and hall church. The main complex with its four aisles is preceded by an unusually large galilee. The two outer bays, when related to the nave, result in a ratio of bays of 3:3. The double-crossed transverse arches extend far down into the interior – a characteristic more often found in Armenian architecture. It might have been introduced to Northern Italy after the Second Crusade.

Nuns' gallery

The high gallery opening towards the nave is constructed over an aisled, low western hall. Nuns' galleries can often be found in convent churches of Benedictine nuns, for example in the convent church of Lippoldsberg in Hesse (now the Protestant parish church).

◄ Western choir, two-storey

The two-storey western choir of the church of St. George in Cologne (twelfth century) projects from the square central section of the western hall and is spanned by a domed ceiling. The wall system is articulated by means of pilasters and round arched windows. On the top storey, there is a corridor behind the wall. In the western section; the top storey used to function as a gallery.

Western transept with gallery ►

The Schottenkirche (Scots church) in Regensburg (St. James', eleventh/twelfth century, right), an aisled columned basilica, features a western transept. A gallery, which was used by choristers, was put in front of the southern and northern termination of the transept.

Western gallery, single-storey

An imposing effect is created by the interior of the westwork of the abbey church of Essen (eleventh century). The high gallery forms a striking contrast to the thick-set arches of the ground-floor and is probably inspired by the Carolingian Palatine Chapel in Aachen.

The interior Construction of the nave

The design of the wall of the nave in Romanesque churches is often conceived as a multi-storey system. One or two stages (triforium or blind triforium) and/or a clerestory were constructed above the arcades, depending on the size and proportions of the building. The bays comprised either one or two arches.

This structure is continued in the upper storeys. Such a concept is dependent on the overall building plan. One system uses the crossing square as its basic proportion, which is repeated in the bays of the nave. Each bay has its own vault, the thrust being taken by the pillars. Sometimes the nave is articulated by a rhythmic alternation of pillars and columns. Such a design lends movement and expression to an interior.

Single-tier construction

Fontenay, former Cistercian abbey church of Notre Dame (from 1139). The single-section wall construction does not allow for a clerestory, which would have been the nave's light source. Two rows of semi-circular headed windows in the western wall were inserted for that purpose. The wall section above the arcades is articulated by means of lesenes.

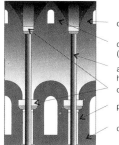

clerestory
clerestory window (light zone)
attached or half column   pilaster
capital
pier
chapel

Double-tier construction

If the wall construction is in two stages, the high nave is divided by means of a clerestory with a row of semi-circular headed windows and by the arcades. Pilasters or attached columns without structural function are inserted in front of the arcades in order to articulate the wall space. The groin vaulting of the individual bays is framed by transverse arches which radiate from the capitals of the pilasters and attached columns in the clerestory. In both cases the church in question is a groin-vaulted arcaded basilica with nave walls resting on pillars, a type particularly common in twelfth-century Germany. The picture on the left shows a bay containing an arcade and a clerestory window, while the second example illustrates a bay housing two arcades and two clerestory windows.

The Church of St. Gertrude in Nivelles/Belgium (around 1000–1046) is a typical example of a wall constructed in two stages.

Four-tier Construction

The four-zone wall construction is layered from bottom to top as follows: arcades, galleries, blind triforium, and clerestory. The bay is separated from the gallery level by a lesene.

Three-tier construction

This type of wall construction is likely to occur in large Romanesque cathedrals, such as the one in Worms. The central section is reserved for the gallery or the triforium. While in most cases it is used for a gallery, there are some churches which do not utilize the space behind this central section. In such cases a blind triforium is applied purely for reasons of surface articulation which can be structured by arcades.

1 side aisle
2 nave
3 buttress
4 gallery
5 clerestory
6 vault

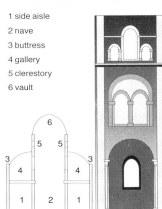

Such a blind triforium can be seen in the wall elevation of Winchester Cathedral (1080). The strictly horizontal layering of the various building sections is typical of English architecture. In order to try and relieve this emphasis on the horizontal, slender arcades and flat, articulating pilasters were installed.

Rhythmic alternation
Three-tier construction

Durham Cathedral in northern England was begun in 1093 and finished in 1128. Its monumental pillars are constructed onto cruciform bases and surrounded by attached columns which lead up to the vaulting where they branch out. Alternating with these half-columns are columns placed within the bay.

Assigned to each of the two arcades within the bay are one double window in the gallery and one single semi-circular headed window in the clerestory. The gallery window "repeats" the structure of the two arches integrated by the bay. The clerestory windows are already part of the vaulted section which starts above the gallery.

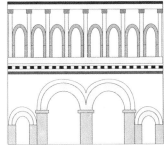

Three-tier construction with gallery

Saint-Lazare in Autun was begun in 1120 as an arcaded basilica with side aisles after the model of Cluny. The elevation of the nave shows a three-tier construction with a gallery above the high nave arcades. Roman city gates served as models (see illustration above), with their pilasters placed between the gallery windows. The beads and reels and rosette friezes are further references to Classical antiquity. However, there is only one clerestory window per bay.

Choir
and crypt

The choir

Originally the choir denoted the place where the singing in church took place. Soon it was designated the liturgical center around which the church interior or the basilica developed. The simple early choir was extended by the chancel square and the apse or chevet. From the thirteenth century onwards, the border area between the monks' and the lay church has been marked by the chancel or choir screen which also serves as a platform for singers or as a lectern. The size of the choir is usually dictated by the width and height dimensions of the nave, except where partial closure of the crossing allows a narrowing of the choir.

1 chancel square
2 apse
3 triumphal arch

1 chancel square
2 apse
3 ambulatory
4 choir screen
5 sanctuary rail

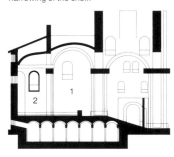

Chancel square and apse
(on one level)

In the church of San Michele of Pavia (twelfth century) steps lead up from the crossing to the elevated chancel square (1) and on to the apse (2). The apse is constructed on one level.

The crypt

The crypt was originally the place where a martyr was laid to rest (confessio). Later on, the crypt served as last resting place for both secular and spiritual dignitaries. Above the crypt would be constructed the east choir and later the whole of the church. The tunnel crypt, consisting of individual chambers, has its origins in the early Christian catacombs.
The dominant type in ninth-century Italy was the hall crypt which was designed to include aisles and was vaulted. The heightened ceiling made it necessary to raise the choir above.

Ambulatory crypt

In the crypt of Flavigny-sur-Ozerain, Saint-Pierre, the confessio (2) is surrounded by a rectangular ambulatory (1) which leads into the chantry chapels or oratories (3). An adjoining aisled arm (4) leads on into a hexagonal Lady Chapel (5). This complex ground plan was conceived in the ninth century.

Single- and multi-pillared crypts

Depending on the scale and the design, crypts are distinguished according to aisles and supports. The single and four-pillared types have frequently been constructed with a groin vault. The short shafts of the columns absorb the vertical thrust of the vaulting, while the outward thrust is diverted into the outer walls. These crypt interiors are characterized by massive cushion or acanthus capitals (Corinthian capitals). Additional transverse arches are often found in hall crypts with two, three, or four aisles.

Hall crypt

The hall crypt of Speyer is often called "the most beautiful crypt in the world." Indeed, it creates a magnificent impression, with its 8 mighty piers, its massive walls, and its 14 corner piers, 36 engaged columns and 20 free-standing columns (right).
The groin vault is articulated by transverse arches. Extending from the heavy cushion capitals or the imposts of the piers, they divide the crypt into three almost square spaces lined up along the transverse axis, so that three naves are formed, each with three bays. Each of the side rooms is extended in its eastern part by three altar recesses. The bases and the cushion capitals suggest that building was begun around 1030.

Basic choir forms

The basic type of the early Frankish aisle-less church consists of a simple hall or basilica-type space with an adjoining rectangular sanctuary (2).
Aisle-less churches are also found in northern Italy, for example in Pavia and in Sirmione. The Italian type also comprises a simple, undivided hall with apses and flanking apses or apsidioles attached on the eastern end.
These church forms are referred to as t-shaped "basic type", with the English portico church constituting a special form.
Also conceived along the t-shaped ground plan are the closed or open halls (porticos) arranged around the central hall and serving as last resting places for the donors. One example is Reculver in the Canterbury area (seventh century).

Chancel square and apse
(on two levels)

In Great St. Martin, Cologne, twelfth century, the apse adjoining the chancel square is divided into two levels. The lower level consists of blind arcading with columns and recesses opening up behind them. The level above has a peristyle with large semi-circular headed windows.

Rectangular choir

Rectangular choirs are often found in early churches of the t-shaped type, ie there is no chancel square in front of the apse. There are two different types: those with a flat ceiling (for example in Goldbach on Lake Constance, around 1000), and those with a vault (Soest, St. Maria zur Höhe/Hohnekirche, thirteenth century).

The interior vault and dome

The flat ceiling taken over from the early Christian basilica was gradually replaced by a simple barrel vault. The pilasters attached to the front of the aisle columns are continued in the vault by transverse arches. The intersection of the transept and the nave vaults result in groins from which the groin vault takes its name. These groins were reinforced by means of ribs which often sprang from the column capitals. In the course of time and in different regions, this so-called groin vault was adapted and developed in a variety of ways.

Outward and vertical thrust of the vaults

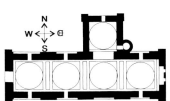

Two types of thrust are created in a vault: the vertical and the outward thrust. The main impact of the outward thrust is absorbed by the exterior walls of the aisle and by the buttresses.

Construction of dome and vault

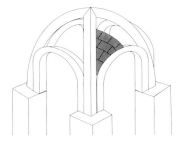

Four arches facing one another are domed by two arches at right angles to each other, creating four spherical triangles, or pendentives (concave spandrels), which are walled up.

Domed churches

A special feature of the Périgord region is the domed churches, their domes usually rising up above pendentives (Périgeux, St-Étienne-de-la-Cité/St-Front). Particularly impressive is the domed church of Cherval (see photo and ground plan) dating from the twelfth century: here, four domes have been arranged one behind the other (3 bays in the nave and the choir).

Curved vault above a lunette

The construction type of the pilgrimage church reached its climax in the church of Saint-Sernin in Toulouse (1080–1150). Its barrel vault spans a nave that consists of eleven bays and has galleries divided into two parts. The transverse arches spring from the capitals of the engaged columns which span a succession of bays.

Pointed vault and groin vault

A typical feature of the Romanesque cathedral of Salamanca (twelfth century) is its pointed vault. The vault tapers to a point at its vertex, thus forming groins (see groin vault).

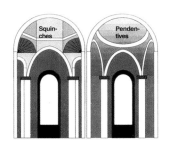

Dome resting on a tambour or drum

San Tomaso in Lemine in Almenno San Bartolomeo (twelfth century) is a round church and is used as a baptistery or a memorial chapel (right). The interior of this rotunda features an inner circle of columns which forms arcades and supports a ring which is transformed into the dome. This tambour (Fr.=drum) or tambour circle has windows which allow light into the dome. The dome itself opens out into a lantern, a small round turret, which also has windows. Visible from the outside, the tambour is often articulated by pilasters, lesenes and blind arcading. Tambour circles are used in centrally planned buildings with circular ground plans.

Groin vault

The intersection of two barrel vaults at right angles above a square results in the formation of arched diagonals or groins within the vault. This is how the vault above the crossing of a barrel-vaulted church nave with a barrel-vaulted transept was created. The piers of the crossing mark the outer corner of the groins and of the vault.

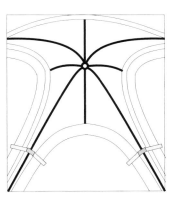

Domical vault

In many cases there was a desire to "raise" the crossing by means of a vault without the construction of a dome. The groin vault was then extended across the level of the arcades, thus emphasizing the direction of both the nave and the transept by means of ribs.

Dome resting on squinches and pendentives

If a dome is erected over a crossing, a solution must be found for the transition from the square into a circle. Squinches are used to bridge, by means of small vaults (which have the appearance of ears or horns), the corners of the square, thus creating an octagonal space which can then carry the circle of the dome. Pendentives are spherical concave triangles which bulge out between the arcades (ie. they "hang" out into the space) and carry the circle of the dome.

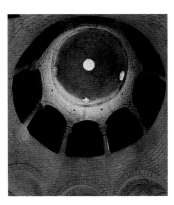

Church doors and windows

Church doors

Romanesque religious buildings have three different types of entrance: 1. the simple round-arched entrance; 2. the recessed or stepped portal; 3. the recessed portal with columns. In the case of 2 and 3 in particular, there is a variety of stylistic detail in construction as well as in ornamentation. The columns included in some of the recessed entrances already anticipate the columned portal. Tympana (a), capitals (b) and archivolts (c) are developed and are often used to display decorative elements. The recessed and the columned portals anticipate the design of the heavily recessed funnel-like portal of the Gothic period.

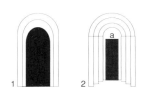

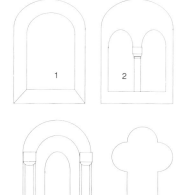

Arles, St-Trophime (western portal)

Semi-circular headed windows with mullion

With its rich ornamentation, its figurative sculptures, its consoles and its apex mask, the apsidal window of the Walterich chapel in Murrhardt (thirteenth century) takes its place amongst the most distinctly Romanesque windows in Germany.

Recessed columned portal with shallow projecting porch

Built between 1190 and 1200, the western portal of Saint-Trophime in Arles is amongst the portals of French Romanesque architecture most richly decorated with figurative sculpture. It appears to have detached itself from the structure of the building in as far as it "veils" the basilica elevation. Figuration was thus more important than architectural organization. Portal and porch are fused into one medium for the communication of a meticulously composed iconographical program. The central theme is the expectation of salvation associated with the Last Judgment, as illustrated in the tympanum, the archivolts, the lintel, and the impost area (above the capitals). Unlike later Gothic architecture, the central column does not yet depict a theme by featuring a figure (in this case it would have been Christ as the ruler of the world) but the apostles and saints along the walls reinforce the universal message of salvation.

Windows

The Romanesque window is a simplified miniature version of the Romanesque portal. There are four different types: 1. the simple semi-circular headed window; 2. the coupled semi-circular headed lights with central colonette; 3. the stepped semi-circular headed lights with dividing colonettes; 4. the trefoil-headed window. The last-named can vary as far as the Gothic rose window. The third frequently occurs with lavish ornamentation, while the second can have three or more lights. With type one, the intrados is often decorated.

Iconographical program

The tympanum shows the central theme, while the accompanying secondary themes are depicted in the archivolts (for example, Old/New Testament or allegorical scenes). The lintel often depicts a scene related to the central theme in the tympanum. The same applies to the capital area. The plinth area below the wall sculptures depicting saints often contains allegorical scenes.

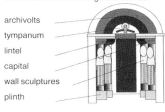

archivolts
tympanum
lintel
capital
wall sculptures
plinth

Semur-en-Brionnais:

on the threshold to the Gothic period

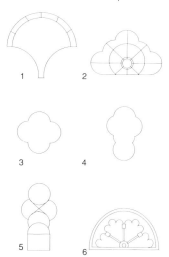

1 simple fan-shaped window

2 cinquefoil window

3 quatrefoil window

4 elongated quatrefoil window

5 stilted trefoil window

6 half-wheel window

Recessed or stepped entrance

One of the most distinct examples of this type of entrance is the recessed portal of the cathedral of Speyer (eleventh century). Stepped towards the central axis, and banded in contrasting stone, the segments of the arch form the shape of a funnel.
This type of portal can be regarded as the prototype of the later decorated portal, since the recesses often include columns which depict figurative scenes.

Stepped entrance with columns
(left)

The lavishly decorated porch of Semur-en-Brionnais (St. Hilaire, twelfth century) represents a transitional stage, in which the steps are "disguised" by decorated columns. The scenes depicted on the lintel (Hilarius scenes), and the Christ in Majesty in the tympanum, place it well into the Gothic era, as do the distinct archivolt ribs and the "pointed" semi-circular arch.

Fan-shaped windows, cinquefoil and stilted

Amongst the Romanesque windows most diversified in form are the fan-shaped and the trefoil windows, both belonging to the category of the multi-foil window. The fan window of St. Quirin in Neuss (dating from the thirteenth century) has a rectangular stilting (stem) from which the individual segments radiate, the so-called foils or fans.

Piers and capitals

Piers

The vertical thrust of the vault is absorbed by a system of pillars, the outward one by the outer buttresses. The pillar and wall construction in a Romanesque religious building exists in that static relationship of tension. Pillars are classified according to the five ground plans as follows: 1. the circular pillar; 2. the quatrefoil pillar; 3. the cruciform pillar; 4. the respond, or pier with engaged pillar; 5. the cruciform pier with engaged shafts, or compound pier. The respond and the compound pier share the basic shape of the cruciform pillar. The latter has attached shafts which often end in capitals. The narrower three-quarter shafts jut out above the capitals and form the transverse arches of the vault.

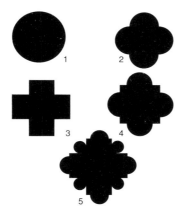

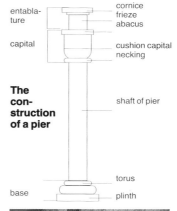

The construction of a pier

entablature — cornice, frieze, abacus
capital — cushion capital, necking
shaft of pier
torus
base — plinth

Rectangular piers

The simple rectangular piers of St. Cyriakus in Sulzburg (eleventh century) cannot yet be regarded as an independent architectural element. They are part of the supporting wall structure and merely flank the round-arched arcades.

Circular pillars

S. Abbondio in Como (eleventh century) is a typical arcaded basilica with the nave walls resting on pillars. The circular pillars are constructed from brick and are topped by monumental cushion capitals. The main function of the pillars is to support the aisle walls and the flat ceiling.

The capital

The development of the Romanesque capital can be traced from the simple cushion capital (2) to the figural capital (5). One variant of the cushion capital, the so-called pyramidal capital (1), might well be the Romanesque "prototype." The Ionic capital with its volute or spiral scroll (3) is an early adaptation. Embellishments such as stylized leaves or shields transform the cushion capital into an ornamental capital (4). The decorative elements show great imagination and include spiral motifs and floral patterns, creating ever new variations. These were followed by masks and animal shapes and finally by figurative scenes, all of which culminated in the figural capital.

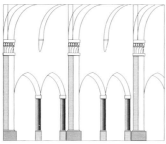

Engaged or attached pillar
(see above)

Talant, Notre-Came (thirteenth century). The octagonal attached nave pillars are of the fourth type. Responds projecting beyond the arcades support the transverse arches of the tunnel vault. Note the support provided by an alternation of pillars and columns.

The respond

The former priory church of Anzy-le-Duc in Burgundy (twelfth century) is characterized by a system of responds. Oriented towards the nave, the half-columns (responds) are attached to rectangular pilasters. They terminate in capitals from which spring the transverse arches.

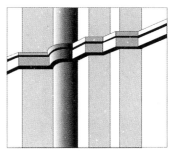

Continuous string or band courses
(see above)

Cornices or string courses are continued around architectural elements such as engaged pillars or pilasters.

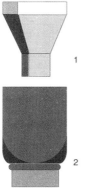

◄ Ornamental or decorated capital

At the former Premonstratensian monastery church in Spieskappel there are capitals which show a combination of ornamental patterns and imaginary creatures. Some of the capitals also depict figurative scenes.

Cushion capital ►

The heavy capitals counter-balance the pressure originating from the arcades which is transmitted onto the shafts of the pillars of St. Maria im Kapitol in Cologne.

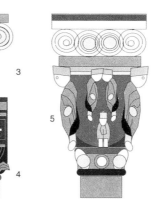

Figural capital

The figural capitals in the nave of the former priory church of Anzy-le-Duc in Burgundy (twelfth century) combine decorative mask shapes with figurative scenes.

31

Wolfgang Kaiser

Romanesque architecture in Germany

Pre-Romanesque architecture of the Carolingian period

The decline of the Roman Empire was marked by turmoil and a mass migration of peoples. As a result, the Merovingian kings, who reigned well into the eighth century, were able to contribute little to the architecture of central Europe. Trade declined and the towns were impoverished. Any building was usually constructed in wood. Only a few towns were able to retain the important role they had once enjoyed under the Roman Empire. Tours, in the west of the Frankish Kingdom, and once the sphere of activity of St. Martin, became a shrine for the Franks. In contrast, one of the most important towns in the declining Roman Empire, the old imperial town of Trier, largely lost its significance in the following centuries.

A monumental style of architecture was able to revive only under the Carolingians and Charlemagne, who strove for a renewal of the Roman Empire (*Renovatio Imperii Romanorum*), uniting central and western Europe under his rule in a Frankish Empire. Imperial monasteries and schools promoted the cultural unity of the Empire. Initially it was a matter of experimentation, and casting about for a valid form of expression. In these earlier days many ideas were tried out, and a multiplicity of building styles developed side by side. Simultaneously there was a development of basilicas, both with and without transepts, hall churches with rectangular choirs and one or three apses, and, finally, centrally planned buildings according to the function and requirements of the client. It was the emperor and nobility, as well as clergy drawn from noble families, especially bishops and abbots, who promoted building and granted the large commissions. Of all the buildings constructed during the Carolingian period, the number surviving barely reaches double figures.

Centers of Charlemagne's court architecture

Since 796 Charlemagne had been building his prestigious Palatine Chapel (photo, opposite). Supervised by the Frankish master builder, Odo of Metz, the prestigious building project brought in craftsmen from all over the Empire – "from all areas this side of the sea," as it was described. In 798, just before the coronation of the Emperor, the shell of the building was completed, and in 805 the chapel was consecrated by Pope Leo III to the honor of the Saviour and the Mother of God. The central structure stood as part of four connecting building complexes on the southern side of the Imperial Palace. It was connected to the hall of justice via a long wing, halfway along which was a passageway to the Aula Regia. The core of the latter is to be found today in the City Hall in Aachen. The Aula Regia was a monumental hall with two lateral conches and a western apse. The huge hall served as Charlemagne's throne room. The Palatine Chapel has not come down to us entirely unchanged, for the rectangular choir from Charlemagne's time has had to give way for a late Gothic choir. The main space of the chapel describes a regular octagon, around which is laid a sixteen-sided ambulatory with galleries. The interior of the octagon, crowned by a cloister vault of eight sections, appears astonishingly steep. Eight massive structural piers, angled in on themselves to form the corners of the octagon, define the perimeter of the central space.

Aachen, Charlemagne's Palatine Chapel.
Inner view of the octagon. Completed
798. Room fittings are 19th Century

Aachen, Charlemagne's Palatine Chapel.
Ground plan, originally with narthex and
rectangular choir

The arcade openings appear as though cut out of the wall. A strong horizontal string course leads the eye from the massively heavy lower storey to the light and graceful galleries in the upper level. The large gallery openings are steeper and higher in proportion than the arcades. Within each opening there are two levels of arches supported by Corinthian columns, one level set upon the other. The classical Corinthian columns are spoils, and were brought from Ravenna to Aachen on the instructions of Charlemagne himself. It is not only these spoils that link the two cities, as San Vitale in Ravenna is one of the possible prototypes for the Aachen Palatine Chapel (photo, p. 77). Built in the sixth century under the Emperor Justinian, S. Vitale is also an example of an octagonal central space on three storeys, ringed however by an octagonal ambulatory. This is not the only difference between the early Christian model and the Aachen Palatine Chapel. In Ravenna the piers are much slimmer and narrower in design, and do not give the appearance of being an integral part of the walls. The columns in the arcade openings curve back in a semi-circle and give the room a wonderful feeling of breadth. In Aachen, by contrast, the effect is of a steeply-sided shaft. In his Aachen Palatine Chapel, Charlemagne strove to create a central structure in the image of the early Christian imperial chapels such as he had seen at Ravenna. This architecture was designed to symbolize the role of the king as the advocate of his people and as the mediator between the secular and the spiritual, this world and the next. Thus the square as a symbol of the worldly is combined with the circle as the symbol of the divine. The resulting octagon is regarded in number symbolism as synonymous with eternity. S. Vitale in Ravenna was not the only model for Aachen: also important was the church of SS. Sergius and Bacchus in Constantinople, which has an octagonal central room encased in a square, and was built as a palace chapel under the Emperor Justinian in the third decade of the sixth century. Particular architectural prominence was given to the west gallery behind the throne of the emperor by means of a tower-like construction, all four sides of which jut out. This tower, protruding from the façade, was a new development, conceived in the Carolingian period, but not at that time consistently exploited. Facing the former atrium, the entrance façade with its high round-arched recess draws attention to the Roman motif of the triumphal arch and lends an imperial monumentality to the façade. This entrance recess and the small pilasters with imitation classical capitals are the few exterior Carolingian forms which remain from the originally plastered exterior of the Palatine Chapel. The small pilasters were designed only as decoration and serve no structural function.

The finest preserved example of a Carolingian exterior is the gate house of the former monastery at Lorsch (photo, p. 34). Erected around 774, presumably as a three-part triumphal gateway, it marked the boundary of the atrium of the church to the west.

The Lorsch gate house looks back historically to classical antiquity, but the idea of the triumphal gateway was modified by making the three archways the same height and size, and not emphasizing the central arch in the classical manner. Use of the classical idiom is made in the columns with the entablature, the pillars with round arches, the fluted pilasters and the

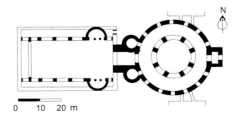

0   10   20 m

Lorsch gatehouse. Erected 774

St. Gallen, Collegiate Library, monastery plan, completed on the island on Reichenau in the early ninth century

1 House for the retinue of noble guests 2 Domestic offices 3 Noble guests 4 Outer school 5 Abbot's building 6 Domestic offices 7 Infirmary building 8 Doctor's house and apothecary 9 Herb garden 10 Bell tower 11 Porter 12 School head 13 Library 14 Bath and kitchen 15 Hospital 16 Cloister 17 Entrance 18 Reception hall 19 Choir 20 Monastery church (basilica) 21 Servants' quarters 22 Sheep pens 23 Pigs 24 Goats 25 Mares 26 Cows 27 Kitchen 28 Hostel 29 Pantries and wine cellars 30 Cloister

monastery. They guaranteed the self-sufficiency of the organization which operated not unlike a small independent state. The monastery church forms the center of the whole, and attached to it are the enclosure with chapter house, refectory and dormitory. Around this central area are grouped the domestic offices, the living quarters for the lay brothers, the guest house, stables and other livestock buildings, larders, hospital and gardens. There is a striking precision in the planning of the whole complex, above all in the church in which the square is already being used as the unit of measurement of the ground plan. This principle was fully exploited only in the following centuries. It is in this respect that the church of the St. Gallen monastery plan differs from the old Christian basilicas such as S. Maria Maggiore in Rome which had no defined system of proportion.

In the church of the St. Gallen monastery plan the nave is built up out of a series of squares, whilst the aisles measure half the width of the nave. That means that each square nave bay is equivalent to two square aisle bays . The square crossing, the point of intersection of the nave and the transept, determines the unit of measurement for the whole. The whole ground plan of the church is derived from this square, and thus each part of the building is placed in a direct relationship to every other part. Although this development of a quadratic scheme was hardly exploited in the Carolingian period, it was to form one of the most important principles for the sacred architecture of the following century.

form of the bases and capitals. On the other hand the facing of the wall with a colorful textile-like surface is Byzantine in conception. The triangular gables of the upper floor come from the northern tradition. The combination of columns with round archways is medieval and inconceivable in classical antiquity, in which only a horizontal entablature was possible above columns. Seen in its totality, the gate-house at Lorsch is an edifice of extreme refinement. Although it stands at the beginning of western medieval architecture, it is at the same time an exquisite late-comer, an almost decadent building.

The St. Gallen monastery plan: instructions for the ideal monastery layout
The gate-house at Lorsch once stood at the entrance to a large monastery complex which has now disappeared and is known to us only through excavations and a few remains. All the other Carolingian monasteries have suffered the same fate as Lorsch; they have been converted, modified or eventually destroyed. The only way we have of conceiving of the layout of a Carolingian monastery is from a parchment plan which originated on the island of Reichenau on Lake Constance, and which is now kept in the library of the St. Gallen monastery. This monastery plan is the earliest architectural plan of the Middle Ages still in existence. The distribution of the individual buildings is in harmony with monastic life which developed according to the rule of St. Benedict. Around the church are grouped a mass of monastic buildings, small courtyards, gardens and paths. The facilities which surrounded the church were of vital importance for the survival of a

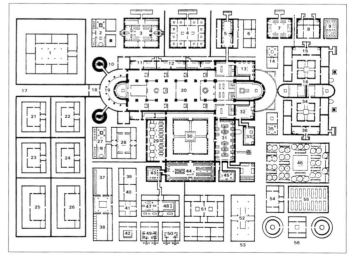

31 Dormitory and calefactory 32 Sacristy 33 Host bakery 34 Cloister 35 Kitchen 36 Novices' school 37 Horses 38 Oxen 39 Cooper 40 Wood turner 41 Storehouse 42 Malt kiln 43 Kitchen 44 Refectory 45 bathhouse 46 Cemetery 47 Brewery 48 Bakery 49 Pestles 50 Mill 51 Various artisans 52 Threshing floor 53 Granary 54 Gardener's house 55 Vegetable garden 56 Poultry houses

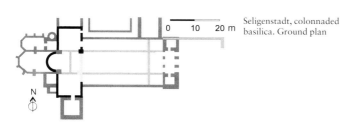

Seligenstadt, colonnaded
basilica. Ground plan

Müstair, Graubünden, Monastery church
from the south-east. Around 800

The search for form – centrally planned buildings, basilicas, one-aisled churches

Included in the small number of centrally planned buildings of the Carolingian period are the aforementioned Palatine Chapel in Aachen, the circular Michael chapel in Fulda, erected by the Abbot Eigil between 820 and 822, and Germigny-des-Prés, built near the Loire according to the quadratic ground plan under Theodulf, Bishop of Orleans, a relative of the Emperor Charlemagne, and consecrated in 806. These isolated examples of centrally planned buildings apart, the dominant structure which developed was the basilica with a nave and two aisles, transept, forechoir bay, and semi-circular apse. The surviving Carolingian churches did not follow the clear and precise quadratic scheme of construction given in the St. Gallen monastery plan. The aisles were mostly much narrower than half the width of the nave. The transept was not yet a balanced structure which intersected the nave at right angles creating a separate square area. This distinct area of intersection, which opened out to all four sides through four equal-sized arches, presupposed a nave and transept of equal height and breadth. This pattern was as yet unknown in Carolingian architecture. In the Carolingian style the crossing was not fully developed, that is to say, the transverse arms were much lower compared to the nave and gave the appearance of having been added later. The transepts were accessible only from the crossing via small openings. These transepts separated from the square by partial walls were, for example, to be found in the basilica in Steinbach near Michelstadt in the Oden forest built in 827 by Einhard, the biographer of Charlemagne. Today only the nave with its semi-circular apse and the northern wing of the transept remain standing. The basilica erected by Einhard in Seligenstadt-on-Main (see ground plan above), on the other hand, had a continuous transept, which was separated from the nave by a large semi-circular arch. The Seligenstadt church was however no more a true fusion of the nave and transept than was Steinbach. It is not a basilica with a nave supported by piers as at Steinbach or Seligenstadt, but a basilica with columns which has been preserved at St. Justinus in Höchst near Frankfurt. The building with its impressive reeded capitals was built in the first half of the ninth century. In addition to the pier and column basilicas, Carolingian architecture also produced simple one-aisled churches with one or three apses at the eastern end of the building, as, for example, at St. Benedict in Mals or St. Prokulus in Naturns in South Tirol. Churches with three apses were a feature above all of the Alpine region, such as Disentis, Mistail and Müstair in Graubünden. The church of the Benedictine monastery at Müstair (illustrated right) was built around 800 from a foundation of Charlemagne. With its ceiling, originally flat and vaulted only in the late Gothic period, the church is impressive for its eastern triapsal termination. Each apse is framed with high blind arches, the middle one being somewhat larger and thus emphasized.

Conflict with Rome – the abbey church in Fulda

Before its rebuilding in the Baroque style, the abbey church in Fulda was one of the most monumental large buildings of the Carolingian period. Between 791 and 819 an existing church was replaced by an enormous new structure under Abbot Ratgar. The basilica, with nave and two aisles and a semi-circular apse at its eastern end, had a huge west transept with a broad west apse. Nowhere else in Carolingian architecture is such a massive west transept to be found, its model being Old St. Peter's in Rome. In the Carolingian period the abbey at Fulda was one of the most important spiritual centers north of the Alps, and as early as 751 was subordinated to the power of Rome. It is therefore not surprising that Fulda sought to emulate St. Peter's church in Rome. It was a common feature of all basilicas and hall churches in the Carolingian period that they had flat ceilings or at least open roof trusses.

ABOVE LEFT
Fulda, St. Michael's Catholic Chapel,
round crypt. 820–822

ABOVE RIGHT
Steinbach Michelstadt/Odenwald.
Completed 827.
Tunnel crypt

BELOW
Constance, Cathedral of Our Lady,
crypt. 780 and 890

Crypts

Only centrally planned buildings or crypts were vaulted. The latter had been erected as tombs since the late eighth century, mostly under the high altar. The main reason for this was the desire to create a place for the venerated relics of the saints and to make them accessible to everyone. Various ground plans were selected depending on the architectural possibilities of the particular building: a ring crypt, a barrel-vaulted, semi-circular passageway such as in Seligenstadt, or a cross-shaped passage or tunnel crypt as at Steinbach (photo, left). When in the post-Carolingian period the cult of relics assumed ever greater importance, the passage or tunnel crypt was enlarged. Rooms were built with one, four or more supports. Gradually crypts developed into centers of cult worship in their own right. Impressive constructions were created such as the hall crypt of Speyer cathedral: a church below a church as it were (photo, p. 46).

The westwork – *Ecclesia militans*

One of the most significant developments in the Carolingian period was the abandonment of the exclusively squat, earthbound nature of the extended early Christian basilicas in favor of the increased use of towers. The abbey church at Centula/Somme, begun by Angilbert, a son-in-law of Charlemagne, has none of this horizontal tranquility, but is characterized by groups of towers at the east and west ends. The tower structure of the westwork was designed either as a means of highlighting a separate devotional space for an additional church patron, or as a part of the building attached to the church and reserved for the emperor. An impressive example from the Carolingian period survives in the monastery church of Corvey (822–848). This westwork, added between the years 855 and 873, underwent no further alterations and still conveys the full power of the Carolingian concept of architecture (photo, p. 37). Rising above the low, heavy basement, whose groin vaults are supported by piers with mock classical capitals, without transverse arches or bays, is the quadrum. This is a steep, open, central space surrounded by an ambulatory with three arcades on each side, and each with a gallery above. A semi-circular arch, opening out onto the center of the western gallery, allowed an uninterrupted view of the emperor's throne.

The main function of the westwork was to draw attention to the emperor or ruler, even if he was not there in person. The westwork embodied the power of the state and the sacrosanct nature of the ruler. The westwork church encompasses two distinct areas of significance within it: firstly, the actual church to the east dedicated to the saints, the *Ecclesia triumphans*, and, secondly, the bulwark-like westwork, symbol of the *Ecclesia militans*, the place of the ruler as the protector of the church. This explains the large number of westworks in Saxony, which had been conquered by Charlemagne. They proclaimed unambiguously the strength of the emperor's right to rule this area.

The westwork as a structure influenced architecture well beyond the Carolingian period and underwent many modifications in form. The end of the tenth century saw the westwork at St. Pantaleon in Cologne with its group of three towers. In 1090 the westwork of the collegiate church at

ABOVE LEFT
Corvey, abbey church, ground
floor hall of westwork

BELOW LEFT
Corvey, abbey church,
westwork interior with
imperial gallery, 873–885

RIGHT
Corvey, abbey church, west
front. Above the Carolingian
westwork are two towers from
1146. Ground plan

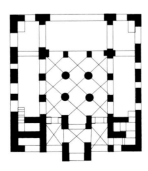

Freckenhorst was completed, a group of three towers of quintessentially Westphalian character. In the middle of the twelfth century the westwork dating from the first half of the tenth century at the cathedral in Minden was rebuilt into a Saxon transept. Similarly in Gernrode in the Harz in the first half of the twelfth century, a westblock was erected around the existing Ottonian round towers (see photos, pp. 38–39).

Cologne, St. Pantaleon, westwork. Late
tenth century

Freckenhorst, parish church of
St Boniface.
Former collegiate church, western end.
Around 1090

Gernrode, former convent church of
St. Cyriakus. Western end. First half of
the twelfth century

Minden, cathedral parish church of
SS. Petrus and Gorgonius. Western end
from the first half of the tenth century.
Converted to a perpendicular block in
the mid twelfth century

Gernrode, former convent church of
St. Cyriakus. Nave looking east, begun in
961

Hildesheim, St. Michael. Nave looking
east. 1010–1033

Early Romanesque Architecture of the Ottonian Period

Under the successors to Charlemagne, the Frankish Empire split into three: a western, a central and an eastern part. The power of the emperor was weakened and a dark age followed. Great wars brought devastation to the land, and building activity largely came to a standstill. The Hungarians engulfed The Frankish Empire from the east and from the west the Normans brought ruin and destruction to town and country. It was not until the tenth century that the crumbling empire was reconsolidated under the first Saxon emperor Henry and above all under Otto the Great. From the East Frankish Empire evolved the Holy Roman Empire of the German Nation and from the West Frankish Empire came France. Both parts of the Empire now began to lead a life of their own, a development which was soon mirrored in their architecture. The political and artistic centers in the East Frankish Empire shifted eastwards, to Saxony, the homeland of the Ottonian Emperors. Everywhere architecture began to flourish. Around the beginning of the new millennium most bishoprics consecrated new cathedrals, for example Mainz, Trier, Regensburg, Bamberg, Basel, Strasbourg and Constance. Today, however, there are only isolated fragments of Ottonian architecture still remaining. The buildings in the Ottonian domain now developed a style of their own. It was no longer merely a matter of imitating and reshaping Classical and early Christian antiquity, but also of finding a new, independent approach. So it was that around the year 1000 a distinctly new type of church was developed, the transept basilica with nave and two aisles and a square crossing separated from the nave and transept by four arches.

In 955, the year of the victory over the Hungarians at Lechfeld, Otto the Great commissioned the building of the cathedral at Magdeburg, which was to become the metropolitan church of the new archbishopric. Otto the Great wanted to emulate the Carolingian tradition, and, for the building of this church, he had magnificent columns with marble and granite shafts brought from Italy. After the fire at the Cathedral in 1207 these columns were built into the wall screens of the chancel as a sign of reverence for Otto the Great.

Gernrode and Hildesheim – the capitals of Ottonian architecture

St. Cyriakus in Gernrode in the Harz is the oldest preserved large building in the Ottonian style. The nunnery was established in 961 by Margrave Gero. Apart from some remains of late Romanesque cloisters, the monastery buildings have been lost. The church itself was changed in the twelfth century by the construction of a west choir and the heightening of the west towers. The exterior parts in the Ottonian style which are still preserved are hardly articulated. It is only the large round-arched windows which alleviate the heaviness of the eastern apse. The important characteristic of the architecture of this period is the lack of a plinth, although because of the changes made in the nineteenth century this fact can only be appreciated in the eastern apse. This typical early design characteristic makes the edifice appear to rise very abruptly out of the ground.

The ground plan of the church consists of a nave and two aisles with a slightly kinked axis. The originally continuous transept in the eastern part

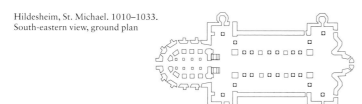

Hildesheim, St. Michael. 1010–1033.
South-eastern view, ground plan

Essen Cathedral, the former collegiate
church Sts. Cosmas and Damian. Western
apse modeled on Aachen. Mid eleventh
century

Reichenau, Oberzell, former collegiate
church of St. George. Looking down
nave in easterly direction with Ottonian
murals

does not quite join at right angles to the nave, suggesting a certain inaccuracy on the part of the builders. Originally the crossing was not regular in shape. Today's regular shape is the result of a nineteenth-century restoration. Access from the transept is gained via steps to the elevated choir, with its forechoir bay and semi-circular apse, and to the hall crypt situated under the choir. Two small apses in the two east walls of the transept wing complement the east choir. Compared with the architecture of the Carolingian period, the interior of St. Cyriakus is endowed with a superiority and a greater generosity of shape and proportion (photo page 40, top left). Both forms of support, the column and the pier, find much greater use, and support the arcade arches which open up the nave to the aisles. By the use of columns and piers a clear rhythm is brought into the construction of the nave wall. Halfway along the nave a rectangular pier divides the arcade into two. On both sides of the pier there are two archway openings with columns. By means of the central rectangular pier not only the wall but also the whole interior of the nave and aisles is divided into two areas of equal size. The gallery area, too, mirrors this division of space, although the openings there are smaller.

Each of the double arcades in the galleries is surmounted by a single large semi-circular arch, although the gallery storey has a different rhythm than the arcade zone. Three double arcades of the galleries correspond to one double arcade of the arcade floor. What is similar is the strong division of the wall by means of a central pier. This system of division is not continued right up into the uppermost storey, the clerestory. Its windows are set into the wall without any alignment to the storeys below. The

inconsistency in the construction is strongly reminiscent of the Carolingian with its variety of experimental styles. Just as with the clerestory windows, so it is with the opening of the eastern apse, which is cut very abruptly out of the eastern wall of the forechoir. The clear and sure division of the nave walls, on the other hand, is emphatically not Carolingian. The Ottonian architecture no longer conceives of the nave walls as continuous rows of arcades. The arcading is now interrupted, the wall has a rhythmical repeating pattern and particular parts are emphasized. In Carolingian architecture it is only on the exterior that we find the tendency to stress particular elements by the projection of certain features. In the interior, the inclusion of galleries was new, and furthermore characteristic of nunneries, where the sisters of the order had special separate rooms reserved for their use. The prototype for the galleries is probably to be found in Byzantine architecture. The capitals in the arcading are still beholden to the style of the classical Corinthian column, although they are already showing a certain independence in their representation of human heads, until then an unusual feature.

Ottonian architecture reached a peak in the former Benedictine monastery church of St. Michael in Hildesheim (photos, pp. 40–41). In 996 the Hildesheim Bishop Bernward, a keen patron of the arts, brought Benedictines from Cologne to Hildesheim and in 1010 began the construction of a church dedicated to St. Michael. The building was completed in 1033. It is assumed that Bishop Bernward, who had traveled widely in France and Italy, himself participated in the planning of the church. Later reconstructions have interfered with the original structure of

Ottmarsheim, Alsace, former nunnery church,
from the third decade of the eleventh century.
View from the south-east (above),
interior view of the octagon (below)

this building even more severely than is the case in Gernrode. Moreover the edifice experienced the most severe destruction in the Second World War, and today's structure is the result of the post-war rebuilding. The basilica, which has a nave and two aisles, a double choir and two transepts, is attractive for the balance of its construction, which culminates in towers at both its eastern and western ends. Compared with Gernrode, St. Michael in Hildesheim is much more balanced in its design. This balance can even be perceived in the ground plan: transepts are added to both the eastern and western ends of the nave. As the nave and the transepts are of the same width, their point of intersection, the crossing, is square in form. The crossing square is repeated three times in the nave, making it the basis of the proportioning of the building. This regular square crossing opens out to all four sides with the same height and breadth. The nave and transepts with their crossing arches with alternate masonry layers thus achieve a completely new spatial relationship one to another. Although the essential features of this design conception were present in the Carolingian period in the St. Gallen monastery plan, it was only implemented for the first time in St. Michael in Hildesheim. Nevertheless, the fact that the side aisles are considerably broader than half the width of the nave shows that the quadratic concept has not been carried out in its purest form. The corner points of the three ground plan squares in the nave are marked by piers. Each pier is connected to the next by three semi-circular arches resting on two columns. By this arrangement of piers and columns, an alternation of supports is achieved, which in this form, pier-column-column-pier, is known as Saxon alternating supports. The alternation in the form pier-column-pier, on the other hand, is known as the Rhenish alternation of supports after the area where this form mainly occurs. The inscriptions on the imposts, each with the names of the three saints, are intended to convey the idea that the saints, symbolized by the columns, support the kingdom of heaven, symbolized by the church. This symbolism is also to be found in the Magdeburg cathedral of Otto the Great. By means of the alternation of piers and columns the space is broken down into regular patterns and split into three areas.

Here it is different from Gernrode, where the nave wall is divided in two parts by a single pier. In Hildesheim a horizontal reglet runs above the arcade and above this a smooth area of wall ascends up to the clerestory, whose windows are also not aligned to the arches below. A flat ceiling closes off the evenly proportioned nave.

The few remaining capitals from the time of Bishop Bernward are so-called cushion capitals in clear simple forms, which no longer hark back to classical tradition, but which represent a new development in Ottonian architecture.

A notable feature of the Ottonian period is the predilection for flat walls. The walls were as uninterrupted as possible by features such as openings and windows. The spaces were clearly delineated and the surfaces sparingly articulated. The most important decorative feature was the different layers on all the arches in the church, where the architecture was accentuated by alternating red and light-colored stones on the arch intrados.

OPPOSITE LEFT
Soest, collegiate church of St. Patroklus.
West tower. Around 1200

OPPOSITE RIGHT
Paderborn, Cathedral of St. Maria,
SS. Liborius and Kilian. West tower.
Around 1220

The incorporation of Carolingian architectural concepts in a new idiom

How the exterior was incorporated into the articulation in the Ottonian period is impressively demonstrated by the westwork of St. Pantaleon in Cologne (photo, p. 38). St. Pantaleon was begun in 964 by Archbishop Bruno and consecrated in 980. This archaic-looking building with its broad, squat nave and subdued transepts had a steeply towering westwork added to its western end, an almost centrally dominated space with a square ground plan. The steeply rising central spaces are surrounded on the west, south and north sides by galleries. The space opens out east towards the nave in a high wide semi-circular arch which is built in alternating layers. In St. Pantaleon the Carolingian idea of the westwork finds its Ottonian descendant.

Apart from the basic concept of the westwork there are no other traces of the Carolingian. The traditional westwork was completely translated into the Ottonian. This is evident from the exterior which reveals a desire for a new articulation. Each storey of the façade of the westwork is articulated by means of lesenes, which are connected to one another by friezes of semi-circular arcading. These small semi-circles, which are laid on the wall like a flat relief, appear somewhat lacking in boldness. They simply protrude from the wall, not on consoles as became customary later. The blind articulation and the arcade frieze represent the beginning of medieval architectural articulation. The exterior is thus endowed with a fine relief which can be used to decorate all the way round in a new idiom.

Carolingian designs are also employed in the former convent church in Essen. It was begun at the end of the tenth century by the Abbess Mathilde and consecrated in the middle of the eleventh century. Whilst the west block from the Ottonian period has remained intact (photo, p. 42), the nave was converted into a hall church. Even if the exterior of the Essen monastery gives the appearance of a westwork, it is in reality a west choir, the end of a church nave or aisle. This is a new feature: the combination of the westwork and the west choir. In this case the west block encloses the west choir, whose interior elevation is modeled on the octagon of the Palatine church at Aachen. The ground plan describes three sides of a hexagon, around which are grouped various small, randomly placed rooms in the ground and gallery storeys. Based on the Aachen model, the piers with their inwardly angled faces have arcade openings. Above these, and separated by a cornice, there are high semi-circular openings with columns inserted in them, as in Aachen. Similar to St. Michael in Hildesheim or St. Pantaleon in Cologne the arch intrados are built alternately. A light semi-dome spans the apse. The return to the architecture of the Aachen Palatinate Chapel was deliberate. This is shown not only by the whole composition of the west choir, but is also evidenced by the small details such as the classical Ionic or Corinthian capitals.

A further, indeed even clearer, exploitation of the Aachen architectural conception is to be found on the Upper Rhine, in the former nunnery church in Ottmarsheim in Alsace. In its ground plan and elevation Ottmarsheim is a simplified imitation of the Palatine Chapel of Charlemagne. The octagonal, centrally planned building, erected in the third decade of the eleventh century, is also encircled by an octagonal ambulatory. In the west there is a single-tower front, whilst the east has a small rectangular choir with a gallery. Although both buildings, Aachen and Ottmarsheim, have similar interiors, the detail at Ottmarsheim reflects the *Zeitgeist* of the Ottonian, and has abandoned any vestiges of the classical idiom. The columns have cushion capitals, and the individual vaulted sections are clearly separated by transverse arches. The impression of space has become much more balanced and tranquil. The central space and ambulatory have been given a strong interrelationship. Overall, the building appears much simpler and more cube-shaped.

Towers and groups of towers

Inspired by the Aachen model, the western end of the church at Ottmarsheim was given greater prominence by means of a tower. It was not only at Ottmarsheim that towers were built during the Ottonian period, but also at many other churches such as the small former monastery church of St. Cyriak in Sulzburg and the St. Luzius church in Werden. Under Abbot Berno the west block of Reichenau-Mittelzell was built after 1006, a quadratic tower structure, which is articulated by long lesenes and semi-circular arcade friezes. At Trier cathedral under Archbishop Poppo around 1040, the towers and apse were combined to form a west block (photo, p. 23). The result was a complex, richly articulated structure with four towers and central gable, in which the huge apse is framed by solid four-cornered towers with round staircase turrets attached.

One of the most impressive towers is surely that of the Ottonian cathedral of Bishop Meinwerk in Paderborn (photo, p. 45). According to the latest research the whole west end was developed around 1220, and not in the late Ottonian period, as had previously been assumed. However, the tower clearly reproduces a previous Ottonian tower in structure and outer appearance. Designed to draw attention to the choir and the cathedral, the powerful tower ascends dramatically without a plinth from the ground up into the sky, flanked on either side up to half its height by round stairway turrets. Above all it had a symbolic function, advertising the importance of the bishop's church far out into the surrounding countryside. This mighty edifice dominates the skyline of the town, almost threateningly proclaiming who was the ruler over its inhabitants.

The collegiate church of St. Patroklus in Soest was also endowed with just such a mighty single tower shortly before 1200 (photo, p. 45). This was, however, not erected by the canons, but by the citizens who had grown wealthy by means of trade and built to assert the independence of the town from the canons. The tower contained the town armoury, and in its narthex was the court porch and above it the council chamber. Single tower fronts, constructed particularly at the west end, were characteristic of parish churches in the following centuries. Bishops' or monastery churches almost always had fronts with double towers or west choirs.

The towers, which rose high above their surroundings, were able to send a powerful and visible message. Dominating their area, they were considerable status symbols, proof of who had the greatest influence in a town. The citizens, by whatever means they had become rich, erected a tower as a sign of independence from church domination of the land.

Speyer, Cathedral of St. Maria and St. Stephan. Nave looking east. 1027/30–1061

Speyer, Cathedral of St. Maria and St. Stephan. Hall crypt. Around 1030

OPPOSITE
Speyer, Cathedral of St. Maria and St. Stephan. View from the north-east

High Romanesque architecture from the Salian period

The architecture developed under the Ottonian Emperors was further consolidated under the Salians. The great creative act of Ottonian architecture, the development of a characteristic ground plan, was taken further. Indeed, a new independent style evolved, which clearly differed from the Ottonian. The problem of vaulting was one of the most important architectural challenges to be overcome. Never before or since have buildings of such monumentality been constructed as in the course of the eleventh century under the Salian emperors or at the monastery of Cluny in Burgundy. In the architecture of these two important sacred buildings of the eleventh century, Speyer cathedral, started by the Salians, and the abbey church of the Burgundian reform monastery at Cluny, there is a clear expression of the struggle between papacy and empire over the problems connected with the Investiture Contest. Speyer, an edifice of unprecedented monumentality, became the embodiment of unlimited imperial power, a testament to the self-esteem of the Salian emperors. The cathedral was the expression of the idea of Christian world domination, an expression of a style of rule, which, according to Stefan Weinfurter is characterized by "the all-pervading power of the Empire, the creation of imperial unity with a firm hand, the strict control of the imperial church and the increased magnificence of its rule through the dignity of the Emperor."

The imperial cathedral at Speyer – a pioneer of vaulting in Germany

According to Ordericus Vitalis, Speyer under the Salians became the "Metropolis Germaniae," one of the most important places in the medieval German Empire. Four Salian Emperors and two of their consorts found their last resting places in the cathedral. The monumental Speyer Cathedral was begun between 1027 and 1030 under Emperor Conrad II and was completed under Henry IV. After the heavy destruction inflicted in the seventeenth century the building remained a ruin until the end of the eighteenth century, when Ignaz Michael Neumann reconstructed the west block in Classical-Romanesque style. However, in 1794 the cathedral was devastated again, and in the early nineteenth century was even earmarked for demolition. It was only saved from destruction by a decree from Napoleon. In the nineteenth century Heinrich Hübsch carried out its restoration, replacing the western end with the westblock which still stands today and which is faithful to the original Salian conception.

New research has established interesting information about the history of the building of the medieval sections. The oldest part of the church, begun between 1027 and 1030, is the east crypt, to which the towers flanking the choir and the foundations of an initial transept were added. By around 1035 the above-ground construction was probably underway with the completion of the sanctuary and transept. Between 1035 and 1040 the piers of the nave, initially designed to be short, were erected close together, and the outer walls of the aisles and the barrel-vaulting of the chancel were constructed. Only after 1045/47, after the death of Conrad II, was the nave extended to its present length under Henry III. At its consecration in 1061 the nave section, the west front and the towers must

Mainz, Cathedral of St. Martin and St. Stephan. View from the east. 1081–1137

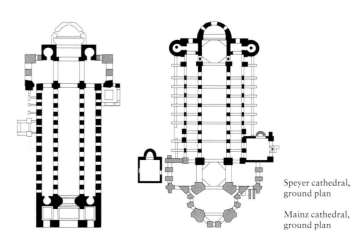

Speyer cathedral, ground plan

Mainz cathedral, ground plan

already have been completed. Until recently it had been assumed that the original Speyer Cathedral was designed only to have vaulting in the aisles, but the latest research suggests that the building begun by Conrad II would have had a huge transverse barrel vault, spanning almost 45 feet, if technical problems had not prevented its execution. The planned transverse barrel vault with windows at its base was modeled on the monastery church at Tournus in Burgundy. The reason for the architects' failure was the excessive width of the nave. As the execution of the stone barrel vaulting was unsuccessful, the building is likely to have been spanned with a wooden vault, for only cross vaulting and relief would have closed off the interior in a manner which was convincing and appropriate to the design and construction of the nave walls.

Problems with the unstable underlying ground in such close proximity to the Rhine must soon have led to damage to the building, as Emperor Henry IV was forced to undertake fundamental renovation of the cathedral soon after its consecration. The bishops Benno of Osnabrück and later Otto of Bamberg were appointed to carry out the imperial commission. In the second phase of building the choir and transept were rebuilt, although the original dimensions were entirely preserved. The major achievement was above all the successful vaulting of the nave. Strong lesenes were attached to the wall projection on every other pier to carry the barrel arches of the vaults. Broad semicircular columns with Corinthian capitals were in turn placed on the lesenes and from these sprang the transverse arches dividing the individual vaulted sections. The nave is thus divided into six bays, each nave bay corresponding to two aisle bays. This relationship of the nave to the aisle bays is known in German as the "gebundenes System." To the eastern side of the nave are attached the transept, the forechoir, flanked by staircase turrets, and the semi-circular apse, and to the western side is the westblock, rebuilt in the spirit of the Salian design concept.

Compared with St. Michael's church at Hildesheim (photos, pp. 40–41), Speyer Cathedral has walls of unprecedented solidity and weight. The walls with their strong relief are richly modeled and powerfully developed in all dimensions. Piers, which are terminated by a simple cornice, carry the nave arcading, over which the clerestory windows are for the first time brought into alignment. Even the windows of the aisles are on the same axis. Such consistent articulation had been absent in Ottonian architecture. The step of bringing into alignment all the windows from the clerestory to the aisles was of the greatest significance for subsequent architecture as it was only then that the vaulting of a whole nave became possible. This arrangement of windows along an axis implied a move towards a more vertical form of articulation and a decline in the significance of the horizontal.

The large, flat semi-circular arch recesses which surround the arcades and windows also emphasize the vertical articulation. These arch recesses are repeated thirteen times in the nave. On the piers between the individual bays there are semicircular projections which rise from plinths with Attic bases. The semicircular pillars terminate in cushion capitals from whose entablatures spring round arches framing the flat blind recesses of the

Mainz, Cathedral of St. Martin and St. Stephan. Nave looking east

Mainz, Cathedral of St. Martin and St. Stephan. Dwarf gallery on the eastern apse

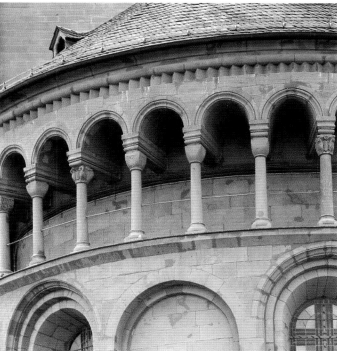

wall. By dint of this system of articulation the nave walls take on a relief of measured and sculptured volume. In this scheme the blind recesses serve to highlight the steepness of the upwardly striving nave.

Modeling of the walls – blind recesses and dwarf galleries

Despite the small alterations undertaken, the east parts of Speyer Cathedral are still amongst the most impressive examples of medieval architecture in existence today. Responds which articulate the apse rise above a high plinth. The responds support semi-circular arches above which there is a dwarf gallery, an uninterrupted row of small column arcades which run in front of a passageway just below the edge of the roof. The dwarf gallery resumes above the transepts and the nave walls. Here, however, it is divided rhythmically by sections of wall which mark the bay separations. Plinths, responds, blind arches and dwarf galleries all serve to model the walls and detract from the heaviness of the upper parts of the building. Previously a central portal opened out from the nave into the west block. It was not simply cut out of the wall, but was recessed and narrowed towards the center (see p. 30). This recessed portal segmented the wall into several layers and served clearly to emphasize the solidity of the masonry. This was the first use of such a recessed portal, but this design subsequently appeared on almost all larger churches.

In 1081 under Emperor Henry IV the cathedral at Mainz was built, a basilica with a nave, aisles and groin vaults. The old cathedral, erected by bishops Willigis and Bardo, had burnt down in 1081. The new structure was consecrated in 1137. The appearance of the Salian western end of Mainz Cathedral is not known. It is unclear whether there was a similar structure on the site of today's late Hohenstaufen west choir. At the east end the nave terminates in a semi-circular apse, whilst the aisles have flat ends with flanking stair turrets from the first cathedral. In front of the apse is built a square bay surmounted by a sail vault. This appears as a tower on the exterior of the building. This ground plan arrangement, similar to a crossing, suggests a transept, but in fact the two aisles are continued on both sides. Each of the five bays in the nave corresponds to two slightly transverse rectangular bays in the aisles. Groin vaults span the aisles. Originally the nave was similarly vaulted, but the Salian groin vaults were replaced by Gothic rib vaults. At Mainz vaulting of the nave was part of the plan from the very conception. This is clear from the clerestory windows, which are not aligned with the arcades. Instead they are clustered in pairs and thereby take account of the vaulting. The nave walls of Mainz Cathedral are articulated by shallow round-arched recesses which rise above the nave piers and extend to just below the clerestory windows. On every other pier there is a semicircular pilaster, which supports one of the transverse arches of the nave vaulting. In comparison with Speyer Cathedral the articulation is much flatter and relief-like, and as

Hersfeld, ruins of the former Benedictine monastery church of St. Wigbert, St. Simon and Judas Thadäus. Built after 1038. Transept and apse

a result the impression of space does not achieve the tension and liveliness of Speyer.

Twin-towered fronts – status symbols of great bishops' and monastery churches

In 1015 a Salian reconstruction of Strasbourg Minster was begun under Bishop Werinher. It was a long, colonnaded basilica with nave and two aisles, attached transept and semi-circular apse. Parts of the choir and the underlying spacious and monumental hall crypt are all that now remain of this building. The long, colonnaded basilica had its origins in early Christian buildings, but its length corresponds to today's Gothic construction. Remains of Salian walls in the Gothic west front suggest that already in the eleventh century there was possibly a twin-towered front with a portico in between. The Cathedral of Our Lady at Constance, and Basel Cathedral begun under Emperor Henry II, both episcopal churches, likewise had twin-towered fronts. This type of front was characteristic of cathedrals and great monastery churches.

From around 1025, at about the same time as the construction by Conrad II of Speyer, the cathedral church of Limburg-on-the-Haardt was begun. The church, whose west front also had a twin-tower, was completed in 1045 and is today an impressive ruin (photo, p. 51). Still preserved are the outer walls of the nave, parts of the column bases in the nave, and the crypt and walls of the choir in the east. The basilica with a nave, aisles and east transept has a crossing separated from the nave and transept by four arches. Instead of a semi-circular apse, the eastern end of the chancel is flat. In the architecture of the Upper Rhine the flat chancel end was a common feature, and was indeed developed in this region. This type of chancel is already to be found in Reichenau-Oberzell and Constance Cathedral. In both buildings a semi-circular apse was covered

by a rectangular wall. Later the flat chancel end was to become one of the characteristic features of the so-called Hirsau School of Architecture. The side aisles of the monastery church of Limburg-on-the-Haardt were not vaulted as at Speyer, but closed by flat ceilings, thereby remaining truer to the tradition of the monastery church. There was a conscious decision not to adopt the modern architectural form of the vault. The eastern parts of the church are richly articulated. Shallow recesses, showing less relief than in Speyer, rise above a plinth. Both its rich exterior articulation over a plinth which runs around the building, and the twin-tower front, make the monastery church of Limburg-on-the-Haardt a typical example of Salian architecture. The whole building is given a monumental quality by expansive articulation comparable to Speyer Cathedral. Nothing remains here of the tranquil prostrate shape of Ottonian architecture, it has made way for an upward striving for height.

After a catastrophic fire the monastery church in Hersfeld was rebuilt from 1038 onwards. Destroyed in the eighteenth century, it is amongst the most impressive monastery ruins in Germany (photo, left). The basilica with nave and two aisles has a projecting Roman transept in the east with side apses, behind which the nave extends to form a long choir with a semi-circular apse. The nave was separated from the side aisles by nine round-arched column arcades, whose arches rested on heavy cushion capitals. In the west an elevated choir rose up, its raised apse situated above a rectangular entrance hall. The entrance front and west choir were perhaps combined here as a reference to the old concept of the westwork. The nave of the church had a flat ceiling.

That is only one of several features of an older style present in the Hersfeld church. Features which look back to previous ages, such as the Roman transept, are not just explained by the re-use of parts of the old walls, but are a conscious borrowing from the past. Just as in Hersfeld, the cathedral in Strasbourg had a long projecting transept, which was reminiscent of the early Christian basilicas. The concept of the colonnaded basilica is furthermore very much in the early Christian tradition. Even though many of the features of the Hersfeld monastery church may be borrowings from the past, it is nevertheless very much a church of its time, and a creation typical of Salian architecture. Isolated motifs which refer back to the past do not hide the fact that the essential overall nature of this architecture is one which addresses us in large forms which clearly relate to one another.

Rhenish School of Architecture – triapsal choirs in Cologne and the Rhineland

The Rhineland became one of the most important centers for innovation in architecture in the eleventh century. In particular, the old bishop's seat of Cologne developed into a significant center of architectural creation with St. Maria im Kapitol as one of the principal artistic highpoints (photo, above). The construction of this church stands at the beginning of what became known as the Rhenish School of Architecture. The most striking feature of this church, which suffered heavy destruction in the Second World War, is its ground plan which was conceived with an

Limburg-on-the-Haard, ruin of the
former Benedictine abbey. 1025–1045.
Interior view, view from the air (above
right), view from east (below right)

Cologne, St. Maria im Kapitol, view of
the triapsal choir.
1040–1049, or 1065

Cologne, St. Aposteln, first third of the
eleventh century. Eastern parts after
1192. View from the north-east

unprecedented completeness of form. Of particular note is the so-called
triapsal choir, which is attached to a nave and two aisles. In this building
there is not only an apse at the eastern end, but the semi-circular apse is
also repeated in the south and north instead of transepts.

The ground plan is therefore trefoil-shaped. The three semi-circular
apses are integrated by means of an ambulatory joining them together, so
that the apses and crossing all appear part of a united spatial whole. This
ambulatory leads into the side aisles of the nave. It may be that the trefoil
pattern created by the three apses is a reference back to the Roman burial
site, and yet the unity achieved by the continuation of the ambulatory into
the aisles is above all a Salian concept which seeks to integrate everything
into one context. Here the transept has developed into part of the choir
and has become a fundamental part of the sanctuary. The aisles and the
ambulatory of the triapsal choir are groin vaulted, whilst the three arms of
the cross in front of the apses are barrel vaulted. The crossing is crowned
by a sail vault, a type of vaulting later often found in the Rhineland. The
nave originally had a flat ceiling. The vaulting existing today dates from
the late Romanesque period, or represents, as do many other parts of the
building, a reconstruction after the terrible devastation of the war. In the
choir there are columns with cushion capitals with a more cube-shaped
and taut form compared with those in Hildesheim. The western side of the
church of St. Maria im Kapitol probably dates from an earlier period and,
with its rectangular projecting structure and stair turrets placed at the
corners, is reminiscent of St. Pantaleon (photo, p. 38). Despite war
damage, the Salian wall articulation is still to be found in the lower parts
of the choir, where a high plinth is terminated by a powerful cornice.
Above the plinth, shallow recesses articulate the wall. The parts of the wall
above this are attributed to the Hohenstaufen period. A sense of free space
and a melding of the individual parts of the interior characterize this
building, which has a very early example of a choir ambulatory. This
concept of the choir ambulatory was borrowed from France (St. Martin in
Tours) and was only taken up again much later at St. Godehard in
Hildesheim (see p. 25).

A golden age of late Salian architecture on the Upper Rhine

The monastery church of Murbach in Alsace (photo, p. 55) is one of the
greatest achievements of late Salian architecture. The nave and the aisles
with their flat ceilings were demolished in the eighteenth century. The
eastern parts which adjoined them, and still stand today, date from the
eleventh century. The transept is only apparent from the exterior as it is
obscured by the chapels built in the interior. The nave extends, uninterrupted by the transept, right up to the choir with its flat termination. The
main choir is flanked on both sides by side chancels, which open out onto
the former with double arcades, a feature borrowed from Cluny. The main
choir and side chancels both end with a flat termination typical of the
Upper Rhine, and square towers are built above the transept wings. Like
the eastern end of Speyer, the east choir of Murbach is truly monumental
in its effect. The lower level of the main choir and side chancels are
articulated by high, steep blind arcades. Deep windows have been cut into
the stone of the blind recesses. Each layer has been worked out of the wall.
Towards the middle the articulation is accentuated with the central
window slightly higher and broader than the lateral windows, producing
the effect of a delicate rhythm. The area above the upper windows is from
the Hohenstaufen period, and dates from as late as the second half of the
twelfth century. The individual parts are fine and created with the greatest
care and attention. Particularly splendid and of monumental effect is the
accurately layered ashlar or square hewn masonry. Originating in
Burgundy, it is one of the earliest examples of its kind in Germany. In
Alsace this type of masonry is also to be found at Marmoutier
(Mauersmünster), where one of the latest Romanesque western ends has
been preserved (photo, p. 54 left).

53

Marmoutier (Mauersmünster), Alsace,
western end, mid twelfth century

OPPOSITE
Murbach, Alsace, former monastery
church.
East parts, around 1130

BELOW
Calw-Hirsau, owl tower (left) with
sculptural decoration (detail right).
Early twelfth century

Hirsau School of Architecture

The Benedictine Order underwent a profound renewal in the tenth century which was inspired by the monastery of Cluny in Burgundy. The main centers for this reform of the Order in Germany were the Black Forest monasteries of Hirsau and St. Blasien, and in Switzerland the monastery of Einsiedeln. The full effect of the reform became felt in the second half of the eleventh century, and its spiritual ethos was reflected in the architecture by a return to the early Christian. This was evident in the construction of Cluny II, where at the end of the tenth century arcades of columns were erected in the style of the early Christian basilicas. It was in the same spirit that parts of the Hirsau reform monasteries were designed and built for the liturgy, albeit with some regional variations. From 1059–1071 a basilica with nave and two side aisles, twin-tower front, transept and chapels in echelon was built in Hirsau over the tomb of St. Aurelius. Only the nave of this church is still extant. Its choir termination with three echeloned apses has been uncovered and recorded in excavations. In the twelfth century the church was rebuilt, and columns and heavy cushion capitals added.

A new monastery complex including the St. Peter and Paul church was begun under Abbot Wilhelm in 1082 and consecrated in 1091. In 1692 the monastery was destroyed. Only the northern west tower of the antechurch was spared, and this actually dates from the first half of the twelfth century. Nevertheless the ground plan of the church is still clearly visible. St. Peter and Paul was another example of a colonnaded basilica with a nave, two side aisles and transept with small apses constructed on the east side. A square choir bay with lateral choirs on both sides adjoined the

crossing. The lateral choirs represented an extension of the aisles across and beyond the transept. The main choir had a flat termination. In the nave, the crossing square provided the basis of the proportioning of the edifice. After the crossing the columns of the nave do not resume immediately, but to the west of the cross-shaped crossing piers there is a further pair of columns on a cruciform ground plan. In the area of this first nave bay the aisles were barrel-vaulted, whilst the other areas of the church had flat ceilings. This pronounced bay in front of the crossing is peculiar to the Hirsau churches, indeed it is a typical characteristic of other buildings based on the Hirsau style such as Alpirsbach in the Black Forest (photo, p. 56 above), All Saints in Schaffhausen or Paulinzella in Thuringia (photo, right). The spatial discontinuity of the first nave bay can be understood as the architectural expression of liturgical functions. It was here that the area reserved for the monks, namely the choir, ended. The easterly choir area, which included the transept and crossing, was where the monks took part in the church service, and is known as the "chorus maior." The "chorus minor" adjoins the latter in the direction of the nave. In churches of the Hirsau School, it is recognizable by the piers in the nave. The "chorus minor" was probably also marked off from the nave by a sanctuary rail. The "chorus minor" was a part of the Cluniac church layout and was determined by the liturgy, for it was here that the monks not involved in the canonical office participated in the service.

The monastery churches of Alpirsbach, Allerheiligen (All Saints) in Schaffhausen and the monastery ruin in Paulinzella are impressive expressions of the spiritual ethos of the Hirsau Reform Order and its school of architecture. These churches exemplify the monumental architecture of this order. Decorative details are almost entirely dispensed with, but it is in the very absence of this decoration that the effect of this architecture lies; it appears monumental rather than merely sober. In their steep proportioning, these box-like naves correspond to the spatial conception of the great imperial cathedrals of Speyer and Mainz.

Common to all church architecture of this period in Germany is the sheer steepness of the inner spaces, together with a monumentality which is the very essence of Salian architecture. The spiritual tension between the emperor and the papacy is all-pervasive in this age. It finds its clearest expression in the opposition of two buildings such as the cathedral at Speyer and the monastery church at Alpirsbach. Both buildings represent highly sophisticated architecture, but are quite different in character. Speyer is the monumental imperial claim to authority down to the smallest detail and decoration, whilst Alpirsbach, Schaffhausen or Paulinzella encapsulate the greatest possible clarity and simplicity.

Worms, Cathedral St. Peter, west choir,
end of the twelfth century

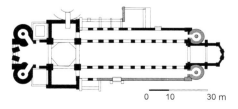

Worms, St. Peter Cathedral. Ground plan

Late Romanesque architecture in the Hohenstaufen age

The Staufen period includes the whole twelfth century and the early thirteenth, and its artistic masterpieces are to be found in Germany and Italy. The nobility and the knights were now beginning to be the patrons of culture. In Germany the artistic centers continued to be on the Rhine, as they were during Carolingian and Salian times. It was in Cologne, the middle and upper Rhine, as well as the Saxony of Henry the Lion that the pioneering buildings of the new style were developing. Initially still very much rooted in the Salian style, it was not until the later stages of the Staufen period, the early thirteenth century, that the Staufen style reached its peak in an intensive dialogue with the architecture of French vaulting. The exterior structures are often dominated by tower groupings of equal weight at the eastern and western ends, and the fronts are articulated with a much greater sense of depth and three-dimensionality. The main elements of articulation are small pairs or rows of arches, which in their turn are spanned by larger arches. The lines of the walls are broken down by means of blind arches and rows of columns which are recessed inwards in several individual stepped layers.

Maria Laach – the embodiment of a Staufen monastery church

The very essence of the fully formed Romanesque church has been preserved at the Benedictine abbey of Maria Laach (founded in 1093) in the Eifel (figure, p. 59). The west choir, nave and crypt were completed in 1156, whilst the east choir did not see completion until 1177. The atrium in front of the west choir, moreover, is an addition of the thirteenth century. The basilica has a nave with five transverse rectangular bays, two side aisles each with five rectangular bays, and double transepts. This differs from the system where the proportions are based on the crossing square as module (the "gebundenes System," see p. 48). The church was designed right from the beginning to incorporate vaulting, although the vaulting of non-square bays did cause problems. The vaulting has the appearance of a longitudinal barrel, into which curved undersurfaces for lunettes have been cut. Compared with Speyer Cathedral, the interior space is noticeably heavy and low. Arcade arches and clerestory windows are cut abruptly into the walls with no articulation in between. Characteristic of the early period of Staufen architecture is the sturdy, powerful elevation and the strict uniformity of the walls. The exterior is a typical structure with its tower groupings above the east and west choirs, each carefully balancing the other. Slim, high towers over square ground plans rise in the spandrel between the east choir and transept. An octagonal broken tower crowns the crossing. Round towers are attached to the ends of the western transept, and above the crossing stands a square tower, crowned by a roof of four rhombi. Both choirs have been consciously designed to stand out with their massive, clustered, towering structures. The result is a rich contrast of varying stereometric forms. Narrow, flat lesenes subdivide the surfaces of the exterior into upright rectangular areas terminated at the top by round arch friezes. Their Staufen character can be clearly seen in the round-arched friezes which do not simply project from the walls as in Salian architecture, but rest on small corbels. There is an obvious pleasure

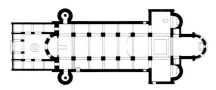

Maria Laach, Benedictine monastery
church. View from the northwest,
ground plan. 1156 and 1177 (east choir)
completed

Rosheim, Alsace, parish church of
St. Peter and Paul. Third quarter of
the twelfth century.
View from the southwest

here in enlivening the surface with small decorative detail. Each individual shape or group, whether lesenes, round-arched friezes or blind arches, is integrated into a unit of great strength and tension.

Masonry as a plastic material

This fondness for groups of towering structures is taken further in Worms Cathedral, which was built shortly after 1120–30 (photo, p. 58). The whole building must have been completed by 1181 except for the west choir. The smallest and last of the three imperial cathedrals to be completed, it is the most unified stylistically and the clearest example of the late Staufen concept of architecture. The basilica with a nave and two aisles is erected using the crossing square as a basis for the proportioning of the building, that is to say, that there is a ratio of five square nave bays to ten side aisle bays. In the east there is a transept, which continues into a quadratic forechoir bay with a narrower, semi-circular apse. The east apse is not visible on the exterior, because the east choir is closed off by a straight wall and flanked on the edges by round towers. In the west the nave ends in a polygonal choir termination, which is also flanked by round towers. The latter lie in the line of the side aisles. The polygonal choir termination was a new feature, as until this time there had only been semi-circular apses or flat terminated choirs. The polygonal choir is an architectural feature originating in France which only became widespread

in Germany at the beginning of the thirteenth century. The immediate prototype for Worms is taken to be the choir of Basel Cathedral. Despite the relatively short period of construction, the interior of Worms Cathedral is not uniform, but this does not detract from the effect of space. Its elevation is based on the imperial cathedrals of Speyer and Mainz. The interior space is dominated by the massively heavy piers and the great quadripartite rib vaults which spring from torus capitals with richly molded cornices. Angular and rounded responds afford the wall a strong relief. The influence of Alsace and Burgundy is evident in the east choir with its stone band rib vaults, and in the later molded band rib vaults of the nave. It is in the west choir that the latest stage of Staufen architecture is to be found. Here masonry has been developed to its maximum potential. The stonework has evolved into a substance which can be sculptured, and in which individual parts are modeled. Even more striking is the fondness for decorating breaks in the wall and for covering uniform parts of the exterior wall with ornament.

The surface of the building is characterized by a skilful play of light and shadow, brought about by the strongly sculptured execution of the individual parts, particularly the dwarf galleries. For all that, the wall is not supposed to appear lighter in effect, rather the power of the wall was to be emphasized. It is an almost unarchitectural late style which is embodied in the west choir of Worms Cathedral and is equally charac-

Bamberg, Cathedral St. Peter and
George. Consecrated in 1237

Basel, minster, former cathedral St.
Maria, today Protestant
parish church. After 1185. Nave, wall
elevation

teristic of the west choir of Mainz Cathedral. The sculpturally modeled
walls are broken up by means of recesses and galleries, penetrated by
windows, but nevertheless retain their solidity. These examples of late
Romanesque architecture date from a time when the great high Gothic
cathedrals were already being erected in France.

Centers of Staufen architecture in the southern upper Rhine

In Alsace, one of the heartlands of the Staufen emperors, there were many
new churches built in the twelfth century, common to all of which was the
use of rib vaulting. A characteristic feature of the architectural landscape
was the contrasting relationship between the interior and exterior. Whilst
the interiors of the churches in Alsace appeared relatively heavy and
compact, the exteriors were rich in articulation and ornament. Twin-
towered fronts, already present in the Salian period, were developed
further in the twelfth century. Under the influence of the cathedrals of
Strasbourg and Basel, twin-towered fronts were built in Sélestat,
Lautenbach or Guebwiller. Parallel to this was the popularity of crossing
towers, a large number of which were erected in Alsace, for example the
multi-storeyed, octagonal crossing towers in Sélestat, Haguenau, Rouffach,
Guebwiller and Rosheim. The ground plan selected was always the basilica
with nave and two side aisles, transept, choir bay, main apse and side apses
on the transept wings. In the nave the crossing square was used as the basis
for the proportioning of the building, and an alternate supporting rhythm
employed.

St. Peter and Paul in Rosheim was constructed in the third quarter of
the twelfth century and is acknowledged as one of the most beautiful
Staufen churches in Alsace (photo, opposite left). The basilica with nave
and two side aisles, transept, choir bay, and semi-circular apse is very
richly articulated and ornamented on the exterior. A multiple molded
plinth, blind recess and round-arched friezes over lesenes covered the
whole of the exterior. The transverse façade in the west and the main apse
are particularly heavily ornamented. The building has a high octagonal
crossing tower, which was renewed in the Gothic period. Just as in
Guebwiller or Sélestat there are human figures on the crossing tower on
the slanting parts near where it meets the roof. The interior is
characterized by a strict uniformity of the walls. The nave is rib-vaulted
whilst the side aisles are groin-vaulted. Cruciform piers and squat columns
on very high plinths with heavy, block-like, ornamented capitals alternate
along the arcade.

The Staufen eastern parts of Strasbourg Cathedral are of monumental size.
Its east choir and transept were built over the old Salian ground plan from
the late twelfth century onwards. The semi-circular apse, which joins directly
onto the transept, is encased in a rectangular wall as at Worms. High plinths
support huge piers, which in turn carry the high vaults and crossing dome.
Despite their pronounced steepness, the east parts seem to weigh heavily
on each other and are characteristically Staufen in style. They exhibit a
heavy monumentality, typical of the late period of Staufen architecture.

Similar in its heavy, powerful appearance is the interior of Basel
Cathedral, which was rebuilt after a fire in 1185 (photo, below right).

Halberstadt, Liebfrauenkirche.
Around 1140. View from the east

Quedlinburg, collegiate church St.
Servatius.
1070–1129. Nave looking west

In this church, galleries have been inserted between the arcade level and the clerestory. Each gallery has three arcades resting on a pair of colonnettes, each contained within a flat round-arched recess. Many influences coincide in Basel, as the upper Rhine tradition here merges with the influences from France and Italy. In this way something distinctive has emerged: a heavy, powerful space which is typical of the Staufen architecture of the upper Rhine. The galleries of Basel cathedral indeed influenced the cathedrals in Strasbourg and Freiburg. The latter is indebted to Basel for its Romanesque east parts.

Bound by tradition – the centre and east of Germany

In 1237 the imposing new Staufen cathedral at Bamberg with its many towers was consecrated (figure, p. 61 above). The cruciform basilica with an eastern crypt and western transept has a double choir. Whilst in the east choir late Romanesque forms are able to express themselves freely and the masonry is articulated with typical sculptural richness, the western choir has adopted forms from the early French Gothic. The east apse, nave pediment and slim eastern towers are built up over a high plinth. Semi-circular in its lower area and polygonal above, the richly articulated apse has wide windows on each side of the polygon. In the molded window intrados there are colonnettes with astragals winding around the arches. The hollow moldings of the window intrados are filled with spheres and rosettes. These small, corporeal forms of decoration model the walls and lend great expressive power to the building. The nave, whose proportioning is based on the crossing square module, is vaulted with six or four part ribbing. The heavy uniform areas of wall combine with the vaults to form a space which conveys considerable power and might. The interior thus has an austere, serious character compared to the exterior which projects joyfully upwards.

Around 1140 the Liebfrauen church in Halberstadt was rebuilt, although the older parts in front of the nave which resembled a westwork were preserved (photo, above). The building exhibits some architectural motifs, which are indebted to the Hirsau style of architecture, such as an east choir with chapels in echelon, or the pier arcades, which do not join directly to the crossing, but are separated from the crossing arches by a short strip of wall. The basilica with nave, sides aisles and transept has a square forechoir which is accompanied by side choirs. Semi-circular apses are attached to the main choir, the side choirs and the east walls of the transepts. The walls of the nave with its flat ceiling rest on piers which have an almost imperceptible rhythm. Both square and rectangular piers are used, creating a very subtle alternation of supports. Moreover, there is very little wall articulation. Only the east parts of the church are vaulted. The still persisting traditions of Ottonian architecture, such as the alternation of supports and flat ceilings, are combined with southern German influences, such as, for example, in the eastern parts of the church with the architecture of the Hirsau School. That this variant of southern German architecture should be emulated is significant, since it is this monastic architecture which kept alive the flat ceiling basilica. The same applies to the collegiate church of St. Servatius in Quedlinburg (figure, opposite,

Königslutter, former Benedictine abbey church of St. Peter and Paul. From 1135 to the late twelfth century. East view (below), round arch frieze on the main apse (above)

Königslutter, cloister

bottom) which used the same Saxon alternation of supports seen at St. Michael in Hildesheim.

The basilica of St. Godehard in Hildesheim, built from 1130 to 1172 with a nave and two aisles, also uses the double alternation of supports of St. Michael. Of particular architectural importance is the choir (photo, p. 25), since this was the first time in Germany that an ambulatory with apsidal chapels (chevet) was built surrounding the choir. The sources of inspiration for this ambulatory are to be found in French architecture, where the chevet had been known since the tenth century. St. Godehard remains a unique example of this in Germany. It was not until the Gothic age that ambulatories of this type were used again, and then it was under the direct influence of French architecture.

Late Staufen Architecture on the Rhine – the interaction with France

A late stage of Staufen architecture is exemplified by the monastery church of St. Peter and Paul in Königslutter, built between 1135 and the late twelfth century by Emperor Lothar (photo, above left). The choir and transept are groin vaulted. On the one hand, the ground plan with two lateral choirs flanking the main structure follows the pattern of the Hirsau School, that is an anti-imperial concept of building. On the other hand, the rich articulation clearly shows the will of the imperial client commissioning the building. The detailed articulation of the main apse in the east is typical of the late style of Staufen architecture. The articulation is generously endowed with responds and round-arched friezes, and the walls are sculptured in their style. The imperial authority is expressed in the classical ornamentation, which, as in Speyer Cathedral, was created by Lombardian stone masons.

St. Klemens in Schwarzrheindorf near Bonn was originally built by the Cologne archbishop Arnold von Wied as a palatine chapel around 1150, but

Beuel-Schwarzrheindorf, palatine church
of St. Klemens, 1150 and 1173. Exterior
from the north-east

Cologne, St. Martin the Great, former
Benedictine monastery church.
1150–1172. View from the south-east

OPPOSITE
Limburg an der Lahn, cathedral, former
collegiate and parish church of St. George
and St. Nicholas. 1215–1235. View from
the north-west

was converted to a nuns' church in 1173 (photo, above left). The ground
plan is based on the Godehard chapel in Mainz cathedral, although St.
Klemens is cruciform. Towards the east, in the direction of the apse, the
interior opens up on both floors to form a broad space. It was here that
not long before 1173 the first ribbed vaulting in the Rhineland was
erected. The exterior is endowed with a rich, taut articulation. The lower
walls of the chapel are largely restrained in their decoration, but the upper
part, on the other hand, is all the more opulent in its ornamentation. There
is a dwarf gallery, running around the whole church, and covered by a
narrow roof. Above the gallery the main part of the church rises up and
reaches a peak in the shape of a powerful tower over the middle of the
building.

The rich surface is much more highly developed than, for example,
Maria Laach, another church of the same period. The shaping of the

windows on the upper level of the building has acquired a style of its own.
The windows are no longer simply round-arched, but quite unusual in their
forms, almost mannerist in style, and quatrefoil or fan-shaped. In the later
architecture of the Lower Rhine such window shapes are commonly taken
up again and variations created.

The exterior articulation of the minster at Bonn (photo, p. 66) shows
further development and perfection. Its east choir with semi-circular apse
was completed in 1166, whilst the construction of the transept, nave and
semi-circular west choir enclosed in a rectangular wall took until 1224.
The towers and apse rise from a single high plinth, which together with the
blind arches of the two storeys above lend a unity to the eastern end. The
top of the apse is crowned by a dwarf gallery. In the interior the east choir
appears low and heavy, whilst the nave in contrast is graceful and well-lit.
This is achieved by the addition of a blind triforium between the wide-

Bonn, St. Martin Minster. 1166 (eastern parts), 1224 (nave and west choir). View from the east (left), tripartite wall elevation (center)

Limburg an der Lahn, cathedral, former collegiate and parish church of St. George and St. Nicholas. 1225–1235. View in crossing with quadripartite wall elevation

spanned arcades and the tripartite clerestory windows. The triforium is offset from the wall, but cannot be used as a passageway. The double-layered effect of the two lower storeys is continued in the clerestory, where small columns with pointed arches stand proud of the wall. As regards the construction of the wall in the minster at Bonn, the inspirations gained from Sainte Trinité in Caen are modified to a late style, almost over-fragile and thin in its construction. This pattern of three storeys, consisting of arcades, triforium and clerestory, became widespread in the religious architecture of the Rhine. A frequent alternative to the triforium was the gallery, used for the first time in St. Ursula in Cologne. Gallery storeys from the late Staufen period are also to be found on the Rhine at St. Gereon in Cologne, Bacherach, Andernach and Neuss.

There was a further development at the collegiate church of St. George (photos, pp. 65 and above), which had been begun in 1215, consecrated in 1235, but not completed until the middle of the century. Both types of elevation, triforium and gallery, were combined by creating four storeys, a design inspired by the early French Gothic style at Laon. The triforium storey was inserted between the galleries and the clerestory. Overall, however, the quadripartite elevation appears heavier and more solid than its French forerunner. Of particular note also is the charming landscape setting on a rocky outcrop which was used to maximize the striking impact of this church with its multiple towers.

These architectural ideas attained their full flowering in St. Aposteln (photo, p. 53) and St. Martin the Great (photo, p. 64) in Cologne. The architectural origins of these sacred buildings are to be found in the Cologne tradition, as is evident in both churches; for example, the idea of the trichora (cloverleaf pattern) from St. Maria im Kapitol was taken up again. The former collegiate church of St. Martin the Great was built in place of the church burnt down in 1150 and was consecrated in 1172.

The three conch apses with their short barrel-vaulted forebays are grouped around the square crossing, over which the massive tower rises with its four accompanying slim octagonal staircase turrets. Before the extension of the cathedral towers in the nineteenth century, this tower dominated the skyline of Cologne. The nave and side aisles appear as a mere annex in comparison to the huge eastern end with its high towers. Round-arched blind arcades divide the conch apses into three storeys. Dwarf galleries over a plate frieze, which run all around the eastern parts, unite the different parts of the building. The richness of the articulation increases towards the top of the building. Characteristic of these generously articulated Cologne churches is their two-layered wall construction, which shapes both their interior and exterior. The heavy walls are thereby afforded their necessary solidity, but at the same time appear light. This effect of lightness is increased at the crossing and towards the ceiling by the use of recesses or passageways behind arches. This kind of wall

Ratzeburg, protestant cathedral church, formerly St. Mary and St. John the Evangelist, 1160/70–1215/20. View from the south

Jerichow, former Premonstratensian collegiate church of St. Mary and St. Nicholas. Nave after 1144

articulation was influenced by Norman architecture and lends a grace and elegance to the interior space which is unusual in Staufen architecture.

The influence of Henry the Lion. North German brick Romanesque architecture

The center of Lower Saxon art was Brunswick, the stronghold of the Guelph Duke Henry the Lion. The cathedral in Brunswick was rebuilt between 1173 and 1195 in a uniform style. With its monumental dignity and austerity, and heavy, almost unarticulated external appearance, the building seems somewhat antiquated. The cross-shaped basilica, whose proportioning was strictly based on the crossing square, was designed for vaulting throughout. Its nave has an alternating system of supports, although its intermediate supports are not columns, but piers without responds, which appear simply as part of the walls. Thus they combine with the barely lit clerestory and the barrel vault to produce a heavy, almost cavernous interior. This powerful but heavy interior is complemented by an exterior constructed from bare, undressed stone, and relieved only by a few lesenes or round-arched friezes. Northern reticence in Brunswick and southern opulence in Worms both go to make up the very wide spectrum of style that is Staufen architecture.

In the north of Germany brick became the favorite building material in both religious and secular architecture. After initial use of dressed stone, brick was used in the Premonstratensian church in Jerichow, begun soon after 1144. This was a building with a flat ceiling and ascetic, restrained forms in the spirit of Hirsau (photo, right). Since the late classical period the techniques of brick building had not been used in their pure form, until the Premonstratensians and Cistercians resorted to its use because of the lack of dressed stone in the north.

Maulbronn, former Cistercian abbey.
Second half of the twelfth century.
Aerial view

Maulbronn, former abbey church.
Nave looking east

The architecture of the Cistercians

The secularization of the old ideals of the Cluniac order, mostly noticeable in the extravagantly splendid abbey at Cluny, prompted a group of the monks to found a new monastery in Cîteaux in the twelfth century where life was to be led according to strict ascetic monastic rules. In 1113 Bernard of Clairvaux entered the order and within a very short time led it to great prominence. More than 500 new Cistercian monasteries were founded under Bernard, all of which were imbued with the same ascetic spirit. These buildings were all simple, plain and austere, in line with the ideals of the Cistercian order. The construction of towers was not allowed. Only a ridge-turret was permitted, which was used for the bells, and could only project slightly above the ridge. A Cistercian church is therefore generally a low building without any towers or projections. Decorative detail in the interior is largely dispensed with.

The Cistercian monastery at Maulbronn has been preserved almost completely intact. The complex with its main and auxiliary buildings is not uniform in its style or age. The center of the monastery is made up of the church and the adjoining enclosure, that is the areas which were reserved for the monks. Slightly apart from this were the domestic offices, gardens, cemetery and infirmary. The whole monastery was enclosed in a circumvallation (circumference wall), closing it off from the exterior. The basilica with nave, aisles, transept and flat terminated choir was originally covered by a flat ceiling similar to that in the church of the Cistercian monastery of Bebenhausen. The vaulting was added later.

Eberbach in the Rheingau exhibits the same type of ground plan as Maulbronn, although the proportioning of the building was based on the square crossing, and the building was groin vaulted. The church of the monastery, founded in 1135, was built between 1150 and 1178, and has remained intact and without any subsequent alterations, apart from the addition of Gothic chapels in the side aisles. Rectangular responds, which rise up from corbels which are set in the wall at the height of the imposts, carry the transverse arches between the groin vaults. Each bay has two clerestory windows, a clear indication that right from its initial design the building was designed to accommodate groin vaulting. The characteristic features of Cistercian design are evident in this building, namely, very simple articulation, a relative lack of decoration and the clarity and simplicity of the interior. Particularly characteristic of the Staufen period is the low and heavy interior and the uniformity of its surfaces, which breathe an austere grandeur.

Maulbronn, former Cistercian abbey,
monastery area and galilee

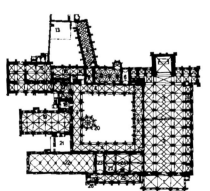

Maulbronn, ground plan of the
abbey church (top), interior of
galilee (right)

Ruin of the imperial palace at Gelnhausen. Second half of the twelfth century. Palas, gate house with chapel and tower

Ruin of the imperial palace at Gelnhausen. Arcades of main living quarters

Ruin of the imperial palace at Gelnhausen. Wall detail

Secular Romanesque architecture

Residential and defensive buildings were amongst the most important items of medieval secular architecture. Their austere character originated in the fortified towns and castles, where the areas of residence and defense were brought into maximum functional harmony with one another. Since the early Middle Ages rulers of the empire had preferred palaces as places of residence. The German expression for these residences, "Pfalz" also originates from the Latin "palatium." These imperial or royal palaces with their generous halls, roof-covered promenades, chapels and atria were widespread throughout the empire, as at this time the emperors led a peripatetic life with no fixed seat of government. These palaces would all be visited in their turn over the years. The domestic offices attached to the palaces would provide for the needs of the emperor's court. The arrangement of the buildings relative to one another has its origins in Roman, Byzantine and Germanic prototypes.

The imperial palace of Charlemagne in Aachen and the extent and nature of its functional buildings is already well known in all its essential features. At Bodman on Lake Constance and the Carolingian palaces at Ingelheim and Nijmegen, excavations have revealed useful information about their structure and function. The imperial palace at Goslar (figure, opposite) was built in the first half of the eleventh century under Otto III and Henry III; the hall structure partly dates from this period. Extensive restoration work and reconstruction in a romantic style in 1865 account for its present appearance.

The ruin of the imperial palace at Gelnhausen (photos, above), first mentioned in 1158, is regarded as one of the most beautiful and artistically

important imperial palaces in Germany. Frederick I received it before 1170 as a fief. Several German emperors are known to have resided here, and on occasions it was used to hold the imperial diet. The ruin was restored in the nineteenth century.

The principles of castle building were determined by the nature of the landscape. In south and west Europe there was the attempt to achieve as standard an overall design as possible. In northern Europe, in contrast, particularly in Germany, the castle was an organic part of the landscape, as it were, and its defensive capability was adapted to the prevailing topography. The ring castle, the rings of which consisted of walls and buildings, would be situated on a site which was protected equally on all sides. On flat terrain the castle would be surrounded by a moat, whilst on a hill top it would easily be protected by the steep slopes. A keep, which usually stood separately, would tend to serve as a last refuge rather than first defense. Therefore the upper floors of the main towers were sometimes built as residences. The 'palas' would house further residential quarters, including a hall and a number of living chambers which could be heated. The construction of castles was therefore one of the most significant artistic achievements of the Staufen era. In the eleventh century castles still served almost exclusively functional purposes. It was only in the twelfth century that large independent types developed. The starting point had been the "Turmburg" (tower castle) which was comparable to the "donjon" in France (pp. 174 ff). In the Staufen castle individual parts were added to make an extended group. Designed as round, square or polygonal, the keep represented the fortified central part of the Staufen castle.

Landsberg, Alsace, castle ruin, main
living quarter with chapel oriel

Goslar, former imperial palace,
eleventh–thirteenth century. So-called
imperial house. 1868–79 renovation to
its present form

Goslar, palatinate area with so-called
imperial house, chapels and collegiate
church. Artist's impression

Ceremonial rooms and living quarters were located in a separate building, the 'palas'. It was generally situated in the innermost castle courtyard under the protection of the keep and the circumvallation (circumference wall). As the castle did not serve residential purposes alone, but was above all intended for the representation of the court, the design and layout would be arranged and decorated to fulfill these functions. The chapel and the chambers which could be heated and used as living accommodation complete the composition of a typical castle. This basic structure was standard for all castles, whether imperial palace, ministerial castle, or the castle of a sovereign prince. Beyond the functional requirements there was a striving towards clear ground plan forms, although this was always subordinate to topographical considerations. In this context a distinction may be drawn between two types of site: those sited on high ground and those situated on low-lying ground. Those on hill tops or rocky ledges represented the most widespread type. Some might be situated on the summit, whilst others would be sited on the slope. In the latter there would be a ditch in front of the castle, with a huge wall shielding the castle and residential quarters. The summit was of course the most secure site for a castle. The 'palas', residential and domestic buildings would be situated in the inner side of the rectangular or polygonal circumvallation, the shape of the latter being dictated by the nature of the

OUTER LEFT
Regensburg, "Baumburg Tower."
Residential tower. Third quarter of the
thirteenth century

Karden, Romanesque house (above),
Bad Münstereifel, Romanesque house
1167/68 (below)

Freiburg, town founded by the Zähringer
Dukes. First half of the twelfth century.
Merian engraving of 1643

Freiburg im Breisgau, Villingen, Murten and Fribourg. It was not until the middle of the twelfth century that the Staufer followed their example with towns such as Schwäbich Gmünd, Reutlingen and Haguenau. In their turn the Guelphs created Ulm, and Henry the Lion founded Lübeck.

The Zähringer towns were planned in the shape of a large oval, surrounded by strong walls with gateways and towers. A wide market street, or two main streets intersecting each other at right angles, determined the layout of the town. At the ends of these streets stood the town gates. Parallel or perpendicular to the main streets were the side streets, behind which in turn lay the tradesmen's alleys. The main streets were of course used to hold large markets. Finally, space was left between the houses for the church and its graveyard.

Few Romanesque dwelling houses remain preserved, as they were largely of half-timbered construction. A small number of buildings made of stone or wood have survived, allowing us at least a small insight into the house building techniques of the time. Amongst the oldest are the so-called Romanesque house in Bad Münstereifel (photo, left above), which dates from 1167/68, and the former hall courtyard in Oberlahnstein from 1160/70. Also of interest is an imposing stone house on the pilgrim route at Obernai in Alsace, with groups of double windows with trefoil arches, which dates from around 1220. Yet another example is the so-called Romanesque house (late twelfth century) at Rosheim in Alsace which is a tower-like construction with embossed corner-stones. In some German towns impressive residential towers from the late Romanesque period have survived, such as in Regensburg where the so-called Baumburg Tower (photo, left) dates from the third quarter of the thirteenth century. The Yellow House in Esslingen, a four-storey late Romanesque tower with a square ground plan, was constructed around 1260. Its embossed stone façades boast windows with pointed arches. Finally, certain half-timbered houses in Esslingen, Bad Wimpfen and Schwäbisch Hall have been shown to date from the late Romanesque period. This was proved by employing scientific techniques to determine the age of the wood used in their construction.

site. The embossed stone masonry, which lent the buildings their monumental and defensive appearance, is very typical of most Staufen castles. The castle at Landsberg in Alsace was constructed around the middle of the twelfth century and is largely walled in embossed stone (photo, left).

The upper floor of the 'palas' ruin has a series of four small round-arched windows and an oriel with a round-arched frieze. The ground plan at Ulrichsburg at Ribeauville has been completely adapted to the mountainous site. Extended in the twelfth century with the addition of, amongst other things, a keep, it ranks as one of the best examples of Staufen castle building (photo, opposite).

Town architecture is just as much an important feature of the late Romanesque period as castle construction. Until the early twelfth century there were few towns in Germany. They mostly owed their existence to a bishop's seat or important merchant settlement. These towns had grown up over long periods of time without any deliberate planning. This changed at the beginning of the twelfth century, when for the first time since antiquity new towns were founded and erected according to clearly designed plans. The most important princely families of the time, the Staufer, the Guelphs, and the Zähringer, founded new towns to consolidate their territories and endowed them with rich privileges. The most impressive towns were those founded by the Zähringer, which included

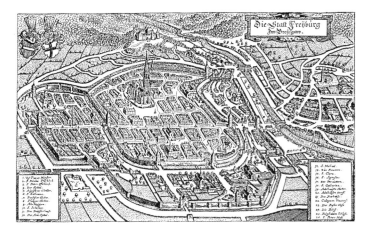

Ribeauville, Ulrichsburg. Early twelfth–thirteenth century

Castle ruin of Trifel at Annweiler, the "finest royal fortification of the Staufen age" and for a time the place where the imperial jewels were kept. Well tower (extreme left), chapel oriel (near left)

Alick McLean

Romanesque architecture in Italy

In 1026 Teodaldo, bishop of Arezzo (1023–36), sent Maginardo to Ravenna to study San Vitale as a model for completing the cathedral of Arezzo, completing the training of this architect whom the bishop esteemed as *arte architectonica optime erudito*. What little documentation remains of the resulting building, which was destroyed in 1561, indicates that Maginardo did indeed integrate aspects of San Vitale. What he adopted is significant for understanding the development of Romanesque architecture throughout Italy. He fused the central, palace-chapel plan of San Vitale with a basilical plan, and thereby infused his cathedral complex with an imperial character.

Maginardo and Teodaldo's intentions in developing this hybrid cathedral and palace chapel are made clear in reference to another copy of San Vitale, 200 years earlier, across the Alps, Charlemagne's Palatine Chapel in Aachen. This earlier Carolingian structure was less compromising than Teodaldo's, beginning with a purely centralized plan that was remarkably true to the Justinianian model. With his palatine chapel Charlemagne had asserted architecturally the same link to the last great Roman Christian emperor, Justinian, that he had asserted politically when he had himself crowned, on Christmas Day, 800, as Emperor of the Western Roman Empire. Teodaldo's return to this same model suggests his own ambition to link himself to Imperial Roman Christianity. The overlaid longitudinal plan of the basilica suggests, however, a slightly different intention from that of his Northern imperial predecessor: the palace church is fused with a building capable of ministering to a far larger congregation than a centralized church alone. San Vitale is therefore not a religious attachment Christianizing a secular imperial palace, but rather an imperial religious structure fusing secular and religious authority at the traditional seat of a bishop.

The repetition of similar overlays of centralized and basilical forms in Romanesque Italian churches in the eleventh century, whether in Ancona, Montefiascone, or, most notably, in Pisa, indicates how ambitious Italian bishops were in their building programs and their symbolism, to the point of competing not only with past Holy Roman Emperors, but also with their present-day successors. Their consistent reference to models at Ravenna, even more than to Roman models, indicates that Rome was by no means the sole font for Romanitas. The remains of Imperial Roman architecture were still visible throughout the peninsula as well as across the Alps. In some cases, especially in Ravenna, they were in better condition than in Rome itself. The quality of Ravenna's late antique buildings, amongst the best preserved in the peninsula, helped to establish the importance of Ravenna in Italian Romanesque architecture. Their dating to the Christian era of Roman antiquity was another factor. Furthermore, the monuments of Ravenna are not only Roman and Christian. They are also imperial, and therefore ideal models for constructing institutions with aspirations to follow the Christian Imperial tradition so dramatically asserted by Justinian in both Ravenna and Constantinople. The characteristic designs of Ravenna's buildings, from the time immediately preceding, during and after Justinian's rule, also made them easy to recognize, even in copies. They are composed of plan

Ravenna (Emilia Romagna), mausoleum of Theodoric. First quarter of the sixth century

Ravenna (Emilia Romagna), Orthodox baptistery. Fifth century. Mosaic decorations in the interior of the circular-plan building

BOTTOM
Ravenna (Emilia Romagna), mausoleum of Galla Placidia. *c.* 425–450

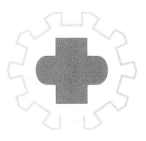

Mausoleum of Theodoric, ground plan

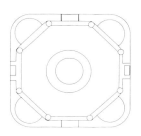

Orthodox baptistery, ground plan

elements and details that include simple volumetric massing and the open or blind arch, for instance at the Mausolea of Theoderic (photo, top left) and Galla Placidia, and unornamented exterior buttressing piers, such as at San Vitale. Their interiors and exteriors are similarly decorated with arcading, such as at the Baptistery of the Orthodox at Ravenna (photo, top right), and with mosaic work. The latter continued to be executed in Italian Romanesque and even Gothic churches up to the thirteenth century and beyond, due to the influence of the mosaic workshop tradition in Justinian's other, and primary, residence, Constantinople, and through the western Byzantine offshoot of that workshop, the mosaicists of San Marco in Venice.

The argument here is not, however, that Ravenna was the exclusive font of Romanesque Italian architecture, but rather that there was a plurality of recognizable sources from diverse moments and places in antiquity. Types originating from the city of Rome itself, whether the basilical section or cruciform plan of St. Peter's, or even earlier pagan temple facades and circular, Pantheon plans, were often overlaid over one another, as in Arezzo Cathedral. A third distinct source was also present, that of another great city of Christian antiquity, Jerusalem.

The story that follows explores the variety of ways that different patrons adopted, mixed and transformed these prototypes over time and across the diverse landscape of the Italian peninsula, Sicily and Sardinia. Again, as at Arezzo, the final package produced from this assortment of heterogeneous models appears to have been driven not only by formal or

OPPOSITE
Venice, St. Mark's. Begun 1063. Mosaic
decorations in the interior of the church

BOTTOM
St. Mark's, main portal with mosaics.
1204

Ravenna (Emilia Romagna), Saw Vitale.
526–547. Exterior view, ground plan

technical interests, but particularly by symbolic ones. As Hans Sedlmeyer and Richard Krautheimer have made quite clear in their studies of architectural symbolism and iconography, the religious structures of Romanesque Italy not only housed congregations, but also spoke to them, telling them specific messages that varied according to the admixture of scale, models, and overall composition. And few buildings were static entities, but were themselves changed by successive generations of patrons and architects in order to modulate their architectural-symbolic messages according to the composition and importance of their congregations. These messages followed their architectural sources loosely but consistently, declaring the connection of local religious and even lay institutions to three fundamental sources for political, religious or moral order that provide the cultural framework for the architectural history in these pages: Imperial roots, Christian Imperial authority, and the Apostolic mission. These three symbolic worlds combined, and often conflicted, in the mentalities of eleventh- through thirteenth-century Italian bishops and priests, emperors and lords, abbots and monks, merchants and artisans.

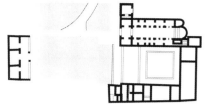

Pomposa (Emilia Romagna), monastery church. Ninth–eleventh century. Narthex and campanile from the west (left), nave and choir (below), ground plan of the monastery complex (right)

Northern Italy

The area to the north and west of Ravenna proved to be the starting point for the revival of Roman and Ravenesque architecture in Italy. Patrons and architects adopted and transformed diverse forms over time in response to divergent patrons and publics. The city that retained the strongest ties of any Italian city with Byzantine culture, Venice, shows in its architecture simultaneous tendencies linking it to Justinian and earlier antique traditions and also of establishing a distinctly local character, not only regarding construction and forms, but even in the programs of its buildings. The primary church of Venice was, and still is, not a cathedral, but rather the palatine chapel for the elected secular ruler of the city; the Doge's chapel of St. Mark's, begun in 1063. Its plan and interior (figure, p. 76) show a fusion of the clarity of the centralized scheme of San Vitale with the multiple domes of Hagia Sophia and particularly of Justinian's five- and six-dome Greek cross designs for the Holy Apostles in Constantinople and for St. John the Evangelist in Ephesus. The significant difference from any model is the relation of the church to its setting, Piazza San Marco, visible in the 1204 depiction of St. Mark's the entry portal mosaic (photo, bottom left). Not only does it draw a broad screen of inviting arches across the east end of the great space, but it then communicates its constellation of interior cupolas across the city with the quincunx of domes projecting high above the rooftops of the adjoining urban fabric. Both inside and out, the church appears as a glistening reliquary, appropriate for the recently stolen relics of St. Mark, whisked away from Alexandria in the ninth century by Venice's true source of power, its merchant adventurers (pirates). The accessibility and visibility of these relics, around which the new church was built, made them and the church the common identity of the entire city, not just of its ruler or bishop.

The unique program and open, inviting character of St. Mark's is a hint at the sort of the fusion of architectural, social, political and religious innovations that was to be repeated in institutional architecture in Italy. These innovations, together with the funds for Romanesque Italian building campaigns, can largely be attributed to the growing number and importance of merchants throughout the eleventh and twelfth centuries. The early and forceful presence of merchants along the Adriatic coast even led the region's monasteries to be constructed and administered as much for the laity as for the cloistered monastic brethren, in marked contrast to contemporary abbeys across the Alps. South of Venice, by the mouth of the Po, Benedictine monks constructed a settlement at Pomposa (photo, top), between the ninth and eleventh centuries. As in the earlier

Cividale (Friuli), Tempietto Santa Maria
in Valle. 772–76 (?). Sectional drawing
showing the lavish interior decoration

development of Carolingian monasteries in the north, the Benedictines of Pomposa built for themselves a monastic complex as the command center for managing extensive agricultural holdings, for studying the abbey's rich library of antique and Christian texts, and for the musical composition and chanting of psalms, greatly aided by the codification of musical notation by Pomposa's own Guido d'Arezzo in the early eleventh century. The prominent role of the monastery in the regional economy and culture is clearly broadcast in its architectural forms, with its richly decorated porch and tall, multi-level Lombard campanile. It even had a structure given over to the laity, its Venetian-style Palazzo della Ragione. The brickwork, blind arcades and buttressing piers of the church show the debt to nearby Ravenna, now overlaid with a triumphal arch motif opening the porch to the west, decorated not with antique spoils, but with Ravenesque majolica plates and geometric ornamental patterns stemming from both merchant trade sources and regional Lombard decorative traditions. The echo of the triumphal entry of Old St. Peter's at the porch of Pomposa appears to be more than a coincidence. During the very years that the Pomposa porch was under construction, Abbot Guido, although himself from Ravenna, succeeded in securing the abbey's autonomy from the bishop of Ravenna, placing it under the direct authority of St. Peter's in Rome. Guido built the image of the mother church at his own abbey.

The brickwork, the arched corbel tables and primitive ornamental forms, and the campanile of Pomposa recall another architectural school that was as influential in the construction and decoration of Italy's Romanesque churches as Rome, Ravenna and Jerusalem were in their symbolism. This is the school of the Lombards, the Germanic tribe that descended from the north-east, beyond the Alps, with the conquests of the Lombard King Albonio in 568–72, establishing centers north of the Venetian lagoon, at Cividale and Aquileia, and surrounding the Byzantine Exarchate with territories along most of the western Po, and as far north as Como and as far south as the foot of Italy. The remarkable Tempietto of Santa Maria in Valle at Cividale (photo, right), from c. 762–76(?), is an early example of the richness of Lombard decorative work, fusing Byzantine and even Saracen influences, which would have been communicated through the southern Italian territories of the Lombards. More typical is the architecture originating around Milan and Pavia around 800, known as "the first Romanesque" in Europe. It is best seen in the Milanese basilica of San Vincenzo in Prato, renovated in the eleventh century, though with few deviations from the original structure from c. 814–33. It is a simplification of architectural forms derived from the Byzantine Exarchate, not only adopting them from the religious structures mentioned above, but also from the Palace of the Exarchs, erected for the governors of Byzantine Ravenna after 712. From the latter comes the upper-storey blind arcade corbel vault, whose columns are either abstracted into stiffening pilasters or, for intervals of open wall, abandoned altogether. At the main apse of San Vincenzo in Prato these arcades become windows, forming an arcaded gallery that, together with the blind arcaded corbel vault, was to become the signature of the Romanesque apse, from Southern Italy to Lombardy, across the Alps to

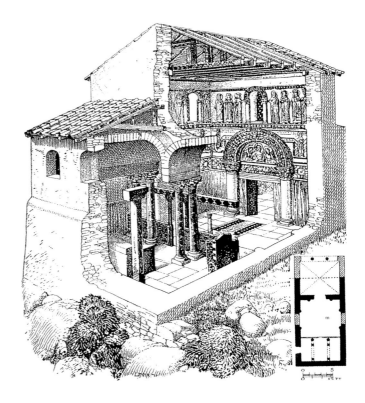

Northern Spain, the Rhine valley, eastern France and Normandy, and even as far afield as Hungary and Dalmatia.

The success of Ravenesque galleries, blind arcades, corbel tables, buttresses and brickwork under and after the Lombards was based on a mixture of pragmatic, political and symbolic reasons. Although records or remains of extensive building programs initiated by the Lombard kings and dukes are scarce, from early on the precocious governing apparatus of the Lombards out of their capital at Pavia showed a clear respect for, and willingness to protect, the building profession. In 643 the Lombard King Rotharis registered the privileges of builders. In 714, King Liutprand promulgated a graduated list of prices to be paid for buildings and construction work. These legal provisions indicate a support for new construction and renovation across the Lombard kingdom, which by King Liutprand's reign included nearly all of Italy. Such legislative protection favored the development of what King Rotharis called the "magistri comacini," or building masters, as a coherent, trained corps of Lombard builders. These master masons would not have been limited to those originating from Como, from which the term "comacini" may derive, but

rather to masons from across the peninsula, steeped in a still present Roman tradition of brick and stone construction, whom the Lombard kings respected and helped to organize legally into what appears to have been the equivalent of a guild.

It was this legal organization of long-established but decaying Roman building crafts that literally revived the building industry in Italy as early as the seventh century, not only in major centers, but, through bands of itinerant masons under their masters, in small towns and even the countryside. However, their masonry techniques were distinctly different from those of their Roman predecessors. While the latter used long bricks or square stones to reinforce and stiffen rubble and mortar or concrete walls, the Lombard masons used the higher-profile Byzantine-type bricks to construct entirely brick walls, without rubble infill. This technique simplified construction considerably, eliminating the necessity for form-work. It was appropriate for smaller-scale construction, but was also effective for large buildings, and could be executed with dressed or even carefully selected undressed stones in place of bricks. The tendency of Lombard walls to be thinner than traditional Roman walls led to the elaboration of the various vertical buttresses, seen as early as San Vitale (photo, p. 77), which stiffened the area of wall planes, while arched corbel tables helped to reinforce their upper edges.

The market for well-organized Lombard mason teams constructing both urban and rural brick structures was greatly enhanced by the new politics of the papacy beginning in the early eleventh century. As in the case of Pomposa, popes began to sponsor monastic foundations which were independent of local bishops as a means of achieving new goals of spiritual reform and temporal jurisdiction. Because many abbots, such as the Lombard William of Volpiano, either moved to new posts at other abbeys or held churches and monasteries under a mother abbey, Lombard building techniques and mason teams moved rapidly across not only Italy, but elsewhere, such as in William's abbey church in Dijon, France, begun in 1001, and even as far as his satellite abbey of Fécamp in Normandy. A capillary system of simple, well-built, and recognizable abbeys and churches began to populate areas of Italy and the north that had previously been bastions of the Holy Roman Emperors and the bishops they appointed. It should not be surprising that as tensions began to grow between the papacy and the empire in the later eleventh century, emperors began to respond with their own building programs, adopting the Lombard Romanesque techniques and style to their own territorial and symbolic ends.

The area of Italy where the Lombard Romanesque style developed earliest and remained most pure is along the Po, extending from the Adriatic just east of Pomposa up the river's 337 miles of navigable waterway. At centers both large and small the red Po valley bricks were used to create the wall, arch and vaulting systems. This constructional system in turn was used to articulate institutions with larger-scale symbolic forms, such as the porch of Pomposa discussed above. At Vigolo Marchese, a small rural community far upstream along the Po, the local feudal lord, Marchese Oberto, had the new abbey of San Giovanni constructed with two such forms, combining a traditional monastery with

Milan (Lombardy), Sant' Ambrogio.
Ninth–twelfth century. View from nave
eastwards, ground plan

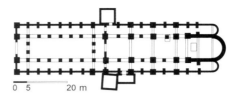

OPPOSITE
Milan, Sant' Ambrogio. Atrium and view
from the west

0   5   20 m

a structure apparently directed towards the local populace. Besides the abbey church of San Giovanni stands the circular baptistery of the same name, adopting its plan from the Orthodox Baptistery of Ravenna, from San Vitale, and possibly from the round-planned Holy Sepulcher in Jerusalem (photo, page 81). The function of this circular structure remains a mystery: the rareness of monastic baptisteries makes some scholars consider it an oratory. The record of an early baptismal font within, however, suggests that this rural monastery, although turning its portal away from the nearby village, welcomed its children and converts into the Church.

The other symbolic form at Vigolo Marchese, less cryptic in its use, is the bell-tower, similar to that of Pomposa. These towers, like their numerous counterparts throughout Romanesque Italy, combine multiple stories of Romanesque blind arches and pilasters with the square plan made famous in the eighth-century belfry of Old St. Peter's. A papal bull of Innocent II from 1134 accounts for this early reference to the Vatican: like Pomposa, San Giovanni di Vigolo Marchese belonged exclusively to the Patrimony of St. Peter's.

One of the largest-scale and most important of the churches that fused Lombard Romanesque construction with forms from St. Peter's was the great monastic basilica of Milan, Sant' Ambrogio. The church began as a martyrial basilica for the remains of the martyred saints Protasius and Gervasius. It was constructed under St. Ambrose, who consecrated the church in 386. Upon his death in 397 St. Ambrose was himself buried in the church, giving it its current name. In 784 Peter, archbishop of Milan, established a new Benedictine foundation at the basilica, which was confirmed in 789 by Charlemagne, who added to the establishment a college of canons as well, who were to minister directly to the urban lay congregation. The new institutions associated with the basilica, together with the growing community of Milan, led to the construction of a new presbytery and crypt at the east end, which in turn provided an appropriate setting for the altar of gold donated by bishop Angilberto II between 822 and 849. Shortly afterwards the campanile was added to the south of the church. Its square plan, material, construction and decoration make it the earliest surviving Lombard belltower to base its design on the recently finished campanile of St. Peter's. Between 1018 and 1050 composite pilasters replaced the antique fourth-century columns, allowing for the vaulting of the aisles, without ribs, and of the nave, with ribs, to be erected over the following century. The same period saw the construction of the present atrium, with the second, taller campanile added between 1128 and 1144. The collapse of some of the western bays of the church led to their construction and reinforcement in the late twelfth century; the entire church was restored in 1863. The complex and continuous building history of Sant'Ambrogio indicates how its monastic and canonical institutions periodically redefined themselves architecturally for the ever-growing community of this great center of administration, trade and communication at the threshold between Italy and the North.

By the late eleventh century Lombard structural innovations and Romanesque architectural vocabulary were well established throughout the Po valley and began simultaneously to diffuse both south and north

Como (Lombardy), Sant' Abbondio. 1027–95. Interior of the columned basilica (left), exterior view from the south west

and to be adapted and varied, even in the regions of Lombardy, Emilia Romagna and the Veneto. Sant'Abbondio in Como was reconsecrated as a Benedictine abbey church in 1095, concluding the construction of an all-stone version of Lombard Romanesque architecture (photo, opposite). It was begun as early as 1027 with an ambitious five-aisle plan and a deep, precociously rib-vaulted apse. Its twin towers anticipate the second tower of Sant'Ambrogio by at least three decades, though their symmetry shows that they were not looking only to Rome, but also to the great contemporary French monastery of Cluny.

Pavia's San Michele, built between c. 1100 and 1160, is another variation on the regional architectural vocabulary (photo, opposite), with its large pediment spanning the entire façade, as at Sant'Ambrogio, but again rendered in stone, richly sculpted on the façade, and with deep arcades following the slope of its roofline. This same model is followed at the twelfth-century cathedral of Parma, with its octagonal twelfth-/thirteenth-century baptistery deploying an even more plastic rendering of its elevations and interior, with multiple stories of trabeated galleries surmounted by elegant arcades defining the termination of its eight wall surfaces. The single-bay porch of the cathedral of Parma compresses the elaborate sculptural figuration of Pavia into a remarkable representation of the months of the year, repeated at the baptistery. Similar porches and sculptural schemes appear as well at Modena's Porta della Pescheria and Ferrara's Porta dei Mesi, to mention a few.

The strongly sculptural nature of eleventh- and twelfth-century Romanesque churches along the Po valley should be seen in the same light as their counterparts in the north, such as Hildesheim's St. Michael or Autun's Saint-Lazare. Façades, portals, bronze doors, interior capitals and even floors and ceilings were articulated with vegetal, monstrous, and narrative sculptural schemes directed to the growing lay population of cities whose monastic and episcopal administrative centers attracted merchant communities. Innovations in agricultural tools and techniques and increasingly successful stewardship of agricultural holdings, particularly by monastic houses, provided crop surpluses capable of feeding not only serfs, tenant farmers and their feudal administrators, but also urban dwellers. Urban dwellers in turn provided local laborers and manufacturers of agricultural tools, clothing and luxury goods as well as traders importing similar goods. The trade successes and increasingly sophisticated monetary instruments of Venetian and, especially, Tuscan merchants, who are treated later in the text, made it possible for this new class, many of whose members had recently been serfs or peasants tied to the land, to wander further and further from their local origins. Travel in turn begot increased worldliness, sophistication and wealth, and freemen and women began to aspire in their own tastes to goods and ways of life previously reserved to their episcopal, monastic or noble lords. We have already seen the first stage of this transformation in architecture, with religious buildings addressing broader publics both with architectural iconographies, such as the towers and porches reflecting features of Old St. Peter's, and also with alluring figural extravagances, with monstrous creatures straight out of the pagan imagination. The scenes of the months at the portals of Parma, Modena or Ferrara represent a shift from images of fantasy and fear to a more sophisticated, narrative content, precociously represented in Hildesheim's bronze doors, but now even more

BOTTOM
Pavia (Lombardy), San Michele. *c.* 1100,
1160. West façade

Verona (Veneto), San Zeno Maggiore.
1023–1035. West façade

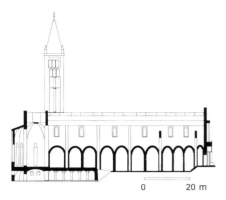

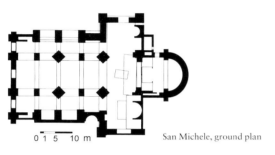

San Zeno, elevation of the nave and side
aisles

San Michele, ground plan

empathetic, with their scenes of the daily activities of both peasant and
village.

The shift in sculptural figuration from the fantastic and even
threatening figures of the eleventh century to the more empathetic ones in
the twelfth was paralleled by changes in architectural design. The use of
pilasters and blind arcades that had characterized earlier Romanesque in
Italy became more complex, developing more and more from a structural
system to one expressive of harmonic order. Such a shift was consistent
with changes in musical composition at the time and with the culture of
trade, no longer barter, but based on abstract, proportional systems of
major and minor monetary values, such as lire, soldi, and denari.

One architectural example of this development is Verona's San Zeno,
an urban Benedictine monstery and church built in its current form
between 1123 and 1135 (photo, top left). Its historiated bronze doors and
flanking marble relief panels contain, subdivide and control figurative
scenes into narrative sequences relating stories of the Old and New
Testament, Ostragothic kings and Carolingian sagas. The vertical pilasters
and piers of the façade, the side elevations and the campanile similarly
subdivide the exterior walls, providing three levels of phrasing and
rhythm, from the three bays of the main façade, to the four- and eight-bay
rhythms of the side and central bays, to the horizontal striation of the side
elevations and campanile. San Zeno is the logical development of the
Lombard Romanesque structural innovations, now transformed from the
simple readings of planes, gables, roofline arcades, atria and towers into a
complex layering of major and minor themes. Like the musical notation
developed by Guido d'Arezzo at the nearby Benedictine house of Pomposa
100 years earlier, the horizontal and vertical marks of San Zeno provide an

Parma (Emilia Romagna), west façade of
the cathedral, campanile and baptistery

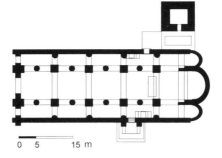

OPPOSITE
Modena (Emilia Romagna), cathedral.
Begun 1099. West façade, ground plan
(left)

0 5   15 m

This magnificent ensemble consisting of
the cathedral, campanile and baptistery
was not built at the same time: construction
work on the cathedral is thought to have
started *c*. 1090. The extent of the damage
caused by the earthquake of 1130 is
disputed. It was probably not too great,
because the cathedral was completed by
1130. In 1170 it was vaulted and a few
years later Benedetto Antelami directed
the "riforma del pontile," alterations to
the transitional area of the nave and side
aisles, crypt and choir. He was also
responsible for the low relief Descent
from the Cross, dating from 1178, which
was designed for the cathedral's pulpit (p.
305) and is now in the church's southern
transept arm. Antelami came to Parma
for a period eighteen years later in order
to direct the building of the baptistery
(1196–1216). Finally, the campanile was
built between 1284 and 1296. The
expansion of the cathedral's southern
side chapels also dates from this time.

Parma, baptistery, portal. Detail of the
archivolts (top), detail of the tympanum
(above)

Modena (Emilia Romagna), cathedral.
Begun 1099. Rood screen and ambo

ordering matrix that is capable of organizing both architectural and sculptural composition at once abstractly and narratively.

The planar abstractions of San Zeno's elevations become spatial once inside the church, in the poly-rhythmic subdivision of the nave, and in the vaulted bays of the crypt. The scale of the crypt and of its endless field of columns would have returned monks, the local faithful and pilgrims to a more primitive world of architectural composition and prayer. The crypt's absence of phrasing rhythms induces an oscillating reading between the individual and infinity that echoes the relation between the worshiper and the gold relics of the church's patron saint. What remarkable progress is evident in the layered composition of the nave and exterior by no means precludes the building's capacity to continue to transmit the pre-urban, pre-merchant messages of the church, whether in the crypt's atavistic capitals or in its ancient cult of an early-Christian saint, who offers salvation not to labor, virtue or sophistication, but to physical intimacy and to an irrational, unquestioning faith in the presence of spirit in body parts and in the building housing them.

The exterior of San Zeno suggests that the church designers were eager to draw the laity into their holy precinct with a mixture of abstraction and narration tuned to their increased sophistication. The presence, design and effect of the crypt suggest that once having lured the laity into the core of the church's body, the designers willingly abandoned the world of structure and order, excavating at once their own architectural archaeology and the archaeology of faith, displacing reason with sensation and magic and exhuming the faithful's most primitive instincts of pantheism, fear and credulity.

To the south, not far from the confluence of the Adige passing by San Zeno with the Po, the cathedral of Modena was built between 1099 and 1184 with a rather different relation of outside to inside. In place of San Zeno's grid of horizontal and vertical piers and stripes, the elevations of Modena's cathedral are integrated by piers supporting blind arches, integrating these two traditional elements of Lombard Romanesque. Subdivision occurs within the curvature of the single arches, with triple-window galleries lining the entire circumference of the church and then penetrating the interior. Once within the body of the church, however, the outer layer of pilasters shifts to a rhythm of every two arches, their sequence less ordered than that of the Gothic vaulting. Single arches still frame triple-window galleries, but now as incised curves into an apparently continuous skin of brick wall surface which slides behind the giant order pilasters sustaining the vaults. At the end of the nave one last triple sequence of arches, framed now by the breadth of the nave, leads the visitor past a richly historiated pulpit and sanctuary screen (photo, above), past the ferocious sentinels of lions supporting the screen columns, and into the field of columns and arches sustaining the triple apse crypt vaults. Even here the logic of one to three remains, ordering and harmonizing the competing animalistic and Classical capitals of the crypt columns.

The subterranean, atavistic world of San Zeno discussed above is also present in Modena's crypt, but in tension with the church's dominant

Rome, San Paolo fuori le mura. 1200.
Cloister arcades

Rome, Santa Maria in Trastevere.
c. 1148. View from the west

BOTTOM LEFT
Rome, Santa Maria in Cosmedin.
c. 1200. View from the north west

BOTTOM RIGHT
Sant'Angelo in Formis (Campania).
c. 1075. View from the west

Rome. Old St. Peter's. Atrium. Begun
c. 320

Rome, San Clemente. *c*. 1100. Interior
view

Rome, San Paolo fuori le mura. 1200.
Detail of mosaic in the cloister

Florence (Tuscany), San Miniato al
Monte. Eleventh–thirteenth century.
Chancel

rhythm of threes, which organizes the crypt's cult of Saint Geminiano, the city's first bishop. The order, and even classicism, of Modena Cathedral tell of the continuous settlement of the area and strong connection to the Roman past – a past also present at Verona, but less explicitly at San Zeno. The linkage of the crypt of Modena to its elevations leads the church to forge a different relation with its public from that at San Zeno, less surprising the laity with the world of the crypt than advertising its entire sacred iden-tity to all the spaces surrounding the church. An extra-ordinarily rich documentation of the cathedral's construction process suggests why Modena Cathedral may have had a different relation to the laity: from the beginning of its construction process they appear to have been involved. By shortly after 1115 the laity had established a free commune and were voting in their consular meetings on matters regarding the construction of the cathedral. The product of their joint efforts with the clergy, the architect Lanfrancus, sculptor Wiligelmo, and their countess, the famous Mathilda of Canossa, established a new paradigm for the region, perhaps on the basis of its stylistic innovations, but more likely for practical reasons: it appears to have been the only church along the Po valley, albeit incomplete, to have withstood the great earthquake of 1117, which damaged severely or destroyed the cathedrals of Cremona, Piacenza, Parma, and most of the other structures that we have examined in the region.

Rome and Tuscany

The use of arches at Modena links it to contemporary and earlier churches built across the Apennines, in Tuscany, before and under the rule of Mathilda of Canossa, who controlled Tuscany and much of Emilia Romagna from 1069 to 1115. Like San Miniato al Monte in Florence, Pisa Cathedral, and numerous other Tuscan churches of the time, Modena

Florence (Tuscany), San Miniato al
Monte. Eleventh–thirteenth century.
West façade

San Domenico di Fiesole
(Tuscany/Florence), Badia fiesolana.
1025–1028 and later. Façade

Florence, Baptistery of San Giovanni.
Eleventh–thirteenth century. Exterior
and interior views

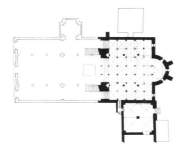

Monte Siepi near Chiusdino (Tuscany), Chapel of San Galgano. *c.* 1185. Interior and exterior views

Pistoia (Tuscany), San Giovanni Fuorcivitas. Mid twelfth century. Detail of the façade

adopts elements of the atria present at Pomposa, Sant'Ambrogio, and contemporary and earlier Roman churches, whether Santa Maria in Cosmedin, Santa Maria in Trastevere (photo, p. 90), or Old St. Peter's. With its Tuscan counterparts, Modena compresses the atrium arcades from the detached façade of the atrium directly onto the church's main west façade, registering the atrium depth and rhythm in the relief of its blind arcades. The result was the presentation of an entry iconography within the thickness of the single façade, which was therefore capable of projecting its symbolism directly, yet abstractly, into the surrounding space. As in Florence's baptistery, Pisa Cathedral, San Martino and San Michele in Foro in Lucca, San Giovanni Fuorcivitas in Pistoia, and Santo Stefano in Prato, the imagery of triumphal entry arcades is echoed on all visible façades of the church, in both tall blind arches and in gallery-level corbel arch friezes or recessed arcades. The result was indeed a more robust wall construction, thickening and reinforcing the wall along the same lines as earlier Lombard designs, but more dramatically and, considering Modena's good fortune during the earthquake, with greater seismic robustness. The good fortune of Modena Cathedral in 1117 appears to have ratified the style of Tuscan blind arcaded churches, which are more classically composed than their northern Italian counterparts, designed with carefully harmonized fugues of relief arches sustained with sometimes elaborately carved Corinthian or composite capitals. Tuscany's Romanesque churches in most cases present even more elaborately and

Empoli (Tuscany), Collegiata Sant' Andrea.
New Romanesque building from 1093
onwards. West façade

Prato (Tuscany), Santo Stefano. First half of
the twelfth century. Cloister

richly articulated elevations to facing streets and piazzas, using the same
precious marbles visible in the pulpit, sanctuary screen and portals of
Modena for all exterior surfaces. The result is a series of churches which
rival Roman temples, triumphal arches and amphitheaters in the richness
and composition of their elevations, appearing in the case of the baptistery
of Florence (photo, p. 92, top right) so convincingly classical that
subsequent generations, as early as Giovanni Villani in the early fourteenth
century, considered it to be an antique Temple of Mars.

It is remarkable that the Tuscan churches pictured in these pages even
surpassed their Roman contemporaries in the classical materials and
compositions of their exteriors, and so resemble the designs of fifteenth-
century Florentine churches to be dubbed "Proto-Renaissance" by architectural historians of a more teleological bent. Rome's eleventh- and
twelfth-century monuments were elaborated similarly to those in Tuscany,
but more on the inside than outside, such as in the cloister of San Paolo
fuori le Mura (photo, p. 89), in the nave columns, choir and apse of San
Clemente, or in the cosmatesque floors of these and many other
contemporary Roman churches. However, the porches or atria of these
Roman churches buffered jewel-like interior sacred precincts from their
urban surroundings within the same tradition that we have seen in Milan
or Pomposa, a tradition that was equally present south of Rome, at
Sant'Angelo in Formis (photo, p. 90, bottom right) or at the abbey of
Montecassino.

The significance of the Tuscan compression and enrichment of the
porch façade is clearly evident in the building history of San Miniato al
Monte in Florence. The earliest portion of the church on record is the
crypt, from the early eleventh century, built by and primarily for the rather
corrupt bishop of Florence, Hildebrand and his consort, Alberga. The
columns and capitals are rich in their spolia, framing the bichrome intarsia
altar housing the supposed remains of the patron saint, Minias, gleaming
at the back of the crypt. By mid-century an alliance of local bishops,
popes, and, by 1069, Countess Mathilda made Florence into the center
point of the era's great reform movement. The architects of San Miniato
pushed attempts to attract the laity yet further than church institutions
north of the Apennines. They began to elaborate the crypt entrance, presbytery and lower façade of San Miniato with identical forms, projecting
the interior iconography of their saint's precinct and of the sanctuary from
the façade across the city. The five bays of the sanctuary are defined with
polychrome arches placed on Corinthian capitals on rich green Monte-
ferrato marble; this same schema is repeated at the sectional shift between
the presbytery and the nave, where stairs lead up along the side aisles and
down along the nave axis to the crypt. The five bays of the lower façade
provide the final recapitulation of this imagery of framing and passage,
alternating blind arches with the three portals providing entry to the
church itself. The iconography of these repeated five polychrome classical
bays is made explicit in the upper façade of San Miniato. It is composed of
an abstracted classical temple front, with a mosaic figure of Christ, St.
Minias and the Virgin guarding the window, which, at the base of the
pedimental temple front, appears as a door to its figurative cella. Like the

Pisa (Tuscany), cathedral, baptistery and
campanile on the Campo dei Miracoli.
1063–1350

Pisa, cathedral. 1063, 1089–1272.
Interior view

Pisa, baptistery. 1153–1265

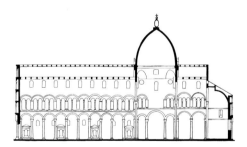

Pisa, cathedral. Elevation
of the nave and side aisles

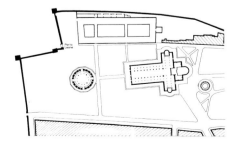

Pisa, Campo dei Miracoli.
Plan of the entire complex

presbytery within the nave, this temple door is visible to the faithful, but appears unreachable, hovering above and out of reach. Only the nave of the church and the crypt remain accessible, providing the intercessionary powers both of St. Minias and of the clergy celebrating the Eucharist in the presbytery above his altar. The message both within and outside the church is the same: salvation is rich and beautiful, but accessible only through the hierarchy of the church and the veneration of saints.

The imagery of a splendid paradise – of the Celestial Jerusalem – rendered in classical arcades and rich polychrome marbles became the common theme of churches along Tuscany's own major river valley, the Arno. It also appears in Florence in the Baptistery, in the Vescovado, in Santo Stefano al Ponte, and in the church of SS. Apostoli as well as in the Badia in Fiesole. As it proceeds along the valley it becomes fused with other motifs, whether the zebra stripes of San Zeno or the deeply sculptural rendition of surfaces characteristic of Pisan Romanesque architecture. In each case the effect is to animate the cityscape with the same conflated images of classical antiquity and salvation that had previously been contained within the apses or crypts of earlier or northern churches. Even the remote chapel of San Galgano at Monte Siepe, built around 1185, projects its interior striping onto the cylindrical drum of its exterior (photo, p. 94, top), constructing the same richness of its marble neighbors with alternating bands of brick and white stone.

The largest-scale expression of Tuscan Romanesque is at Pisa's cathe-

Arezzo (Tuscany), Santa Maria della
Pieve. Before 1008, renovated from 1111
to the end of the twelfth century. Interior
view

Lucca (Tuscany), San Michael in Foro.
Façade

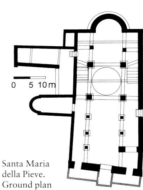

Santa Maria
della Pieve.
Ground plan

dral complex, known as the Campo dei Miracoli, or "Field of Miracles" (photos, pp. 96 and 97). As the name implies, the rich, highly sculptural architecture of the cathedral comprises an entire site, consisting in a co-ordinated array of buildings built between 1063 and 1350. The first element in the complex was the cathedral with its baptistery, which was originally located to the north of the church. The cathedral was begun in 1063, possibly as an *ex voto*, honoring the Virgin upon her delivery of a dramatic victory of the Pisan navy over the Saracens off Sicily. A contemporary façade inscription records that funds for the building enterprise came from the spoils of victory, celebrating Pisa's emerging role as one of the two dominant naval powers of the Tyrrhenian Sea, together with Genoa. In the first decades of the next century the Pisans extended the façade of the cathedral to the west, and then, in 1153, replaced the original baptistery with a new, circularly planned structure on an axis with the new cathedral entrance. Plans for this remarkable interlocking of church with baptistery, similar to that at Florence but more precisely on axis and with a purer geometry of circle and cross, may date from the time when the archbishop of Pisa was serving as patriarch of the newly established Latin Kingdom of Jerusalem, contemporary with the extension of the cathedral façade in the first decades of the twelfth century. Pisa's strong connections with Jerusalem at this time, both through its archbishop and through its recent conveyance of crusaders to the Holy Land, explain the startling similarities between the Campo dei Miracoli

and Jerusalem's most sacred site on the Temple Mount. The circle and line composition of Pisa's baptistery and Cathedral echoes that at the Temple Mount's Haram-al-Sharif, or Noble Sacred Enclosure, where the centrally-planned Dome of the Rock, known to the Pisans and crusaders as the Temple of the Lord, aligns with the basilical Mosque of Al-Aqsa, then called the Temple of Solomon. At the time of its completion the Pisan complex would have even been more splendid than its Holy Land prototype, with its polychromatic intarsia, marble and richly sculpted elevations gleaming like that other Jerusalem of Revelation, the Heavenly Jerusalem, which John describes as studded in precious stone. The other structures added to the complex only amplified the Campo dei Miracoli's gold presence, transforming an entire area of the city into an outdoor reliquary with the endless arches of the 1174 leaning tower, and with earth, excavated and transported by the Pisans from Golgotha, lining the burial ground of the 1278 Campo Santo.

The power of Tuscan Romanesque churches assured their adoption beyond the boundaries of the region. Both Pisan traders and Camaldolese and Vallombrosian missionaries transported the rich classicizing elevations and polychrome interiors to port cities on the Tyrrhenian sea as far as Sardinia, whether at San Pietro Sorres in Borutta or Nostra Signora di Tergu at Castelsardo (photo, p. 99). San Pietro Sorres in Borutta was erected between 1170 and 1190 on the foundations of an earlier church from the previous century. It fuses Pisan motifs of rotated squares in arches

Porto Torres (Sardinia), San Gausho

Castelsardo (Sardinia), Nostra Signora di
Tergu. West façade, nave and side aisles

Bulzi (Sardinia), San Pietro del
Crocifisso. West façade

Borutta (Sardinia), San Pietro Sorres.
1170–90. Apse

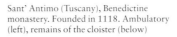
Sant' Antimo (Tuscany), Benedictine monastery. Founded in 1118. Ambulatory (left), remains of the cloister (below)

OPPOSITE
Sant' Antimo. View from the south east

Benedictine monastery of Sant' Antimo

Sant' Antimo was the swan song of the great mediaeval Italian monasteries that lived according to the Benedictine Rule. Though it was followed in this region by other masterpieces such as the Cistercian San Galgano dating from the beginning of the thirteenth century, none of them can even begin to approach this building for its effect of unity, power and size. Signs of the imminent decline of this era can be seen on the façade of Sant' Antimo, which was never finished. Despite later efforts on the part of the Cistercians, social and religious changes started the trend of moving from the country into the cities; many parishes, of whatever size, had assets similar to those of an abbot, and invested them in building churches and cathedrals.

San Pietro in Valle (Umbria), former Benedictine monastery. Tenth–twelfth century

with bichrome striping and geometric intarsia characteristic of Pistoia, Prato and Florence (photos, pp. 92–5). The connection to Tuscany was probably through the Benedictine monastery of Camaldoli, which by early in the century controlled properties nearby in Saccargia and elsewhere in its judicial and administrative region, the Giudicato of Torres. The Abbey at Saccargia was also a conduit for Tuscan design motifs for Nostra Signora di Tergu, which was itself an abbey church, and which also had strong connections with Italy's original and most powerful Benedictine seat, Montecassino. It appears to have been constructed in two phases, with an early church begun in the early twelfth century, and then the remarkable façade added a century later, using the rich local stone mixed with marble to achieve its rich bichrome effects.

The diffusion of the highly plastic Romanesque style of Pisa was not limited to the Tyrrhenian sea. The Pieve of Santa Maria Assunta in Arezzo adopted a flattened portico entry similar to that at Pisa Cathedral (photos, pp. 96–7). Although geographically closer to Florence, where a similar blind porch frames three portals, the high relief of the Pieve's second- and third-level arcades and fourth-level gallery shows a stronger debt to Pisa. The same applies to the treatment of architectural details, where the builders relied exclusively on sculpture for their articulation, abandoning polychromatic intarsia or the planar harmonic subdivision of San Miniato or the Florentine baptistery.

It would be a mistake to look only west for influences, however dominant Pisa and Florence were at the time of the Pieve's interior and new façade, which were executed in the twelfth and early thirteenth century. Rather, this extraordinary flat-roofed elevation and the later, early fourteenth-century tower show traces from one of the earliest sources of Italian Romanesque architecture, Ravenna. While it is possible that the similarity of the façade of the Pieve to the Palace of the Exarchs in Ravenna and of the tower to towers such as that of Pomposa are due to a direct Ravenesque influence, this author suggests that the source for these forms may have been the very buildings built by the architect Maginardo for Teodaldo after 1026, after his visit to Ravenna, namely, the cathedral of Arezzo and the bishop's palace. Within its rectangular urban site the architects of the Pieve inserted a cross-shaped plan surmounted with a dome which, however, remains incomplete. The apse and side walls are lined with upper-level arcaded galleries which, apparently Pisan, may again derive from the now destroyed cathedral and its original Ravenesque sources, which would have included the second-storey arcade, now fallen, of the Mausoleum of Theodoric. What is extraordinary about the Pieve is the apparent fusion of the cathedral's domed cross plan with the flat-roofed, galleried façade of the Palace of the Exarchs, which may have been visible, in copy, at the bishop's palace in Arezzo. The Pieve is a religious monument that looks like a civic structure. The secular reading is reinforced by the heavily fortified appearance of the massive later tower. It is at once temple, cathedral and *palatium*, although in reality it is none of these, but the relatively modest institution of a parish, second in importance to the famous cathedral of Teodaldo.

By the year 1200, however, parish churches in Tuscany were capable of monumental expression, as in Prato's Santo Stefano or similar institutions at the Collegiata of Empoli and San Gimignano (photo, right). Each of these canon churches thrived due to its distance from cathedral seats in other towns. While the local bishop's seat seems to argue against a similar situation at Arezzo's Pieve, it turns out that the cathedral of Arezzo was unusually distant from the town, situated within its own fortified enclosure on the suburban Pionta hill. It was so remote, in fact, that the bishop was forced to move into the town center, and to build a new, more central cathedral seat, beginning in 1277. In the meantime the Pieve of Arezzo had begun to cater to the religious needs of the urban population through its presence at the *Platea Communis*, documented since 1008 as the official town marketplace. The Pieve, etymologically the church of the people, grew in scale and monumental articulation from that date to the early fourteenth century, paralleling the increase in the merchant population of Arezzo. Consistent with its counterparts to the north of the Apennines, the stages of its growth are marked by a transition of its architectural sculpture from grotesque figures to narrative scenes, including its own cycle of months, now with both agricultural and urban vignettes. The architectural equivalent is the reorganization of the interior into a vast open space clearly delineated by Gothic structural forms, articulated with the round arches and mouldings that remain true to the long-standing Romanesque – or rather Ravenesque – tradition of the town.

As if in counterpoint to these urban developments, another religious institution began to take shape during this same period south of Arezzo, in the wine-rich countryside overlooked by the citadel of Montalcino. Sant' Antimo, as pure a Benedictine monastery as any in Europe, was begun about 1118 (photos, pp. 100–1). It is closer in spirit and in architecture to Burgundy than to any Tuscan or Northern Italian monuments. Its Toulousian style sculpture, its radiating apse chapels and ambulatory and its remote setting all confirm a Cluniac influence. So does its scale, as one of Italy's largest, wealthiest and most powerful Romanesque monastic complexes. Its status, however, derived from quite a different source than that of Cluny: unlike its Burgundian counterpart, Sant'Antimo was an imperial foundation, reminiscent of Carolingian monasteries, even in the title of the abbot as "Conte Palatino."

Despite its obvious wealth and the vast expenditure on its construction, Sant'Antimo never developed to the extreme scale and excess of either the early Carolingian monasteries or Cluny III. If architecture can indeed communicate religious ideals, then the design and construction of Sant' Antimo codify in stone a sensibility consonant with the spiritual aspirations of eleventh and twelfth-century monastic reform. Though its plan and sculpture show clearly Burgundian influence, the purity, even muteness, of its vast expanses of unarticulated wall, anticipate another Burgundian architectural tradition, that of the Cistercians. The resemblance is less in structural systems than in concept: architecture, not sculptural figuration, is the primary means of representation. Sant' Antimo achieves this expression without suppressing sculpture, but simply by the primal force of its architecture. It has the same layering of single arches over double-arched windows at the apse and interior gallery that

Assisi (Umbria), Cathedral of San
Rufino. Begun *c.* 1134. West façade

Spoleto (Umbria), Cathedral of Santa
Maria Assunta. Begun *c.* 1175. West
façade

the Cistercians were to use, but where the Cistercians and later Gothic architects were to elaborate this layering through vertical structural units interlaced by ribs and rib vaulting, the architects of Sant'Antimo render their layers as so many peeled away skins of smooth stone. The side elevations are supported with Lombard, even proto-Gothic piers, rapidly proceeding between each window as they move to the apse. As they arrive, however, something extraordinary happens: the wall surface breaks free from the structural rhythm, supported rather by the most fundamental architectural reinforcement, the curve. The ground-level radiating chapels provide the only visible buttressing for the ambulatory's vast sensuous arc, above whose terracotta roof tiles rises the sanctuary's exposed semi-cylindrical form.

Sant'Antimo is the swan-song of the great medieval monasteries of the Benedictine rule in Italy. Though followed in the region by other masterpieces by the Cistercians themselves, such as San Galgano in the early thirteenth century, none matches the unity, force and scale of its impact. Signs of the waning of its era are already visible at Sant'Antimo's façade, left incomplete to this day, with one of its elaborate portals placed instead, according to Raspi-Serra, at the nearby church of San Quirico d'Orcia. Despite the subsequent efforts of the Cistercians, the tide of social and religious change was away from the countryside and increasingly

towards the city, where many communities of all sizes were investing the equivalent of an abbot's wealth in the construction of their local churches and cathedrals.

Umbria

The churches of Assisi and Spoleto (photo, top) are a few examples of the development of Romanesque architecture in Umbria, to the south and east of Tuscany. The chronology of San Ruffino at Assisi reflects the history of Umbrian Romanesque architecture and intimates the eventual displacement of Italian Romanesque by the Gothic. The church dates from a "parva basilica" from the eighth century, which provided a modest setting for the remains of the town's patron saint, the third-century martyr Rufino. Around 1028 Bishop Ugone replaced this with another structure and, by 1035, established it as the cathedral of Assisi. One hundred years later, around 1134, Bishop Clarissimo hired Giovanni da Gubbio to replace this basilica with the far larger one that stands on the site today. The façade of the church registers the work of Giovanni da Gubbio at its lower portion, with a triple rhythm of larger bays subdivided by a second triple rhythm in each bay. The horizontal and vertical subdivisions of the façade plane recall the designs of San Zeno, which was begun eleven years earlier, although the verticals dominate the latter more dramatically and

OPPOSITE
Tuscania (Latium), San Pietro. Begun towards the end of the eleventh century. Detail of the façade

Spoleto (Umbria), Sant'Eufemia. Second half of the twelfth century. Nave wall

BOTTOM
Valenzano (Apulia), Ognissanti di Cuti. Begun after 1060. Exterior view of the domes

with a consistent rhythm. San Rufino instead has an equivalent bias of horizontal and vertical divisions, which form a grid that seems to run as a layer behind the more structural vertical buttresses providing the major façade subdivisions. This grid is similar to that employed at San Pietro fuori le Mura at Spoleto, though again the latter is more regular in its subdivisions, neatly framing its remarkable sculpture (photo, p. 307). At the lower façade of San Rufino the sculpture is concentrated on the portals, with the wall surfaces ornamented only by the superimposed grid. Rather than serving as frames for figures, the panels of this grid respond to the size of the portals, which push for themselves a wider space at the center of each of the three main façade panels. As at Sant'Antimo, architecture is the primary expressive medium, not sculpture. Instead of layering skins, San Rufino develops layers of Lombard bay systems, pushing it beyond the abstract consistency of San Zeno into a similarly expressive language as at Modena or San Miniato in Florence. In each of these churches, a syncopated rhythm of threes reinforces the primary function of the west façade: the expression of passage.

The classicism of this rhythmic system is repeated on the later upper façade and echoes a similar clacissim within the earlier church crypt. The three Gothic rose windows vary in size from edge to center, and align precisely above their respective portals, as if to recapitulate the imagery of passage by penetrating the church with circular arc of light. The pointed arch framed within the tall pediment crowning the façade is again Gothic, but with broad dimensions that are in character with the spacious proportions of the rest of the façade. The two dividing corbel tables and miniature blind-arcade galleries restrain any vertical potential in the upper-storey Gothicism and maintain the clear overall image of a temple front overlaid with a ground-storey triumphal arch entry. It is not necessary to look as far as San Miniato or Empoli's Collegiata for the source of this imagery, but rather to the nearby market piazza, where the Corinthian columns and pediment of the ancient Roman Temple of Minerva stand to this day as an explicit model for the overall form and abstracted portico of San Rufino's façade.

The earlier crypt of San Rufino is even more explicit in its classicism, with most of its columns classical spolia, and even the seat of the bishop, according to tradition the burial place of San Rufino, a Roman sarcophagus. The magic of San Rufino and of so much Umbrian Romanesque architecture is that this classicism in composition and in details by no means excludes the homunculi of sculptural imagination, but rather freely accommodates them, as does the upper Gothic façade. Figurations of the Evangelists are painted in the early Ugonian crypt and then repeated in sculptural form around the central rose window. They confuse any easy notion of progress from figure to abstraction, and rather emphasize that even at the time of the construction of the basilica of St. Francis, when the upper façade was completed, creatures from the primitive world could share and even support the International Gothic. A close look at the base of the central rose window reveals, indeed, one of two famous Romanesque Umbrian reinterpretations of classical caryatids.

The other caryatids support another rose window at another Umbrian

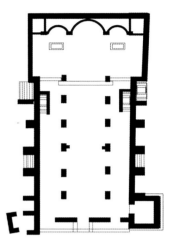

cathedral, that of Spoleto, south-east of Assisi. That these two statues are framed by carefully carved miniature Corinthian columns and capitals makes it clear that Umbrian sculptors and architects were well versed in their antique models already in the twelfth and thirteenth centuries. As at Assisi, with its Temple of Minerva, the patrons and artists of Spoleto were blessed with impressive antique models, the Temple of Clitunno and the paleo-Christian church of San Salvatore. The early thirteenth-century mosaic of Christ above this rose window reveals the same instinct that guided the architects of the last phase of San Miniato al Monte in Florence, who similarly broadcast an image of Christ for the entire town to see. The diverse sources for the design of the cathedral, from Assisi to paleo-Christian to Roman and Ventetian mosaicists suggest a rich, vibrant artistic culture in the city during the Romanesque period, which only grew in intensity after the sack of the town by Frederick Barbarossa in 1155. A continuous classical building tradition in the area from distant antiquity made such a culture possible. This building tradition was in turn sustained, as at Milan and Pavia, by the active presence of a powerful Lombard seat in the Duchy of Spoleto. By the tenth century the advent of the Carolingians led to the shift of power from the Lombard dukes to imperially and papally appointed bishops, who even occupied the same palaces as their secular Lombard predecessors up to the thirteenth century.

The Lombard history of Spoleto is best recorded architecturally in the gem-like church of Santa Eufemia (photo, top left). Here, in the middle of Umbria, stands a twelfth-century church that serves as a text-book example of Northern Lombard design principles, from the triple apses to the pilaster strips and corbel tables stiffening the exterior elevations. Its

Umbrian lineage is hinted at by the simple biforate window above the portal and the subtle designation of a triple rhythm with the two side windows on either side of it. The interior reveals the archaeology of Spoleto's Romanesque sources, with paleo-christian columns, piers and capitals interwoven between abstract semi-columns supporting taut, perfectly composed lower and gallery arches and vaulting that echo in miniature the nave and side aisles of Sant'Ambrogio in Milan.

Puglia

As one proceeds far enough south and east along the Italian peninsula to reach the Adriatic coast, another set of influences appears, from Byzantine sources. The eleventh-century monastic church of Ognissanti di Cuti by Valenzano, in Puglia (photo, p. 105, bottom), has the same triple apse termination as Santa Eufemia and so many other early Romanesque churches, but the three square protrusions in the nave roofline indicate an utterly different organization of the interior space. Here, three bold domes spring from tall piers and pendentives, subdividing the interior like that of San Marco in Venice and its early-Christian and Byzantine sources. However, as so often, more local sources may have been equally important to the designers, in this case the corbelled domes, or trulli, typical of utilitarian buildings in the area since the Etruscans. Similar domed forms are visible in the octagonal cupola of the centralized church of Santa Caterina by Conversano, built in the twelfth century following a plan typical of Syrian quatrefoil churches.

The oldest large-scale monument of the region, San Nicola at Bari, built around 1089, appears more Lombard in its design than Byzantine, with links in layout and interior details to Pisan and Florentine architecture as

Bitonto (Apulia), Cathedral of San
Valentino. Begun after 1175. View from
the south west

well. The reason for such northern influences so far south in the heel of Italy is simply the ocean, which provided rapid conveyance to and from areas far more remote than the Po or Arno valleys. Indeed, the patrons of San Nicola at Bari were perhaps the most capable and far-ranging seafarers in the world, namely Norsemen, or Normans, from their recently established Duchy of Normandy. By 1041 they had arrived at the shores of Puglia, by 1059 the Norman Robert Guiscard was anointed Duke of Puglia and Calabria, and by 1063, his Normans had extended their territory to include Sicily. Their Norman French origins, however, are less present in their Apulian and Sicilian architecture than other influences. The first and most important inspiration in the case of Bari was Saint Nicholas himself, whose remains the Normans transported from Asia Minor in 1087. Two years later they began his church, applying to the façade a triple division adopted from Lombard churches such as San Zeno or Modena. Its vertical proportions, steep roof and two flanking towers link it to the spires, westworks and tall narthex entries of Norman churches of Jumièges, Mont-Saint-Michel, and Caen, all from the mid eleventh century. It is in the interior that the Tuscan influence is evident, with the horizontal arched screens, grouped piers, triple rhythms, triforia and clerestory echoing San Miniato and Pisa Cathedral.

The cathedrals of Trani (begun 1098) and Bitonto (begun after 1175)

share sufficient characteristics with San Nicola in Bari to indicate that the latter spawned an Apulian school of architecture (photos, top right and pp. 108–9). Both are unencumbered by the double towers of Bari. Even though the tall, slender tower of Trani is nearly coplanar with that church's façade, it detaches itself as an apparently separate form above the ground-storey arch. The west elevation of Trani breaks from its model at Bari by providing a continuous, smooth surface without the reinforcing piers breaking Bari and Bitonto into a triple rhythm. The only rhythm is that of entry, where a compressed and extended version of the Tuscan porch, flattened from its original protrusion from the façade, frames three portals above a dramatic double stair. The single-tower composition of Trani is particularly well-suited to its site: the tower is counterbalanced by nothing less grand than the Adriatic, reflecting in its azure blue the bright white stone and elegant proportions of the church.

The same balance of similarity and difference between the architecture of Trani and San Nicola of Bari is present in their cults. The cathedral of Trani is also dedicated to a St. Nicholas, but not the same one as at Bari. Rather, the Trani St. Nicholas was a pilgrim boy from Greece, who took up a cross and bore it to holy sites in Greece, Dalmatia and the Adriatic coast of Italy, singing incessantly "*Kyrie eleison*" up to his death near the original cathedral of Santa Maria at Trani. The sanctification of this young pilgrim in 1094 led archbishop Bisanzio to found a new church on the site of the earlier, ninth-century cathedral. Beneath the entire complex the Tranesi constructed a vast new crypt, perhaps the source for later double-churches, such as San Francesco in Assisi, which shared San Nicola's necessity of accommodating throngs of pilgrims without disturbing services. The giant, vertical transept, with its tall exterior apses spanning

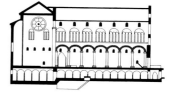

Trani (Apulia), cathedral. Begun in 1098. West façade (far left), nave to the west (left), view from the south east (opposite), elevation (below)

the two interior levels, symbolically interlinks nave and crypt with the site's traditional and new cults. The transept's large thirteenth-century Gothic rose windows illuminate the terminus of both the eucharistic sacrifice and the pilgrim saint's journey to death and salvation at the center of the tall church crossing.

The cathedral of Troia (photo, left), begun shortly before Trani in 1093 by Bishop Girardo, proclaims clearly its independence from the school of Bari. Unlike San Nicola or Trani's cathedral, Troia is designed with broad proportions and with a blind façade arcade punctuated by inlaid decorative motifs within its arches. They derive from Tuscan Romanesque architecture, particularly from the elevations of Pisa's cathedral, dating from 1063 to approximately 1108. The latter date corresponds to the date of the second major building campaign at Troia, between 1106 and 1119, when Bishop Guglielmo II completed most of the church. The tell-tale Pisan inset rotated squares and circles in the blind arcades date from one of these two early building campaigns. The link to late eleventh-, early twelfth-century Tuscany is due to the political status of Troia, which was directly under the patronage of St. Peter's in Rome, which, in turn, had its strongest ally on the Italian peninsula in Tuscany's Countess Mathilda of Canossa during these very years. Either direct visits by local architects to Mathildine architecture in Pisa, Florence, Pistoia, Lucca or even Modena, or contact with Tuscan builders through pilgrimages or the first crusade, which departed from the area in 1096-7, led to the adoption of these motifs at Troia. The presence of other Tuscan planning ideas in the interior of Bari's San Nicola suggests the latter. The explicit presentation of distant Tuscan motifs at Troia, on its main elevation, emphasized how important uniqueness in Apulian religion and politics was to the bishops constructing and inhabiting the cathedral seat.

Sicily

The mixture of Byzantine, Islamic, Norman and papal Roman styles present in Norman Puglia is even more extreme in the other kingdom

established by the Normans, just beyond the tip of Italy, on the island of Sicily. The recent and powerful presence of Islam on the island and the Normans' tolerant attitude to it, as well as to Byzantine and to Roman Christianity, led to an extraordinary receptiveness to combining Islamic and Byzantine architectural forms for Latin-rite churches. The simultaneous presence of the Normans in North Africa assured continuous influences from African Islamic traditions throughout the Romanesque period. The Normans arrived in Sicily from France in 1061, and won control over the island over the next thirty years. As in Normandy, England and Puglia, these "Northmen" transformed themselves from restless Viking marauders to permanently settled citizens of a highly organized political kingdom. One of the primary vehicles for this radical change in identity was their adoption of Latin Christianity, which not only led to a normalization of relations between the Normans and the Europeans they once terrorized, but also provided an ideal means for the Normans to pacify and unite the areas they conquered and settled. Just as Charlemagne had used a mixture of palace, cathedral and monastic construction to stabilize and extend the Carolingian empire two and a half centuries beforehand, the Normans, beginning with William Longsword at Jumièges in Normandy, William the Conqueror at Hastings in England, Robert Guiscard at Venosa in Puglia and Roger II at Palermo in Sicily, engaged enthusiastically in building campaigns to establish their presence in each region in stone.

As if to confirm the parallel between Carolingian and Norman architectural policy, Roger II constructed himself a palace and attached palatine chapel, dedicated to St. Peter, in Palermo. The chapel was completed between the year of Robert's coronation, 1130, and 1143. Like its contemporaries in Normandy and the Italian peninsula, it has a triple apse. Its two side aisles are screened from the nave by marble columns supporting classicizing Corinthian-composite capitals. The tall pointed arches these capitals sustain are typically Islamic, as is the stalactite ceiling, while the rich mosaics, dating from 1143 and 1189, are Byzantine. The dissolution of the wall and ceiling by mosaics and

Palermo (Sicily), Palatine Chapel. Completed between 1130 and 1143. Mosaic decorations in the interior of the chapel

Palermo, cathedral. 1069–1190. View from the east

elaborate non-structural vaulting patterns undermines the simple geometric clarity of the rectangular space of the nave, anticipating the more complex spatial arrangement of the sanctuary's triple apses and their sectional projection into the screening arches and dome of the crossing. The ensemble creates a similar sense of hieratic awe as that of the great Imperial churches of Justinianian Byzantium at Hagia Sophia and San Vitale, on a more modest scale.

Similarly rich, hybrid church complexes sprang up across Palermo during the twelfth century, including the Martorana, (Santa Maria dell' Ammiraglio), San Giovanni degli Eremiti, San Giovanni dei Lebbrosi, San Cataldo, and Santo Spirito. The largest of the Norman building projects in Palermo was the Cathedral, built between 1069 and 1190 by the Archbishop Walter of the Mill (Gualtiero Offamilio) of Palermo (photo, top). Its apse and side elevation are the best evidence for how the entire complex would have originally appeared. The interlocking major and minor pointed arches of the former and the wave-like array of stepped windows and crenellation of the latter are both Islamic in origin. The four corner towers were added in a new phase of Sicilian architecture, under the Hohenstaufens, starting in 1094, while other elevations and the interior, which serves to this day as the Pantheon for Norman and Staufen kings and emperors, were changed later, especially after 1781.

Cefalù (Sicily), cathedral. Begun in 1131.
View from the south east

Cefalù

Roger II originally planned and began construction of another cathedral to house the tombs of the Norman kings of Sicily, not at Palermo, but to the east at Cefalù. The transept and sanctuary date from Roger's time, but his successors and the Hohenstaufens completed the nave and façade, between 1180 and 1240, on a more modest scale, focussing instead on Palermo Cathedral as their Pantheon. The difference between the original and completed version of the complex is evident at the side view, where the scale drops dramatically past the interlaced arches of the apse, side chapels and transept. Traces of this complex ornamental treatment of arches are still present in the newer nave walls, visible from the cloister, but are more contained and internally layered, rather than interlocked. They reappear at the upper west façade, but are tamed by the smoother ashlar of the triple-arch porch and the powerful, monolithic towers framing the entry. The interior is similarly simplified, with the regular rhythm of the unadorned nave arches leading up to a sanctuary whose only uniquely Norman feature is the extraordinary Byzantine mosaic of the semi-dome.

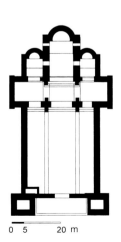

Nave and side aisle (right), cloister gallery (far right), ground plan (above)

0 5   20 m

111

Monreale (Sicily), cathedral.
1147–82. Part of the choir from the
south east (top left), interior view to
the east (top right), cloister (bottom)

Monreale

The dominance of Palermo, and particularly of the bishop at its cathedral, was so strong by 1172 as to lead King William to establish a competing church, palace and monastery nearby at Monreale. He finished most of the church by 1182 and the vast twenty-five-bay square cloister by 1200. William's goal of counterbalancing the bishop of Palermo succeeded with Pope Lucius III's elevation of Monreale to an episcopal seat in 1183. Like his counterparts in Puglia, he was open to Tuscan influences, in this case the sculptor Bonanno of Pisa, whom he commissioned to execute bronze doors for the main portal, which were installed in 1185. Another set, sculpted by Barisone of Trani, was added to the portal to its north five years later. As at Cefalù, a series of interlocked arches extends above the east portals, framed by two short, apparently incomplete towers. Similar Islamic arches cover the exterior of the apse and transept of Monreale, more relentlessly than in the transept of Palermo Cathedral or Cefalù, with the effect of dissolving the exterior planes of the structure.

A similar dematerializing effect is achieved within the church by its mosaics. As in Palermo's Palatine Chapel, these Byzantine mosaics deny the structure of the pointed arches and classicizing Corinthian columns supporting their walls. The linguistic variations in the inscriptions accompanying the mosaic scenes help to decipher their intended effect. Along the narrative scenes on the nave walls they are in Latin, which would have been more familiar to the laity and Norman court, while at the apse, surrounding the remarkable mosaic of Christ, they are in Greek, with the exception of the text in Christ's hand. The Latin words and accompanying mosaic vignettes along the nave draw the worshipper toward the crossing, where narration and motion are stopped by the Greek text and the giant, otherworldly vision of Christ dominating the apse.

Though extreme in the diversity of its sources, the multivalent character of Monreale only dramatizes the multiple functions that Romanesque architecture throughout Italy was built to fulfill: to attract the laity with imaginative or empathetic scenes, and then to overwhelm them with the awesome power of divinity. The mediators between daily existence and eternal salvation were the permanent inhabitants of the church. These holy residents, the saints, clergy, and, at Monreale, the kings, proclaimed in architecture their readiness to intercede on behalf of those members of the laity who were willing to honor them and to abide by their laws.

OPPOSITE
View of the nave and side aisles from the
cloister courtyard

112

Secular architecture

Monumental secular architecture in Romanesque Italy derived from the same sources as those of religious architecture. The fifth-century Palace of Theodoric and the early eighth-century Palace of the Exarchs in Ravenna transmitted examples of Imperial palace design to both episcopal and lay builders of governing palaces. Their lower arcades and upper-level galleries were copied at such geographically diverse sites as the Palazzo della Ragione in Pomposa, the Zisa in Palermo (1164-80), possibly the Pieve of Arezzo, and the town halls of Bergamo, Milan and Orvieto, all built between the early twelfth and mid thirteenth centuries. These structures established a town hall type, with a lower-level arcade supporting a glazed rectangular second-storey meeting hall, which became widely diffused between the twelfth and fourteenth centuries.

The unprotected arcade made this urban palace type inappropriate for rural residences of emperors, kings or their vassals. Feudal strongholds in Italy, as in the North and along the Crusade routes, tended, rather, to be built of multiple rings of fortification, first around an entire settlement, then around the castle, and finally forming a prominent tower. Usually on hilltop sites, such as at Frederick II's castle at Assisi, such fortresses generally conformed more to the topography in their layout than to the laws of symmetry. Frederick II was the only castle-builder at the time to develop as well an alternative to these rather crude expressions of defense and power, in a series of symmetrical, centrally planned castles ranging from Castel del Monte in Puglia (photo, top) to the Palatium Imperatoris at Prato in Tuscany. Both examples fuse the image of impenetrable fortress with the iconography of Roman imperial palaces by situating classically pedimented portals between twin towers, just as at Diocletian's Imperial palace at Split.

When the growing wealth of Romanesque Italian cities began to attract rural lords to build near their marketplaces, the nobility imported their rustic castle and tower forms and adapted them to entire blocks or sectors of towns. The Tuscan town of San Gimignano (photo, p. 115, top) provides an example of how most Romanesque Italian cities would have looked, literally bristling with towers constructed by both the nobility and by powerful merchants emulating them. Even papal Rome had its share of towers, occupied by its powerful families such as the Caetani at their Torre delle Milizie (photo, p. 115, right).

As the civic governments of Italy's cities grew in wealth, population and military aspirations, they began to compete with the tower-house complexes of the nobility on two scales. One was by constructing towers of their own, often grafted onto more urban public palaces such as those discussed above. The other was by encircling their towns with city walls protected by regularly placed towers and gates, which in many cases had previously protected only individual monuments in the cities, such as the originally fortified eleventh-century cathedral and palace complex of the bishop of Arezzo. In Florence, Prato and numerous other cities, the construction of city walls, in most cases by the mid twelfth century,

OPPOSITE
Castel del Monte (Apulia). Begun *c.* 1233

BELOW
Sectional drawing of a medieval housing complex, viewed from the inner courtyard

ABOVE
San Gimignano. Residential towers from the twelfth and thirteenth centuries

RIGHT
Rome, Torre delle Milizie. Beginning of the thirteenth century

Florence's densely populated town
centre, viewed from above. Detail from a
fourteenth century painting

Milan, Palazzo della Ragione. Equestrian
statue dating from 1233

coincided with the building of civic palaces and with the formation of
secular civic governments to reside within them.

The moment most communes built city walls their populations quickly
filled them, leading to densely packed spaces and narrow streets that
seemed all the more cavernous due to the frequency of tower houses. This
busy, noisy, cramped and dangerous environment made the ornamented
façades and vast interior spaces of urban Romanesque houses of worship
all the more splendid. The aura of religious architecture was so powerful
that nearly all town halls of the twelfth century were built adjoining the
principal churches of communities, and were articulated with decorations
adopted from church windows and portals. The common architecture and
interests of church and state are clearly visible, for instance on the façade
of Milan's Palazzo della Ragione (photo, p. 116). Between the ground-
storey arcade and upper-level triforate windows a single arch frames an
equestrian statue of Oldrado da Tresseno (photo, top right), the city's
podestà, or governor, in 1233. The inscription reads: *catharos ut debuit
uxit*, "he burned heretics as he ought to." It was only with the revolution
of the mendicant orders, in the mid thirteenth century, that the
concentrated monumentality of the Romanesque city began to diffuse
throughout townscapes, leading to the spread of monumental arcades,
such as those in Bologna, along all major thoroughfares, and to the
multiplication of mendicant churches and piazzas disseminating a new,
popular piety with what was to become the architectural equivalent of the
vernacular, the Gothic.

The heavenly Jerusalem. Detail from a ceiling painting in the abbey church of Saint-Chef (France)

developments in Syria, Ireland, Italy and Northern Europe. By the sixth century two clear strands existed in the West. One was Irish monasticism, where the scale of communities founded by monks such as St. Patrick remained as small as possible and the settings remote and desolate. Irish acetic extremism developed to the point of monks competing with one another in self-denial, bringing upon them the critique of wild individualism by St Benedict of Nursia. St. Benedict's own monastic foundation represents the other strand. Benedict codified a monastic rule which regulated every aspect of daily life, providing a military-like organization that guaranteed a pious life and a capacity to

live harmoniously. Benedictine monasteries became oases of stability, order and even agricultural and economic productivity within a harsh, chaotic world.

Under Charlemagne and Louis the Pious, Benedictine monasteries became the core of a policy of reevangelizing the countryside and organizing agriculture, learning and the training of the court. The clearest architectural expression of Carolingian monasticism is in the plan of St. Gall, from around 820, which was literally a blueprint for the construction of monasteries throughout the Holy Roman Empire. The scheme is organized around it most significant innovation, the cloister, which became the focal point for all monastic architecture since.

The three great monastic houses of the Romanesque period were all based on the Carolingian plan of St. Gall. The first was Monte Cassino, Benedict's settlement in

The monastery as Heavenly Jerusalem

Early Christian and medieval architecture and urbanism derive their emotive strength from their capacity to express in earthly materials the promise and durability of the heavenly afterlife. The first architectural expression of the world after death was St. John the Divine's literary description of the Heavenly Jerusalem in Revelation. He tells of a place that is at once a city and not a city, built with walls, foundations and gates, yet floating down from the sky, built of durable materials, yet of transparent gems, not opaque stone. The number of gates, twelve, reveal that the image is as much a community of apostles and tribes of Israel as it is a physical place. At the center John tells us there is not a temple, but Christ the Lamb himself. Architecture is no longer necessary in the city of salvation, and yet the only way to describe that city is in architectural terms.

The paradox of St. John the Divine echoes in the architecture of monasteries up to the Reformation. The first monastic settlements in Egypt were no more than assemblages of hermit retreats, organized by nothing more than their proximity and their walls, which were as much to keep hermits in as to keep the evils of the world out. And yet already by the time of St. Pachomius, in his coenobium of the early fourth century, a more architectural organization of buildings and activities was developing. Architecture was the most effective means for expressing at once the individual retreat of each hermit and the growing sense of common mission and needs which the hermits shared. They organized an ideal city for themselves, dividing themselves into smaller groups according to trade. Each fold had its own architectural unit, with a series of cells and a common room. The tension between individual retreat and life in common persisted in monastic

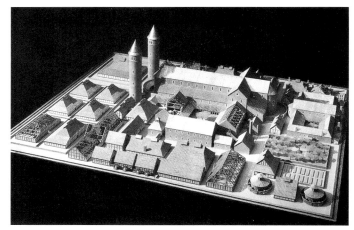

Model of the St. Gallen monastery after the plan made c. 820

Cluny III, monastery church and part of the monastery. Section of model

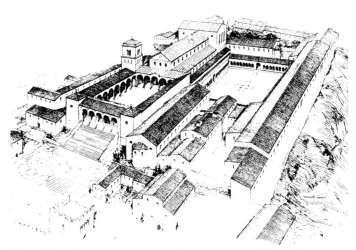

Abbey of Monte Cassino. Reconstruction of the monastery c. 1075 (after K. J. Conant)

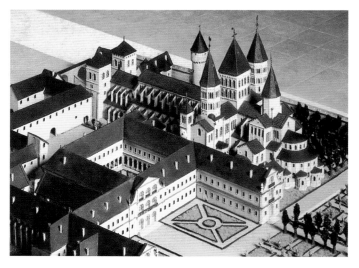

118

Campagna in the sixth century. It was rebuilt by Abbot Desiderius in the eleventh century. Masons from the nearby seafaring town of Amalfi introduced Islamic pointed arches and groin vaults into the mixture of early Christian and Lombard traditions at the site.

One visitor to Monte Cassino, in 1083, was Abbot Hugh of Cluny. By this time Cluny had established itself as another of the most important monastic centers in Europe. When Hugh returned to Burgundy he began, by 1088, to build Cluny III. It is through Monte Cassino and Cluny III, according to Kevin Conant, that innovations in Romanesque engineering techniques made their way across Burgundy and France.

By the late eleventh century the scale and beauty of Monte Cassino and Cluniac monasteries were matched only by the magnificence of monastic life. Monks were serviced by serfs providing them with the best in food and wine. Their sole labors were prayer, illumination and the chanting of psalms. The relation of worldly to spiritual became so unbalanced that, already in 1075, the first of a series of Cluniac monks fled to establish a more ascetic retreat. By 1119 Pope Calixtus II had approved their new monastic charter, establishing the Cistercian Order at the third great monastic house of Europe, named after its remote valley, Cîteaux. The best preserved Cistercian abbey is Fontenay in France, sited far from any urban center, along a stream that the monks channeled for power and sanitation. The architecture eschews all figurative excess, elevating the layering of structural elements, the quality of surfaces and joints, and the admission of pure white light to an expression of paradise. The separation of activities and setting assured the insulation of church and cloister from the profane world, restoring the settlement at once to the ordering principles of Benedict and the acetic isolation of the Egyptian and Irish hermits.

Fountains Abbey. Aerial view of the monastery ruins

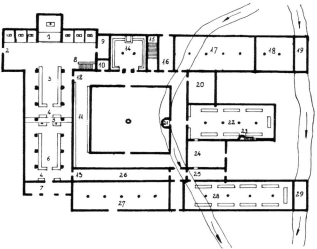

LEFT
Ideal plan of a Cistercian monastery (after W. Braunfels)

1 Sanctuary	15 Dormitory steps
2 Dead gate	16 Auditorium
3 Monks' choir	17 Monks' hall
4 Invalids' benches	18 Novitiate
5 Rood screen	19 Monks' latrine
6 Lay brothers' choir	20 Warming room
7 Narthex	21 Well
8 Dormitory steps	22 Monks' refectory
9 Sacristy	23 Pulpit
10 Armarium – monastic library	24 Kitchen
11 Mandatum – stone benches for reading and washing feet	25 Cellarer's consulting room
	26 Lay brothers' passage
	27 Storehouse
12 Monks' gate	28 Lay brothers' refectory
13 Lay brothers' gate	
14 Chapterhouse	29 Lay brothers' latrine

Bernhard and Ulrike Laule

Romanesque architecture in France

The establishment of the French Kingdom after Charlemagne

After the death of Charlemagne in January 814, the huge empire fell into the hands of Louis the Pious, only to be split up in 843 amongst his three sons in the Treaty of Verdun. Louis II received East Francia. Lothar gained the imperial crown and the Middle Kingdom, which included a broad strip from Friesland to Provence dividing East and West Francia, Lombardy, Friuli and Italy as far as the Duchy of Benevento. Charles the Bald was granted West Francia which, with the exception of the easterly areas, and Normandy and Brittany in the north west, corresponds to the France of today. He also received parts of what are today Belgium and the Netherlands. By 875, however, Charles was able not only to obtain the imperial crown for West Francia, but also to extend his imperial boundaries as far as the Rhone, the Duchy of Vienne including the towns of Vienne and Arles, and part of the Jura and Burgundy including the towns of Basle, Geneva and Besançon.

These boundaries remained stable for a long period, and the young French kingdom, whose roots stretched back to the pre-Carolingian period of the fifth century, was able to consolidate its position.

The Roman occupation of Gaul had brought Christendom to the area by the second century, and the Frankish kingdom soon had a close relationship with the Church. King Clovis I (481–510) converted to the Catholic faith and was baptized during the Christmas of 497. This alliance of Church and kingdom was to prove its worth in the following centuries.

Sources in the ninth and tenth centuries report the founding of numerous monasteries, whilst many towns saw the building of the new cathedrals of the early Christian period. It must be remembered that these churches were still in the Roman tradition: large basilicas, naves with flat ceilings and transepts with semi-circular apses. The prototype was still Old St. Peter's in Rome.

The development of Romanesque – new spatial forms in the choir and nave

Many of the early Christians of the Frankish Empire were now canonized, and new saints were continually being created. Reports circulated of miracles at their graves, which often lay within monasteries or even led to the founding of new ones. The faithful made pilgrimages to these monasteries, and important new pilgrimage routes developed. The growth in pilgrimages, which brought large numbers of pilgrims to the monasteries, created a need for lodgings and particularly for devotional objects of all kinds. It increased their income considerably, but required an efficient organization. Ways were sought of directing the pilgrims so that those coming in and out of the church did not cause disturbance detrimental to the liturgy of the monks in the choir. It was below the main altar that the saint's tomb would almost always be situated.

From the middle of the ninth century onwards, rectangular ambulatories were created in Auxerre and Flavigny-sur-Ozerain. These led around the saint's tomb in the crypt, allowing the pilgrims to descend the stairs from one side aisle and return up via the other. In both these churches the ambulatory was extended to include a round or octagonal lady chapel behind an aisled approach. Before the middle of the ninth century the crypt at Saint-Philibert-de-Grandlieu on the Atlantic coast was extended to house the relics of St. Philibert, later taken to Tournus. The crypt had a rectangular ambulatory with echeloned chapels on its eastern arm. The first crypt at Tournus, which was built in the years after 875, must have been similar. These first ambulatories were gradually adapted to the curvature of the end of the choir. Early examples are the choirs of Clermont-Ferrand and Saint-Maurice-d'Agaune. During the second half of the tenth century the monks in Tournus erected just such an ambulatory with rectangular radial chapels, which enclosed a chapel in front of the confessio with a nave and two side aisles. The first fully developed ambulatory with semi-circular radial chapels was the one at St. Martin at Tours. It was built around 1000, but largely demolished after the French Revolution.

It was the monastery of Cluny and its priories which were to remain influential in the development of the nave over the following century. In 948, only a few decades after the completion of the first church, the monks of Cluny began the construction of a second, larger church (Cluny II). It was not consecrated, however, until 981, probably because of difficulties encountered in the construction. Its form is only known from excavations and written sources. It had a nave with two side aisles, and a projecting transept. It also had a choir with chapels in echelon, the first example of its kind and one which was at first widely imitated. The function of the individual rooms has never been completely explained. The echeloned chapels in Cluny II consisted of seven symmetrically arranged apses. The central three had a semi-circular termination, and were slightly staggered one to another. Their deep, probably barrel-vaulted forebays were connected with each other by colonnades. On each side of these three chapels, and set back slightly, there was a chapel with a rectangular termination. Finally, on the very outside of each of these there was a small apse on the transept wall. The elevation of the nave must have had two storeys. Above the arcades was a barrel vault without transverse arches. Small windows pierced its base, making it the first known example of a vaulted church with an illuminated vault.

Thus it was that by around the year 1000 both architectural features characteristic of Romanesque architecture had been developed, namely the ambulatory with radial chapels and the illuminated vault. The latter was then still in its early stages of development, and over the following century was to undergo continual improvement and perfection. It was not until about 120 years later that the barrel vault was superseded by other forms of vaulting, including those based on Gothic design principles.

Several buildings from the years after the turn of the millennium have either survived or are known about in sufficient detail: the great basilica of Saint-Bénigne in Dijon with its curious choir apex rotunda and the small church of Saint-Vorles in Châtillon-sur-Seine, both in the territory of the duchy of Burgundy; in northern France the basilicas of Montierender, Sainte-Gertrude in Nivelles and Saint-Rémi in Rheims and, in the deep south of France in the former province of Narbonensis, Saint-Martin-du-Canigou.

Burgundy – the problem of barrel vaulting

In 1001 William of Volpiano, the abbot of Saint-Bénigne in Dijon, commissioned a replacement for the huge basilica which had been built in 535 over the tomb of St. Benignus (d. c. 274). In 989 the monastery of Cluny had been reformed, and it may be assumed that William of Volpiano knew and appreciated the vaulted basilica which had just been completed there. Nevertheless, he decided on an "old-fashioned", unvaulted construction. This was partly because of lack of space, but it must also be remembered that Saint-Bénigne was already 500 years old, possessed numerous relics and was a famous destination for pilgrimages – in other words, a place of tradition. The result was an enormous basilica with a nave and four side aisles, transept and a choir with five radiating chapels. The central apse was, however, substituted by a huge choir apex rotunda dedicated to the mother of God (figure, p. 122). It is only the rotunda that remains of this construction dating from the beginning of the new millennium, as the nave was damaged in 1137 and 1271 and in both cases was replaced by more modern structures.

It is a three-storeyed rotunda with a nave and two aisles. The continuous central shaft opens upwards into a circular opening at the apex. Eight columns enclose this central shaft, whilst there are sixteen between the first and second ambulatory and twenty-four engaged columns on the outer wall. Both ambulatories are barrel-vaulted. In the outer ambulatory the semi-circular barrel vault is interrupted in every third bay by a groin vault. In the last storey there is a single wide ambulatory, vaulted with a quarter circle barrel vault. In the north and the south, semi-circular projecting staircases are added to the exterior of the rotunda. In the east, a small chapel is added, the forerunners of which are said to date from the sixth century and stood on the Gallo-Roman cemetery.

The atmosphere in this rotunda is that of a giant crypt and the impression of space is confusing and mystical because of the multiplicity of aisles and storeys. It would not be right, however, to draw a comparison with the Holy Sepulcher in Jerusalem as there is too little harmony in the building. It is more likely that this particular design solution was dictated by the presence of the centuries-old tombs of saints and dedications to patron saints. Similar situations are known to have arisen at other places and, as with the example of Saint-Bénigne, they were not imitated because of the individual nature of their solutions.

The ground floor of the rotunda was like an extensive crypt underneath the whole transept and half of the nave. Here, in a prominent position on the dividing line between the transept and choir, was the tomb of St. Benignus.

The nave may have had three storeys: arcades above square piers, galleries, clerestory and flat ceiling. Even this nave initially found no imitators. The second church at Cluny had shown that illuminated barrel vaults were possible, albeit with a limited width of nave and minute windows. However, it was to be several centuries before Cluny, with its third church, once again dared to vault the huge nave and four aisles with barrel vaults over the clerestory.

Vault constructions after Cluny II

Around the year 1000 the bishop of Langres, Bruno de Roucy, commissioned the complete renewal of what was probably a Carolingian construction in Châtillon-sur-Seine. A nave and two aisles with four bays is still standing, as well as a projecting barrel-vaulted transept and the remains of a chevet with five chapels, also with the original barrel vaults. Today there is groin vaulting in both nave and aisles, the former dating, however, from the seventeenth century. Originally there must have been a barrel vault here, possibly with small openings at the base of the vault. The exterior, which would once have been very attractive with its clearly demarcated parts, is dominated by a crossing tower; but only the first floor remains with its blind arches between flat lesenes.

Between 1020 and 1030 the monks of Saint-Philibert in Tournus had a new nave and aisles built. In 1007/8 their church had been damaged by the Hungarian invasions, but was repaired again and consecrated by 1019. In the mean time the monks must have found their broad nave with its flat ceiling quite old-fashioned, and they decided on the construction of a narrower nave with vaulting. The eastern parts were narrower than the older nave, and so they began in the west in front of the church with three bays of a nave, which was adapted to the width of the choir. The nave bays, with giant round pillars at their corners, were square, whilst the side aisle bays were the corresponding rectangular shape. When these first bays

were complete up to the level of the arcades, it was decided to leave the old outer walls standing, and to try to vault a wider nave. The narrower bays which had just been erected were to become the narthex. Because, however, the very long rectangular aisle bays were difficult to span with groin vaults, the groin vaulting was used in the square nave bays and the side aisles were covered with a quarter-circle barrel vault. It is possible that the original nave project was abandoned because there was greater confidence that they would be able to vault a wider nave. It is equally probable that the monks realized that their bay divisions with square nave bays was unsuitable for a barrel vault.

This experience was to benefit the small church of Saint-Martin in Chapaize, a priory which was independent of Tournus (photos, p. 123 below). The ground plan and shape of the piers, as well as the dimensions of Saint-Martin, are virtually identical to those of the narthex of Tournus. The bays on the other hand are so constructed that they form transverse rectangles in the nave and squares in the side aisles. This means that the powerful piers stand closer together. The elevation is of two storeys: arcades, pointed vaults with small windows which pierce the barrel vault, and groin vaulting in the side aisles. Semi-circular responds over round piers articulate the upper wall and carry the transverse arches. In the twelfth century the original round barrel collapsed (the upper walls are still remarkably slanting even now) and was replaced with the pointed barrel still existing today. The transept is as low as the side aisles and three apses, the central one of which is larger, form the choir. Saint-Martin is also articulated on the exterior by round-arched friezes, and the high crossing tower with two bell storeys, one over the other, is visible from a great distance. In Saint-Martin in Chapaize, built around 1030, shortly after the narthex ground floor at Tournus, there is a clear sense of the greatness and influence of a Cluniac church of the eleventh century. Today it stands empty, except for simple rows of benches and a small altar.

The pretty little church of St. Peter and Paul also has dimensions incredibly similar to those of Cluny II and the Tournus narthex. This church is to be found in the upper reaches of the small river Nozon, in the area of Burgundy now in Switzerland.

Gregory of Tours reported that St. Romanus and his brother, Lupicinus, had founded a small monastery which after an eventful history was made over in a will to Cluny in 928. It was not until a century later, after two smaller preliminary constructions, that a new building was constructed in Romainmôtier under Abbot Odio of Cluny. With its nave and two side aisles with round piers under round-arched arcades, it echoes Tournus and Chapaize, and probably more directly Cluny II. One example of an advance in Romanesque architecture is the broad supporting pieces in the arcades. The aisles support barrel vaulting which is pierced on both sides by lunettes, whilst the nave has been rib-vaulted since the late thirteenth century. The lower transept, projecting only slightly, still has the original vaulting. This explains the features on the upper wall, where there are traces of the arches which used to spring from the still existing small corbels. It is apparent that there was a desire to avoid windows which pierced the barrel vaults, and so the high windows in the transept are

BELOW
Chapaize (Saône-et-Loire), former priory
church Saint-Martin. Around 1030.
Nave and tower from south-west
(left), nave wall (right)

Romainmôtier (Switzerland), former
monastery church St. Peter and Paul.
Around 1030/40. Nave looking west

placed beneath broad curved undersurfaces which spring from small
corbels on the upper wall and pierce the round barrel. These arches at the
same time reduce the radius of the barrel by at least a yard. Deep barrel
forebays, connected by two colonnades, were situated in front of the semi-
circular apses. The latter were altered in the Gothic age and their original
forms are only just recognizable. The articulation of the exterior is typical
of the first half of the eleventh century with its blind-arched friezes
between flat lesenes and a beautiful crossing tower with two storeys. The
double-storeyed narthex with its nave and two aisles with cruciform piers
and groin vaulting over supporting beams in both nave and aisles dates
from around 1100. The upper storey has round piers with sculptured
imposts. The ground floor has groin vaulting throughout, and in the eastern
part there is a small semi-circular recess which extends into the nave.

Around 1050 the monks of Saint-Philibert in Tournus had modernized
and vaulted their old nave (photos, p. 125). The nave was wider than
originally envisaged when it was constructed between 1020 and 1030,
making the bays square. Narrow and very steep round arches spring from
strong round piers. The ceiling is a round barrel vault with small windows
at its base. As in Chapaize, engaged columns are fitted to the wall above
the imposts of the piers, which supported the transverse barrel arches, in
alternately laid bricks.The side aisles were groin-vaulted with the inner
cells towards the nave slightly sloping in order to support the barrel vault.
The nave has not survived in this form as the barrel vault collapsed very
soon after its construction. Around 1070/80 the collapsed transverse
arches were renewed or replaced without alternately laid bricks (the old

Payerne (Switzerland) former abbey
church. Around 1040/50. Nave looking
east

arches are therefore still recognizable) and the nave was covered as a temporary measure with transverse barrel vaults. The impression of space which resulted is extremely unusual, and must have seemed so even to contemporaries. Although the nave is certainly significantly brighter, as the transverse barrel vaults are pierced by large windows, nevertheless the continuity of the space, the even progression of identical sections along the nave, is significantly interrupted. Despite all the different attempts to explain them, the transverse barrel vaults at Tournus can really only be seen as a solution to a particular problem. They found no imitations elsewhere.

Between 1040 and 1050, contemporary with the first nave vaulting at Tournus, another large church was built in this mould; the second abbey church at Payerne (figure, left). Odilo of Cluny cited Adelheid, the daughter of Rudolf II of Burgundy, as the founder of this tenth century abbey. In her second marriage she married Emperor Otto the Great and since 991 had been the regent for her grandson Otto III who was not yet of age. It cannot be discounted that it was her parents who founded the abbey, for the grave of Adelheid's mother Bertha was at Payerne, where one of the monks' duties was to pray for the salvation of her soul. The new imperial monastery was subordinate to Cluny. The whole royal family of Burgundy, which spanned the Jura mountains, had long had close ties to Cluny. In the second quarter of the eleventh century and under the influence of Cluny, a new west front was constructed for a building which was initially planned to be narrower. The change in plan must have happened quickly. A westblock with one bay was erected with the Michael chapel in the upper storey, and the old tenth-century nave was enclosed. For this reason the north and south walls of the nave do not follow the axis of the building. The square nave piers were then constructed, and powerful projecting columns added. Stepped responds in the side aisles echo these projecting columns. Initially the crossing was planned for the sixth bay, but finally it was built in the seventh. The final stage of the building was the square crossing and the high projecting transept with its chevet of five chapels. All the previous examples of this type of elevation discussed either collapsed or were modified. This is therefore the oldest preserved example of the barrel vault above high, slender arcades and windows which pierce the foot of the vault. As at Tournus, the barrel vault has transverse arches. However, the transverse arches at Payerne are supported underneath by responds, whilst at Tournus they spring from the imposts of the round piers. These rectangular responds influenced the decision to use square piers with projecting columns instead of round piers. This nave elevation is continued into the long choir and allowed a double row of windows in the main apse, which makes the interior very high and bright compared to other buildings of that period. The exterior is reminiscent in its articulation and decoration of the other churches discussed, but has been modified by later additions.

The abbey church of Payerne is one of the last perfectly preserved buildings of its type, and synthesizes the experience of almost a century of the work of the Cluniac architects. For the first time a consistent rhythm has been achieved in the nave which, together with the smooth transition from the responds to the transverse arches, foreshadows the Gothic style.

Tournus (Saône-et-Loire), former abbey church Saint-Philibert. After 1020. Nave west towers from south-east (left), Nave looking east (right)

A dedication has survived from the year 1120, which refers to the repair of the eastern parts whose more modern forms were built up over the old ground plan.

Tournus (Saône-et-Loire), former abbey church St. Philibert. After 1020. Cloister (left), ground plan (right)

Barely older than the nave is the surviving north wing of the cloisters, whose wide arcades are articulated by strong semi-circular responds. Abbot Ardain was laid to rest here in 1156. He commissioned the building of the ground floor of the narthex and the nave, and was later canonized.

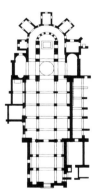

La-Charité-sur-Loire (Nièvre), former priory church Sainte-Croix-Notre-Dame. 1056–1107. Interior view of the choir, and ground plan

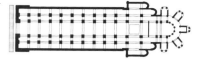

Nevers (Nièvre), former abbey church of Sainte-Etienne. 1063–1097. Nave and choir

The models for the third church at Cluny

The nave of Tournus and the abbey church of Payerne had long since been planned and completed when Hugo of Semur ascended the abbot's throne at Cluny in 1049. His new church of Sainte-Croix-Notre-Dame at La Charité-sur-Loire was inspired by Cluny priory, but is nevertheless very much a product of its own age (photos, p.126).

In 1056 the Duke of Nièvre founded a monastery which lay in a very favorable position on the pilgrims' route to Santiago de Compostela. Documents from 1107 and 1135 have survived referring to a first church in the style of Cluny II and a modification in the style of Cluny III. The only parts surviving from the Middle Ages are the transept (today with pointed barrel vaults above a clerestory) with its squinch cupola, the four outer apses of the chevet (which originally had seven), an ambulatory with chapels and a west tower. If one knows those buildings which were constructed under Cluniac influence during the eleventh century and one is also aware of Hugo's ideas for Cluny III, these few remaining parts are sufficient to imagine the original church.

In line with the customs of the time, a chevet with seven chapels was erected initially. As in Payerne, there were colonnades in the forechoir, a two-storey clerestory in the main apse, and the narrow, steep transept with windows high up under the barrel vault. Without doubt, the second church of Cluny was the inspiration for La Charité. The ground plan of the nave, probably with four aisles, extended westwards with ten bays. With its size it is clearly recognizable as the immediate forerunner of Cluny

III. Similar to Cluny III, La Charité must have had a three-storey elevation right from the outset, consisting of arcades, blind triforium and clerestory; it is not, as was mistakenly assumed, the result of a reconstruction in the first half of the twelfth century referred to in the consecration document of 1135. It is surely unlikely that such a recently constructed building would be rebuilt from the foundation walls upwards.

It has often been asked why, in contrast to other abbots and bishops, Abbot Hugo did not start the construction of the new church until he had been in office for forty years. Apparently he wanted to test out the architectural concepts for his great and ambitious new project, and, as we shall see, in several places at once, before he finally felt able to show his contemporaries the greatest and most perfect building in Christendom. In La Charité after 1107 it was only the three central apses which were replaced by an ambulatory and side chapels and consecrated in 1135.

In Nièvre, not far from La Charité, the building of the abbey church of Saint-Etienne (figure, above) started in 1063 and the consecration took place in 1097. Nièvre was also a significant station on the pilgrims' route to Santiago and was also a priory of Cluny. It is therefore no surprise that the building constructed in Nièvre differed from the traditional type of Cluny II. A nave and two side aisles with six bays is attached to a projecting transept with a square crossing, a semi-circular apse on each side and an ambulatory with three chapels.

One forebay is missing. The elevation once again has three storeys. Over the comparatively low arcades there are gallery arches of approxi-

126

Saint-Benoît-sur-Loire (Loiret), former
abbey church Saint-Benoît.
Around 1070/80–mid twelfth century,
western view of narthex (antechurch
tower)

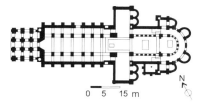

Saint-Benoît-sur-Loire (Loiret), former abbey church
Saint-Benoît. Ground plan (left),
Choir (above), Columns of narthex (below)

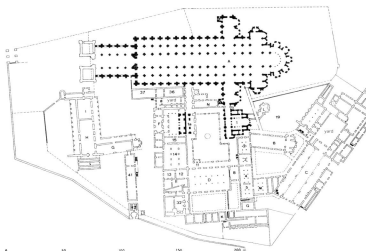

Cluny (Saône-et-Loire), former monastery church Saint-Pierre-et-Paul (Cluny III). 1089–1131/32
Southern transept

Ground plan of whole site, reconstruction of its state around 1150

A   Monastery church
B   Lady chapel
C   Infirmary
D   Refectory
E   Pantry
F   Palace court
G,H,I   Hospices and stables
K   Novitiate
L   Cemetery chapel
M   Extension to dormitory (?)
N   Abbot's chapel

1   Old church
1a Old Galilee
2   Chapter house
3   Parlour
4   Camera
5   Dormitory above
6   Latrines
8   Calefactory
11 Well
12 Monks' kitchen
13 Lay kitchen
14 Cellar
15 Room of the almoner
19 Cemetery
32 Bakery
36 Guesthouse for women
37 Guesthouse for men
41 Stable and store house
42 Latrines

mately equal height, into which large tympana are set, leaving only narrow openings. A small window with a steeply sloping sill in each bay forms the clerestory. Evidently they did not yet have great faith in their vaulting techniques. The piers are cross-shaped, but on each side of the square central part, engaged columns are fitted which in both the nave and the side aisles link smoothly to the transverse arches and in the arcades to the supporting arches. Groin vaulting is used in the side aisles, whilst in the galleries there is quarter barrel vaulting which is supported by the nave walls. The transept wings are separated from each other by a strainer arch which is lower than the crossing arches. A set of five arches breaks through the wall above, a motif which is reminiscent of Carolingian buildings such as Germigny-des-Prés and one which was imitated and can still be seen today in the Romanesque transept of the cathedral of Saint-Cyr-et-Sainte-Juliette in Nièvre. On each side of this strainer arch two rows of windows pierce the walls of the transepts. The choir also has three storeys, but the high galleries have been replaced by sigificantly lower blind arches. Colonnettes highlight the high windows.

The exterior is different to elsewhere. Whilst it is still true that the composition of the building is predominant, and that was to remain so for the whole of the high Middle Ages, it is not the only determining feature in a building. Small block friezes articulate the building horizontally and surround the round arches of the ever larger windows. A set of blind arches on short colonnettes, a dwarf gallery, decorates the high wall of the end of the choir, behind which is the vaulting. The crossing tower is low

and octagonal, whilst both the west towers were destroyed in the French Revolution.

Although Nièvre is an example of a perfect basilica with a clerestory, Abbot Hugo chose the elevation with the blind triforium, since he wanted a ceremonial, elegant architecture, and therefore a continuity of space which was not to be broken by too many strong contrasts of light and shadow. The wide galleries of Saint-Étienne were to be influential, on the other hand, in the churches along the pilgrims' route to Santiago.

After vaulting had been successfully executed in 1097 in Nièvre and by 1107 in La Charité, the monks of Tournus tried out this technique in the upper floor of the three-bayed narthex. The side aisles were completed with quarter barrel vaults as in Saint-Étienne, where there are two windows in each bay and a round barrel vault. The intermediate floor was dispensed with and the upper floor of the narthex may only have been built towards the end of the eleventh century. At the same time the construction of the two splendid west towers was completed. These rise above the high front and have become the symbol of the town.

It is more than likely that these two new buildings in Nièvre and La Charité encouraged the Abbot at Saint-Benoît-sur-Loire to carry out a modernization of his church which dated from the first half of the tenth or beginning of the eleventh century (photos, p. 127). Saint-Benoît had been founded in 651 and since around 672 had been in the possession of the relics of St. Benedict of Montecassino. These relics were amongst the noblest treasures in France in this period. Odo of Cluny (927–942) had reformed this monastery during the first half of the tenth century. Several buildings, repairs and modernizations had followed upon each other, before Abbot Guillaume (1067–1080) began the construction of new parts in the east from 1070/80 and, at the same time, the erection of a massive fortified tower in the west of the church. An ambulatory with only two radial chapels and a deep forechoir bay was built over a crypt. This ambulatory is flanked by two chapels, each with an east apse and crowned by towers. In front of the long choir there is a projecting transept with two apses in the east wall. Above the square crossing is a dome resting on squinches. As at Saint-Étienne, the elevation of the choir has three storeys: arcades, blind triforium, windows framed by colonnettes and a round barrel vault. The ambulatory and side aisles of the long choir are also barrel vaulted. In its ground plan and elevation it strongly anticipated the choir of the third church at Cluny, which had been under construction since 1089. It is only the transverse arches under the barrel of the forechoir, which strongly articulate and give rhythm to the interior, and the absolute perfection of that concept that are still lacking here. For that reason there can be no doubt that it was not only the will of Abbot Guillaume that was instrumental here. Saint-Benoît is the third large building on which Hugo of Cluny was testing his architectural concepts. The result proves the viability of this method of procedure: all the details and motifs, all the shaping of the interior volume are to be found in the "test buildings." Yet no other church even approaches the third church at Cluny in effect, perfection of execution, or consistency of conception.

In 1108 the east parts of Saint-Benoît were consecrated, whilst the nave was not completed until around the middle of the twelfth century. The latter differs only slightly from the choir. The slope of the ground was compensated for by an area of wall between the arcades and blind triforium, which remained empty. Like the long choir barrel vaulting, the vaulting of the nave remained unarticulated and had only one transverse arch which was not complemented by any responds on the nave wall immediately below. The massive two-storey west end of the church is enormously impressive. On the ground floor there is a hall opening in three directions with nine bays and massive piers supporting groin vaults. The church is above all famous for its capitals and small reliefs on the exterior. The upper floor is similarly articulated, but is closed and has three apses sunk into the east wall.

In 1089 Abbot Hugo (1049–1109) finally began the building of the third church at Cluny. Already in 1095 Pope Urban II was able to consecrate the main altar and three further chapel altars. The final consecration was completed by 1131/32. The narthex with its nave and two side aisles was not completed until 1225. However, by 1258 the once powerful monastery was converted into a sinecure. In 1790 this was dissolved and in 1798 the building was sold for demolition. This began in 1811 and left only the south arm of the transept, the choir capitals and a few other individual parts still standing.

There was a nave and four aisles (total length 614 feet, length to transept 242 feet, transept 237 feet, height of nave 97 feet, width of nave 49 feet), eleven bays, a transept with the same width as the nave and with

Cluny (Saône-et-Loire), former monastery church Saint-Pierre-et-Paul (Cluny III). East view of church in sixteenth century. Lithograph by Emile Sagot (after 1789). Paris, Bibliothèque Nationale, small collection of copper engravings

two eastern apses to each arm, a long choir, also with four aisles, and an ambulatory with five radiating chapels, which was flanked by a second lower transept, also with two eastern apses to each arm. We know what the church must have looked like from extensive excavations, a large number of picture sources and, not least, from both the churches that anticipated it and the churches that were to emulate it subsequently. The details, however, are still very much a matter of debate.

The elevation of the nave had three storeys: slim arcades with pointed arches, a blind triforium with three arches in each bay, and a clerestory with a similar pattern. In the case of the latter, the arcades formed the frame for the arches of the outer aisles and for the windows of the inner aisles. Recessed piers with semi-circular or fluted responds supported the transverse arches of the pointed tunnel vault and articulated the interior volume evenly and harmoniously. The square crossing was crowned by a small blind gallery with a cupola. This in turn was surmounted by a square crossing tower. The steep transverse arms, which extend over nine bays, were each surmounted in the second and eighth bays by two towers over domes on squinches. The elevation of the two outer bays was similar to that of the nave. Only the tower of the southern transept and the adjoining southerly bay escaped demolition (figures, p. 128). Towards the east, and adjoining the first transept, were two choir bays which repeated the pattern of the nave elevation. Adjoining this in turn was the second transept with another square crossing and a further octagonal tower above

129

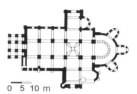

Paray-le-Mondial (Saône-et-Loire), former monastery church of Notre-Dame. First half of eleventh century. Nave and choir (left), ground plan (right), view of exterior from north-east (below)

0 5 10 m

a dome resting on squinches. In the second transept it was only the central three bays which were as high as the nave or the large transept. The two adjoining bays on either side were low and must have had the appearance of chapels. The eastern termination of the church was formed by a further bay with the same elevation as the nave and the ambulatory, and with an annular barrel vault and lunettes. Only flat fluted responds decorated the wall between the arcades and the clerestory and there was no blind triforium.

This church could therefore be divided into two zones: on the one hand, the nave which bordered on the gigantic, but which was clearly structured, and on the other hand, the eastern parts with their incredibly complex juxtaposition of a whole variety of spaces and structures. It was, of course, the eastern parts which were reserved for the use of the monks. Both zones were held together conceptually by the uniform elevation throughout.

The decoration must have been of a truly magnificent splendor. Apart from the utterly beautiful capitals, which everywhere attracted the eye, all the arches, windows and cornices were surrounded by sculptured ornamental strips and all the responds were fluted. In addition there would certainly have been murals, carpets, colouring of all the architecture, huge radial chandeliers which shed a mystic light, figures of saints, incense, golden liturgical vestments, and gleaming golden or silver ornaments set with precious stones. Above all there was the singing which must have been such an essential part of the liturgy, even at the time of Cluny II, but certainly during Cluny III.

It is necessary to have some idea of how the people lived in the early and late Middle Ages in order to understand the intoxicating effect of such a multi-faceted work of art which would have appealed to all the human senses. Light and warmth only came from the sun, as firewood and candles were expensive and only available to the few. Music was unknown, save for the shepherd's flute and the simplest songs, and pictures of any kind only existed in monasteries. Colorful clothing was not permitted to the ordinary people, and their living quarters were dark and gloomy. Not even the lower nobility on their country estates lived a much more privileged or comfortable way of life. It is therefore not surprising that the faithful saw in Cluny an image of the heavenly Jerusalem, and considered it all to be a miracle.

No secular building of the period could even bear comparison with Cluny. On the one hand, secular rulers were constantly obliged to invest large sums of money in soldiers and military equipment, and on the other hand, the Church forbade the faithful from accumulating wealth or splendor. As a result, large and generous donations were made to the Church and monasteries.

The third church at Cluny, much as it impressed its contemporaries, was not emulated by many. One reason for this was the founding of the Cistercian Order which scorned pomp and ornamentation and returned to simplicity and work. Another reason was that although the question of barrel vaulting had been solved and the form perfected, the future belonged to the rib vault and the Gothic style. Already before the consecration of Cluny III, the perfect sexpartite vault had been built in

Anzy-le-Duc (Saône-et-Loire),
Sainte-Croix-et-Sainte-Marie.
2nd half of eleventh to early twelfth
century.
Nave with crossing tower (below),
nave wall (right)

Caen, and between 1140 and 1144 Abbot Suger in Saint-Denis erected the first Gothic building. Nevertheless, with its strict structuring of all the parts and with its constant repetition of the basic unit of measure, the third monastery church at Cluny already possessed one of the essential properties of the Gothic.

The successors to Cluny III

Notre-Dame in Paray-le-Mondial (photos, p. 130) is a miniature version of Cluny III, and it will come as no surprise to learn that its architect was none other than Abbot Hugo of Cluny. Founded in 973, the monastery at Paray-le-Mondial came into the hands of Cluny in 999, and Abbot Odilo consecrated a small church here in 1004, possibly the same type as Cluny II. In the first half of the eleventh century the surviving narthex with its twin tower front was added. In 1090 Abbot Hugo began the existing building, a nave and two aisles with three bays, a projecting transept with apses, a square crossing with a dome resting on squinches, forebay and ambulatory with radiating chapels. The elevation of Notre-Dame proves its descent from Cluny III, even if the latter was completed considerably earlier. Here also are to be found arcades with pointed arches on stepped piers, three-part blind triforium and clerestory, pointed barrel vaulting with transverse arches, fluted responds, ornamental bands, a steep transept and the absence of a triforium in the chancel. Nevertheless the similarity is restricted to the formal. The building has not been able to emulate to any great extent the tremendous sense of space and finely articulated elegance of Cluny III.

Freer in it details, yet much closer in its effect to the prototype is Saint-Lazare in Autun (photo, p. 132). Bishop Étienne de Bâgé, who was an enthusiastic supporter of the Cluniac reform and liturgy, began this building around 1120 to replace a canonical foundation from the ninth century. On the occasion of a visit by the pope a dedication was transferred, although the relics of St. Lazarus could not be brought to the church until 1146, when the narthex was still under construction. The narthex has a nave and two aisles and both its bays correspond in width and height to those of the nave, whose seven bays extend eastwards. The crossing is square, as are the transepts. The latter squares are divided in two by supporting arches which are extensions of the outer nave walls. Two forebays make the transition to the choir with three apses. Saint-Lazare therefore dispenses not only with an ambulatory, but also with transepts. Despite the disturbing chapel extensions, the interior comes over as festive and full of vitality. The recessed piers support arcades of pointed arches. On all four sides of the piers there are fluted responds attached, which in the nave reach up to just under the transverse barrel vaults. In the blind triforium the middle of the three arches is open, and in the clerestory there is only one window in each bay in contrast to the three at Cluny. Above each bay there is barrel vaulting. Autun still has very important Roman remains, so it is not surprising that the classical decoration of the responds and courses is very sculptured and calculated to exploit the effects of light and shade, and that the capitals are incredibly fine and realistic. This elegant festiveness of the interior volume and the calculated absence of the transepts in favor of a continuity of space are the aspects of Saint-Lazaire which bind it more closely with Cluny III than any other building.

Autun (Saône-et-Loire), Saint-Lazare.
1120–1146. North wall of nave
(opposite), ground plan (right)

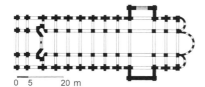

Vézelay (Yonne), Sainte-Madeleine.
After 1120. Nave looking eastwards with
Gothic choir (above), view of exterior
from south-west, ground plan (below)

Experimentation with groin vaulting

Parallel to the large buildings of La Charité, Saint-Étienne and Saint-Benoît, which were erected under the patronage of the monastery at Cluny, there were several smaller churches, such as Sainte-Trinité, Sainte-Croix and Sainte-Marie in Anzy-le-Duc. The construction of Anzy-le-Duc was begun in the second half of the eleventh century and probably not completed until the early twelfth century (photos, p. 131). It was a priory of Saint-Martin in Autun, and in its ground plan follows the model of Cluny II: a nave and two aisles, a projecting steep transept, an echeloned choir with five chapels with a semi-circular lady chapel at the main apse, this being a special feature of Anzy-le-Duc. The elevation does, however, take account of progress. On all four sides of the cross-shaped piers there are engaged columns. In the arcades, these carry the underarch supports, whereas in the nave and aisles they combine with the underlying responds to carry the stepped transverse arches. It is possible that barrel vaulting was intended here with windows at the base, but the plans were subsequently changed, and the nave and aisles were groin vaulted. In this way it was possible to retain the genuine basilica cross-section whilst putting larger windows in the upper wall. This is also an unwitting (?) anticipation of the Gothic design principles.

The transept and main apse are barrel vaulted whereas the forebays of the subsidiary apses, opening out onto the main apse, act as an extension of the side aisles and are groin-vaulted.

What had been obvious a century earlier during the vaulting at Tournus between 1020 and 1030 had now been recognized at Anzy-le-Duc, namely that groin vaulting in the nave solves all the problems of the clerestory. Nevertheless it is only a small group of buildings in Burgundy which exploit this discovery. The most important are Saint-Lazare in Avalon and Sainte-Madeleine in Vézelay (photos, right).

The nave of Saint-Madeleine at Vézelay was rebuilt immediately after a fire had destroyed it in 1120. Founded in 858 by Girard de Rousillon, this monastery, like Cluny, was directly subordinated to Rome. In 1104 the eastern parts of the Carolingian structure were replaced with a new structure, followed in 1120 by the nave which still stands today. Together with the narthex which fits exactly to the nave, there are thirteen bays, two more than at Cluny III. The elevation is different, however, and is similar in appearance to Anzy-le-Duc. Cross-shaped piers with engaged columns on all four sides carry the underarch supports of the arcades and the transverse arches of the vaulting in both the nave and aisles. Square responds demarcate the semi-circular columns from the wall and make the bay articulation clearer. A horizontal course, which follows all the wall articulations, marks the top of the first storey. In the smooth wall above there are windows, framed by the wall ribs of the groin vaulting.

Like Anzy-le-Duc, Sainte-Madeleine is groin-vaulted in both the nave and aisles. Because of the bigger windows the interior is considerably brighter than with barrel vaulted naves. The transept which is aisleless is only Romanesque in its lower parts, the upper parts belonging to the same period as the Gothic ambulatory.

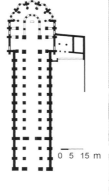

The anti-Cluniac movement under Bernard of Clairvaux

In the course of over two centuries the monastery community in Cluny had achieved great wealth and, with their third church, had clearly demonstrated their power to all the world. Inevitably this drew the attention of the critics. The most telling of them was Bernard of Clairvaux. He severely criticized Cluny for its opulence, the distractions caused by the numerous pictures, and the continual masses which kept the monks from their physical work. Just as the Abbot of Cluny had once sought reform, so Bernard wanted to return to the original rules of St. Benedict. *Ora et labora*, prayer and physical work, and abstinence from all luxury, indeed from any decoration even of the church, were his credo. In Burgundy he founded four new monasteries, the first of which, Citeaux, gave the name to the new order of St. Benedict, the Cistercians. Only one of these four monasteries has retained its original appearance, Fontenay. Construction of this monastery church began after 1139. Decoration was entirely dispensed with. In deliberate contrast to Cluny, Bernard of Clairvaux returned to simplicity and work. However, that such simplicity need not deprive an interior of its impact is amply demonstrated by the church at Fontenay. Following the typical Cistercian ground plan, it consists of a nave and two aisles with eight bays, a projecting transept with two square chapels on the eastern wall of each arm and a somewhat deeper angular choir. Square piers with attached columns support the arcades of pointed arches. The wall above is smooth and undecorated and is separated from the pointed barrel vaulting by a simple cornice. The powerful transverse arches sit on semi-circular responds. Each arch of the aisle has barrel vaulting which is perpendicular to the axis of the nave. Each bay of the aisle opens out to the next through a low connecting arch. High windows on the exterior walls as well as the west wall are the only sources of light. The stone of the interior space truly embodies the Cistercian rules: a reduction of the building to its absolute essentials by rejecting vanity and striving for clarity, dignity and sobriety. It is only in the choir area that there is an altar with a few decorative items, including the graceful and charming Madonna of Fontenay.

The peaceful and equally empty cloister also belongs to the Romanesque style. Here also the impact rests exclusively on the use of few forms and a single material.

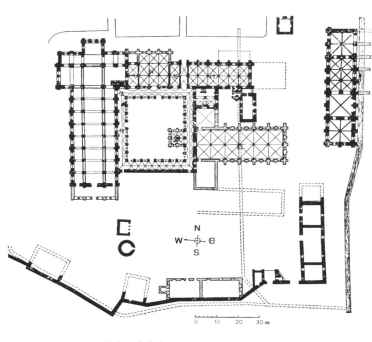

Fontenay, ground plan of whole site

Fontenay (Cote-d'Or), former Cistercian monastery. Founded in 1118, transferred to the present site in 1130. Church under construction from 1133.

Interior of church (opposite),
west front and choir from exterior (left),
views of cloisters (below)

134

Northern France – the absence of vaulting

In northern France a whole range of buildings have survived from the
first half of the eleventh century. All of them have flat ceilings. Until the
end of the century barrel vaulting set clear limitations to the width of a
nave. The builders chose wide and high naves with large clerestory
windows and thus dispensed with vaulting. The church of Montier-en-der,
which was already complete by the year 1000, is the earliest surviving
example.

The year 1000 also saw the building of a new church at Nivelles to
replace the old complex structure which had been destroyed by fire (figure,
right). The double-ended church was consecrated in 1046 in the presence
of Emperor Henry III. It was divided into two parts by (reconstructed)
strainer arches in the high and spacious nave. The eastern area has four
bays of the nave, a wide projecting transept and a choir with a flat
termination with subsidiary rooms and chapels above an extended crypt.
Like its predecessor this eastern area is dedicated to St. Peter, whilst the
western end of the nave, with its much narrower and shorter transept, is
dedicated to St. Gertrude. Extensive rebuilding in the twelfth century has
made the west choir into a complex structure with many storeys and an
imperial chamber on the upper floor.

As with the two-storey colonnaded nave with its flat ceiling, the
western transept is also virtually without ornamentation. However, in the
choir and the eastern transept there is a large range of blind arcades and
recesses typical of the period.

The same structure and spaciousness as at Nivelles are also to be found
at Saint-Rémi in Reims, although the ground plan and elevation are much
more elaborate (photos, p. 137). The first church on this site, consecrated
in 852, had been built by Archbishop Hincmar to the honor of St.
Remigius. A new building was begun by Abbot Airard after 1005, and was
completed according to a slightly simplified plan by Abbot Thierry some
time after 1034. Modifications in the Gothic style were made in the
twelfth century, namely the responds in the nave, the pointed blind arches
above the galleries, the rib vaulting and the ambulatory. Subsequent
additions are probably also the tympana on the slim colonnades which are
placed in the gallery openings.

There was clearly a very devoted following to St. Remigius, and Abbot
Airard acknowledged this in his new building to the saint. The significance
of St. Remigius predated the feverish popularity of the pilgrimage to St.
James which spread throughout Europe and established Santiago as the
most important goal for pilgrims. The interior must once have been very
impressive: clusters of slender columns supported the arches of the thirteen
nave arcades, above which were the galleries whose openings were almost
as large as the arcade openings themselves. High up above a wide empty
area of wall were the windows of the clerestory. Above this was the flat
ceiling which must have been as colorful as all the walls; one has only to
think of Reichenau Oberzell or the minster at Constance from the same
period. Bright light from the windows of the clerestory, galleries and aisles
must have flooded into the nave, whose heavy walls were lightened by the
large gallery openings.

The eastern parts are a real revelation. The aisles with their galleries
continue along the west side, and previously also along the front of the
very slim projecting transepts. On the eastern side there are five
interconnecting chapels, four of which have semi-circular terminations.
This must be an adaptation of the Cluniac choir with radiating chapels,
which evidently must have been necessary as the galleries continued over
these chapels. In this way an interior was created which was clear and yet
subtle in its impact. The end of the chancel formed a large semi-circular
apse with a forebay. A similar ground plan, although with a nave and four
aisles, was to be found at Orleans cathedral, the forerunner of this
building and also dating from around 1000.

The church at Vignory, too, belonged to this category. In the deed of
gift of 1050 it is described as having just been completed, but this must
only refer to a repair or a partial rebuilding, as nearly all the parts of the
unvaulted church would already have been finished in the first quarter of
the eleventh century.

Rheims (Marne), Saint–Rémi. 1005 to
mid-eleventh century. Nave wall (right),
ground plan (left)

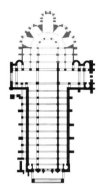

The nave leads directly into the choir, only a strainer arch marking the boundary between the two. The windows arranged in two zones in the gable over the strainer arch are an unusual feature.

The church consists of a nave and two aisles, extending over nine bays. Arcades of differing heights, and without the under arches, rest on unornamented square piers. Above each of these is a parallel opening with a strong column in the middle and square piers on the sides. The arches are not grouped, resulting in a continuous row of arches with alternating supports. The clerestory consists of a large simple window in each bay beneath an open roof framework. The architecture is all reduced to the tension between the wall and opening. The almost complete absence of sculptured ornament and articulation causes the nave to appear archaic and austere. At the same time, however, the interior is surprisingly well illuminated.

The choir consists of two forebays without galleries or windows, a semi-circular column capital and a vaulted ambulatory with three radiating chapels.

Articulation in the upper nave walls

An alternative style of wall articulation under flat ceilings has survived at Notre-Dame in Bernay (photos, p. 139). At some time after 1015 a monastery church of relatively modest proportions was erected there. It is the oldest of a whole group of Norman churches with the same concept of interior design. To the vaulted east parts were added wide, unvaulted naves and aisles with three-storey elevations and flat ceilings. It is as if the flat ceilings were taken into account, not only because of the light from the clerestory, but also because the possibilites of developing the upper walls of the nave had been recognized. Furthermore with the opening up and increased articulation of these areas of wall, it was not only the light and shadow effects that could be exploited, but useful spaces could be created in the upper storey, which could be reached by the increasingly popular west towers. As in Cluny, this development would certainly have had liturgical justification, as it was almost always the projected use of a space or object which determined its shape and form.

Jumièges (Seine-Maritime), former
abbey church of Notre-Dame.
1040–1067. Nave, ground plan (above),
west front (below left),
nave interior (below right)

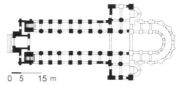

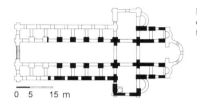

0 5   15 m

In Bernay there are only small openings in the dark roof structure complementing the piers and arches below. Next to each window is a blind recess. Above this is the clerestory and a flat ceiling, which was soon replaced by a wooden barrel vault. The barrel vault was certainly regarded as the finest type of ceiling. At Bernay it was chosen for the projecting transept and for the almost exact copy of Cluny's chevet with five radiating chapels. The small galleries in the transept walls and the choir were used, but the windows were dispensed with for the time being. A tower crowned the crossing, but its collapse between 1080 and 1090 also resulted in the renewal of the choir and transept. In the choir the barrel vaulting was abandoned in favor of a clerestory. The transept was also given windows and the barrel vaulting of the ceiling renewed.

A significant advance in the design of the nave walls was achieved in the abbey church of Notre-Dame in Jumièges (figures, p. 138), which was begun some time after 1040 and consecrated in 1067. Today it is an impressive and picturesque ruin surrounded by meadows. The richly articulated twin towers, which soar steeply into the sky, are one of the earliest surviving examples of a twin tower façade with a central gable. It was here that a particular scheme of proportioning was used for the first time, in which one square nave bay was equivalent to two aisle bays, and in which the aisles were half the width of the nave. This scheme had been already used at Saint-Rémi in Rheims, but in that church there were originally no responds which would have grouped pairs of arches together to form a square. In Jumièges these responds were present, reaching from floor level virtually up to the window sills of the clerestory, and at one time supporting the strainer arches. Also for the first time we find an alternation of supports. The "strong" piers are square with four engaged columns, whilst the "weak" supports are simple columns. Each arcade corresponds to a set of three arches, grouped together in an arch-shaped recess in the second storey and a single window in the clerestory. Above this was the flat ceiling.

The whole appearance of the interior space changed with the introduction of responds. The nave no longer appeared so box-like and the openings were "anchored" more securely. The responds furthermore created a vertical counterweight to what had previously always been a very horizontal articulation. They brought the space together and divided it into sections, each resembling the next, and reproducible in any number. They also emphasized the vertical, a deliberate effect at Jumièges, for the nave was increased to an unprecedented height of 78 feet (Cluny III was only 18 feet higher).

This building also had a projecting transept and an ambulatory with radiating chapels. In the fourteenth century the latter unfortunately had to make way for a new building which was attached directly to the west walls of the transept. The ground plan of the first choir was excavated and shown to have two forebays with capitals, an ambulatory and three radiating chapels. By all appearances, the elevation of the nave was continued in the choir, albeit with a reduced height, and its nave and galleries had barrel vaulting. In the transept a sort of bridge over two arches linked the galleries of the nave with those of the choir. This is a clear indication that these areas were used.

On the west walls of the transepts there is an interesting feature. A thick wall has subsequently been built in front of the inner wall, suggesting that vaulting had been planned. It is possible that this was an attempt to reduce the width which the vault would have to span. Of greater significance, however, for the development of Norman design is the passageway at the level of the windows, which was made possible with the building of the second wall. In this way the concept of the window passageway was born. It led not only to the abandonment of choir vaulting, but also to the breaking down of the continuity of the wall around the high windows.

The eastern parts of Jumièges were built only slightly later than the chancel and transept of Mont-Saint-Michel. The construction of the nave of Jumièges, on the other hand, just preceded the nave at Mont-Saint-Michel (photo, p. 1.40).

The builders of each church were fully aware of what was happening at the other. Mont-Saint-Michel had a polygonal ambulatory built over a gigantic substructure crypt, but, because of the sloping terrain, the

139

Mont-Saint-Michel (Manche), former
monastery church Saint-Michel. Around
1035 ff. Nave wall and wooden barrel
vaulting

ambulatory had no chapels. There was also a transept, which, together with the ambulatory, had the same elevation as Jumièges. The eastern parts were moreover modified in the late Gothic style. The nave is more richly decorated and is not proportioned in the same way as Jumièges. All the piers are identical and the bays are oblong. One arch in the arcades corresponds to two gallery arches, each of which has double openings and one slender clerestory window above. The strongly projecting responds do not support strainer arches and extend to the edge of the wooden barrel vault. It may be that strainer arches were rejected because they would have reduced the light from the clerestory windows. Moreover, the vertical articulation afforded by the responds was now perhaps considered indispensable. Nevertheless, this makes the wooden barrel vault at Mont-Saint-Michel look out of place above the nave. The supporting arches,

supported by the responds, are absent here. Two different concepts of the interior space meet here unintentionally: the older concept found in Nivelles and Rheims, and the newer one whose impact rests on powerful vertical divisions.

The perfection of Norman architectural Ideas

Only a few years after Jumièges and Mont-Saint-Michel, the building of the two abbey churches of Saint-Étienne and Sainte-Trinité in Caen was begun. The architectural rivalry between these two churches over decades saw the perfection of the Norman style (figures, pp. 141ff.). The bene-factors were William the Conqueror and his wife Mathilde. William was laid to rest in Saint-Étienne in 1087. It is possible that the monastery had always been conceived of as his place of final rest, but the immediate reason for the endowment was that the marriage of William and Mathilde was disputed by Rome.

The construction of both churches began between 1060 and 1065. Both have a powerful twin-towered west front, a nave and two aisles with a three-storey elevation, and an aisleless transept. The original chancel in Saint-Étienne had to make way for a Gothic ambulatory. Although excavations have given no firm evidence, analogous structures at Cerisy-la-Forêt (inspired by Saint-Étienne) and Sainte-Trinité strongly suggest that it was a chancel with chapels in echelon of the Bernay type.

Saint-Vigor in Cerisy (photo, p. 143) also gives us clues about the elevation of the chancel. Because the clerestory was supposed to be two-layered and include a passageway, as at Jumièges, there was no vaulting in the eastern parts. Above the arcades of the forechoir there must have been a double-arched opening in each bay. In the main apse, which had no articulation on the ground floor, these double arches were offset from the wall allowing room for a narrow passageway between themselves and the wall. Both zones of the apse were illuminated by windows. The forechoir, which similar to the nave had a three-storey elevation, may have had sets of two or three arches in front of the passageway and windows. More likely would have been a simple arch, which framed the window and pierced the wall in front of the passageway.

The transept, also with a passageway in front of the windows, has survived intact. The construction of the nave began in the years after 1070. With the subsequent addition of a sexpartite rib vault, the original appearance of the clerestory has been modified. The arcades have been retained, however, together with the almost equally large gallery openings above. The piers in the nave are complex, consisting of responds and engaged columns, and forming an alternation of "strong" and "weak" supports. The responds, which used to reach to just under the flat ceiling, also alternate, but today now only extend upwards as far as the edge of the vaulting. The wide gallery openings may have had tympana above a colonnette.

Tracery balustrades would certainly not have been used here. It is known that sets of three arches were constructed in front of the passageway.

The articulation of the wall, not only in the gallery area, but also in the clerestory, had, on the one hand, made barrel vaulting impossible, but, on

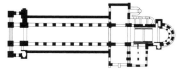

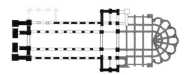

the other hand, had lent the interior a whole new quality. The wall did not have the ethereal quality of the later Gothic, yet the articulation in the clerestory is a clear step in this direction. The nave and the end of the chancel were now well-illuminated, generous spaces, whilst the arches, whose number increased in the upper parts of the cathedral, rested on delicate colonnettes and were backlit by the increased strength of the light.

The story of the construction of its sister church of Saint-Étienne, the convent of Sainte-Trinité, is very similar. Sainte-Trinité also originally had a chancel with chapels in echelon, which was raised slightly because of the underlying crypt. As the nuns had to be kept from view, the main apse with its two forebays was closed to the side chancels. Of the original structure only the ground floor of the long chancel with the blind arcading remains. There must have been just such a row of arches in the main apse too, and above it simple windows and a barrel vault, whose central transverse arch is still in place today. The transept may have been low, as is suggested by the northerly and southerly crossing arches.

Next came the nave (figure, p. 142). In contrast to Saint-Étienne there is no alternation of supports and it has a blind triforium instead of galleries. This significantly changed the spatial proportions of the interior. The present clerestory has been modified in its form, as the original at the time of building (1075–85) must have been lower, perhaps the same height as the lateral arches of today's triple arcatures, which probably belong to the original structure. The central arch, which framed the deeper-lying window,

may have been just as high, as it may be assumed that there was a passageway in front of the clerestory such as at Saint-Étienne. Above the clerestory would have been a flat ceiling, perhaps even a wooden barrel vault. Two towers form the west front.

It is quite possible that the barrel vault in the long chancel, which, after all had a span of almost 24 feet, was soon threatened with collapse. At all events it was dismantled between 1100 and 1110. The long chancel now had a double-walled clerestory added, albeit with very low lateral openings. The windows in contrast are very high. This elevation was groin vaulted. It was known from Burgundy, Anzy-le-Duc and Vézelay that groin vaulting, which had, after all, been used extensively in the aisles, allowed a significant increase in the size of the upper windows. This was successful at Sainte-Trinité, even over a double wall. The interior of the apse was given an inner layer consisting of two superimposed column arcatures, causing the elevation to be double-layered.

Once the rib vaulting of the long choir had been successfully mastered, it might be assumed that this form of vaulting would establish itself everywhere. England, where William had been king since winning the Battle of Hastings in 1066, had led the way in experimenting with rib vaulting since about 1100. The future clearly belonged to rib vaulting, and between 1120 and 1125 the idea was brought to Normandy, where it was used to vault Saint-Étienne and Saint-Trinité (photos, p. 142). It is one of the unsolved mysteries why rib vaults were sexpartite at the beginning.

Caen, Saint-Étienne. Sexpartite rib vaulting above altered clerestory. Around 1120

Caen, Sainte-Trinité. Sexpartite rib vaulting. Around 1120

They group two bays together and span them diagonally in what is approximately the form of a round arch. A third arch, similar to a transverse arch, spans the nave and intersects the other two at a crossing point in the center. The alteration of supports in Saint-Étienne suited this type of vaulting, indeed seemed almost designed for it. Sainte-Trinité on the other hand had no alternation of supports.

The height of the clerestory at Saint-Étienne, which was determined by the height of the galleries, caused difficulties with the vaulting. The transverse ribs intersected the outer arches in each double bay. The whole inner layer of wall was taken down right to the base of the clerestory zone and a new triple arcature was planned, this time with low and narrower arches at the sides. Apparently they were still too high in the area of the transverse ribs, as subsequently both the outer arches in each double bay had to be filled in with masonry. The result was the well-known asymmetrical clerestory.

At Sainte-Trinité the initial situation was more favorable. The clerestory was significantly lower because of the blind triforium and could remain the same apart from the windows which were altered. The clerestory was extended upwards by the height of today's windows and the nave was covered with sexpartite vaulting as at Saint-Étienne.

With the introduction of rib vaulting, the Norman architects had made the great breakthrough which allowed them to vault their naves so that

they were wide, well lit and presented an elevation with a variety of articulation and openings right up to the ceiling. For decades they had made do with wooden barrel vaults, limited themselves to vaulting of the eastern parts, or even abandoned vaulting altogether in order to break up and lighten the uniformity of a plain wall. The dimensions of the naves give a clear indication of their intentions. All of them are between 29 and 36 feet in breadth, far in excess of what could be successfully spanned up until 1100 with a barrel vault. Cluny III was the first to break this barrier with the construction of a pointed barrel vault with a width of about 36 clear feet.

With the two abbey churches at Caen, Norman architecture had reached the zenith of its achievement. Both Cluny III and the churches at Caen represent the almost simultaneous perfection of an idea which architects had been grappling with for more than a century.

After this period Normandy lost its way as an inspiration for artistic ideas and sank into oblivion. Its achievements were taken up elsewhere, for the world was now on the threshold of the Gothic age, both chronologically and architecturally speaking. It was the Ile-de-France which was to be the cradle of the Gothic.

The few buildings which were built in Normandy after 1065 to 1070 are the descendants of Saint-Étienne or Sainte-Trinité: namely Lessay,

Cerisy-la-Fôret (Manche), former priory
church of Saint-Vigor. Around 1080/85.
Choir with apse, transept, central tower
and two nave bays

Tournai (Belgium), cathedral. From
1130. Nave and group of east towers

Saint-Martin-de-Boscherville and Cerisy-la-Forêt. Especially the last,
Saint-Vigor in Cerisy-la-Forêt, has retained much of its original character,
and is still surrounded by the same meadows and apple orchards (photo,
p. 143). It was indeed built as part of the priory of Saint-Étienne between
1080 and 1085, but in contrast to its mother building, it was never
vaulted. The chancel, a chevet with radiating chapels like that of Bernay,
has three storeys, as has the apse. The five ground floor windows in the
apse have no counterpart in the two choir bays where there is only smooth
wall with doors to the choir aisles. It may be that the arcades, which one
might have expected here, were filled in later with masonry. In the second
level the galleries have two arches in each bay and are continued into the
apse as a low colonnade in front of a narrow passageway. The clerestory is
also double-layered with three slender arches in each bay, the central arch
being fractionally higher. The windows of the passageway have been made
smaller by a subsequent change in the aisle roofs. The passageway continues
past the apse windows and it is striking that here at Saint-Vigor the three
levels are all more or less the same height.

The transept is very high and crowned by a tower. In its outer bays
there is a tribune placed transversely over a central support and groin
vaulting. Only one and a half bays remain of the nave. Their elevation
resembles that of the choir: arcades, double arches in the galleries grouped
together by larger arches, and three slim arches on columns in front of the
clerestory stairs. The strong piers carry strainer arches, whilst the weak
piers serve only to articulate the interior space.

On the threshold of the Gothic age
The cathedral at Tournai is a mixture of styles. On the one hand it draws
on Norman models, but on the other hand it is one of the first examples of
a typical early Gothic elevation, that is, it has four storeys. The new
building, which superseded a church constructed in the early Middle Ages,
was begun in 1130 with the erection of the nave. Tournai did not, however,
become a bishopric until its separation from Noyon in 1146.

The huge nave aisles have the characteristic Norman piers with the
cross-shaped center and engaged columns. Once the capitals were complete
there must have been a change in plan. The flat responds and the engaged
columns in the nave, which must have been intended to support the
vaulting shafts or the strainer arches, now carry the outer arch of the
arcade, which is recessed with two sub-arches. The galleries above, of
equal height and width as the arcades, also have triple recessed arches, the
outermost being supported by a slender colonnette. The next level is the
blind triforium, modeled on Sainte-Trinité, and situated above the gallery
elevation borrowed from Saint-Étienne. Small openings into the roof truss
interrupt the double recessed walls under the wall rib of the colonnade
which has a rhythm double that of the galleries below. The windows of the
clerestory are surprisingly large. The nave now has a baroque groin vault,
but it must originally have had a flat ceiling. It may have been the decision
to include galleries and triforium which motivated the builders to dispense
with the originally-planned vertical articulation and vaulting, and instead
to raise the nave to an enormous height. This was yet another step towards
early Gothic ideas, which since Suger's choir in Saint- Denis, had been
exclusively four-storey elevations, although they did include vertical
articulation and vaulting. The nave at Tournai may therefore have been
one of the most important inspirations for Suger's Saint-Denis.

The transept, which terminates in an apse at each end, is therefore a
building from the very early Gothic period, and is closely related to the cathedrals of Soissons, Noyon and Senlis. The choir was completed between
1242 and 1245 and is a beautiful example of the high Gothic style.

Pilgrimage churches and the Auvergne
About halfway between the first assembly point on French soil and the
Spanish border, a so-called pilgrimage church was built along each of the
four great pilgrims' routes to Santiago de Compostela. They were the
churches of St. Martin in Tours, St. Martial in Limoges, St. Fides in
Conques, and St. Saturninus (St. Sernin) of Toulouse. The most important
one was, of course, the church of St. James in Santiago. Of Saint-Martial
in Limoges nothing has remained, and of Saint-Martin in Tours only the
foundation walls have survived. Founded around the year 1000, Saint-
Martin in Tours was the oldest of the five great pilgrimage churches and
the one with the earliest fully-developed ambulatory with radiating
chapels. In fact, it established the prototype of the five-aisled church with a
three-aisled transept which was later repeated in Toulouse and Santiago.

Conques (Aveyron), former abbey church
of Sainte-Foy. Around 1050–1130.
Exterior view from the north (left);
ground plan; wall of nave (right)

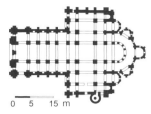

The transept aisles with their four chapels in the east are only the logical continuation of the ambulatory. They offered not only more space for further chapels, in which devotional images could be displayed, but also the possibility of an uninterrupted procession which did not interfere with the closed-off area for the clergy in the sanctuary and in the central aisles of the transept and nave. Such a layout must have been highly welcomed by the monasteries along the pilgrim roads.

The first beginnings of an ambulatory around the end of the chancel are found in the monastery church of Saint-Philbert-de-Grandlieu dating from the first half of the ninth century. About half a century later, the monks from Saint-Philbert appear to have applied this chancel layout in the monastery church of Tournus. A fully-developed ambulatory with radiating chapels, albeit rectangular ones, was built there just after the year 1000 and has survived until today.

There appears to have been a parallel development with regard to the three-aisled transept and the nave in Tournus and at Saint-Rémi in Rheims. Since building work started almost at the same time, it cannot be established which was the model for the other. It would therefore be of great interest to see the elevation. The early building date makes it highly unlikely that the forechoir, the nave and the transept aisles would have had vaulted ceilings. The church is most likely to have been a basilica with galleries and a flat ceiling, similar to that of Saint-Rémi.

Around the year 1050, half a century after work had begun at Tours, the construction of a new church was started in Conques (figure, above). The church took over eighty years to complete and is dedicated to Saint Fides whose statue made from gold and jewels and dating from around 1000 is still an object of veneration (photo, p. 361). The statue is one of the earliest examples of large-scale sculpture in the western world. The oldest part of the church is the chancel area, and both its interior and exterior constitute a highly complex and impressive work of art. A groin-vaulted ambulatory with three semi-circular chapels leads around the three-storey chancel end. There is room for one window between each of the chapels. The gallery has no source of daylight and, seen from the outside, appears as a low, closed, semi-circular structure with a lean-to roof.

Above it, and below the calotte, is the clerestory which projects beyond the wide lower storey and is articulated by blind arches outside.

Looking at the ground plan, however, it looks as if the initial intention had been to build a chancel with seven semi-circular apses in echelon, similar to those built in La Charité-sur-Loire after 1056. But at Conques, this plan must have been changed even during the building work, for, in order to deal with large numbers of pilgrims, an ambulatory provided a much better solution than a choir with chapels in echelon which were, after all, intended to provide places of quiet contemplation for the monks. The transept, too, must have been altered and now had the appearance of

OPPOSITE PAGE
Conques (Aveyron), view of the village
and of the church of Sainte-Foy from the
south-east

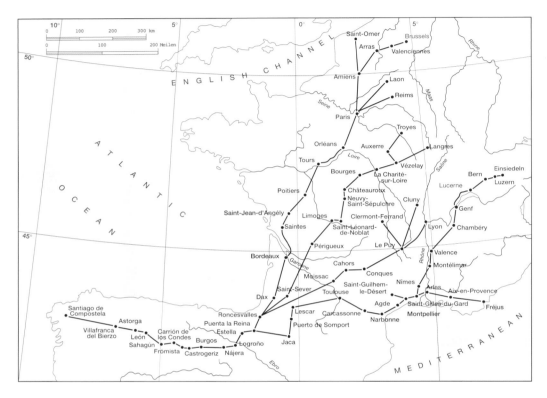

The pilgrimage to Santiago de Compostela

The *Legenda aurea* has it that, after the apostle James was beheaded in Judea, his disciples took his body and secretly put it on a boat. They then boarded the boat without any oars, crossed the sea and reached the coast of Galicia. There, the saint is said to have been laid to rest in a marble tomb. Later, the tomb of James must have been forgotten, probably because the whole peninsula was under Moorish occupation. It cannot have been an accident that its rediscovery coincided with the reconquest of Spain by the army of Charlemagne. According to the legend, an angel appeared to the hermit Pelagius in 813, showing him the site of the apostle's tomb. When the bishop of Iria Flavia (today Padron) heard of this, he had the site dug up and did indeed find the tomb. The news of the rediscovery of St. James's grave added a tremendous impetus to the Christian army's eagerness for battle. After centuries of occupation its site had to be freed. Nevertheless, this

famous campaign suffered a tragic defeat, and Spain remained under Moorish rule for the time being.

During the second half of the eighth century, the relics must have been brought to Santiago de Compostela. It was not until the turn of the millennium, however, that the road to Santiago became accessible to pilgrims. Nevertheless, it took only about 100 years to establish four major routes through France, along which the pilgrims from all parts of France would join together in large groups. They would then make their way to Santiago, stopping frequently for prayer. The first of the four roads was the Via Tolosana which started in the east and led via Saint-Gilles-du-Gard, Saint-Guilhem-le-Désert, and Toulouse. The second, the Via Podensis, ran almost parallel to the Via Tolosana, starting in Le Puy and running through Conques and Moissac, whilst the third, the Via Lemovicensis, started in Vézelay, passed through Limoges and Périgueux, and joined the Via Podensis at Ostabat. The last one was the Via Turonensis which started at the Channel coast and passed through Tours, Poitiers, Saintes and Bordeaux before reaching Ostabat where it also joined up with the two aforementioned roads. The pilgrims on the Via Tolosana finally joined this main route in Puente la Reina where all four routes combined for the rest of the way to Santiago.

Within a very short time, Santiago de Compostela had become one of the three most important places of pilgrimage in the whole of Christendom. The other two, Rome and Jerusalem, had been the focus for Christian pilgrims ever since the first century and were dedicated to Christ the Redeemer and St. Peter, the first of the Apostles. Far from being first of the apostles, St. James was the patron saint of Spain and of the poor. It was mostly the latter who undertook the arduous and dangerous journey. It lasted several months and led them over hundreds of miles of toil and privation. They could never be sure of arriving at Santiago safely, let alone of ever seeing their homes again.

It therefore comes as no surprise that the pilgrims also paid visits to other saints on the way, asking for their help and resting for a few days before continuing the journey to Santiago. For this reason, a large number of monasteries flourished along the route at this time.

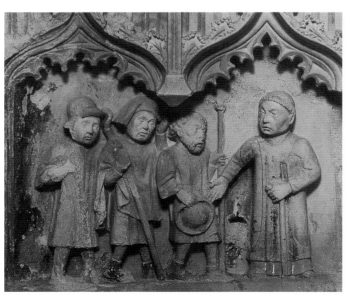

San Juan de Ortega, depiction of pilgrims

Toulouse (Haute-Garonne), Saint-Sernin.
1080–mid twelfth century. Choir,
transept and central tower (right),
ground plan, nave wall (below)

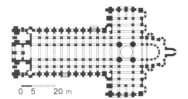

Clermont-Ferrand (Puy-de-Dôme), former monastery church of Notre-Dame-du-Port. Started around 1100. East section and central tower (below), nave and chancel area (bottom)

Oreival (Puy-de-Dôme), former monastery church of Saint-Austremoine. View from the east.

an aisled pseudo-basilica, with the roof supports of its wide side aisles nearly reaching up to the eaves of the nave roof. The two-storey elevation of the transept consists of arcades and high galleries divided into two sections. The clerestory was omitted to make room for the barrel-vaulted ceiling of the nave. The room is lit by the windows of the side aisles and the galleries. The eastern side aisle makes a right-angle turn and continues into the bay of the forechoir where it blocks out the clerestory.

The semi-circular responds of the cruciform-based piers support the recessed arches of the arcades and the vaults respectively. The nave has only four bays and has the same ground plan and elevation as the transept. Only the shape of the supports varies in every second bay. A spacious crypt, more or less echoing the ground plan of the chancel area, was intended to house the relics and to display the monastery's considerable treasures which has been preserved at Conques.

The experience gained at Tours and Conques was combined and perfected in the pilgrimage church of Saint-Sernin in Toulouse (photos, p. 148). Building work started in 1080 and was not completed until the middle of the twelfth century. The ground plan is consistently based on one unit of measurement even down to the last detail. The side aisles continue in the same shape around the nave and transept and continue around the choir in the form of the ambulatory. The piers at the crossing are breath-taking, carrying a bold tower consisting of five storeys of arcades, tapering towards the top, and finishing with a high balustrade. The five-aisled nave comprised eleven bays, compared to the ten of Saint-Martin. Viewed from the divided entrance bay between the towers, it appears to continue into infinity.

The three-storey choir area is very similar to that of Conques, consisting of arcades, gallery, and clerestory, and supported in the extended bay by the side aisles that extend up as far as the beginning of the ceiling. Additional features are the oculi which are set between the roofs of the ambulatory chapels and illuminate the gallery above the choir. The decoration, too, is in a much more lively vein: the elements articulating the wall vary in shape from section to section, the windows have multiple recessed intrados and colonnettes, and the outlines of arches and imposts are emphasized by ornamental friezes. Saint-Sernin, too, has a vast crypt, a mysterious complex of spaces on different levels housing an immeasurable wealth of relics. It is therefore all the more regrettable that the whole crypt appears more like a museum than a place of devotion.

Between Saint-Nectaire and Issoire – the monasteries of the Auverge
Between the Via Lemovicensis and the Via Podensis lies the mountainous region of the Auvergne. There a group of monastery churches began to emerge from the late eleventh century onwards that were inspired both by the pilgrimage churches and by the church of Saint-Étienne in Nevers. The most famous amongst this group of buildings are Saint-Nectaire, started probably around 1080, Notre-Dame-du-Port in Clermont-Ferrand, dating from around 1100, Saint-Austremoine in Orcival, also begun in the early twelfth century, and Saint-Paul in Issoire, built around 1130 (photos, pp. 150ff.).

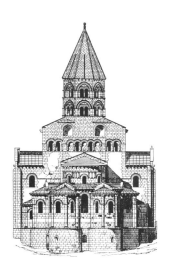

Issoire (Puy-de-Dôme), Saint-Paul.
Started around 1130. View of the richly
ornamented walls of the east section
(below), detail of wall (bottom), ground
plan (right)

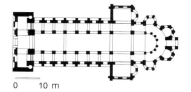

0   10 m

There are striking similarities between the four churches. They all have a low ambulatory with four radiating chapels and a deep extended bay. Above the stilted arcades of the chancel bay is a clerestory. The extended bay is formed by a wide arch and is probably windowless because of the support of the barrel vault. The aisle-less transept consists of five parts and has two apses in the eastern wall. It increases in height from the projecting transept arms which correspond to the choir, via the two steep, diagonally placed intermediate bays, towards the central dome. The effect of this increase in height is, however, considerably reduced by the two strainer arches framing the crossing at the level of the chancel arch. The upper section of the choir wall is broken up by a triple arcature. There is no doubt that this motif was inspired by Saint-Étienne where the arms of the transept, also in five sections, are separated by similar strainer arches. Another such arch is used to separate the higher nave from the crossing.

This nave has two storeys, with arcades surmounted by galleries and a barrel vault, as in the pilgrimage churches. The proportions are different, of course, and the triple gallery openings are low, similar to those of Saint-Étienne. Nevertheless, none of the builders of the four monastery churches risked including a clerestory.

What is most surprising, however, is that there is no vertical wall articulation. It had been a well-known feature in Normandy since 1040, in Nevers since 1065, and in Conques since the 1080s at the latest. In Saint-Nectaire, the oldest church of the group, the absence of any vertical wall articulation could still be explained by the fact that circular piers were used. In Notre-Dame in Clermont-Ferrand, however, there are already square piers with three semi-circular responds, but none facing the nave. The responds are attached only to the second pair of piers from the west and end at the gallery. A similar situation exists in Saint-Austremoine and also in Saint-Paul: in both churches, the pair of piers with the responds is placed in the centre of the nave, but neither has a transverse arch under the barrel vault. It appears that in all three churches a deliberate decision had been made not to use any vertical articulation in their naves, despite the fact that it exists in the side aisles. The reason for this might be an attempt to achieve a particular spatial effect, which caused the monks to draw on two different sources and freely adapt them to their purpose.

The ideas underlying the construction of the monastery churches of the Auvergne are very individual and can be appreciated more by analyzing the exterior rather than the interior. The chancel apse rises only a little above the roofs of the ambulatory and the chapels and therefore appears squat and earthbound. The roofs of the transept arms are the same height as the roof of the choir apse; but the effect of the intersecting roofs of the eastern section is interrupted by the projecting central transept bays which form a powerful, block-like mass, from which the tower rises. This block stands solidly between the choir and the nave, and dominates the whole eastern view. Its stepped arrangement, culminating in the central tower, is further emphasized by the lean-to-roofs. This motif is shared by all four churches, as is that of the four radiating chapels that leave out the central axis. During the course of the century it was only the ornamentation that became richer. The original structure and articulation was, however, retained.

Saint-Nectaire (Puy-de-Dôme), former
monastery church of Saint-Nectaire.
Started around 1080. View of the whole
compact and monumental complex

Saint-Savin-sur-Gartempe (Vienne).
1065/80 and 1095/1115. View through
the columned nave (1095/1115) into the
old choir ambulatory (1065/80), ground
plan (right)

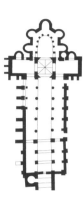

Cunault (Maine-et-Loire), Notre-Dame. Around 1100/10–around 1180. Façade, hall-type nave, tower above the north aisle

The west of France

In the west of the Frankish empire, the region between the Loire and the Dordogne, we find Romanesque buildings of very differing characters. Two main groups can be distinguished: the hall churches and the domed churches.

The hall churches

Saint-Savin-sur-Gartempe (photos, p. 152) appears to be the oldest hall church of the Poitou region, with the choir and transept dating back to between 1060 and 1085 and the nave to between 1095 and 1115. The church has a narrow, groin-vaulted ambulatory with columns, which is adjoined by five, almost completely circular, ambulatory chapels of differing sizes, the ones closest to the Lady Chapel being the largest ones. The two-storey elevation shows arcades on the lower level, with the clerestory and the calotte above them. Set in front of the choir area is a three-part transept with a square crossing and an eastern apse on each arm. In these features the building type differs little from the monastery churches of the Auvergne. Entering the nave, however, the visitor is in for a surprise: the groin-vaulted side aisles are just as wide and almost as high as the central nave with its high colonnades spanned by a barrel vault. This barrel vault is smooth as it extends from the east over the first six bays. In the last three bays, the vault is articulated by supporting arches which made it necessary for the ground plan of the piers to be altered. The sixth pair of piers from the east consists of a square core with semi-circular attached columns, while the two last pairs of piers have a trefoil ground plan. And whilst the responds on the nave side of the first pair of supports extend as far up as the beginning of the barrel vault, the responds of the two following pairs have their capitals all at the same height. In the nave, the capitals and the starting point of the vaulting arches are connected by means of a short vertical element attached to the wall. Thus a wide, well-illuminated space is created whose separation into individual aisles is hardly noticeable, thanks to the width of the side aisles and the slenderness of the supports. The extensive remnants of the original painting on the piers and the vault give a clear idea of the lively character of Romanesque churches.

The development begun at Saint-Savin is continued at the church of Notre-Dame-la-Grande in Poitiers which was built probably during the second quarter of the twelfth century. The ambulatory has three radiating chapels along its polygonal exterior wall. Because it is only one storey high it is fairly dark. Darkness also characterizes the narrow, projecting transept, with its crossing crowned by a central tower. The nave is governed by different proportions to the aisles in both width and height. The central nave is now noticeably wider than the side aisles and, owing to an extra section of wall above the arcades, distinctly higher. The barrel vault no longer receives its light from high side windows as in Saint-Savin. Instead, there is an atmosphere of subdued semi-darkness. The supports are modeled on the sixth pair of piers in Saint-Savin: the square core has been adorned with semi-circular responds, with those in the central nave extending as far as the beginning of the barrel vault and carrying a supporting arch. The nave of Notre-Dame-la-Grande is governed by different proportions and thus illuminated differently. The more pro-

nounced rhythm makes its hall character far less obvious and emphasises the central nave as opposed to the side aisles. This development is already seen in the last few bays of Saint-Savin and the changes of the piers and the introduction of the supports under the arches. It was to continue in the churches of Chauvigny and Aulnay.

The extravagant joy in ornamentation that marked the Romanesque style of western France left a further example in Poitiers – namely the façade (photo, p. 269). The whole wall surface is a virtual pattern book of architectural sculpture. Hardly a stone in the whole façade has not received of ornamental treatment. On the ground level there is the main entrance accompanied by three archivolts and framed by two wide blind recesses with a twin arcade set in each. The spandrels above are taken up by figurative scenes bordered at the top by blind arcading. Along two zones the high central window is flanked by niches with inset figures, followed by a second frieze of blind arcading which continues beyond the higher central window. The tympanum features ornamental stonework and a large oval area containing a figurative scene set within an ornamental framework. The façade is framed by two round turrets surrounded by compound responds. These terminate in a series of windows beneath a high, conical roof. There are façades with similar articulation in the Poitou region, for instance in Civray (photo, p. 267) or in Échillais, but none equals the richness in ornamentation and figurative sculpture of Notre-Dame-la-Grande.

Cunault (Maine-et-Loire), Notre-Dame.
Around 1100/10–around 1180. View of
the nave towards east

One of the lightest and, at the same time, most imposing hall churches is Notre-Dame in Cunault, situated very close to the Loire (figures, p. 153 and above). Notre-Dame was founded in the Carolingian period, while the present church was built during the first half of the twelfth century in response to a pilgrimage that attracted ever more pilgrims. Cunault was the site of the relics of Saint Maxentiolus, the engagement ring of Mary and dust from the birthplace of Christ in Bethlehem. The immense complexity of the layout of the building suggests that its design changed more than once. Building work started around 1100/1110 with the construction of the ambulatory with three unusually large radiating chapels. While the ground plan and decoration recall the choir area of the nearby monastery of Fontevrault, in Cunault the clerestory in the choir area was omitted, and the barrel vault of the chevet was supported by the groin vaults of the side aisles and the ambulatory respectively. The first change of plan seems to have occurred after the construction of the third forechoir bay, and the choir was completed with a fourth and deeper bay. Adjoining this is a four-aisled nave with side aisles all of the same height.

The two outermost aisles terminate in two semi-circular apses. Had this project been completed, the result would have been the most unusual Romanesque church imaginable, with a four-aisled hall of a height and lightness otherwise encountered only in the late Gothic period.

However, this plan, too, was abandoned after a further two bays had been built, and the nave now possessed just two aisles. Up to this time, between 1160 and 1170, the idea of a barrel-vaulted central nave had been considered essential, so it followed that the side aisles were lower than the nave. But now the last three nave bays were rib-vaulted and therefore of the same height as the side-aisles. These so-called Angevin vaults, built in a dome-shape and articulated by eight very slender columns, relieve the interior of all weight and sense of direction.

There are a small number of places in the church interior where the remains of painted decoration from the Gothic period can be seen. Part of the original decoration is represented by the strikingly beautiful capitals which have fortunately survived the last few centuries with very little damage and little need for restoration.

Talmont (Charente-Maritime), Sainte
Radegonde. First quarter of the twelfth
century. View from the east (with the
Atlantic Ocean behind)

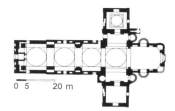

Angoulême (Charente), cathedral of Saint-Pierre. Started around 1120/30. Interior with domed vaulting (below), ground plan and richly decorated façade (right)

0 5   20 m

The domed churches

At the beginning of the twelfth century, the west of France experienced the sudden and unexpected blossoming of the art of the domed vault, a feature that might well have had its origin in the Middle East. It is more likely, however, that the inspiration came from Venice where the construction of the domed church of St. Mark had begun in 1063. Consecration occurred no later than 1094. The most famous domed churches of western France are the convent church of Fontevrault, Saint-Pierre in Angoulême, Saint-Front in Périgueux, and, in its renovated form, Saint-Hilaire in Poitiers.

Around the year 1110 Robert d'Arbrissel was given some land in the valley of Fontevrault for the purpose of establishing a convent there (figures, p. 157). By 1117, the choir area had been built, and on September 15, 1119, Pope Calixtus II consecrated all the completed sections. Robert d'Arbrissel had another choir with an ambulatory built that included three chapels and was terminated in the west by a five-part transept with two eastern apses and a crossing with central tower. An unusual feature of this choir is the enormous height of its arcades: they take up more than half the overall height. Above them is a series of low, blind arcading, followed by small windows set beneath a tunnel-vaulted roof. The steep ambulatory is spanned by an annular barrel vault. The original plan must have made provision for an aisled nave to complete this east section. It is possible that such a nave would have been identical in elevation to the choir area, although it is more likely to have been a hall-type nave. The later option is supported not only by the size and positioning of the windows but also by the presence of the pier buttresses on the exterior nave wall which suggest an interior compartment comprising eight bays. It remains unclear what caused this project to be abandoned at a stage when work had already been begun on the exterior walls. In any case, what was actually built was an

aisleless church with four square bays spanned by domes resting on pendentives. They are supported by relatively low transverse and lateral transverse arches, respectively attached to the outside walls, and their height remains below the apex of the tunnel vault of the choir. The resulting nave space is wide and somewhat oppressive. The dark pointing of the very regular stonework appears clumsy, whilst the capitals, on the other hand, are of a very high quality. The side walls of the ground floor are articulated by blind arcading, and above that each wall has two windows flanked by colonnettes.

The nave of the cathedral of Angoulême (figures, p. 156) which was begun around 1120/30 appears to be a faithful imitation of the convent church of Fontevrault. In contrast to the latter, there is no ambulatory at Angoulême; the choir consisting only of another apse with three semi-circular chapels. The transept consists of five parts. The square crossing is covered by an octagonal dome resting on a tambour. Extending outwards from the crossing, there is a narrow intermediate bay with an eastern apse on each side, the last feature reminiscent of the traditional transepts. On each side of the transept, this intermediate bay is followed by a square bay covered by a smaller dome. Both transept arms were intended to carry a tower, but only the north tower was actually built: four storeys high, it exceeds even the height of the dome.

The cathedral's remarkable feature is the façade. Similar to the west-front of Notre-Dame-la-Grande in Poitiers, it is almost completely covered with decorative elements. The façade consists of three storeys of differing heights and is subdivided into five sections by means of half-columns. These are linked by semi-circular arches which in turn span smaller side recesses with figures. In no storey does the height of the side arches correspond with that of the central arch; this is a façade with no horizontal

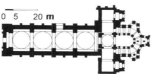

Fontevrault (Maine-et-Loire), founded in 1110. Ground plan and domed nave (left), sculptured tomb effigies: Richard the Lionheart and Eleanor of Aquitaine

From 1189 to 1204, the convent church of Fontevrault was the burial site of the kings of the Plantagenet dynasty. A total of six of its members are laid to rest here: Henry II and his wife Eleanor of Aquitaine, their son Richard the Lionheart and his sister Joan of England, their son Raymond, and finally the widow of John of England, Isabella of Angoulême. Origi-

nally the tombs were arranged in such a way that the children were always placed at the feet of their parents. The position of the burial sites in the church is, however, no longer known. What has remained are the four beautiful tomb effigies of Henry II, Richard the Lionheart, Eleanor, and Isabella.

Fontevrault, bird's eye view of the whole site (left), kitchen quarters (above)

Périgueux (Dordogne), Saint-Front.
From around 1120. View of the domes

BOTTOM RIGHT
Saint-Front before the restoration of its
domed roofs (photograph dating from
the nineteenth century)

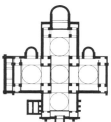

Saint-Front, ground plan.
From around 1120

St. Mark's (Venice), ground plan.
From 1063

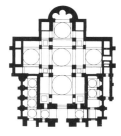

continuation. The clearest structural feature is the vertical division of the lower level into five parts, suggesting a five-aisled nave. It is therefore all the more surprising to enter a well-lit domed interior.

If the two hall naves of Fontevrault and Angoulême with their strings of domes are not enough to convince the viewer of their Venetian influence, then surely the cathedral of Périgueux (figures, p. 158) must dispel any remaining doubts. The cathedral is a large building in the shape of a Greek cross with five domes. Built on the site of a small rectangular church from the tenth/eleventh century which was destroyed by fire in 1120, it was now a kind of antechurch. Like St. Mark's in Venice, the cathedral's domes rest on pendentives set on short barrels. The powerful piers on the corner of each square are pierced by passages which are either groin-vaulted or covered by small domes in the Venetian style. Blind ornamental articulating elements run across the exterior walls. Above, each exterior wall has a group of three windows. The five domes are each pierced by four windows. The eastern end of Saint-Front has an apse on the northern and the southern arms of the cross, and a larger one on the eastern arm. A low forebay establishes the connection between this last apse and the eastern section of the barrel vault. Two levels of the apse are also decorated with blind arcading, the upper one containing windows.

What distinguishes Saint-Front from St. Mark's is the degree of decoration. Today, the cathedral of Périgueux is completely bare. Apart from blind arcading along the exterior walls, it lacks responds, capitals, decorated cornices and colonnettes adorning the openings. Also absent are the columned screens which in St. Mark's appear to divide the crossing arms on the ground floor into three aisles. There is no trace of decorative painting, an indispensable feature of medieval churches. The five sections of the interior are curiously lifeless, with arches and windows that seem as though cut out of the walls. The combination of stereometric shapes and the absence of any ornamentation suggests a product of the Revolutionary style.

Our last example of a domical construction in western France is the converted church of Saint-Hilaire in Poitiers (photo, right). Dating from the first half of the eleventh century, the interior of the building was completely reorganized from around 1130 onwards, when an ambulatory with radiating chapels was added, as well as two new side aisles on each side. The original narrow, projecting transept with its two eastern apses remained, as did the upper walls of the nave and its wide apse.

In the nave, trefoil plan piers were built which create aisles in the former hall (?), and support the transverse arches. Their spandrels contain masonry squinches which form the connection to the octagonal domes. The latter follow in the tradition of the earlier central domes. The piers and the transverse arches of every bay are supported by two bridge-like arches placed above one another. On account of the width of the domes, the load-bearing piers of each are supported in eight places. Including the four outer side aisles, the church has a six-aisled, basilica-type interior in which diverse elements are unusually combined. Whether or not this was an improvised solution to a problem, Saint-Hilaire has no equal in French Romanesque architecture.

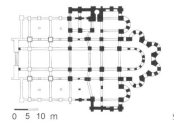

0 5 10 m

Saint-Hilaire, ground plan

OPPOSITE PAGE
Saint-Juste-de-Valcabrère (Haute
Garonne). Late twelfth century. View
from north-east

Saint-Bertrand-de-Comminges (Haute-
Garonne), cloister arcades

Saint-Guilhem-le-Désert (Hérault), former convent church of Saint-Guilhem. Tenth century, third quarter of the eleventh century, around 1100. View of the apses (built during different stages of construction), the nave (consecrated in the tenth century) and the west tower

Saint-Martin-du-Canigou (Pyrénées-Orientales). Supported by bold retaining walls, the mountain monastery is situated in a picturesque location below the summit of the Canigou in the eastern Pyrenees.

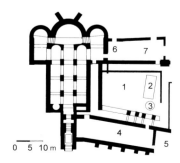

Saint-Guilhem, ground plan

Saint-Martin-du-Canigou, isometry of the two-storey church

Saint-Guilhem-le-Désert (Hérault),
former convent church of Saint-Guilhem.
Tenth century, third quarter of the
eleventh century, around 1100. Cloister
and nave from the south

center and three identical apses. Originally the supports had three pairs of granite columns which were encased during the construction of the upper church. Today, only the eastern pair survives. The lower church is connected neither to the trapezoid-shaped narthex in the west section, nor to the upper church of Saint-Martin.

Saint-Martin also has a nave and two aisles, all barrel-vaulted. Two bays of the lower church correspond to one bay of the upper church, but the latter is displaced more towards the east relative to the lower church: the building begins above the second nave bay and projects at its eastern end over the lower church by one and a half bays. The strikingly high and broad arches under the barrel vaults are supported by thick column shafts with clumsily decorated cushion capitals. The interior is divided into half by a pair of cruciform-based piers with transverse arches. The space is terminated in the east by three semi-circular apses, the central one of which is wider because of the broader central nave. There is no clerestory at the base of the barrel vault as at Cluny II. It is conceivable that the omission of windows was deliberate after the experience gained in the lower church.

A massive bell tower is situated in the north-east, articulated by beautiful blind arches similar to the ones in the apses of the upper church. In the south-west there is the trapezoid-shaped cloister which has been greatly altered by restoration work.

The monastery church of Cluny must have influenced developments in the south quite early on and also encouraged builders to experiment with barrel vaulting. A whole century before such a style had gained ground in the west of France, a barrel-vaulted hall church of the same type as Saint-Savin-sur-Gartempe or Cunault was built on the Canigou. In the region west of the Rhône, three further barrel-vaulted hall-type naves were built during the first half of the twelfth century: in Corneilla-de-Conflent, Carcassonne, and Marcevol. East of the Rhône, this style had already been taken up around the middle of the eleventh century, first in Saint-Donat, and later in Saint-Rémy-de-Provence, Embrun, and Hyère.

The development of the religious architecture of Burgundy took place almost exclusively under the patronage of Cluny. That it nevertheless provided the main impetus for developments in the south throughout the eleventh century is testified to by the churches of Quarante and the former Benedictine abbey of Saint-Guilhem-le-Désert (photos, pp. 162–4). The church of Quarante was consecrated in 1153 and, as in Cluny II, has a barrel-vaulted central nave with windows in the barrel base. Saint-Guilhem is situated in the Gorge of Verdus and was established by Count Guillaume of Toulouse, a comrade-in-arms of Charlemagne.

Between 1962 and 1970 a square crypt was excavated which presumably dates back to the late tenth century. It might have belonged to the aisle-less church from which the first bay of the existing church and the two tiny apses in the transept originate. It is likely that even the foundations of the nave supports and parts of the transept are of the same origin.

Today the church of Saint-Guilhem, consecrated in 1076, has an aisled nave comprising four bays, and a very prominent aisled transept with three apses from around 1100. The nave has two storeys; broad rectangular piers with responds on the sides facing the nave, and the side

Roussillon and Provence

The second church of Cluny was just under construction in Burgundy when in the year 975 seven bishops consecrated a church in Saint-Michel-de-Cuxa which had been established by Seniofred, Comte de Cerdagne. The church has a nave and two side aisles and a very prominent transept to which were attached five or seven apses in a staggered arrangement. The central apse was of rectangular shape. In the early eleventh century, its famous builder, Abbot Oliba, arranged for the addition of a vaulted ambulatory around the main apse, with three further apses on the east side. He also had the nave extended and soon afterwards built the round church of Notre-Dame-de-la-Crèche in the eastern part of the site. In order to do this, the central ambulatory apse, which had only just been completed, had to be destroyed. The originally unvaulted ceilings of the basilicas in Arles-sur-Tech (from 1064) and Elne (first quarter of the eleventh century) suggest that initially the nave of Saint-Michel would also have had a flat ceiling.

In contrast, the church of Saint-Martin-du-Canigou is vaulted throughout. The church belongs to the monastery established by Seniofred's son Guifred and used as the family's burial site. It is situated in a remote area in the eastern Pyrenees, below the 9188 feet high Pic du Canigou (photo, p. 163), the building has two storeys. The lower church Notre-Dame-la-Souterraine has barrel-vaulting in the nave and aisles. Its nave has six bays of equal size followed by another bay situated in between the aisles and later bricked off. Finally, a groin-vaulted choir has aisles as wide as the

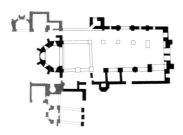

Alet-les-Bains (Aude), former convent church of Sainte-Marie. First half of the twelfth century. Nave, central nave, apse (left), exterior view of the apse

aisles carry the arcades with their recessed supporting arches. Above the arcades and under the barrel vault there are large windows. The responds initiate the supporting arches of the barrel vaults and also serve as vertical elements of articulation. The exterior of the nave is articulated by a rhythmical arrangement of blind elements.

The windows of the single-storey choir area are placed below a row of wide blind arcades. The building work must have extended over a prolonged period: whilst the southern apse still shows the typical blind arches between the lesenes, the northern apse is articulated by a low blind arcade underneath the eaves into which small windows are inserted. The wide central apse, supported by unusually strong pier buttresses, even has large windows with flanking colonnettes. Below the eaves is a continuous row of arcades through which one can see the calotte. A similar blind arcade is found in Saint-Étienne in Nevers. The basilica-type elevation of the nave with the clerestory underneath a barrel vault is also recalls that building. There is, of course, no gallery.

Burgundy was not the only influence, however: the pilgrim churches, too, occasionally left their mark on the Roussillon region. When the Benedictine abbey of Sainte-Marie in Alet-les-Bains received a new church in the first half of the twelfth century, the Abbot Raymond decided that the seven-bay nave should be built in the style of the pilgrim church, whilst the eastern section consists only of one apse as wide as the central nave. The building is now a ruin (photos, above). The piers, now largely altered, are

likely to have had cruciform bases, and between them arcades and galleries of more or less equal size were set underneath a barrel vault. The galleries must have been covered by barrels with a quarter-circle profile and had large windows framed on the outside by colonnettes and ornamental friezes; there might also have been some oculi. Apart from the double entrance in the west, a recessed portal still exists in the south. At the level of the fifth bay from the west, high, slender stair turrets were attached to the outside of the nave. These may also have been bell towers, since the top storey of the north turret shows traces of arcades to release the sound.

The central apse has five recesses flanked with columns and three calotte windows. The polygonal, triangular exterior is supported on the corners of the lower storey by pier buttresses. Between them, the broad, rectangular forms of the recesses project and carry a slender, tripartite blind arcade over a smooth plinth area. The upper storey, behind which the calotte is situated, is furnished with corner columns and a three-part architrave endowed with lavish ornamentation.

In addition to the "imported" styles, the Roussillon region developed its own: the longitudinal nave. This emerged during the eleventh century and later spread widely throughout the south: the longitudinal nave. At first, it did not have a vaulted ceiling; examples are the churches of Monastir-del-Camp (1064/87), Serrabone (end of the eleventh century), Caunes-Minervois (after mid twelfth century) and Saint-Génis-des-Fontaines (consecrated in 1153).

Montmajour (Bouches-du-Rhône),
former convent church of Notre-Dame.
Around 1140–1153: crypt, choir and
transept; from 1160: nave and aisles.
Diagonal view into the choir (top), view
of the whole site (bottom)

The late Romanesque style of Provence

Little was built in the region east of the river Rhône before the twelfth century. At that time, Romanesque architecture had reached its zenith in Burgundy and in the north of the country with the construction of Cluny III and the two monastery churches in Caen. East of the Rhône, there was no record of a church being consecrated until 1103. The cathedral of Aix-en-Provence had been restored and now it, too, had an aisle-less nave without vaulting but with round-arched niches in the side walls. Almost at the same time, the (admittedly narrower) nave of Saint-Martin-de-Londres was spanned by the first barrel vault. Thus the vaulted aisle-less nave with recessed niches was born. It was not until after 1200 that the barrel vault was replaced by the rib vault, which at that stage in Provence was still a powerful and heavy structure. Rib-vaulted aisle-less naves can still be seen in Castellane, Fréjus and Grasse.

In the south, the preferred type of vaulting was the barrel vault. Although it had been possible to barrel-vault a basilica since the last quarter of the eleventh century, it was nevertheless still a highly complicated task. There are therefore only four barrel-vaulted basilicas in the whole of Provence: Saint-Trophîme and Saint-Honorat-des-Aliscamps in Arles, Saint-Victor in Marseille, and the cathedral of Vaison-la-Romaine, all dating from the second half of the twelfth century.

An aisle-less nave is accompanied either by a transept and three eastern apses, or, in the case of churches without a transept, by one apse. The space was unsuitable for an adjoining ambulatory with chapels. The only churches of this type to have an ambulatory are the church of the monastery of Saint-Gilles, which was subordinate to Cluny, and the foundation crypt of Montmajour. These interiors are strikingly dark and austere. Dark because the only places where windows could be situated were the west wall of the nave and the apse. The austerity is more difficult to explain. Admittedly, there were no column capitals in the nave and ambulatory that could have been decorated; but ornamentation has also largely been omitted on the blind articulating elements in the chancel area and on the responds between the niches. The interiors thus remained austere at a time when Roman architecture experienced its first major Renaissance. The wonderful sculpture made its appearance almost exclusively on the porches and in the cloisters.

One of the many aisleless churches in Provence belongs to the former monastery of Notre-Dame in Montmajour (photo, p. 166). The foundation crypt, built on the rockface of the Mons Major, could be reached only by boat until the marshes were drained. The crypt was consecrated together with the east sections of the upper church in 1153. The building has a domed confessio as in a central planform, with one antebay in the west, and surrounded by a barrel-vaulted ambulatory with five radiating chapels. In front there is transept-like tunnel with two eastern apses and an access ramp in the central axis. The walls are made from large, carefully smoothed ashlars adorned with stone mason's marks; but there are no responds, supporting arches, cornices, or capitals.

With the exception of the ambulatory and the chapels, the eastern sections of the church follow the design of the crypt. Here, a wide apse,

Saint-Gabriel (Bouches-du-Rhône),
Chapel. Around 1200. Westfront with
entrance porch

BOTTOM
Saintes-Maries-de-la-Mer (Bouches-du-
Rhône), pilgrimage church of the Holy
Maries. Around 1170/80, around 1200.
View from south-west

semi-circular on the inside and polygonal on the outside, opens onto the oblong crossing. Flat ribs in the shape of a solid stone band articulate the renovated calotte. The arms of the transept are lower than the nave and the apse. They are barrel-vaulted and, as in the lower storey, have apses in the east. The building of the nave began around 1160, and only two of the five planned bays were built. The bays are articulated by strongly recessed transverse arches which support the pointed barrel vault that starts above a narrow cornice. Above it, the recessed niches open up. Even the upper church is marked by an almost Cistercian austerity; the apse alone is decorated by a pair of columns with simple crocket capitals. Between 1190 and 1200 part of the building collapsed, so that the east section had to be rebuilt and the crossing vault modernized. The cloister, which dates from the last quarter of the twelfth century, used to house important works of Romanesque sculpture, most of which are today kept in museums. Some beautiful tombstones can still be seen in the galleries of the church.

The pilgrim church of the Holy Maries in Les-Saintes-Maries-de-la-Mer was built in the decade after 1170 and is one of the most famous monuments of Provence. It, too, is a aisle-less church with five bays and with recessed blind arches articulating the exterior walls (photo, p. 167). A sixth bay in the shape of a trapezoid leads over into the semi-circular apse. As early as 1200 the building was extended to form a fortified church. Battlements were added above the machicolation, and the chancel area was crowned with a polygonal tower. The apse windows were closed so that the already dimly lit interior became even darker. Apart from the flat blind arches on the apse wall, the exterior of the pilgrim church is completely devoid of ornamentation. As a result, the parapets, with their battlements rising above the row of semi-circular arches on the machicolation, and the closed "keep" above the apse appear all the more threatening. The apse and the two adjoining bays had to be raised so that the crypt, donated by René d'Anjou, could be accommodated.

Not far from Tarascon is the delightful chapel of Saint-Gabriel (photo, p. 167). Built around 1200, it is one of the most important Romanesque buildings in Provence. It too has no aisles and a pointed barrel vault. Its interior is notable for its recessed blind arches and lack of ornamentation. The nave has three bays, short, chapel-like extensions in the east, and a low, semi-circular apse. The westfront is reminiscent of a Roman triumphal arch. The façade is divided into two sections which correspond to the wall section and the vault section of the interior. The pointed arch on the gable has an oculus set in a framework of ornamental bands imitating classical forms. Around it at the four points of the compass are the Evangelists' symbols. A wide semi-circular arch framed by an egg and dart pattern opens up underneath, framing a slightly recessed portal flanked by two columns and with a triangular pediment with a small relief plaque. The apex is crowned by a lamb. The entrance between the columns also has columns, a tympanum with carved figures, and archivolts; the door lintel no longer exists. A centrally placed flight of stone steps leads to a platform supported by a wall. This feature adds further to the enchantment of this beautiful west front.

Vénasque (Vaucluse), so-called
baptistery. Eleventh century. View of the
interior with the octagonal water basin
and the altar in the eastern apse

Montmajour (Bouches-du-Rhône), Chapel
of Sainte Croix, ground plan (right)

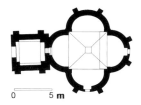

Centrally Planned Buildings in the South of France

Aix-en-Provence, Fréjus and Riez all have beautiful baptismal chapels dating from the fifth and sixth centuries. Whilst their exterior is based on a square ground plan, their interior is octagonal, with niches and ambulatories. The centrally planned building was probably rediscovered during the twelfth century, along with a renewed appreciation of the beauty of classical Roman form. Thus the chapels built in Vénasque, Rieux-Minervois, and Montmajour are centrally planned, but unlike the early baptisteries do not all follow the same ground plan.

The oldest is Vénasque (photo, p. 168). Said to have been built in the eleventh century, it is regarded as a proper baptistery. Its interior consists of a rectangular central space, about 20 x 33 feet, and four apses: the north and south-facing ones are horseshoe-shaped, whilst the east and west-facing ones are semi-circular. They have a rectangular exterior casing and are decorated inside with a row of blind arches set on columns. The bases, shafts and capitals were taken from other buildings and reassembled. An octagonal water basin is set into the floor of the central interior.

The chapel of Rieux-Minervois (photo, below) was built between 1150 and 1175 and has a very individual character. Its heptagonal center consists of four cruciform piers alternating with three columns and is surrounded by a fourteen-sided

ambulatory decorated with blind arches set on colonnettes, and spanned by a quarter-circle barrel. The central space is crowned by a dome. Almost the entire chapel is surrounded by an untidy arrangement of additional chapels and sacristy buildings. New plans in 1839 added a tower to the dome and another fourteen independent chapels opening out onto the ambulatory. The high quality capitals include an Assumption of the Virgin by the Master of Cabestany.

The chapel of Sainte-Croix in Montmajour (photo, above) is a cemetery chapel based on a four-sided apse. It differs from Vénasque in the degree of architectural perfection, which had reached its zenith by the late twelfth century. Like the crypt and upper church of the abbey church, Sainte-Croix is a perfect ashlar building in which the pointing is hardly noticeable. The central interior is high and square and has four lower apses attached to it, one along the entire width of each side. Adjoining the western apse is a square entrance hall. The unornamented rooms rely for their magnificent effect on the combination and proportioning of the architectural elements, the precision of the stonework, and the details. An unobtrusive yet highly effective feature is the continuation of the corners between the apses towards the central structure. Instead of being by the ridge of the cube, the hollow molding is continued so that the four sides of the cube are drawn forwards by an inch or so to suggest a Greek cross. Equally delightful are the four gables above the sides of the cube with the intersecting saddleback roofs and the lantern.

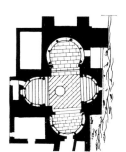

Vénasque, "baptistery," ground plan

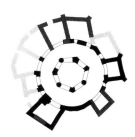

Rieux Minervois (Aude), round church of
L'Assomption-de-Notre-Dame. Around
1150–75. Interior view and ground plan

Cistercian churches in the south of France

Amongst the most spectacular buildings from the Romanesque period in France are the Cistercian monasteries in the foothills of the Alps and the Pyrenees. They were built in the second half of the twelfth century. Similar to the slightly older church of Fontenay (photos, pp. 134–5), the Cistercian churches of Provence are simple, clearly structured spaces made from stonework of the highest quality. Again as at Fontenay, they rely for their effect largely on their idyllic setting and on the peace and serenity of the nature surrounding them.

Sénanque

The monastery of Sénanque was established in the remote valley of Sénancole by the Bishop of Cavaillon in 1148. The construction of the church itself began around 1150, and its eastern section is in the typical Cistercian tradition, albeit in the style more popular in the south. The rectangular chancel area is replaced by an apse which is as wide as the nave and situated behind a transverse arch. The arch has a function similar to that of an extended bay. The side chapels have developed into apses with rectangular

outer casing and extended bays. In front of these extends a three part, projecting transept with barrel vaulting and a domed central crossing. The aisled nave is higher than the transept. It is spanned by a pointed barrel vault above a clerestory, but without supporting arches. Such arches are, however, used in the side aisles under the quarter-circle barrel vaulting. The responds are semi-circular in shape and carry plain crocket capitals. Seen from the west the transept is hardly noticeable behind the large broad façade.

Seen from the east, however, it is an individual structure encompassing the nave and accompanied by a side-aisle. The extended horizontal shape of the transept is effectively broken up by the wide apse.

The western part of this church, oriented north, contains a delightful cloister bounded by the other monastery buildings which, in their unadorned simplicity, also follow Cistercian tradition. The exception is the chapter house, vaulted at a later date.

Sénanque (Vaucluse), former Cistercian monastery. Established in 1148, monastery church from 1150. East view (left), wing of cloister, and interior courtyard (right)

Silvacane

Silvacane (= silva cannorum, reed wood) is first mentioned in the year 1030 in connection with a settlement of hermits. More than a century passed, however, before the Cistercian monastery was established in the valley of the Durance. The monastery enjoyed the highest protection and had Otto, a half-brother of the emperor Konrad III, as its first abbot. The monks came from Morimond. The church was finally built around 1160 and has survived almost unaltered. The building work lasted several decades, and the square chancel with accompanying rectangular chapels was not completed until 1191/92. The transept arms with their pointed barrel-vaulted ceiling were then built, followed by the crossing spanned by a rib vault. The nave must initially have been planned as a three-aisled basilica with pointed barrel vaulting in nave and aisles; this is suggested by the vaulting in the eastern bay of the northern side aisle and by the window in the upper wall of the nave. But the plans were altered, resulting in deeper, almost square nave bays with barrel vaulting over recessed transverse arches. The side aisles were fitted with pointed barrel vaults of varying dimen-

sions whose apex is shifted strongly towards the nave. The church was not completed until about 1230. Again, there is very little ornamentation, although the supporting arches of the barrel vaults and the arcades rest on half-columns with plinths and crocket capitals, similar to the arrangement at Sénanque. In keeping with the steep down gradient of the site towards north, the level of the three aisles has also been staggered towards that side. This creates the impression of closed-off rooms connected by windows. They allowed themselves a hint of decoration on the nave entrance with its multiple recesses, but the columns no longer exist.

Like the monastery buildings, the cloisters date back to the second half of the thirteenth century.

Silvacane (Bouches-du-Rhône), former Cistercian monastery. Established around the middle of the twelfth century, monastery church from 1160 to around 1230. South wall of the nave (opposite), side aisle and nave (left)

Fontefroide

Situated in the foothills of the Pyrenees south-west of Narbonne, the monastery of Fontefroide was founded towards the end of the eleventh century by Ayméry I, Vicomte de Narbonne. In 1146 it joined the then young Cistercian Order. The money for the building of the beautiful monastery church was donated by Ermengarde, the granddaughter of the founder, in 1157. An aisled pseudo-basilica with five bays and a transept consisting of three squares were built. Opening onto the transept are a polygonal central apse with an extended bay, two smaller chapels, and two side apses, also of polygonal shape. A pointed barrel vault spans the nave and is flanked by the quarter-circle barrel vaults of the side aisles. The three transept bays and the extended bay of the apse, on the other hand, already have quadripartite rib vaulting, since they were not completed until the early thirteenth century. By the second half of the thirteenth century, the cloister galleries, the chapter hall and the dormitory were built, as well as the building for the lay brothers in the west and the elegant abbot's chapel in the south-eastern part of the church. The row of chapels on the south side is an addition from the late Gothic period.

As in all Cistercian churches, the apse and the extended bay are considerably lower than the nave. This opened up the possibility of providing additional lighting from the east for these naves were relatively dark on account of their quasi-basilica elevations. In the eastern wall of

Fontenay there are five round-arched windows, following the line of the choir pediment. In Fontefroide, on the other hand, this group of windows has developed into a five-part tracery window that takes up the whole of the upper wall above the forechoir bay (photo, below). The choir itself is also more complex. At Silvacane, the choir is in the pure Cistercian tradition, having

one almost square room, while at Sénanque and Le Thoronet that space is semi-circular. In contrast, Fontefroide boasts a choir divided into an extended bay and a polygonal apse. Here, one becomes distinctly aware of a gradual relaxation in the austere Cistercian style, which had found a perfect model in the large-scale and straight structures of Romanesque architecture.

Fontefroide (Aude) former Cistercian monastery. Founded end eleventh century. Monastery church from 1157. Aerial view of the site (top). Nave of the church (below left), cloister early Gothic period (below right)

Le Thoronet (Var), former Cistercian monastery. Founded in 1136, monastery church 1150/60 to around 1200. View of nave towards east

Le Thoronet

Despite the fact that building work on the fourth Cistercian monastery in southern France began later, Le Thoronet was actually completed earlier than Fontfroide. The church and monastery buildings are still imbued with the traditional Cistercian simplicity and dignity. Founded in 1136 by Raymond de Saint-Gilles, Comte de Toulouse, the monastery was first situated near Tourtour and moved to its present site between 1150 and 1160. Work on the church and monastery building must have begun immediately after the move, and was completed around the year 1200. By 1514, only seven monks were left at Le Thoronet. Nevertheless, the choir was rebuilt in the baroque style at the beginning of the eighteenth century. The present state of the building is due to the restoration work by Revoil.

The wide, squat central nave is flanked by narrow side aisles. The pointed barrel vault continues across the crossing so that the lower transept arms appear like chapels attached to it. Standing in the nave, all one notices are the slightly higher arcades in that area. The apse behind the crossing is preceded by an extended bay which also has a pointed barrel vault. Four chapels with rectangular casing open out into the transept arms. The church interior is well lit despite there being no clerestory in the nave, as enough light can enter through the windows in the main apse, the southern side aisle, the western wall, and above the apse.

The plain, barrel-vaulted cloisters in the northern section of the church are unusually large, their sides measuring 142 feet. They are surrounded by the monastery buildings according to the usual pattern. They, too, are rather austere, with the sole exception of the chapter house in the east which was rib-vaulted at a later stage.

View across the cloister towards the church (left), cloister with pump-room (bottom left), ground plan of the monastery

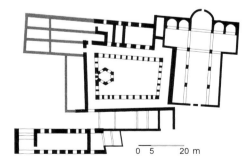

0 5   20 m

Secular buildings

The keep – a residential building and symbol of power in the high Middle Ages

At the end of the first millennium, at a time when a completely new style was developed in French religious architecture, secular architecture also set out on a new path. Until this period, the castles and seats of the rulers had consisted mainly of so-called mottes, that is to say, conical mounds of earth combined with irregular wooden enclosure walls. The residential and domestic quarters seem to have been built exclusively from non-durable materials. Excavations have discovered the foundations of multi-storey, rectangular wooden or timber-framed buildings on the platforms of the mottes.

Around the year 1000, wood was increasingly replaced by stone for the construction of these residential towers. On the one hand, the reason for this change might have been the desire for greater security: stronger barriers were needed to withstand the ever-growing dangers of improved war and siege techniques. On the other hand, there was also a change in society which enabled individual rulers to build stone towers. Therefore the keep became not only a fortified residential building but also a symbol of power.

The earliest examples found in France are the keep of Doué-la-Fontaine, Maine-et-Loire, dating from around 950, and the keep of Fulk Nerra, Count of Anjou, in Langeais, which has recently been dated to 1017. Both are rectangular, with their

originally thin walls supported by responds attached to the walls at regular intervals. Recent research has shown that both keeps were initially used more for residential rather than defensive purposes, and that they were only fortified around the year 1100 when the windows were walled up and the walls reinforced.

Around 1070, Humbaud d'Huriel in Huriel (Allier) had a keep built according to the same plan, but with a much more pronounced fortified character. A space measuring about 20 x 27 feet is enclosed by walls 6½ feet thick, each wall having four flat pier buttresses attached to its exterior. Of the original five storeys, only the lowest one has a vaulted ceiling, whilst the other storeys have flat ceilings resting on the exterior walls which become thinner towards the top of the building. The inhabitants probably used ladders to get from one storey to the next. Two entrances were placed on the second and the third floors. Below them are beam holes suggesting that there must have been wooden passageways and arcades which could be set on fire and thrown off in an emergency.

Guillaume le Roux is also said to have begun building a fortification in Gisors (Eure) during the last years of the eleventh century. Today only its high motte remains, around which Henry Plantagenet (Henry I) built rings of walls and crowned with a "shell-keep" in the early twelfth century (photo, above). The "shell-keeps," the ring-walls on the plateau of the mottes, were invented by the Anglo-Saxons and were not widely used in France. Normally the shell-keeps housed the residential and domestic quarters, the stables and the chapel. In Gisors, however, Henry II built an octagonal keep around 1170 which provides a spectacular crowning feature for the concentric wall circles. Both the shell-keep and the keep are articulated by pier buttresses.

In terms of defense technology, the introduction of the circle or the octagon, as at Gisors, represented progress. It eliminated the blind spots that existed around the corners of a rectangular defense layout, and offered less space for attack by projectiles. In spite of these advantages, the circular form never became fully established in its own right,

Houdan (Yvelines), keep. First quarter of the twelfth century

OPPOSITE PAGE
Provins, castle with octagonal keep from the early twelfth century

LEFT
Gisors (Eure), castle. Shell-keep from the early twelfth century, keep around 1170

and rectangular keeps continued to be built throughout the thirteenth and, indeed, until well into the fifteenth century. One of the strangest fortifications is the keep of Houdan (Yvelines, photo, bottom left). It was built by Amaury III, Seigneur of Montfort and Comte d'Évreux, in the first quarter of the twelfth century. Its more or less square interior space with bevelled edges is enclosed by a circle of irregular shape, to which massive, semi-circular responds are attached facing the four points of the compass. One of these tower-like responds has a spiral staircase. Such a staircase within the wall was a sign of enormous progress, not only because it was convenient, but also because it was easier for the noble lords and ladies to keep away from their retinue. Now, the individual floors were independent of one another, and each room could be reached without having to cross another one. The pretty biforia of the second floor probably express the inhabitants' desire for homeliness and exclusivity in their noble quarters. The ground floor, too, has small openings – probably an indication that the keep of Houdan must once have been protected by strong court walls.

The development begun at Houdan was continued by the keep of Étampes (Essonne) which was built between 1130 and 1150. It is laid out on a quatrefoil plan, so that each of its four towers of semi-circular section takes up the entire width of an interior square. The result was a keep with five separate rooms on every floor and with several spiral staircases, a real palace within a tower. It is, however, doubtful whether the quatrefoil shape was defensively advantageous. The round and polygonal towers, which since the middle of the century had become no less important than the rectangular ones were more advantageous. Another keep with octagonal ground plan and four semi-circular towers was built at roughly the same time as the keep of Gisors: the Tour César in Provins (photo, p. 175).

OPPOSITE PAGE LEFT
Saint-Antonin, town house of the Granolhet family. Second quarter of the twelfth century. Front looking onto the street

OPPOSITE PAGE RIGHT
Auxerre, former bishop's palace. Around 1120/25. Gallery wing

Druyes-les-Belles-Fontaines (Yonne), castle. Begun around 1200

Set on a high and steep motte there is a square substructure measuring 67 x 67 feet and supporting the keep and the towers which are massive at ground floor level. About halfway up the building the exterior wall recedes, making room for a defensive passage leading through the towers. A second defensive passage used to run along behind the battlements on the top storey. Inside, there were two domed halls. Again, such a complicated layout, consisting of so many parts, raises the question of the effectiveness of the building's defense. The Tour César was brilliantly protected by walls and moats, and the motte meant that it was raised far above the level of any attackers. However, the style of construction of the latter must surely also have had something to do with the desire for prestige.

The quatrefoil ground plan was once more taken up at the end of the twelfth century in Amblény. Here, however, a straight stretch of wall remains free between the semi-circular towers. The whole complex consists of large, care-fully smoothed ashlars. As with most keeps, it was modernized in the late Middle Ages when the keep was rediscovered as a residential building. Today, the keep of Amblény is a mere ruin. The beginning of the twelfth century saw a fundamental change in the building of castles in France: the enclosure walls, which for centuries had enclosed a terrain of irregular and arbitrary shape, became narrower and more regular. Around the year 1200, this style was introduced into France by two buildings: the old Louvre in Paris and the castle of Druyes-les-Belles-Fontaines (Yonne), commissioned by King Philippe II Auguste and his cousin Pierre II de Courtenay, respectively. Whilst the Louvre of the early thirteenth century is today known only from excavations and old pictures, Druyes-les-Belles-Fontaines still exists as a picturesque and impressive ruin, set high up on a natural rock ledge (photo, above). The corners of the square structure are protected by circular towers. The living quarters were situated above the steep rockface overlooking the valley. Unusually for the period, they extended along the whole front and had regularly spaced twin openings.

The mighty gate-tower with its pointed archway and pier buttresses in the centre of the reverse side has survived almost intact. In contrast to the enclosure walls, the gate-tower is built from high-quality ashlars. At the top, it terminates in machicolations set above multiply recessed and moulded corbels.

This type of fortification remained in constant use in France for more than two centuries, the only changes being in the decoration of the living quarters.

(1115–1136) on the east wall of a building that had previously stood on this site. One of the best-preserved examples of Romanesque city architecture is the town house of the Granolhet family in Saint-Antonin, dating from the second quarter of the twelfth century (photo, left). The three-storey façade had three distinct levels. On the ground floor, pointed arches open out into a vaulted hall. On the second floor, the whole width of the façade is taken up by a window set in a framework of delicate molding. Similar to the technique used in cloisters, the division into three sections is achieved by two piers with superimposed figures. Each section has three twin colonnettes with richly decorated capitals. The top storey, finally, has three twin openings whose outlines are traced by string courses.

Whilst the architecture of the Romanesque period focused mainly on religious and secular buildings, it was also becoming aware of the technological tasks which it could perform: there is, for example, the famous kitchen in the monastery of Fontevrault (photo,

p. 157), but there are also mills, canals, brickworks, mines, roads, and bridges. It is in their nature that hardly any of these constructions were built to last, with the exception of the wooden and stone bridges which have survived here and there, at least partially. The best-known Romanesque bridge is the Pont-Saint-Bénézet, or the Pont d'Avignon. Legend has it that building work on it was begun by Saint Benedict who was laid to rest in 1185 in the chapel of Saint-Nicolas which is situated on the second pier of the bridge. During a heavy military siege in 1226 the bridge was seriously damaged and was rebuilt at a slightly raised level. Further repairs were carried out in the fifteenth century, but from the seventeenth century onwards the bridge has been incomplete. All that remains now are three wide, flat arches and three piers. The burial chapel of Saint Benedict with its polygonal apse and barrel-vaulted nave is set on one of these piers. The chapel was divided into two storeys at a later date.

Town residences of the bishops and the nobility

In the cities, the defensive potential of individual houses was of no consequence. Rather than developing particular building types, architecture would concentrate on the decoration of the façades, resulting in magnificent frontages featuring arcades, galleries and twin openings.

Many houses have suffered badly not only from the passage of time, but also from the restoration efforts of the nineteenth century, and often only parts of them have survived. The former palace of the bishop of Auxerre, for example, still has a delightful arcade (photo, top right), albeit below a somewhat disfiguring balustrade dating from the nineteenth century. Delicate twin colonnettes with lavish and varied shaft decoration carry semi-circular arches with hollow moldings decorated with stone balls. This arcade is part of a gallery wing built by the bishop Hugues de Montaigu

Avignon, Pont-Saint-Bénézet. Around 1170/75

Bruno Klein

Romanesque architecture in Spain and Portugal

Historical background

In Spain and Portugal, the origin and development of Romanesque architecture took a course different from that in most other countries of western and central Europe. The historical background was different there, as nearly all of the Iberian Peninsula had been under Moorish rule since 711. It was not until the Romanesque period that the "Reconquista" – the re-conquest under the Christian banner – achieved its first great success. The movement started in the Asturian mountain region which had never fallen completely into Moorish hands. In 924, the kingdom of the Asturias became the kingdom of León, and later of Castile and León. The Reconquista developed also in the Franco-Spanish border region of Catalonia (from 795) and also in the kingdoms of Navarre and Aragon. The local rulers there managed to turn the conflict with the Muslims into an issue which involved the whole Christian community. These efforts found their most significant expression in the organization of the pilgrimage to Santiago in Galicia, a journey which in the tenth and eleventh centuries was still advocated as a kind of crusade; the first crusade to the east, to Jerusalem, did not start out until the year 1096. In the late eleventh century, after the immediate threat posed by the Muslims had been eliminated, at least from northern Spain, the journey to Santiago took on the characteristics of a proper pilgrimage. Pilgrims made their way to the grave of St. James in the cathedral of Santiago in order to solicit the Apostle's intercession for the salvation of their souls, now that this salvation could no longer be achieved primarily by the use of weapons against the Moors.

It is true that the consolidation of a Christian Spain initially depended on the military success against the Muslim enemy. From the eleventh century onwards, however, the military effort was increasingly supported by cultural developments. The few, widely spaced hospices that had been set up along the route of the pilgrimage in order to provide a base for the travelers on their dangerous and arduous journey to Santiago soon grew into sizeable settlements. The local rulers encouraged this development further by means of active population policies, which meant that they granted extensive privileges to immigrants who were prepared to settle there. Parallel to this development, a series of religious reforms were introduced, culminating in the introduction of the Roman liturgy to replace the local Mozarabic one. A number of monastic communities took care of both the mental and physical well-being of the pilgrims, while their spiritual needs were met by the construction of new religious buildings.

The development of Romanesque architecture on the Iberian Peninsula must be seen in the context of the historic and cultural developments occurring at the time, which can be only briefly and roughly outlined here. The proximity of Al-Andalus, the southern, Muslim part of the Iberian Peninsula, as well as the Reconquista and its immediate aftermath, all brought their influence to bear on the development of an architectural style which was independent only at its outset. It soon came more and more under the influence of an architectural culture shaped by mainland Europe, and by France in particular. By the end of the twelfth century, it showed pronounced regional tendencies.

Oviedo, Monte Naranco, San Miguel de Liño. Mid ninth century

Oviedo, Monte Naranco, San Miguel de Liño. Mid ninth century

Oviedo, Monte Naranco, Palace auditorium from the time of King Ramiro I. (842–850)

Of course this does not necessarily mean that architecture in twelfth-century Spain lost any originality by following foreign trends, but that Spain became increasingly integrated into a broader European context whilst not losing its own identity.

The conflict between the various Muslim rulers in the south, whose base was at Córdoba, and the Christian rulers in the north, brought about a cultural division of the Iberian Peninsula into two parts: evidence of Romanesque architecture is therefore found only in the north, while in the south Muslim architecture continued to be cultivated, in some parts until well into the fifteenth century. Whilst it is true that the fiercely contested borders gradually moved further south, the starting point of Romanesque architecture, however, must always be looked for in the extreme north of Spain.

Pre-Romanesque architecture

Only fragments have survived of the earlier Christian architecture in northern Spain from the time of the kingdom of the Asturias. The most significant monuments are found near the old capital of Oviedo: here, King Ramiro I (842–850) built a palace complex with audience chamber at the Monte Naranco (photo, top, right), which was extended by his successor Ordoño I with the construction of a church, San Miguel de Liño (photo, top, left). Both buildings feature a remarkable wealth of architectural articulating elements, such as pilaster strips, blind arches, and cornices, and many ornamental shapes in relief. While the palace audience

chamber is unique for its period, the church – only parts of which have survived – can more easily be connected in typological terms with other contemporary churches. The main space is subdivided into several short aisles. The transepts, which hardly project beyond the width of side aisles, is adjoined by rectangular, cell-like chambers used as side chapels and to house the altars.

Before long this building style underwent a decisive change, triggered by the emigration of the Christian "Mozarabic" population in the Moorish part of Spain, coming under increasing pressure and moving northwards, where their influence brought about the development of a new architectural style. This was characterized by the fusion of older local traditions with Moorish elements which, in turn, still contained traces of Roman and Byzantine style. This type of "Mozarabic" architecture had existed at an earlier date in Al-Andalus. Presumably, the most important examples were situated in Toledo: none of the works there have, however, survived. Instead, there is a whole series of buildings extant in the Christian north of Spain in which the earlier Asturian style is mixed with novel elements. While the churches tend to be based on a simpler layout, they are endowed with arcades and apses with horseshoe arches and central domes. The older type of the square-ended apse often remains intact, but only as an outer wall-casing surrounding a horseshoe-shaped interior chamber, and there is an increasing wealth of architectural ornament.

Soon afterwards, this building style followed in the Christian areas of the Iberian Peninsula was replaced by Romanesque architecture.

One can hardly describe this process as a gradual change from the old to the new – it was more like a complete break. One reason for this was probably the culmination of political events in the late tenth century. The Moorish ruler Almanzûr "the victorious" conquered parts of the kingdoms of northern Spain, and in 985 destroyed Barcelona, in 988 León, and in 997 Iria Flavia, the future Compostela, where a church had already been erected above the tomb of the Apostle. However, before long Almanzûr himself suffered a defeat near Calantañazor, and soon after his death in 1002, the once powerful caliphate of Córdoba disintegrated into several small principalities called taifas, which one by one fell prey to the Reconquista. So, in a sense, a "tabula rasa" had been created at that time for the construction of new buildings, which were now to be built in the spirit of a strengthened Christian identity. Almost simultaneously, a reform within the monastic order began in France, led by the Benedictine monastery of Cluny. In Italy, too, efforts were made to reform the Church. The architectural results of these efforts can be seen in a widespread return to early Christian building forms.

The development of Romanesque style in Catalonia, Aragon and Navarre

It was almost as a matter of course that the first buildings in the new style were constructed in the Catalonian region on both sides of the Pyrenees. Formerly under the sway of Charlemagne, this region had been independent since 865 and was ruled by the counts of Barcelona. Its proximity to the Christian mediterranean countries of France and Italy made it a natural melting-pot for the Moorish and Christian cultures. Moreover, the counts of Barcelona had obviously found a way of peaceful communication with the Moorish

kingdom of Córdoba. During the tenth century, the counts probably had to pay dues to Córdoba. After the Moorish invasion at the end of the century, however, which was soon followed by the decline of the Moorish empire, the situation was reversed, and the counts of Barcelona were able to demand allegiance and tribute from the small Moorish principalities.

The abbot Count Oliva Cabreta of Bedalú and Cerdaña played an important political role, which was also to have great impact on architecture, at that stage of Catalonia's economic development. Like several others of his official colleagues, the aristocratic prelate had traveled to Italy where he had encountered the new reforms. He was abbot of two monasteries in Catalonia: Saint Michel de Cuxa situated in the French Roussillon region, and Santa María in Ripoll. Adaptations following the new style were carried out on both churches. From the year 1018, Oliva Cabreta was also bishop of Vic.

Today no more than a ruin, Saint Michel de Cuxa was one of the most important building complexes in the Mozarabic style dating from the tenth century. Oliva Cabreta commissioned major extensions both eastwards by the addition of a new chancel area, and also at the west end by a new façade with two towers. At Ripoll, there was another church built in the older style which had been consecrated in the late ninth century. In the course of the tenth century, that building had been extended twice and had finally ended up featuring a five-aisled hall layout with a matching number of apses. Even when he was already Bishop of Vic, Oliva Cabreta had this building altered again, this time arranging for the construction of a broad transept that would terminate the nave and aisles. The apses – whose number had now risen to seven – were joined to the east wall of the transept (photo, below). The re-consecration of the church finally took place in 1032, the same year as the dissolution of the caliphate of Córdoba.

It might appear as if the shape of the church of Ripoll was arrived at more or less by chance and gradually, by the series of alterations and

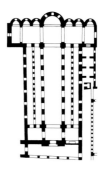

Ripoll (province of Gerona), abbey church of Santa María. Newly consecrated in 1032. Eastern section with seven apses, ground plan

Sant Pere de Rodes (province of Gerona),
abbey ruins

BOTTOM
Sant Pere de Rodes: interior of the
monastery church consecrated in 1022,
projecting columns mounted on high
plinths

extensions described. Nevertheless, we can assume that the work done in the
eleventh century was largely the construction of a new building in which
only a few foundations, a few parts of wall, or a few capitals were reused.
The layout of the new church is reminiscent of the Roman-early Christian
style: the five-aisled hall layout, unusual in itself, and the addition of the
prominent transept had brought the church in line with the Constantinian
basilica pattern of Old St. Peter's in Rome which had the same characteristic
features. These were repeatedly copied throughout the whole of the Middle
Ages, though it should be noted that their overall number is so small that in
every single instance one must assume a special direct relationship to the
church of Old St. Peter's in Rome. In Ripoll, that relationship was embodied
in the person of the client who had traveled to Italy. What is, however, of far
greater importance to the history of architecture is the fact that Santa María
in Ripoll was a building which represented a clear move away from the
traditional regional models in the Iberian Peninsula.

After Ripoll, very few Mozarabic elements were integrated into the
new type of architecture which was now dominated by Roman forms – or

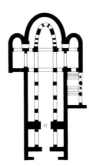

OPPOSITE
Saint-Michel-de-Cuxa (France, Eastern
Pyrenees), abbey church. Completed
around 1040. Ground plan

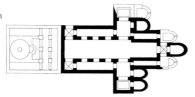

TOP
Tahull (province of Lérida), San
Clemente. Consecrated in 1123

BOTTOM
Serrabone (France, Eastern Pyrenees),
Notre Dame. Consecrated in 1080,
extension completed in 1151

at least such forms as were then associated with things Roman in the widest sense. In other words, with the work in Ripoll, Spanish architecture rejoined the mainstream of European style from which it had become more and more isolated owing to the special status and political development of the Iberian Peninsula. Given the great significance of the church at Ripoll, it is all the more deplorable that today – after repeated acts of destruction, particularly during the nineteenth century – the building remains no more than a half-hearted, poor quality pastiche.

This is not the case with the monastery of Sant Pere de Rodes (photo, p. 181) situated in an impressive setting high above the sea. Consecrated in 1022, this building is also in a state of ruin today. Nevertheless, it has retained much more of its original character than Ripoll, the victim of over-restoration. Beyond its projecting transept arms, the three-aisled church has an ambulatory flanked by chapels. The very high side aisles with their barrel vaults prop the vault of the central nave which is supported on strong transverse arches. These, in turn, spring from projecting columns located one above the other in double rows on very high plinths. Further projecting columns on the square pier-reveals support the arches of the arcades, the overall result being a very three-dimensional structural form. Despite this, the upper wall sections and the chancel area (whose arcades are carried not by columns but by pilasters which appear to have been cut out of the solid wall) are dominated by flat wall surface.

The variety of all these elements is also reflected in their stylistic origin. The columns placed one on top of the other demonstrate that the builder of Sant Pere de Rodes was familiar with the Moorish architecture found in the south of the country, where this motif could be studied above all in the mosque of Córdoba. The brilliant sculpting of the capitals also points in that direction. The ambulatory, on the other hand, is an element largely unknown and very rarely employed in Spanish Romanesque architecture, and its origin must definitely be regarded as French. The same is likely to apply to the shape of the piers with their diagonally placed projecting shafts. The basilican spatial construction, on the other hand, as well as aligning compartments of different height along the central axis, is a feature typical of Mozarabic architecture. After all, the barrel vault with transverse arches had already been known in Asturian architecture of the ninth century.

We can therefore appreciate that Sant Pere de Rodes does not follow the Roman pattern anywhere near as closely as the slightly earlier building of Ripoll. It becomes obvious, nevertheless, that the Catalonian clients no longer looked for inspiration only from local sources, but that they self-confidently tried to amalgamate highly demanding elements from very different regions. Even in its vast scale, this church building far surpasses anything that had been built before in the country, and competes with other buildings in southern Europe.

At that time, Catalonia experienced an extremely fecund period of architectural activity, attested by a number of extant buildings which, however, cannot all be discussed here. The cathedrals of Girona, and especially that of Vic, must however be mentioned. The latter was consecrated in 1038, while Bishop Oliva who, as we know, had a great

Cardona (province of Barcelona), San
Vicenç. 1029–*c*. 1040. View from north-
east. Ground plan

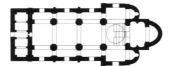

OPPOSITE
Cardona, San Vicenç. Nave with chancel
(top left),
wall of central nave (top right),
crossing (bottom left),
side aisle (bottom right)

interest in architecture, was in office. Unfortunately only few remnants from the eleventh century have survived from both buildings.

However, the particularly impressive church of Sant Vicenç in Cardona (photos, above and on p. 185) has fortunately been preserved. Built between 1029 and around 1040, even the ground plan of this building is distinguished by an unusual regularity and clarity. There are three more or less square bays in the nave behind a narthex which supports a gallery. Extending from the crossing are short transept arms with tall apses. The chancel area, corresponding in width to the transept arms, is situated above the crypt and is likewise terminated by a large apse. The building is completely vaulted: a dome set on squinches rises above the crossing; chancel, transept arms and central nave are all covered by barrel vaults which are echoed in the side aisles by three small groin vaults in each bay. This feature had been unknown in Spanish architecture before this date. Walls and piers are decorated in a novel kind of relief work. The interior walls of the chancel are hollowed out with a series of deep niches which have stepped openings rather than being directly cut into the plane of the wall. Where two recesses conjoin, they are separated by a slender respond supporting a blind arch above both of them. The same subtlety employed in the design of the wall relief can also be observed in the western sections of the church where no niches are integrated into the wall. There, the main piers of the nave and aisles at first appear to have been cut out of the solid wall. They do, however, have imposts added on their narrow sides from which spring the stepped arches of the arcade. Along the arcades there are double-step imposts, with the lower ones ending just above arcade level, while the upper ones support the stepped transverse arches of the barrel vault. A similar construction occurs on the side aisle faces of the arcades.

The exterior of the building is marked by lavish architectural decorative elements such as pilaster strips and blind arches.

The stepped arrangement of wall relief is one of the main stylistic features of European Romanesque architecture. At that time, the principal concern was no longer the mere fitting together of individual spatial compartments that were hardly articulated in themselves, but the addition of some architectural decoration. The aim was to devote just as much care and attention to the design of the spatial boundary, in other words, the wall, as to that of the sequence of chambers.

Traditionally, this new form of wall articulation is ascribed to master builders from Lombardy who were active in Catalonia, and who are also mentioned in written sources. Indeed, similar forms are found around the same period in northern Italy where they must be regarded as a further development of the earlier Byzantine and early-Christian architecture in that region. These influences from Lombardy should, however, not be overrated, for the corresponding richness in form and shape emerges in Catalonia only slightly later than in Italy itself, and there underwent not only parallel but also individual development. It is therefore natural to see the specific layering of relief in Cardona in the context of a general renewal of the repertory of form that can be observed in many places in southern Europe during that period. After all, even the innovative wall treatment which places Cardona on a par with other foreign examples cannot hide the fact that in typological terms the building is grounded within the regional architectural tradition. This is demonstrated by such features as the high side aisles and barrel vaults supported by transverse arches, already known from Sant Pere de Rodes, but not usually employed in Italy.

From now on throughout the eleventh and twelfth centuries, Catalonian architecture on both sides of the Pyrenees remained largely faithful to the models it had found, with only a few exceptions. This is demonstrated by the church of Serrabone (photo, p. 183) on the French side, but becomes much more impressively obvious in the rebuilding of the cathedral of La Seu d'Urgell, begun in 1175 (photo, p. 186). Here, the mighty nave flanked by very wide side aisles leads to projecting transepts. Each arm has two small apses cut into its eastern wall. Further extensions of the transepts, maintaining their overall width, provide a massive tower on each side. The church therefore has an east wall whose continuity is broken only by the apse, creating a monumental effect.

We are already familiar with the structure of the nave and aisles from the example of Sant Vicenç in Cardona. There, too, cruciform piers support the groin vaults of the side aisles and a barrel vault with transverse arches above the nave.

Here, the nave vault springing is a little higher than at Cardona, leaving room for small round windows above the arcades which provide direct light for the nave. The dome above the crossing and the barrel vaulting in the transept are also familiar features. The way in which the apses have been integrated into the eastern transept wall is, however, completely original: since their height is less than half the height of the transept wall, there was enough space left above the apses for windows below the springing level of the barrel vault. These openings high up in the wall are

La Seu d'Urgell (Lleida/Lérida),
cathedral. From 1175. View from the
east. Ground plan

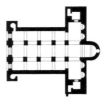

San Salvador de Leyre (province of
Navarre), monastery church consecrated
in 1057. Ground plan of the crypt (right),
interior view of the crypt (below)

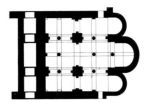

its ornate group of windows above are also reminiscent of the same Italian building, and maybe even of S. Abbondio in Como dating from the late eleventh century (photo, p. 84). It is unlikely, on the other hand, that the unusual layout with two massive towers on the extended transept arms was modeled on the Italian cathedral of Aosta. It proves, rather, that even at the end of the twelfth century the Catalonian church of Saint-Michel-de-Cuxa (photo, p. 182) on the other side of the Pyrenees was regarded as the aspirational model for the cathedral of La Seu d'Urgel, since they both share the same plan. To this extent it is out of the question to suggest that Catalonian architecture in the eleventh and twelfth centuries constituted an "offshoot" of the so-called Lombardic architecture. After all, despite any connections with Italy which can be proved, Catalonian architecture remained independent in the form of its buildings, while any corresponding features apply almost exclusively to surface decoration. Another typical example is the church of Tahull (photo, p. 183) which was consecrated in 1123. All this goes to show clearly that Catalonian architecture took its inspiration not merely from traditional regional models, but was also capable of integrating other elements.

There was no comparable wide-ranging architectural development in the province of Navarre situated further to the west although there, too, some new buildings were constructed.

The most significant amongst them is probably the monastery church of San Salvador de Leyre (figures, p. 186) which was also used as the burial chamber for the kings of Navarre. The kings of Aragon had a corresponding burial site in the Monastery of San Juan de la Peña (photo, right) with its impressive setting beneath a large ledge of rock which provided effective protection from the Moorish troops. All that is left of San Juan de la Peña are a few ruins, and the building had never been on a particularly large or ambitious scale. It was different in Leyre: the building there has a nave with single aisles dating from the thirteenth century, with an adjoining three-

much larger than the small apse windows that seem like slit windows by comparison. Seen from outside, the transept gives the impression of lighting a palace-like upper storey of the church. The design of the large main apse is also unusual. The principal opening has the usual recessed arch articulation, but at the far end is an opening into a three-quarter circular chapel set within the solid wall, which features an arrangement of niches and a domed vault. This is hardly noticeable when viewed from the outside because the central chapel can be recognized only by one tiny window. Above it, a much larger one with deeply recessed reveals provides light for the main apse. By looking at the exterior wall structure of that apse we can clearly see that the master builder, Raimundus Lambardus, was familiar with the architecture of Lombardy: the minor articulation of the wall cylinder by means of several pilasters ending at a cornice surmounted by a dwarf gallery strongly calls to mind the corresponding sections of S. Michele in Pavia, Italy (photo, p. 85), which was probably built in the second quarter of the twelfth century. The west front of La Sue d'Urgell with its three deeply recessed entrances abated at either side, and

San Juan de la Peña (province of Huesca).
Eleventh and twelfth centuries. Ruins of
the monastery

aisled chancel area consecrated in 1057. The crypt underneath counts amongst the most peculiar monuments of that epoch: it is situated exactly under the two eastern bays of the church above. Under their narrow, single side-aisles the crypt also has corresponding aisles, but the section situated beneath the wider central nave has two aisles surmounted by the familiar Mozarabic tunnel vaults with transverse arches. Their thrust is in this case not transmitted directly to the floor of the crypt, but they rest on very slender and extremely short columns with very broad and prominent capitals. At first glance it appears as if the floor had been raised considerably at a later date, so that the columns seem to have sunk into it. A closer look reveals, however, that here we see the result of an attempt to combine two systems of architecture that are obviously difficult to reconcile. On the one hand, the builder did not want to do without columns and capitals which were always regarded as ennobling elements. The vaulting, on the other hand, was necessary to carry the floor of the upper church. Moreover, a completely vaulted building was considered particularly ambitious and prestigious. It was not possible to have a less pronounced vault due to the fact that the barrel vaults covering the space are carried by arches separating the nave and the side aisles and stretching from capital to capital. Admittedly, some crude attempts were made to imitate vaguely Classical shapes in the ornamentation of the capitals. There is, however, no trace of any understanding of an architecture based on the rules of antiquity, which would have demanded completely different proportions.

During the Moorish raids in the ninth century, the monastery of San Salvador de Leyre was used temporarily as the royal residence and as the seat of the bishops of Pamplona. Even after that it retained its religious and political importance until well into the eleventh century. Under the reign of Sancho Garcés III (1000–1035), king of Navarre and Aragon, the rules of the orders of both San Salvador de Leyre and San Juan de la Peña had been reformed according to the example of the powerful French monastic center of Cluny. This demonstrates clearly that the Spanish provinces west of Catalonia, encouraged by their rulers, began to model themselves more and more on the French cultural example. The pilgrimage to Santiagode Compostela was largely responsible for this. The journey was organized along rigid, disciplined lines, unusual for the Middle Ages. What the pilgrims encountered along the way – including, of course, any architectural features – was imbued predominantly with French culture. It is for this reason that the buildings discussed in the following pages – in contrast to those in Catalonia – are distinguished not so much by Italian or "Lombardic" elements, but rather have to be considered in the context of contemporary French architecture. Far from suggesting that Spanish architecture at that time was a mere offshoot of its French counterpart, this observation is just a reminder that its course developed in a direction different from that of Catalonian architecture.

Architectural features along the pilgrims' route to Santiago

The closing years of the tenth century saw a new sense of piety amongst the population reflected in the ever-increasing significance of the pilgrimage to the shrine of St. James at Santiago de Compostela. Initially the Apostle had been hailed as a legendary fighter against the Moors. Gradually, however, the journey became more and more attractive as a pure pilgrimage from which those taking part hoped to gain forgiveness of their sins. In some cases the journey was imposed as an act of penance. Apart from the fact that, except for the Roman examples, the shrine of St. James was the only one of an apostle which could be reached within Europe, its attractiveness was strengthened further by several reports of miraculous events. A number of contemporary sources provides us with information about the nature of the pilgrimage, the most important being the so-called "Pilgrim's Guide" dating from the second quarter of the twelfth century. Not only does it mention a whole series of Romanesque churches and shrines of saints, but it also gives a relatively detailed description of the route itself. Admittedly, details of the individual stages of the journey are

Puente de la Reina (province of Navarre).
Bridge on the pilgrims' route dating from
the late 11th century

San Juan de la Peña (province of Huesca).
Two capitals of the cloister

somewhat sketchy, obviously in order not to deter potential pilgrims from the undertaking. Four main routes started in France: in Saint Gilles in Provence, in Le Puy, in Vézelay, and in Tours, and groups of pilgrims from further east met up along these routes. The three western ones joined together before they reached the Pyrenees and crossed the pass of Roncesvalles together. The eastern route was the only one to cross the Somport before joining the others in Puente de la Reina (photo, above). From there, the combined route led on to Santiago in Galicia.

The course that the pilgrims' road took made it quite natural for French influences to find expression in some of the architectural features along the Spanish section of the route. This appears to have been a quite deliberate development, and for two reasons. On the one hand, it was to ensure that there would be some familiar features for the French pilgrims who traveled to a foreign country in order to see the shrine, and who are likely to have accounted for the majority of the pilgrims to Santiago. On the other hand, the policy of encouraging foreigners to settle along the "Camino" was sometimes promoted by granting special privileges. Again, these were taken up mainly by French settlers, some of whose colonies lasted until the end of the Middle Ages. The fact that occasionally an almost identical artistic style can be detected in the westernmost corner of

Galicia and in various places in southern France is therefore surprising only at first glance. While this observation applies primarily to sculpture, it was much the same with the architecture.

Popular in France as well as in Spain was the so-called "pilgrimage church," a type of building that included an ambulatory with chapels, projecting transept and tall galleries extending up as far as the barrel vaulting of the nave. Examples north of the Pyrenees are the churches of Saint-Martial in Limoges and Saint-Martin in Tours, both of which were destroyed in the aftermath of the Revolution. Sainte-Foy in Conques (photos, p. 145) and Saint-Sernin in Toulouse (photos, p. 148) have, however, survived. In Spain, the corresponding architectural style is exemplified in the cathedral that marked the destination of the pilgrimage to Santiago – the cathedral of Santiago de Compostela itself. Correspondence of architectural styles does not prove that the same architects and builders were always active in different places. This would have been impossible simply because of the different dates at which the various churches were built, and there are also quite obvious differences in some of the details. It does, however, seem unlikely that one building would have been constructed without knowledge of the other. Rather than manifestations of a homogeneously propagated architectural type, the so-called pilgrimage churches must be regarded more as evidence of a highly mobile society in the regions of northern Spain and southern France whose culture was co-determined to a high degree by the pilgrimages.

It is generally assumed that the ceremonial laying of the foundation stone of the cathedral of Santiago de Compostela was a joint performance by the Bishop Diego Peláez and King Alfonso VI (see ground plan on the right; photo, p. 190). They are also depicted together on two capitals found in the Lady Chapel of the chancel. The overall layout of the church follows the building plan established at the time, with the exception of the west entrance which will be discussed later. In the initial building stages, progress was slow and sometimes interrupted altogether, due to a series of problems. To start with, there were difficulties with financing the building, and then Bishop Diego Peláez was arrested in 1088. While Santiago was without its spiritual leader, Diego Gelmirez held the position of administrator of the diocese several times, but he was not ordained bishop until the year 1101. Parts of the still unfinished cathedral caught fire during a revolt by the inhabitants of Santiago against their bishop in 1117. Despite all this upheaval, it had been possible to consecrate the chancel chapels during a peaceful spell in 1105.

Initially, the building project was led by a man called Bernardus. Presumably he was the administrator of the project, while the actual architect must have been the "mirabilis magister Bernardus senex" who drew up the definite plan which his successors followed. This layout features a three-aisled church with a transept, also three-aisled, and a chancel area around which the side aisles were arranged to form an ambulatory. Attached to the outer wall of the chancel are five chapels, the central one being square-ended as opposed to the apsidal form of the other four. Two chapels are also placed on the eastern wall of each transept arm. Situated in the center of the sanctuary is the high altar, and below it the crypt where the actual bones of the apostle were kept, which represented the real destination of the pilgrims. The whole building is fitted with tall galleries, even the interior façades of the prominent transept. Thus the internal elevation of the cathedral shows two levels. According to the aforementioned "Pilgrim's Guide," the cathedral is reminiscent of a palace, thanks to its galleries. The central aisles of both main church and transepts are spanned by barrel vaults strengthened by transverse arches which spring from the piers.

The cathedral of Santiago de Compostela is not only the largest Romanesque church building in Spain, but also ranks amongst the biggest in Europe. But despite its monumental dimensions, its architecture is distinguished by particularly slender articulation of the individual elements. This becomes especially apparent when it is compared with French buildings of the same architectural type. The piers are relatively thin and high, with cruciform-plan piers alternating with ones whose cruciform plan has rounded quoins: these have circular plinths, whilst the cruciform piers are supported by square ones. In this way rhythmic variety is introduced into the arcade which helps to avoid a sense of monotony within the vast building. The pier faces all have engaged semi-circular responds from three of which spring the transverse arches of the side aisles

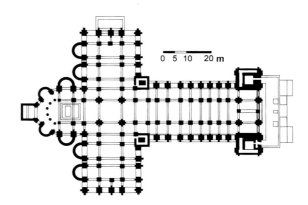

and the main arcades, whilst the fourth one rises up as far as the base of the vault, interrupted only by a narrow cornice. The tall main arcades are echoed at higher level by the gallery arcade: paired columns placed one behind the other are used to subdivide them into twin openings set within a single blind arch.

Light is admitted only via the windows of the side aisles and the galleries and via the central tower, which means that it does not directly illuminate the mighty nave of the church. The space therefore lies in a diffused semi-darkness which provides an even more effective atmosphere for the controlled architectural articulation. The chevet alone has its own ring of windows, which must have made a major contribution to the almost mystical illumination of the sanctuary and of the shrine of the martyr. Because of later alterations the original daylighting arrangements can, unfortunately, no longer be reconstructed completely.

The exterior of the cathedral has also been subjected to a series of changes. Here the rebuilding of the towers in the eighteenth century should be mentioned, and the contemporaneous rearrangement of the forecourt. Except for the transept gables, all the other parts of the cathedral have been almost completely obstructed by later additions. The modern visitor to the building is therefore all the more impressed and surprised by the powerful interior. Originally, the skillful overall design had been visible also from the outside. The walls of the north and south façades with their high-level galleries are articulated by robust blind arcades not unlike plain aqueduct construction, whilst the east end with the chancel appears richer and more detailed. At low level the chapels are dominated by frequent responds interspersed with deep, molded window openings, while the two upper storeys of the chancel area are enclosed by blind arcading. In contrast, the eastern walls of the wide transepts give more of a flat impression, apart from the chapels. The large windows at the upper level suggest that it might have served as the model for the cathedral of La Seu d'Urgell which was not built until the late twelfth century.

Thanks to the diversity of its exterior decoration, the pilgrim to Santiago was able to comprehend even from afar the individual signifi-

OPPOSITE
Santiago de Compostela (Galicia),
cathedral. First stage of building 1075–c.
1125. View along the southern transept
to the crossing (left). Central nave (right)

Jaca (Aragon), cathedral. 1036 (?)– after
1094. Nave with gothic vaults

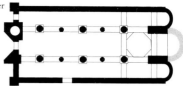

cance of the various elements of the cathedral. The transept gables,
designed along the lines of triumphal arches, played a special part in this,
the northern one more than the southern one, which was not completed
until later; for it was through this side that the pilgrims, approaching from
the north, entered the building above the shrine of the apostle. According
to a pilgrimage leader's report, there was a forecourt with shelter and a
large fountain decorated with lions in which the pilgrims washed before
entering the sacred site.

The cathedral of Santiago is without doubt the outstanding Romanesque church in Spain whose architecture demonstrates the closest links to
French architecture of that period. Coupled with this, it should be realized
that, despite its undoubted significance on a purely Spanish level, Santiago
also plays a very important international role. Situated between the Pyrenean
mountain passes and the pilgrims' goal in Galicia are other churches, some
of which had begun to be built even before the cathedral. But, unlike
Compostela, these churches mainly follow regional building traditions.
The most prominent amongst them feature a number of noticeable stylistic
similarities which again apply not only to the architecture itself but also to
the sculptures.

The first large-scale religious building the pilgrims on the other side of
the Somport pass would come across was the cathedral of Jaca (photo,
right). The town had been the capital of Aragon before it could be moved
further south to Huesca during the progress of the Reconquista. Despite its
close proximity to France, the kings of Aragon seemed to find it necessary
to promote this town by granting special privileges to new settlers. The bill
of rights of Jaca was later transferred to other cities.

Even today, the exact date at which the cathedral was built is still
disputed. There are sources which state that construction had already
begun under the king of Aragon Ramiro I who died in 1063: that year saw,
at any rate, a solemn consecration ceremonial in which several bishops
participated. On the other hand, we know that substantial building works
had been commissioned by Doña Sancha, Ramiro I's daughter who died in
1094. Attempts have been made to account for the time discrepancy by
suggesting that the earlier dates referred to the eastern sections of the choir
and the transept, while the later dates applied to the nave, which was
completed in a somewhat modified version as compared to the original
plan. The architectural sculpture in both the supposedly older and newer
sections is, however, stylistically so indistinguishable that it is difficult to
believe that the individual pieces could have been created over such a long
period of time. It is therefore more likely that the relatively small-scale
cathedral of Jaca was subjected to a far smaller amount of foreign
influence than the large cathedral of Santiago. Thus it appears that at
Jaca an earlier architectural style managed to survive what was probably
a somewhat hesitant start to a building program which only gained
momentum towards the end of the project.

Thus, the layout of the choir and the transept – which does not project
beyond the alignment of the aisle walls – basically still follows the earlier
Mozarabic style which had already been adapted in the early Romanesque
architecture of Catalonia. One of the characteristic features of this style is

the flat central dome similar to the one we have already seen at Cardona.
At the same time, the exterior articulation of these elements already shows
many similarities to the cathedral of Santiago. In contrast, the nave
arcades alternate between robust piers stepped on plan (like the ones
known from Cardona) and slender columns with exquisitely carved
capitals. Such an arrangement was unusual in Spain at that time. Owing to
the rather uncertain history of the building, it must remain the subject of
speculation as to whether this kind of arcade should be interpreted as an
allusion to the much less pronounced one in the cathedral of Santiago (in
both buildings there are also circular plinths), or whether it was the other
way round, with Santiago adapting the model of Jaca. It is perhaps more
likely that the large-scale building should have served as a source of
inspiration for the smaller one.

The comparison between Jaca and Cardona, which was built about half a
century previously (photos, pp. 184–5), provides a good opportunity to

LEFT
Loarre (province of Huesca), castle.
Eleventh-thirteenth centuries

OPPOSITE
Frómista (province of Palencia), San
Martín. Before 1066 (?) – after 1100.
View from south-west (top), nave and
choir (bottom left), view from south-east
(bottom right)

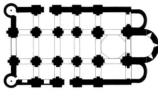

illustrate the entrenched building tradition of the church of Aragon, and also highlights more clearly the innovations. To start with, the piers in both churches are so similar that on the sides facing the central nave they even have the same kind of redundant projecting pilasters which simply stop part-way up the wall. The question remains open as to whether or not Jaca was at one time meant to have a barrel vault similar to the one at Cardona or at Sant Pere de Rodes. It is, however, important to remember that, in contrast to those older buildings, the piers of Jaca have additional, very slender projecting columns. These contribute to the unity of the building's architectural design and do not appear to be "added on," again in contrast to Sant Pere de Rodes.

It is no longer known what the main apse of the cathedral of Jaca, reconstructed in the eighteenth century, looked like in its original state. What is fairly certain is that it would have been the most lavishly decorated part of the church. Its design was probably similar to that of the fortified chapel of Loarre. This chapel forms part of a castle built in a commanding position high up on rocks between Jaca and Huesca, whence it overlooks the plain extending towards the south (photo, above). The oldest part of the complex is perched precariously on a steep rockface dropping away towards the west. In the thirteenth century an outer ring, consisting of walls with ten towers, was added to the castle, defending it from the south-east.

The natural topography made any strong fortification on the western side appear superfluous, while, seen from the east where the ground rises more gradually, its high walls give the castle an even more powerful and massive appearance. Integrated into that part of the complex, the chapel takes up the south-eastern corner of the castle. Steps underneath the chapel lead to a recessed portal and through it into the main courtyard of the castle. Above the portal one can see the rudimentary remnants of a figurative frieze depicting a scene from the Last Judgement. In order to even out the different levels between natural rock and chapel floor, it was also found necessary to construct a small crypt.

The religious building takes up an unusually large proportion of the overall castle complex. The main element of the chapel consists of a semicircular apse, a square, domed bay, and a short nave ending in a diagonally placed west wall. Closer analysis reveals that this single space was conceived as a reduced version of a multi-aisled building with transepts. The side walls of the central bay, whose dome rises above doubly-recessed squints, slightly overlap those of the apse. A deep lateral transverse arch further suggests spatial depth. The short nave is spanned by the customary barrel vault resting on blind arches which are also supposed to give the impression of leading into side aisles. The chapel of Loarre can therefore be regarded as a version of Jaca reduced in size but certainly not in artistic ambition. Even the sculpture on both buildings was probably produced by the same artist. It is unusual to find such an obvious and extreme delight in ornamentation in the chapel of a castle which in all other respects appears so austere. This poses the question as to the overall function of the whole complex. Certainly, defense against the Moors should no longer have been a major issue at the time Loarre was built. It seems therefore more logical to assume that it was intended more as a prestigious residence where the kings of Aragon could demonstrate in highly symbolic and effective terms their military commitment to the Reconquista as well as their religious obligations.

León, San Isidoro. Church consecrated in 1149. Interior view towards west. Ground plan

OPPOSITE PAGE
León, San Isidoro, Panteón de los Reyes. Around 1063 – 1100

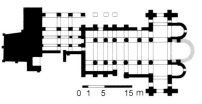

All the buildings along the pilgrims' route we have looked at so far were royal foundations, or at least the king was involved in the ceremonial laying of the foundation stone, which gives us some idea of the lively interest which the rulers of the various kingdoms of northern Spain took in them. After all, not only did they hope to gain economic prosperity from the vast stream of pilgrims, but obviously they must also have expected dividends, both dynastic and spiritual, through their prominent church foundations. This can be seen most clearly at San Isidoro in León, the last major building before one reaches Santiago.

The Romanesque church (photo, top left) was erected on a site where several other churches had stood before it. The last of these had been built during the reign of Fernando I, the first king of León and Castile, and his wife Doña Sancha, the daughter of King Alfonso V of León. Its purpose was to house the relics of St. Isidore of Seville which Fernando I arranged to be brought from there. Partly excavated foundations suggest that the church was originally a plain three-aisled building without transepts. Immediately after its consecration, in 1063, the king died. In the following years Doña Sancha had the so-called "Panteón de los Reyes" built to the west of the church site (photo, p. 195). The Panteón, the burial monument of the kings, is today the oldest part of the building complex. Based upon a 3 x 3 bay ground plan, the supporting columns in the Panteón have free-standing columns to the east and clustered shafts to the west. The building captivates the visitor not only by its finely articulated walls and vaulting, but also thanks to its exquisitely carved capitals. The vaults and lunettes are also decorated with frescoes.

The Panteón, in its capacity as royal and dynastic burial site, proves that the rulers of Castile hoped for the salvation of their souls by choosing to be buried so close to the great Spanish ruler. Another important consideration must have been the intercessions they expected from pilgrims on their way to Santiago. This was presumably the reason why soon after the completion of the Panteón the actual church, too, was rebuilt from scratch by being transformed into a large, completely vaulted, aisled basilica with transepts, terminating in a triple apse. In 1149 the church was consecrated in the presence of King Alfonso VII and several bishops, amongst them the archbishop of Santiago. We know the name of the master builder responsible for the last stage of construction because we have his epitaph on the south-western corner of the church where Alfonso and his sister Sancha had him buried.

The new building of the church of San Isidoro is wider than the older Panteón which had to take into account the dimensions of the narrow building which had preceded the new church. It cannot be established with absolute certainty whether the central nave was intended to have a flat ceiling. This possibility, at any rate, seems to be indicated by the arcade design in the nave, where there is a supporting wall respond only for alternate transverse arches of the barrel vault, whilst the intermediate piers present a flush face to the nave. With this arcade design, it could be said that in essence San Isidoro followed the example of the already familiar cathedral of Jaca, even though the sequence of individual columns is different. In any case, the projecting transepts and the distinctive apsidal

If you travel from Jaca along the pilgrims' route further towards the south for several days, you come to the church of San Martín in Frómista (photo, p. 193). The building is said to have been started before 1066 by Doña Mayor, the widow of the king of Navarre Sancho Garcés III el Mayor. There are, however, so many stylistic features both in the architecture and, particularly, in the sculpture which correspond with those found in later churches – for example Jaca, Léon and Santiago – that it seems hard to believe San Martín could have been completed before the turn of the century. Of course the problem of its dating has no bearing on the evaluation of its quality. Built to a symmetrical plan, six bays rise under three barrel-vaults. Adjoining them flush-gabled transepts lead to the triple-apsed east end. The arcade elevations could almost be regarded as a reduced version of that in the cathedral of Santiago: the shapes of the pillars and the vault are identical, but the considerably smaller church of Frómista does not have an upper level gallery. It would, however, be wrong to consider this church only in the context of the large cathedral that represented the pilgrims' destination, and this view is supported by a comparison with Sant Pere de Rodes. There we already have a very similar arcade design, at least in essence, except that two projecting columns are placed above one another, where in Frómista a single respond is carried up as far as the transverse arch. The exterior massing is handled in a very harmonious manner: small round turrets terminate the west façade, while the crossing is surmounted by an octagonal tower adjoined by the group of apses with their richly worked surface reliefs.

Sahagún (province of León), San
Lorenzo. Twelfth century. View from the
south

termination seem to have more in common with other, more closely
situated buildings, such as the no longer extant monastery church of Santo
Domingo de Silos (consecrated in 1088) which was revealed by
excavations, or by the old cathedral of Burgos (begun in 1075) which is
thought to have had a similar groundplan. It can therefore be assumed that
such buildings, with projecting transepts but without ambulatories, are all
reduced versions of the plan of the cathedral of Santiago. The fact that
close links existed between Santiago and León is further emphasized by the
portal sculpture of San Isidoro which shows great similarities to that of
Santiago.

Regional styles in the mid twelfth century

The analysis of the buildings discussed in the previous chapter shows that
the churches and chapels built along the pilgrims' route to Santiago were
linked to one another in a variety of ways. They form a group of unusual
homogeneity which clearly sets them apart from the other Romanesque
buildings in Spain. It is, however, also important to remember that
the Romanesque style of the pilgrims' route constitutes the second
phase of this style in Spain. It had been preceded by the group of buildings
in Catalonia and was followed mainly by the churches located further
south.

The latter are distinguished by an increasingly regional approach in
their architecture which moves further and further away from the "international style" of the pilgrims' route. Particularly impressive examples of
this are the brick churches typical of Sahagún, known in Spain as
"sahaguinas." The original model was presumably the monastery of San
Tirso in Sahagún (photos, opposite). Situated about 40 miles from León,
this important monastery was one of the main stages on the pilgrims'
journey. In the eleventh century it had been reformed under the influence
of Cluny and appointed not only the archbishop of Toledo but also
bishops in the other dioceses of León and Castile.

Sahagún was also the place where the Roman legionaries Facundus and
Primitivus suffered their martyrdom. The original name of the church
"De Sancto Facundo" was changed to "Santfagund" and finally became
"Sahagún." This name was then also given to the village that developed
around the monastery. In the twelfth century the monastery was rebuilt,
but today little of it remains. In contrast, the church of San Tirso, also in
Sahagún, has survived in remarkably good condition, even if extensive
restoration work has been necessary. It cannot be established with
certainty whether this is the same church mentioned in a document from
1123, although it is very unlikely that the construction of San Tirso began
later than this. The building was started with the main apse, the lower
sections of which consist of dressed stone.

Brick was not used until a height of about ten feet above ground level
had been reached; from that stage on it was used almost exclusively. The
origin of this practice was presumably the "mozarifes," the building
workers who had experience of Moorish architecture on the Iberian
Peninsula where brick building along Classical lines had been practiced for
a long time.

Sahagún (province of León), San Tirso.
Twelfth century. Tower reconstructed
after 1949. View from north-west (left),
view from north-east (right)

When looking at the church exterior it becomes obvious that the original intention had been an apse similar to those of the other churches built along the pilgrims' route. In other words, it would have been articulated with projecting shafts. However, a change of plan occurred in the upper brickwork sections, and the result was a richly articulated pattern of rows of semi-circular arches placed one above the other. A very similar feature is found in the imposing tower, the original of which collapsed in 1949, but the reconstruction closely followed the original design. What is unusual is its position: it is not placed above the crossing, as the church has no transept. Instead, the four-storey tower with its pyramidal-shaped base rises up from a narrow, barrel-vaulted extended bay of the apse. Its ground plan is therefore rectangular and accounts for the fact that, seen from the choir end of the church, the tower almost has the appearance of a façade.

San Lorenzo in Sahagún (photo, p. 196) looks very similar and is built completely in brick. Like San Tirso, it has a nave and broad aisles with three apses in front of a narrow extended bay. Whilst the apses have horseshoe arches, pointed arches can be seen in the chevet. Both elements must be regarded as typical motifs borrowed from Moorish architecture which was to influence Spain's Romanesque style increasingly in the following years.

The Romanesque architecture of Portugal may also be considered as a "regional development." The north of the country, roughly as far down as the river Douro, was re-converted to Christianity fairly soon after the Moorish occupation, whilst the actual Reconquista did not take place until the reign of King Ferdinand I of Castile and León. Alfonso VI gave his son-in-law Henry of Burgundy the province of Portugal as a fiefdom, and Henry's son Alfonso Henrique continued with the Reconquista. After the victorious battle against the Moors near Ourique in 1139, he assumed the title of king of Portugal, which a few years later was recognized by King Alfonso VII of Castile and León. After further successful battles in the Reconquista, the boundaries of modern Portugal were established in a treaty with Castile in 1297.

In the twelfth century, Portugal was only one of several kingdoms on the Iberian Peninsula which, because of its connections to the ruling house of Burgundy, partly looked towards France for its cultural development, whilst at the same time maintaining its strong links with Castile and León and particularly with its neighbor in the north, Galicia.

This is quite obvious in its religious architecture. Portugal's great Romanesque cathedrals in Coimbra, Evora and Lisbon generally follow the same basic plan, a plan that can be regarded as a slightly modified version of that of Santiago. The westblock, usually designed as a west

front with two towers, is adjoined by an aisled nave with galleries above the side-aisles and a barrel-vaulted central nave. Situated further east is the aisleless transept with a central tower and a group of three apses arranged in echelon. The cathedrals of Braga and Porto have also survived, but they have been so extensively altered by restoration or rebuilding work that they no longer reflect the original design.

After a prolonged construction period, the old cathedral of the former Portuguese capital of Coimbra, "Sé Velha," was finally completed in 1180 (photos p. 198, see also ground plan on p. 199). Although it seems natural to assume that the construction of the church began around 1140, that is, immediately after the coronation of the first Portuguese king, there is no evidence to support this view. Seen from the outside, its compact appearance and the ring of battlements surmounting the nave walls give the building the character of a fortified church. At the same time, the choir area is richly decorated with attached semi-circular responds along the walls and a number of carved figurative corbels like those commonly found in the architecture of buildings along the pilgrims' route. There might also be a connection with buildings found in the Auvergne region in France, for example with the church of Issoire: the high walls of the transept continue on their eastern side underneath the central tower where they are intersected by a gallery, a typical feature of Auvergne regional style. The centre of the façade at Coimbra is dominated by a mighty, two-storey entrance porch with the deeply recessed main entrance on the ground level and a window of similar design above it. The interior shows clearly how close the connection is between the cathedral of Coimbra and the churches along the pilgrims' route: it seems like a copy, on a reduced scale, of the cathedral of Santiago.

Very similar in construction and design is the cathedral of Lisbon (figures, p. 199). Its construction had begun as early as 1147, the year in which the city was reconquered from the Moors, and it was built instead of a mosque. The cathedral was, however, not completed until the thirteenth century. The master builders responsible for the construction are thought to have been Robertus and Bernardus. The former might be the same Robertus who had already worked on the cathedral of Coimbra. Only the nave and transept remain from the original building which, in its character of a fortified church, followed the Portuguese tradition typical of its early Romanesque style. The massive twin-towered façade was not completed until the fourteenth century. It is conceivable that this cathedral, too, was intended to have a projecting double-storey portico in the center of the façade. But it was soon integrated into the main line of the façade by the addition of flanking towers. The large gallery in the cathedral of Lisbon is subdivided by double arcades. Compared to the side aisles, it represents a much lower storey which appears grilled off because of an arcade of slender columns. As with the cathedral of Coimbra, here, too, a connection with Issoire in France comes to mind, for there this motif is used in a similar way.

In contrast, the piers are highly unusual: stepped and with three circular supports on each narrow side, they finally merge with the multiple recessed and richly molded intrados of the arcade. At best, the sculptured

Lisbon (Portugal), cathedral. Start of construction in 1147. West front

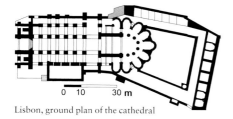

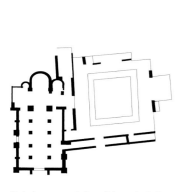

Lisbon, ground plan of the cathedral

Coimbra, ground plan of the cathedral

volume of these piers could be compared to some German churches of the late Romanesque period; but it is too far-fetched to try and establish any direct links here. It is more reasonable to think of connections to the Spanish cathedral of Zamora which will be discussed later; but even there the piers and intrados are far plainer than those at Lisbon.

An earthquake in 1340 caused the collapse of the Romanesque choir. It was replaced by a new choir built in the high Gothic style. But that too was devastated by another earthquake in 1755 so that virtually all that remains are ruins. Parts of the damaged façade also had to be rebuilt at that time.

The youngest member of this group is the cathedral of Evora: construction started in 1186, and the consecration took place in 1204, even though the church was not completed at that stage. It is very similar in design to Coimbra, except that the nave is more elongated and comprises seven bays, as opposed to six in Lisbon and five in Coimbra. The proportions of Evora and details such as the rose windows already anticipate the Gothic style. It is therefore all the more remarkable that the young kingdom of Portugal continued with this historical building style until well into the thirteenth century.

Meanwhile in Spain, the tendency towards regionalism now also made itself felt in the south of the kingdom of León, namely in those regions that had been snatched back from the Moors only a short time previously.

There, the cathedrals of Zamora and Salamanca and the collegiate church of Toro were built around the middle of the twelfth century. All three have a number of features in common, although the similarities between Zamora and Toro are particularly striking (see ground plans of both churches on p. 201). Both Zamora and Toro have relatively short naves and two wide aisles. In the east there are transepts that project slightly beyond the straight row of the side aisles and are situated in front of a group of three echeloned apses. Only at Toro has this feature survived in its original state.

The cathedral of Zamora is the oldest of these churches (photos, p. 200, and ground plan on p. 201). Its construction began under Bishop Esteban in 1151, and the consecration took place in 1174. Here, around the middle of the twelfth century, we can see the beginning of a process of architectural emancipation, a breaking away from the forms traditionally used in the kingdom of León. The structure of the nave piers became more complex, achieving a much more sculptural effect than in the earlier buildings.

The view from the side aisle clearly illustrates the nature of the innovation and highlights the distinctions with the older churches: in principle, the rectangular or square core of the pier, such as is found in San Isidoro in León, in Frómista or Santiago, has been retained. As in the aforementioned buildings, that core continues up into the nave wall or the

Zamora, cathedral. 1151–1171. View
from south-west (left). Interior view of
central tower (right)

groins of the vaults of the side aisles, together forming a homogeneous spatial unit. Sculptural elements are also added, in this case, horseshoe-section columns set on high plinths on the front of every pier. The central column is stronger than the lateral ones. Together they support the transverse arches and the arcades and almost completely conceal the core of the piers. In the nave, the central responds act as supports to the broad transverse arches that separate the individual bays, whilst the responds on the sides lead into the ribs of the groin vault. The whole space is thus articulated both by a flat outer shell and the underlying three-dimensional framework. Instead of the barrel vault usually found in the earlier buildings, the rib vault here means that the ceiling is also integrated into the overall spatial articulation.

Of course, this innovation did not find immediate acceptance, as can be seen in the collegiate church of Toro (photos, pp. 202–3; ground plan, p. 201). Started in 1160, the church of Toro is very similar to the cathedral of Zamora in its overall layout, but instead of the more modern groin vault, the central nave is covered by the traditional barrel-vaulted ceiling. But interestingly, and in contrast to Zamora, groin vaulting has been used in the side aisles of Toro, and each of the two western bays even features an eight-part rib vault.

The third building belonging to this group is the cathedral of Salamanca (photos, pp. 204–5; ground plan, p. 201). In the early sixteenth century a new building of monumental proportions had been constructed

immediately next to the original one, and although the north wall of the latter was destroyed to make way for it, the rest of it remained undamaged. Since then, a distinction has therefore been made in Salamanca between the new cathedral, the "Catedral Nueva," and the old Romanesque one, the "Catedral Vieja." The starting date for construction work on the old one is unknown. The building is first mentioned in a document made in 1152 by King Alfonso VII and dealing with the building workers' pay. It is likely, however, that the construction of the "Catedral Vieja" was started before that date, even if for stylistic reasons the major part of the work was not carried out until the second half of the twelfth century and building was not completed until the thirteenth century.

A cursory look at the ground plans of the three churches suggests that there are few similarities between Zamora and Toro on the one hand, and Salamanca on the other, for the latter has a nave that is considerably longer and has more bays than the two other buildings. The transept is also relatively more prominent, a feature that is reminiscent of even earlier buildings such as the aforementioned churches in Santiago, Burgos or Silos. Another significant factor in this context might be that the building of Salamanca Cathedral was begun before Zamora and Toro and was therefore designed according to a traditional plan.

In the interior, on the other hand, the similarities immediately become obvious. Not only has the cathedral of Salamanca been constructed throughout with groin vaults; it also boasts the mighty, pointed transverse arches in the nave, just as at Zamora. Moreover, at Salamanca they form a particularly prominent sculptural feature in the cathedral interior because of an extra respond. The diameter of the piers was also increased: powerful, cruciform-based clustered piers rise from round bases (similar to those at Santiago) and project so far into the nave that they almost seem to obstruct it.

The transition to the new building style can be appreciated more easily when looking at San Vicente in Avila (photos, p. 206). Commissioned by Count Raimund of Burgundy and his wife Urraca, the construction of the basilica of San Vincente was begun before 1109, and it was erected above the tomb of the eponymous martyr and his sisters. Its ground plan is almost identical to that of the old cathedral of Salamanca, with an elongated nave and aisles, a projecting transept, and terminating in the east with a group of three apses arranged in echelon. This layout shows that Avila was originally intended to follow in the tradition of the great religious buildings along the pilgrims' route. There was, however, a prolonged suspension of work on the church after the year 1109. When construction work was finally resumed, probably not before the middle of the twelfth century, a change of style occurred that can be clearly observed in the nave. The piers are much more massive than those of the earlier buildings, and they rise up from mighty round bases. Half-columns are attached to the cruciform-based piers. It is unclear what kind of ceiling the church was intended to have when these piers were built; what was eventually built is an unusually richly molded rib vault that corresponds to the system of vertical building elements attached to the nave wall. The central half-column supports the transverse arch, and the flat responds at the sides support the diagonal ribs. Capitals placed between the two facilitate the skilful transition from the rectangular edge of the pier to the diagonally placed rib.

The same device is found in French buildings of the late Romanesque or early Gothic periods, for example in the Cistercian church of Pontigny in Burgundy.

After analyzing the interiors of these buildings, it would be inexcusable simply to ignore what the churches of Zamora, Toro and Salamanca have

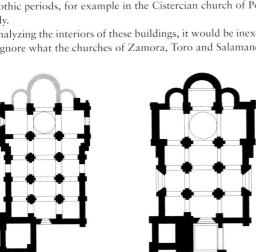

Cathedral of Zamora, ground plan   Collegiate church of Toro, ground plan

Cathedral of Salamanca, ground plan

Toro (province of Zamora), collegiate
church of Santa María la Mayor. Started
in 1160. Interior view of central tower
(top), north entrance (bottom)

OPPOSITE
Toro (province of Zamora), collegiate
church of Santa María la Mayor. Started
in 1160. View from the south

most ostensibly in common: their crossings are each surmounted by a peculiar circular or domed tower known as "Cimborio," the origins of whose shape are difficult to explain. The oldest of these towers is probably the one at Zamora: it rises above pendentives that lead from the crossing square to the circular base beneath the dome. Columns set on high plinths are placed on this round base and support sixteen ribs that intersect in the centre of the dome. Between the ribs are vault cells billowing backwards like wind-filled sails. The lower ring of columns is interspersed with deeply recessed windows set within a richly molded framework. Seen from the outside, the central tower appears even more articulated, because, unlike in the dome interior, the ring of windows does not continue uniformly. Instead, there are additional turrets on the diagonal axes and architectural features on the longitudinal and transverse axes, each crowned by rows of miniature arcades with domes or pediments. All these features contribute to making the exterior of the central tower appear like a greatly magnified example of micro-architecture, such as might, perhaps, be found as a baldachin over some figures, or in a work of art produced by a goldsmith.

And yet this lavish exterior articulation is more than mere decoration. It also fulfils a number of structural functions, since the small corner turrets project exactly above the pendentives in the interior. Thus, they help absorb the sideways thrust of the central tower, while at the same time neutralizing the diagonal thrust of the dome.

In Toro and Salamanca, this type of central tower was modified by the addition of an extra storey, so that there are two rows of windows underneath the domes of these churches. The architect of the collegiate church at Toro, however, simplified the rich articulation evident in Zamora, his model, by omitting the pedimented recesses along the longitudinal and transverse axes, and also leaving out the crowning features on top of the flanking turrets on the diagonals. Moreover, these turrets were set apart from the central circular tower by means of a different decorative style that also varied from storey to storey, with the result that the walls of the central tower now have a far more dominant effect than those at Zamora. In Salamanca, on the other hand, the architect kept closer to the original model, and paid particular attention to the window recesses along the main axes (omitted in Toro) and their lavish and detailed decoration. They therefore represent some of the major factors contributing to the formation of real façades on the four principal sides of the central tower of Salamanca cathedral, named "Torre del gallo" (Tower of the cockerel) after its crowning weathercock. The circular corner turrets are clearly subordinated to these façades in terms of height and sculptural ornamentation. Looking at the tower's interior, one notices a slight increase in decoration from the bottom to the top sections. Here we find a return to the system used at Zamora, namely that of multi-layered wall articulation. But the relatively simple inner ring of colums at Zamora is now transformed into a number of mighty responds with three-quarter circle profiles that firmly clamp the two storeys together.

In contrast, Toro remains much more restrained and makes do without additional architectural elements that would link the two arcaded circles

Salamanca, old cathedral. Before mid
twelfth century – early thirteenth century.
Interior of nave (opposite page). Chancel
and "Torre del Gallo" seen from the
south-east (left), interior view of the
"Torre del Gallo" (right)

together. Neither does it have a dome like those found at Zamora and Salamanca, with their strongly molded ribs and billowing vault cells. The dome of Toro is a simple hemisphere with slender ribs not necessary for its actual construction.

These three very striking central towers constitute special cases within Spanish Romanesque architecture and have therefore been attributed to a regional development. Only one other tower of this kind, albeit with modifications, has been built since, namely in the Portuguese town of Evora. It seems therefore paradoxical that at the same time as classing the towers as a product of regionalism, scholars have tried to find prototypes for them throughout the whole of the Mediterranean region, citing possible models in Byzantium, Amman or Palermo. On the other hand, there are undeniably formal similarities with the architectural style of the region of Poitou in France, where comparable examples of such sculptural articulation can be found, for instance at Notre-Dame-la-Grande in Poitiers (photo, p. 269). These possible links to France can even be supported by

historical facts: King Alfonso VI (1072–1109) of Castile and León was married to Constance, the daughter of the Count of Burgundy. Also married to counts from Burgundy were his two daughters Teresa and Urraca, the latter temporarily holding power after her father's death. In 1170, more or less the exact date when the central towers of Zamora, Toro and Salamanca were built, Eleonor of Aquitaine became the wife of Alfonso VIII (1158–1214). Although it is conceivable that at that time a new influx of French artists came to Spain, this possibility should not be given too much credence. What appears like an unusually rich language of form within the Romanesque architecture of Spain had long been a tradition there. Elements similar to those observed in the aforementioned central towers may already be found in earlier buildings, most notably the upper storey of the southern transept façade of Santiago Cathedral.

Of particular interest here are the "multi-faceted" arches, that is arches whose supports are not continuous but form small arches in turn; these can be seen on all three central towers discussed, either inside or outside.

Avila, San Vicente. Construction started
before 1190, main construction period
2nd half of the twelfth century. View
from the south

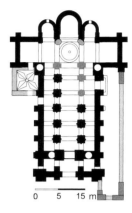

Avila, San Vicente. Ground plan.
Interior of nave

Santiago also manifests the tendency towards wall articulation of a
markedly detailed and ornamental character. At Zamora, in particular, we
realize that the central tower should not be regarded as a feature on its
own but should be seen in the context of other sections of the cathedral. It
becomes clear that the tower is by no means isolated in architectural terms
from the rest of the building. A tendency to the generous use of ornamentation is already obvious in the southern transept façade (photo, p. 201)
including the "Puerta del Obispo" (the bishop's door) and a multiply
recessed wall relief. The archivolts of the portal consist of perforated
voussoirs, like those used in Moorish architecture. The fluted columns
flanking the portal and details such as the inset rosettes are, on the other
hand, elements that evoke Classical antiquity and as such were also
familiar features of the Moorish style.

On the façade of the church of Santo Domingo in Soria (photo, p. 207)
this kind of ornamentation was subjected to a somewhat tighter control
and all obviously Moorish elements were eliminated. Here, there are no
decorative details, and yet the west wall of the church is dominated by a
double row of arcades, almost ornamental in character, and is broken
up in the center by a large recessed entrance featuring a large number
of columns. The other portals of Zamora and Toro also follow a similar
layout. The type of portal which projects just slightly beyond the
outermost wall level, and which has two figures of saints set in the
spandrel areas next to the arch, turns out to be the modernized version of
an earlier type of portal, the kind that was found along the pilgrims' route,
for example at San Isidoro in León.

Again, it is probably pointless to look for concrete examples of French architecture that might have exerted their influence on this design, for that would be to ignore the significance of the regional traditions of Spain itself.

It would, nevertheless, be unwise to exclude altogether the influence which French architecture might have had on these buildings. However, we must look for it, not in the decoration of the buildings, but rather in the design of the interior, which in its clear and almost succinct articulation seems to owe much to modern French architecture. Worthy of mention are, above all, the rib vaults, prepared so logically by the piers; but of course there also are the ubiquitous pointed arches. Most of these elements used to structure the space are fairly simple in their cross-sectional design, with features barely more sophisticated than recessing. In French architecture, such plain forms are more often encountered in buildings of the Cistercian Order. The first Cistercian monastery in the kingdom of León was founded in 1131 in Moreruela, at the wish of King Alfonso VI and his wife Sancha. The Cistercian Order was a strictly organized religious order that spread throughout most of Europe in the twelfth and early thirteenth century, and whose members lived according to strict rules. This does not mean to suggest, however, that the Cistercians alone could have been responsible for the reintroduction of French stylistic elements into Spanish architecture, a cross-fertilisation that had first occurred in the years after 1100 via the pilgrims' route to Santiago. It is more appropriate to regard the Cistercians and their peculiar building style as merely one (albeit important) factor amongst many that explain the very far-reaching adoption of French culture in Spain at that time. Spain is full of examples of this stylistic transfer.

Internationalization versus regional tradition

Whilst the details of the process were, of course, far more complicated than the following simple scheme suggests, it may be maintained that the adaption of the French style in architecture occurred in three main stages. In the initial stages, the international cultural climate that existed along the pilgrims' route repeatedly allowed elements of modern French architecture to take root in Spain. This development must certainly have been supported, if not planned, by the monastery at Cluny. Cluny, after all, was not only committed to the pilgrimage to Santiago, but was connected to Spain and Portugal by a network of monasteries covering the whole Iberian Peninsula.

Presumably the Cistercians were the second important reason for the links with France, so evident in terms of architectural history. In the course of the twelfth century, they were gradually gaining the trust of the population for their care regarding the salvation of the souls of the dead. The Cistercians were therefore encouraged to settle, above all by the rulers of the various kingdoms who then entrusted them with the placing of their bodies in their final resting place. As mentioned above, the Cistercian Order was governed by very strict rules, with all the abbots of the individual monasteries meeting once a year in Cîteaux for the General Synod where the rules were reiterated. The spread of the Cistercian monasteries all over Europe meant, of course, that a constant and lively exchange of ideas took place between the centre of the order in France and its subsidiaries abroad.

Apart from the religious orders, there were other groups which were interested in the promotion of an international culture on the Iberian Peninsula. These included the orders of knights whose principles were based on French culture, and who were a typical phenomenon of the age of the Crusades. It must be remembered here that, as far as Spain was concerned, the knights' first priority was not the recovery of the holy sites in the Middle East, but the re-conversion to Christianity of the population of the Iberian Peninsula. All the members of these influential knightly orders were part of a large, international class of noblemen, even if individual members had strong national interests.

Finally, we must not forget that since the end of the twelfth century, the early Gothic building style of modern France had also begun to be considered exemplary for purely aesthetic reasons. Anyone who wanted to commission or build an ambitious church project could therefore hardly ignore these new French models. Admittedly, there were no actual models of Gothic architecture in Spain before the early part of the thirteenth century. But the so-called "late-Romanesque" style had been increasingly infiltrated by Gothic elements ever since the final years of the twelfth century, especially in the east of the country.

We have therefore established that several reasons for the increasing acceptance of French architecture came together at the same time on the Iberian Peninsula.

These reasons were not all relevant to the same degree in other European countries, so that their Romanesque styles at the end of the twelfth century looked different. But even in Spain, the architecture of that period cannot simply be explained in terms of French influence. This is shown by the example of the cathedral of Zamora: our analysis has demonstrated that the striking style of this building was the result of a number of quite different, often specifically regional architectural developments.

The cathedral of Santiago itself remains the principal example through which to study the confrontation with non-Spanish architecture along the pilgrims' route. Construction work on the cathedral was halted around 1125 after severe disturbances in the city and confrontations between the archbishops and the kings. It appears that the first opportunity to resume work on the still missing nave bays of the western section and on the façade was provided under the rule of Bishop Pedro Gudesteiz (1167–1173). Whilst a contract was signed with construction workers in 1168, the work is likely to have been resumed earlier than that. It was necessary at that time to begin construction with the crypt-like narthex which extended from the westernmost nave bay as far as the façade. This construction was needed in order to even out the different height levels between the floor of the main church and the terrain sloping towards the west. In the lower church of Santiago, the novel French technique of the rib vault was put into practice for the first time. Some elements, such as the cornices which lead around the capitals, make a similar appearance in the early Gothic architecture of Burgundy. Above all, the choir of the abbey church of Vézelay comes to mind, starting point of one of the main pilgrims' routes. The style of the church of Vézelay is further reflected in the entrance porch of Santiago, the "Portico de la Gloria" (portal of glory; photo, p. 298). Several sources name the builder responsible for this porch as Mateo. Since 1161, he had worked in Galicia as a bridge builder, a "ponteador," and it appears he was still alive in 1217. Above the lower church, Mateo built a two-storey entrance porch with an additional narthex between the towers. Today, this ground floor narthex is all that remains, as the exterior façade underwent considerable alterations in the seventeenth and eighteenth centuries. An inscription informs the visitor that the doors were ready to be put into place in 1188. The portal is famous mainly for its sculpture, which is among the most significant work of its kind of the twelfth century. From an architectural point of view, the porch is a perfect example of the respond-rib system developed in France since the middle of the century.

So many shafts are clustered around the piers that their cores can hardly be recognized. Nevertheless it would appear wrong to classify the Portico de la Gloria as a work of the early Gothic period, for Mateo obviously made efforts to adapt his porch to the older parts of the cathedral. To this extent the historical forms are at best modified, but not fundamentally altered.

The Spanish orders of knights were closely connected with the pilgrimage to Santiago. After all, the Christian expulsion of the Moors was fought under the banner of the Apostle James. He had been revered as the personal leader of the Reconquista ever since having been credited with bringing about victories in more than one successful battle against the Moors. The Order of the Hospital of St. John of Jerusalem had established a branch in Spain in 1113, and the Templars had arrived in 1118. Despite their international status, both these orders of knights were strongly influenced by France and French culture. Other orders of knights represented in Spain were those of Calatrava and Alcántara, and later in Portugal the Order of Santiago and the Order of Christ as successors to the Templars. A common characteristic of the older orders is that they not only integrated elements from France and the regions into their architecture, but also attempted to imitate sites in the Holy Land. A truly international style was the result. It is no coincidence that a number of very characteristic buildings constructed by those orders sprang up on the Iberian Peninsula during the twelfth and the early thirteenth century, the very period when it was dominated by a strong international climate.

The largest of these churches is at Tomar in Portugal (photo, p. 208; ground plan, p. 211). In 1159, King Alfonso I Henriques had given a castle to the Order of the Templars in honor of their contribution to the Reconquista. The castle's strategic position was, however, so unfavorable that it was soon moved to its present site. All that has survived from the new fortification are some ruins and the church. Today, it stands in the center of a Castle of the Order of the Knights of Christ, the main part of which was built between the fifteenth and the seventeenth centuries. From 1318, the Order of the Knights of Christ had taken over the Portuguese possessions of the Order of the Templars after the latter's dissolution in 1312.

The Romanesque church, known as "Charola," dates from the second half of the twelfth century. It consists of a centrally planned building with sixteen sides and with a free-standing, octagonal chapel in its center. The observer will be puzzled by the contrast between the fortified style of the exterior and the elegance of the interior: the chapel in the center does not have massive walls like the church exterior, but consists of slender arcades with richly molded piers on the lower floor, and a steep window storey above it. An optical link is established between the two storeys by responds, attached both on the inside and the outside, and from which the ribs of the vault rise. These meet in the center of the building to form a small dome, while the ribs on the outside of the chapel lead into the surrounding walls. Since the latter are sixteen-sided and the central chapel is only octagonal, vault ribs in the shape of solid stone bands run from each corner of the outer walls to the interior wall. Only every second rib is also connected to a respond, whilst the intermediate ones terminate on

corbels above the narrow windows of the upper storey of the central chapel. Despite the fact that generous layers of stucco were applied to the interior of the "Charola" in the early sixteenth century, its original architecture can still be satisfactorily appreciated.

The peculiar layout of the church as a centrally planned building with an ambulatory leading around a chapel in the center might have come about because the building was intended as a copy of the church of the Holy Sepulcher in Jerusalem. A copy in the Middle Ages did not have the same meaning as it does today: it did not have to be an exact reproduction of the original, but was intended rather to remind the viewer of certain basic forms of the original. In this respect, the centrally planned church of Tomar was entirely adequate. The church was built by the Templars, who had founded their Order in Jerusalem in order to protect the holy sites and their pilgrims. It therefore seemed natural that they should try to create a copy of Jerusalem in their most important base in Portugal. Moreover, the period in the late twelfth century when the church of Tomar was built coincides more or less with the loss of Jerusalem to the Arabs in 1187, and also with the unsuccessful attempts by the participants in the third and the fourth Crusades to reconquer the city. It is therefore quite conceivable that the "Charola" was intended to remind the visitors of the lost sites in the Holy Land. This assumption is further strengthened by the fact that at that very time, more and more copies of the church of the Holy Sepulcher appeared.

The "Vera-Cruz" church, or Church of the Holy Cross, near Segovia (photo, p. 210; ground plan, p. 211) is closely linked to the "Charola" of Tomar, both in terms of the date of its construction and its design. Consecrated in 1208, the "Vera-Cruz" was most probably built by the Order of the Canons of the Holy Sepulcher. As in Tomar, there is a central chapel surrounded by a circular barrel-vaulted ambulatory. The two parts of the building are, however, of dodecagonal shape so that there is no discrepancy between the inner and the outer wall circles. In addition, the Vera-Cruz church has a chancel with three apses at the east end, and a heavily recessed entrance in the west. It can therefore be considered both as a building with a centrally planned layout and as one of linear planform. The chapel placed in the center of the building is not as richly decorated as the one at Tomar, but its design is more complex. The chapel is built over a low, crypt-like lower storey and can be reached via a double staircase on the west side. Since the chapel walls are almost solid throughout, the only light sources for the chapel are the windows placed high up, where the chapel pierces the roof of the main church. The chapel itself is crowned by a small dome supported by two pairs of parallel ribs that do not intersect in the center.

A similar vaulting system can be seen in another centrally planned building along the pilgrims' route, namely at Torres del Río in Navarre (photos, p. 211). It cannot be established with certainty whether the church there used to belong to the Templars, although it is certainly dedicated to the Holy Sepulcher. Unlike at Tomar and Segovia, the octagonally laid-out building has no central chapel. But compared to the former buildings, this church is distinguished by its relatively lavish

TOP
Segovia, Vera-Cruz, consecrated in 1208

BOTTOM
Eunate, circular-plan building

ornamentation, both of the exterior and particularly of the interior, where its system of vaulting brings out a truly unusual magnificence.

Instead of two pairs of parallel ribs as in Segovia, Torres del Río has four pairs which support the dome, the center of which is crowned by a lantern. The sculptural articulation of the vault is completed by a number of additional ribs that spring from the responds in the corners of the building. The large windows in the upper storey of the outer building are reduced in the inner building to tiny gaps which allow in only a small amount of light and which are located at the base of the crossing ribs.

In Torres del Río it becomes particularly obvious just how eclectic and international Spanish architecture of the twelfth century could be. The church of Torres del Río has a centrally conceived ground plan and is a church of the Holy Sepulcher and, as such, must certainly be seen as a kind of crusade against the Arabs. Nevertheless, the builders freely combined the decorative style traditionally used for the exterior of the churches along the pilgrims' route with a dome modeled on the second mihrab of the mosque of Córdoba. The church of San Miguel in Andaluz near Soria might have functioned as a possible intermediate stage in this development, since it has a similar dome which is thought to have been built a little earlier than that of Torres del Río. Buildings following the example of Torres del Río can be seen in nearby Eunate (photo, bottom left), and in the Hospital of Saint-Blaise on the French side of the Pyrenees, also situated on the pilgrims' route.

Whilst all these centrally planned buildings are representative of a particular trend within Spanish architecture during the second half of the twelfth century, they were generally of less importance than the buildings erected by the Cistercians. Ever since the last third of the twelfth century, there have been numerous examples of their novel building style all over the Iberian Peninsula. During this period, the oldest Spanish convent in Moreruela built its convent church (photos, p. 213). It is not certain whether this was the building mentioned in records of 1168, especially since it was normal practice for Cistercians to build the eastern sections of the church first to accommodate the choir monks. This part would also be consecrated earlier than the western parts of the church. Moreruela is, however, unlikely to have been built much later than the above date. It was probably built at much the same time as the Portico de la Glória of Santiago, another church influenced by Burgundy.

All that remains of Moreruela are some picturesque ruins. Nevertheless, they give a clear idea of what the building must have once looked like: the cruciform layout included a nave and two aisles with nine bays, and on the other side of the transept there was an ambulatory with radiating chapels. Although very rarely used in Spain until then, the above layout is derived directly from the French mother convent of Clairvaux. At Moreruela the inclusion of the ambulatory with radiating chapels must obviously have caused some difficulty, since the outermost of the seven chapels are placed so close to the transept that there remained hardly any room for the other chapels normally included in Cistercian churches. Two transept chapels were added in spite of the space problem, but they had to be kept unusually small in order not to interfere with the chapels in the chancel area.

Torres del Río (province of Navarre),
Church of the Holy Sepulcher. End of
twelfth/beginning of thirteenth century.
Exterior and interior views of the
circular-plan building

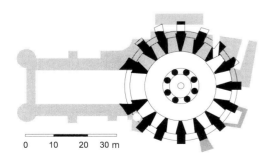

Tomar, Templar church.
Ground plan

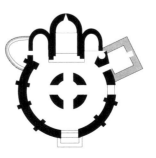

Segovia, Vera-Cruz.
Ground plan

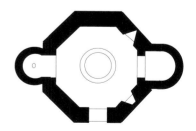

Torres del Río, Church of the
Holy Sepulcher. Ground plan

211

Santes Creus (province of Tarragona),
Cistercian church. 1174–1211

OPPOSITE PAGE
Moreruela (province of Zamora), ruins
of the Cistercian church. After 1168.
Views of the chancel interior (top), view
of chancel and nave from south-east
(bottom)

The overall design of the choir itself is based on the pattern tradition-ally used in Burgundian architecture even before the time of the Cistercians. At Cluny, for example, the low chapels are covered by semidomes and are attached to the higher, rib-vaulted ambulatory whose only light sources are the tiny windows set above the chapel openings. An arcade of columns with pointed arches leads from the ambulatory to the interior choir. The latter has an upper storey with windows which start above a cornice that is engaged with the corbels underneath the clustered vaulting shafts. These compound vaulting shafts rise up between the semi-circular headed windows and support the ribs of the semidome vault above the choir apse.

At Moreruela, Spanish Romanesque architecture achieves a hitherto unknown quality, both in the overall layout and the detail of the extremely subtle design of the choir. Such an achievement would have been impossible without the French influences described earlier. Paradoxically, any contemporary models in France from which Moreruela might have drawn inspiration have all been destroyed. The Spanish abbey church thereby allows an appreciation of early French Cistercian architecture, a pleasure no longer possible in France itself.

The nave and transept of Moreruela are far less well preserved than the choir, but can nevertheless be reasonably well reconstructed: both sections were covered by barrel vaults supported by transverse arches. Although this type of construction may have been directly derived from French Cistercian church building, it had been traditionally used for centuries in Spain itself. The

only modern features were the pointed arches of the barrel vault and the rib vaulting in the side aisles.

The architectural system employed at Moreruela was used once more - probably only a very short time later – in the Cistercian monastery of Poblet in Catalonia, founded by Count Ramón Berenguer IV of Barcelona in 1153. There are two main differences between the two buildings: the bays of the nave at Moreruela are more compressed, so that it has nine bays compared to Poblet's seven. Furthermore, the ambulatory at Poblet has only five radiating chapels, so that there was enough room to furnish the transept with chapels of the same size.

Of somewhat different appearance is the church of the Cistercian convent of Santes Creus (photo left), which is also in Catalonia and was established in the year 1150. As at Poblet, it relied on the support of the counts of Barcelona, and, after their alliance, also on the kings of Aragon. Both monasteries house numerous tombs of counts and kings and were extended in the late thirteenth and early fourteenth centuries to include residential quarters.

It seems that the convent had chosen the wrong site, and had to move twice before building work on the present church could start in 1174. It was finally consecrated in 1211. The elongated nave and two aisles comprise six bays. It is adjoined by a very narrow transept without aisles, on the east side of which there are four rectangular chapels and the large, equally elongated choir without ambulatory. The ground plan of this church is therefore roughly comparable to the German Cistercian convent of Maulbronn (photos, pp. 68–69). The interior, however, is anything but typical of this order. The individual bays and aisles are separated by mighty cruciform piers. The outermost front vertical responds are beveled off on the nave side (a feature often found in Cistercian architecture), so that further up they can carry the powerful pointed transverse arches. Extending between these arches are groin vaults with broad vault ribs in the shape of solid stone bands that start immediately above the corbels without being initiated by responds. No other features articulate the two-storey wall which has arcades and a clerestory, so that the effect of the church interior on the beholder is one of austerity and, at the same time, extreme monumentality. The same impression is conveyed by the exterior of the church with its solid massive wall. A number of buildings belonging to the original convent from the twelfth century are still present, amongst them the hexagonal pump-room with its stone-band rib vaulting, the chapter-house, and the dormitory. Begun in 1191, the dormitory was designed as a continuation of the southern transept arm and features a rising beamed ceiling set above a row of pointed strainer arches. It might well have been the first of a number of similar buildings that were to become a characteristic feature of Gothic architecture in Catalonia.

The earliest and arguably the most impressive example of the late Romanesque style in Catalonia is the church of Santes Creus, a statement of succint monumentality. The other two main examples are the cathedrals of Lleida (Lérida) and Tarragona. Both these churches show a remarkable degree of tradition in their style, considering that the period of their construction continued well into the thirteenth century – a time when France

212

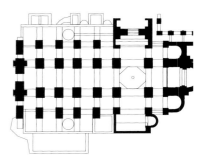

Tarragona, cathedral. Ground plan

was already building cathedrals that were the very embodiment of the high Gothic style. The strongly sculptural articulation of their interiors puts Lleida and Tarragona in the same tradition as Zamora, Toro and Salamanca.

A dated epitaph on the exterior of the choir of the cathedral of Tarragona (photo, p. 214) suggests that building work must have begun before the year 1174. However, the church was not completed until the fourteenth century. The best indication as to the possible appearance of the original design is the cloister in the north-east, since all the western parts, including the façade, were built in the later stages. Plain walls with little articulation, and windows reminiscent of embrasures make the cathedral appear like a fortified castle, creating an effect similar to the Portuguese cathedrals already discussed, or the abbey church of Santes Creus. In the cloister, on the other hand, there is a singular fusion of different elements and predominantly finer, almost filigree-like shapes. Whilst as a whole, the cloister bears all the hallmarks of late Romanesque architecture, some individual columns and capitals are clearly borrowings from buildings of the Classical period. The detailed rosettes above the triple arcades, on the other hand, and also the frieze of multiple arches both betray their Moorish origin.

The aisles of the nave continue on the other side of the transept and terminate in apses of different sizes. Uniformly covered by groin vaulting, the building is articulated by powerful piers, each with a pair of columns of three-quarter circular profile attached to the front side. These attached columns support the transverse and the arcade arches, whilst the more slender responds attached to the corners lead over into the diagonal ribs of the vaults.

The old cathedral of Lleida (photos, p. 215; ground plan, see above) is situated high above the town. Although it was begun later than that of Tarragona, the building was completed much earlier, namely in 1278. During the War of the Spanish Succession, it was converted into barracks. This was in 1707 and was indeed used for this purpose until 1926. As a result, the church interior was not subjected to the type of alterations suffered by most other Spanish churches, and is therefore much easier to analyze. Restoration work on the cathedral of Lleida did not commence until 1946.

The history of the building is well documented. According to a commemorative stone, the ceremonial laying of the cornerstone took place in 1203 through King Pedro II of Aragon and Count Ermengadus of Urcel. It is further known that Berengarius Obicions was responsible for the building administration, and that the architect was Petrus Decumba. Lleida was not reconverted to Christianity until 1149, and the cathedral was built on a site that had formerly been occupied by a mosque. This might explain some peculiarities with regard to its layout. The position of the cloister in the west, in front of the church, is reminiscent of the outer court traditionally found in mosques. The unusual overall width of the church and the relatively short nave (comprising only three bays) are due to the re-use of the foundation walls of a mosque with its traditional broad layout. On the other hand, it should not be forgotten that there was a tradition in Catalonia of churches with projecting transepts, such as at Ripoll and La Seu d'Urgell; this feature was moreover found in the churches along the pilgrims' route. It is no accident that the side entrances of the church at Lleida, with their corbel-decorated porches, are reminiscent of the older porches normally found along the pilgrims' route.

Lérida, old cathedral. 1203–78. View of
the exterior from the south-west (top),
interior of nave (bottom)

Lleida however lacks the recesses in the Moorish style which would flank the entrances of these churches.

There used to be five apses all increasing in depth towards the central axis. Now, only two of them survive in their original state, allowing us to appreciate just how thick the walls of the building are. The piers too are enormous and are fitted with coupled columns on the front that support the mighty transverse and arcade arches, similar to the arrangement at Tarragona. At Lleida, however, the transverse arches are attached to an additional supporting element, the edge of which is further strengthened by a respond placed next to the one which supports the diagonal rib. This arrangement means that the piers of the cathedral of Lleida have one extra step compared to those of Tarragona. As a result, they project further out into the nave, whilst the walls, despite their thickness, appear as though they had been stretched between them. A similar effect had already been achieved in the cathedrals of Zamora, Toro and Salamanca. Their interior spaces moreover share another feature with Lleida: the clerestory windows are set above a cornice which is linked to the capitals of the piers. As in Salamanca, the capitals at Lleida are endowed with extremely rich sculptural decoration.

All these Catalonian cathedrals of the late Romanesque period clearly have close affinities to the French Gothic style regarding their structural articulation and rib vaulting. Individual elements such as the rose windows, for example, are further clear indications that the Gothic style must have been known in Catalonia. Nevertheless, these buildings cannot be classed as "Gothic." For one thing, the structure of their walls and vaults is not based on the system of support and load; the powerful piers tend to fulfil an optical function rather than a static one. The reduction of wall thickness, on the other hand, had made much greater progress in the architecture of the high Romanesque period, as is shown by Santiago. It is more appropriate to view these Catalonian churches as part of a regional tradition, enriched by modern stylistic elements, rather than as a transitional style. Indeed, the transition from Romanesque to Gothic style was not a gradual process in Spain. The new architectural style did not really start there until well into the second decade of the twelfth century, but when it did arrive, its impact was immediate and widespread.

The first examples of the new style were the cathedrals of Toledo and Burgos, almost exact copies of certain Gothic buildings in France. Its arrival also coincided with the final settlement of the conflicts surrounding the succession to the throne. These conflicts had flared up again and again during the eleventh and twelfth centuries, causing continual splits within the country. Only the three kingdoms of Portugal, Catalonia and Aragon, and Castile and León now remained. The kings of Castile and León attempted to introduce an autocratic and centralized government modeled on the example of France. The new style of the Gothic cathedral served as a seemingly adequate means of expressing their ambitions. All these developments heralded the beginning of a new era, one that turned its back on the traditional, regional and also international values that had been the hallmark of the Romanesque period in Spain.

Heinfried Wischermann

Romanesque architecture in Great Britain

Before the Norman Conquest

One faces considerable problems when trying to produce an outline of the English Romanesque. Research in the field is still unsatisfactory – despite the efforts of the British Archaeological Association since 1975.

Although the term "Romanesque architecture" was coined by William Gunn as early as 1819, the terminology used in Britain to describe the Romanesque is still undeveloped. Gunn's term has not been universally accepted, and English authors fluctuate between "Norman" and "Anglo-Norman."

In addition, it is difficult to date the start to the Romanesque period in Britain. The first decades of the new millennium, under the rule of Ethelred II (978–1016), were turbulent, and those churches that were built have more in common with late Anglo-Saxon architecture. Political unrest, such as the invasion of the Danes in 1013, and the economic shortages associated with it, evidently prevented Britain from immediately adopting the styles of the early Romanesque period, which started on the continent at the turn of the millennium. The Danes were led by Canute, who was king of England from 1016–1035. He made England the center of his northern kingdom, but built little. His most important foundation, St. Edmund's in Suffolk, was consecrated in 1032; it has yet to be excavated. The church was probably in the style of Aachen's palatine church.

A new wave of building started during the reign of King Edward the Confessor (1042–1066). In 1050, Bishop Heremann of Ramsbury wrote to the Pope, saying that England was gaining new churches day by day, even on sites where none had stood previously. From about 1045, long before the Norman Conquest of 1066, modestly-sized Anglo-Saxon churches without aisles began to be replaced by buildings with aisles and round arches, attempts at vaulting, several sections at the east end, towers over the crossing and west end, and external ornamentation consisting of blind arcades and series of round arches.

Canute died without an heir in 1042, so the crown passed to Edward, son of Ethelred and Emma, daughter of Count Richard I of Rouen. Edward had grown up in exile in Normandy, and, as a result, was familiar with the culture of western France. He brought continental bishops and architectural styles to Britain.

Despite unreliable sources and numerous undated buildings, the influence of the continent on English early Romanesque can be traced with varying degrees of confidence to four examples:

After a visit to Rheims in 1049, Abbot Wulfric built an octagonal ambulatory in Canterbury, the oldest monastic center in England; it was situated between the old Peter and Paul church and the church of St. Mary. The building was not completed after his death in 1059, and was excavated at the beginning of this century (figure, p. 217, left). Adding a new section to revered old buildings is a typically English tradition, though the models were continental: St. Bénigne in Dijon and Ottmarsheim. In Sherborne, Dorset, Bishop Aelfwold II (1045–58) built a new church right against the old one, which continued to be used. It has to be said that we know little more about it than that it had a massive western tower and a

Canterbury, abbey church. After 1049.
Wulfric's octagon, ground plan

London, Westminster Abbey.
Consecrated 1065. Church of Edward
the Confessor, ground plan

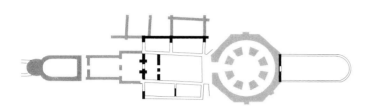

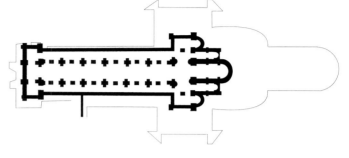

distinctive portal which led into a south-facing portico. In Stow, Lincolnshire, the crossing, which is separated from the nave and transept by four arches, and the transept arms still remain of a collegiate church built (c. 1053–55) by Duke Leofric of Mercia. The strong relief of the arches at the crossing, and the way the church is composed of individual cubes, show the influence of the continental Romanesque style.

The first truly Romanesque British building was commissioned by none other than Edward the Confessor. From 1045/50, he had various old buildings (next to his London residence) belonging to the Abbey of St. Peter (founded in 730/40) demolished and replaced by a large-scale building (figure, p. 217, right). It is possible, with reference to a contemporary description, pictures on the Bayeux tapestry and a few excavations, to produce the following reconstruction of the building: the two towers at the west end connected to a nave with twelve bays and an alternating system of supports, a projecting transept with a tower over the crossing and tribunes in each arm, and finally a choir with chapels in echelon. The length of the nave alone (140 feet) is enough to demonstrate the royal claims of the building; it copies the churches of Normandy, from which Edward had just returned. Norse invaders had settled there from 911 onwards, and from the beginning of the eleventh century they started building a series of large churches to demonstrate their power and daring.

The most important early building in Normandy was the abbey church of Jumièges; it was begun in 1040 by Abbot Robert Champart, the very man who was made Bishop of London by King Edward in 1044, then became archbishop of Canterbury in 1051, and returned to Jumièges in 1052. Champart was probably responsible for the identical elevations of the monastery church of Jumièges, now in ruins, and Westminster, of which only the ground plan remains. Both churches were attempts to realize the same goal, a monumental vaulted basilica. The church of Jumièges and its successors were decisive in the creation not just of Westminster, where England's monarchs are buried, but of the majority of high and late "Anglo-Norman" Romanesque buildings in Britain; because of this, the reader is referred to the in-depth study on pp. 140ff.

It is likely that King Edward's Westminster Abbey, which was consecrated in 1065, was not the only pre-conquest building to exhibit clear signs of Romanesque influence. Romanesque thinking is reflected in buildings in places such as Wittering in Nottinghamshire, Wareham in Dorset, and Great Paxton in Cambridgeshire – though that influence is rather more visible in the three-dimensional subdivision of the supports and walls than in any clear articulation of the different sections of the buildings. They suggest that there was more than just the one example of Romanesque in Britain to work from.

It would seem sensible to date the start of English high Romanesque from the Norman Conquest. From that time, people who commissioned buildings adhered more rigidly to the recommendations of Goscelin de St. Bertin, who came to England in 1058: "If you want to build something better, you have to start by tearing down what is already there." The new buildings were "magnificent, marvellous, extremely long and spacious, full of light and also quite beautiful."

The episodes of the Conquest – though not the background to it – are narrated on an epic scale on the Bayeux tapestry, a piece of needlework over 240 feet long, though just 20 inches wide. Colorfully embroidered pictures tell of the preparations for invasion and end (the last section is missing) with the Battle of Hastings; events that happened concurrently are depicted as occurring in sequence. The scenes are amazingly vivid and full of figures; each one was created using various colors of wool on a bleached canvas. The style is the same throughout, figures being presented in outline, skilfully composed but without any attempt at producing a sense of perspective. The detailed Latin text was probably written for William's half-brother, Bishop Odo of Bayeux, by the "Canterbury School," an important center of book illumination. It is an extraordinarily wide-ranging source of information on many aspects of cultural history, such as architecture, weapons, warfare, clothes and military equipment.

The Battle of Hastings and its political consequences

The background to the Battle of Hastings, one of the great turning points in English history, is quickly dealt with. Edward had no children, and, as a consequence, the question of a successor was very much on his mind. He exiled his father-in-law Godwin, and at the same time, in 1051, named William of Normandy as his heir. When Godwin died in 1053, he was succeeded as earl of Wessex by his son Harold. In the same year William, the designated heir, married Matilda, daughter of the count of Flanders and a descendant of Alfred the Great. This connection supported William's claim to the throne. In 1064 Harold (Godwinson) was captured by William and was forced to swear to support his claim to the English throne; this is one of the most important scenes on the tapestry.

Whether this oath was actually made or not, Harold clearly did not consider it to be binding. When Edward was on his deathbed he named Harold as his heir, and the latter was duly anointed king in January 1066. William appeared to have little prospect of disputing his possession of the throne. It was an enormous amount of luck combined with exceptional energy that helped him gain victory. He declared war in the firm conviction of the justice of his claim, and with the moral support of the pope. Two further events aided him, the weather and an invasion by the king of Norway, who Harold successfully fought at Stamford Bridge. On October 14, 1066, William met Harold at Hastings.

Harold fell in battle, and English resistance against the invaders collapsed. William was crowned at Christmas 1066 in Westminster Abbey, Edward's new building.

The victory at Hastings did not bring with it peace and security for the invaders. The Normans remained an army of occupation for more than five years, and met with considerable problems in the north of England and Wales.

At first, William attempted to maintain the type of state and government system that Edward the Confessor had set up – and to do so with the co-operation of the Anglo-Saxons. But this attempt was frustrated by localized revolts and the demands his followers made for appropriate rewards; in its place, an authoritarian system gradually emerged with a centralized royal household, feudal aristocracy, a Great Council and a

reformed Church. The emphasis of William's policies was on continuity – an example is his first decree to the city of London, giving the assurance that "it is my desire that you should retain your laws and customs as they were in King Edward's days." But he also intended to record and organize the new wealth and property that he had acquired. This was done by means of the famous Domesday Book, which was a systematic description of the country carried out between 1066 and 1087 by travelling commissioners; it recorded the property in each manor and every county.

It is unlikely that Duke William II (crowned William I) turned his thoughts to building churches much before 1070. The priority was to build and man as many castles as possible; they were needed both to combat military threats and to safeguard his regime. But William was not the only person in a position to commission buildings. He had placed a variety of noblemen in positions of power in England, and they intended to have a say in the country's future, whether as secular or church dignitaries. The pre-Conquest noblemen were replaced by the Continental invaders. By the end of William's reign, a mere 8 percent of land was still owned by Anglo-Saxon noblemen. A fifth of the land belonged to the king, a quarter to the Church, and nearly half to William's relatively small band of followers from Normandy, Flanders and Brittany.

The church hierarchy underwent the same process as the aristocracy, Normans being given positions formerly occupied by Anglo-Saxons. With the agreement of the pope, William the Conqueror removed Stigand as

OPPOSITE
Bayeux Tapestry. Battle scene around a
motte-and-bailey (top). Harold swearing
an oath before William that he will help
him gain the English crown (below).
Wool embroidery on linen. Height 20
inches, length more than 240 feet. From
1077 to 1082. Tapisserie de Bayeux.
With the special permission of the town
of Bayeux

archbishop of Canterbury and replaced him in 1070 with Lanfranc, an Italian who had been a trusted advisor of William's ever since his time as Abbot at St. Etienne (St. Stephen's) in Caen, the church William had built to be buried in. Lanfranc united the English Church and reformed the monasteries. The Normans now controlled three church provinces, Rouen, Canterbury and York. In 1070 Thomas of Bayeux was made archbishop of York, and a result of this was continuing conflicts for the primacy in England. The most important part of the reforms was the moving of several bishops' sees and a new version of English canon law.

Revisions to the dioceses had started during the reign of Edward the Confessor. Leofric's see had been moved from Crediton to Exeter in 1050. In 1070, London's ecclesiastical council shifted the see of Elmham to Thetford, and then to Norwich. In the same year, the see of Lichfield was moved to Chester, Selsey went to Chichester, and Sherborne to Salisbury. Finally, in 1072, Remigius also moved his see, from Dorchester to Lincoln.

While he was revising canon law, Lanfranc discovered a curious arrangement: four English cathedrals were governed by monks. They were Canterbury, Sherborne, Winchester and Worcester. Monks at several other cathedrals were being encouraged to adopt a community life similar to a monastery, with vows of celibacy, dormitories and refectories. A monk himself, Lanfranc was in favor of making monks bishops. Three more cathedrals received monastic constitutions; they were Norwich, ruled by Herfast, Rochester, ruled by Gundulf, and Durham, ruled by William. But Sherborne/Salisbury rejected this arrangement. It was decided that Chichester, Exeter, Hereford, Lichfield, Lincoln, London, Salisbury, Wells and York should be governed by cathedral chapters or canons, a system comparable to that in Normandy; these nine cathedrals were known as the "Old Foundation."

Each of these cathedrals was led by four prelates (dean, precentor, chancellor, treasurer). The position of high-ranking clergymen within England's system of government was abundantly clear: they were directly subordinate to the archbishop and, being powerful feudal lords, were an important part of the country's military structure.

By 1080, Wulfstan of Worcester was the sole remaining Anglo-Saxon bishop. All the rest – with the exception of Giso of Wells, from Lorraine – were Norman either by ancestry or education. All abbots of the thirty-five independent Benedictine monasteries that existed in 1066 were replaced within the first six years, as they were hostile towards the conquerors. Despite some mistakes, the majority of abbots that William appointed won high praise; they included Paul of Caen in St. Albans, Simon from St. Ouen in Ely, Serlo from Mont. St. Michel in Gloucester, and Vitalis from Bernay in Westminster.

English high Romanesque

However much the Church and its architecture may have changed, William's priority, and that of his Norman followers, was nonetheless continuity. Norman monastery and bishop's churches, which had served as the models for Edward the Confessor's Westminster Abbey, continued to influence Britain's large-scale buildings until well into the twelfth century.

This is confirmed by the following chronological summary, covering the period from the first monumental stone building, Battle Abbey, to the early Gothic revision of Canterbury Cathedral.

The first church William the Conqueror built was Battle Abbey in Sussex (figure, below). He founded a Benedictine monastery shortly after 1066, on the site where he defeated Harold; its church, which was begun by 1070 and consecrated in 1094, did not survive the Reformation. Whether William indeed swore an oath on the eve of battle, as legend would have it, to build a monastery if he were victorious, or whether he was attempting to atone for the bloody invasion he had started, is not clear. Whatever the case, the abbey was a means of safeguarding the coastal region which he had just conquered.

We are familiar with the ground plan of the church, its altar placed above the spot where King Harold was killed. It had an aisled nave, was over 240 feet long, making it as long as monastery churches in Normandy, and was almost certainly a galleried basilica like its Norman counterparts; it had a transept with apses and – probably for the first time in Britain – an ambulatory with radiating chapels. The abbey was generously endowed by its founder, and before his death he bequeathed it his cloak, relics, and a portable altar he had taken with him on his campaigns; but he was not buried there. William, the founder of the Anglo-Norman kingdom, was buried in St. Etienne in Caen.

His defeated opponent, Harold, was buried beneath the high altar of the church he had founded, Waltham Abbey in Essex, to the north of

Battle Abbey (Sussex). Consecrated 1094. Ground plan

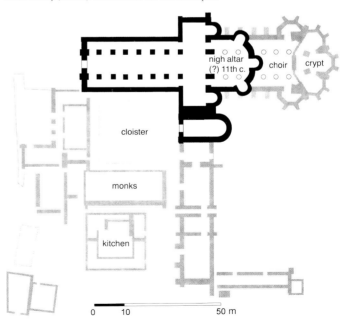

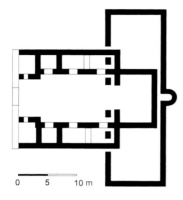

Waltham Abbey (Essex). Consecrated 1060. Ground plan

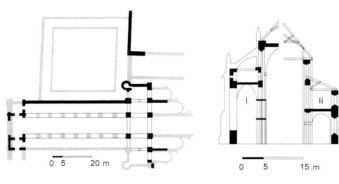

Canterbury Cathedral. Completed before 1089. Built by Lanfranc, ground plan

Elevation of the nave and side aisles, I: present condition, II: Lanfranc's times

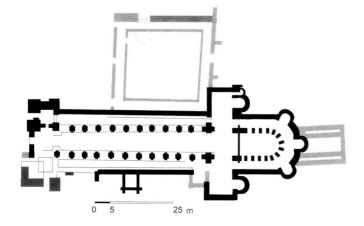

Canterbury, St. Augustine's Abbey. New Abbey of Peter and Paul. Started between 1070 and 1073. Built by Abbot Scotland, ground plan

London; it was begun in 1053 and consecrated in 1060. The ground plan (figure, top) of its antiquated church (a continuous transept and single tiny apse) was revealed by excavations some years ago. It is quite likely that the plan of the church, which Harold showered with relics and gold ornaments, was deliberately old-fashioned, showing the influence of Old St. Peter's in Rome, or St. Denis in its archaic appearance – a reaction to the "Normanizing" influence of Westminster Abbey.

The first monumental buildings of the English Romanesque were built from 1070 in Canterbury, the city where St. Augustine had become England's first bishop in 601. From the summer of 1070, Lanfranc, an Italian, was its archbishop. In 1045, he had left Pavia to become the prior of the monastery of Le Bec. William sent for him to take charge of his new monastery in Caen, and then promoted him to Canterbury. In the period around 1060/63, Lanfranc started, and possibly even designed, the largely preserved church where William was buried. He applied its form to his new cathedral, Christ Church in Kent, whose Anglo-Saxon predecessor burnt down in 1067. We are familiar with the ground plan of this church (figure, center), which was completed before Lanfranc's death in 1089; the original north-west tower was replaced when alterations were made to the cathedral in the early nineteenth century. A façade with two towers was connected to a nave with pillars and eight bays, a three-part transept with galleries in the projecting sections, and a five-part choir with chapels in echelon and a crypt underneath the main apse.

The elevation can be largely inferred: groin-vaulted aisles flanking a three-storey nave (arcade, gallery, clerestory with a walkway and three windows in each bay). The galleries in the transept were also supported by groin vaulting. The groin vaulting in the aisles on either side of the choir, and the barrel vaulting in the upper storeys of the outer apses suggest that the intention was to vault the main choir. There was no evidence for vaulting above the nave and side aisle galleries, and as a result it is unlikely that there was a stone barrel vault over the nave itself. Given previous failed attempts to vault the nave (in churches such as Caen), Lanfranc almost certainly decided to use a wooden vault in the transept and nave; it would have been a visually quite adequate substitute.

An important rival of this cathedral was the rebuilt Abbey of Peter and Paul, which was built by Abbot Scotland (1070–87) outside the east walls of the city (figure, bottom). This was where St. Augustine had founded a monastery in 598, hence its later name of St. Augustine's Abbey; it was used as a burial site for the first archbishops and the kings of Kent. Scotland was the first Norman abbot (from Mont St. Michel), and started on his large new building between 1070 and 1073. It was not only a few meters higher than the cathedral, but even copied its basic shape (façade with two towers, columned nave and aisles without alternation, projecting transept with apses, though no tribunes) though it replaced its chapels in echelon with the rather more extravagant solution of surrounding the choir with an ambulatory and radiating chapels over a spacious crypt. Clearly, the requirement to venerate the relics of St. Augustine had suggested a choir with ambulatory, a form which Scotland was familiar with from Mont St. Michel. The ground plan of the church, which was

Lincoln Cathedral. 1073/74–1092.
Central part of the west façade, built by
Remigius (detail), ground plan (bottom)

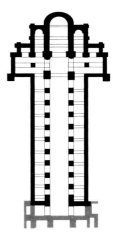

221

Old Sarum (Salisbury) Cathedral.
Completed 1092. Reconstruction of the
exterior view, ground plan

Rochester Cathedral, Kent. West façade

 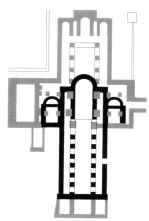

statement that Remigius had built a church "in loco forti fortem, pulchro pulchram, virgini virginum."

The people building churches at this time must have felt a pronounced need for security. This view is supported by the transfer of the episcopal see of Sherborne and Ramsbury to Old Sarum to the north of Salisbury, carried out in 1075 by Bishop Herman the Fleming, formerly the court chaplain to Edward the Confessor. His new cathedral (illustration, left) was not built in the town, but on a broad hill in the shadow of a large Norman castle – meaning that even water shortages were an acceptable trade-off for safety.

The cathedral was completed in 1092 by St. Osmund, but five days before it was due to be consecrated it was destroyed by a storm. The foundations, which were excavated in a field in 1912/13, show that the building had little in common with churches in Normandy, possibly because of the person who commissioned it. A cross-section façade was connected to a nave and side aisles with pillars; the transept and towers,

destroyed from 1538, can be made out in the ruins which were excavated in a Canterbury meadow, and its elevation would have been similar to models in Normandy, and the slightly older Canterbury Cathedral.

The next English successor of St. Stephen's in Caen was the Anglo-Norman cathedral in Lincoln which, like so many of its contemporaries, was extensively rebuilt during the Gothic period in the Early English style. Remigius, who had previously been the almoner at the monastery of Fécamp, was made bishop in 1067. In 1072, as part of the reforms made to the dioceses after the Norman Conquest, the bishop's see of Dorchester on Thames was moved to Lincoln; the cathedral was built on the fortified Lincoln Hill, above the River Witham. The Cathedral Church of St. Mary, which was started in 1073/74, was completed by 1092, when it was consecrated. As Remigius died on the eve of the consecration, it was undertaken by his successor, Robert Bloet. All that remains of Remigius's building is the central section of the façade (photo, p. 221), built of hewn stone, and with narrow openings that look like the arrow-slits on a castle. Because of excavations, it is possible to make a reliable reconstruction of its appearance: a two-bay façade with twin towers was connected to a nine-bay columned nave and aisles, a projecting transept with tribunes that was initially in two sections, and a choir composed of five chapels in echelon. The rectangular sides of the side apses were a common feature in churches in Normandy. The cathedral itself must have been a galleried basilica. There is evidence to support there being groin vaulting in the side aisles, underneath the tribunes and in the four outer chapels in echelon. The central part of the choir was probably roofed by a barrel vault. The transept and nave would have had wooden vaults. Nothing is known about the shape of the crossing tower. In 1911, John Bilson quite rightly praised the building for its "logical precision, clearly defined structural organization, and feeling for monumental form." Its most remarkable section was the façade area, shaped like a triumphal arch; if this section was really – as R. Gem suggested in 1982 – originally conceived as a fortified church without towers, it would explain Henry of Huntingdon's

St. Albans Cathedral, Hertfordshire.
Nave

St. Albans Cathedral, Hertfordshire.
Exterior view with Romanesque crossing
tower

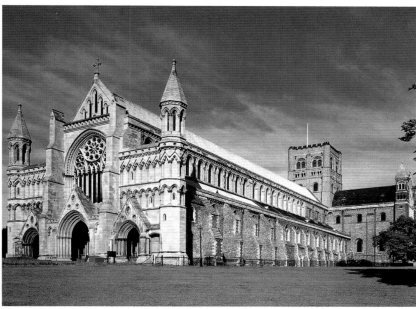

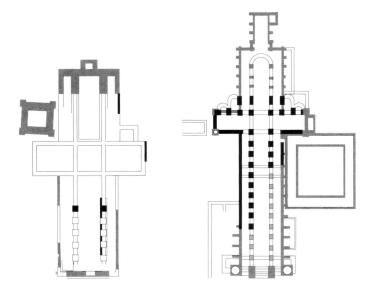

Rochester Cathedral. Built by Gundulf

St. Albans, monastery church. Built by
Paul of Caen

which are remarkably similar to Murbach in Alsace (cf. p. 55), were
followed by five apses in echelon.

Rochester Cathedral in Kent (photo, p. 222 and figure, bottom left) was
started by Bishop Gundulf (1077–1108) soon after he was made bishop,
together with a Benedictine convent; it, too, shows that defense was still an
important consideration. It is possible that Gundulf, who came from Le Bec
like Lanfranc, incorporated an older fortified tower which filled the area
between the northern transept and the choir of the new cathedral.

We know the basic shape of this building which, like its Anglo-Saxon
predecessor, was dedicated to St. Andrew and was the second-oldest bishopric in England (founded 604). The two west bays of the groin-vaulted
crypt remain, together with the walls that separated the three aisles of the
rectangular choir (83 feet). The small eastern rectangular chapel probably
contained the relics of St. Paulinus, one of Rochester's seventh-century
archbishops. The transept projected, and it is possible that a tower stood
over a square bay in the south transept, as a counterweight to the fortified
north tower. The interior decoration of the two galleried aisles and nave
was altered in the middle of the twelfth century; like Old Sarum, it ends
with a cross-section façade. There is conspicuously little similarity to the
ground plans of St. Etienne in Caen or Christ Church in Canterbury – even
though Gundulf worked alongside Lanfranc on both of those buildings.

It is easy to explain the clear dependence of the abbey church (a
cathedral since 1877) of St. Albans in Hertfordshire (photos, above), built

223

at the same time as Rochester, on William's church in Caen. In 1077, Lanfranc sent the monk Paul of Caen to the town on the River Ver near the ruins of Roman Verulamium; it was here that St. Alban, the first British martyr, was beheaded in about 304, and a Benedictine monastery was founded here in 793 by King Offa of Mercia.

Using bricks from the Roman ruins that had been gathered by his predecessors, Paul built strongest Anglo-Norman building still extant, over 410 feet long. Large parts of Paul's basilica still stand: it was a church with pillars and ten bays, a very wide transept and seven chapels in echelon. As in Rochester, the aisles on either side of the choir chapels did not open into each other. The use of plastered brick masonry may go some way to explaining why the nave and aisles, with their stepped arcades, low galleries and clerestory with one window in each bay, appear to be so archaic, massive and ponderous. The sober interior would have been softened by paintings, however. Like the chapels, the side aisles were groin-vaulted, and the central choir chapel would have been barrel-vaulted. The projecting pillars in the nave would probably have supported the chords of a wooden vault. Because of the enormous thickness of the walls, there is every reason to believe that the original plan was to vault the nave with stone or bricks, but that this was not possible because the nave was too wide – even the galleries are not vaulted. The open galleries of the nave are replaced in the transept by low double arches in front of a narrow passageway, underneath a high-arched clerestory. The crossing tower, which is crenellated like a battlement, is the only such eleventh century tower remaining on an English church; it is likely that the original plans included a façade with twin towers. The church was consecrated in 1115.

The mighty White Tower (photos, left, and p. 250) fulfils many roles: it is a defensive structure, residence and prestigious building, and at the same time the symbol of William the Conqueror's rule of London. It also plays an important part in the history of England's Romanesque sacred buildings. Gundulf, the bishop who already had experience of building in Rochester, had the White Tower constructed for his king from about 1078, and personally equipped the rather bare St. John's Chapel for its function as a private chapel; it can be identified from the outside: a semi-circular projection at the southern end of the east side of the building. It occupies the third and fourth storeys of the building. It is an aisled galleried chapel without a clerestory, with round pillars and an ambulatory, and its dimensions (55 feet x 31 feet) are roughly equivalent to the choir in a large church such as St. Augustine's in Canterbury. Particularly noteworthy is the stone vaulting throughout the chapel; the nave is barrel and the aisles groin-vaulted, and the galleries are covered by semi-circular vaults. This chapel demonstrates on a small scale what the Norman architects were attempting to achieve: a building made completely of stone, in this case without light sources in the nave. Given that the nave in the Tower was only 15 feet wide, the fact that the builders decided against adding a clerestory shows just what bad experiences eleventh-century architects must have had in their attempts to put stone vaults on larger basilicas.

York Minster (illustration, p. 225, top) is second only to Canterbury. Its archbishop controls fourteen dioceses. He is the "Primate of England,"

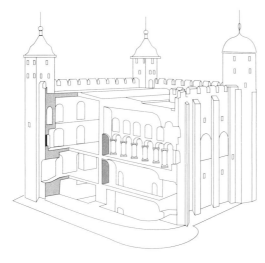

White Tower, cross-section with chapel

York Minster. Begun around 1079 (?) by
Thomas of Bayeux. Reconstruction from
the north-east, ground plan

Winchester Cathedral. Northern transept
arm, interior view

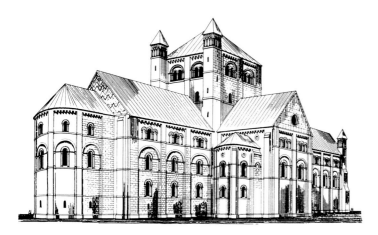

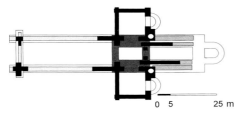

the north side aisle) have made it possible to reconstruct the exterior, which would have been divided by tall blind niches and several rows of windows.

York Minster remained very much an exception. In Winchester, Hampshire, Bishop Walkelyn (1070–98) of Rouen replaced the last Anglo-Saxon bishop, Stigand. Walkelyn, who had been the king's chaplain, started work on a new cathedral in 1079 (photo, bottom and figures, p. 226); it was built "a fundamentis," from scratch, and shows that the Normans were using Canterbury as a model, though with some differences and embellishments.

On a hill above the River Itchen, Walkelyn built what was at the time the largest church in northern Europe, until Cluny III. Its very length of 533 feet was an expression of the importance of a city which had witnessed the coronations and funerals of kings and was the destination of a pilgrim route to the grave of St. Swithin. In 1093, the Benedictine monks

but the archbishop of Canterbury is the "Primate of all England." The minster, in the center of the city that the Romans called Eboracum, has always been a cathedral; there was never a monastery here. York had its first bishop in the fourth century. At Easter 625 Bishop Paulinus baptized King Edwin of Northumbria in a wooden church; in 634 he was promoted to be the city's first archbishop.

The last Anglo-Saxon cathedral to stand on this site, St. Peter's, was destroyed during the last Danish invasion of 1075; its replacement was begun by Archbishop Thomas of Bayeux (1070–1100) in about 1079, and the first stage was completed by the time he died. York Minster must be viewed as a rival of Canterbury Cathedral, and that would go some way to explaining the peculiar shape of the 366-foot-long church, which Derek Philipps excavated between 1967 and 1972. Like Angers Cathedral, it had a mighty, 154 foot nave that was over 58 feet wide. Over the projecting transept was a sturdy crossing tower and it had stair turrets to the east and apses; the long choir had aisles and ended in a semi-circular main apse with a small crypt underneath. Sections of this substructure, which was over 5 feet wide, can be viewed underneath the crossing. The lower courses of stone, bootied pieces from Roman buildings, were built on an oak frame. The present-day pillars in the nave stand on the foundations of the Romanesque nave, so the cathedral built by Thomas had a lasting influence on the newer Gothic building which was started in about 1215. Remains of Romanesque walls, complete with their original plaster, and the painted ashlar of the crossing tower (above

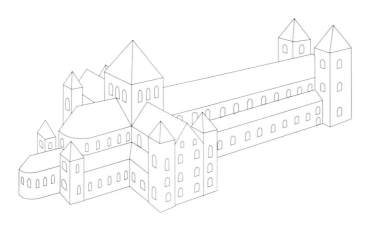

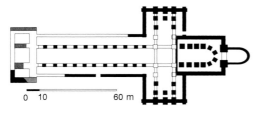

from the nearby Old Minster were able to move into the completed east section. In 1107 the crossing tower collapsed, but was soon replaced with the aid of stronger pillars. Repairs also had to be made in the bays of the transept, most noticeably to the capitals. The church was completed in about 1120.

The façade, which was guarded by two towers, was connected to a nave and aisles with eleven bays, which retains its late Gothic cladding up to the gallery. The most impressive part is the transept, incorporating new continental ideas. It was redesigned in about 1085, giving it side aisles, so that the aisles to either side of the nave continued into the wings of the transept. Towers – two at either end of the transept – were intended to be temporary alternatives to a crossing tower. It was clearly modeled on the galleried transepts found in pilgrimage churches such as Toulouse and Santiago. The choir, raised above a powerful crypt in several parts, also had side aisles. The end of the choir was surrounded by a semi-circular ambulatory, and an apse-like Lady Chapel was attached to its rectangular termination. A rhythmic alternation of pillars and columns, together with vertical supports in front of the strong walls, suggests that a stone barrel vault was planned for the central aisle at the beginning of the choir. The idea was abandoned in about 1085, at gallery level.

The transept (photo, p. 225, bottom) was almost untouched by the Gothic alterations made at the end of the twelfth century (which started with a retro-choir); it gives one the opportunity to experience at first hand

the imposing power of these large high Romanesque buildings. Massive, sharply stepped pillars flank openings on three levels that become progressively lower higher up the building: a sunken arcade, gallery openings with small columns and tympanums, and a clerestory which contains certain irregularities, a result of the small towers which were planned for either end of the transept. The transept is reinforced throughout, indicating that it was supposed to be vaulted. The arcades from the side aisles continue along the front side of the transept, but on the other side are open tribunes which support the ambulatory vault.

Soon after 1079, Robert de Losinga (Lorraine), bishop of Hereford from 1079–95 and brother of the builder of Norwich Cathedral, decided to rebuild his cathedral of SS. Mary and Ethelbert (figure, bottom photo, p. 227). A church on this site, built by Bishop Aethelstan (1012–56), had burnt down in 1054; despite being repaired, it clearly did not meet Norman requirements.

The ground plan and elevation of the east section, which was consecrated in 1110, followed what had become a well-worn pattern in England: a nave and side aisles were connected to a projecting transept. The east wall of the southern transept arm remains. Its construction (blind arcades, triforiums and clerestory with passageways) shows that the building was re-planned and changed on several occasions and that – like pilgrimage churches – a barrel vault may well have been planned for the galleries of the original central choir aisle. The oldest part of the east wall of the transept is the outer area, from the clearly visible vertical line between the different sections. The gallery bay bordering the crossing is old in its form, but was evidently restored in the twelfth century, probably after the crossing tower collapsed around 1110 (which also made it necessary to repair the choir). The remaining three bays and two storeys of this choir, which had lavishly stepped pillared arcades, low galleries and broad vertical supports in the central aisle, would have been roofed either by means of a barrel vault or – more likely – by a groin vault over a clerestory.

Groin vaulting in the nave would have been an early example of the modern form of four-point vaults, earlier ones being Speyer II and the choir of the Trinité in Caen. The eastern towers over the first bays in the side chancels are also reminiscent of Speyer. Bishop Raynelm (1107–15) was responsible for the planning of these sections, and on his tombstone he is referred to as the "fundator ecclesiae." The nave and side aisles – the round pillars in the ground floor are still Romanesque – were not completed until the rule of Robert de Béthune (1131–48), and the church was consecrated in 1142 and 1148.

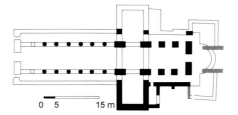

Hereford Cathedral. Begun around 1080. Built by Robert de Losinga, ground plan

OPPOSITE
Hereford Cathedral. East wall of the southern transept

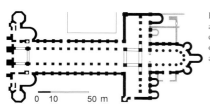

Bury St. Edmunds, abbey. Begun after 1081. Tower above the entrance hall (right), ground plan of the monastery church (left), aerial view of the abbey (below)

In the 1080s, several important monastery churches were begun, quite apart from the cathedrals of Worcester, London and Gloucester. Unfortunately, it is precisely the most remarkable ones that fell victim to the Reformation.

Some informative ruins (photo, top left) remain of the 500 foot long abbey church which Abbot Baldwin of St. Denis (1065–97) had planned for the wealthy Benedictine establishment founded in 633 near the grave of St. Edmund (d. 870), the last king of East Anglia. The project to build Bury St. Edmunds in Suffolk started soon after 1081. This was the year in which William the Conqueror released the abbey from the control of the bishopric. It is possible to make out the ground plan and – next to one of the crossing pillars – even the beginning of each storey of the church's ruins, which are spread out over a large green area.

A transept with a side aisle to the east and chapels, a three-storey galleried nave and aisles and a 247 feet wide west transom with three towers was connected to an ambulatory with radiating chapels, which in size even outdid its model of St. Augustine's in Canterbury. It was possible to move the relics of Edmund into the new building as early as 1095, and the entire complex was finished by the end of the century. On the occasion of the transfer of the relics, the monk Hermann (*Miracula Eadmundi*) praised the marvellous vaulting over the new choir, which he compared to the temple of Solomon. Doubtlessly a major factor in the decision to build the new church was the desire to increase the number of pilgrims coming to St. Edmund's grave.

Ely Cathedral. Begun after 1081.
Structure of the nave wall (top), ground
plan of Simeon's building (right), towers
and nave and aisles from the south-east
(bottom)

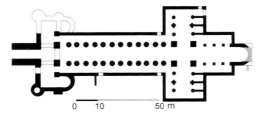

One can still get an idea of what the west front of Bury looked like by examining Ely in Cambridgeshire (photo, p. 229). The wide façade of this cathedral, which was dedicated to the Trinity, was evidently built in direct competition with Bury. A monastery founded in the early Middle Ages – by St. Etheldreda, the Queen of Northumbria who died in 679 – was the starting point at Ely, as it was at Bury. With the aid of the monks, King William was able to defeat one of the last pockets of Anglo-Saxon resistance in the marshes around Ely. In 1081, the office of abbot was conferred by William upon Simeon, a Norman who had been prior of Winchester and was the brother of Bishop Walkelyn.

Simeon started work at Ely soon after he was made abbot, and the original building remains, except for the crossing and choir. Like St. Albans, the choir had aisles and three storeys, and probably terminated in a semi-circular apse. The transept, as at Winchester, had three storeys. The mighty octagon over the crossing, built between 1322 and 1344, disturbs the regularity of the slim Norman bays quite considerably. The east section was probably completed when the relics of the monastery's founder were transferred in 1106. In 1109, the church was elevated to the rank of cathedral, and the Breton Abbot Hervé became its first bishop.

The journey from the high to the late Romanesque period can be made by passing from the oldest section, the south arm of the transept with its plain storeys without responds (alternating system of supports in the ground floor, galleries, triplets (windows with three lights) with a walkway, the latter probably built after the crossing tower collapsed in 1111), via the northern transept which has a clear vertical structure due to elements placed in front of the pillars, the nave and side aisles with thirteen bays (alternating system of supports in the arcade storey and gallery, triplets with a walkway, photos, left), to the façade. The walls of the open west transept arms, dating from the late twelfth century, are richly decorated with sequences of blind arches. The nave is magnificent; though it took a long time to build, it remained remarkably true to the original design. The horizontal sequence of its storeys, which are proportioned in a 6:5:4 ratio, is broken by the narrow responds which, instead of the broken wooden ceiling, almost certainly supported a wooden barrel vault. As in Peterborough and Norwich, this is high Romanesque articulation of a building carried out to a beautiful degree of perfection. The exterior of the nave and side aisles is more lavishly decorated than the interior, and includes a sequence of blind arcades.

Bermondsey Abbey in Surrey (figure, p. 230, top) was a Cluniac priory like Lewes in Sussex and Wenlock in Shropshire. Its eastern section, which has only been known since recent excavations were made, is curious and until now was difficult to interpret, just like the solutions to building the choir in Rochester and York. The building had a transept with four apses, and it was connected to a sanctuary that was a good 65 feet long, surrounded by five apses on the eastern side. The church, which was probably begun in 1082, was an unusual successor to Cluny II.

Only sections remain of the monastery church that was founded in 1083 by Roger de Montmorency for Benedictines from Séez. The three bays in the nave and aisles, built around 1100, have round pillars and the

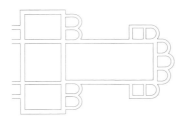

Bermondsey Abbey.
Ground plan of the
eastern section

usual tympana in the galleries, but the clerestory does not have a walkway in front of the windows.

The Cathedral of St. Mary in Worcester (photo, below) is especially informative where the continuous relationship between architects in Normandy and Norman architects in England is concerned, and it has been quite unjustly ignored in publications on the European Romanesque period. While the large building, built of reddish sandstone, is largely Gothic, important sections of its Norman predecessor (crypt, base of the façade, arches, responds) still remain. The town was made a bishopric in 680, and the then church of St. Peter was under the care of secular canons. St. Wulfstan (1062–95), who was the only Anglo-Saxon bishop to remain in office after the Conquest, demolished the late tenth-century church, which had been built by St. Oswald and subsequently damaged by the Danes, and started work in 1084 on a church, the large size of which had become necessary due to growing numbers of monks. By 1089 the building work had progressed so far that the clerics were able to move from Oswald's old church into the new cathedral. After the translation of the relics of Oswald, Wulfstan had the old building demolished; it probably stood near the present nave. Wulfstan kept records that show that a synod took place in 1092 in the crypt which he had built and

dedicated to Mary. In 1095 Wulfstan died, and despite statements to the contrary by William of Malmesbury, it is unlikely that he lived to see his cathedral completed. After a series of fires in the first half of the twelfth century, a collapsing tower in 1175, and the completion of the two western nave bays towards the end of the twelfth century, the cathedral was finally consecrated in 1218.

Wulfstan's building had aisles and a transept and ambulatory with polygonal radiating chapels. Because it was the most distinguished church in the diocese, it is likely that it was not just the clerical, but also the artistic center of the "Severn Group" in the west of England. Being the head of this group, to which the Benedictine monasteries of Great Malvern (c. 1085ff.), Tewkesbury (1087/92), Gloucester (1089ff.), Pershore (1092ff.) and Evesham (twelfth century) belonged, it is probable that it left its mark on the remaining sections of the younger members of the group, enabling one to theorize about its elevation.

The two storeys of the original choir elevation that remain in Gloucester (figure, p. 231, bottom right) can be used by way of comparison for the choir elevation in Worcester. An abbey had existed in Gloucester since the seventh century, and in 1088 the church that was dedicated to St. Peter in 1058 burnt down. As Abbot Serlo (1072–1104)

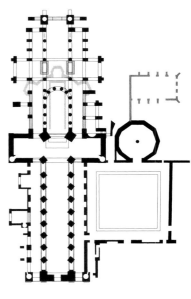

Worcester Cathedral. Begun 1084. Built by Wulfstan, ground plan

Worcester Cathedral. Crypt

230

laid the foundation stone of the new building in July 1089, it is safe to
assume that he was working to a model.

St. Peter's in Gloucester – a cathedral since 1540 – is an aisled basilica
with a transept, ambulatory and radiating chapels. There is a crypt with
several aisles which extends for the entire length of the choir, just as in
Worcester. The polygonal main choir has arcades over round pillars. The
ambulatory is groin-vaulted, and above it are barrel-vaulted galleries.
Their round pillars originally had four semi-circular responds, of which
three remain. Those facing inwards disappeared when the choir was
renovated during the late Gothic period. The first two storeys are the same
height, and above them is a late Gothic clerestory. The aisle-less, five-bay
transept with chapels to the east is Romanesque in its ground plan and in
parts of its elevation. Compared with the choir, the nave and side aisles
have a completely different elevation now. Above round pillars without
responds, pseudo-galleries open out onto a walkway. The clerestory was
rib-vaulted in the thirteenth century, but underneath this are clear traces of
its former shape: stepped triple arcades, walkway, central window. The
side aisles are rib-vaulted, and the exterior walls have alternately three and
five responds.

The galleries of the two remaining Romanesque storeys of the choir
provide important information for a reconstruction of the former superstructure. They have semi-domes, which must have been intended to
support a vault over the central choir. There are six possible solutions for
the superstructure, and if the intention was to vault the aisle with stone, it
is likely that the third storey was a triforium with a walkway, with or
without tiny windows.

Such a solution would have appeared quite strange to anyone brought up
on the French Romanesque style. But it is the very one that can be proved to
have existed in two other barrel-vaulted buildings belonging to the Severn
Group. They are the churches in Tewkesbury, Gloucestershire, and Pershore,
(Hereford & Worcester, photos, p. 232). In the eastern sections of both
churches were vaults over the central aisle, covering galleries and a triforium
and walkway; this was a three-part elevation, not the four-part one that Jean
Bony reconstructed in 1937. The transepts of Tewkesbury and Pershore used
to be barrel-vaulted in stone, and give clues to the elevations of the choirs,
which in both cases no longer exist. As both churches belonged to priories
that were subordinate to Worcester and Gloucester, they probably had
corresponding elevations at the first stage of planning, but the intention to
use stone vaulting failed, probably because of the width of the nave, despite
the novel elevation. Worcester and Gloucester were presumably replanned,
and the stone vault was replaced with a wooden vault with girders, the only
form of roofing that corresponded to the desired spatial effect.

It is easy to reconstruct the transepts in Worcester and Gloucester. Both
of them, like the better preserved transepts in Tewkesbury and Pershore,
had one aisle and five bays. They had two-storey eastern chapels and
towers with staircases at the corners. They had a three-storey elevation
and stone vaults were planned, and possibly even built.

There are very sparse remains left to aid a reconstruction of the
Romanesque nave and side aisles in Worcester. They do, however, prove

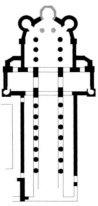

Gloucester, abbey church. Built by Serlo,
ground plan

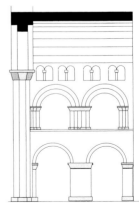

Gloucester, abbey church. Built by Serlo,
elevation of the choir

231

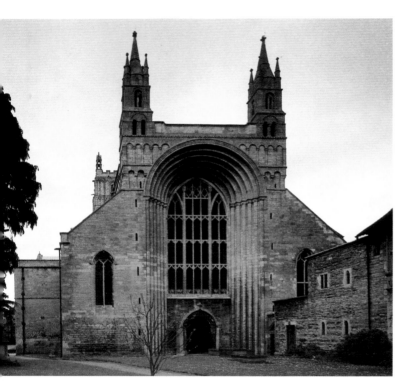

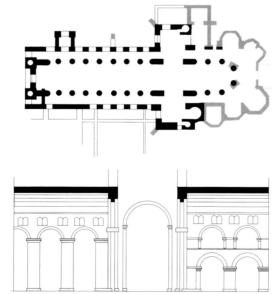

Tewkesbury,
ground plan
(above), elevation
of nave and choir
(right)

that Worcester did not simply have round pillars like Gloucester and Tewkesbury. The elevations of their naves and side aisles are quite different from the eastern sections of the buildings, and have excessively high arcades and a low triforium and walkway; the triforium had started replacing galleries from about 1110, as they were no longer considered structurally or liturgically necessary. In Gloucester, construction work was started later, and around 1120/30 the openings of this intermediate storey were grouped in the center of the arcade beneath; this clearly shows that the intention was to use what, at that time, was the most modern form of vaulting, namely the six-section rib vaulting that had been invented in Normandy (see photos, p. 142). It is probable that the plans in Worcester were changed to an alternating system of supports in the nave and side aisles, in order to avoid the obvious break between the substructure and vaulting evident in Gloucester.

Due to the combination of vaulted galleries and triforiums with walkways underneath a vault, the Severn Group occupies a special position in the English Romanesque period. The main architect of the Group must have been aware that a stone vault could not be executed over a basilica's elevation if the span was more than ten meters. It can only have been possible to realise his solution to this problem in smaller buildings.

The bishop's chapel in Hereford, which was demolished in 1737, had a

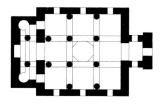

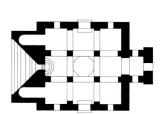

Hereford Cathedral. Bishop's chapel. Reconstruction by Drinkwater

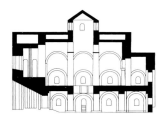

Longitudinal section, ground plan of upper storey (above left), ground plan of lower storey (below left)

similar system of vaults to Tewkesbury. Contemporary sources refer to it as the successor to Aachen's palatine chapel, and it was a two-storey central-plan building (figure, top left) erected by Bishop Robert of Lorraine (1079–95). It can easily be reconstructed: the bottom storey was similar to a crypt and had a groin vault supported by pillars, and above it was a bright superstructure with a vault and a central tower in the nave and semi-domes in the side aisles. The relationship between this chapel and the chapel of St. Emmeram by Speyer Cathedral and the Church of Our Lady in the palace at Goslar proves that the architects' clients had introduced Salian and, possibly, Burgundian influences to Britain by the late eleventh century.

Astonishingly enough, neither the two Norman bishops Robert and William, who had been appointed by Edward the Confessor, nor King William's first bishop Hugh de Orival (1075–85) started work on a new version of St. Paul's Cathedral in London (figures, bottom right). It was not until an extensive fire in 1087 that Bishop Maurice (1086–1107) was given the opportunity to do this. Another fire in 1133 led to restoration work on the church which had probably been completed before 1127, and this lasted right into the second half of the twelfth century. The outlines of the ground plan of the predecessor to today's Baroque building are known. The cathedral had a hall crypt, and above it probably an ambulatory with radiating chapels, such as that at Bury. Connected to it was a transept that projected unusually far, and a nave and side aisles with pillars which were powerfully articulated by means of twelve bays; its condition, complete with galleries, clerestory and Gothic rib vaulting, was recorded by Wenzel Hollar in the seventeenth century. If small square towers did indeed flank the cross-section façade, they would not have been added until the late twelfth century.

In the last decade of the eleventh century, work was started on some Cluniac monastery churches, as well as the cathedrals. An example is the priory church in Castle Acre, Norfolk (photo, p. 234; figure, p. 235), which was begun soon after the priory's foundation in 1089 by William I of Warenne; six bays of the nave and side aisles, and the façade (middle of

the twelfth century) with its typically English sequences of blind arches, still stand. The church of Lewes Priory in Sussex (figure, p. 235) was also started after 1090; this was another priory founded by William I of Warenne, in 1078/81. The church, which has been excavated, was a successor to Cluny III, begun in 1088: like it, the English daughter-house had two transepts and an ambulatory with radiating chapels.

The first cathedral built during this decade was Chichester in Sussex (figure, p. 235). The cathedral, dedicated to the Holy Trinity, was part of a bishopric founded around 681 in Selsey by St. Wilfrid, a former abbot and bishop of York. In 1075, the decision of the Council of London to move the "village sees" to cities led to the bishopric being shifted to Chichester (Noviomagus). Stigand was the first bishop (1070–87) at this new site; he probably started work around 1080 on a new building to replace the church of St. Peter's, which was used on a temporary basis. That would explain why this large building, of which large parts survived the Gothic modernization (despite a fire in 1187), appears rather old-fashioned. The

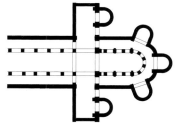

London, St. Paul's Cathedral. Built by Maurice, ground plan (left)

233

cathedral was commissioned by Bishop Ralph Luffa (1090/91–1123), and William of Malmesbury reported that Luffa built "a novo." The eastern sections (ambulatory with three chapels, aisle-less transept with two-storey east chapels), which were started soon after 1091, and the four east bays of the nave and side aisles, were probably completed before the consecration in 1108. The elevation of the choir, which can be reconstructed, is important in the history of the building's development. It was only 26 feet wide, meaning that it is possible that a stone vault, such as the one in the Tower of London's chapel, or in Winchester, could have been intended; this suggests that the building was planned during Stigand's time as bishop. The vault would have been supported by the arcade of pillars in the ground floor and the galleries which were strengthened by stone arches. In 1114, the town and cathedral were destroyed by a fire, and the eleventh-century remains are still visible in the crossing and bordering transept bays. Luffa resumed work on the building. He built the Lady Chapel, a nave arranged as a three-aisled basilica with pillars, eight bays, a powerfully articulated, three-storey elevation (the arcades, the unvaulted galleries and the exterior sides of the triple-arched clerestory are still Romanesque) and a façade with twin towers (consecrated in 1184).

The reddish sandstone building dedicated to St. Werburgh near the city walls of Chester in Cheshire (a cathedral since 1541) was extensively reno-vated in the Gothic style from the middle of the thirteenth century. Previously there was a collegiate church on this site, built soon after 907. In 1092, Hugh Lupus, earl of Chester and nephew of William the Conqueror, made it an abbey of Benedictine monks. Bishop Richard of Le Bec (1093-1117) started work on a new building, of which parts remain on the north side of the cathedral (wall of the side aisle, north transept), but it cannot yet be reconstructed.

There is no way of categorically deciding where the new idea of rib vaulting first appeared, whether Worcester in the 1120s or Gloucester after the fire of 1122. Both examples of rib vaulting – and also the one which we can assume to have existed in Lincoln – predate that of Durham, which continues to be wrongly connected with the date of 1093.

Durham Cathedral was built next to the bishop's castle at the highest point of the city within a loop of the River Wear; it is one of the purest embodiments of Norman architecture (photos, pp. 236–27). It is the symbol of the Normans' strict safeguarding of ecclesiastical and secular power, a symbol of authority for their subordinates and a bastion against Scotland. It was preceded by a monastery church, which was begun by Bishop Aldhun in 993 and consecrated in 998; the relics of St. Cuthbert (d. 687, bishop of Lindisfarne) were kept there.

The present large-scale building – a basilica with aisles and an alternating system of supports, porch to the west, façade with two towers, transept with two aisles, choir and rectangular chapel at the east end, replacing the three Romanesque apses – was begun by Bishop William of St. Carileph (Guillaume de St. Calais, 1081–96) in 1093, and the work was continued by Ranulph de Flambard (1099–1128). The east section was probably completed by 1104, and that is when the relics of St. Cuthbert were transferred there. In about 1128, the church was completed

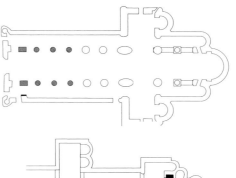

Castle Acre (Norfolk), former Cluniac priory church. Ground plan

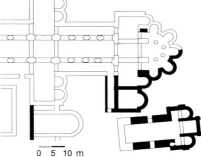

Lewes Priory (Sussex), monastery church. Begun after 1090. Ground plan

0 5 10 m

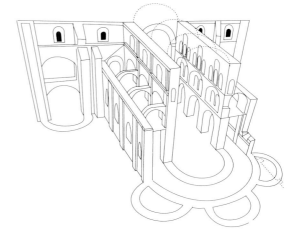

Chichester Cathedral, Sussex. Begun around 1080. Built by Luffa, elevation of the choir

Durham Cathedral. Begun 1093. View of nave towards the east (left), view from the west (opposite)

with the addition of galleries, a clerestory, groin vaulting in the east section and probably a wooden vault in the nave. There is no justification for the frequently expressed opinion that the rib vaulting was planned and built from the outset.

Rib vaulting the nave was not "invented" until 1120/20 in Normandy – St. Étienne in Caen to be precise. The earliest plans of this church had intended the monumental basilica to have a stone roof, but at the time the width of the spans meant that it was not possible to realise these plans with a stone vault; rib vaulting meant this was now possible after all. William the Conqueror's mortuary church had an alternating system of supports, which is why the first example of monumental rib vaulting, which corresponded to its system of vertical building elements, is in six sections. In Durham the four-part rib vaulting lacks all reference to the elevation, and was quite evidently added later (from 1128/33 to around 1160), being put up on consoles over galleries with concealed buttressing. During the course of this, the clerestory was modified, and the interior was given a more lavish decoration in keeping with the late Romanesque style. Naturally the ribs in the side aisles, such as one sees on many occasions in England, had groin vaulting pushed underneath them at a later date.

Another thing which speaks out against the early dating of Durham's rib vaulting is the fact that this type of vaulting was not yet known in the buildings (such as Norwich, the choir built by St. Anselm in Canterbury

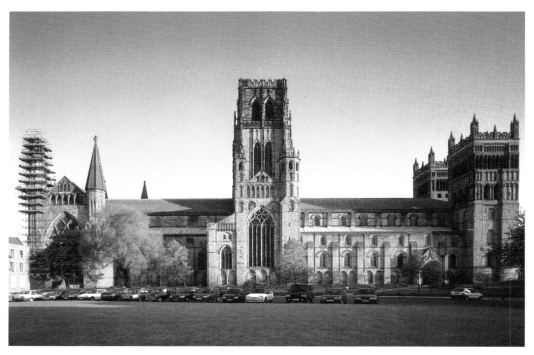

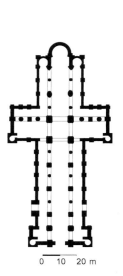

Durham Cathedral. View from the north (right), ground plan (William of St. Carileph's building)

236

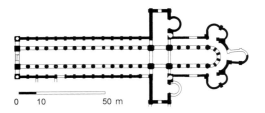

Norwich Cathedral. Begun 1096.
Ground plan of Herbert de Losinga's
building, view from the south-west (left),
structure of the nave walls in three zones
(center), view of choir towards the east
(right)

Cathedral, and Peterborough) started shortly before and after the turn of the century. Rather, Norwich and Peterborough both finally decided against attempting to vault the nave. Instead, their designers perfected the 'aqueduct system' of the nave walls. This pre-Gothic structure, which removes all the heaviness from walls, finds its most magnificent expression in these buildings.

The bishopric of East Anglia probably dates back to a see that was founded in Dunwich, Suffolk, by St. Felix of Burgundy around 630. In about 955, it was combined with North Elmham in Norfolk, and the see was moved to Thetford in 1075. It was not until 1094 that Bishop Herbert de Losinga (1091–1119), who had previously been prior of Fécamp and abbot of Ramsey, moved to Norwich, which was safer. Losinga had evidently bought his office from William Rufus, the avaricious son of the Conqueror. He had a part of the Saxon city torn down and started work on a mighty new building in 1096 (photos, p. 238). He lived long enough to see the east sections (a three-storey choir with ambulatory and three chapels, aisle-less transept, and first double bay of the nave) completed. The sanctuary, like that at Ely, is strikingly long, and the elevation follows that of St. Etienne in Caen in other respects: the arcade supported similarly high, unseparated galleries, and there was a walkway in front of the clerestory and a triplet. Double responds in front of the galleries show that the structure was stabilized by stone arches, like Durham. The late Gothic rib vaulting, in several sections, was probably preceded by a wooden vault. The supports in the ground floor are conspicuous: they swing out to the

east and west like segmental arches, as if round and edged pillars had been merged. A typically English feature is that the east and west sides of the transept (which has its original two-storey chapels) are different.

By the time he died, Bishop Eborardus (Everard de Montgomery, 1121–45) had completed the nave, fourteen bays long, and finished it off with a simple cross-section façade.

We will pass over the medium-sized monasteries built around 1100, which are well worth seeing: they are Lindisfarne in Northumberland (1093ff., photo, p. 239), which is now in ruins but which was rebuilt with rib vaulting at the instigation of the Benedictines in Durham; Christchurch Priory in Hampshire (1094) which has late Romanesque patterned arcade spandrels and was founded by Ranulph Flambard, later bishop of Durham; Binham Priory in Norfolk (c. 1091ff.), of which just one hall remains and whose pointed roof suggests that the upward thrust of the double responds must have supported a barrel vault; the mighty arched walls of Colchester Priory in Essex (c. 1095ff.), which was the first Augustinian settlement in England and is now in ruins; and the two Romanesque nave storeys of Wymondham Abbey in Norfolk (1107ff.), which was founded by William de Albini as a daughter-house of St. Albans.

The architectural climax of these years must have been the choir of Canterbury Cathedral, of which only the outside walls still stand (photo, p. 239). The building was begun in 1093/96 by Anselm (1093–1109) and his prior Ernulph (1096–1107), and eventually completed by Prior Conrad (1108–26); they replaced Lanfranc's three apses with a choir so long that it

Lindisfarne (Holy Island), ruins of the
monastery church

Canterbury Cathedral. Choir built by Anselm.
Begun 1093/96

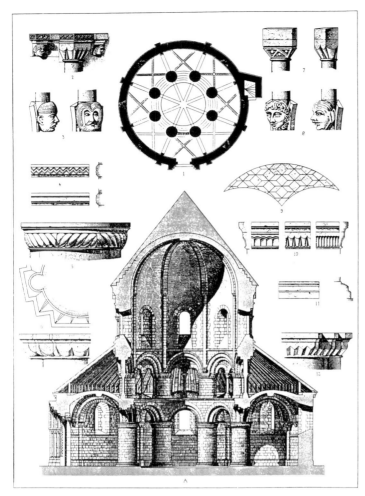

Cambridge, Holy Sepulchre. Begun around 1120. View from the west (below), cross section, ground plan and types of architectural sculpture (left)

nearly doubled the length of the cathedral. In the east was a transept with two chapels in each arm, and an ambulatory with two tangentially connected radiating chapels as well as a rectangular Lady Chapel; they were built over the extended crypt and were able to house numerous new altars. The elevation of the extension, which was consecrated in 1130, would have been round pillars supporting a weakly lit gallery and a clerestory with a walkway. Gervasius of Canterbury writes that the ceiling was painted.

The most remarkable of the few central-plan buildings in England is the round Church of the Holy Sepulchre in Cambridge (photo, above), which was begun around 1120; we do not know why it was built. It is a copy of the Church of the Holy Sepulcher in Jerusalem, and while it was renovated by the Cambridge Camden Society from 1841, its forms are nonetheless trustworthy. Eight round pillars surround a central space which is roofed, via unvaulted galleries and round arch windows, by an eight-section dome. Its powerful ribs have as little in common with the original plan as those in the ambulatory.

Apart from renovations to choirs such as those in Old Sarum, Wiltshire (c. 1110–30) and Rochester (1111–25), the first third of the twelfth century also saw the start and extension of several important monastery and bishop's churches: in Waltham Abbey, Essex, a new building (IV) with an ambulatory and transept was built between 1110 and 1160, and the

galleried nave and side aisles still stand, complete with the patterned round pillars and arcade arches that were influenced by Durham. The transition to the Gothic period can be seen at Selby Abbey in Yorkshire. The choir with chapels in echelon, which was started around 1100, was later replaced by a late Gothic building, but the Romanesque aisle-less transept with its low crossing, and the two east bays of the nave and side aisles, still remain. From the second double bay onwards, individual Gothic forms appear in a quite bizarre shape. We only know the outlines of the ground plan of the monastery church at Chertsey in Surrey, which was built from 1110 onwards. And little more is known, other than the two mighty towers over the transept arms, of the cathedral church in Exeter, Devon, which was begun in 1114 by Bishop William Warelwast (d. 1137) and consecrated in 1133.

The churches of Chertsey and Old Sarum, as well as Southwell Minster in Nottinghamshire (photos, p. 241) which was begun by Archbishop Thomas II of York (1108–14) as a collegiate church, and Romsey Abbey in Hampshire (photo, p. 241, built c. 1120–1250 for Benedictines), are amongst the earliest buildings to have rectangular choirs or ambulatories. This type of ambulatory, which appears to be an invention of the English Romanesque period, can be traced back to continental ambulatory crypts of the late Carolingian period. The best preserved is the choir of Romsey Abbey, which only lost its probably two-

Romsey Abbey (Hampshire).
c. 1120–1250. Ground plan, west façade

Southwell Cathedral, Nottinghamshire.
Begun 1108–14. View of nave towards
the east

Southwell Cathedral, Nottinghamshire.
Ground plan, west façade

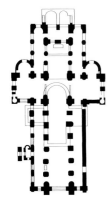

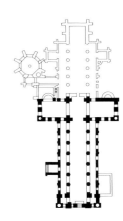

storeyed east chapel. The naves of the two collegiate churches are variations of the English high Romanesque period that are full of character. In Southwell, three storeys that decrease in height (arcade with round pillars, gallery without a tympanum, round window behind a walkway) support a wooden vault (!), and the side aisles have an early rib vaulting that is inserted on consoles. Romsey also has the typically British "aqueduct system" with three storeys, and another wooden vault! While Southwell avoids any vertical emphasis, in the first bay it looks as though the massive round pillars were rising through to the gallery, creating a "colossal order" such as that in Oxford or Jedburgh.

Both buildings belong to a group which around 1120 replaced the stone vaults planned in the eleventh century with wooden vaults; they distinguished themselves by means of their alternating systems of supports and increasing use of decorative features, as well as the repeated later inclusion – though only in the side aisles – of the increasingly fashionable ribs. The type of façade also changed: Romsey has a cross-section façade, while Southwell has elegantly proportioned twin towers.

The most important large building (478 feet long) at the end of the high Romanesque period is Peterborough Abbey in Cambridgeshire (photo, p. 242). It was started around 1118, elevated to the position of cathedral in 1541, and the Benedictine abbey's church was dedicated to Peter, Paul and Andrew. Abbot Jean de Séez (John de Sais, 1114–25) replaced the original church, which was consecrated in 972 and burnt down in 1116; the monastery was founded shortly after 653 by Peada, king of Mercia. He perfected the pattern set by Ely and Norwich and – during the period when the early Gothic had started in France – managed, to a large extent, to

Peterborough Cathedral,
Cambridgeshire. Begun around 1118.
View of nave towards the east

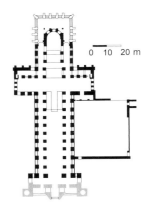

Ground plan of Jean de Séez's building

dissolve the walls as well as illuminate the interior. By 1143 the choir, whose three aisles ended in apses and which had an alternating system of supports consisting of octagonal and round pillars, was ready; the ribs in its side aisles were added later. The main twin-shelled apse, which governs the sequence of storeys in the choir, is extremely important, and it has windows in all three storeys. The double-aisled transept, which has three storeys (as in the choir and nave, arcades, galleries with tympanums and trioles), has a proper screen composed of responds and cornices across it. Abbot William de Waterville (1155–75) also started work on the nave and side aisles, which did not have an alternating system of supports or vaulted galleries, and work was finished by Abbot Benedict (1177–99) before 1193, in accordance with the original design. The polygonal broken wooden ceiling in the nave, which dates from the thirteenth century, was almost certainly preceded by a wooden barrel vault. The western side of the church is Gothic, and would have been completed, with its little corner towers and the gigantic niches reminiscent of Lincoln, by the time the building was consecrated in 1238.

The English high Romanesque period concluded towards 1135 with the end of the reign of Henry I. Henry's main work was the abbey of Reading, in Berkshire, which has disappeared, except for a few remains of the transept at the end of Forbury Gardens. The monastery was founded in 1121, and its church, which Becket consecrated in 1164, is where the king was buried. Cluniac monks came from Lewes to guard his tomb in front of the high altar.

One can get an idea of this church by looking at Leominster Priory in Hereford & Worcester (figure, bottom left). It was a daughterhouse of Reading, and was an austere aisled building with a transept, crossing tower and radiating chapels, built after Henry I gave the Anglo-Saxon foundation to the mortuary church he had had built in Berkshire. Only the

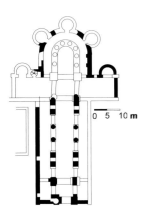

Leominster Priory (Hereford & Worcester), ground plan

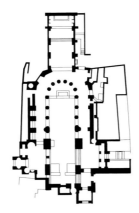

London, former abbey church of St. Bartholomew. Ground plan of the choir and transept

nave, which had a lavish stepped portal, and the northern side aisles survived its dissolution in 1539.

The priory church of St. Bartholomew-the-Great in London (figure, p. 243, bottom right), which was built in 1123 by Rahere, a favorite of Henry's, also had an ambulatory and radiating chapels. Rahere had started a pilgrimage to Rome, and when he became ill vowed to found a hospital. He was the first prior and died in 1143; it is unlikely that he lived long enough to see the completion of the church, which was looked after by the Augustinian Black Canons. The aisled choir, with its sturdy round pillars, gallery and clerestory, is impressive.

From the outside, Wimborne Minster in Dorset looks completely Gothic; but inside are significant remains dating from the decades after 1120. The nave is reduced to two storeys, and the round pillars are covered with Late Romanesque chevrons. The Church of St. Kyneburgha in Castor, Cambridgeshire (photo, above) is dominated by a magnificent crossing tower, the only remaining Romanesque section of the building; its crossing pillars are decorated by some low relief capitals.

Patrixbourne (Kent), Romanesque
church. Last third of the twelfth century.

The English late Romanesque period

The English late Romanesque period runs roughly concurrently with the reigns of three kings, Stephen (1135–54, Stephen I of Blois), Henry II (1154–89) and Richard I (1189–99, Richard the Lion-Heart), though the Gothic style arrived in England during the reign of Henry II with the building of the Temple Church in London around 1160. No large scale buildings were erected during the late Romanesque. The period was spent adding decorative features to the large churches that had already been started (such as the western end of Ely) and in building a few small treasures.

Amongst the more impressive are the parish church of Kilpeck in Hereford & Worcester, which is a hall with a square choir and apse and a lavishly decorated south portal dating back to around 1150 (photo, p. 323); the former Augustinian priory church (Christ Church) in Oxford with its self-consciously decorated arcades; the nave and aisles of Worksop Priory in Nottinghamshire, which has an alternating system of supports consisting of round and polygonal pillars; the lavishly figured south portal of the nave of Malmesbury Abbey in Wiltshire; the structure of the walls (dating to 1160/80) of the rectangular chapterhouse of Much Wenlock in Shropshire; the chapterhouse of Bristol Cathedral; and the Lady Chapel of Glastonbury Abbey in Somerset which has interlaced blind arcades which also appear, around 1200, in the church of St. Cross Hospital on the outskirts of Winchester. Prime examples of this late Romanesque delight in ornamentation are the portals of the small churches in Iffley, Oxfordshire (photo, p. 245, top left), Barfreston, Kent (photo, p. 245, right), and Patrixbourne, Kent (photos, pp. 244 and 245, bottom left), dating from the last third of the twelfth century.

Cistercian abbeys

While England's cathedrals and Benedictine monastery churches followed the pattern of churches in Normandy, from 1120 the Cistercians introduced the influences of a different French cultural landscape to Britain. By 1160, the reformed order already had fifty-one abbeys in Britain. While the majority of the churches have been destroyed, in most places it is possible to recognize that the churches and monasteries (photos, pp. 246–7) were modeling themselves on Burgundian Romanesque buildings. During the period of St. Bernard of Clairvaux (d. 1153), five model monasteries were built which formed an ideal (Fontenay, see photos, pp. 134–5) that most of the Cistercian buildings in Britain attempted to emulate. Their churches had either three (Waverley in Surrey, founded in 1128), five (Tintern Abbey in Gwent, founded in 1131, or Roche Abbey in Yorkshire, founded in 1147), or seven (Rievaulx Abbey in Yorkshire, founded in 1132, or Fountains Abbey in Yorkshire, founded in 1135) rectangular apses, transepts and an aisled nave. They had no towers, very little ornamentation, were discreetly articulated, but – as far as we can tell – were, in contrast to their French models, rarely vaulted in stone. The sober peace of these ascetic buildings can no longer be properly experienced in Britain, as all these churches have survived only as picturesque ruins. In Tintern and Fountains, Kirkstall in Yorkshire and Buildwas in Shropshire,

Iffley (Oxfordshire), west façade of the
Romanesque church. Last third of the
twelfth century (top)

Patrixbourne (Kent), Romanesque
church. Detail of an archivolt (bottom)

Barfreston (Kent), Romanesque church.
Last third of the twelfth century. Exterior
view (top) and detail of the portal
(bottom)

245

Fountains Abbey (Yorkshire), former
Cistercian monastery. Founded in 1135.
Exterior and interior views of the ruins of
the monastery church.

OPPOSITE
Rievaulx Abbey (Yorkshire), former Cistercian
monastery. Founded in 1132. Exterior views of the
remains of the walls and the monastery church

Byland Abbey, ground plan

Cashel (Ireland), Cormac's Chapel.
1127–34, tower façade

the hallmarks of the Burgundian Cistercian style are the ground plans, the shapes of the pillars, the pointed arch arcades, and the cleanly cut stone. France was also the inspiration for the pointed vaults in the side aisles and choirs, though the pointed vaulting which is typically found in the windowless naves of continental Cistercian buildings does not seem to have found favour. The naves appear to have had wooden roofs, though Kirkstall and Buildwas had early rib-vaulted choirs.

Those Cistercian buildings that were started in the late twelfth century – Byland in Yorkshire, Roche in Yorkshire, Furness in Lancashire and Jervaulx in Yorkshire – show that the strict architectural rules of the first half of the century were being relaxed in Britain. Byland Abbey (figure, p. 248, top left) had a transept with aisles, and an ambulatory, and Roche Abbey was showing signs of the Gothic style from the region around Laon as early as the 1170s.

While rural parish churches kept to Romanesque models until around 1200, the rebuilding of the choir of Canterbury Cathedral following a fire in 1174 led to the first large-scale building to follow continental early Gothic models, such as the cathedral in Sens, in all its details.

Sacred buildings in Wales, Ireland and Scotland

In comparison to the impressive sequence of sacred buildings in England, the churches of Wales, Ireland and Scotland play a rather more modest role. Not enough buildings have survived in any of these countries for one to be able to reconstruct a clear development in style. Norman influences

are visible everywhere: such as the dreary nave and side aisles of the Welsh cathedral of St. David's (1190–98), which is nestled in a hollow.

Worth mentioning in Ireland, which was part of the Norman kingdom from around 1170, are the barrel-vaulted hall of Cormac's Chapel (1127–34) on the Rock of Cashel (photo, top right); the ruins of the Cistercian abbeys of Mellifont (only the foundation walls remain of the church which was consecrated in 1157) and Jerpoint, which dates from the second half of the twelfth century; the slender, 93-foot round tower of Ardmore; and the cathedral of Clonfert, whose portal is studded with numerous heads. The continued existence of the small stone churches belonging to the early Irish monks is demonstrated by St. Kevin's church in Glendalough, which is a tiny stone building with a steep roof and round tower.

The most important Romanesque churches in Scotland date back to the reign of King David I (1124–1153). The Benedictine abbey of Dunfermline in Fife, founded around 1070, was the burial place of eleven kings and queens. The arcades of the three-storey nave and side aisles of the church (illustration, p. 249, bottom), which was consecrated in 1150, clearly copy Durham, and its exterior reminds one of models such as York (built by Bayeux). Equally late Romanesque (1180–1200) in style is the mighty ruined tower at the western end of Kelso Abbey in the Borders, which was founded in 1126. In the countryside nearby, the monks of the reformed orders built the "Border Abbeys," magnificent ruins from the twelfth century, which were a source of inspiration to Romantic painters. The Cistercians founded Melrose in 1136, the Augustinians founded Jedburgh

Jedburgh Abbey (Scotland), former
Augustinian monastery church.
Monastery founded in 1138

in 1138 (photo, top) and the Premonstratensians founded Dryburgh in 1140; the Cistercians' abbey served as a model for the other orders' buildings. The ground plans of the churches and their individuality show that there can hardly have been a "Scoto-Norman" style. That is also shown by the few remaining Romanesque sections of the cathedral of St. Andrews, which was started in 1160/70; its choir, in an ambitious project for the far north, was vaulted in stone.

Secular buildings

Military conquerors such as the Normans had to pay more attention to the building of fortifications (castles, city walls) to protect their rule of the cities and countryside than to building castles to God. They covered Britain, in particular its southern coastline and cities, with monuments to their military aristocracy. These are intimidating demonstrations of the sovereign's power, and the elemental force of their appearance served to perpetuate the system of rule that had been imposed on the country. It is possible to interpret the sacred buildings as the expression of the unity of "regnum" and "sacerdotium" that the conquerors dictated, in which case the defensive buildings are clearly the architecture of power. Alternatively, if one considers the Romanesque churches to be representations of the social and religious world order, as a transcendence of the real feudal world, in which conquest by the sacred and worldly power of the invaders is viewed as something worthwhile, then the fortifications, which were often built and governed by bishops, are the safeguards of rulers in a foreign land, and positions from which it was possible to exercise economic, political and cultural control over the natives. Ordericus Vitalis (1075– c. 1142), who was a Norman historian from St. Evroul, recognized that it was the castles his countrymen built that enabled them to settle permanently in England. "The Norman fortifications called castles," he wrote, "were unknown in the English provinces, and that is why the English – despite their courage and pugnacity – were able to put up little resistance to their enemies." And the Anglo-Saxon Chronicle of 1137 complained: "They were burdening the unfortunate country folk with forced labour at their castles. Once they had finished building them, they filled them with devils and bad men."

The earliest fortifications which the conquerors built in England were the so-called "earth-and-timber" castles. Excavations have shown there to be two main types, dating mainly from the late eleventh and twelfth centuries, "motte-and-bailey" castles and "ringworks." There were far more mottes (as the first variety was named, after its most important feature, an earthen hill) in England and Wales (about 750) than ringworks (about 190), but it is not clear what influenced this. Ringworks could certainly be built much more quickly and cheaply, but motte-and-baileys could be defended with far fewer people. Motte-and-baileys consisted of four sections: a usually artificial mound, about 16 to 35 feet high, a wooden tower on top of the mound, a ditch and walls, and one or more outer courts (baileys), which were protected by earth walls and palisades and which contained the living quarters and stables. Contemporary pictures of such mottes are on the Bayeux Tapestry (photo, p. 218): it not only shows

Dunfermline Abbey (Scotland), former Benedictine monastery church, reconstruction of exterior. Monastery founded in 1070

London, White Tower. From around 1078. Exterior view

LEFT TO RIGHT

Goltho (Lincolnshire), castle layout

Abinger (Surrey), motte and tower

Ashley (Hampshire), circumvallation

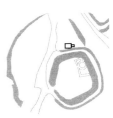

As in France (see pp. 174ff.), stone buildings were used as well as wooden towers. While stone donjons (residential fortified towers) first appear in France in about 950 (Doué-la-Fontaine, Maine-et-Loire, Langeais, Indre-et-Loire), they were not built in Britain until William fitz Osbern constructed a great rectangular keep in Chepstow, Gwent, in 1067/70.

There is, as in France, a large series of remaining examples which enables us to trace the development from square or rectangular keeps such as those in Canterbury (figures, p. 251, bottom right), Carlisle and Hedingham, Essex, via round keeps such as Conisborough in Yorkshire (photo, p. 251) and polygonal ones such as Athlone in Westmeath, to the tall towers with many rooms of the late Middle Ages, such as Tattershall Castle in Lincolnshire. Well-preserved examples include the White Tower (photo, p. 250, left), which William instructed the Bishop of Rochester to build by the River Thames from around 1078 as a fortress, palace and place of government. The same talented bishop, Gundulf, is thought to have built Colchester Castle in Essex. The exterior decoration of the towers, with niches, series of blind arches, arch friezes and portals, copied that of the churches – compare Castle Rising in Norfolk. The same architects were probably responsible for both groups of buildings.

We know of numerous Romanesque residences from royal itineraries and descriptions (Inver Forest in Staffordshire), but very little actually remains. A royal hunting lodge was excavated in Writtle, Essex. The country seat of Castle Acre, in Norfolk, met with an unusual fate. A lightly fortified two-family house dating from the late eleventh century was turned into a keep several storeys high around 1140/50. The oldest remains of an aisled rectangular hall, which served as the starting point of the lord's residence, are preserved in the Norman castle in Leicester. The wood frame construction dating from the middle of the twelfth century is surrounded by stone enclosure walls.

There are hardly any Romanesque town residences still in existence. Two examples are Moyse's Hall in Bury St. Edmunds, Suffolk, and the bishop's palace at Ashby de la Zouch in Leicestershire.

Romanesque secular architecture ended in about 1200. As on the Continent, foreign influences (such as buildings in the Orient), new architectural techniques (rib vaulting), new methods of attacking and defending buildings (projecting towers and arrow-slits to enable archers to shoot along the sides of a fortress) and increasing demands (for prestige and comfort) altered the face and interior of these buildings.

the raising of the motte at Hastings, but also views of mottes at Dol, Dinan and Rennes in Brittany and Bayeux in Normandy. Well researched examples are Gotho in Lincolnshire (illustration, p. 250, top right) and Hen Domen in Montgomeryshire, which was probably built by Roger of Montgomery from 1071. The wooden structures on the mottes varied considerably. Some were simple lookout towers, such as Abinger in Surrey (illustration, p. 250, top right), while others were fortified residential towers with more than one storey, such as Rhuddlan in Clwyd.

The ringworks also varied in size and shape. Most of them were circular. They consisted of ditches and walls which were fortified with wooden palisades; within were various buildings. Ringworks were not invented by the Normans, for Ireland has numerous examples dating back to the sixth century. An illustration of Ashley in Hampshire (p. 250 top right) should be sufficient.

In numerous cases, the Normans placed their strongholds within older fortifications: sometimes in Roman forts (Portchester in Hampshire, figure, p. 251 top right), or in Anglo-Saxon villages such as Pleshey, Essex. In the towns and cities (York, Norwich, Lincoln etc.) whole quarters were destroyed to make way for their fortresses.

Conisborough, circular donjon, fortified
with towers. 12th century

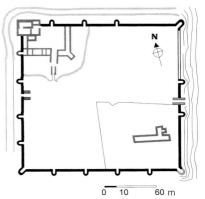

Portchester Castle, ground plan

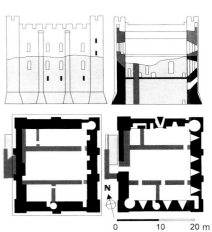

Canterbury Castle.
Exterior elevations (top),
ground plan of first floor (bottom left),
ground plan of second floor (bottom
right)

251

Trondheim Cathedral. Three-section structure of the walls of the north transept arm

The Romanesque period in Scandinavia

The history of architecture in Europe cannot simply be described in terms of the architectural heritage of western Europe. For this reason, at least the main representatives of the northern and central European Romanesque style should be dealt with. Unfortunately, it is not possible within the confines of this volume to deal with the Orthodox buildings of eastern Europe (Serbia, Macedonia, Bulgaria, Romania, the Ukraine and Russia west of the Urals).

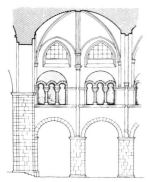

Ribe Cathedral. Elevation of the nave wall

Denmark

In Denmark, the Romanesque period did not begin until after the Viking Age (800–1060) towards the end of the eleventh century. Until then wood had been the only building material, but at that point stone and brick came into use. During the reign of Valdemar the Great, the cathedrals of Ribe (figure, p. 252, top left, built between 1150/70 and 1225, an aisled galleried basilica with towers at the west end, Early Gothic rib vaulting around 1250) and Viborg (built as a sister church of Lund in Sweden and finished around 1150, only the aisled crypt survived the Neo-Gothic renovations of 1864/74) in Jutland were built, very much under the influence of Lower Rhine churches. The Romanesque sections of the cathedral of Århus in Jutland (c. 1200-1250), which was rebuilt after 1400 in the Gothic style, are remarkable, as is the Benedictine church of Ringsted in Zealand (basilica built of brick from 1160), modeled on churches in Lombardy, the Cistercian church of Sorø in Zealand (basilica with transept, after 1161), and the five-towered central plan castle church at Kalundborg in Zealand (figure, p. 252, bottom left, 1170/90).

The well-known round churches with several storeys also date from the second half of the twelfth century; they were both places of worship and defensive buildings. Four of the seven that remain are on the island of Bornholm (Nyker, Olsker, Nylarsker and Østerlarsker).

The Gothic period started late in the North: from about 1200, the brick cathedral of Roskilde in Zealand (figure, p. 252, bottom left), which Bishop Absalon had started c. 1170, and which was to be the mortuary chapel of several kings, was replanned in the forms of northern France's early Gothic style. It was a church with galleries, replacing its predecessor, which has been excavated and was built between 1040 and 1084 as Denmark's first stone church.

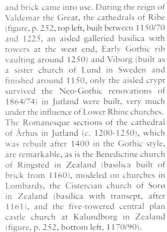

Kalundborg, Vor Frue Kirke. Ground plan

Roskilde Cathedral, Denmark. Elevation, 1175– c. 1240

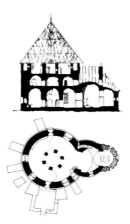

Østerlarsker, Øster Lars Kirke. Cross-section and ground plan

Norway

While the Christianization of Denmark and Sweden had been completed from northern Germany in the ninth and tenth centuries, that of Norway did not start until the late tenth century. It was not finished until 1030 with the fall of Olaf II in the battle at Stiklestad, who also reunited the country after a short period of division.

The two most important cathedrals in Norway owe much to Danish and German Romanesque architecture. Stavanger was started c. 1130 by an English bishop, which is why the aisled nave has typically English round pillars, as does the ruined cathedral church of Hamar. The flattened choir of the Nidaros Cathedral in Trondheim (photo, p. 252, top right), which was started in the eleventh century and is the longest church in Scandinavia (347 feet), is connected to an octagon containing the grave of St. Olaf (d. 1030); it is reminiscent of the Church of the Holy Sepulchre in Jerusalem and the Capella of Charlemagne at Aachen. All that remains of St. Mary's Church in the community of Bergen, formerly a Franciscan church, is the late twelfth-century façade with its two towers. Two additional churches worthy of mention from among the numerous small stone churches built shortly after 1100 are the Gamle Akers in Oslo, Tingelstad and the Hove Church in Vik in Sogn.

The most splendid contribution that Norway made to Scandinavian art in the Romanesque period are the 28 (of originally 1000) preserved stave churches built in the eleventh and twelfth centuries. Stave churches are a form of wooden church found only in northern Europe; they were built using upright planks fitted between rounded corner posts which reached up to the roof truss of the main area. The exterior is frequently surrounded by an arcaded walk, and has several levels of double-sloped roofs. The most magnificent examples are the Urnes (figure, p. 252, bottom right, c. 1130), Lom with its pointed tower (twelfth century, enlarged 1630), and especially Borgund (photo, p. 253, left, c. 1150) with its elaborate carvings on the portals and gables of dragons and other legendary motifs, as well as runic inscription and six levels of double-sloped roof.

The most beautiful medieval secular building in Scandinavia is King Håkonís Hall in Bergen, which was completed in 1261 using Gothic forms.

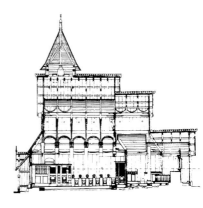

Urnes, stave church

Sweden

The only remaining stave church is Sweden is the rather plain church in Hedared in Västergötland, dating from around 1500. A rubble church was built in Sigtuna, Uppland, which was the seat of a bishop at a royal court from around 1100. It is not certain whether the cruciform ruin of St. Per was in fact the bishop's church.

The church of Husaby in Västergötland was larger, and also situated at a royal court; it has been called the "cradle of Swedish architecture," because in the early twelfth century a stave church dating from around 1020 was replaced with a stone church. Another large church was the cathedral in Skara, Västergötland, which was replanned on several occasions; its crypt dates back to the eleventh century. If the church in Gamla Uppsala, of which the choir and crossing remain, really dates from c. 1130, it would be the oldest bishop's church in the country.

In 1145 – in what was Denmark at the time – the east sections of the cathedral of Lund in Malmöhus were consecrated. The building is a basilica with an alternating system of supports, projecting transept, choir and façade with twin towers, and was begun c. 1110 by King Niels (1104–34) and Asser, the first archbishop (d. 1134). It is the most important Nordic successor to the imperial cathedral of Speyer. The powerful relief of the outside of the apse and the many columns of the hall-like crypt underneath the altar and transept are magnificent. Despite the largely renovated vault, the overall effect of the nave and aisles is one of most agreeable harmony.

A variety of influences can be detected on Swedish architecture at the end of the twelfth century. The Cistercians introduced Burgundian monastery layouts to Alvastra in Östergötland (founded in 1143 by Clairvaux, ruins of the church consecrated in 1185 remain), to Nydala in Småland (also founded in 1143 and in ruins), to Varnhem in Västergötland (founded in 1150 as a daughter-house of Alvastra, rebuilt after a fire in 1234 as a rib vaulted basilica with nave walls resting on pillars) and to Roma in Gotland (daughter-house of Nydala founded in 1164, now in ruins). The mendicant orders imported brick from northern Germany, a material that was first used in the groin vaulted hall of Gumlösa in Malmöhus, which was consecrated in 1191/92.

Finland

South-west Finland was not converted until about 1150. In 1156 Henrik, the Bishop of Uppsala, was killed while undertaking missionary work, and was buried in the predecessor of the present church in Nousiainen. Finland probably did not receive a missionary bishopric until the early thirteenth century, and the first normal bishopric, with a see in Turku, dates back to 1276. None of its secular and sacred wooden Romanesque buildings has survived. Most of its stone buildings (there are about 125 medieval stone churches) are built of rubble, meaning that they have very little ornamentation and are therefore difficult to date. The predecessor to the cathedral in Turku was a Romanesque wooden church dating from the first half of the thirteenth century. The churches of Åland have a rather Romanesque appearance; examples include the rough stone hall in Hammarland, dating from the late fourteenth century, and the stone sacristy in Finström (second half of the thirteenth century), which was part of a wooden church.

Borgund, stave church

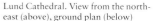

Lund Cathedral. View from the north-east (above), ground plan (below)

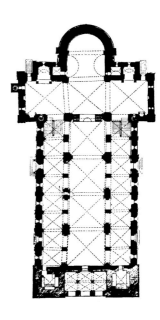

253

The Romanesque period in Central Europe

The Romanesque period produced several important buildings in central Europe. There are, however, so few in each country (Hungary, Bohemia, Poland), and the buildings were the result of such diverse influences, that it is scarcely possible to reconstruct any independent development in these countries. There are also no unmistakable characteristics that might lead one to classify buildings as Hungarian, Bohemian or Polish Romanesque.

Hungary

The Árpád Duke Géza (972–997) attempted an amalgamation of the Magyar tribes into a sovereign state; his son Stephen I (998–1038) was to succeed where the father had failed. He was crowned in 1001, organized his country into administrative counties and created two archbishoprics (Esztergom/Gran and Kalocsa). The Benedictine order was brought to Pannonhalma from Bohemia. The Roman Catholic Church replaced the Greek Orthodox Church that had prevailed until that time. Stephen formed connections with his neighbors, in particular those in the west, which to some degree explains the strong influence of Bavarian and German architecture on Hungary's early Romanesque style. Not until the second half of the twelfth century did Italian and French influences predominate.

The Hungarian early Romanesque architectural style expressed itself in numerous forms. The round churches of Esztergom and Veszprém (St. George's Chapel) have been excavated and probably date back to the late tenth or early eleventh centuries. Those early bishop's and collegiate churches that have been excavated were hall churches without transepts or – usually – basilicas with three apses, such as the cathedral in Székesfehérvár which was built for coronations and royal funerals; its ruins are behind the bishop's palace, and the

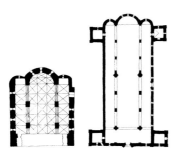

Pécs Cathedral and lower church (left), ground plan

Zsámbék, former monastery church

church was founded between 1018 and 1038 by King Stephen. Other similar churches are the cathedral in Kalocsa (rebuilt between 1735 and 1754 with a large apse and west tower instead of a hall), Gyulafehérvar (Roman Alba Julia, briefly part of Romania, but restored to Hungary towards the end of the twelfth century), the Benedictine monastery church in Tihany (founded in 1055, church consecrated in 1060 and replaced, all but the hall crypt, between 1740 and 1754) and Szekszárd (where King Béla I was buried, 1060–64). The parish church of Feldebrö, dating from the first half of the eleventh century, is reminiscent of Byzantine architecture; only the crypt remains. It was a Greek cross form church with a dome over the central section. In Pecs, the old church burnt down in 1064; its replacement was a three-aisled lower church and above it, the oldest existing example of a three-aisled basilica without a vault or transept, but with three apses and towers (figures, p. 254, bottom left), a type of building that was widespread in the twelfth century – others include the cathedral of Eger, which was renovated from 1831, and the church in Boldova, which has two east towers.

A pair of towers and a gallery for the rulers at the west end has, since the second half of the twelfth century, been the hallmark of monastery churches built by noblemen for their own use; examples include Akos (Acîs in Romania) and Kapornak.

The royal palace at Esztergom (c. 1200), in particular its east wing and chapel, is the high point of late Romanesque architecture as supported by the court, clergy and aristocracy.

The Cistercians' original buildings in Zirc (founded 1182), Pilis (founded 1184) and Szentgotthárd (founded 1183, rebuilt 1748-64) have disappeared almost without trace. They influenced the monastery church, consecrated in 1224, of the Benedictine

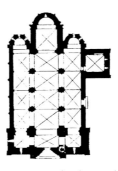

Ják, former monastery church, ground plan

abbey of Pannonhalma, which was established in 996.

The Benedictine monastery church of Lébény was attached to the Györ family, built at the beginning of the twelfth century and frequently rebuilt; the Benedictine church at Ják (figure, p. 254, top right) was founded around 1210 by Márton Nagy of Ják; and Zsámbék (figure, p. 254, top left), a Premonstratensian church, was built by the Ainard family from 1220 ff.: all of these were three-aisled vaulted hewn-stone buildings with twin tower façades and lavish external ornamentation. In the time before the devastating Mongol invasions of 1241/42, further important late Romanesque churches were built, such as the Premonstratensian church in Óska (first documented in 1234, influenced by Burgundian early Gothic), the second cathedral in Gyulafehérvár/Alba Julia (started at the end of the twelfth century, best preserved Romanesque cathedral) and the Benedictine church of Vertésszentkereszt (c. 1200–1231, in ruins).

Poland

Poland became Christian with the baptism of Duke Mieszko I in 966. While early buildings (such as the cathedrals in Kraków, Gniezno, Poznán) date back to the Ottoman period, Romanesque architecture that was strongly influenced by Germany began with the founding of the archbishopric of Gniezno in 1000. From then on, until the Cistercians started spreading the Gothic style c. 1250, numerous cathedrals, monastery and collegiate churches were built, as well as castle churches such as that at Inow (hall with western round tower, late eleventh century). Sections remain of some secular buildings, such as the Piast castle in Bolków. None of Poland's cathedrals has retained its original Romanesque form. The Cathedral of St. Wenzel and St. Stanislaus, on the Wawel in Kraków, is the Gothic replace-

ment for the Romanesque church of St. Gereon (1018–1142). All that remains of the latter (a double-ended basilica with nave walls resting on pillars and two towers at the west end of the nave) is the western crypt. From 1342, Gniezno Cathedral was rebuilt in the Gothic style, but its important bronze doors, dating from the second half of the twelfth century, are from the older Romanesque cathedral.

Between 970 and 977, Mieszko I built the original church at Posnán on a heathen ceremonial site. In 999, the year he was canonized, the relics of St. Wojciech (Adalbert of Prague) were moved there. Mieszko I chose Posnán as the first Polish bishopric and center of the Piast dynasty's rule. The remains of the pre-Romanesque and Romanesque bishop's churches (figure, p. 254,

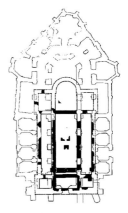

Poznán Cathedral, ground plan

right) still exist underneath the Gothic cathedral of Peter and Paul.

While all that remain of the monastery churches in Wrocław (the Augustinian monastery "Our Lady of the Sand," and the Benedictine or Premonstratensian monasteries) are the tympana dating from the twelfth century, there are presentable monasteries in various other places, even though they are somewhat antiquated when compared to other works from the same period. The church of St. Andrew is the most beautiful sacred building in Kraków (figure, p. 255, bottom left). The complex, which in the eleventh century was first used both as the sovereign's and as a parish church, was made a monastery church later. Its original hall was renovated in 1200, as a short basilica with a choir at the east end; the side apses have been excavated. The smooth façade is flanked by two polygonal towers. The Premonstratensian church in

Strzelno, famed for its columns with figures, was probably begun around 1175 and completed by 1220/33. It is a three-aisle basilica with a transept and has an unvaulted columned nave and aisles and – equally unusual in Poland – an aisled choir. In the third quarter of the twelfth century, a simple basilica with two towers at the front was added to the Augustinian abbey of Czerwinsk, founded between 1148 and 1155; the basilica's most remarkable section is a stepped portal decorated with reliefs. In Trzesmeszno, the Augustinians took over an old Benedictine abbey at the beginning of the twelfth century. Their basilica was built between 1130 and 1146 and had a transept and façade with twin towers; in the eighteenth century, it was replaced by a late Baroque church.

Poland's Romanesque collegiate churches were also unvaulted. In Kruszwica is a basilica with nave walls resting on pillars and dedicated to Peter and Paul; it has a flat roof, transept and three apses (1120/40), and was restored to its former glory after the Second World War. The Church of St. Martin in Opatów dates from the middle of the twelfth century, and is also a basilica with nave walls resting on pillars and a flat roof. And it also has a transept and three apses, and a façade with twin towers. The exterior, built of large hewn stone, is decorated with lesenes and round arches. The parish church of Thum, dedicated to Mary and Alexius and restored after sections were destroyed, is the most elaborate building in this group (photo, p. 255, bottom): it is a double-ended church with galleries over the side aisles. The nave

has a wooden roof; at its east end it adjoins a barrel-vaulted choir with side apses, and at the west end is an apse flanked by towers. Rib vaulting was introduced to Poland by the Cistercians in the first half of the thirteenth century; it can be seen in the churches of the monasteries of Sulejów (founded in 1176, church consecrated in 1232), Wachok (founded in 1179), and Koprzywnica (founded in 1185, church begun in 1207).

Bohemia

Numerous wooden buildings have been excavated in the region that used to be called Czechoslovakia. But none of these seems to date back to the country's early history, such as the rise to power of the Premysl dynasty towards the end of the ninth century. In 921 Václav I became Duke of Bohemia. He increased the pace of Christianization, until he was murdered by his brother Boleslav I in 929. In 973, the Saxon Benedictine Thietmar was made the first bishop of Prague.

The oldest Christian stone churches in Bohemia (dating from the middle and second half of the ninth century) were excavated in and near Prague (Hradschin, rotunda of Hradcany Castle) and in Southern Moravia (Mikulcice). Foundations are all that remain, even of the oldest large-scale buildings in Bohemia. Underneath the Gothic Cathedral of St. Vitus, on a hill next to the castle, is the Rotunda of St. Vitus (926–930, two-storey round building with four apses) and the Basilica of St. Vitus (c. 1060, double-ended building with a chancel with three apses and two crypts).

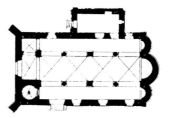

Tismice, Church of St. Mary, ground plan

The political dependence of the Dukes of Bohemia on the Holy Roman Empire continued after 1068 (when Duke Vratislav was made king by Emperor Henry IV). Correspondingly, there is also a large degree of architectural dependence on German models.

The large buildings can be divided into two groups. Basilicas with three apses but no transept, of a type found in Lombardy or southern Germany, were built in Stará Boleslav (Basilica of St. Wenzel, consecrated 1046), Tismice (Church of St. Mary, the best-preserved basilica in Bohemia, built at the end of the twelfth century, figure, p. 255, top), Prague-Strahov (Premonstratensian monastery founded in 1148) and in Diakovce (Benedictine abbey church, consecrated in 1228). Basilicas with transepts – usually in accordance with the system of architectural proportions based on the crossing square as a module, and with an apse and twin towers at the front – were built in various places including Kladruby (Benedictine church, completed in 1233) and Doksany (Premonstratensian monastery founded in 1144).

There are three distinct types of small churches in Bohemia: the chancel square church, which is founded throughout north-west Europe (Mikulcice, Kyje near Prague); the apse hall with a gallery for the nobility (Stará Boleslav, St. Clement, after the middle of the twelfth century; Jakub, consecrated in 1165; Mohelnice, Church of St. Mary, end of the twelfth century; Dazovice, St. Michael, c. 1200); and the – rare – chancel tower church such as that in Topanov. Besides galleried hall churches, another type of church built for the nobility that is particularly noteworthy is the palatine chapel type, found in Cheb (palatine chapel, after 1167) and Zábori on the River Elbe (middle of the twelfth century). "Bohemian rotundas," small round churches with an apse, were particularly widespread: there are examples in Rip (after 1039, completed 1126), Znojmo (before the middle of the eleventh century), Prague-Wischerad, Church of St.

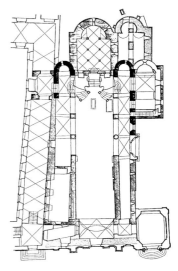

Prague, St. George's, ground plan

Martin (twelfth century) and Holubice (1224/25).

The most important remaining large-scale buildings are characteristic of the diversity of forms used in Bohemia. St. George's in Prague (974/976, figure p. 255, top right) is a Saxon galleried basilica with an alternating system of supports, restored after 1142. The Premonstratensian monastery church in Milevsko (founded 1184/87) is a basilica whose nave walls are supported only by columns. In Teplá, one of the oldest hall churches outside Bavaria was consecrated in 1232. In Trebic, a Benedictine church was built in 1225/50 with domical vaults in the choir similar to those found in Anjou.

The Cistercians, who were brought to Bohemia by King Vladislav II (1140–72), introduced the Gothic style to the country. They first settled in Sedlec in 1142/43, and those buildings were renovated in the Gothic style. The church still stands at Plasy, founded in 1144/45; it was originally an unvaulted basilica with nave walls resting on pillars and a transept. While the monastery church of Velehrad (founded in 1205, church built 1218/38) and the monastery of Ossegg (founded in 1191) are still largely late Romanesque in style, Oslavany (after 1228) and Tisnow (founded 1232/33) show that the rib-vaulted Gothic style was finally gaining acceptance.

Kraków, St. Andrew's Church, ground plan and elevation

Thum, collegiate church

Uwe Geese

Romanesque sculpture

Introduction

Isolated new beginnings in large-scale sculpture appeared during the tenth century, but it was not until the construction activity that began suddenly in many regions around the year 1000 that sculpture became more wide-spread; Romanesque sculpture, with very few exceptions, is firmly tied to architecture. And this first spreading of a style, through Roman and Christian Europe, that was uniform in terms of form and content is the reason why, for the first time since the Classical age, art historians feel justified in talking of an era.

Given that sculpture depended so strongly on architecture, it mainly appeared in the form of a relief, and this was a decisive difference from the free-standing and anatomically correct sculpture of antiquity. Though they are traditionally considered to be part of sculpture, reliefs occupy a middle position between painting, which is flat and tied to a surface, and spatial, corporeal sculpture. It is special due to the synthesis of haptic and optical values, which the eye perceives as being genuinely three-dimensional. Depending on the distance between the background and the protruding figure, reliefs are classified as either low relief (also called bas relief), middle relief or high relief. All these forms appear in Romanesque art in various contexts. While low relief is normally a feature of the pre- and early-Romanesque periods and was used later for decorative work, the narrative scenes in tympanums and capitals were normally carried out in middle or high relief.

The earliest sites of Romanesque sculpture are usually simple architectural elements, such as the corbels in Frómista in Spain (photo, opposite) and the surfaces, similar to metopes, between them, or the door lintel in Roussillon (photo, p. 258). While corbels bore secular motifs in the widest sense, door lintels were more suited to a row of figures such as that at the Last Supper. Soon, tympanums started to appear vaulted above door lintels; they were initially no more than the one in Arles-sur-Tech, which was an arch filled with sandstone (photo, opposite) containing a cruciform representation of Christ in Majesty. During the following period, the tympanum became the central and most prominent site for Romanesque sculpture.

The capital was the upper part of a column and supported the vault. The column's symbolic content derives from its origins in the shape of trees. And just as trees have roots and a crown reaching for the skies, columns have bases and capitals. This correlation has never quite disappeared in the sacred sphere. In addition, the column and vault bore the symbolical form of the cosmos, where God lived. And between them, an architectural intermediary between the support and burden, was the capital: at the bottom it was still earthly, but above it faced the heavens. This is the context within which the contents of Romanesque sculpture on capitals developed.

Romanesque sculpture was strictly hierarchical, where its form and content are concerned; it followed strictly laid down, decidedly ceremonial and frequently rigid forms that had developed out of religious traditions. As a result, the folds in clothing and position of bodies, as well as the depictions of hands, feet and faces, had certain generalized features that

TOP
Frómista (Province of Palenzia), San
Martín. Pediment with console figure.
Last third of the eleventh century

CENTRE
Arles-sur-Tech (Western Pyrenees), abbey
church of Sainte-Marie-de-Vallespir.
Tympanum. After 1046

BOTTOM
Chauvigny (Vienne), former collegiate
church of Saint-Pierre. Capital in the
ambulatory: Adoration of the Magi,
signed. Second half of the twelfth century

can be recognized as hallmarks of Romanesque sculpture on a national
and even international basis. In addition, Romanesque art had countless
symbolic contents which are frequently no longer accessible in our modern
world (cf. pp. 328). These do not just include the wide-spread representations of animals and hybrid creatures; the symbolical importance of
numbers and gemstones was equally varied.

But who were the sculptors who worked on all these things? There is a
widely accepted prejudice about Romanesque art, which states that artists
remained anonymous intentionally, as their works were dedicated to
the glory of God. While the majority of artists have indeed remained
unidentified, there are hundreds of artists' signatures, primarily in France,
Spain and Italy, which show that there can be no talk of a conscious
decision to remain anonymous. The name that appeared was usually that
of the master in charge of the workshop that had produced a tympanum,
or perhaps the capitals of part or all of a cloister.

Attempts have been made to explain the significance of these
signatures, and the thought that they could be requests for observers to
include the artists in their prayers suggests a lack of inspiration in coming
up with alternatives to the prevailing view that artists wanted to remain
anonymous. The reason for this anonymity is more likely to have been that
artists were at first held in little esteem as craftsmen. This theory is
supported by the conspicuous increase in artists' signatures in areas where
more political, economic and social progress had been made. In the sense
that the person commissioning a work, whether for secular or ecclesiastical reasons, wanted to express his pride in that work by engaging
an important master or a famous workshop. The detailed inscribed
acknowledgement of Master Wiligelmus of Modena appears to support
this. During the historical period that saw the first signs of the bourgeoisie
and urbanization, artists gained increasing self-awareness and pride about
their abilities and the quality of their work, and they wanted to express
this by using signatures. One should not, however, forget that names
which have "fecit" – "he made this" (photo, bottom right) added are frequently only naming the client, not the sculptor.

There are also groups of works which share stylistic characteristics that
suggested they belong together, but whose sculptors are unknown. Art
historians use invented names for them, which normally refer to the home
of one of the main works. So, for example, the "Master of Cabestany" is
named after Cabestany, a small suburb of Perpignan in southern France,
because that is where there is a tympanum whose stylistic features are
similar to many others throughout a large area.

Romanesque sculpture in France

Monumental sculpture was not the way Romanesque sculpture first
manifested itself in France. Rather, there are a series of set pieces which
probably were not even created in their original architectural context.
As an example, Bernhard Rupprecht considers the famous door lintel
of Saint-Genis-des-Fontaines (photo, p. 258, left) to be the work of a workshop in the Pyrenees which produced other sacred decorative pieces. And it
is indeed the case that this door lintel belongs to an entire group of related

St-Genis-des-Fontaines (Western Pyrenees), abbey church of Saint-Genis. Door lintel: Christ between angels and saints. Marble. 1019/20

Tournus (Saône-et-Loire), former abbey church of Saint-Philibert. Gerlanus arch in the upper storey of the western side: mask. Second quarter of the eleventh century

Tournus (Saône-et-Loire), former abbey church of Saint-Philibert. Gerlanus arch in the upper storey of the western side: man with a hammer. Second quarter of the eleventh century

works from the eastern Pyrenees, including the door lintel in Saint-André-de-Sorède, a neighboring town to Saint-Genis, and the tympanum cross as well as the window frame in Arles-sur-Tech, which are all related stylistically. The door lintel in Saint-Genis has an inscription which gives its date of origin as the twenty-fourth year of the reign of King Robert the Pious, which started in 996. This dates the lintel precisely to the year 1019–20, making it one of the oldest examples of Romanesque stone sculpture.

In the center Christ is enthroned in a mandorla, held by two angels. On either side are three apostles in arcades with horse-shoe arches. At this point the connection between the figures and the architecture is still very tight, and this is demonstrated by the silhouettes of the apostles, who are not shaped as normal figures but according to the form of the arcades. Despite the similarity of the figures, there are substantial differences in the bearing and movement of the figures in Saint-André.

All these reliefs and the framing decorations are worked in extremely flat chip-carving, and contemporary models for this would hardly have been found in antique sculpture. It is more likely that two-dimensional frescoes or small pieces of art such as ivory reliefs, illuminated manuscripts and goldsmith's art served as models, and Rupprecht quite rightly comments: "Format and mobility meant that this piece was less a precursor of monumental architectural sculpture, but rather an enlargement of workshop art."

During the same period the new abbey church of Saint-Philibert was built in Tournus in Burgundy, together with what its inscription called the Gerlanus arch (photo, right). Capitals, coarsely chip-carved with ornaments and plants, each support a thick slab with a sort of impost block. One of them bears a mask-like bearded man's head, while the other shows a man carrying a hammer. The latter is frequently considered to be Gerlanus the architect himself. While there is no way of verifying this interpretation, there is still something quite sensational about it, as it would be the first individualizing portrait of an artist in Western art history. But in contrast to Roussillon, these earliest examples of Burgundian Romanesque show that stone and its material consistency were problems that had not yet been overcome in the search for artistic expression, so that "the effort as well as the work and imagination, which the frequently indistinct wrestling with the block of stone caused," are quite visible.

Toulouse

The undisputed center of the Romanesque in south-western France was Toulouse, which had three great cloisters, all of which fell prey to the iconoclasm of the Revolution. Since 1792, the remnants have been looked after in the secularized Augustinian friary, now the Musée des Augustins. The collegiate church of Saint-Sernin still exists; after Cluny III, it was the largest sacred building of the French Romanesque period. The sculptures inside this church are a highly innovative ensemble in the artistic development around the turn of the eleventh and twelfth centuries, and at least three stylistically different workshops can be identified at work here. The famous table altar, which was probably consecrated on May 24, 1096 by Pope Urban II, not only for the first time shows the direct influence of the Classical period in Languedoc, but also makes use of the three-dimensional possibilities of the relief, by using light and shadow as new means for giving spatial structure to a work. The slab bears a quite long inscription, which ends with the artist's signature: BERNARDVS GELDVINVS ME FEC. ("Bernardus Gelduinus made me"). Other works by him, or from his workshop, include the seven reliefs dated around 1096 in the ambulatory, which did not all originally belong to that place. Even though the way the figures – Christ, angels and apostles – are formed does not seek to deny their origins in small sculptural pieces or goldsmith's art, their enlargement to half life-size nevertheless marks an important turn towards monumental sculpture.

TOP
Toulouse (Haute-Garonne), collegiate
church of Saint-Sernin. Porte Miègeville,
tympanum: Ascension of Christ, door
lintel: apostles. Before 1118

BOTTOM
Toulouse (Haute-Garonne), collegiate
church of Saint-Sernin. Capital on the
Porte des Comtes. *c.* 1100

Two portals on the south side of Saint-Sernin are further milestones in the development of Early Romanesque sculpture. Even if the quality of the capitals of the Porte des Comtes (photo, bottom), in the south transept and dating from around 1100, does not compare with that of the other workshops, it is still the first time that an iconographical program appears on a portal, a feature that was later to become a central theme of Romanesque sculpture in general. Even more important in the development of Romanesque portals is the Porte Miègeville, the entrance to the southern side aisle. Its name, which derives from *media villae*, center of the village, describes its central position within the town. It was probably completed before the consecration of the church in 1118, and together with the Spanish examples in Léon and Compostela is one of the first portals in which all the important elements in the structuring of a portal, such as the tympanum with a lintel and archivolts, columns with figured capitals set into the stonework, sculptured consoles and reliefs on the façade of the structure, separate from the rest of the church architecture, are gathered together in a united ensemble.

The tympanum of the Porte Miègeville (photo, top) is the earliest in Languedoc; its theme is the Ascension of Christ, who occupies the center of the scene. Two angels are carrying the standing Christ towards Heaven. His raised arms, and his slightly raised left leg, which subtly correspond to his raised head and the way he is looking upwards, form a motion which had never been seen before in this way, the upward movement of a stone figure. As if the sculptor had not dared trust his own genius, he placed the two angels on either side to assist the process. A string course with carved vine foliage separates the area within the arch from the architrave, thereby also separated the heavenly events from the earthly ones. Below are the apostles, their heads twisted upwards in order to see what is happening. On either side of the tympanum are two large upright reliefs, on the left St. James the Great, a reference to the Via Tolosana, one of the main pilgrimage routes to Santiago de Compostela. On the right is St. Peter, in connection with the Ascension; at his feet is a relief showing the fall of Simon the sorcerer.

Moissac

As young Adso in Umberto Eco's novel *The Name of the Rose* steps into the entrance of the church, he is dazzled by "the silent speech of the carved stone" and plunged into a vision. And his report is in a type of double past tense. He is writing as an old man, but at the same time he is writing of a vision the memory of which had been burnt directly into his religious spirit. Before his eyes he still saw the portal he had just walked beneath. The reason Eco's description of the portal at Moissac (photo, p. 261) is so extremely impressive is that it enables us to understand how it would have been experienced by monks at the time. And indeed, the tympanum at Moissac is a vision. Or more precisely, the vision of St. John as described in his Revelation.

Enthroned in the center is the crowned figure of Christ, majestic, unapproachable, transported beyond terrestrial humankind, on its own embodying the order of Heaven. He is surrounded by a tetramorph, the symbols of the four Evangelists, themselves flanked by two angels with

259

Moissac (Tarn-et-Garonne), former abbey church of Saint-Pierre. South portal, eastern side of the trumeau: the prophet Jeremiah, detail. 1120–1135

Moissac (Tarn-et-Garonne), former abbey church of Saint-Pierre. Western side of the south portal's narthex, detail: the soul of the rich man is tormented by devils. 1120–1135

OPPOSITE
Moissac (Tarn-et-Garonne), former abbey church of Saint-Pierre. South portal. 1120–1135

260

TOP AND CENTRE
Moissac (Tarn-et-Garonne), former
abbey church of Saint-Pierre. Cloister
gallery. 1100

BOTTOM
Moissac (Tarn-et-Garonne), former
abbey church of Saint-Pierre. Cloister,
two pillar reliefs. 1100

scrolls. They are the sole reference to the Last Judgement. The rest of the area is taken up by the twenty-four elders, two on each side in the top register, three on each side below, and the remainder underneath the "sea of crystal," the waves at the feet of the sublime one. The unusual meander pattern growing out of the mouths of beasts at the edge of the tympanum has been interpreted as the bonds with which Hercules tied up Cerberus, the dog from Hades. Below the tympanum is the door lintel on which wheels of fire symbolize the fires of Hell in the Apocalypse. It is all supported by two mighty door posts, whose edges are unusual, like waves pointing inwards; on the left one is a very long relief statue of Peter, the patron saint of the abbey, and on the right there is one of Isaiah.

"What were they and what symbolic message did they communicate, those three criss-crossed pairs of lions rampant, like arches, each with hind paws planted on the ground, forepaws on the back of his companion ... ?" With some license, Adso's vision describes the exterior of the trumeau, and his question is the same as anyone looking at the portal would ask. What do these lions mean? The Physiologer (cf. p. 339) describes their sides, the ones relating to Christ. Here too they seem to mean strength, as they are carrying the lintel. But on the trumeau they appear in front of a background of the rosettes of hellfire on the architrave, and this – in an extremely high quality piece of work – creates a whiff of evil. This example demonstrates the enigmatic ambiguity of Romanesque visual idiom, and the menacing proximity of Good and Evil which it frequently reveals.

Of exceptionally high sculptural quality are the figures on the sides of the trumeau, on the left the apostle Paul, on the right the prophet Jeremiah (photo, p. 260). The latter, in particular, is the sculptural peak of the works at Moissac. The figure is very long, to match the pillar, upright and quite twisted, again scarcely conceivable given the patterns of figures described in Classical writings. The figure appears to be standing firmly on both legs, but they are crossed in a peculiarly wide manner, the left over the right, so that he almost seems to be dancing. His twisted hip protrudes slightly from the pillar but his upper body is sitting rather rigidly on top. His head is bent down in a strong counter-movement, and his hands are holding a scroll across his upper torso, though nothing can be read on it. The finely structured elegance of the head in particular, with its long hair and beard, is the direct model for the Isaiah in Soulliac (photo, p. 265). The side walls of the portal entrance each have a double arcade with scenes in two registers; above them are friezes with complementary scenes. To the left is the story of Lazarus connected to the damnation of Avaritia and Luxuria (cf. pp. 344), while on the right are scenes whose theme is the Life of Christ.

According to the inscription, the cloister of Moissac was completed in 1100, and it is the first one in which biblical stories and other scenes appear on the capitals. There are ten marble reliefs on the corner pillars, and 88 capitals, making it the largest decorated Romanesque cloister to have survived. As there is an alternation of single and coupled columns, the scenes themselves vary in their proportions, and in between the capitals bearing figures others are interspersed with patterns of flowers or ornaments. The cloister is further broken up by the corner pillars bearing reliefs and the rectangular pillars in the middle of each side.

TOP
Moissac (Tarn-et-Garonne), former
abbey church of Saint-Pierre. Two
capitals in the cloister. 1100

BOTTOM
Moissac (Tarn-et-Garonne), former
abbey church of Saint-Pierre. Cloister
gallery. 1100

TOP LEFT
Souillac (Lot), former abbey church of
Sainte-Marie. Relief on the inner western
wall. 1120–1135

BOTTOM LEFT
Souillac (Lot), former abbey church of
Sainte-Marie. Trumeau, detail: sacrifice
of Abraham. 1120–1135

Souillac (Lot), former abbey church of
Sainte-Marie. Trumeau, now against the
inner western wall. 1120–1135

Souillac (Lot), former abbey church of
Sainte-Marie. Relief on the inner western
wall: the prophet Isaiah. 1120–1135

Souillac

The former abbey church of Sainte-Marie in Souillac, built between about 1075 and 1150, had suffered extensive damage during the Huguenot wars. The extensive figured portal was affected extremely badly, and the remaining pieces were put back in position in the seventeenth century. Nowadays these fragments are on the inner western wall.

The former trumeau of the lost portal (photo, opposite, right) has intertwined griffin-like fabulous creatures depicted on its outer side, and lions fighting other animals. At the very top, a man is being swallowed by a beast. In a fashion similar to the trumeau at Moissac, the bestial tumult is brought under control by the symmetrical manner in which the fabulous creatures are arranged; chaos and order are confronted with each other in such a way that they balance each other out – thus obeying one of the most dominant stylistic principles of Romanesque art. If one only takes this approach, the trumeau in Souillac can be considered the prototype of bestial columns (cf. photos, p. 336). The left side depicts the sacrifice of Abraham (opposite, bottom left).

The Theophilus relief (photo, opposite, top left) is possibly a later amalgamation of various fragments in the form of a triptych. The figures at the sides have been interpreted as Peter and Benedict, and probably flanked the original tympanum in a way similar to the figures of Peter and James who flank the Porte Miègeville in Toulouse. The central relief shows the legend of Theophilus who was the administrator of the bishopric of Sicily in the sixth century. Angered at being relieved of his office, Theophilus enters into a pact with the Devil in order to be reinstated. In his remorse he turns to Mary, who returns the paper with the agreement to him in a vision. The legend is told in three scenes. The first is the pact with the Devil which is shown at the bottom left. The scene next to it on the right shows the Devil attempting to grab Theophilus. Above them, in the third scene, is the figure of Mary, the patron saint of the church. She is really the main figure in the relief, and that explains why the story being told here is not of a saint but of a sinner. Stylistically, the center of the Theophilus relief has more in common with the prophet Isaiah (photo, right) than the saints flanking it.

The depiction of Isaiah is not only arguably the main work in Souillac, but also the most important depiction of a prophet in Romanesque art. In style it is directly dependent on the figure of Jeremiah in Moissac. However, there is one main difference: the figure of Jeremiah is standing still, whereas the figure of Isaiah almost seems to be moving. Isaiah is now walking, and this, together with his swinging garments, gives the figure a kind of new dynamism. Nonetheless, there is no sense of anatomical unity, and if the figure were truly walking one would expect the feet and the right hand to be in different positions relative to the body. Another significant detail is the wide cloak with its rich braid trimming, which fills the background of the relief and in the process creates a new means of structuring sculpture. The unusually violent and lengthy movement has encouraged some critics to talk of an "expression of visionary dynamism." Perhaps the relief expresses the moment when Isaiah was called by God.

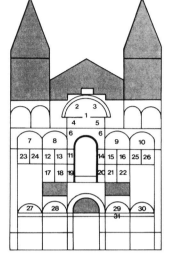

Angoulême (Charente), cathedral of Saint-Pierre. Scheme of the façade (according to Droste):

1	Christ in the mandorla
2	Eagle = the Evangelist John
3	Angel = the Evangelist Matthew
4	Winged lion = the Evangelist Mark
5	Winged ox = the Evangelist Luke
6	Angels
7–10	The Elect
11	Mother of God
12–22	Apostles
23	The Damned
27–30	Apostles
31	Mounted battle (illustration of the Song of Roland?)

The West

The landscapes in the mid-west region of France, roughly between Poitiers in the north and Puypéroux in the south, possess the richest remaining Romanesque sacred buildings and sculptures. A number of characteristic peculiarities developed here in the way façades and portals were structured, the most obvious difference from the portals in other regions being the lack of a tympanum. In places other than Angoulême and Poitiers, where the entire façade is a showpiece, the sculptural decorations are restricted mainly to the archivolts. Occasionally, in sites such as the archivolt portal in Aulnay, sculpture and architectural elements were treated as equivalents.

Angoulême

The most extensively planned façade in Romanesque art is on the cathedral of Saint-Pierre in Angoulême (figures, top). It was produced between 1115 and 1136 under Bishop Girard II, and expounded a complicated iconographical program that was probably conceived during two different periods, dividing into the ground floor with the portal tympanum and the high arcades, and the upper floor with the central area and angels. The central area is almost like a very high tympanum in the way it stretches above the portal and large window. In the centre Christ is standing in a mandorla protruding from the façade, and around him the Evangelists' symbols have been let into the wall in flat niches. The varying degrees to which the sculptural elements are graduated with relation to the façade wall display a special characteristic of Angoulême, which is repeated in the forms of the angels above the window. The four angels between the frieze and the arch are, like the Evangelists' symbols, set into niches and face Christ. In contrast, the angels in the spandrel project

from the wall and face outwards. This creates a complex structure of relationships which does, however, open out as regards content. Standing in front of the wall, the two spandrel angels are formally related to the mandorla with the standing figure of Christ; above him is a cloud which has cleverly moved beyond the wall, issuing forth from the church and covering the peak of the mandorla.

What has been depicted is the precise beginning of the process in the Acts of the Apostles (1, 9), where it is written: "As he said this he was lifted up while they looked on, and a cloud took him from their sight." The two angels are those "two men in white" (1, 10) who turn to the apostles and say: "This same Jesus (…) will come back in the same way" (1, 11). On first sight the framing of a mandorla depicting the Ascension with the Evangelists' symbols appears unusual, but it is nothing other than an allusion to his prophesied return, the Last Judgement, of which the four angels in the niches are part.

In this respect, we are dealing with an almost word for word conversion of an important New Testament passage into stone. As a result, the relevant biblical figures are collected in the side arcades: within the arched areas are the Chosen of Judgement Day, in the double arcades underneath the apostles present at the Ascension. They are joined, in the middle register to the left of the window, by the Madonna. There is scarcely another example in Romanesque art which demonstrates such a single, self-contained meaning. And as the apostles are also present to witness the Last Judgement, they are accompanied on either side by devils and the people they are tormenting.

While the equestrian statues of St. George and St. Martin underneath the inner double arcades and by the tympanum of the central portal are nineteenth century additions, the tympanums in the blind arcades on

Civray (Vienne), former priory church of Saint-Nicolas. West façade. Second half of the twelfth century

Poitiers (Vienne), former collegiate church of Notre-Dame-la-Grande. West façade, detail: Birth of Christ, bathing the baby, Joseph. Around the middle of the twelfth century

either side are the originals. While they stylistically predate the rest of the façade's sculptures, they also relate to the theme of the Ascension, for they show the apostles making their farewells. The frieze in the blind arcade to the right of the portal shows battles between horsemen that have been interpreted as scenes from the Song of Roland.

Poitiers

The three-storey façade of the former collegiate church of Notre-Dame-la-Grande in Poitiers (photo, p. 269) is similar to Angoulême, being determined by pronounced vertical lines; these are formed by a central portal, a window above it and an immense mandorla in the gable storey, all accompanied by corner towers. Despite this, the scheme of the façade's structure is not unified. While the lower storey with its central portal and blind arcades is related to a building with several aisles, the upper storey, divided into two registers with figured arcades, is shaped like the enlarged wall of a sarcophagus or shrine.

In contrast, the iconographical program is simple. The mandorla which projects from the gable wall contains a standing Christ and the Evangelists' symbols, and it is accompanied by the twelve apostles in the upper storey. They are shown sitting in the eight arcades of the lower register, while the four apostles above are standing. It has been suggested that the two bishops standing in the outer arcades could be Saint-Hilaire, Saint-Martin or Saint-Martial. The figural ornamentation of the lower storey is restricted to the area between the upper storey's arcade string course and the portal arches. Above the highest point of the left blind portal arch are the four prophets of the Old Testament: Moses, Jeremiah, Isaiah and Daniel, next to them on the left is King Nebuchadnezzar and in the left spandrel is the Fall of Man.

On the prophets' right is the Annunciation, the stem of Jesse, and on the right side of the portal the Visitation of Mary. In the right spandrel of

the right blind portal arch (photo, top) the Birth of Christ, the bathing of the Child and Joseph sitting are depicted. Capitals, arches and archivolts are, more even than in Angoulême, covered with such lavish decoration that it forms an exciting contrast with the figural sculpture. Nonetheless, there are many stylistic inconsistencies within the entire ensemble of the façade.

There are no written sources relating to the foundation of the building, but it is thought that the construction of it started towards the end of the eleventh century and was completed by around the middle of the twelfth century. The façade also dates from this period, which is the late part of the French Romanesque period.

The façade of the church of Saint-Nicolas in Civray (photo, bottom) is structured much the same way as that in Poitiers. There are two storeys with three equally high arcades. The central ones are real arcades with the one at the bottom containing a portal and the one at the top containing a window. While the blind arcades to either side of the portal themselves contain blind double arcades, the upper ones, on the other hand, house pieces of sculpture. On the right, the arched area is separated from the area beneath and contains the four Evangelists. Underneath them is St. Nicholas who offered protection to three girls whose father was about to abandon them to prostitution.

Opposite them is an equestrian statue but only fragments of it now remain. The archivolts and arches in particular are completely covered with sculptural decorations. And finally, the degree to which the great variety of Romanesque forms was gradually beginning to break up and lose itself in increasingly tightly packed decorations can be seen in the choir polygon of Notre-Dame in Rioux.

Rioux (Charente-Maritime), Notre-Dame. Exterior wall of the polygonal choir. Last third of the twelfth century

OPPOSITE
Poitiers (Vienne), former collegiate church of Notre-Dame-la-Grande. West façade. Around the middle of the twelfth century

268

Aulnay-de-Saintogne (Charente-Maritime), former collegiate church of Saint-Pierre-de-la-Tour. South transept portal. After 1130

Saintes (Charante-Maritime), former abbey church of Sainte-Marie-des-Dames. West façade. Second third of the twelfth century

BELOW
Portal archivolts

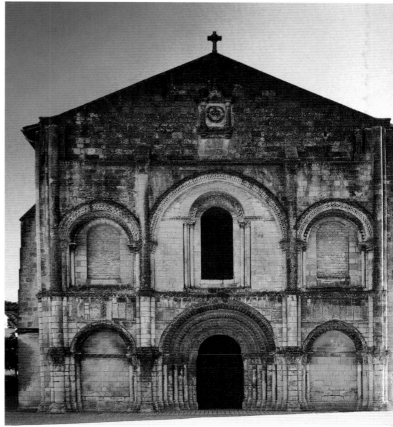

Aulnay

The immediate sense of architecture and sculpture having merged with each other, which is a characteristic of the Romanesque in the west of France, is expressed most succinctly in the archivolt portals of Aulnay-de-Saintogne (photo, opposite) and Saintes (photos, top). There are four archivolts in the portal of the south transept of the pilgrimage church of Saint-Pierre in Aulnay, and the three outer ones show a large number of small figures arranged radially. As each figure was carved separately from a single stone, every stone in the archivolts has two functions: decorative, and supporting the arch.

This agreement of construction and decoration is not applied on the inner archivolt. Here there are only animal and vine ornaments twisted across the arch. Above them are twenty-four figures with haloes, holding books and containers and probably representing apostles and prophets. In the third archivolt, however, there is a serious conflict between biblical tradition, the aesthetic arrangement and the requirements of architectural construction. The crowned figures are holding instruments and containers and allude to the Elders of the Apocalypse. But only twenty-four are mentioned there, and here there are a total of thirty-one figures. For aesthetic reasons, the figures could only be a little larger than those in the arch below, and in order to do justice to the architectural construction of the arch, the number of stones, and with it the number of figures, was increased to thirty-one. All the figures in these two archivolts are supported at the bottom by little atlantes, which are only visible from

below. In the fourth archivolt are numerous animals, fabulous and hybrid creatures, of which a few, such as the sphinx and the sirens, date back to Classical times. Others refer to local legends and myths or, like the donkey with the instrument, are an allusion to the vices. The entire arch is framed by a torus, on which animals are arranged "tangentially," with their body axis touching the arch, facing towards the center.

Saintes

The façade of Sainte-Marie-des-Dames has two storeys and is divided into three sections, meaning that it was following the scheme used throughout western France. The remaining sculpture is concentrated around the main portal, and its archivolts are formed by animal and vine friezes. Here, too, the sculpture is arranged both radially and tangentially. On the inside, six angels are moving tangentially towards the highest point, where two of them are holding a medallion with the hand of God. In the second archivolt are the Evangelists' symbols surrounded by vines, and at the top is the Lamb of God. There are many figures in the third archivolt, each of them on its own voussoir, and they show the Massacre of the Innocents in Bethlehem, while the number of the Elders of the Apocalypse is increased in the fourth archivolt, in accordance with the number of voussoirs, to fifty-four.

271

RIGHT
Charlieu (Loire), former priory church of
Saint-Fortunat. Tympanum of the west
portal. End of the eleventh century

BOTTOM LEFT
Semur-en-Brionnais (Saône-et-Loire),
former priory church of Saint-Hilaire.
Tympanum and door lintel of the west
portal. After the middle of the twelfth
century

BOTTOM RIGHT
Saint-Julien-de-Jonzy (Saône-et-Loire),
church of Saint-Julien. Tympanum and
door lintel of the west portal. Mid
twelfth century

OPPOSITE
Charlieu (Loire), former priory church of
Saint-Fortunat. Tympanum and door
lintel of the north side of the narthex; to
the right next to it, the lintel, tympanum
and archivolts over the window on the
north side of the narthex. Mid twelfth
century

Burgundy

Burgundy always enjoyed a special position amongst the Romanesque
artistic landscapes of France, for the reason that this section of country,
between the Saône and Loire, offered both external security and internal
stability. It is therefore no coincidence that this was the place where
monasticism revived at an early period and Cluny was built, the largest
and mightiest monastery in the western world. This had a considerable
impact on Romanesque art, in particular sculpture.

Burgundian tympanums

There are two reasons why the west portal of the abbey of Saint-Fortunat
in Charlieu (photo, top right) occupies an important position in art
history. It is the oldest remaining columned portal, in which all parts of the
portal are decorated with sculptures. And in addition, this is the first place
where Christ appears "in Majesty" in the mandorla, a means of representation which was later used for the Last Judgement. That this innovation
should have taken place in Burgundy has been explained by Bernhard
Rupprecht as a specific adoption of the Classical period, in which attention

was paid chiefly to the monumental "combination of architecture and
sculpture," considered to be "an imperial gesture and pretension." The
Cluniac reforms, which became an ecclesiastical political movement in the
eleventh century, finally led to fundamental confrontations between
spiritual and worldly power, between the pope and emperor for dominion
in western Europe. It therefore seems reasonable to suggest that the lordly
figure of Christ in Majesty was a visualization of these feelings about power.

Built in the second half of the eleventh century, Saint-Fortunat was torn
down after the French Revolution. All that remain are the western section
with the tympanum, and the narthex in front of it, built in the first half of
the twelfth century with two openings to the north. We have this circum-
stance to thank for providing us with examples from the beginning and
end of the Burgundian Romanesque period of sculpture on one building.

The entire height of the tympanum of the west portal, dating from
about 1090, is taken up with the figure of Christ enthroned with a
cruciform halo in a mandorla, supported by two angels. The earliest large-
scale sculptural representation of the type, it displays a statuesque calm
and balance which allows the monumental nature of the piece to be

comprehended as regards content. This hieratic moment is heightened by the row of apostles enthroned underneath arcades in the lintel.

This type of scene in a tympanum was frequently repeated right until late Burgundian Romanesque sculpture, and underwent considerable stylistic developments. If one compares the early west portal tympanum of Charlieu with the late one on the north portal (photo, top), it is conspicuous just how flat the relief of the former is. The bodies of the figures are only slightly curved and smoothly shaped, the contours of each figure being mainly accentuated by linear elements. The relief background and the archivolts arching over the tympanum are completely plain. This gives the composition within the tympanum a peculiar sense of dead weight, expressed mainly by the angels holding the mandorla. They are leaning slightly inwards and supporting the curved sides of the mandorla, but their lower legs, bent equally slightly outwards, act as a visual support for the mandorla which is delicately balanced on its tip. Then there are the wings of the angels, which lie at the edge of the tympanum and vault the entire scene. The message for the observer – here the true lord, the Lord of Heaven, is enthroned.

The structure of the north portal in the narthex, which dates from much later, in the middle of the twelfth century, differs very little from its predecessor. Columns and pillars set into the stonework support the curving archivolts, and the tympanum is carried by a sturdy lintel. Nonetheless, the observer gains a completely different impression when looking at it. All the architectural elements are covered with ornamentation to such a degree that they almost seem to dissolve into it. Ornaments even appear amongst the figures, causing the two to blend. The figure of Christ in Majesty in the tympanum, to which the Evangelists' symbols have been added, is in considerably higher relief than that on the west portal. Instead of linear drawings on the figures, there are plastic ridges formed by the folds of the garments, which both cover the bodies and take on an ornamental role. There is an even clearer change in the movements of the figures. Christ in the mandorla is no longer sitting enthroned in a frontal hieratic position, but is moving on his seat, almost a variation of a standing position. The violent movement of the angels, constrained by the addition of the Evangelists' symbols, goes beyond anything seen until then, by incorporating and dividing two directions of movement in one scene.

273

TOP
Autun (Saône-et-Loire), cathedral of
Saint-Lazare. Choir capital: Dream of the
Magi. 1120–1130. Autun, Musée "Salle
Capitulaire"

BOTTOM LEFT AND RIGHT
Cluny (Saône-et-Loire), former abbey
church of Saint-Pierre-et-Saint-Paul.
Ambulatory capitals: the four rivers of
Paradise and the first four notes of
Gregorian chant. 1115/1120. Cluny,
Musée de Farinier

TOP LEFT AND RIGHT
Autun (Saône-et-Loire), cathedral of
Saint-Lazare. Two capitals: Flight into
Egypt (left) and suicide of Judas.
1120–1130. Autun, Musée "Salle
Capitulaire".

BOTTOM LEFT AND RIGHT
Saulieu (Côte d'Ore), former abbey
church of Saint-Andoche. Two nave
capitals: First Temptation of Christ (left)
and The Angel Blocking the Path of
Bileam and His Ass (right). Mid twelfth
century.

For the hands that are positioned to support the mandorla are inconsistent with the position of the angels' bodies. They seem to be pulling apart, almost as if they are trying to open the mandorla. There are further examples of this late style in Saint-Julien-de-Jonzy (photo, p. 272, bottom right) and Semur-en-Brionnais (photo, p. 272, left), and art historians have invented the term of Romanesque "Baroque" to classify them.

Even though the early tympanum in Charlieu predated that in Cluny, it was finally Cluny, the most powerful center of Christianity after Rome at the time, which was to spread artistic impulses in all directions. For its tympanum, later destroyed, also contained Christ enthroned in a mandorla supported by angels.

Burgundian capitals

The influential importance of Romanesque sculpture in Burgundy was also expressed in the design of figured capitals. Created around 1100, the capitals of the former abbey church of Saint-Pierre-et-Saint-Paul in Cluny were preserved quite by chance; they distinguish themselves through their self-contained reference to ancient Corinthian capitals. This appears particularly clearly in the two capitals bearing the eight personifications of the notes of Gregorian chant (photo, bottom). While the basic form of the Classical model is adhered to, the sides are opened up by mandorla shapes, which are not used here for the glory of the figures but in order to provide them with a bowl-like area in which to be displayed. The Corinthian volutes at the corners were lost from the musical capitals when they were forcefully dismantled, but remain in other places, such as the capital with the Fall of Man; they clearly show a characteristic stylistic feature of Burgundian capitals. The tension between the architectural interrelations and figural elements develops into an extra-ordinarily plastic design, which relates the individual sides of the capitals to each other.

One of the greatest sculptors of the Middle Ages was Master Gislebertus, who inscribed his name on the tympanum in Autun. The majority of the capitals in the interior of Saint-Lazare are also ascribed to him; most of them are on pilasters and therefore remain firmly connected to the surface. His sculptures are some of the most human, touching works that exist in Romanesque sculpture. The vision of the Three Kings (photo, top), originally on the east side of the north-east crossing pillar, shows the three crowned figures together under a large, round cover. Two of them are still asleep, but the third has already been woken by the movingly gentle touch of the angel who is pointing the star out to him. The Flight into Egypt (photo, opposite, top left), on the pillar opposite, is sometimes thought to be by a different sculptor; it shows Mary who is looking at us in an almost personal manner, showing us her child. She seems to be floating on the donkey rather than sitting on him, a position similar to the enthroned Madonna and Child. But the sculptor has given his own interpretation to the hieratic "sedes sapientiae"; the mother's head is slightly bowed, and her arm, laid protectively around her child, creates a scene of human profoundness and sensitivity. In contrast, the suicide by hanging of Judas (figure, opposite, top right) is a scene of anger and terror

OPPOSITE
Vézelay (Yonne), former abbey church of
Sainte-Madelaine. Main portal. In the
tympanum: the miracle of Pentecost.
1125–1130

Vézelay (Yonne), former abbey church of
Sainte-Madelaine. Main portal. Detail of
the lintel: Panotians with large ears.
1125–1130

of evil, which Gislebertus depicted in the tympanum with just as much vividness as the more positive emotions of mankind. The betrayal of Christ was inspired by the Devil, and two other devilish figures appear here, helping Judas to hang himself. Nonetheless, the triangle formed by their heads gives the composition a sense of balance which expresses the human misery of despair in devastating fashion.

A further development of the style of capital found in Autun, and at the same time the "end phase of north Burgundian figured capitals," as Rupprecht notes, can be found in the few examples which have been preserved in the nave and side aisles of the former abbey church of Saint-Andoche in Saulieu. The close relationship with Autun is particularly visible in the stylistic transposition of the tree and Satan in the capital showing the first Temptation of Christ (photo, p. 275, bottom left). Due to the way they are placed on half-column responds, the capitals in Saulieu develop greater spatiality than the pilaster capitals in Autun, and this creates an increased sense of drama. As an example, the depiction of Bileam's ass, who shied away three times from the angel's sword (photo, p. 275, bottom right) varies from deep recesses in the relief to its entirely three-dimensional head, turned away in fear. While the figures in scenes such as the Flight into Egypt remain completely connected to the relief, both Bileam on his donkey and the angel protrude from the capital, and are as it were placed in front of the Corinthian plant motifs, which are correspondingly reduced in extent.

Vézelay

At the beginning of one of the four main pilgrimage routes to Santiago de Compostela, the "Via Lemovicensis" (the Latin name for Limoges), Vézelay was the place where innumerable pilgrims gathered in order to start their journey together. The town first gained importance in the eighth century, due to the legend that the relics of Mary Magdalene were kept there; as a result, Vézelay itself became a destination for pilgrimages, and these increased sharply after it gained papal recognition in 1103.

In 1104, a new church dedicated to St. Mary Magdalene was built by the former abbey church of Sainte-Madeleine, but it was destroyed by fire in 1120. Afterwards, another new church was built, to which a narthex (photo, p. 276) was added around 1140/50, and this is where an historical event took place at Easter 1146, which affected the entire contemporary Christian world: before an immense crowd that included numerous secular princes, Bernard of Clairvaux called for people to join the Second Crusade. Hence, Vézelay was a focus for both Europe's pilgrims and crusaders.

In the center of the tympanum, Christ is enthroned in a mandorla with his legs twisted to the left. On either side, beneath his outstretched arms, sit the Apostles holding books and in the process of receiving the Holy Spirit, represented by rays coming from Christ's fingers. Like Christ, the Apostles are not facing the observer directly and are no longer arranged in the traditional row. This creates a strong sense of individuality in the figures, and their increased corporeality causes them to stand out from the background of the relief, something that is clearest in the robed figures.

In accordance with the Acts of the Apostles (2, 5 ff.), the radiating coffers depict the nations that need to be converted; some of them depart from normal human appearances, an idea that goes back to Ancient Greece. On the right side of the lintel, led by the Apostles Peter and presumably Paul, is a procession of large-eared Panotians from Scythia (photo, top), Pygmies and Giants. On the left is a heathen scene showing the sacrifice of a bull, and behind it are Romans and Scythians, as representatives of pre-Christian peoples. The affinity between the Old and New Testament is indicated by the monumental figure of John the Baptist which is on the trumeau in the same axis as Christ.

The theme of the Vézelay tympanum, sending the Apostles to be missionaries to the world, and also the cosmological dimension of the signs of the Zodiac and Labours of the months in the surrounding archivolt, is an extremely demanding theological conception. This is one reason why it is likely that the sculptures, which are usually dated around 1125–30, were actually, given the iconography of this tympanum, produced in the context of preparations for the Crusade around 1146.

The figured capitals inside reproduce images of Good and Evil, frequently with a degree of iconographic complexity; Old Testament themes in the nave and aisles are interpreted as predictions of the New Covenant, and New Testament themes complement them in the narthex and on the façade. The person behind the comprehensive encyclopedia of knowledge realized in this cycle of capitals (whose sculptural quality is less exalted) is thought to be the brother of Abbot Ponce, the Prior Pierre de Montboissier, who as Abbot of Cluny, under the name of Petrus Venerabilis, was to become one of the most famous figures of the twelfth century.

TOP
Serrabone (Western Pyrenees), former
priory church of Notre-Dame. Tribune
for the choir. After the middle of the
twelfth century

BOTTOM
Elne (Western Pyrenees), former
cathedral of Sainte-Eulalie. Romanesque
gallery in the cloister. After 1172

TOP OPPOSITE
Serrabone (Western Pyrenees), former
priory church of Notre-Dame. Coupled
capital of the choir tribune. After the
middle of the twelfth century

BOTTOM OPPOSITE
Serrabone (Western Pyrenees), former
priory church of Notre-Dame. Details
from two capitals in the choir tribune.
After the middle of the twelfth century

Roussillon

The earliest Romanesque sculptures in France can be found in this southern landscape near the Golfe du Lion. This region also saw the emergence of a number of artistic impulses, mainly as a consequence of the developing fortunes of the monastery of Saint-Michel-de Cuxa. These were impulses which were to have a significant effect on the entire region for a long time to come.

Serrabone

Far off the main roads of Roussillon, on a northern arm of the Pyrenees to the east of the Massif du Canigou, lies the Church of Notre-Dame. The church belongs to the former priory of Serrabone; since the monastery complex to which it was connected was destroyed, the Church of Notre-Dame has become a lonely building that dominates the surrounding countryside. Its relevance to Romanesque sculpture lies mainly in one sculptural feature – the sculptural design of the southern gallery and tribunes (photos, top left and opposite).

Erected around 1150 in the west part of the church, the tribunes were moved to the center of the church in either the seventeenth century or the nineteenth. They consist of three arcades spanning the nave, and they form two bays and are supported by pillars, columns and coupled columns with figured capitals. The vaults are supported by sturdy, round rib vaulting. The western face is covered all over with reliefs; those on the arcade arches are flowers and vines, and in the spandrels are Christian symbols. Between the northern and central arcade is the winged lion of St. Mark and the eagle of St. John, in the spandrel to the right of the central arcade is the Lamb of the Eucharist and the angel of St. Matthew, while St. Luke's bull appears in the spandrel by the south wall of the nave.

Separated from the shaft by toruses, the capitals are in high relief, and the impost blocks are surrounded with rosette, palmette and vine ornaments. The figures depicted consist of a variety of grotesque creatures which are standing on the toruses. The heads of these figures are mostly facing outwards, underneath the corner volutes; in many cases they flank a human head or mask. Their content is predominantly set within the limits of a traditional iconography depicting the battle between Good and Evil.

Presumably this structure is intended for the singers in a choir. Built from a reddish-white marble, the structure forms a fine contrast to the otherwise plain interior. Like the sculptures on the capitals in the south gallery, those on the tribunes are of high sculptural quality, which suggests that two masters were at work here. At the same time, it is assumed that the sculptors who worked here were the same sculptors who worked on the cloister in the nearby monastery of Saint-Michel-de-Cuxa. It is possible that the entire tribune was produced in the workshop there, transported to Serrabone in individual pieces and then finally assembled there. Similar procedures probably happened in other places, whose sculptures closely copy those in Cuxa. In general, this choir tribune can be considered a peak of High Romanesque sculptural art in Roussillon.

The "Master of Cabestany"

While the sculptures in Cuxa reveal a certain stylistic uniformity, the very opposite is the case with the work of a sculptor whose name has remained unknown to this day. His personal style is so individual that his works are easily identified everywhere, and they are widely dispersed, from Italy, through France and into Spain, from Tuscany via Roussillon down into the Basque country. The invented name he has been given derives from a tympanum (photo, top left) which can still be seen in the church in the small town of Cabestany near Perpignan. Rolf Legler quite rightly wrote that: "The Master of Cabestany is one of the most distinctive and fascinating artistic personalities in the entire Romanesque period, similar to Gislebertus of Autun, Gilabertus of Toulouse and Antelami of Parma."

This tympanum contains several scenes describing the Ascension of Mary, and unusually begins on the right with Mary waking from the sleep of the dead. The central scene depicts Mary giving her belt to doubting Thomas, who after his doubts about the resurrection of Christ did not want to believe in the Ascension of the Mother of God either, and was given a belt by her by way of proof. The sculptor's unconventional style becomes apparent here, because his figures always have large heads with flat foreheads, long massive noses and oblique almond-shaped eyes. Other characteristics include oversize hands with long fingers, and robes folded in the Classical style. In none of these characteristics, however, is there any suggestion of the intentions of creating a Classical effect that are found in the sculpture of places such as Provence.

The Museo di Arte sacra in San Casciano Val di Pesa to the south of Florence, which was renovated a few years ago, contains a small column which is surrounded with reliefs (photo, top right). At the bottom is the Annunciation, and above it the annunciation to the shepherds – the angel is holding one shepherd by his beard. Like the scene showing the Assumption of Mary into Heaven, this one shows a human intimacy such as is rarely discovered in Romanesque sculpture, though occasionally it is manifest in the works of Gislebertus. Above it are further scenes from the Birth of Christ; firstly, the baby in swaddling clothes twisted backwards around the stele, as if resigned to its future fate; next, the baby in the stable with the ox and ass, and in the final scene the baby is shown being bathed.

TOP
"Master of Cabestany," tympanum: Ascension and Mary Lowering her Girdle. Cabestany (Western Pyrenees), parish church of Notre-Dame, western wall of the north transept. Second half of the twelfth century

RIGHT
"Master of Cabestany," sculptured column of a font: scenes from the Birth of Christ. San Casciano Val di Pesa (Tuscany), Museo di Arte sacra. Second half of the twelfth century

"Master of Cabestany," or colleagues, group of capitals. Rieux-Minervois (Aude), church of L'Assomption-de-Notre-Dame. Second half of the twelfth century

"Master of Cabestany," relief: death and martyrdom of St. Saturninus, detail. Saint-Hilaire-de-l'Aude (Aude), former abbey church. Marble. Second half of the twelfth century

BOTTOM
"Master of Cabestany," male head with inlaid eyes from San Pedro de Roda. Marble, height 12 inches. Now in Perelada Castle, Mateu collection. Second half of the twelfth century

There is a peculiar magic about this sculpture, which conveys both the Nativity and a sense of perfection, but avoids being easily placed in any art history category. Its iconography suggests it could be the stele of a font.

The Saturninus sarcophagus (photo, top) in the small church of Notre-Dame-de-l'Assomption in Saint-Hilaire-de-l'Aude, which could alternatively be a predella, is one of the main Romanesque sculptural works in Roussillon. It narrates the martyrdom of St. Sernin, the first bishop of Toulouse, in all the energetic vividness characteristic of this master's visual idiom.

His identity is nonetheless a mystery. It is generally assumed that he was a traveling sculptor from Tuscany, who produced most of his works in Roussillon. As he did not have to follow any models, he could translate his own visual ideas into sculpture; this has recently led to the speculation that he was a heretic who was working in Cathar regions during the period of widespread heresy in the last quarter of the twelfth century.

Saint-Gilles-du-Gard (Gard), abbey
church of Saint-Gilles. West façade.
Second quarter of the twelfth century

Saint-Gilles-du-Gard (Gard), abbey
church of Saint-Gilles. West façade, main
portal, northern jamb: James the Great
and Paul. Second quarter of the twelfth
century

Saint-Gilles-du-Gard (Gard), abbey
church of Saint-Gilles. West façade, main
portal, southern jamb: John and Peter.
Second quarter of the twelfth century

Provence

The name of this Mediterranean landscape on the left and right banks of the Rhône goes back to the original Roman term for this region which in classical times extended far to the west, "provincia gallia narbonensis." Though the countless pieces of art remaining from Roman times were important models for medieval architects and sculptors, Romanesque art blossomed here relatively late, albeit unusually maturely. It is no surprise that two of the main works of Provençal Romanesque are portals formed in the shape of Roman triumphal arches.

Saint-Gilles-du-Gard

Similar to Vézelay, Saint-Gilles was not just a place of pilgrimage – to the legendary founder of the eighth century monastic community, the wealthy Athenian merchant Aegidius – but also the place where French pilgrims to Rome set sail from, and a place where pilgrims to Santiago gathered, most of them having traveled from Italy via Arles, before continuing their journey to Spain along the "Via Tolosana." The multi-functional nature of

this place ensured its importance, in turn reflected by its large population: at the beginning of the thirteenth century around 40,000 people lived there, compared with 9,000 today.

The façade of the former abbey church (photo, opposite) is unique within the Romanesque period, and is divided into three sections by walls set between the widely separated portals which are flanked by massive corner towers. The central portal is emphasized by a raised lintel, a higher tympanum and a trumeau. Here, the adoption of Roman triumphal arches is mixed with the effect of Classical theater architecture, such as the stage façade preserved in Orange.

The complex stepping of the entire structure is accompanied by a frieze which stretches over the entire front and is picked up in the side portals by the lintels one level lower. Many figures are portrayed in what is both the first complete, and the most extensive, cycle showing the Passion in medieval sculpture. It starts in the left jamb of the north portal with the preparations to enter Jerusalem, and with the entrance itself on the architrave, continues on the northern partition wall with the payment of

Saint-Gilles-du-Gard (Gard), abbey
church of Saint-Gilles. West façade,
detail of the frieze: Washing of the Feet.
Second quarter of the twelfth century

Judas and the expulsion of the dealers from the temple and concludes with the prophecy to Peter in the north jamb of the central portal. Its architrave shows the washing of the feet (photo, top) and the Last Supper, and in the south jamb is Judas's kiss and the arrest. The scene before Pilate, and the Flagellation (photo, opposite), appear on the southern partition wall and the carrying of the Cross, badly damaged, starts right next to them; the Crucifixion itself is spread out across the southern tympanum. In contrast, the frieze in the south portal shows the events after Christ's death. Some scenes are added that are not part of the Passion and are therefore rather curious; they are the raising of Lazarus, in the section of wall between the northern partition wall and jamb of the central portal, and the anointing of Jesus's feet by Mary Magdalene in the jamb of the south portal. Hans Fegers explains these additions, which are subdivided into various scenes, as the desire to incorporate the Provençal saints, the three Marys of Les-Saintes-Maries-de-la-Mer, Lazarus and Maximinus, into the cycle.

The rectangular niches in the partition walls and the jambs of the central portal contain twelve life-size figures, some of which can be identified as Apostles due to the inscriptions still visible on their haloes. The Apostle in the first niche of the northern partition wall is presumably Matthew, next to him is Bartholomew, followed by Thomas and James the Less. In the southern jamb are John and Peter (photo, p. 283, right) and opposite them are James the Great and Paul (photo, p. 283, left); the remaining four Apostles in the southern partition wall can no longer be identified. In the outer northern niche St. Michael is depicted killing a dragon, and in the southern pendant an archangel is fighting devils.

Unlike the seventeenth century tympanum in the central portal which shows Christ in Majesty and the Evangelists' symbols and possibly repeats what the Protestants destroyed in 1562, the tympanums in the side portals are original. The relationship of the Apostles in the niches to the content of the frieze seems to be as witnesses to Christ's Passion, their presence as it were confirming that event's real historical basis, but the tympanums are removed from this scenic sphere. The theme of the Crucifixion, which was

omitted from the frieze, takes on the character of a *Christus triumphans* in the southern tympanum, and the addition of Ecclesia, the symbolization of the Roman Catholic church, and the synagogue supported by an angel, the symbol of Judaism, raises this to the level of a depiction of the Christian doctrine of salvation. It has been suggested that this very scene was produced in the context of the heresies of Pierre de Bruys, who was burnt to death in 1143 in Saint-Gilles; that would, probably not without good reason, mean that it was intended as a piece of contemporary propaganda. The enthroned Mother of God in the northern tympanum is also in accordance with the hieratic symbolic content of the Crucifixion scene, and it is separated from the narrative depictions of the Three Kings to the left and the dream of Joseph to the right by flanking columns.

There have been lengthy debates about the dating of the work, and Richard Hamann's early dating of its completion by 1129 has since been rejected. The issue is clouded by a sculptor's signature on the background of the relief of the apostle Bartholomew, saying BRVNVS ME FECIT ("Brunus made me"); it has been connected with documents from 1171 and 1186 which mention a person called Brunus. There are a number of arguments to do with the style, suggesting that of all those sculptors working here, the master who produced the archangel Michael was the most influential in the design of the frieze and tympanum, but none of them provide a satisfactory explanation. Today it is thought that the sculptures were started during the second quarter of the twelfth century. The wider relevance of Saint-Gilles results from the entire complex, and it is assumed that there were many changes of plans while it was being built; the debate continues.

Arles

The most extensive sculptured portal after Saint-Gilles is attached to the former cathedral of Saint-Trophime in Arles (photo, p. 287). Designed in imitation of ancient single-arch triumphal arches, such as that in nearby Saint-Rémy, the portal is not set into the wall as is usual, but placed in front of the otherwise undecorated façade. The entire ensemble has been remarkably well preserved, and the restoration work, which was finished in the summer of 1995, has restored it to its original condition.

The iconographical program alludes to the Last Judgement, without having the urgency of that in Moissac or Autun. In the tympanum Christ is enthroned in a mandorla, accompanied by the Evangelists' symbols; he is surrounded by hosts of angels in the inner archivolt. There is a continuous large frieze at lintel level; in the lintel itself the Apostles are depicted sitting. Starting at the northern outside edge, the Fall of Man is depicted, followed on the front of the façade by the Chosen, facing the center, whose souls are being laid to rest in Abraham's bosom in the jamb. In the jamb opposite, the Passion of the Damned starts; they are moving away from Christ, pushed through the gateway into Hell. A small frieze underneath shows scenes from the Birth of Christ. The apostles standing in the jambs are Peter and John on the left and Paul and Andrew on the right, while James the Great and Bartholomew are in the box niches on the northern outer wall and James the Less and Philip in those to the south. To the side of the door on

Saint-Gilles-du-Gard (Gard), abbey
church of Saint-Gilles. West façade,
detail of the frieze: the Flagellation.
Second quarter of the twelfth century

TOP
Arles (Bouches-du-Rhône), Saint-
Trophime. Cloister gallery. Second half of
the twelfth century

BOTTOM
Arles (Bouches-du-Rhône), Saint-
Trophime. Cloister capital. Second half
of the twelfth century

the left is the church patron Saint Trophime, and opposite him is the stoning of St. Stephen. The relics of the latter were kept in Arles.

The portal complex, which dates from the second third of the twelfth century, has an extremely united appearance, due to its reduction to a single portal. In addition, the frieze, which runs through all the levels, is a strong visual link due to the almost monotonous uniformity of its rows of figures. Nonetheless, this shows the Romanesque power of expression beginning to ossify, and it has frequently been pointed out that there is an element of stylistic dependence on the Chartres Early Gothic style.

The monastery of Saint-Trophime also possesses the most extravagant and lavish sculptured cloister in Provence. The north and east wings are the only remaining Romanesque sections, dating from between 1150 and 1170, or possibly towards the end of the twelfth century. The iconographical themes of the scenes on the figured capitals in the north wing concentrate on the Passion, and Old Testament events are interspersed between them, as they are between the scenes from Christ's childhood in the east wing. This, and the small frieze on the façade, gives increased substance to the Christian idea of redemption.

One feature peculiar to Arles, and differing from Moissac, is that each of a pair of coupled columns has its own capital, and the pair is connected above it by the impost block in order to be able to support the weight of the arcade. As a result, the figures can take up the entire height of the capital, and ornamentation, similar to that on the portal, no longer occupies the area containing the figures but adopts an independent function, primarily as a frame. These are the aspects emphasized by the special nature of the adoption of Classical forms during the Provençal late Romanesque period.

There are also clear signs in Arles that there were intensive exchanges of ideas with Romanesque sculptors in Italy. At the same time, the lions that support columns and pilasters, as they do in Saint-Gilles, are merely an iconographical motif. Clearer evidence in favour of this theory is the capital showing the vision of the Three Kings and the Flight into Egypt in the east wing; it has been recognized as an early work by Benedetto Antelami, who was to become one of the principle identifiable masters of the Italian Romanesque.

Compostela (Galicia), cathedral of Santiago. Puerta de las Platerías on the south transept. Western jambs of the left door: King David, the Creation of Adam, Christ giving his blessing. Fragments of the north portal moved to this site. Last decade of the eleventh century

Compostela (Galicia), cathedral of Santiago. Puerta de las Platerías on the south transept. Completed in 1103.

Romanesque sculpture in Spain

The study of Spanish art, particularly that of the Middle Ages, spent a long period in the doldrums due to the political isolation caused by Franco's fascist regime. Added to this was a desire for art historical hegemony, which was expressed by French research in particular, and according to which the art of the Spanish early Romanesque period had to be seen as dependent on the French Romanesque style. In contrast, a new generation of art historians has succeeded during the last two decades in freeing Spanish art history from its isolation and returning it to the level of international research. This caused international medieval art historians to turn their attention to the Spanish Romanesque, and they brought some surprises to light as a result.

Horst Bredekamp, for example, has proved in several investigations that an independent center for producing sculptures was already established in Frómista and its courtly and artistic surroundings around 1070, and that this can be "experienced in the history of the development of art as a quite individual break with the past and as a clear leap forward." The scholarly importance of such a statement is contained chiefly in the fact that it releases the Spanish early Romanesque style from its dependence on France and recognizes its independent genesis.

The emergence and development of the Spanish Early Romanesque style have to be seen in terms of two basic factors. First of all, it was the royal families of León, Castille and Aragón whose close dynastic connections gave rise to some important churches with appropriate architectural sculpture being built as early as the second half of the eleventh century. Besides the church of San Martin de Frómista, which was started in 1066, are the churches of Santa Maria in Iguácel (1072), San Isidoro de Dueñas (after 1073), San Isidoro in León (after 1072), the cathedral of San Pedro in Jaca (c. 1085) and San Pedro de Loarre (after 1080). They display a wide spectrum of self-contained Spanish sculpture, and research in this area, with the exception of nationalistic pieces, is still in its infancy. Secondly, it is a fact that architectural sculpture was mainly distributed along the edges of the pilgrimage routes to Santiago de Compostela.

TOP
León, Colegiata de San Isidoro. Puerta del Cordero, tympanum. Early twelfth century

BOTTOM
León, Colegiata de San Isidoro. Puerta del Perdón. Early twelfth century

Spanish sculpture around 1100

After pilgrims had covered hundreds, and even thousands of miles, they were eagerly anticipating what they would encounter at their goal. Here, in Santiago de Compostela, the target of numerous pilgrimage routes throughout Europe, is where work was started on a cathedral in 1077/78. The work of the stone masons, and this includes sculptural work, was directed by the "admirable master" Bernard, who in more recent literature has been called "the elder" in order to differentiate him from a later Bernard. His workshop employed fifty stone masons, and one of his assistants was a certain "conscientious Robert."

Besides the capitals in the interior which are an adaptation of ancient Corinthian foliage, it is the large portals that contain the important works of the Spanish early Romanesque period. It was not possible to complete the west portal that was originally planned, though, and its present appearance is a work of the Spanish late Romanesque. The northern portal of the transept, the Puerta Francigena, was destroyed in the eighteenth century. The side portal in front of the north transept, the Puerta de la Azabachería, was destroyed by a fire started during a revolt as long ago as 1117. All that remains of it is a very artistic section of a column. The only portal still in existence is the Puerta de las Platerías – the portal of the silversmiths – in the south transept (photo, opposite, right), which was completed using some fragments from the other portals. Put together from quite varying slabs, the two tympanums of the double portal completed in 1103 have quite disparate appearances. In the right portal, in the center of the lower register, is the Flagellation of Christ, and next to it, on the left, the Crown of Thorns and the healing of the blind, and in the upper register, badly damaged, is the Adoration of the Magi. Depicted in the left tympanum, that was put together from even more disparate pieces, is the Temptation of Christ in the desert. Most of the reliefs are, at least in French research, considered to be stylistically dependent upon Conques, while the healing of the blind displays references to the sculpture in León.

Those reliefs set into the jambs of the Puerta de las Platerías widened as far as the pier buttresses, which date from the last decade of the eleventh century (photo, opposite, left), were probably originally part of the destroyed Puerta Francigena. The depictions of King David playing a musical instrument, and the Creation of Adam, are of particularly high sculptural quality, and the latter scene, in which the Creator has laid his right hand on Adam's heart in order to bring him to life in God's image, radiates a simple and sublime dignity.

Two portals were built on the south side of the Colegiata del San Isidoro in León around 1100; they are the Puerta del Perdón (photo, bottom) – the portal of forgiveness – in the south transept and the Portal del Cordero, which grants access to the building from the southern side aisle. The tympanum of the latter (photo, top) shows the sacrifice of Isaac by Abraham together with details, some of which are not mentioned in the Bible, such as Isaac getting onto his mount or taking off his shoes and clothes once they have reached their destination. This extension of the story emphasizes that Abraham's son had surrendered himself to divine providence and accepted his fate willingly.

Frómista (Province of Palencia), San Martín. Capitals on the half-columns between the nave and side aisle. 1066–1085/1090

Frómista (Province of Palencia), San Martín. Capital: The Fall of Man. 1066–1085/1090

Frómista (Province of Palencia), San
Martín. Interior. 1066–1085/1090

Jaca (Aragón), cathedral. South portal
capital: Bileam and his ass. *c.* 1100

Jaca (Aragón), cathedral. South portal
capital: The sacrifice of Isaac. *c.* 1100

BOTTOM
Jaca (Aragón), San Salvador y San Ginés.
Sarcophagus of the Infanta Doña Sancha:
display side. *c.* 1100

One particular detail refers to the contemporary history of the Christian Reconquest. The two figures on the left edge are Hagar, the Egyptian maid of Abraham's wife Sarah, and her illegitimate son by Abraham, Ishmael, who is described in Genesis (16, 12) as "a wild-ass of a man." Both of them were sent away into the desert, and that is the origin of the Christian term for the descendants of Mohammed as "Ishmaelites," or outcasts. The figure of Ishmael riding out of the scene, his turban being a reference to Arabic culture, is pointing his arrow to the Lamb of God above the sacrifice. This expresses a deep condemnation of all things Arabian, not surprising given that Spain was engaged in the Reconquista, fighting the Moors during the period this tympanum was created.

Other pieces created around the turn of the century are two archivolt capitals (photo, top) opposite each other on the portal on the southern side aisles of the cathedral in Jaca. The one on the left shows Bileam and his ass, and on the right, again, is the sacrifice of Isaac by Abraham. This is one of the most popular themes of the Romanesque period, because it symbolized a humble submissiveness to one's personal fate as determined by God. This capital is exceptional in two respects. First of all, it shows the sacrifice at its most dramatic moment; Isaac is standing there fearfully, but obedient and ready to make the sacrifice, his hands tied behind his back, and Abraham about to carry out the worst deed of his life as a man and father. In this instant, God's angel seizes his sword and releases him from his pious deed.

Secondly, the sculptor is making a direct reference to Classical nude figures. Isaac is standing naked on the capital's torus, and Abraham is also naked, through draped in a large cloth. Ancient corporeality clearly continues to have an effect here, though the style is Romanesque. Here, too, Frómista serves as a model, because the sculptor there designed a paradise scene as a direct copy of an ancient Orestes sarcophagus in the abbey of Santa Maria in Huzillos, now in the Prado in Madrid, in which the classical figure of Orestes became the Romanesque figure of Adam.

One of the most important works of the Spanish Romanesque period not connected to an architectural structure is the sarcophagus of Doña Sancha, daughter of King Ramiro I and the widow of the Count of Toulouse (photo, bottom); it used to be kept in the convent of Santa Cruz de la Serós not far from Jaca. On the front, underneath arcades, are two scenes in memory of the countess who died in 1097: on the right Doña Sancha herself is depicted between two nuns or maids, and on the left is her burial. In the center, the soul of the dead is shown by two angels within a mandorla, an image of salvation. On account of his sympathetic, naive simplicity, Durliat calls the sculptor the "Master of Doña Sancha." The reverse of the sarcophagus shows a tournament divided into three arcades; it too is simply and powerfully vivid, but is clearly the work of a different sculptor.

Pamplona (Province of Navarra), cathedral. Four sides of a capital in the cloister: the Passion of Job. *c.* 1145. Pamplona, Museo de Navarra

The middle of the century

Around the middle of the twelfth century, sculpture connected to pieces of architecture was established throughout Europe, and in Spain it had become one of the favorite types of artistic depiction. This can be gauged not least in the high quality of sculptures produced during that period. In two genuinely Spanish sculptures dating from the middle of the twelfth century, the sufferings of Job (photos, top) are compared to the Passion of Christ. Two coupled capitals in the former cloister in the cathedral of Pamplona employ a method of narrative that includes all four sides of the capital and relates the episode chronologically and in sequence. Even a modern comic could scarcely be more vivid and direct. The first narrow side of the Job capital shows, on two levels, the conflict between God and Satan, which led to their "wager" regarding Job's fear of God, and his sons' banquet. The following double side shows one message after the other reaching Job: at the bottom is the theft of his herds, and on the second narrow side the collapse of his house and death of those inside. The second double side is divided vertically and shows the discussion between Job, who has been afflicted with leprosy, and his wife and friends, none of whom can understand that he continues to profess faith in God, despite all the evils that have befallen him. Job appears a second time, almost like a copy, but this time in order to be finally redeemed by God's blessing. The naturalistic wealth of detail and powerful and dramatic expression of the

individual scenes make these reliefs one of the greatest achievements of European sculpture in any period.

Another sculptor, called the "second Master of Uncastillo" by Marcel Durliat, displayed his skill on the south portal of the church of Santa María in Uncastillo, Zaragoza, which was started in 1135. Instead of a tympanum, this portal has an archivolt comprising several arches, and on it the master depicted numerous secular scenes with examples of crude excesses and acts of violence (photo p. 294). Its marked tendency to burlesque and droll exaggeration contrasts rather sharply with the religious scenes on the capitals that support the archivolt, and this makes it difficult to interpret the scene iconographically.

Probably the most comprehensive Christian iconographical program of this age, however, is on the west façade of the abbey church of Ripoll in Catalonia (photo, p. 295). The regrettable damage to the sculptures was a result of a fire in the monastery in 1835. The portal has no tympanum, and is stepped with seven archivolts supported by pilasters and columns, some decorated with leaves, flowers and Romanesque depictions of animals. The third archivolt is supported by the column statues of the Apostles Peter and Paul, and shows a number of scenes from the life and martyrdom of the two saints. It is followed by an arrangement of curved staves, and then there is an archivolt covered with ornamentation. The next archivolt with figures tells the stories of Jonah and David. The last

Uncastillo (Province of Zaragoza),
church of Santa María. South portal,
archivolt by the "Master of Uncastillo,"
detail. Mid twelfth century

OPPOSITE
Ripoll (Province of Gerona), abbey
church of Santa María. West façade and
portal: detail. Second quarter of the
twelfth century

The end of the century

The capitals and reliefs on the corner pillars of the cloister of Santo Domingo de Silos (photos, pp. 296–97 and p. 338), to the south-east of Burgos, are some of the most remarkable Romanesque sculptures in existence. Started around the middle of the century and spread out over two storeys, it took a quarter of a century until the lower gallery was completely finished. The coupled capitals, which are the most important artistically, are in the east and north wings.

Many of them are covered with foliage and fruits, and exhibit a sort of blocky completeness, though at the same time showing a tendency to break up similar to that in the other capitals. They depict constantly changing collections of fantastic birds and Harpies, foul creatures from Greek mythology with the heads of old women and the bodies of birds. On other capitals are the heads of animals, birds or deer-like creatures, entangled in foliage. While these works seem to have been created by one particular master, some of the capitals in the south wing are quite different and seem to be governed by a wild, demonic means of depiction. The animals appear to be bound by the foliage, and the women with the bodies of birds have changed into devils' brats.

The reliefs are the most conspicuous and important works, from the point of view of art history, in this cloister. A feature that had appeared for the first time more than half a century before in Moissac, and that subsequently spread throughout southern France, was the decoration of the corner pillars with Biblical scenes. The cycle of the death and resurrection of Christ starts on the northern side of the north-east pillar with the Descent from the Cross (photo, p. 296, top left), a theme that was frequently preferred to the Crucifixion in Romanesque art as it demonstrated the power of Christ and his surmounting of death. The beam of the Cross is inserted between the capitals of the flanking columns like a cross strut. It divides the earthly scene of mourning, connected with the descent of the dead Christ from the Cross, from the heavenly and cosmic area in the tympanum.

Beneath the feet of those in the scene is a stylized representation of Calvary, the site of the Crucifixion, from the Latin translation of the Hebrew Golgotha "the place of skulls." In the center, beneath the feet of the Crucified Jesus, Adam, the progenitor of the human race, is opening the lid of his coffin for the Resurrection. And the tympanum, which Christ's head projects into, mirrors this process. Angels are holding censers, while the anthropomorphic faces of the sun and moon are holding out cloths. Integrated into this generalization of the Resurrection and presence of Heaven, the depiction of the dead Christ appears at the same time to be the iconographical transition from Christ triumphant to Christ the Redeemer, from the Pantocrator to the Salvator.

The relief on the eastern side of the same pillar is even more complex; it shows the Resurrection integrated with the burial (photo, p. 296, top right). This double scene starts in the center, where Christ is being placed into the sarcophagus by Nicodemus and Joseph of Arimathea. The open lid of the tomb bisects the upper part of the relief diagonally, thereby not only creating a two-dimensional division of the areas, but also giving the

arch, which is architecturally an arcade, depicts the Labours of the months in the jambs and, at the top, the figure of Christ in Majesty surrounded by angels.

The façade which surrounds the portal is extremely richly decorated with figures, and is subdivided into six registers, which are supported by a socle featuring monsters and medallions showing the cardinal sins. In the center of the register that continues across the top of the portal archivolts is the largest figure on the façade, a Christ in Majesty surrounded by angels and the Evangelists' symbols of John and Matthew, and the twenty-four elders of the Apocalypse on either side. In the archivolt spandrels of the register beneath it are the symbols of the other two Evangelists, Luke and Mark, each followed by a row of saints.

Pedro de Palol interprets these two upper registers as the symbolic representation of the "Church triumphant," while below them is the "quarreling Church." Both registers contain stories from the Bible, and the way in which these scenes are depicted is strongly influenced by Catalan eleventh-century Bible illustrations. The next register, second from the bottom, is divided into five blind arcades on either side. On the left is King David with his musicians, and on the right is Christ blessing people thought to be Count Oliva Cabreta of Besalú and Cerdaña, his son, Abbot Oliva and a further person. In the bottom register, the scenes are quite demonic and awful. The entire portal has a triumphal structure of a type familiar from ancient triumphal arches and possibly conveyed by Carolingian miniatures.

OPPOSITE
Silos (Province of Burgos), monastery of
Santo Domingo. Cloister, reliefs on the
corner pillars, top left: Descent from the
Cross, right: Burial and Resurrection,
bottom left: Christ as a pilgrim to the
shrine of St. James in Emmaus, right:
Doubting Thomas. Mid twelfth century

Silos (Province of Burgos), monastery of
Santo Domingo. Two views of the
cloister and two capitals. Mid twelfth
century

297

Compostela (Galicia), cathedral of Santiago. Pórtico de la Gloria. Central portal and entrance to the nave. Work of Master Mateo. 1168–1188

Right jamb of the central portal with the apostles Peter (left), Paul, James the Great (Santiago) and John (right)

scene a sense of spatial depth. While the corpse's left arm is lying on the floor of the sarcophagus, the right arm is lying along its lid and points to the top left. Up there is the angel of the Resurrection. And behind the tombstone, to one side but nonetheless very much present, the three Marys of the Resurrection appear. Below the sarcophagus, occupying precisely one third of the height of the relief, are the sleeping guards at the tomb.

The scene of the Resurrection is followed on the western side of the north-west pillar by a depiction of doubting Thomas (photo, p. 296, bottom right). In accordance with older Romanesque principles of design, the sculptor arranged the Apostles in three horizontal rows. The rows are stepped one behind the other. There is a subtle rhythm worked into the representation of their heads, for they are focusing attention concentrically on the events in the foreground to the left. The scene unfolding there is the famous one in which Thomas was invited to place his fingers into the wound in Christ's side in order to convince himself that Jesus had really risen from the dead. This scene culminates with Christ saying: "You believe because you can see me. Happy are those who have not seen and yet believe" (John 20, 29).

While as usual the figures in the back row are reduced to mere busts, it is possible to make out the legs and feet of some of the apostles in the second row in the small gaps between the complete figures in the front row. This naturalism, which is also expressed in the treatment of the legs and standing positions of the figures in the front row, reappears in the everyday topic of the area above the arcade arch. Behind a crenellated wall and bordered by towers are the figures of four musicians, two men blowing horns and two women with tambourines. This secular framing of one of the principal scenes of the Christian faith appears rather unusual. In one of the most fascinating essays on Romanesque art, Meyer Schapiro points out that this represents the secular power of the new urban surroundings of the monastery, which confronted the absoluteness of faith with empirical knowledge, a new historical quality of knowledge, a factor the Church had to react to.

Without necessarily appearing as its representative, Thomas follows Christ's instructions and touches the wound in his side with his index finger, an event that is not actually directly described in St. John's Gospel. He supports his faith through a sensory perception of the risen Christ. The sculptor has, however, placed his antithesis in the very center of this picture. Paul, who was not even present on this occasion and never knew Jesus when he was alive, is standing on the left next to the over life-size

Ávila (Castile), Basílica de San Vincente. Grave of San Vincente. Reliefs: Executioners tearing the bodies of the three saints apart (top). While angels carry the souls of the saints up to Heaven, their heads are being crushed by the executioners (bottom). *c.* 1190

Christ, so that his head is occupying the center of the entire scene. He represents exemplary faith, and by being depicted next to the Apostles is a counterpoint to doubting Thomas. At the same time, this figure represents the reaction of the Church to the new urbane search for knowledge. The three remaining reliefs show Christ as a pilgrim to the shrine of St. James in Emmaus with the disciples, the Ascension and the miracle at Pentecost.

At the end of the period of Romanesque sculpture in Spain is the exceptional work of Master Mateo in Santiago de Compostela, the Pórtico de la Gloria (photo, opposite, left). Its construction, which included architectural tasks, took nearly half a century. From February 22, 1168 Mateo was in receipt of a high life annuity from King Ferdinand II; out of this he not only had to support himself but also bear the costs of manufacture. The work was finally completed in 1211, the year the church itself was consecrated.

A substructure similar to a crypt was built to suit the terrain, and over it a monumental narthex which surrounded the actual Pórtico de la Gloria and the three entrance portals. Only the central portal is covered by a tympanum which is supported by a compound column with many parts. In front of the trumeau is a further column whose shaft is decorated with the Tree of Jesse, and its capital depicts the seated apostle James the Great, the patron saint of the church. A banderole in his left hand says "misit me dominus," the Lord sent me.

In the center of the tympanum the figure of an oversize Christ is enthroned. This figure is surrounded by the Evangelists and their symbols; his hands bearing the stigmata are raised, and his robe is open to reveal the wound in his side. On either side angels display the "arma Christi" which are the symbols of his Passion. Above are the heavenly hosts of the Redeemed. In the archivolt framing the scene the twenty-four elders of the Apocalypse are arranged in a row. They are facing each other in pairs and playing musical instruments.

The side portals do not have tympanums, and develop their visual programs in three archivolts each. Various interpretations consider Christ to be shown on the left amongst the Chosen or the Jews, and on the right amongst the Damned or the Gentiles. The reason for this difference of opinion is that the entire program can be interpreted either as a depiction of the Last Judgement, or as the triumph of the Redeemer over death and sin. However, if one considers that a large amount of space in the tympanum is taken up by the *arma Christi*, an interpretation of the scene as a Judgement becomes less tenable. It is more likely that this is a fundamental change in the way the Son of God is perceived, from the Judge to the Redeemer of mankind. The extent to which this portal heralded the dawn of a new era of forms in the Spanish Middle Ages is shown by the sixteen statues taking the place of the column shafts in the jambs.

Romanesque sculpture in Italy

Northern Italy

As elsewhere, the development of Romanesque sculpture in Italy was connected to the flowering of contemporary architecture. Nonetheless, sculpture here was not dictated to by the structural requirements of architecture to the same extent as it was in France, as the demands were more of a liturgical nature. Instead, early works display strong decorative intentions, with the use of animal ornaments and abstract interlaced patterns derived from Lombard art.

The church of Santa Maria in Pomposa was built in the second quarter of the eleventh century; its façade, placed in front of an atrium, has retained its original form to the present day. It is rather low and wide, and constructed of many different colors of brick; the end result is highly decorated, and in the center the wall is broken up by three entrance arcades (photo, above). Their inner archivolts are decorated with friezes of vine foliage, and on the front side these are framed by archivolts made of radially and tangentially arranged bricks. The three horizontal areas of the façade are produced by two long bands of terracotta; the lower one is interrupted by the arcades, and the upper one stretches along the entire length of the wall, above the highest points of the arches. The uniform vine foliage, larger than in the archivolts, twines around numerous figures, and is also used to form two crosses which penetrate the upper band above the spandrels. The two arcade arches at the sides are crowned by two fabulous creatures, and over the central one is a small marble cross. The side walls are broken up by oculi, and next to them inscribed stone tablets are let into the wall. The tablet on the right is signed by the artist, Master Mazulo, though he unfortunately did not date his work. It is thought that the master and his craftsmen came from Ravenna, as the structure of the façade is so Oriental, even Byzantine, in style.

Around 1100, the influence of the Languedoc region started to make itself felt, particularly in the person of Master Wiligelmus, who worked from 1099 for the cathedral architect Lanfranco in Modena. We know his name due to the inscription which he left over one of the four façade reliefs whose theme is essentially the Book of Genesis (photo, opposite, top right). If considered in its original order as a continuous frieze, it started with the depiction of God, in a mandorla held by two angels, holding an open book. Next was the Creation of Adam by God touching his head, the Creation of Eve by means of Adam's rib, and finally the Fall of Man. The second section shows God's judgement of the sinners, their expulsion and fate tilling the soil. In the third relief is the story of Cain and Abel, their offering, the fratricide and Cain being called to account in front of the Lord for his brother's whereabouts; the fourth section continues with his death, which is only described in the Apocrypha. The last two of the twelve scenes are of Noah's Ark. These four reliefs and their powerful expressiveness are, as it were, the starting point of Romanesque sculpture in Italy, and the return to the Classical style is characteristic of Wiligelmus's figures.

The design of the two-storey portal, whose columns rest on ancient lions (photo, opposite, bottom left), has led the American art historian Arthur Kingsley Porter to make a fascinating assumption. He thinks that the two lions were found in Roman ruins, and were spoils used by Lanfranco and Wiligelmus to support the columns, and this in turn, quite by chance, led to the construction of a wider portal of the type which one finds frequently both in the plains of the River Po and also in Saint-Gilles-du-Gard in Provence and Königslutter in Germany.

OPPOSITE
Pomposa (Emilia-Romagna), Santa
Maria. Detail of the façade. Brick,
marble, terracotta. Second quarter
of the eleventh century

BOTTOM
Modena (Emilia-Romagna), cathedral of
San Geminiano. Lion portal on the west
façade. Beginning of the twelfth century

Modena (Emilia-Romagna), cathedral of
San Geminiano. Relief on the west
façade: Creation of Adam and Eve, Fall
of Man. Work by Wiligelmus. Beginning
of the twelfth century

At the end of the nave, bordering the choir, is the choir screen whose present position is a fairly precise reconstruction dating from 1920. The barrier-like wall is formed of five variously sized and painted marble reliefs, supported by six columns, most of which have figured capitals, and four of which are supposed by lions. The reliefs depict scenes from Christ's Passion, starting on the left with the Washing of the Feet. Next to it, occupying a wide area, is the Last Supper, and Judas's kiss. The last two slabs show Christ before Pilate and the flogging, followed by the carrying of the Cross.

Art historians have identified at least four different masters at work on this important Italian Romanesque work, which has been dated between 1160 and 1180; Anselmo da Campione is considered to have been the main master at work on the reliefs. He is the first of the few Romanesque sculptors belonging to the famous Campionese group, from Campione on Lake Lugano, who we actually know by name. These architects, sculptors and stone masons are credited with preserving and developing ancient methods of construction, and with being responsible for a large proportion of the development of Romanesque architecture that took place in northern Italy, France and even Germany. Campionese sculpture is distinctly reminiscent of Provençal sculpture, and was probably modeled on works in Saint-Gilles and Arles. The round ambo, built later between about 1208 and 1225 on the left in front of the Pontile, is also thought to be a Campionese work, and according to an inscription in the lapidarium the work is by a Master Bozarinus. The reliefs show Christ surrounded by the symbols of the four Evangelists', the Fathers of the Church and the Calling of St. Peter.

It is nonetheless worth casting an eye over the epigraph which sings the praises of the sculptor which was carved as a postscript to the inscription over the foundation date on the cathedral's façade: INTER SCULTORES QUANTO SIS DIGNUS ONORE, CLARET SCULTURA NU[N]C WILIGELME TUA – "How greatly you are respected amongst sculptors, Wiligelmo, is now shown by your work." This is an example of "sculptural outdoing," as Albert Dietl puts it, making the person being praised stand out amongst "all his competing professional colleagues." This does, however, presuppose that sculptors had, due to the growing prestige of their work and products, already managed to distance themselves from the traditionally undervalued crafts such as those of the stone masons, a group in which sculptors tended to be included.

A portrait of a sculptor on the Porta dei Principi in Modena Cathedral, described by Dietl as "a self-portrait of an anonymous sculptor from Wiligelmo's own circle," testifies to the way in which artistic self-awareness was able to express itself around 1100. The creation of a self-portrait, insofar as one can speak of such a thing, was subordinate to the theology of the universal act of creation as carried out by God with regard to Adam; like a sculptor, he formed him from clay according to his own image. Because the tablet bearing the praise of Wiligelmus is held by the prophets Enoch and Elijah, who never died but were translated into

Ferrara (Emilia-Romagna), cathedral.
Detail of the baldachin in front of the
main portal: Telamones on a lion. Work
of Niccolò. End of the twelfth century

TOP OPPOSITE
Fidenza (Emilia-Romagna), cathedral.
Niche figures, David (left), Ezekiel
(right). Ascribed to Benedetto Antelami.
End of the twelfth century

BOTTOM OPPOSITE
Fidenza (Emilia-Romagna), cathedral.
Façade, portal area: baldachin supported
by two lions, niche figures and side
portals. End of the twelfth century

Heaven, the sculptor is also, as it were, being translated into an eternal sphere and can expect a special life in the next world. It is a special phenomenon that most Romanesque artists' names have been found in Italy, though research into this field is still in its infancy. Peter Cornelius Claussen considers the reason for this to be that "the thirst for glory and obsession with prestige of the Upper Italian cities … turned individual artists into heroes, even in the Middle Ages."

In Ferrara in the north east of Emilia-Romagna, towards the end of the 1130s, Master Niccolò signed the cathedral façade, dated 1137; it is assumed that he had been a pupil of Wiligelmus' in Modena previously. Niccolò's works seem to be inspired less by the Classical period than by his predecessor, though they scarcely match his power of expression. Nonetheless, his figures have a special vividness which also comes through in the garments they wear. Niccolò also worked in Verona; pieces in the church of San Zeno, and in particular the jamb figures on the cathedral's portal (photo, p. 304, bottom) are ascribed to him and his workshop. The latter figures, like those in Ferrara, have a strange, largely unexplained affinity with the Early Gothic jamb figures in France.

On the portal of the church in Fidenza are a group of sculptures and reliefs (photos, p. 303) whose stylistic similarities to those on the Baptistery of Parma have suggested links with Benedetto Antelami and his workshop. The structure of the portal area, in a clever system of horizontal and vertical lines, together with the three projecting portals, gives the façade a complex three-dimensional quality. The side portals are separated from the main portal by two sturdy half-columns placed in front of the wall. The main element in the horizontal structure is the relief frieze, which runs from the capitals over the northern half-column to its counterpart to the south, and narrates the story of the life, martyrdom and miracles of St. Donninus.

The figures and scenes are extremely vivid and full of life and display a considerable closeness to the style of Benedetto Antelami, so that the "Master of St. Donninus" should be viewed as an exceptional pupil of his, apart from the possibility that Antelami himself worked on the project. The two prophets' statues flanking the central portal, David on the left and Ezekiel on the right, are ascribed to him with a considerable degree of confidence. They are standing in niches and are very rare examples of three-dimensional Romanesque sculpture.

The name of the most important High Romanesque Italian sculptor is known to us only from his two signatures; the more detailed of the two is on the relief of the Descent from the Cross (photo, p. 305) in Parma Cathedral and it is dated: ANNO MILLENO CENTENO SEPTUAGENO OCTAVO SCULTOR PATUIT MENSE SECUNDO ANTELAMI DICTUS SCULPTOR FUIT HIC BENEDICTUS – "A sculptor appeared in February 1178; this sculptor was Benedetto, also known as Antelami." It is not certain whether the additional name Antelami is actually a family name, but at any rate it is a name rich in tradition referring to a group of architectural experts from the Valle d'Intelvi between Como and Lake Lugano, called the "intelvino"; the extended term, "Magistri Antelami," dates back to Roman times and was used to mean architect.

TOP LEFT
Lodi (Lombardy), cathedral. Portal figure: Eve, detail. Last quarter of the twelfth century

TOP RIGHT
Florence (Tuscany), San Miniato al Monte. Pulpit with a support made up of a lion, man and eagle. Second half of the twelfth century

RIGHT
Verona (Veneto), cathedral of San Zeno. Detail of the left portal jamb: figures of prophets. *c.* 1135

Parma (Emilia-Romagna), cathedral.
Benedetto Antelami, Descent from the
Cross. High relief. Marble. Height
40 inches, width 84 inches. 1178

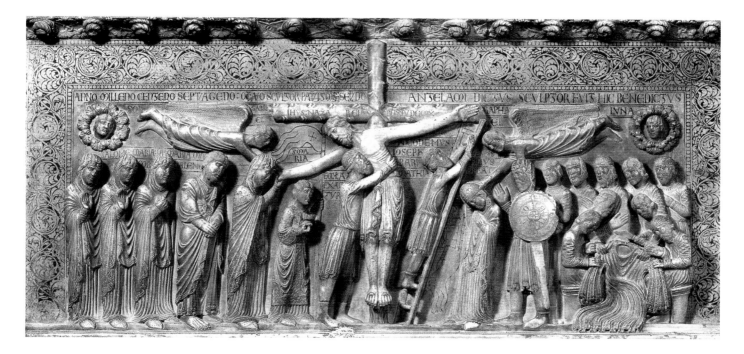

This is the capacity in which we meet him in Parma, where he is thought to have designed the Baptistery. The sculptural decorations, whose program depicts the importance of the Birth of Christ for humankind's salvation, are also by him and his workshop. The relief of the Descent from the Cross, originally part of the cathedral's choir screen or pulpit, is the earliest work of his that we know of. The scene is framed by a broad, damask-like vine scroll band in the niello technique. The picture divides into three groups, the central one being the recovery of the body. On the left, lined up in the manner of a procession, are the mourners together with the personification of Ecclesia, and on the right, stepped in two levels, is a procession of male Jews, and in front of them soldiers with Synagoga, throwing dice for Christ's robes.

The strict arrangement in a row is, in particular, what reminds one of the portal frieze in Arles, and this is generally where Antelami's stylistic sources are to be found. Antelami's work constitutes an important body of Romanesque sculpture in Italy. Aspects of his stylistic innovation have been imitated on several occasions and whose legacy can be found in the work of Nicola Pisano and his pupil Arnolfo di Cambio.

The cathedral façade in Lucca (photo, p. 306, right) was strongly influenced by the architectural school of Pisa; according to an inscription it was completed by Giudetto da Como in 1204 and is the oldest remaining section. In the ground floor, three large arches open into a narthex containing the actual portals. Above it are three galleries, whose columns and arcades, in contrast to Pisa, are richly decorated with sculptures and stone inlay. Older pictures show the equestrian statues of the patron saint, St. Martin, in the right arch spandrel of the narthex, in the act of cutting his robe in order to give half to a beggar. For a long time this legend was felt to be so moving that the statue was clothed with a cape and hat made of valuable materials on feast days. Today it has been replaced with a cement cast dating from 1950, and the Romanesque original has been moved inside. Its main importance in sculptural history is that it belongs to a series of famous Italian equestrian statues.

One of Lucca's most exceptional Romanesque sculptures is the font in San Frediano, produced around 1150 (photo, p. 306, left). The richly sculptured basin rests on a shaped round base, and in its center is a column in the form of a flame with little devils. It supports a round vase with a tempietto. Several sculptors worked on this piece, including one Master Roberto, who left his signature on the edge of the basin. He produced the figures of the Good Shepherd and the six prophets influenced by the Byzantine style. Another sculptor, probably taught in Lombardy, produced the series of Moses episodes, which narrate stories from the Pentateuch using simple but vivid figures without an architectural framework.

The reliefs on the façade (photos, p. 307, top and bottom left) of the church of San Pietro fuori le mura in Spoleto, Umbria, were probably produced around 1200. There are sixteen rectangular reliefs spread out across the entire façade, and the central section around the main portal is one of the oldest remaining parts. Above the portal is a horseshoe-shaped lunette with Cosmati mosaics and flanking eagles above decorative strips.

Lucca (Tuscany), San Frediano. Font.
Sculptors working with Master Roberto.
c. 1150

Lucca (Tuscany), cathedral of San
Martino. Façade, detail. Completed by
Giudetto da Como. 1204

The entrance is framed by vine scroll decorations, and is surrounded by arcades several storeys high, decorated with flower patterns and stylized animals. On each side are five reliefs depicting stories from the Bible and animal fables. On the slab at the top right is the death of the penitent sinner who freed St. Peter from his bonds. Above him a demon is angry, the reason for which is explained on a sign: "I am angry because he was mine before this."

The parallel folds of the angel's robes show the influence of Lombard sculpture, in particular of Benedetto Antelami. The second tablet shows the death of the sinner who did not repent, being tortured by demons. He is head over heels in boiling water, and to one side the Archangel Michael is leaving with the scales. The three reliefs underneath show events with lions. The first one shows a woodcutter who has trapped the paws of a lion in a tree trunk, and this is meant to show man's superiority over animals. Further down in the second relief, a man is kneeling in front of a lion, and in the last relief a soldier is being attacked by a lion. According to a Tuscan bestiary, in which the lion is compared to God, this depicts the theme of repentance. The lion spares the humble, but not those who continue to

hold fast onto worldly things. On the right at the top are the Washing of the Feet and the Calling of St. Peter and St. Andrew, and underneath it two wolf fables. At the very bottom is another lion, the symbol of Christ fighting a dragon.

The great columned portal of the collegiate church of San Quirico in Orcia (photo, p. 307, top right) is rather oversize in its proportions compared with the façade. It was created during the late twelfth century, and is a well-preserved example of Lombard portals in the province of Siena. Its characteristic features are a projecting structure supported by two columns knotted together, which in turn stand on lions positioned parallel to the façade. On either side of the entrance the jambs are formed out of groups of columns. Above the columns are the archivolts. While most of the capitals are decorated with foliage, two of them depict animal heads. In the tympanum is a Byzantine statuette which is thought to represent Pope Damasus II (1048). It is above all the battle between two demons in the architrave which enables this Tuscan portal to convey that terrifying dimension which is so familiar from the great portal of the French Romanesque period.

TOP AND BOTTOM LEFT
Spoleto (Umbria), San Pietro fuori le
mura. Façade relief, details. *c.* 1200

RIGHT
Orcia (Tuscany), collegiate church of San
Quirico. Portal supported by knotted
columns. Late twelfth century

Rome, central and southern Italy

In Rome and Latium, it was, above all others, the Cosmati who took care of the artistic decoration of churches from the beginning of the twelfth to the start of the fourteenth centuries. Apart from architecture, the fields they preferred working in were sculpture and mosaics. The term Cosmati is a collective name for a series of Roman families of sculptors who frequently bore the name Cosmas. We know about them because they occasionally left their signature and date on works. In addition to the Cosmas, other well-known artistic families included the Mellinis and the Vassalettos.

Some of the most remarkable products of these workshops are the monumental Easter candle stands, dating from about 1190, which can still be seen in Gaeta Cathedral or the Romanesque church of San Paolo fuori le mura (photo, opposite, center). The latter stands on a base decorated with sphinxes and people, and its column is divided into several registers

in a manner reminiscent of ancient triumphal columns. Created by Pietro Vassaletto and Niccolò di Angelo, its visual program, comprising the Passion, Resurrection and Ascension, is centred on Easter. The similar Easter candle stand in Gaeta also depicts scenes from the Passion, though it includes other scenes from the childhood of Christ and the life of Erasmus, the patron saint of Gaeta.

Roman workshops did not just work for the churches and monasteries of Rome. They also prefabricated sections that could be exported to other places in order to be assembled there. The first section of the cloister of Santa Scolastica in Subiaco, between Tivoli and Anagni in Latium, for example, was signed by Jacobus Romanus, and his sons confirmed its completion: "Cosmas and his sons Lucas and Jacobus, three Roman citizens and master artists in marble, created this work during the rule of Abbot Landi." The best preserved and most important Roman cloisters, those of San Giovanni in Laterano and San Paolo fuori le mura (photos,

OPPOSITE
Rome, Lateran Palace. Cloister gallery
with lions supporting the columns next
to the entrance. Below: Detail of a
twisted column covered with mosaics.
The work of Vassaletto and his son.
1215–1232

BELOW
Rome, San Paolo fuori le mura. Easter
candle stand, detail. Work of Pietro
Vasseletto and Niccolò di Angelo.
c. 1190

Rome, San Paolo fuori le mura. Entrance
arcade to one of the cloister galleries.
Work of mosaic artists in the Vassaletto
family. 1205–1241

top and opposite, right), were built in the first half of the thirteenth
century by the Vassaletto family. There is evidence that the father and son
were the masters who produced the cloister of the Lateran Palace, which
was constructed between 1215 and 1232 and some of whose arcades are
supported by variously twisted coupled columns. They are frequently
covered with delicate mosaics, and at the entrances to the inner courtyard
are supported by animals. There are numerous sculptural figures decorating the gutter cornice, the arch spandrels and the capitals. Above the
arcades facing the inner courtyard is a decorative mosaic frieze, characteristic of the Roman Romanesque style. The cloister of San Paolo fuori le
mura, built between 1205 and 1241, may be smaller, but is even more
lavishly decorated.

Situated on the threshold between the Orient and the Occident, Apulia
produced a wealth of art from the eleventh century onwards, and apart
from architecture, the main objects were sacred pieces of equipment. The

Bitonto (Apulia), cathedral of San
Valentino. Pulpit eagle. Including
remains of a pulpit by Master Nicholas,
c. 1220. Eighteenth century

Bari (Apulia), San Nicola. Throne of Elia.
Marble. End of the eleventh or beginning
of the twelfth century

OPPOSITE
Moscufo (Abruzzi), Santa Maria del
Lago. Pulpit from the workshop of
sculptors Robertus and Nicodemus.
1159

throne of Bishop Elia in San Nicola in Bari (photo, p. 310, right) is of
exceptionally high quality, and its seat is supported by three entirely three-
dimensional atlantes. The main weight is carried by the two figures on
either side, the central figure playing a minor role. The stave he is carrying
proves him to be a pilgrim, and this is thought to be a reference to the
pilgrim route to San Nicola, which was a significant "support" for the new
importance of Bari and Bishop Elia. It has recently been suggested that the
work could date from the third quarter of the twelfth century, though
traditionally it was assumed to have been produced immediately before
1105.

Other liturgical church furnishings of the Italian Romanesque period
include the magnificent ambos, predecessors of the pulpits. In Bitonto,
Apulia, the remains of the Romanesque pulpit by Master Nicholas have
been preserved (photo, left), and in the eighteenth century they were
combined with fragments of the ciborium dating from 1222, giving them

their present form.

In the church of Santa Maria del Lago in Moscufo is an important
example of Italian Romanesque ambos (photo, opposite). It was produced
in 1159 in the workshop of the sculptors Robertus and Nicodemus, and is
the only complete Abruzzi pulpit remaining in its original location. On
three sides of the square pulpit box are lecterns, and underneath them
convex surfaces bearing the Evangelists' symbols, which also take on a
liturgical function: this is where the New Testament stands in the light of
the church service. Next to the Evangelists are figures from the Old
Testament. "But the greatest narrative pace is developed in the depiction of
the story of Jonah on the sides of the staircase," Roger Willemsen writes.
Truly surprising, however, is the depiction of the Boy Extracting a Thorn.
This is to be found on one of the corner pillars, an unusually early and
direct adoption of Classical sculptures, as this was not a general feature
until the Renaissance.

Gernrode (Saxony-Anhalt), former convent church of St. Cyriakus. Holy Sepulchre. Western outer wall of the burial chamber (top). Interior of the burial chamber, martyr and bishop Metronus in the niche of the west wall (bottom). 1100/1130. Head of Metronus from the end of the eleventh century

Romanesque sculpture in Germany

In contrast to the Mediterranean countries, Germany did not enjoy a continuous developmental history of Romanesque sculpture. It started with mainly sacred pieces of equipment in churches, such as the Ottonian bronze works of the Hildesheim workshop under Bishop Bernward at the beginning of the eleventh century, or the metalwork pieces of other Ottonian centres. Even where stone sculpture did appear in the twelfth century, it mainly provided objects for the interior. Plants, animals and other figural decorative forms gradually appeared on the originally undecorated cushion capitals. At the same time a clear Italian influence is noticeable in this, which is a result of many Upper Italian sculptors being called to Germany. "In around 1100 almost the entire range of architectural ornamentation in the German-speaking region was dependent upon Upper Italian forms," is how Rainer Budde summarizes the situation.

There was probably a quite different situation in the Rhineland with Cologne as its center, because there was still a direct confrontation with the remains of Classical sculptures there, and this also explains the actual availability of tried and tested techniques, such as those for working stone, in the eleventh century. An independent sculpture high in quality developed here relatively early.

The once rich sculptural works on the Holy Sepulchre in the former convent church of St. Cyriakus in Gernrode were also of high quality, as is shown by those remnants that have been preserved (photos, left). The west wall, in particular, of the chambers built in between the two eastern bays of the southern transept is decorated so extensively that it is frequently called a prayer in stone. A central area with three niches is framed by a double frieze. In the central niche a plaster tablet with the figure of Mary Magdalene is set in, flanked by two columns standing in semi-circular niches. The outer narrow frieze consists of a band of vine foliage that is being disgorged by masks and animal mouths, while the inner and wider one contains actual scenes which are also framed by vine foliage. In the top left corner is John the Baptist, and opposite him on the right is Moses; both of them, as Christ's predecessors, are pointing to the Lamb of God, which is in the center of the upper part of the frieze. Both figures are accompanied by lions, and the bunch of grapes that the one on the right is carrying in his mouth show them to be good lions. After them, and flanking the Lamb of God, are two birds, the one on the left a phoenix and on the right an eagle, both symbols of the Resurrection. The theme of the upper section is the Resurrection and Salvation, but the lower one, with the animals of the Physiologer, presents us with symbols of human strengths and weaknesses.

This visual program on the west wall of the Holy Sepulchre also informs us about its liturgical importance. The "Sepulcrum Domini," the imitation of Christ's sarcophagus in Jerusalem that existed in many Romanesque churches, was used to keep Christ's corpse in; it was taken down from the Cross during the Good Friday service and laid to rest in the sarcophagus in the inner chamber. During the celebration of the Resurrection on Easter Sunday, it would be brought out ceremoniously and presented to the community. Produced in the period from about 1100

BOTTOM LEFT
Riesenbeck/Tecklenburg (North Rhine-Westphalia), St. Calixtus. Tombstone of Reinhildis. Sandstone c. 1130/1135

BOTTOM RIGHT
Merseburg (Saxony-Anhalt), former cathedral of St. John the Baptist and St. Lawrence. Tombstone of Rudolf of Swabia (d. 1080). Bronze. Before 1100

Externsteine near Horn (North Rhine-Westphalia), Holy Sepulchre group. Depiction of the Descent from the Cross. Relief on rock. First quarter of the twelfth century

to 1130 at the latest, the Holy Sepulchre in Gernrode is probably the oldest example of its type in Germany.

The most important form of medieval grave is the tombstone made out of stone or bronze, which would be placed on the floor of a church covering a grave below, or onto a sarcophagus-like tomb. While early Romanesque churches and crypts were at first used exclusively to bury martyrs and saints, members of the clergy were gradually also buried there, and eventually even secular lords or the founders of the churches.

In the crossing of Merseburg Cathedral is the grave of Rudolf of Swabia (photo, bottom right), who was killed in 1080 at the Battle of Elster. As the anti-king to Emperor Henry IV, he was furnished with the insignia of the imperial orb, sceptre and stirrup crown, though he was not actually entitled to these. In addition, his bronze tombstone was originally gilded, giving it a noble quality that led to heavy criticism from contemporaries, in particular Henry IV's supporters. The important feature for art historians is that this is probably the earliest figured tombstone. The reason for its appearance within a church, which until then was the

preserve of members of the clergy, is given in the surrounding inscription as being that this person died battling for the Church and had therefore earned the right to be buried in this place.

The trapezoid tombstone of Reinhildis in the village church of Hörstel-Riesenbeck near Tecklenburg (photo, bottom left) was possibly originally the lid of a sarcophagus. The scene, framed by a band of foliage, shows, as the inscription tells us, "… the virgin Reinhildis, who was the heir of her deceased father and who was murdered by her mother at the instigation of her second husband. She soon ascended in order to assume her seat in Heaven, and has become a devout joint-heir with Christ. Gerhard." The young woman has a halo and is wearing a Byzantine dress with wide sleeves and a headscarf. Her arms are raised as she looks upwards, where an angel is bearing her soul to Heaven in the form of a child. The slab was originally dated around 1189, as this was the year in which Bishop Gerhard of Oldenburg took over the Osnabrück diocese, and his is the same name as the person who donated the tombstone. Its style is, however, more consistent with a date around 1135, meaning that the bishop has to be ruled out as a possible donor.

One of the most unusual phenomena in the German Romanesque period is the relief of the Descent from the Cross, eighteen feet high and more than ten and a half feet wide, in the Externsteine (Extern rocks) near Horn in East Westphalia (photo, top). This is a monumental piece of free-standing sculpture which seems to have more in common with the huge Presidents' heads carved into the rock at the Mount Rushmore National Memorial in South Dakota than Romanesque sculpture, which one would normally only expect to find in connection with a man-made piece of sacred architecture. And it is indeed an ancient heathen ceremonial site; the Benedictine monastery of Abdinghof in Paderborn gained the property rights in 1093, as Abbot Gumpert wanted to build a hermitage there. It was finally the Paderborn Bishop Heinrich of Werl who decided to have an

Gelnhausen (Hesse), Protestant parish
church, formerly St. Mary's. Choir
arcade, console: man in vine foliage.
c. 1240

imitation of the religious sites in Jerusalem carved into the rocks here. The cave-like chapel, which is behind the relief and is considered to be an Adam chapel, was consecrated in 1115 according to its inscription. This date also suggests the date of origin of the Descent from the Cross, which is occasionally thought to have been produced at the same time as the chapel was consecrated. Budde, however, considers it to be closer in style to the Freckenhorst baptismal font, dated 1129, which would date the relief to around 1130.

In the center of the relief, which presumably served as a scenario for Easter festival productions, is a mighty cross, in front of which the actual events take place. Joseph of Arimathea and Nicodemus are depicted recovering the body of Christ, and his mother is standing on the left edge of the relief. Opposite her, on the right side, is John holding a book. At either end of the beam of the Cross are the sun, on the left, and the moon, on the right. Beneath all of this, with the serpent twined around them, kneel Adam and Eve. Above the left side of the Cross beam is a bearded figure with a cruciform nimbus, who is holding the banner of the Cross in his left hand and pointing his right hand to Mary in blessing. This figure has been interpreted as either the Resurrected Christ, or possibly as God himself.

With a few exceptions, there are no counterparts to the extensive visual narratives on the capitals in Spain, southern France and Burgundy in German churches. Most of the capitals only have geometric shapes, animals and plant decorations, masks or monsters. The sculptors were not, however, any less self-aware, as is shown by the signature on the famous Hartmann column in Goslar: HARTMANNUS STATUAM FECIT BASISQUE FIGURAM – "Hartmann made the column and the figure on the base" (photo, opposite, bottom right).

Romanesque portals

The Gallus gate (photo, p. 316) which appears on the north transept of the Basel Minster of Our Lady looks as if it is set within a Roman triumphal arch. The structure, which was built towards the end of the twelfth century, has been restored and altered on many occasions during the course of the years. Part of the original Romanesque structure are the upper part of the tympanum and the figures in the jambs. In the tympanum Christ is enthroned as a judge, holding the open Book of Life with his left hand against his thigh; the Cross in his right hand is a later addition. He is accompanied by Peter on his right and Paul on the left. In the right corner, a bearded man is kneeling holding an architectural model, and Paul is leading a male and a female figure by the hand to Christ. In the left jamb are the Evangelists John and Matthew, and on the right are Mark and Luke. Their symbols are added over their heads in a type of lower capital underneath the actual capitals.

Following an earthquake in 1356, during the course of which the east side of the cathedral in particular was heavily damaged, it was necessary to carry out extensive restoration work. The figures of the wise and foolish virgins in the architrave probably date from this time, as do the columns which make it difficult to see the jamb figures. The portal area is flanked

Quedlinburg (Saxony-Anhalt), former
convent church of St. Servatius. Nave,
cushion capital with figural decoration.
Before 1129

Spieskappel (Hesse), former
Premonstratensian monastery church of
St. John the Baptist. Nave, capital with
bearded mask and heads. c. 1200

Hildesheim (Lower Saxony), former
Benedictine monastery church of St.
Michael. Nave, capital with foliage and
heads. Before 1186

Goslar (Lower Saxony), former collegiate
church of SS. Simon and Jude. Capital of
the Hartmann column with mask and
dragons. Third quarter of the twelfth
century

Basel, minster of Our Lady. Gallus Gate,
stepped portal with jamb figures
(bottom). The Evangelists Matthew and
John with their symbols (left). End of the
twelfth century

showpiece wall covered with reliefs, and which is structured by vertical and horizontal elements. The height of the lower zone matches the jambs, and underneath the three arch blind arcades to the left of the portal is the enthroned Madonna and Child, and on the right another ruling figure is enthroned, considered to be the antagonist to the Mother of God, and which in medieval opinion was the Antichrist. Both of these figures are accompanied by symbolic representations of Good and Evil, some of which accord with the animal allegories of the Physiologer. The upper zone, around the archivolts, is split into two areas with blind arcades, the lower of which is supported by caryatids. One of the figures on the right has been identified as Luxuria. This identification arises from the snakes on her breasts, and as a result the other figures are also considered to be personifications of the Vices; the figures opposite, on the Madonna's side, are thought to be the Virtues. Above the upper archivolt a relief row with thirteen figures is let into the wall, and the central one is easily recognized as Christ, due to his raised right hand and the depiction of the Book of Life. He is accompanied to the left and right by the Apostles, and the row of figures is bordered on either side by larger reliefs containing depictions of Mary and John the Baptist.

The theme of this wall is the conflict between Good and Evil with regard to the Last Judgement, and the portal and its tympanum, which again depicts Christ, are placed between the figures of James the Great and

by three tabernacles on each side, arranged one above the other, containing representations of merciful deeds. Above them is a type of aedicule architecture with taller tabernacles containing the figures of John the Baptist on the left and the deacon Stephen on the right. At the very top, on either side, is an angel blowing the last trumpet, and the one on the right dates from the early sixteenth century. Small reliefs next to them depict the resurrected dressing themselves. A profiled entablature with a palmette frieze forms the upper conclusion to the portal. The Gallus gate was noticeably influenced by Italian and French styles, predominantly the latter. The Evangelists' robes in particular display a debt to Burgundian sculpture, even if not entirely specific.

The entire layout of the north portal of the former Benedictine abbey church of St. James in Regensburg is also reminiscent of an ancient triumphal arch (photo, opposite, top). The actual portal is fitted into a

TOP
Regensburg (Bavaria), former
Benedictine abbey church of St. James.
North portal. *c.* 1190

BOTTOM
Freiberg (Saxony), minster of Our Lady.
Golden Gate. *c.* 1230

John the Evangelist. His right hand is raised and he is holding the Book of Life, and Rainer Budde considers him to be Christ the teacher proclaiming the message of salvation. In each of the jambs are three ornamented columns placed in front of the inward grading, and between them, at the top and bottom, are small crouching figures, one of which, with a point, can be identified as a stone mason.

Despite its unity, this portal, unique in the German Romanesque period, shows vague influences from other regions such as Upper Italy and southern France, and also from the Anglo-Saxon sphere. It is assumed that it was constructed towards the end of the twelfth century, though this can not be conclusively proved.

One of the last Romanesque portals in Germany is the west portal of the parish church of Freiberg near Dresden (photo, opposite, bottom), known as the Golden Gate. The jambs of the portal are graded in eight steps, and combine a whole variety of influences both in its structure and the style of its figures, and these can, above all, be traced to the style of Gothic cathedrals that had been developing in France from the middle of the twelfth century.

The theme of the entire ensemble is the glorification of the Mother of God and the Child, and she appears in the center of the tympanum as the enthroned Queen of Heaven with the baby Jesus. She is accompanied on the left by an angel carrying a scepter and Joseph, and on the right by the Magi. The glorification of Mary is aided by the eight figures in the jambs, which are depictions of typological predecessors of Christ and Mary. In the left jamb is Daniel, who because he survived the lions' den is considered to be proof of the virginity of Mary. The High Priest Aaron, opposite him, should be understood in the same context. The two women's figures standing opposite each other, Bathsheba and the Queen of Sheba, correspond to each other in their meaning, which is as the Old Testament allusion to Mary. The Kings Solomon and David from the Old Testament appear as the predecessors of Christ. The inner figures in the jambs, to either side of the portal, represent as it were the life of Christ, with John the Baptist on the left and John the Evangelist on the right.

The theme continues in the four archivolts over the jamb figures. The inner one shows Christ, accompanied by archangels, crowning Mary. At the highest point of the second archivolt the souls of the Chosen are being brought to Abraham, and his lap is meant as the symbol of Heaven. At the sides are two angels and four apostles. At the crown of the third archivolt is the dove of the Holy Ghost, also accompanied by angels and the remaining eight Apostles. The depictions of the Angel of Judgement and the resurrected leaving their graves in the outer archivolt has been used to argue that the theme of the portal was the Last Judgement. Budde quite rightly points out that the most important elements, such as the heavenly Judge, the Damned and the jaws of Hell, are missing, and that, in addition, the theme of the Last Judgment would rule out that of the glorification of Mary. "Furthermore," he writes, "the resurrected in the archivolts should be seen as the Blessed being led into Paradise by the Angel of Judgement [Michael]."

317

OPPOSITE
Bamberg (Bavaria), cathedral. Mounted
king, known as the Bamberger Reiter
(Bamberg Horseman), on the first pillar
of the north side of the George's Choir.
Sandstone, height 93 inches. Before 1237

Freudenstadt (Baden-Württemberg),
Protestant church. Font. On the base a
man and lion as supporting figures, and
basilisks and bearded masks on the bowl.
c. 1100

TOP
Canterbury (Kent), cathedral. Capital in
the crypt. 1100–1120

BOTTOM
Avebury (Wiltshire), church of St. James.
Font. Stone. Twelfth century

Romanesque sculpture in England

There was a rich Anglo-Saxon tradition of art in England from at least the eighth century, which included influences from the Celtic predecessors of the Anglo-Saxons, as well as traces of the Romans. This was suddenly interrupted by the Danish invasions around 1000. It was not until the Danish King Canute had consolidated his position of power in England and become a Christian that new artistic creativity, in particular in the field of sacred architecture, was able to develop. Another cultural change was brought about by the arrival of the Norman William the Conqueror in 1066. In the end, Romanesque sculpture in England developed under a whole range of widely differing influences, and native forms combined with Scandinavian and Continental styles to form a distinct Anglo-Norman artistic style. Indeed, the Romanesque style is generally known in England as 'Norman'.

The remaining capitals in the cloister of the Benedictine abbey founded in 1121 in Reading, the county town of Berkshire to the west of London, are partially ornamented with beaded bands twisted around each other; some also bear figurative decoration, such as a rather disconcerting angel. One capital has what is thought to be the oldest remaining Coronation of the Virgin. These capitals were preceded by the capitals in the south transept arm of Worcester Cathedral and those in Romsey Abbey, which in turn referred to those in the crypt of Canterbury Cathedral, which were produced between 1100 and 1120 at the latest (photos, top and center). What they all have in common is that their point of departure was Anglo-Saxon models, metalwork and illuminated manuscripts such as those in the scriptorium in Canterbury.

Numerous baptismal fonts remain of the church furnishings that were produced, and though some of these were made of lead, most were produced using stone. The stone basin from St. James's, in the village of Avebury in Wiltshire in the south-east of England, has a flat relief; in the lower part a garland of tightly interlaced blind arcades circles the body of the font (photo, bottom). This motif was extremely popular and can often be found as an architectural ornamentation in English Romanesque churches. Above it are vines of varying lengths. Here, as on the other stone fonts, Anglo-Saxon elements are clearly visible.

In Chichester Cathedral in Sussex are two reliefs which originally were probably part of the rood screen (photo, opposite). One of them shows the meeting of Jesus, Mary and Martha in front of the gates of Bethany, and the other shows the raising of Lazarus who was an intimate friend of Jesus. Both scenes are thematically related, because before Jesus entered the village near Jerusalem, Lazarus's sisters Martha and Mary came to him one after the other, telling him of their great sadness at their brother's death and also complaining that if Jesus had been there, their brother would not have died. His answer, that he would call Lazarus back to life, was understood by the women to mean their brother's resurrection on Judgement Day, and this was little comfort. This is followed by the shortest verse in the Bible, which is also one of the most touching: "Jesus wept" (John 11, 35).

The scene depicted in this relief combines the two successive encounters

Chichester (Sussex), cathedral. Relief:
Raising of Lazarus. 1120–1125

Chichester (Sussex), cathedral. Relief:
Mary and Martha meeting Christ by the
gates of Bethany. 1120–1125

into one event. Both women are kneeling before Jesus, begging him to really restore their brother to life in this world. The relief is damaged, and of all places the areas affected are the left hand and right arm of Christ. The damage seems so calculated that one feels justified in assuming that this is a deliberate act of iconoclasm, perhaps in order to remove the personal and binding nature of the friendship John writes about. The relief of the raising of Lazarus was probably displayed very close by, for the two reliefs are also related stylistically. The high lines of the robes' folds are emphasized by deep cuts, and the structure of the two scenes with Christ in the center, either sitting or standing, dividing the events taking place in front of him from the Apostles behind, is identical.

Begun in 1091, the choir of Chichester Cathedral was consecrated in 1108. Georg Zarnecki considers the rood screen to have been created during the period of office of Bishop Ralph de Luffa, who died in 1123 and was presumably German. This would explain certain stylistic similarities to Ottonian works in Hildesheim and Cologne. The reliefs probably dated from between 1120 and 1125.

The tradition of Norman architectural ornamentation led to some extraordinarily magnificent English Romanesque portals. The one in the southern narthex of St. Mary and St. Aldhelm in Malmesbury, Wiltshire, between London and Bristol, is not only the main sculptural work in this church, but is also one of the most exceptional and unusual examples of its type anywhere.

The narrow columns border the archivolts directly, without being interrupted by capitals. Four arches, separated from each other by narrow ornamental strips and surrounded by another at their outer edges, contain round and almond-shaped medallions containing figures from the Bible. On the side walls of the narthex are two lunettes opposite each other, each containing six seated Apostles, and an angel floating above their heads holding a banderole (photo, p. 323, top). The elongated figures are reminiscent of Burgundian works around 1130, and their quality is the equal of the sculptural works in Autun.

The portals of Ely and Kilpeck also demonstrate the special British love of rich decorative work. The Prior's Door of Ely Cathedral in Cambridgeshire, which was made a bishopric in 1108, is the most lavishly decorated of the three entrances from the church's Romanesque cloister

TOP OPPOSITE
Malmesbury (Wiltshire), church of St.
Mary and St. Aldhelm. Lunette on one of
the side walls of the south portal narthex.
c. 1155–1170

BOTTOM LEFT OPPOSITE
Ely (Cambridgeshire), cathedral. The
Prior's Door. Before 1139

BOTTOM RIGHT OPPOSITE
Kilpeck (Herefordshire), church of St.
Mary and St. David. South portal with
animal columns. *c.* 1140

(photo, p. 323, bottom left). The columns are supported by figures that can no longer be identified, though at least one of them appears as a lion in older engravings, a motif familiar from Italy. While the architrave is carried by its very own support, the columns and the pillars flanking them continue into the archivolts they support, separated by bead moulding. While the outer archivolt is covered with a flat acanthus strip to match the flat relief of the pillars, the inner archivolt curves inwards towards the tympanum, corresponding to the columns that bear it.

The depiction in the tympanum is of Christ in Majesty in a mandorla held by angels; while this iconography derives from French models, it is developed here in an unfamiliar manner. This is because the bottom tip of the mandorla and the lower legs of the angels penetrate the entire height of the lintel, and more than half its width, so that it was not possible to place an independent scene there.

This also shows one of the unusual features of English Romanesque portal sculpture, in that countless small figures are given space in equally countless ornamental medallions which are actually vine scroll decorations, while the large-scale relief, in contrast, is afforded little room. The Prior's Door encapsulates this conflict between the native traditions and Continental influences.

The south portal (photo, opposite, bottom right) of the church of St. Mary and St. David in Kilpeck, Herefordshire, has a different vocabulary of form. Georg Zarnecki considers it to be the best preserved example of an entire series of works, such as architectural sculpture and fonts, produced by an influential school of sculpture in western England, which worked during the second quarter of the twelfth century along the border with southern Wales.

The church of Kilpeck occupies a special position in that its founder, Oliver de Merlemont, presumably did not just return from his pilgrimage to Santiago de Compostela with the intention – or even vow – to found a church, but probably brought back sculptors with him who were familiar with Continental forms. Nonetheless, the latter were largely drowned out by the decorative idiom of the English Romanesque, and little can be established of their provenance.

Narrow pillars that can best be described as a type of animal column are covered with snake-like monsters, and these form the outer frame of the portal. At the top, angled inwards, they form the capitals of the richly ornamented columns on the inside next to them. Massive impost blocks which project outwards to either side support the two equally mighty archivolts, one row wider than the supporting columns, and which contain rows of medallions with depictions of animals. The core of the inner archivolt is formed by a rounded pole which animals and demons are sitting on, like birds on a perch, and underneath each one is a console. At the crown a flying angel is depicted with a banderole. The architrave, which is formed by a zigzag band, supports the tympanum which contains a stylized depiction of what is probably a Tree of Life. Dating from between 1135 and 1140, the portal is one of the later English Romanesque works.

Barbara Deimling

Medieval church portals and their importance in the history of law

It is June 18, 1209. Very few inhabitants of the town of Saint-Gilles du Gard, in southern France, stayed at home on that day, because none other than Duke Raymond VI of Toulouse was making his way through the streets to the portal of the abbey church. In this case, however, it was not his magnificent robes that attracted the attention of the curious spectators, but rather the remarkable fact that Raymond was not wearing any clothes at all – he was approaching the church portal stark-naked; "adductus est comes nudus ante fores ecclesiae," as it was reported in a contemporary chronicle. This humiliating walk was the penance the church authorities had laid upon him for murdering the papal legate,

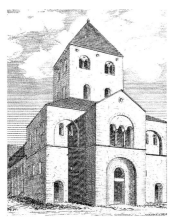

1. Werden, Westphalia, church of St. Salvator with westwork. Perspective view from the north-west

Peter of Castelnau. In this way it was possible for him to become reconciled with the Church and be readmitted to its communion. Before the duke walked through the abbey church's portal, he would have had to see the relief on the tympanum above the main entrance, presenting the Second Coming of the Lord to him and illustrating the value of penance and reconciliation. It was the apocalyptic vision of St. John with the *Majestas Domini*, surrounded by the four beasts of the Apocalypse. The wide

2. Strasbourg Minster, south portal

circulation of this scene meant that the eschatological message for medieval observers such as Raymond was inescapable. It is a fact that the apocalyptic visions of God, as well as the explicit representation of the Last Judgement, were favorite topics for medieval church portals in western Europe.

The frequency with which both scenes appear has to be seen in the context of the most important events regularly to take place in front of the church portal: secular and ecclesiastical trials. Numerous legal records still exist that tell of judgements and the arbitration of conflicts taking place at the entrances to churches, whether "in galilea" (Perrecy-les-Forges, 1108), "sub portico" (Ferrara, 1140), "in atrio" (Regensburg, 1183), "ante gradus ecclesie" (Frankfurt, 1232), "ante portam" (Frankfurt, 1248) or "in rufo ostio" (Goslar, 1256). This legal tradition can be traced back to the Ottonian and Carolingian eras. In 813, a royal edict was issued forbidding legal judgement of secular issues to take place in the atrium in front of the main portal of churches; this reflects just how widespread this convention was. The decree even had to be repeated on various occasions. This is why a document dating from 943

4. Frankfurt Cathedral, the red door walled up in a side chapel

5. Paderborn Cathedral, the red door

3. Bernhard Jobin, engraving showing the south portal of Strasbourg Cathedral, 1566

reported that the newly constructed westwork in front of the main portal of the church of St. Salvator in Werden, Westphalia, had been built specifically for holding synods (fig. 1).

The practice of carrying out secular and ecclesiastical legal business by church portals was common throughout the Middle Ages. In Strasbourg, in the thirteenth century, the town council's court was set up near the south portal, beneath the statue of Solomon, the Old Testament king and judge (fig. 2). A decree in 1200 commanded that "if an

argument breaks out amongst citizens … no one should straightaway reach for their weapons, but instead appear before the councillors outside the Cathedral of Notre Dame." Their precise position outside the cathedral's south portal is clarified in another document. The portal was at one time protected by a roof and surrounded by barriers, as shown in an engraving by Bernhard Jobin dating from 1566 (fig. 3). These measures meant that the legal proceedings were protected from the elements and crowds of people.

A further example of a church portal used as a secular place of judgement is the cathedral of León in Spain. Between the central and right entrance in the church's entrance hall is a statue of Solomon, and beneath it the inscription "Locus Appellacionis" (place for making petitions), together with the coats of arms of Castile and León. While the heraldic elements can be dated to the thirteenth century, the inscription is eleventh century. The words distinguish the entrance hall as a place of royal jurisdiction.

There is a place in Spain where court sessions take place by the church portal to this very day. It is Valencia. Farmers meet every week by the large main portal of the Baroque cathedral; the judges they have chosen step up to the Water Court and hear disputes over irrigation waters.

It was frequently the color of the door which indicated its use as a place of judgement. In numerous cases, the portals in front of which legal proceedings took place were framed in red, a tradition that can be proved to have

6. Autun, Saint-Lazare.
Detail from the tympanum in the west portal

7. Stefan Lochner, The Last Judgment,
Cologne, Wallraf-Richartz-Museum, *c.* 1435

existed mainly in northern Europe. The monk Roger of Helmashausen, who was an artist, devoted an entire chapter in his treatise on the techniques of various arts, the "Schedula Diversa Artium" written around 1110–40, to the subject of "how to give doors a red frame." Red doors used as places of judgement have been shown to have existed at the cathedrals of German towns such as Frankfurt, Paderborn, Münster, Würzburg, Magdeburg, Bamberg and Erfurt. In Frankfurt (fig. 4), documents dating from the first half of the thirteenth century state that contracts used to be entered into in front

of the "rode dure," the south portal which has since been bricked up. In Paderborn, judicial acts were still being sealed as late as 1452 outside "dei roden Doer" on the north side of the cathedral (fig. 5).

Since ancient times, the color red had been considered to be the symbol of power and status associated with dignitaries, and in the Middle Ages it was a color much used in connection with legal matters. Thus, the emperor carried out the enfeoffment of his jurisdiction by handing over a red banner, and this process was recorded as taking place in

1195, when Henry VI enfeoffed the town of Cremona with his regalia. The color red was to an equal extent an allusion to the potentially bloody execution of legal judgements. As a result, the highest court in the Middle Ages, which had to decide on matters of life and death, was called the Blood Court, and its law books were the Blood Books. There were also blood stones, the *lapides sanguinis*, sometimes called red stones, and these are recorded as existing in Frankfurt, Passau and Worms. That is where judgements were announced and sentences executed in the early Middle Ages, and the name of the stones is evidently a reference to the blood that was spilt. Because of these traditions and customs, red became the symbol of jurisdiction. It was the color favored by jurists and judges, and even Christ wore a red garment in pictures of Judgement Day. This can be seen in Stephan Lochner's picture on this theme (fig. 7). As a result, in the Middle Ages there were not only red church doors, but also red towers, benches, city gates and trees, and in each case the color was a reference to the original function of those sites as places of judgement.

Besides the color red, another way of indicating the legal functions of portals was the widespread depiction of a pair of

10. Oloron (Pyrénées Atlantiques), Sainte-Marie. Detail of portal: maneating monster

lions on either side of church entrances (figs. 8, 9). The lions were often connected with the throne of Solomon, which was flanked by two lions. As Solomon was the most exemplary judge in the Old Testament, the two lions were generally connected with jurisdiction and symbolized judicial power. This is how the French monk Pierre Bersuire explained it in his "Repertorium Morale," a moralizing interpretation of the world dating from 1362: "The judge is associated with two lions, which are set up on many of the flights of steps and

8. Bolzano, Trentino-Alto Adige.
Cathedral portal

9. Ferrara Cathedral, reconstruction of the destroyed Porta dei Mesi

11. Worms Cathedral

flank the entrances of buildings. They make it more difficult to walk through, and because of this they are placed wherever judges sit to punish greedy people." And there are indeed many acts of justice that were decided *inter duos leones*, (between two lions). One definite example is Werden in Westphalia, at the Church of St. Nicholas which was later destroyed; two columns were placed in front of it, each with a lion on it. Right into the eighteenth century it was the custom of the abbey judge to carry out official business between these two columns, and his acts closed with the phrase *actum inter duos leones*. A similar interpretation can be made of the pairs

of lions which lined the porticoes of north Italian cathedrals. In the 1140s, numerous legal cases were concluded at the Porta dei Mesi (which was later destroyed) of Ferrara Cathedral; it was flanked by two lions and overlooked the market square (fig. 9).

The legal activities that occurred at portals were not just restricted to court sessions. The portal was also used as the place to swear an oath. From the eighth century onwards, and particularly in the North, the legal custom of taking an oath "on the threshold" or "by the church doors" became widespread. In the documents of the Cluniac priory of Rüeggisberg in Switzerland, for example, there is a report that the Bernese church advocate Petermann of Krauchthal swore an oath to protect the Church and all people belonging to the province; he took the oath by "taking the ring which hung on the church door in his left hand and repeating the stipulated oath with his right hand raised." Taking an oath at the church door can also be found in a literary source, the "Nibelungenlied," which was written around 1200. When the two queens Kriemhilde and Brünhilde failed to sort out the quarrel that had broken out between them in the women's chambers of the palace, they transposed it to the portal of the cathedral in Worms, normally considered to have been the north portal (figs. 11, 12). There they called upon their husbands Siegfried and Gunther as witnesses, and Siegfried finally offered to swear an oath on the church doors. This literary evidence has a more fundamental character than any

12. Worms Cathedral, north portal

historical documents could have, because these tragic protagonists are idealizations of queens, kings, heroes and heroines, just as the church doors are an archetype which lifts the legal function of the Worms portal into the realms of myth. The legal importance of this portal is underlined by the fact that it is the very spot to which Frederick Barbarossa nailed the privileges which he bestowed upon the city in 1184.

In the Middle Ages, the church portal was also a place to seek asylum. Many contemporary reports tell of fugitives seeking asylum at church doors. Legally, grasping hold of the door ring was the decisive act. This right of asylum at church doors was also codified in law books. In the "Sachsenspiegel," a collection of laws from southern Germany, the earliest version of which appeared around 1215, the following decree can be found: "if a person cannot get into the church, and instead touches the ring on the church door, he should experience the same feeling of tranquillity that he will have inside the church."

The signing of contracts also took place by church portals, and that includes the marriage contract. In the Middle Ages, weddings took place in front of the church doors, and it was not until they were married that the bride and groom would be taken inside the church to mass. This tradition explains the occasional references to portals as the "bride's gateway" which one finds in churches in Bamberg, Brunswick, Mainz and Nuremberg. For this reason, the

13. Robert Campin, The marriage of Mary and Joseph (detail), Madrid, Prado, *c*. 1420

painters of the age often pictured the marriage of Mary and Joseph as taking place in front of the entrance to a temple or church. Robert Campin, for example, portrayed the wedding as taking place in front of a church portal that was lavishly decorated with sculptures, in a painting which he created around 1420 (fig. 13).

Trade agreements were also concluded in front of church portals. The many markets that remain at and around churches testify to this tradition (fig. 14). In many cases, the official measurements still remain at church entrances. One of the most extensive examples is the Minster in Freiburg; various measures, and the year in which they were decreed, are engraved on the walls of the tower's entrance hall. They include the prescribed sizes of loaves of bread and rolls for the years 1270, 1313 and 1320 (fig. 15), and the measurements for corn, wood, coal and bricks, together with the right, granted by King Ruprecht, to hold a fair twice a year.

The legal significance of the church portal in the Middle Ages also explains the penitential walk of Raymond VI, which was mentioned earlier. The public rite of repentance took place by the church portal as it was also a judicial act that comprised the punishment and reconciliation of the sinner. According to the rules of the rite of repentance, those sinners upon whom this punishment had been laid were driven out of the church on Ash Wednesday, "just as Adam was driven out of Paradise." The parallels drawn between the sinners and Adam

15. Freiburg Minster, prescribed measurements for bread and rolls for the years 1270, 1313 and 1320

14. Heidelberg, Church of the Holy Ghost and market

explains why Raymond was required to go to the portal naked; it was not just a question of publicly humiliating him, but of illustrating his connection with Adam. The public act of repentance culminated in a rite of reconciliation on Maundy Thursday. The sinners had to come to the church portal, where the priest would take them by the right hand and lead them back into the church. This act illustrated the reconciliation of the sinners with the Church, and their readmittance to the community of the faithful. This process was frequently reproduced in works of art, above all in scenes of the Last Judgement. One example is a detail of the tympanum in Conques (fig. 16), showing an angel who has taken one of the Blessed by the hand in order to guide him through the gateway to Paradise. In medieval symbolism, the church portal was equated with the gates of Paradise, allowing the faithful entrance into the church, or the heavenly Jerusalem. In Stephan Lochner's painting of the Last Judgement, which has already been mentioned (fig. 7), the entrance to Paradise is painted as a church portal.

But why did the church portal acquire this important legal significance in the Middle Ages? The answer is complex, but one aspect which should be singled out concerns the legal function of the portal in historical and theological terms. The custom of carrying out legal business at a public gateway can be traced back a long way. In the Old Testament, the city

gates were the place where the elders dispensed justice, as is shown on numerous occasions. God commanded the Israelites: "Hate evil, love good, maintain justice at the city gate" (Amos 5, 15); Boaz went to the city gates in order to discuss the legalities of his marriage to Ruth with the elders (Ruth 4); and Absalom would "stand beside the road leading to the gate … whenever a man with some lawsuit had to come before the king's court" (2 Samuel 15, 2-6).

In the Middle Ages, the church portal was treated as the equivalent to the city gates. For example, when a church was consecrated, its doors were described as city gates. The comparison of city gates and the church portal can also be seen in Giotto's representations of *Iustitia* (Justice) and *Iniustitia* (Injustice) in the Arena Chapel frescoes in Padua (figs. 17, 18). The personification of Justice is sitting on a throne, the back of which appears to be open, enabling one to see the blue sky beyond. The painted architectural forms are reminiscent of a church portal whose doors are wide open. In contrast, the personification of Injustice is sitting in front of locked, ruined city gates. The city gates are a reference to the Old Testament. The Old Covenant, which God entered into with the Israelites, has been superseded by the New Covenant with Christ, in this case symbolized by the figure of Justice. In many paintings of that period, the personification of the synagogue, with a

17. Giotto, personification of Iustitia, fresco, Padua, Arena Chapel, *c.* 1305

18. Giotto, personification of Iniustitia, fresco, Padua, Arena Chapel, *c.* 1305

broken lance and crown fallen onto the floor, a symbol of the Old Covenant, would be set against with the victorious figure of *Ecclesia*; here, instead, Justice and Injustice appear as the antitheses of the Old and New Covenants. The locked, ruined city gate is contrasted with the open portal. The open door is a symbol of Christ, who said "I am the door. Anyone who enters through me will be saved" (John 19, 9). Therefore, Christ is the gateway to Paradise, open to all who believe in Christ and lead an upright life. This is also the sense in which the medieval church portal should be interpreted: it is the place of judgement, the gateway to Paradise which is open to the just.

16. Conques, Sainte Foy, detail of the tympanum showing the Blessed

Beaulieu-sur-Dordogne (Corrèze), abbey church of Sainte-Pierre. South portal, tympanum: The Last Judgement, door lintel: creatures from Hell. 1130–40

Image and significance

The Last Judgement

Before a medieval believer entered the church, the House of God, he encountered the most terrible and severe event which his powers of imagination could conjure up, namely the end of the world. The threat which continued to make itself felt, and was sensed with even greater presentiment in the early Middle Ages, was the Old Testament threat of the God of Vengeance. This God was now enthroned as the New Testament Judge of the World over church portals, within the new tympanum, and constitutes one of the central and most important inventions of Romanesque sculpture. The Last Judgement was the main theme of this new type of Romanesque portal sculpture.

Life in the Middle Ages was always lived in a state of direct confrontation with death. The average life expectancy was thirty to thirty-five years, with a high infant and child mortality rate and numerous illnesses and epidemics; as a result, death was a constant and powerful companion, an ever-present aspect of life. As Otto Borst writes, "There was no other course of action for someone living in the Middle Ages than to walk hand in hand with Death, as if it was a companion, shyly, flinching, but in the knowledge that it was ever-present and a part of life on earth … Death was the foundation of life." And man's fear of death, as physical and vital as it was, was above all a deep-rooted religious fear. For death was not the end of life, which would – according to the doctrine of the two worlds – continue in the life beyond. Every dying person was therefore faced with the burning question of whether he would receive mercy from Heaven or be condemned to the torments of Hell. The judgement that would make this decision would take place on Doomsday, which was thought of as the end of all ages.

In the tympanum above the west portal of the abbey church of Sainte-Foy in Conques-en-Rouergue, which was produced in the second quarter of the twelfth century, Christ is enthroned in the center, surrounded by a gloriole (photos, pp. 329–31). That in turn is surrounded by a wreath of clouds and stars as a reference to the heavenly position of the enthroned figure. In this sphere four angels are also depicted, two of them holding banderoles on either side of his head, and the other two, by his feet, carrying torches.

In accordance with the vision of the Last Judgement as narrated by Matthew, after Christ has placed the sheep on his right hand and the goats on his left (Matt. 25, 33), he will with his outstretched arms divide the world beyond into Paradise on his right and Hell on his left, a division of the world into Good and Evil which dominates the entire Christian art of the Middle Ages and has been a determining factor in culture right until the present.

In the tympanum of Beaulieu-sur-Dordogne (photo, opposite), which was created at roughly the same time, Christ is also enthroned in the center. But he lacks a gloriole, and is only accompanied by two horn-playing angels. His arms are extended horizontally, creating an obvious allusion to his death on the Cross which is held behind his right arm by two angels. They are assisted by a third, who is presenting the cross nails behind Christ's left arm. Together they are showing the *arma Christi*, the objects which tell of his Passion and the triumph over death. They are rather unusual in depictions of the Last Judgement, and should be interpreted as symbols of that triumph and Christ's majesty, which is confirmed by the angel above the right row of apostles who is arriving carrying the judge's crown. The entire design is a reference to the Parousia, the Second Coming of Christ, which will usher in the Last Judgement. For the Weighing of the Souls, the actual process of judgement, still lies in the future. At the end of time the living and those who have risen from the grave will gather at the foot of the Throne of Judgement.

The architrave, which is divided into two registers, depicts demonic beings at the bottom, including the seven-headed monster from Revelation. While this is clearly a depiction of Hell, there are dis-agreements as to how the upper register should be interpreted. It is, on the one hand, also considered to belong to Hell, showing the Damned being swallowed by monsters, but there is an alternative view that these events could correspond to the "Hortus deliciarum" or Garden of Delights of Herrad of Landsberg (1125/30–1195), in which it is written that "At God's bidding the bodies and limbs of people once swallowed by wild animals, birds and fish will be brought forth again, so that the intact limbs of the saints will rise again from the holy human substance." Earlier sources also demonstrate the contemporary topicality of this idea, accord-ing to which being swallowed can also be understood as being disgorged,

an idea more in line with the Parousia.

In contrast to Beaulieu, Christ in Conques is a strict judge who divides the world beyond into Paradise and Hell. The vertical dividing line runs through the trunk of the Cross, in front of which is the gloriole and throne, and through the Weighing of the Souls below. Christ's right upper arm is stretched out horizontally, with his lower arm bent vertically upwards. In this position Christ is, as it were, representing the co-ordinate system where the order of Paradise is to be found. Mary, Peter and perhaps the founder of the monastery are approaching him from that direction in an upright posture, followed by further saints who cannot be clearly identified, though presumably including Charlemagne. Immediately on his left are four angels, one of whom is holding the Book of Life up for him to see, and another of whom is swinging a censer. The two angels facing away from him are armed with a shield and pennanted lance in order to protect him from the Hell which borders the scene.

In the lower register is a structure of arcades covered by a pediment, representing the House of Paradise in the New Jerusalem from the Apocalypse. In the central arcade Abraham is to be found seated with two figures who have been redeemed, and in the side arcades one can see pairs of holy men and women. In the left spandrel the Hand of God is stretched

Details of the tympanum: the damned being pushed into the jaws of Hell (top). The Devil enthroned in Hell and meting out punishment (bottom)

OPPOSITE
Conques-en-Rouergue (Aveyron), abbey church of Sainte-Foy. West portal, tympanum. Second quarter of the twelfth century

out towards the begging St. Fides – Sainte Foy. Behind the figure of the saint are images of chains hanging from arcades. These are the chains which bound the prisoners who were spared on her recommendation. In the right spandrel angels are opening the graves which the dead are rising from, in order to gain admission to Paradise or Hell following the Weighing of the Souls. The doors to both of the next worlds are wide open; they are particularly noticeable due to their naturalistic mountings and locks, and are separated from each other by a sturdy wall.

The Judge's left arm is pointing diagonally down towards the Damned in hell: "Go away from me, with your curse upon you, to the eternal fire prepared for the devil and his angels" (Matt. 25, 41). The order of Paradise is contrasted with the chaos of the underworld. And sticking through the gates of Hell are the open jaws of Leviathan, who is swallowing the Damned and throwing them into Hell (photo, top). This monster, which originated in Phoenician mythology, was, in the Bible, the monster of chaos. It was this monster which God defeated at the outset of creation, but the same monster could easily be woken and break out of captivity if a curse was uttered against the existing order. In the Conques portal showing the Last Judgement, he is depicted as the jaws of Hell, behind which the Devil reigns. Crowned, and seated under the pediment as a symmetrical counterpart to Abraham, he is holding a second hellish judgement, in which he allocates torments according to the severity of the sins committed.

The hanged man with a bag around his neck to his left is a reference to Judas, while an exposed woman and a monk, in other words a man of the Church, are awaiting their hellish tortures. And behind them a knight and his horse are being thrown head first into Hell. It is not, however, just the torments of Hell that are being put on view; each of these tortures of the human flesh is also an exemplary punishment for human vices and sins. The fallen knight embodies arrogance, and the monk and naked woman are symbols of fornication. In the register above it, there is even a bishop being accused of the misuse of his ecclesiastical office, and a glutton is being hung up by his legs.

In Autun in Burgundy, where the relics of St. Lazarus had been brought in the eighth century, the Cathedral of Saint-Lazare was built between 1120 and 1146. Here, too, the Last Judgement is on display in the tympanum, and in its center Christ is enthroned in a gloriole held by angels (photo, p. 332). Each of the sides is split into two registers with the architrave underneath. The upper one shows the enthroned Virgin Mary and two apostles as observers of the judgement. In the lower register, to the right of Christ, eight apostles stand, facing the enthroned figure in the manner of petitioners. St. Peter with the keys is guarding the entrance to the heavenly Jerusalem, which is represented as an arcaded structure, and into which the resurrected are laboriously trying to squeeze with the assistance of an angel.

On the opposite side, in one of the most graphic scenes in Romanesque sculpture, the Weighing of the Souls is taking place between the Archangel Michael and the Devil, and behind them stands Luxuria with snakes at

her breasts (photo, p. 333). Behind Michael's back, facing Christ, is the twelfth apostle, who is opening the Book of Life that is being weighed for the Judge. The architrave depicts the resurrected being separated into the Redeemed and the Damned by an angel in the center. The procession of the Elect on the left, which includes two pilgrims, contrasts with the army of the Damned on the right. This frightened crowd is apprehensively and fearfully moving towards the spot where the poor sinners are grasped by the hand of the Devil and pulled into a dreadful Hell. The medallions on the outer archivolts, with the labors of the months and signs of the Zodiac are a reference to the larger cosmic context of the Last Judgement.

The tympanum in Autun is especially vivid due to the elongation of the figures which, depending on the proportions, almost revokes their corporeality. Added to this is a sense of drama in the contrast of Good and Evil, for instance in the Weighing of the Souls, which could scarcely be

more graphic. The archangel wrapped in silk – worked in stone using a filigree technique – stands opposite frightful and grotesque devils with long, skinny limbs. It is scarcely possible to imagine a more urgent way of visualizing the last days when there will be no going back, no repentance, when turning back will no longer be of any use. The Last Judgement, at the end of time, really is taking place in this tympanum, at the feet of the enthroned Judge. And anyone who walked through this portal in the knowledge of his sins would have had a good idea what was in store for him.

And strategically located right in the middle of the Last Judgment of Autun, in the area at the bottom of the mandorla where it touches the architrave, at the feet of Christ and yet above the angel separating the Elect and the Damned, the sculptor inscribed his signature: GISLEBERTUS HOC FECIT – "Gislebertus made this." Placed here right in the visual center of the tympanum, his signature elevates him – and his exceptional work – into a divine sphere.

OPPOSITE AND BELOW
Autun (Saône-et-Loire), cathedral of
Saint-Lazare. Main portal, tympanum:
Last Judgement. Detail below: the
Weighing of the Souls. 1130–1145

The sculptural wealth of capitals

The extremely exciting display of God on the portals goes hand in hand with the mysterious wealth of symbols of Romanesque sculptured capitals in the interior of churches. Apart from monstrous animal shapes, there are most puzzling forms which are scarcely intelligible to modern observers and whose roots lie not only far back in the history of Christianity and the Classical world, but even in the countries of the Near East and Africa. Christianization and early monasticism caused those visual worlds to be incorporated into Christianity without being understood, and to be passed on until they were given a new sculptural expression in the Romanesque churches of France, Spain and Italy. There was a similar pattern to the handing down and interpretation of heathen images incorporated into the Christian imagination in the countries north of the Alps, and sculptural items there owe more to the magical wealth of images of the Celts and Teutons.

On the other hand, direct use was also made of ancient art. While the traditional school of thought holds that the "antiquarian cord" between the so-called Carolingian Renaissance and the adoption of Antiquity in the twelfth century had been broken, Horst Bredekamp has recently pointed out that in northern Spain, "as early as the 1080's, an adoption of ancient forms had started, and their boldness and originality goes far beyond anything that took place in the twelfth century." This realization is highly important to art historians in that it contradicts the traditional thesis that the French Romanesque period was historically pre-eminent over that of Spain. Additional factors are the high degree of mobility and "iconographical playfulness" of sculptors, and these contributed to the development of an enigmatic and iconographically open visual idiom which cannot be tied down to particular unambiguous meanings simply by consulting contemporary texts. This more recent research into this fascinating aspect of art history is in its infancy, however, and wherever one question is answered, many others spring up in its place.

The great pilgrimage routes of the Romanesque period led countless people right across Europe to the famous reliquaries, to the graves of the Apostles Peter and Paul in Rome, and to the grave of the Apostle James the Great in Santiago de Compostela in the extreme north-west of Spain. And the First Crusade of 1095 to 1099 meant that Jerusalem was also once more accessible to Christians. Like modern tourism, these "travelers" played a large part in the exchange of cultures in the Middle Ages. What they saw on church portals, capitals and consoles when, for example, they came to Spain from the North did not just shock them, but was taken home with them as soon as they returned. And if the people concerned were painters or sculptors, they would incorporate what they had seen into their own visual language in order to give those images new life in the places where they worked.

But above all these, and incorporated in all sermons, was the penetration of Creation by the work of Satan and his hosts, which lay in wait for mankind wherever demons could find a home. There were many such opportunities: rough forests and ravines, storms and threatening dark clouds, illnesses and famines, and also the temptations of sins of the flesh and transgressions of the Christian Virtues. Whenever a pilgrim walked

Chauvigny (Vienne), former collegiate church of Saint-Pierre. Four capitals in the ambulatory. Second half of the twelfth century

The Devil displaying his altar with the symbol of death

Dragon (symbol of death) swallowing a Christian

Eagles carrying souls to Heaven

Griffin with a tail hand

Bonn (North Rhine-Westphalia), minster
of St. Martin, former collegiate church of
St. Cassius and St. Florentinus. Choir
stalls, side wall with the Devil (left). Side
wall with an angel (right). Limestone.
c. 1210

into one of the new churches, he would be confronted with the demon who would give him no peace until it had penetrated him and consumed his heart and soul. St. Matthew's Gospel gives many examples of how Jesus dealt with demons, by driving them out using Beelzebub (Matt. 9, 34; 12, 24–27). Romanesque sculptors made use of this countermeasure in their sculptures. "Demons were attached to churches in a stone form, the intention being that they would recognize themselves, as in a mirror, and be scared off by their own appearance," is how Bredekamp puts it.

Many of these people suddenly recognized their unending loneliness in the face of Creation and as a result developed something whose existence has been disputed especially since the early nineteenth century – their individuality. The many Romanesque artists' signatures are proof of this. Many finally took refuge in the religious movements and sects that were springing up in many places.

Even if the sculptured capitals of Saint-Pierre in Chauvigny do not reach the high quality of the Toulouse workshops and their surroundings, they are nonetheless some of the most expressive works of the French Romanesque period (photos, opposite). They rest on the columns between the choir and ambulatory, and present a bewildering universe of biblical

and demonic figures and scenes in over thirty sculptures. The Devil himself, wearing a scaly garment, stands with his legs apart on the northern crossing pillar holding a magical symbol of death. Between his legs the fires of Hell, burning on an altar, are visible. Another scaly demon is turning towards him from the left, and on the other side a smooth-skinned demon is bringing him one of the Damned (photo, top left). On the southern crossing pillar two eagles, symbols of renewal and resurrection, are beating their wings and holding little naked human figures in their claws and beaks. These are the souls of the Dead which have been redeemed and are being carried up to Heaven (photo, top right). Every sinning Christian was haunted by the terrors of the inexplicable powers in this world and plagued by premonitions of an impending terrible punishment, and would therefore have seen the picture of the winged dragon swallowing the naked souls of the Damned as representing his own fate (photo, p. 335, bottom left). The griffins, in contrast, which are a mixture of lions and eagles with human hands growing out of their tails, are an enigma (photo, p. 335, bottom right).

The sculptor in charge also left his signature behind in this ensemble. Similar to Conques, he carved it into the highest ranking religious sphere,

Freising (Bavaria), cathedral of St. Mary and St. Corbinian. Crypt, animal column. Height 102 inches. *c.* 1200

Kilpeck (Hereforeshire), St. Mary and St. David. South portal, animal column. Mid twelfth century

Silos (Province of Burgos), monastery of
Santo Domingo. Three coupled capitals
in the cloister. *c.* 1085/1100

the edge of the impost block of the capital showing the Adoration of the
Magi: GODFRIDUS ME FECIT – "Godfridus made me" (photo, p. 257).

But the Devil was omnipresent. He appears noting down man's sins on
the stone side wall of a choir stall (photo, p. 336, top left) in the Minster of
St. Martin in Bonn, the former collegiate church of St. Cassius and St.
Florentinus. While the demon's head attached to a human or apparently
human body was meant to fend off the Devil, at the same time his book-
keeping was meant to remind members of the clergy who used these stalls
of their own sinfulness. Next to it was something more comforting, however, because the same choir stall contained an angel noting down man's
good deeds (photo, p. 336, top right).

Animal columns

Animals in all shapes populated free-standing columns or other supports,
extending the sculptures on the capitals and bases across the entire shaft.
An entire demonic animal kingdom came together there, either engaged in
battles or intertwined ornamentally, and frequently including human
figures. These animal columns are a special form of Romanesque sculpture
found mainly on French church portals, where they form the trumeau or
central support such as the one in Souillac (photo, p. 264, right), which was
moved inside the church of Sainte-Marie following the destruction of the
portal during the iconoclasm of the religious wars; in the rest of Europe,
this form is comparatively rare. There is a little column of this type in the
façade gallery of San Martino e San Michele in Foro in the Italian town of

Rivolta d'Adda (Lombardy), San
Sigismondo. Capital: twin-tailed
mermaid. *c.* 1100

BOTTOM
Sangüesa (Aragón), Santa María la Real.
Detail of the façade: sphinx and fabulous
creatures. Last quarter of the twelfth
century

Lucca. The south portal of the church in Kilpeck, Herefordshire, in
England, contains a similar column (photo, p. 337, right), and the only
example in Germany is to be found in the crypt of Freising Cathedral
(photo, p. 337, left). The latter, dating around 1200, depicts a dramatic
battle between two winged dragons and knights; two of these have already
been swallowed and the remainder are under threat by further snake-like
dragons rising up from below. The iconographical interpretation of this
column in particular, which is executed in a rather coarse style without
close parallels, can at best be made in terms of a general symbolism in
which the dragon-fight is illustrating the battle between Good and Evil.
The eagles in the capital, separated from the earthly sphere by means of a
magical rope, appear to represent Christ. The east side shows the half-
length figure of a woman with plaited hair, which Rainer Budde believes
represents the Apocalyptic female figure of Mary/Ecclesia.

Image and Symbol

The images which people in the Middle Ages created of the things that
surrounded them, of animals, forests and mountains, and of natural events,
were imbued with a variety of quite different meanings. Nothing remained
stuck in its plain physical existence. The great Dutch historian Johan
Huizinga expressed this in a uniquely appropriate way: "It was never
forgotten that every object would be meaningless if its relevance went no
farther than its immediate function and appearance, and as a result all
objects projected quite a way into the next world." As a result, holiness
could appear in almost anything that was visible and tangible, whether it
be a tree, rock or thunderstorm. This was because God was free to assume
any form he wanted in order to reveal himself to mankind. This position
demonstrates the medieval expectation of incarnation, and despite their
heathen origins these hierophants could be "understood as desperate
attempts to visualize the mystery of incarnation before the event," as
Mircea Eliade says, cautiously interpreting them as the expectation of
Christ *per se.*

Apart from simple items, it was the representational world of
sculptures that was full of symbolism, and could contain unambiguous or
many-layered references. Whether good or evil, they always accorded with
the special type of medieval world orientation to which they owed their
existence. Everything was woven together by a network of similarities or
affiliations, and beneath the superficial appearance of a thing, its other
form, of which it was a symbol, lay dormant. Medieval man was constantly
creating links in his understanding between the appearance of an object
and the supernatural world and the higher reality. Yet even these
references are not always clear-cut and the sole valid ones, they can alter at
any time and place, be extended or changed into something else. The
examination of symbolic meanings has to proceed by emphasizing particular features which are related to each other. For example, the light blue
color of a sapphire is a characteristic that can be connected directly with
the light blue of a clear sky, and this gives the gem its role as a symbol of
Heaven. And this is the point from which the symbolic power of the
sapphire can be extended or altered depending on the context.

Mariental near Helmstedt (Lower
Saxony), monastery church. Lion as a
persecutor of the Good, taking a lamb.
c. 1140

Bari (Apulia), San Nicola. Main portal.
Before 1098

What is revealed is a specific peculiarity of medieval thought, which – in contrast to its more normal cognitive means of recognition based on a sequence of cause and effect – is reduced simply to the associations made with particular outward shapes. Umberto Eco describes this phenomenon with reference to a rather shortened ability to visualize things: "In this context people have spoken of a spiritual short-circuit, of a way of thinking that does not seek the relationship between two things in the convolutions of the causal correlations between them, but rather makes an abrupt leap to see them in terms of the relationship between meaning and purpose."

The "Physiologer"

This way of thinking found its expression in what is called the "Physiologer," or "one versed in natural science," one of the earliest exegetic reference works that can be consulted over the world of animals depicted in Romanesque sculpture. Its core was probably written by AD 200, when the canon of New Testament writings was already largely consolidated, and it was, on the one hand, the product of ancient physical science. But it was also constantly reworked over the course of the following millennium, extended and brought into line with the Christian body of thought.

Animals are described in simple language in fifty-five contemplative and edifying stories, grouped according to their particular characteristics and behavior, and these form the groundwork for equating their qualities and behavior with an exemplary Christian lifestyle and even Christ himself, all this narrated in a touchingly naive allegorical style. For example, the nature of the "sun lizard" is described, and it is said that it becomes blind in old age, and slips into a crack in a wall towards dawn in order for its eyes to be healed by the sight of the rising sun. This passage is followed by the following recommendation, addressed directly to elderly people: "When you are wearing the clothes of old age, and the eyes of

TOP
Charlieu (Loire), former priory church of
Saint-Fortunat. Capital depicting an
acrobat. Twelfth century

BOTTOM
La Chaize-le-Vicomte (Vendée), capital
showing a scene with acrobats. Twelfth
century

your reason have become dulled and stupid, go seek the rising sun of righteousness which is Christ," who will open "the eyes of your heart" and take away all the darkness. The Physiologer contains the source of all those famous Christian animal allegories, such as the lion who conceals his tracks and is therefore the symbol of the Saviour who moves unseen amongst men. Another example is the phoenix, wrapped in precious stones, which would fly up to the cedars of Lebanon every 500 years in order to fill its wings with pleasant smells, burn itself in the altar fire and which, when pulled from the ashes by the priest in the shape of a worm, would grow new wings. Like Christ, it could lose its life and then come to life again.

Romanesque sculpture contains numerous depictions of animals and fabulous creatures, which can only be comprehended by means of this enigmatic – and by no means definite – symbolic and allegorical perception, one which has been largely lost to modern understanding except in those cases where it can be deduced by sources such as the one above.

Players, entertainers and acrobats

"Joculatores," as traveling entertainers were called in medieval Church Latin, occasionally appear on capitals. They were people without status, home or honor, which made them "dishonest people." Their social independence also made them outcasts, though people admired their artistic skills at fairs. Ingeborg Tetzlaff believes that depictions of them were used to represent the sins of the mind. "If they symbolize intellectual speculation or 'mental contortions'," she writes, meaning the very contorted positions the acrobats were depicted in, "it comes down to the same thing: the Church's proscription of undogmatic or heretical thinking, mixed with any however involuntary respect for its undeniable spiritual power." While the acrobat whose legs are twisted over his shoulders and whose hands are stroking his beard, depicted on one of the capitals of the Benedictine abbey of Saint-Fortunat in Charlieu (photo, right top), may indeed suggest such an idea, he surely has a more modern purpose. Horst Bredekamp, in a study of the console figures on the roof of San Martín in Frómista near Burgos, has shown just how much these depictions were connected to immediate apotropaic purposes. This church, which was built between 1066 and about 1090, and was the seventh stage on the pilgrim route to Santiago de Compostela that ran south of the Pyrenees, has retained its importance largely due to these sculptures, numbering over 400 in total. Naked acrobats of both genders appear in all sorts of pleasurable contortions, and this is a warning that unbridled behavior is likely to lead to damnation. In addition, the faces of a group comprising a musician, acrobat and two wrestlers in La-Chaize-le-Vicomte (photo, right bottom) are contorted into animal masks, revealing that they are possessed by devils.

Demonization of the sexes

While the proscription of the unbridled body was clearly expressed in the scene depicting music and dancing, acrobatics and illusions, the damnation of sexual matters was turned into a kind of body-search made

TOP
Compostela (Galicia), cathedral of
Santiago. Puerta de las Platerías, left
tympanum: adulteress or Original Sin.
Second decade of the twelfth century

BOTTOM
Aulnay-de-Saintogne (Charente-
Maritime), former collegiate church of
Saint-Pierre-de-la-Tour. Capital in the
apse: Demon with creeping vines.
Beginning of the twelfth century

stone. The character of these sculptures as the "means of warding off
fears," borne by pilgrims in particular, is very sharply defined. The capitals
of many Romanesque churches depict animals or humans in bonds,
mainly formed of coiled vines which were believed by contemporary
theologians to form part of Satan's hunting weapons, and these scenes
sometimes contained sexual and even faecal aspects. In Aulnay, for
example, the vine foliage is being excreted by an anus demon who is
holding his legs up in order to be able to set Satan's bonds on their faecal
way into the world (photo, p. 342, bottom), where they will turn into
devilish snares for sinners.

This idea of devilish machinations was not just conjured up out of thin
air. Pseudo-Hrabanus Maurus considered the world to be a tangled forest
full of demons whose sole purpose was to torment mankind. And in his
Ethymologiae, Isidor of Seville wrote that criminals, whose deeds had in any
case forfeited them to the Devil, had to eat magical plants which transformed them into all sorts of different animal shapes and hybrid creatures.

Just as these creepers, depicted on countless Romanesque capitals,
grew out of demons' orifices, so they could only turn into monstrous
beings if they had taken the same path into this world. This shows that
these flourishes were by no means just some ornamental accessory, but
were rather the "frame and catalyst" within which terms all these demonic
apparitions and demonizations had to be understood.

The demonization of sexuality in the depiction of the sexual organs
themselves is visually crude to the point of grotesque distortion. A naked
monk playing a lute on the northern side of the tower of San Martín in
Frómista, for example, is making a point of displaying his penis. That this
was more than a remote theme depicted in out of the way architectural
corners is proved by its presence in prominent architectural sites. On the
pediments of the same church a phallus man appears two consoles away
from a vulva woman. And at another site in San Martín is another phallus
man, whose penis has been drastically extended to the thickness of his arm
(photo, p. 343, left).

One of the most puzzling and exceptional depictions of a vulva woman
is in Kilpeck, England (photo, p. 343, right); Bredekamp thinks that the
version in Frómista served as a model for this and other examples, such as
a console figure in St-Quentin-de-Rancannes, because the founder of the
church of St. Mary and St. David in Kilpeck, Oliver de Merlemont, built
his church after he had made a pilgrimage to Santiago de Compostela and
had been impressed by what he saw there and *en route*. The figure, dating
from the middle of the twelfth century, is steeply foreshortened and its
head is not female as much as demonic; her arms are folded underneath
her legs, like the acrobat in Charlieu, and she is using her hands to open
and display her vulva. This depiction, called a "Sheela-na-gig," meaning
"ugly as sin," had some counterparts in Romanesque sculpture. The
capital with the twin-tailed mermaid in San Sigismondo in Rivolto
d'Adda, Lombardy (photo, p. 339, top) is also part of this series. These
graphic depictions of female genitalia do in fact date back to the Stone
Age, and can be found in many Asian countries. This image gained
mythical dimensions both there and in Ancient Greece. This must have

Kilpeck (Herefordshire), St. Mary and St.
David. Console figure: "Sheela-na-gig."
Mid twelfth century

made it an even more powerful witness in Romanesque Europe to the obsessions that plagued members of the clergy and monks in particular.

The motif of being swallowed has connotations with the vulva. Being eaten by beasts and demons, one's enemy or opponent, was a widespread image for the entrance to the underworld in the Old Testament, and during the Romanesque period it meant passing through the jaws of the Devil, as depicted on the tympanum in Conques or the capital in Chauvigny. There are countless variations on this theme both on Romanesque capitals and animal columns. Many examples appear in both biblical and contemporary texts, in which this very opening to the Inferno is brought into an intellectual association with the "mouth of the vulva."

The horror of living in a terrible world and knowing through which opening one had entered it had the effect, quite apart from all ascetic reactions, of elevating it to a fiction in which all sexual matters were considered to be demonic. That this opening was at the same time the goal of male desire, under autonomous female control, inevitably led to a deep-seated fear of the vulva, which was expressed in countless pictures as being eaten. Quite apart from the dangers of the journey which every pilgrim traveling through France and northern Spain had to endure, he was also constantly immersed in a range of feelings ranging from fear to terror. This despite the fact that it was the pilgrimage itself that was supposed to free those people taking part from their traditional torment caused by the theological state of sin. For there was no way of telling whether the apotropaic intention of warding off the demonic by means of these stone figures actually worked. The attempt to use it entirely for the purpose of presenting these repressive morals in fact led to the imaginative liberation of sculpture. As Bredekamp puts it, "Having been required to condemn the liberation of the senses, they depicted Evil so convincingly that their sculptural skills ended up drawing out and recording something that should rather have been kept at a distance."

343

Moissac (Tarn-et-Garonne), former
abbey church of Saint-Pierre. Western
wall of the south portal narthex, detail:
the Devil and Luxuria. 1120-1135

This almost archetypal threat is accompanied by moralistic aspects, such as the tympanum of the Puerta de las Platerías in Santiago de Compostela, where a sensuous woman with long, loose hair and a transparent garment is depicted holding a skull in her lap (photo, page 342, top). She is traditionally interpreted as an adulteress holding the skull of her lover, but a more recent view is that she is Eve in the form of the "Mother of Death." Her physical sensuous presence is very noticeable, however, and it reveals how Evil can gain its attraction by the form it assumes. The visual taming of the demon of gender managed, as it were, to force it to be unleashed.

Nakedness and sin

Given the general condemnation and outlawing of everything to do with the body, it is astonishing that so much space in Romanesque sculpture was devoted to nakedness. It was this ostracizing of the flesh that constantly challenged sculptors to come up with new ways of depicting nudity within the ambiguous limits of moral condemnation and sculptural form. And the positions of these images were usually prominent architectural sites, so that one could not help but see the figures when approaching.

One of the most famous depictions of Luxuria is on the western wall of the portal entrance in Moissac (photo, bottom). Integrated into the story of Dives and Lazarus and the sin of avarice, it is the last part of that sculptural program. She is modeled in an impressively naturalistic manner, and the countermovement of her head against the direction she is walking in is extremely expressive; her body is naked, and its sensuousness is further accentuated by her long wavy hair, a true image of voluptuousness. She is followed by the Devil who has a distended stomach and grotesque face and he is gripping her by the right arm which she has raised. Is she his mistress or the victim of his punishments? The reprehensibleness of her actions is certainly symbolized by the snakes, ever-present symbols of evil, which have bitten into her breasts. In addition a toad is attacking her genitalia. This is where the iconographical content becomes more complicated, because since ancient times the womb was often depicted as a toad, and the latter was also occasionally shown helping during births. In the Middle Ages, it was more likely to embody the animal shape of a demon, so several symbolic meanings merge at this point. Despite the considerable damage, the dramatic effect that these figures must have had on contemporary minds is still obvious.

The direct connection between greed and unchastity found in many Romanesque visual programs such as those in southern France is a genuine motif in Romanesque art, or to be more precise, an expression of contemporary social changes. By replacing the theological sin of pride with greed as the source of all evil, a new and growing stratum in society was attacked, one that was about to establish itself as an urban bourgeoisie by means of collecting material wealth through activities such as moneylending, producing goods and trade. The exchange of money and goods increasingly freed the individual from his feudal obligations, as he was more frequently in the position of being able to pay for things that he had previously had to work for personally. Unchastity, considered to be the sensuous, early libertarian counterpart to the economic pursuit of profit, complemented this new freedom of the individual, which tended to withdraw people from the sphere of influence of the Church, and which also led them to question the religious and moral basis of the feudal system of the early Middle Ages. Seen from this point of view, the program of reliefs in Moissac is less of a general religious condemnation of the vices depicted there and more in the way of the resistance led by the clergy against gradual historical change in medieval society.

Nudity was, above all, the condition of mankind in Paradise, a condition free of shame and sin. Betrayed by the cunning of the serpent and the temptation to become godlike and clever, the original woman risked the death of herself and all her descendants. And in the instant of the original sin she recognized herself and her guilt. One capital in Frómista (photo,

344

Autun (Saône-et-Loire), cathedral of
Saint-Lazare. Eve, from the door lintel of
the former north transept portal.
c. 1130. Autun, Musée Rolin

p. 290) acts as a type of snapshot of this process. Adam and Eve are standing dressed in the robes of God's creation on either side of the forbidden tree, and the serpent is winding itself around its trunk. At the very moment that Eve reaches for the apple with her left hand, she places herself and all of humanity into a condition of sin, making her aware of her shame so that they have to cover their nakedness. Adam expresses his horror by clasping his right hand to his throat. And already the demons that will accompany them from now on are present on either side.

The Eve of Autun (photo, top) is sensuous and seductive like no other in Romanesque art. She is presumably also a work of that Gislebertus who signed the tympanum, and is a remaining fragment of the lintel of the north portal of Saint-Lazare. The figure of Adam has been lost. Supported only by her right elbow and knees, Eve is moving through the Garden of Eden as if she were the serpent itself. She is looking towards Adam, to whom she is whispering instructions to do what she has just done, using her right hand, held against her mouth, to amplify what she is saying; her left hand is reaching behind her, in order to pick the apple on a branch which is being bent towards her by the clawed hand of her seducer. The presence of her feminine nudity is heightened further by the anatomically exaggerated way in which her upper body is turned towards the observer.

There is no other example of a figure of Eve lying in such a position, and it would remain a puzzle were one not to consider the contemporary meaning of this position. The liturgy of penance demanded that the penitent should lie stretched out on the floor, supported by his knees and elbows. The sculptor incorporated the penance that could be expected into the process of the seduction, but it is a questionable connection, as the position of penance seems rather like the movement of a snake, culminating in the seductive way Eve is whispering to and looking at Adam. In this way, the meaning of this original example of a mortal sin changes into an enigmatic play on the senses in which Gislebertus expresses something quite outrageous. He uses this theme in order to provoke what he is actually supposed to be warning against.

This figure of Eve is indeed the high point of a highly imaginative epoch in European sculpture, in which the freedoms of the as yet unassimilated power of depiction had been largely exhausted by what were by no means anonymous sculptors. Soon, in the figures on the west portal in Chartres, this freedom would be absorbed by the "spirituality of the virtually lifeless body" and transformed into a weakened and affirmative visual content.

Altarpiece, from Santa María in Taüll.
Wood, painted. Twelfth century.
Barcelona, Museo de Arte de Cataluña

BOTTOM
Alpirsbach, church pew made of turned
round pieces of wood. Twelfth century

Wooden sculptures

Wood was so widely used in the Middle Ages and the proportion of it used in the production of sculptures was so small that it could be ignored were it not for the existence of some outstanding pieces of Romanesque art. Although the wood carvers were quick to distance themselves from other craftsmen, they were still considered inferior to other artists in their field, for usually they only produced the basic model which was later decorated with magnificent colors or gilded with gold or silver. However, those sculptures whose coats of paint have now gone or whose gilding has been gradually removed during restoration work reveal the high artistic standards to which these wood-carvers worked.

Apart from the decoration of the building, the carver's tasks also included the production of church interiors, and the carvings on the doors were most visible to the outside world. This type of sculpture was bound to the surface, and low relief was, as it were, the prescribed means of depiction. In the field of church furnishings, this was developed further to include the production of pieces of high relief as well as almost free-standing figures like the individually carved figures attached to the altarpiece in Santa María in Taüll dating from the twelfth century (photo, top). The famous lectern in the monastery church at Alpirsbach (photo,

p. 350) is a completely free-standing piece of sculpture.

In the early Middle Ages there arose one of the most widely used sculptural forms of the Romanesque period: the enthroned Madonna and Child, representing the *sedes sapientiae*, or throne of wisdom (photos, pp. 351ff.). It is often compared to the icons in Byzantine art because there is a strict hieratic quality to its frontality. Even the child, who either sits or stands in front of Mary, emphasizes this moment of severity which did not begin to disappear until around 1200, with the increasing depiction of Mary turning towards the child. The magnificent way in which they are painted can only lead one to guess at the significance these figures had within Romanesque sculpture at a time when the process of Christianization caused the veneration of heathen mother goddesses, common in numerous regional cults, to be transferred to the central figure of Mary the Virgin Mother. Where figures – with the exception of the flash-tones – were entirely gilded, the intention was to imitate expensive goldsmiths' statues. Since the majority of these statues were easy to move, they could be removed from their usual position on the altar and used in liturgical events, processions and religious plays.

Many colorfully painted crucifixes (photos, pp. 348ff.) were produced in which Christ is usually depicted nailed alive to the Cross. This complied with the contemporary emphasis on the sufferings endured by the Son of God as representing a triumph over death. Depictions of a dead Christ on the Cross are rarer. With a few exceptions the clothes on the figure consist either of a long fitted tunic on the living, and a loin-cloth on the dead Christ. In addition to these, numerous types of crucifixes peculiar to different regions developed, of which several became prototypes for entire series, one example being the Volto Santo in Lucca.

Cologne (North Rhine-Westphalia), St. Maria im Kapitol. Left door, detail: Annunciation to the Shepherds, Birth of Christ, the Three Kings before Herod, Adoration of the Magi. Wood, painted. Entire height of the doors 190 inches, width of this door 91 inches. *c.* 1065

Province of Gerona. Christ in Majesty on the Cross, from the Olot region. Wood. Height of Christ 36 inches. Mid twelfth century. Barcelona, Museo de Arte de Cataluña

OPPOSITE
Cologne (North Rhine-Westphalia), St. George's. Crucifix. Walnut. Height 77 inches. *c.* 1070. Head of the Crucified Christ. Cologne, Schnütgen Museum

OPPOSITE
Lectern, from the monastery church of
Alpirsbach. Upper half. Wood, painted.
Height 55 inches. Mid twelfth century.
Freudenstadt (Baden-Württemberg),
Protestant parish church

Enthroned Madonna and Child, from
Rarogne. Linden wood, painted. Height
36 inches. *c.* 1150. Zurich,
Schweizerisches Landesmuseum

Enthroned Madonna and Child, from
Acuto. Wood, painted with inset semi-
precious stones. Height 44 inches. *c.*
1210. Rome, Museo di Palazzo Venezia

Auvergne. Enthroned Madonna and
Child. Wood, copper, silverplated.
Height 29 inches. Twelfth century.
Orcival (Puy-de-Dôme), Notre-Dame

Enthroned Madonna and Child, "Notre-
Dame-la-Brune." Wood, painted and
partially gilded, painting and gilding
restored in 1860. Height 29 inches.
Second half of the twelfth century.
Tournus (Saône-et-Loire), abbey church
of Saint-Philibert

Enthroned Madonna and Child, from the
church in Ger. Wood, painted. Height 21
inches. Twelfth century. Barcelona,
Museo de Arte de Cataluña

Cologne (North Rhine-Westphalia).
Angel from a Holy Sepulchre group.
Poplar wood, painted. Height 25 inches.
c. 1180. Berlin, Staatliche Museen
Preußischer Kulturbesitz, sculpture
gallery

Bronze sculptures

Bronze is considered the most valuable of the base metals. It is not a single metal, however, but an alloy of copper with either tin or zinc; the proportions used vary according to the date, region and even workshop where the pieces were produced. Bronze is the most popular metal amongst craftsmen because it is relatively easy to work despite its hardness, and because it stands up well to the various effects of the weather. Alloys with high proportions of tin or zinc have the advantage of being particularly fluid in their molten state and can reproduce even the finest of details when poured into the mould.

The usual process for the casting of a sculpture in the Middle Ages consisted of producing a wax model which was covered with a layer of clay or plaster (see the figures on p. 379). The firing of the cast made the wax melt away leaving a hollow core ready to be filled with molten metal. This is known as *cire perdue*, or the lost-wax process. The cast was secured in a bed of sand so that it did not break. Numerous vents ensured that when the molten metal was poured in, the air could escape and the cast would be filled completely.

Inscriptions on two medieval casts summarize this complex process in concise terms. One, on a lion's head door knob on Trier Cathedral, says: "What wax created, fire has taken and bronze has reproduced." What was so rewarding for

the artist and his work about this transformation of a sculpture from one material into another was that it was the result of a successful bronze cast. But there was always an awareness of the expense of this process, for if the casting went wrong, it could not be repeated unless a second wax model was produced. The second inscription, on the tombstone of

Two details from the Bernward door: doorknocker, scenes from the life of Jesus (left), Expulsion from the Garden of Eden (right)

Lion of Duke "Henry the Lion." Bronze copy. Brunswick (Lower Saxony), Castle square. Original also bronze. 1163/69. Brunswick, Herzog Anton Ulrich Museum

Bishop Wolhardt of Roth in Augsburg Cathedral, recalls the division of labor which the production of bronze sculptures involved: "Otto made me in wax and Konrad in bronze." For larger objects bell-founders were usually enlisted, for they specialized in producing big casts and were experienced in dealing with large amounts of molten metal.

Inscriptions such as the one above also tell us specific names, and while we know little more about "Otto" and the bronze founder "Konrad" than we are told there, we nonetheless know of many others including Renier of Huy, who created the famous font in Liège (photo, bottom); or Oderisius of Benevento, who made the bronze doors of Troia Cathedral (photo, p. 359) as well as those of San Giovanni in Capua and San Bartolomeo in Benevento. Barisanus of Trani and Bonanno of Pisa are also worthy of note. The question arises here, though, as it does in the case of inscriptions on capitals, tympanums and other architectural sites, as to what extent we are dealing with artists or whether it was their clients who were trying to leave a memorial to themselves.

Numerous highly ornate bronze church doors have been well-preserved. Amongst them are the Bernward door in Hildesheim, dating from 1015 (photos, p. 354); the eight reliefs on each half of the door depict scenes from the Old and New Testaments. The almost seventeen-foot high candelabra in Brunswick (photo, p.

356) has seven arms spanning fifteen feet, and highlights the installation problems of such objects. Its lions' feet are stylistically similar to the lion statue (photo, top), bearing a strong resemblance to details such as the shape of its ears and mane. The famous Brunswick lion, which was probably based on Italian models, such as the even more famous Roman Lupa or a range of medieval lion statues whose existence is confirmed only in written sources, is the oldest remaining free-standing three-dimensional statue of the Middle Ages.

During the twelfth century, courtly and chivalric ways of life and manners became increasingly refined and sophisticated, especially in the field of table manners; this was reflected in the production of a large number of bronze-cast aquamaniles of various designs, including those in the forms of figures, which were used for washing the hands during a meal.

Font. Work of Renier de Huy. Bronze. Early twelfth century. Liège (Belgium), Saint-Barthélemy

Brunswick (Lower Saxony), cathedral.
Candelabra with seven arms. Bronze,
champlevé. Height approx. 192 inches.
Inserts at the base dating from 1896.
c. 1170–1190

Hildesheim (Lower Saxony), cathedral.
Font. Bronze. Height 68 inches, diameter
38 inches. *c.* 1225

Verona (Veneto), San Zeno. Door of the west portal. Right section, details: the Tree of Jesse, mounted prophet, San Zeno fishing, healing of the princess, salvation of the possessed carter, Galienus and San Zeno. Wood, bronze. Entire height 192 inches, width 144 inches; height of picture panels approx. 17–20 inches, width approx. 16–17 inches. c. 1138

OPPOSITE
Tróia (Apulia), cathedral. Door of the west portal. Oderisius of Benevento. Bronze. Height 146 inches, width 81 inches. 1119

358

Crozier with scenes from the childhood
of Christ and the life of St. Nicholas.
From the area ruled by the Plantagenets
(Anjon?). Ivory. Height approx. 5 inches.
Mid twelfth century. London, Victoria
and Albert Museum

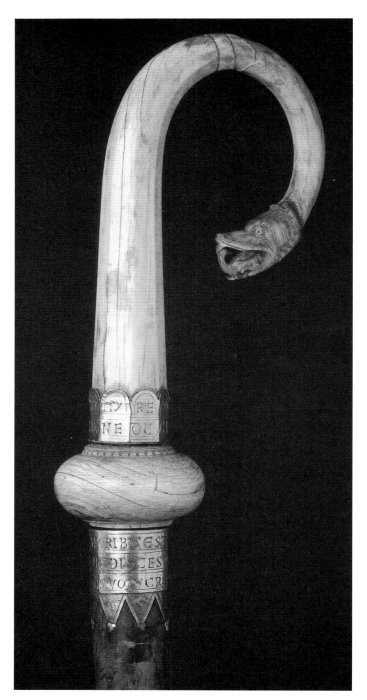

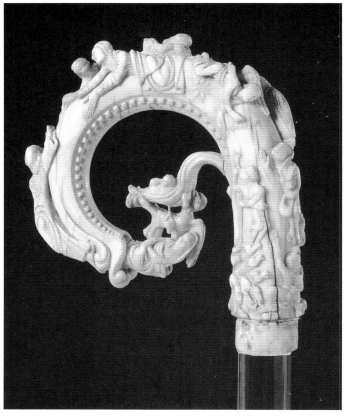

Church treasures

Gold and silver have always been highly valued. In the Middle Ages, however, these precious metals could not compete with the value attached to reliquaries. As a result they were combined to form a single highly esteemed work of art. Gold and silver were the favorite substances used to make the containers of relics. It was certainly important that these metals shone with a sparkle that entranced observers, but even more so that the more of them a monastery or church possessed, the greater was its importance and power. They also, however, expressed the desire to make appropriate receptacles for the bodily remains of saints, and lesser-endowed monasteries had to content themselves with lesser metals like bronze and copper. Because relics were so precious, it was particularly difficult to get hold of them. However, no altar or church could be consecrated without having at least one. The founding of many new Romanesque churches and monasteries caused the demand for relics to grow to incredible proportions. Theft or forgery frequently contributed to the wondrous increase in the number of relics, as did the division of a corpse. Teeth, nails, hair, hands and feet were worth the most as relics. Behind this was the assumption that the saint was present in every part of his body.

Nowadays, one is rather taken aback if one sees a medieval manuscript in which there is a drawing of a bishop cutting the arm off a saint's corpse, for such a thing is unheard of today. In the Middle Ages, however, it would have been quite reprehensible to miss the opportunity to cut a piece off a sacred body in order to give it to one's church or monastery. Bishop Gotefredus certainly had his church or monastery's best interests at heart, for he cut off the whole of

Donzio, Vita of Countess Mathilde of Canossa. Bishop Gotefredus cutting an arm off the body of St. Apollonius. 1115. Città del Vaticano, Biblioteca Vaticana (detail)

Gold statue of St. Fides. Wooden core, gold plated, precious stones. *c.* 1000. Conques-en-Rouergue (Aveyron), former abbey church of Sainte Foy, church treasury

St. Apollonius's arm (figure, p. 361, top right), and then presumably had it placed in an arm reliquary recently added to his church treasures. The arm reliquary of St. Lawrence in the Berlin Kunstgewerbemuseum is an early example of a "talking" reliquary, whose external form makes it clear which part of a saint's body is contained within.

This medieval drawing also shows that the ownership of relics of important saints brought their owners great glory. In 1162 the archbishop of Cologne, Rainald of Dassel, asked Barbarossa, the Staufen dynasty emperor, to let him have the relics of the Three Kings from the conquered city of Milan, as they were "a most precious booty, a treasure which cannot be compared to anything on earth." The special feature of these relics was that they were considered to be the embodiment of the first kings to pay homage to Christ, the King of Kings. Ernst Günter Grimme, who describes them as "political" relics, writes: "They consequently became the incarnation of the Christian kingdom. Whoever owned this Christian Palladium and asked the Kings of the Orient for protection, possessed the authorization of his Christian rule." The archbishop of Cologne was not particularly concerned with the Kingdom itself, rather more with the retention of his right to crown the Emporer. To this end he attempted to acquire the relics of Charlemagne, whose canonization he had himself attended in 1165. As the city of the Three Kings, Cologne has three crowns in its coats of arms to this very day.

Arm reliquary of St. Lawrence. Cedar wood, silver, partially gilded. *c.* 1175. Berlin, Staatliche Museen Preußischer Kulturbesitz, Kunstgewerbemuseum

Léon or Asturias. Relief panel from a reliquary: the journey to Emmaus (top), Noli me tangere (below). Ivory. Height 10½ inches. First half of the twelfth century. New York, Metropolitan Museum of Art, J. Pierpoint Morgan Foundation, 1917

Italy (Salerno or Amalfi). Relief panel from the "Paliotto" of Salerno. Ivory. Height 9½ inches. *c.* 1084. Salerno, Museo del Duomo

Crucifix of King Ferdinand and Queen
Sancha, from S. Isidoro in León. Ivory.
Height 21 inches. *c.* 1063. Madrid,
Museo de Arqueológico Nacional

TOP
Small reliquary box showing the
"Beatitudes," from the Colegiata de San
Isidoro in León. Ivory. 1063. Madrid,
Museo de Arqueológico Nacional

BOTTOM
North-west Spain. Adoration of the Magi
(detail). Relief made of walrus tusk.
Height 13$\frac{1}{2}$ inches. First half or mid
twelfth century. London, Victoria and
Albert Museum

Ivory

A natural product, ivory has been widely
used in the production of small works of
art from the late Classical era onwards.
African ivory imported via Venice and
other Italian ports was the most commonly used. Of equal importance, however, were the teeth of hippopotami,
narwhals, sperm whales and walruses.
Even brown rhinoceros horn was so
similar to ivory that it was considered an
equally valuable resource.
The main source of work for ivory
carvers was early medieval book covers
which were often decorated with miniature
reliefs depicting Biblical stories, and
which were embellished with precious
metals and stones. Due to their work
these liturgical books, which were
available only to a minority of people,
gained a considerable religious importance. Apart from precious metals, ivory
was the favorite material for small works
of art such as three-dimensional figures.
The popularity of medieval carvings and
sculptures in ivory lasted right into the
twelfth century. Apart from the production of small sculptures, ivory found
other uses, but these were mainly
religious ones; even combs, boxes and
other small items were produced for
liturgical purposes.

Cologne. Domed reliquary from the
Guelph treasure. Wooden core,
champlevé on copper, gilded, reliefs and
figures made of carved walrus tusk, floor
section with email brun, feet cast in
bronze and gilded. Height 17 inches,
width 16 inches. *c.* 1175–1180. Berlin,
Staatliche Museen Preußischer
Kulturbesitz, Kunstgewerbemuseum

Palermo (Sicily). Box with painted ivory.
Oak core, ivory panels, bronze mountings.
Height 6$^{1}/_{2}$ inches, width 9$^{1}/_{2}$ inches,
depth 7 inches. Twelfth century.
Berlin, Staatliche Museen Preußischer
Kulturbesitz, Kunstgewerbemuseum

Northern Germany or Denmark. Highly
colorful reliquary box used as the base
for a cross. Oak, champlevé panels.
Height 5$^{1}/_{2}$ inches, width 8 inches, depth
5 inches. First half of the twelfth century.
Berlin, Staatliche Museen Preußischer
Kulturbesitz, Kunstgewerbemuseum

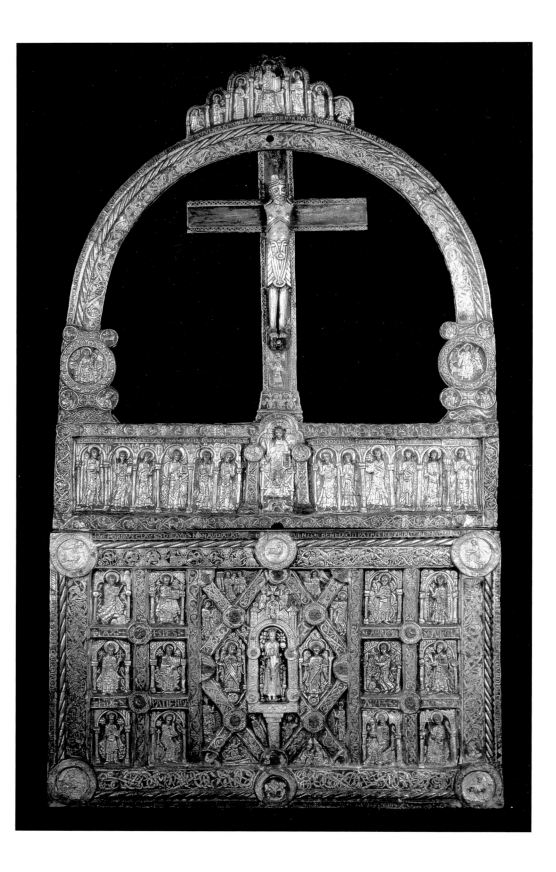

OPPOSITE
Altar, from Lisbjerg. Rolled and repoussé copper sheeting, gilded, ornaments in email brun, Mary and Child in gilded cast bronze. Width 63 inches. *c.* 1140. Copenhagen, National Museum

RIGHT
Triptych of Alton Towers. Copper, gilded, precious stones and champlevé. Height 14½ inches. 1150–1160. London, Victoria and Albert Museum

BOTTOM LEFT
Limoges (Haute-Vienne). Ciborium by Master Alpais. Copper, gilded, engraved gems, champlevé. Height 13½ inches. *c.* 1160–1180. Paris, Musée du Louvre

BOTTOM RIGHT
England. Balfour ciborium. *c.* 1160–1170. London, Victoria and Albert Museum

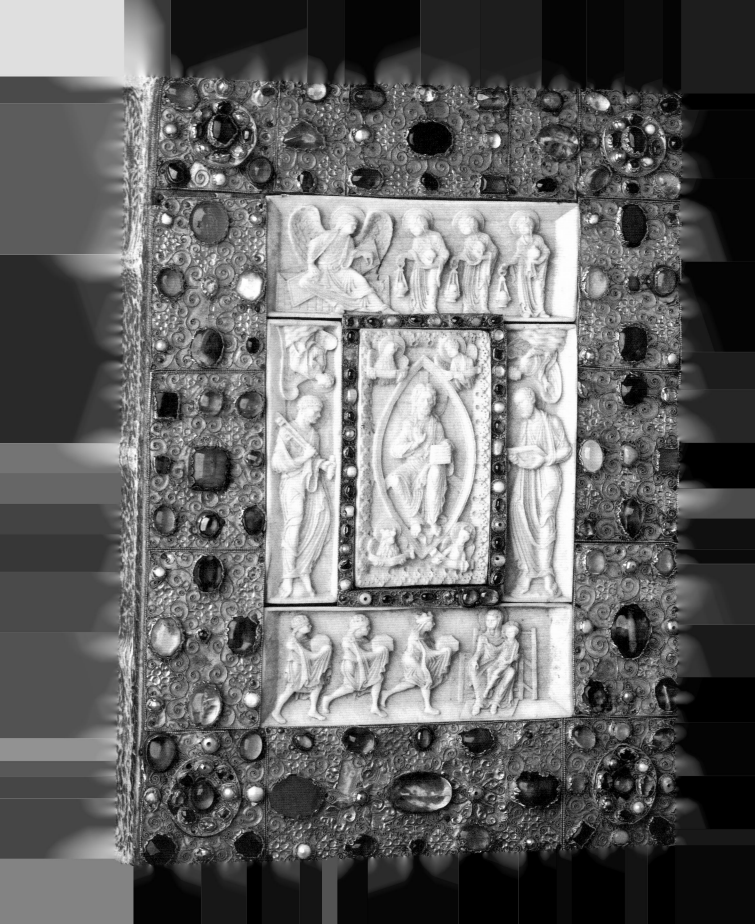

OPPOSITE
Lower Saxony. Book cover of an
evangeliar from St. Aegidien. Wooden
core, silver sheet, gilded, pearls and semi-
precious stones, walrus tusk. Height
12 inches, width 9 inches. End of the
twelfth century. Brunswick, Herzog
Anton Ulrich Museum

Helmarshausen (Hesse). Cover of an
evangeliar. Roger of Helmarshausen (?).
Silver, gilded, semi-precious stones,
pearls, bone. Height 15 inches. c. 1100.
Trier, Domschatz

Santo Domingo de Silos (Province of
Burgos). "Urna" of St. Dominic, detail:
Apostle. Copper, gilded, champlevé.
Between 1160 and 1170. Burgos, Museo
Provincial

Pamplona (Province of Navarra).
Altarpiece, details: the winged lion of the
Evangelist Mark (left), enthroned
Mother of God (right). Copper, gilded,
champlevé and cloisonné. 1175–1180.
San Miguel in Exelsis

Western France, Limousin. Statuette of an angel. Attributes of the Evangelist Matthew, detail. Copper, gilded, champlevé and cloisonné. Height 9½ inches. *c.* 1140–1150. Church of Saint-Sulpice-les-Feuilles

Maas region. Panel with a centaur.
Copper, gilded, champlevé. Height
4 inches. *c*. 1160–1170.
Paris, Musée du Louvre

Limoges (Haute-Vienne). Tombstone of
Duke Geoffroi Plantagenêt (d. 1151),
father of Eleanor of Aquitaine. Copper,
champlevé, enamel. Height 25 inches.
Between 1151 and 1160.
Le Mans, Musée Tessé

Font of an enamel box.
Limoges. Around 1180. London, British Museum

Aachen. Shrine of Mary. Oak, silver
sheeting and copper, gilded, champlevé,
embossed, bronze cast, edged with
stones. Height 38 inches, width
21½ inches, length 73½ inches.
c. 1215-1238. Aachen, Domschatz

OPPOSITE
Cologne. Shrine of the Three Kings. Oak,
gold, silver and copper, gilded,
champlevé and cloisonné, precious and
semi-precious stones, ancient engraved
gems and cameos. Height 61 inches,
width 44 inches, length 88 inches.
c. 1181 to *c.* 1230. Cologne, Cathedral

Ehrenfried Kluckert

Arts and crafts techniques

Gospel from Liessies: Evangelist writing (detail). 2nd quarter of the twelfth century. Avesnes, Musée de la Société Archéologique

"In principio erat Verbum, et Verbum erat apud Deum, et Deus erat Verbum." In the beginning was the Word, and the Word was with God, and the Word was God. "Word" is emphasized three times! God creates the world through language – a unique version of the many myths of the creation of the world. St. John, whose Gospel begins with these words, referred to the Jewish myth of creation. The cultic veneration of the written word, of the text of the liturgy, is the result of a God who reveals himself through the word. The foundation and spread of Christianity goes hand in hand with a high esteem for the written word.

The Gospel from St. Pantaleon (mid twelfth century) depicts St. John energetically putting quill to parchment, about to write down the first words of his Gospel. In this Gospel, the act of writing is treated almost as a subsidiary theme which pays homage to that great art. The individual stages of the preparation and the actual process are illustrated: St. Matthew has just picked up the quill and is sharpening it – an action that took place in all scriptoria prior to any prolonged period of writing. Lifting up his head, St. Mark is inspecting the quill which is now ready for use. Finally, St. Luke dips the quill into an inkpot.

Thus the four Evangelists create the impression of a scriptorium such as would normally have been found on the upper storey of the chapter-house of a Benedictine monastery. It was absolutely vital to pay strict attention to safety regulations here, since materials such as tinctures, paper, wooden panels and wax

were highly inflammable. For that reason the naked flame was prohibited. And of course there was also a ban on speaking, since the scribes had to concentrate on their work. It could be very costly and sometimes very difficult to correct mistakes in the writing. It required the careful scraping off of the ink and the renewed preparation of the writing surface. The black ink, a preparation the recipe for which had been used by the ancient Egyptians, was almost as thick as a paste and was made of blood and soot. Before one could begin to write, the quill had to be moistened with water. The

inkpot was shaped like a small bowl with a rim that curved inwards and was sometimes provided with smaller holes to hold the quills. Many medieval book illustrations depict ink-horns, which were used as an alternative to inkpots.

"Erasing" was another, and easier, method of correction which was referred to as "Stilum vertere," which means "turning round the stylus." The stylus or slate-pencil was usually made of bone, wood or metal and consisted of the point at one end and the spatula at the other. The point was used to scratch into the top layer of the writing surface, and the spatula

was used to smooth the scratched area down again, as required. In order to do this, the stylus has to be turned around. The writing tablet was made out of beech wood, a practice which continued unchanged from Classical Antiquity up to the Middle Ages. The word for "book" derives from the old English name for the beech tree, "boc". This writing tablet was a kind of shallow tray that was treated with a mixture of linseed oil, charcoal and tallow. The tray was then filled with wax which served as the writing surface. In late Antiquity it was customary to combine several wax tablets into a block which later was referred to as the "codex" (from the Latin "caudex"). This term was applied also to bound sheets of parchment as early as the fourth century.

The stylus and the wax tablet were indispensable in any monastery. At least, this is what St. Benedict demanded for his monks.

Medieval scriptoria often had workshops attached to them. In one of them the writing equipment, the inks and the colors were produced. In other workshops the monks prepared hollow molds or matrixes for the molding of reliefs, wax models for bronze casting, or stamps for ornamental patterns. There were instructions and textbooks to guide all these diverse activities. These technical treatises provide for us today an invaluable insight into medieval art and crafts production.

It is possible to look at these writings as a special literary genre which experienced its richest flowering between the eighth

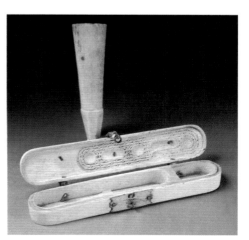

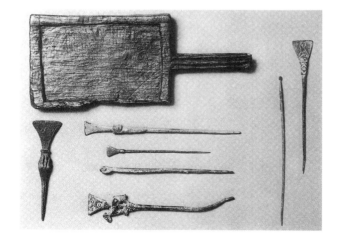

LEFT
Ink horn. Rhineland. ninth – eleventh century. Cologne, Schnütgen-Museum

RIGHT
Writing tablet with handle. Cologne, thirteenth century. Cologne, Römisch-Germanisches Museum und Kölnisches Stadtmuseum (joint property)

Helmarshausen (Hesse). Cover board of the Gospel (detail). Roger von Helmarshausen. Silver, gilded. Semi-precious stones, pearls, bone. Height 37 cm. Around 1100. Trier, cathedral treasure

Round medallion. Limoges. 1st half of the thirteenth century. Cologne, Schnütgen-Museum

maintenance. This serves to emphasize the significance of craftwork in the Middle Ages. And, as if he wanted to give particular encouragement to his readers, the craftsmen, he begins his treatise with the following words: "Well then, my clever friend ... let an even greater artistic sense be aroused in you and let it be the supreme task of your spirit to bring to completion that which is still lacking amongst the tools of the house of God, without which the divine mysteries and the practical execution of the holy acts cannot exist."

The English encyclopedist and theologian Alexander Neckham (1157–1217) also wrote a treatise dealing with technical instructions for the production of arte-facts. His *De utensilibus* was designed for use as a school-book, since many passages deal with the training of the

technical and artistic skills. His desire to teach future generations of craftsmen becomes apparent in references to training. Addressing the master of the workshop, he writes:

"His as yet inexperienced pupil needs a waxen tablet, or rather, one that is coated with either wax or clay, so that he can use it to design or to copy a variety of scrolls. And in order that he should not be deceived, he shall be made acquainted with silver and gold; and he shall learn to distinguish between purified gold, brass and copper so that he will not buy brass instead of purified gold."

and the twelfth centuries. The monks consulted the older encyclopedias, for example those of Hrabanus Maurus or Isidor of Seville. Also consulted were collections of old recipes for making colors or glue and for working glass or metals. One such example is the "Mappa Clavicula" which has been preserved in a codex dating from the twelfth century (Corning, NY, USA, Corning Museum of Glass). Originating from northern France, it is based on an older collection of recipes from the Carolingian period.

This specialist literature is also full of hints as to how a medieval workshop was run. Apart from lists of instructions governing the production processes of various artefacts, we find here lists of tools, and even collections of figurative or ornamental motifs. At the beginning of the eleventh century, the historian Adémar de Chabannes made the following notes regarding certain processes in the production of a crucifix: "Make the measurement of the cross according to the width of one thumb-nail. Make the width from the right hand to the left hand one full Dornus. Also from the toes to the nose, one Dornus, and make a simple cross. From the throat to the forehead, where the hair stops, the length of one thumb-nail, as for the measurement of the cross." (Cod. Voss. lat. Oct. 15, fol. 212r, Leiden, Library of the Rijksuniversiteit).

The most important treatise concerning medieval craftwork was, however, produced by Theophilus Presbyter and entitled *De diversis artibus*. This com-

pendium was made in north-western Germany around 1100 and is also known under the title of *Schedula diversarum artium*. Two early examples have come down to us, one from Vienna (Österreichische Nationalbibliothek, Cod. 2527), and the other one from Wolfenbüttel (Herzog-August-Bibliothek, Cod. Guelf. Gudianus Lat. 2069). It is fairly safe to presume that the monk and priest Theophilus is identical with Roger von Helmarshausen. Consisting of three books, his treatise concerns itself with painting, glass production and metal-work. The first book is dedicated mainly to painting and deals above all with recipes for making colors. A particularly important role is given to gold and silver, since Theophilus distinguishes between genuine and imitation coatings. His recipes often include recommendations as to which colors are most suitable for particular subjects of illustration: "Prepare a mixture from very clear gum and water ... and use this to mix all colors except for green, white lead, minium and carmine. Green containing salt is not suitable for books. To achieve darker shading, add some juice of iris, cabbage or leek."

The subject of the second book is the production of glass. Theophilus explains exactly how the tools are to be made and how the various kilns are to be constructed. The third book is the most substantial: here the author is concerned with the production and working of metals. To start with, he focuses on the workshop itself, its equipment and its

workshop assistants. Furthermore, he gives advice on the purchase of raw materials, which always posed many difficulties. He also provides revealing information about the various tools and how to use them. The author places particular emphasis on the passing on of

Portrait bust of the Emperor Frederick
Barbarossa. A present from the Emperor
to his godfather Otto von Cappenberg.
Bronze, gilded, partly silver-plated.
Height 32 cm. Around 1155–1160.
Cappenberg, Stiftskirche St. Johannes
Cappenburg

Cire perdue or the lost-wax process

First a model is made out of wax with thin rods of wax and a plug attached, so that later the hot wax can escape. The model is then encased in clay (2) from which the rods and wax project. Model and clay mould are then placed in a hot kiln (3). When the hot wax has escaped, molten metal is poured into the mould (4). After the metal has cooled, the mould is broken, and the rods and bung removed.

1

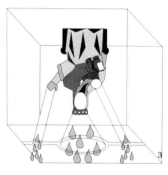

2

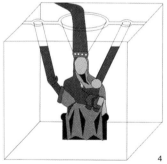

3

4

5

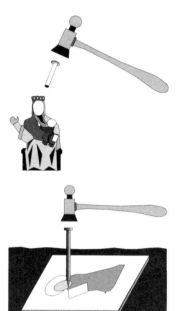

3

Chasing

The process of finishing the surface of either metal casts or repoussé work is done by polishing and removing imperfections that occurred during casting or repoussage, for example when removing rods from a metal cast (1). Repoussé work is corrected and reworked on the reverse side. In order to do this the object is heated and placed on a soft pliable base (2) where it is then worked with hammer and steel punch (3).

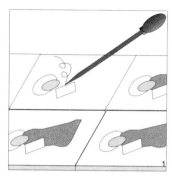

1

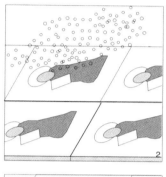

2

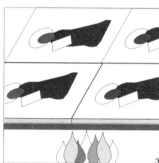

3

Niello

The Italian word "niellare" means "to fill in". Lead, copper or sulfur are rubbed into metal plates with patterns engraved into them. The metallic alloys then form a black pattern on the polished metal ground. After the plates are engraved (1) the metal or sulfide is applied (2) and burned on (3) before the metal plate is polished.

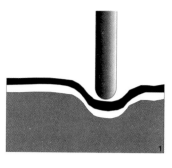

1

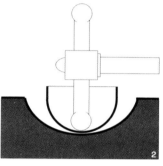

2

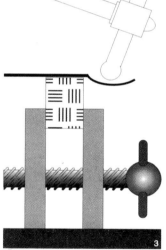

3

Repoussage

A metal plate is placed onto a soft surface (eg a pliable board) and worked with a steel punch (1). The rough modeling is followed by chasing. The initial modeling can also be done with a metal ball hammer. Hollowed-out shapes are made by placing the metal plate over a block of wood with a depression in its surface and working the metal with a repoussé hammer (2). For shallow plate shapes, the metal is placed over a piece of squared timber and then worked with a hammer as required (3).

Ceremonial cross (detail), around 1107, Cologne, Schnütgen-Museum. Probably by Roger von Helmarshausen

Gospel of Henry the Lion, between 1185 and 1188 (Wolfenbüttel, Herzog August Library, Cod. Guelf. 105 Noviss. 2°).

This manuscript is one of the outstanding achievements of Romanesque book production. It underlines the political power and self-confidence of the ruler.

"He is the descendant of Charlemagne. To him alone would England entrust Mathilda, who was to bear him the children through whom Christ's peace and salvation were given to this country. Their generosity surpassed all the glorious deeds of their predecessors. They have exalted this city splendidly; this is proclaimed by rumor throughout the whole world."

Those words are used in the dedicatory poem of the Gospel to praise the glory of the duke and duchess. The final picture of the coronation (illustrated opposite) displays the splendor and the importance of the noble couple while at the same time showing their authority being conferred upon them by the grace of God. The top section of the picture shows Christ surrounded by apostles and saints.

The stylized model of a sphaira penetrates the heavenly zone and sinks down onto the earthly sphere of power of the duke and duchess. "Divine hands" appear with crowns which are received by the couple in humility (they are carrying crosses). This coronation can be understood as expressing the hopes of Henry, Duke of Saxony. His ambition for political power found expression in this artistic representation of his hope of salvation. Surely this "coronation" must also be understood as a "heavenly coronation," as a conscious vision of the hereafter.

The picture showing St. Mark (top right) shows an abundance of ornamentation, pictorial architectural elements, and a decorative script. A striking feature is the combination of different patterns such as meander, rosette friezes or plain framing. The Gospel for Henry the Lion was made in the scriptorium of Helmarshausen. The precious and rich illumination of this manuscript has caused it to be linked with the *Schedula diversarum artium* by Theophilus Presbyter, alias Roger of Helmarshausen, since the techniques of ornamentation and the depiction of the human figure are contained in Theophilus's instructions. Thus the model-ing pattern for a head (above left) as set out in the treatise (volume 1, chapter 1–13) can, for example, be transferred to the head of Henry as depicted in the "coronation picture." In chapters 10–12, Theophilus describes the depiction of hair and beards in the sequence of the ages of man, from boy to man to old age. The distinction between the ages of man is a significant feature of the Gospel: despite the fact that Mark is shown with a beard which establishes his status as a wise and dignified old man, his hair has the light color of a boy. The Gospel of Henry the Lion is the joint property of the federal state of Lower Saxony, the Free State of Bavaria, the Federal Republic of Germany, and the Stiftung Preussischer Kulturbesitz.

Ehrenfried Kluckert

Romanesque painting

Introduction: It began with the "Libri Carolini"

"... with all humility King Charles submitted himself to God and the request of the bishops and of the whole Christian community, and took on the title of Emperor and was ordained by Pope Leo, on the day on which the birth of Jesus Christ our Lord was celebrated. And thus he restored peace and harmony to the Holy Church of Rome, bringing an end to the discord which had existed within it."

These comments were made by the chronicler of the Annals of Lorsch (probably the Archbishop Richbod von Trier) in 801 to describe the imperial coronation of Charlemagne, Charles the Great, in Rome by Pope Leo III on Christmas Eve in the year 800. For the pope, this ceremony represented a first step towards clarifying the situation between Byzantium and Rome. The political balance of power in the Mediterranean had been destablilized by the turmoil surrounding the iconoclastic controversy and the issue of the succession to the throne. Now at last there was one ruler for all the Christian community, including that of the Byzantine Empire: the Emperor Charlemagne. Charlemagne, incidentally, was able to regulate this new situation on a political level as well with the Treaty of Aix-la-Chapelle of 812. In the treaty, he was recognized as emperor by the emperor of Byzantium, Michael I, providing him with a very flattering solution to the "problem of the two emperors." However, he had to pay for it by handing over Venice, Istria and Dalmatia.

The "discord" mentioned by the chronicler was, of course, a reference to the iconoclastic controversy which had been raging in Byzantium since the middle of the eighth century. The Byzantine emperors Leo III and his son and successor Constantine V wanted to ban all religious painting and images. They condemned the worship of God through pictures as heresy and a danger to religion. Furthermore, they wanted to put the monks in their place, since they had profited from the trade in pictures. In 787 the Council of Nicea ruled in favor of those who worshipped through images and icons. Charlemagne later criticized this decision, arguing that the pictures painted by the "Greeks" had been painted "for love of decoration and not out of a desire to do away with it." The "Libri Carolini" (see pp. 422 ff.), the cultural manifesto of the court school of Charles the Great, were drawn up by Theodulf of Orleans. They pass judgement on both the over-enthusiastic icon lovers and the extreme iconoclasts. What the Frankish emperor was concerned about was the "right measure": religious images must not be traded as holy objects but should be treated as guides leading to the true faith by expressing the sacred events and messages of the Bible. Images showing Christ, the Madonna and the Saints were regarded as being close to idolatry and were rejected, although those who used them were no longer persecuted. This decree was not relaxed until after the Synod of Paris of 825 when the "Libri Carolini" were discussed and modified. The number of subjects worthy of depiction was expanded to include, for instance, the representation of Christ as the ruler of the world. Thus the subject which was to become the central theme of Romanesque painting, the Christ in Majesty, had at last become presentable at court.

This "coincidentia oppositorum," the reconciliation of the differing cultural stances of the eastern and western churches, suggests that the beginning of Romanesque painting coincided with the appearance of the "Libri Carolini."

The Carolingian cultural policies as laid down in the "Libri" not only include decisions on fundamental principles regarding the function of images. They also aim at raising the general level of education at court and in the church. Painting now had the specific task of educating its viewers about the truths of Christian salvation. It was thanks to this that painting achieved such a high level of skill and became so widespread.

One could argue that Romanesque painting began with the coronation of Charlemagne. Defining the exact period of time during which the Middle Ages occurred is equally controversial. Ernst Robert Curtius said of such an attempt that it was the "most pointless concept" in historical discourse. Terms such as "early Middle Ages" or "early Christian art" can refer as far back as the sixth century and the beginning of western monasticism; and they refer to painting in the most varied ways. Thus, early medieval painting can consist of Byzantine miniatures, Irish manuscripts, and Carolingian book illustrations and frescoes. As far as the Ottonian epoch is concerned, there is a tendency to assign it to the high Middle Ages. Often this period is treated as separate from Romanesque painting, which – just like sculpture and architecture – began at the turn of the millennium. However, Carolingian and Ottonian examples are cited whenever an attempt is made to define the typology and the design of Romanesque monumental painting. Indeed, it is often said that the subject-matter of Romanesque frescoes cannot be understood without looking at Carolingian painting.

Whether as a separate or an integral part of Romanesque painting, Carolingian and Ottonian art objects belong to it and are relevant to it. Let us therefore include in our observations these two periods which made such rich contributions to our cultural history, particularly since their codices and illustrations are the most distinctive, the best developed, and in the best state of preservation. Unfortunately the same cannot be said of Romanesque monumental painting: what has come down to us is very incomplete and mostly in very bad condition.

The end of Romanesque painting is sometimes said to coincide with "its highest development," i.e. the panel painting of 14th century Italy and artists such as Duccio, Cimabue and Giotto. There are certainly references to Romanesque painting in the work of these artists, albeit more on an iconographical level than a formal one. But these artists also usher in a new artistic epoch, that of the "post-Middle Ages." This applies only to Italy, where the concern with the "figure in space" can already be seen in Giotto's work, and where this exploration of pictorial space was developed into the Renaissance system of central perspective.

As far as the rest of Europe – and particularly France – was concerned, the construction of the first Gothic cathedrals meant the loss of the large wall surfaces required for painting Romanesque frescoes. In Germany the Romanesque style continued to be used for a long time, until about 1250 in fact. A few decades before its final demise, special forms developed, such as the "zigzag style" and the voluminous treatment of the figures of the "Staufen Classicism."

It appears sensible to locate Romanesque painting in the period from 800 to 1250. The "Libri Carolini" refer to "classical models," by which are meant the ancient forms and types of Byzantine art. In addition to Byzantine miniatures, we shall also look at mosaics and codices of the early Hiberno-Saxon school as illuminating comparative examples.

The spread of wall painting
Painting in the Carolingian Empire

To provide an outline account of the art of the Carolingian period, one must ignore national borders. The usual European formula is of little use here. Charlemagne ruled over nearly all of western Europe, including provinces in Italy and northern Spain. His empire was not homogeneous and it had inherited no governmental and administrative structures that had stood the test of time. For these very reasons Charlemagne wanted to found a society which enjoyed a high culture – an almost impossible task given the very modest level of education that existed. The majority of his population were barbarians, many of whom served successfully in his army. His first priority was therefore to promote the sciences and to increase the cultural achievement in his realm. Charlemagne looked to Byzantium and the Arab countries as models. There, a high level of education and culture had been achieved and preserved, thanks to the constant revitalization of ancient scientific practice.

Charlemagne therefore assembled at his court eminent European scholars, including artists from Byzantine Italy. The first humanist scholar to arrive at his court was the Northumbrian Alcuin of York. There was also the Visigoth Theodulf of Orleans, author of the "Libri Carolini" mentioned earlier. The presence of these universal scholars provided a boost for the sciences, the education system and the arts. They were interested not only in the glorification of the Christian faith, but also particularly in the development of an educational program which was as broad as possible. Alcuin, who taught at the monastery at Fulda and who counted amongst his pupils the famous Hrabanus Maurus, designed a building for teaching based on the Seven Liberal Arts: grammar, arithmetic and geometry together with music, astronomy, logic and rhetoric. Later these arts appear as allegories in book illumination and are particularly popular in portal sculpture.

The intense promotion of the arts and sciences, which was due to the presence of such eminent scholars at Charlemagne's court, produced scriptoria which will be described in detail later on. It also resulted in magnificent examples of monumental painting, most of which, however, were destroyed. A comprehensive survey and a detailed analysis of Carolingian wall painting are therefore not possible.

One can proceed from the assumption that every church interior was extensively painted – otherwise it would have been considered unfinished. The dome of the Palatine Chapel in Aachen, for instance, is reported to have been decorated with a splendid mosaic.

The surviving information is incomplete so that today we cannot be certain whether the subject of the mosaic was a Christ in Majesty, a representation of Christ as the ruler of the world within a starry sky, or the

Germigny-des-Prés. Oratory of Theodulf
(apse). The Ark of the Covenant. Around
800

Adoration of the Lamb. According to other documents, Charlemagne's imperial capital was supposed to have been the home of a cycle of historical paintings. Both subject-matter and design are, however, unknown and cannot be commented upon. Nevertheless, even these vague hints suggest that Aachen and the other centers of the Carolingian Empire were treasure-houses of art. One should remember that the scriptoria (see below) and the workshops were busy centers for the production of religious art.

With regard to large-scale painting on historical subjects, more detailed information can be given about the Imperial Palace in Ingelheim on the Rhine. Louis the Pious, son and one of the successors of Charlemagne, commissioned a history of the world which artists painted on the walls of his private rooms. It depicted historical events from early antiquity up to the age of Constantine, as well as scenes from the lives of great men such as Theodosius the Great, Charles Martell, and, of course, the life of his own father, Charlemagne.

Today, there remains only one large work of art from the time of Charlemagne and it has been only slightly restored. It is the mosaic in the oratory of Theodulf of Orleans in Germigny-des-Prés, situated just a few miles east of Orleans, the seat of his bishopric (picture above). This only remaining Carolingian mosaic depicts two angels with outstretched wings who point at the Ark of the Covenant. Theodulf presumably had in his mind a comprehensive plan for the interior decoration of his oratory.

The Caroligian church of St. Germain is not far from Germigny-des-Prés, in Auxerre, and can still be visited today. It was founded in 841 by Conrad, Duke of Auxerre, who was the uncle on his mother's side of Charles the Bald. It is likely that the church had already been completed eighteen years later, in time for the arrival of the relics of St. Germanus. It was then, or possibly later in the 860s, that the frescoes in the upper level of the crypt were painted. Only the scenes from the life of St. Stephen have survived – his condemnation, torture, and stoning. When the paintings were discovered in 1927 they were in good condition, so that one could gain a clear idea of the vivid coloring and the outline and composition of the figures. The colors used were mainly shades of red, yellow ochre, greyish-white and greyish-green. Influences from early Roman catacomb painting and from compositional patterns of Byzantine mosaics in Santa Maria Maggiore in Rome have been detected.

The best-preserved Carolingian fresco cycle can be found in a remote valley in Graubünden, in the monastery church of Müstair. The church is dedicated to St. John the Baptist, and it is generally believed to have been founded towards the end of the eighth century, in about 790, and probably by Charlemagne. His name-day, January 28, is still celebrated today. Moreover, the king is said to have vowed that he would establish a monastery in the valley to offer thanks for his safe crossing of the mountain pass of Umbrail in stormy weather. One can assume that the frescoes were painted soon after the completion of the monastery church. Located in the apses, the paintings remained undiscovered until 1896 and were finally completely uncovered by 1950. Parts of the frescoes had been painted over in the twelfth century by artists belonging to the School of Salzburg.

Charlemagne probably never returned to Müstair and may have forgotten about it altogether, for the artists who executed the paintings did not belong to his court school. Extensive commissions like the one at Müstair were usually taken on by itinerant artists who came from Italy and were trained in the Byzantine style. The Byzantine influence can be found not only in the shapes but also in the treatment of the pictorial narrative, that is the manner in which the individual scenes are emphasized by the articulation of the architectural elements around them.

Quite close to Müstair in the Venosta region of south Tyrol lies the little town of Malles with its simple little Benedictine church. In the Carolingian era, this church and the one in nearby Graubünden belonged together, the church of Malles being affiliated to that of Müstair. A series of paintings were executed much later, probably in about 880, but all that remains in the apses are the figures of Christ standing, of St. Stephen, and of Gregory the Great. On the narrow strips of masonry between the apses there is, amongst other things, the figure of a priest accompanied by the noble donor, who offers a model of the church to God (photos, p. 385). Roman influence has been detected in these frescoes, but their execution and treatment of detail differs significantly from the style of the figures in the Müstair church.

Further down the valley, towards Merano, lies Naturno. Its church of Patroklus, built towards the end of the eighth century, contains a painting of the "flight of Paul" executed in a very simplified manner.

The apostle is depicted above a meander frieze almost as if on a swing, and the figure is executed in a naive and very reduced style. His body consists of the sweeps of his garment; his face appears flat and devoid of contours and modeling with the exception of the eyes, nose and mouth. The meander frieze is the only element that betrays some of the ingenuity

Naturno, St. Proculus, angel carrying a
cross, around 800

Malles, St. Benedikt (apse). Donor figures.
Around 800

of three-dimensional treatment and was undoubtedly inspired by Classical antiquity. It is possible that the picture has suffered through restoration. It is, however, just as likely that the work was produced by badly trained artists. If so, it may help to explain the inconsistent quality of the art work produced within the developing Carolingian Empire. There is no doubt that it was exclusively the imperial court schools that provided the best-trained artists. In remote regions far away from the artistic centers, it was left to the locals to find master-builders, artisans and artists, and this resulted in variable success. As mentioned above, remote Alpine regions depended upon artists from Italy who were traveling through and who were well trained. These could then be engaged provided it was possible to promise them good pay. If money was tight, one had to make do with less talented local artists. The criteria employed here for the evaluation of artistic quality are, of course, contestable since, as has been pointed out earlier, there are no examples for comparison. The only thing that can be of assistance is Carolingian book illustration, and this has survived in unusual quantity and complexity, quite in contrast to monumental painting. Any comments about the quality of the wall painting of the period have therefore to be arrived at only after "consulting" examples of book illustrations done in Carolingian scriptoria.

Our last example of Carolingian wall painting is found in the crypt of the abbey church of St. Maximin in Trier and depicts St. John the Evangelist standing next to the cross. The fresco was probably painted towards the end of the ninth century and in stylistic terms is so closely connected with contemporary book illustration that a direct link with the school at the palace of Aachen has been suggested. The connection between miniature and monumental painting will be reiterated again and again in the appropriate chapters in order to explain the composition and the subject-matter of the frescoes.

The spread of post-Carolingian painting during the Ottonian period and later on up until the mid thirteenth century is easier to treat with reference to specific countries. In artistic terms, the heritage of the Carolingian era was absorbed more readily and developed more richly in

France, Germany and Italy. Following the death of Charlemagne in 814, the empire was repeatedly divided during the ninth century, resulting in a significant change to the political landscape of Europe. Structures began to emerge which laid the rough foundations for Europe as we know it today. Nevertheless, the political and cultural connections between the individual European countries continued to exist even throughout the high Middle Ages. Until the end of the Hohenstaufen dynasty in 1268, Italy remained part of the German empire. In 1033, for example, this connection with Italy was expanded by uniting the kingdom of Burgundy to form the powerful European trio of "Germany–Italy–Burgundy." The monastic orders, too, operated on a European rather than on a national level, in particular the Cluniacs and the Cistercians. The notion of a cultural life organized along strictly national lines during the high Middle Ages is therefore sustainable only to a limited degree.

Saint-Plancard, St.-Jean-le-Vigne. Two details of frescoes: angel, the Fall of Man. Around 1140

Montoire-sur-Cher, St. Gilles. Detail of fresco in eastern apse: angels. Second quarter of the twelfth century

surrounding places such as Tavant, St.-Savin-sur-Gartempe, St.-Aignan-sur-Cher, Montoire-sur-Cher. Their work is characterized as the "naturalistic school" and there has even been a tendency to present their works as the "first naturalistic" phase of French painting.

The coronation of Hugo Capet in Rheims in the year 987 marked the rise of the Capetian dynasty, and with it the appearance of a new architecture and later also a new style of painting in that part of France. It was in the same year that Thibault, Duke of Tours, founded the priory of Tavant. The wall paintings in the crypt of the parish church of St. Nicholas were painted later, probably in the first half of the twelfth century, and deal with an unconventional subject: the battle between good and evil, in parables from the Old Testament and events from the New Testament. One well-preserved scene shows Christ descending into Hell and saving Adam and Eve from the clutches of the devil. This first group of paintings is characterized by sandy-colored paintings on a pale background.

The wall paintings that were executed around 1180 in the collegiate church of St.-Aignan-sur-Cher are of similar appearance. Stylistic similarities are also found in the frescoes of the monastery church of St. Gilles in Montoire, situated a few miles north of Tours (photo below). It is at St.-Savin-sur-Gartempe, however, that the style of this first group can be seen at its best. Found there is what Prosper Merimée described in 1845 as "the most significant and magnificent Romanesque painting in France" (photos, pp. 454–55).

Painted around 1100, this fresco cycle is unusually complete and well-preserved, and is referred to in the chapter dealing with narrative style.

The second group, located in central south-eastern France and centered around southern Burgundy and the Auvergne, is known as the "Montecassino Group." The abbot Hugo or Hugues (1049–1109) had a small

France

Romanesque wall painting reached its peak in France between 1080 and 1150, a period also of great significance for European politics. During those years was decided the fate of the German Empire which, under pressure from the Church, had to give in to Rome. To a considerable extent it was the French Church, under the influence of Cluniac reforms and their swift spread to the north, which supported the papacy in its battle against the secular demands of the German emperors. What finally decided the battle for the leadership of western Christendom were the intense efforts of St. Bernard of Clairvaux to strengthen papal power – efforts which, incidentally, ran contrary to the views of the Cluniac order.

Cluny was the star that outshone all the other artistic centers in Europe in the high Middle Ages. The turmoil of the French Revolution resulted in the almost total destruction of the monastery church – once the largest church in Christendom – and all its treasures. Today we can have only a very rough idea of the effect of this center of art and science upon artists of all kinds all over Europe.

Generally speaking, four groups can be distinguished in France. All four can be defined not only in topographical but also in stylistic terms with reasonable precision. The center of the first group is Tours, with

Lavaudieu, former Benedictine abbey.
Christ in Majesty with symbols of the
Evangelists, including Mary on the
throne with angels and Apostles.
Around 1220

church built for the priory of Berzé-la-Ville, a few miles east of Cluny. The abbot is reported to have retreated to this little church in order to contemplate the approach of death. Along with St. Savin, the monumental paintings of Berzé-la-Ville are among the most important works of art of the French Romanesque period (photos, p. 411). They were probably painted at the same time as those of St. Savin, around 1100, although it is possible that they were not executed until 1120. The style, however, is different, it is more "Byzantine." It is probable that Cluny arranged for artists from the monastery of Montecassino in southern Italy to come to Berzé in order to paint the frescoes there. This does not, hoever, apply to all the frescoes. Only fragments remain of "Christ's Entry into Jerusalem" on the western wall of the church (painted around 1180), but stylistically, this fresco is connected to the first group, the one centered around Tours. Such stylistic variety in the same place runs contrary to a precise topographical classification, especially as so few examples survive. Nevertheless, one may tentatively establish two groups: the dark frescoes with blue backgrounds are typical of southern Burgundy and the Auvergne, while the sandy-colored paintings on a pale background are characteristic of the Loire valley.

Also among the second group are the fascinating frescoes of St. Chef in the Dauphiné region, east of Lyons. An inscription suggests that they were painted in the year 1080. Also belonging to this group are the wall paintings of St. Julien in Brioude in the Auvergne, which date from the beginning of the thirteenth century. The frescoes of Brioude are sometimes seen as being related to those found in neighboring Lavaudieu, and are therefore classified as belonging to the third group. Similar to the paintings of Berzé-la-Ville, the frescoes of the third group have a dark background. They are, however, not connected with Cluny or Montecassino, despite the fact that they exhibit some Byzantine characteristics. These are found in the heads of the Apostles with their distinctive physiognomy, and in the carefully modeled muscles of their faces and hands. The frescoes (photo, right) are in the refectory of a former Benedictine abbey and were painted around 1220. Lavaudieu might well allow us to call this the "Byzantine group."

The fourth group is known as the "Catalan group" since the wall paintings differ strongly from the French type. They have more in common with those found in the Catalan region of Roussillon. The paintings of St.-Martin-de Fénouillar south of Perpignan, executed around 1150, should also be mentioned here, as should those of St. Romain in Caldégas which date from about the same period. Another good example of this fourth group can be found in the frescoes of St.-Jean-le-Vigne in St. Plancard, about 30 miles east of Tarbes (photos, p. 386). These paintings, dating from around 1140, are located in the only church in France that has two chancels and are in two different styles. The often sharp-edged style employed in the figures in the chapel of the chancel suggests a Catalan artist, while the strong emphasis on outlines and the flat faces of the figures in the apses are more reminiscent of a master trained in the east. This treatment of form is found in many, often minor, frescoes in the valleys of the French Pyrenees. They also serve as reminders of the lively cultural exchange that took place between the regions of northern Spain and southern France.

Spain

At the time of the Carolingian Empire, most of Spain was under Moorish rule. It was referred to as the Umayyad Emirate of Cordoba. The narrow stretch of the Spanish Marches in the Pyrenees was partly under Frankish administration, and partly under Frankish influence. During the Reconquista, the Christian states on the edges of the Moorish empire, the kingdoms of Asturia and Navarre, and the county of Barcelona, had to battle against Islam. By the mid thirteenth century, the "moriscos," the Moors, had been driven out of the Iberian Peninsula, with the exception of Granada, which remained the last Moorish state on European soil until 1492.

Today, the majority of Romanesque frescoes and paintings from the Christian areas mentioned above are no longer in their original church setting.

At the beginning of this century, experts began the removal of the monumental paintings from the churches, set in hand their restoration, and then distributed them amongst the three most important museums of Catalonia – Barcelona, Vich, and Solsona.

Spanish Romanesque painting can be roughly divided into two categories: the style influenced by Moorish art, and that influenced by

Frescoes from Tahull (Santa Maria).
Detail: David's victory over Goliath.
Around 1123. Barcelona, Museo d'Arte
de Cataluña

OPPOSITE PAGE:
León, Panteón de los Reyes. Details:
murder of the innocents at Bethlehem,
Christ in Majesty (top); the Annunciation
to the shepherds (below). Around 1180

Byzantine art. The Arab-Moorish influence led to the development of the so-called Mozarabic Christian art. It is characterized by the flat treatment of the figures and their elongated heads. The artists belonging to the "Moorish group" were active in places such as Durro, Gerona and Tahull. The early-twelfth-century Master of Osormort deserves to be mentioned, since he was responsible, amongst other things, for the frescoes in the Church of St. John in Bellcair. The most famous (or, at least, most often cited) frescoes were from Tahull and were made around 1123. Today, they are in the Catalan Museum in Barcelona (photo, p. 388).

The Master of Pedret painted in the Byzantine style. The hair-styles and the arrangement of folds, as well as the decoration of the robes, all show an artistic affinity with Byzantium. Even stylistic elements from northern Italy have been detected in the twelfth-century frescoes of the monastery of Burgal. The Byzantine influence is particularly noticeable in the western part of Catalonia – and not only with regard to formal elements but also to subject-matter: the apse frescoes of San Pedro of Seu d'Urgell show Christ in Majesty, symbols of the Evangelists, and Mary and the Apostles (around 1200). The scenes from the Passion of Christ depicted in San Esteban, Andorra, are also typically Byzantine in their motifs and design. Also likely to be indebted to the Byzantine tradition are the wall paintings from the monastery of Sigena which were badly damaged by fire in 1936. There are, however, shades of ocher and salmon-red, and a light-blue color which is extremely uncommon in Spanish painting. These colors draw attention to another link – a link with English twelfth-century painting. There have been suggestions that the Winchester Bible and the stained glass windows of Canterbury Cathedral might have served as models. The connection between northern Spain and England could possibly be explained by the Crusades. There is evidence that at the beginning of the twelfth century English knights stayed at the Norman court of Palermo where they are likely to have met Spanish crusaders or clergy. Moreover, it is well known that direct ecclesiastical and political contacts existed between Canterbury and Constantinople. It is almost certain that English ships put in at the Atlantic ports of the north-western part of Spain and at the Spanish Mediterranean ports south of the Pyrenees.

The Panteón de los Reyes of San Isidoro in León has been called the "Sistine Chapel of the Romanesque period." This burial chamber of the kings of Castile and León (1054–1067) was decorated by an artist from southern France or from Catalonia who around 1180 painted magnificent frescoes over the walls and on the ceiling (photos, p. 389). Using mainly bluish-grey, red, and deep-brown shades and a typically Byzantine style, the artist depicted scenes from the life of Christ that are enlivened by ornamental plant motifs and animals.

OPPOSITE PAGE:
Canterbury Cathedral. Wall and vault
frescoes in the crypt (Saint Gabriel's
Chapel). Around 1180

Canterbury Cathedral. Saint Anselm's
Chapel. Paul throws a snake into the fire.
Third quarter of the twelfth century

Knechtsteden, former Premonstratensian
abbey church of St. Maria and Andreas.
Group of three Apostles. Around
1170/80

England

The close political contact (mentioned above) between England and the eastern Mediterranean region explains the strong Byzantine influence in English Romanesque painting. Unfortunately, only very few examples of fresco painting have survived. An attempt to construct a topography of Romanesque painting is therefore not possible. The only testimony remaining can be found in the villages of Hardham and Clayton in Sussex, in Copford in Essex, in Kempley in Gloucestershire, and in Winchester Cathedral, as well as in the crypt of Canterbury Cathedral (photo, p. 390).

It has been claimed that the paintings in St. Botolph's, Hardham, and St. John's, Clayton, also show signs of continental influence, including that of Cluny. Presumably manuscripts of the Carolingian court schools reached the island, since in Hardham stylistic elements have been discovered that correspond to those of work from the school of Rheims.

Germany

A strict formalism distinguishes German Romanesque wall-painting of the eleventh and twelfth centuries in stylistic terms from that of other European countries. It is comparatively easy to arrive at a topographical division, since enough examples of monumental painting have been preserved in the individual regions to allow this. The towns which extend along the Lower Rhine valley as far as Westphalia make up one of the main centers. Remarkable paintings were produced there in the twelfth century, such as the wall-paintings of Schwarzrheindorf; the paintings in the chancel of St. Gereon in Cologne; those in the chapter house of Brauweiler; or those in the collegiate church of Knechtsteden (photo, right). There are also the vault frescoes in St. Maria Lyskirchen in Cologne which date back to the mid-thirteenth century and are in very good condition. Fragments of Romanesque frescoes dating back further, to the late tenth and early eleventh centuries, can be found in the chapels and monastery churches of Essen, Werden, and Aachen. The paintings in the Hohnekirche (St. Maria zur Höhe) in Soest were executed around 1250 and are examples of the typically Rhenish late Romanesque style which is often aptly referred to as "softly flowing." This "softly flowing" style takes on monumental proportions in Schwarzrheindorf and would be more suitably described as "Staufen Classicism." There is, however, a second style of late Romanesque painting in Germany – a somewhat affected, "nervous" zig-zag style that heralds the transition to Gothic form. This style will be discussed in more detail in the appropriate chapter (see pp. 414 ff.).

Another center can be identified in Lower Saxony. The best example is the ceiling of St. Michael in Hildesheim (photos, p. 392). The only other surviving example of a painted wooden ceiling is in Zillis, Switzerland, but neither in form nor subject-matter does this have any similarity to St. Michael's.

Other paintings worth mentioning are those in Brunswick Cathedral and in the Neuwerkkirche in Goslar. They belong to the first half of the thirteenth century and show strong Ottonian stylistic influences. Both Rhenish and Westphalian painting had close links with Franco-Flemish culture. Lower Saxony, on the other hand, extended its influence towards

Hildesheim, St. Michael (wooden
ceiling). Partial view and detail. Second
quarter of the thirteenth century

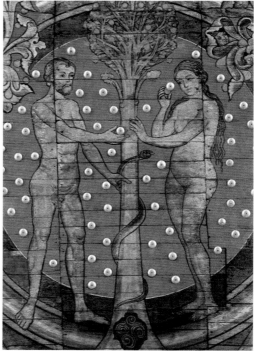

Scandinavia and even the British Isles. The situation was completely
different in south-west Germany, where the so-called "School of
Reichenau" emerged, though its existence is doubted by some scholars. (A
more detailed discussion of this school of painting and the associated
controversy will follow in the section dealing with book illustration.)
Germany is home to a cycle of paintings that has been immensely revealing
with regard to the stylistic development of Romanesque painting in Europe.
The paintings in question are the Ottonian frescoes of the church of St.
Georg in Oberzell on the island of Reichenau on Lake Constance. Despite
careful restoration efforts, they are in a poor state of preservation. What
has remained intact, however, is the cycle of paintings depicting the
miracles of Christ which run along the interior walls of the church nave.
Closely connected to the Reichenau paintings are the Sylvester chapel in
the nearby village of Goldbach and the large wall fresco in Burgfelden in
Württemberg.

Another important center in south Germany was Regensburg. The
Allerheiligenkapelle (All Saints Chapel) in the cathedral (around 1160)
and the Magdalenenkapelle (Chapel of Mary Magdalen) in Sankt
Emmeran (around 1170) have to be seen in context with the paintings in
the monastery church of Prüfening (around 1130). One is struck by the
linear and clearly contoured style that could be influenced by Reichenau,
or by the book illustration of Hirsau. From there, another link can be

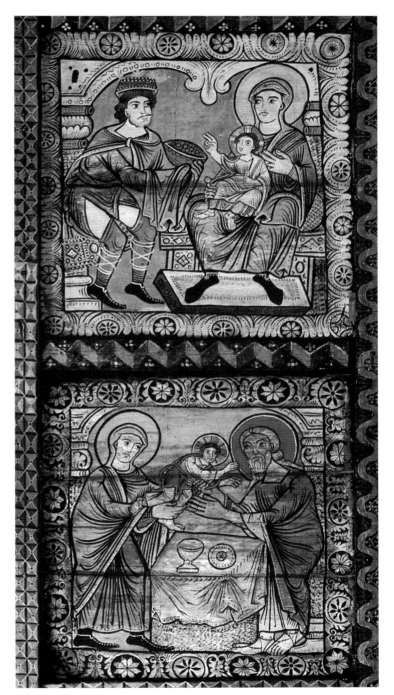

Zillis, St. Martin. Detail of wooden
ceiling. Partial view. Around 1130/40

established, namely to Archbishop Eberhard I of Salzburg who was an enthusiastic patron of art and, indeed, emerged as a keen practitioner himself around 1150. Even today, the frescoes in the convent church at the Nonnberg in Salzburg bear witness to this.

It is very difficult to formulate uniform stylistic characteristics for the various European regions of artistic activity. Although it is possible in the case of France, it is not so in the case of Germany. There are two possible reasons for this: since the second half of the twelfth century, the abundant vocabulary of form of Ottonian art had become exhausted, and the result was an artistic vacuum. Therefore Byzantine culture, which had become a familiar feature thanks to the Hohenstaufen policies towards Italy, could now again exert a stronger influence in Germany. The second reason has to do with the thirteenth century: from the late twelfth century onwards, the Gothic structure and style had become increasingly dominant, first and above all in France, and in due course also in the other, mainly south-western European countries. Germany, however, remained fixed in a strict aesthetic formalism which held on to the traditional design criteria. One example of "evasive action" typical of such a conservative attitude consisted in the development of the so-called "zigzag style", exemplified by the Soest altarpiece, the "Soester Retabel," and its depiction of God the Father (photo, p. 414 below).

Austria and Switzerland

Both countries are closely linked to the artistic development of their neighboring countries: for northern and western Switzerland, stylistic trends were set by Reichenau and Burgundy, while southern and eastern Switzerland looked to Lombardy and the Tyrol for inspiration. In cultural and geographical terms, the Romanesque painting of the Tyrol presents a homogeneous picture. Of particular iconographical interest are the frescoes of Termeno, Lana near Merano, and Bressanone. All these frescoes were painted during the first half of the thirteenth century. Reference has already been made to the Carolingian paintings of Malles and Naturno in Venosta (southern Tyrol) which are closely connected with those of Müstair (Graubünden). Situated above Malles, near Burgusio, is the Benedictine abbey of Marienberg (Monte Maria). The crypt there contains frescoes from around 1160 which are likely to have been influenced by Reichenau. Another artistic center is Styria. The frescoes in the cathedral of Gurk (around 1260) have as their subject-matter "the church as the city of God" and, with their typical zigzag style, are already part of the transitional phase leading to the Gothic style.

The question as to whether Reichenau's influence extended also to the wooden ceiling of the church of St. Martin in Zillis (Graubünden) has already been discussed; it must, however, remain doubtful. The same applies to the dating (around 1130/40) of the works which have been restored several times. They are an impressive cycle of paintings depicting the Life of Christ and his Passion, and also some episodes relating to the life of the church's patron, in 153 main pictures with 43 accompanying marginal pictures (photo, p. 394). The marginal spaces show allegorical depictions of animals and stylized plant forms.

Müstair, monastery church of St. John.
Detail of side apse: the stoning of St.
Stephen. Twelfth century

Venice, St. Mark's. Mosaic in the
narthex: dome of Genesis. Early
thirteenth century

Italy

In Italy there are three centers of Romanesque painting that can be clearly defined in geographical terms: Montecassino in the south, Rome in central Italy, and Milan in the north. Each adopted Byzantine art as their stylistic ideal. At that time the influence of the Byzantine mosaic schools of Trieste, Venice, Ravenna, Rome, and of Cefalù and Palermo in Sicily was overwhelming. Its effect was felt for a long time afterwards not only in the artistic centers themselves, but throughout Italy (photo, left, p. 397). When Desiderius, the abbot of Montecassino during the second half of the eleventh century, wanted to have the Provost's quarters of the monastery of Sant'Angelo in Formis decorated, he even sent for artists and artisans from the Byzantine metropolis, Constantinople. In the case of Rome, particular mention must be made of San Clemente. A fresco dating back to around 1000 can still be seen in the upper church – in the past it used to be situated in the narthex of the lower church. The crypt, the existence of which can be traced back as far as the fourth century, is today regarded as a treasure-house of Romanesque painting. It boasts ninth-century frescoes in the nave, depicting the Ascension of Christ, and in the narthex a cycle from the early twelfth century representing the legend of St. Clement (photo, p. 398). A Madonna painted around the year 500 in the Byzantine style completes the impressive array.

The work done by the Master of the legend of St. Clement and his workshop had a far-reaching effect in Rome and far beyond. The Roman school might even have influenced the paintings of the abbey of Castel Sant'Elia near Nepi (around 1100, photo, p. 399) and in the cathedral of Agnani (around 1200).

Nothing has remained of the artistic center of Milan. One has to look to the neighboring towns and villages, such as Galliano near Cantù (early eleventh century) or Civate (around 1090) north-east of Lake Como, in order to find examples of the characteristic Milan style. The Ottonian influence that affected the places just mentioned will be discussed at a later stage. There are the less well-known frescoes of Sant'Ilario in Revello (beginning of the eleventh century; situated between Cuneo and Turin) and of San Pietro e Sant'Orso in Aosta (around 1150), all of which were certainly painted independently of Milan but are nonetheless remarkable. Aosta could even be singled out as the Piemontese center of painting. Of iconographical interest are the paintings in the oratory of San Siro in Novara which date from the first half of the thirteenth century. In a colorful and lively manner they illustrate miracles and events from the life of St. Sirius. The scenes include elements of both realistic and dramatic design and are enlivened by the use of brilliant blues and pinks.

Scandinavia, Bohemia and Moravia

In art one should not refer to "peripheral works" – at most, one should regard them as works of no particular consequence for future developments. At this point we therefore mention examples from Scandinavia and from Bohemia and Moravia in order to give a geographically complete survey of Romanesque painting and define its eastern borders.

The development of Romanesque painting in Scandinavia is closely linked with the art trade in England and in Lower Saxony.

Florence, baptistery. Detail from the
mosaic in the dome. From 1225

Panel showing the Ascension of Christ
(detail) from the church of Eke. Around
1200. Stockholm, Statens Historiska
Museum

Byzantine influences do not come to the fore until the end of the twelfth century and the beginning of the thirteenth. One can assume that most wooden churches of the eleventh and twelfth centuries were decorated with panel paintings. Unfortunately, only very little of this kind of work has survived. One example is the Ascension of Christ, painted around 1200, from the Swedish church of Eke (photo, p. 397). The panel is now kept in the National Museum in Stockholm.

The earliest wall paintings found in Bohemia and Moravia date from the twelfth century and include the frescoes in the castle chapel of St. Catharine in Znojmo painted in 1134. Work found in the church of St. Klemens in Stará Boleslav suggests a connection with book illumination in Salzburg. The scenes from the life of St. Clement are thought to have been painted around 1180. Amongst the stylistically most mature work of that region are the paintings on the piers in the Mariageburtkirche (Church of the Nativity of the Blessed Virgin Mary) in Pisek. The depictions of the Passion of Christ contain a mixture of Byzantine and early Gothic stylistic elements. This has led to the assumption that the work was done towards the end of the thirteenth century by an artist from the Middle Rhine.

Rome, San Clemente, lower church.
St. Clement celebrating the Mass.
Around 1100

OPPOSITE PAGE:
Castel Sant'Elia di Nepi, Basilica
Sant'Anastasio. Apse frescoes. End of
eleventh/beginning of twelfth century

Book Illumination

Hiberno-Saxon and Anglo-Saxon manuscripts

The significance of Irish book illumination (the origins of which were in Scotland, the home of the Irish) for the development of Carolingian and partly even Ottonian painting was considerable. The main reason for this was the missionary work carried out by Irish monks. Around 590, St. Columba and his companions traveled to France, Germany and across the Alps to Northern Italy. In the Vosges Mountains he founded the monastery of Luxeuil and in Lombardy that of Bobbio. Many of the early monasteries later developed thriving scriptoria. Amongst them are the monasteries of Fulda (Bonifatius), Würzburg (Kilian), Regensburg (Emmeran), St. Gallen (Gallus) and Echternach (Willibrod). Before St. Columba's activity, his father, Columba the Elder, had been involved in founding monasteries in his motherland – amongst them Durrow on the Hebridean island of Iona, and Kells in Ireland. These were the most important centers of early medieval scholarship. They produced manuscripts which were soon to be known at any royal or prince's palace in Europe as well as in all abbeys and in the Vatican. Amongst the famous manuscripts are what are today known as the *Book of Durrow* (seventh century, photo, p. 401) and the *Book of Kells* (around 800). Long after the first Hiberno-Saxon and Anglo-Saxon missionary activity directed south-east had taken place, the artistic tradition of the British Isles was cultivated and continued on the continent. In this way the aesthetic foundations of Carolingian painting had been established.

Around the end of the seventh century the artistic activity of the Irish monks shifted from Scotland to England. The monastery of Lindisfarne was founded in Northumbria. Its unique manuscript, the *Lindisfarne Gospels*, was produced around 700 and inspired artists in German scriptoria to adopt its use of sophisticated pictorial patterns.

In the year 597 the Benedictine monk Augustine arrived in Canterbury from Rome. This marked the beginning of the conflict with the artistic tradition of Rome, i.e. with the Byzantine style the influence of which, it is true, was present only in a restrained way and which was only gradually making itself felt. It is reported that he was carrying out missionary work on the instructions of Pope Gregory the Great and that he had with him various codices from Rome. Another two centuries passed before the Byzantine form was accepted and modified in the course of the eighth century. This assimilation took place mainly in the schools of Canterbury and Winchester. Both writing schools were gaining recognition at that time, inspiring continental artists to develop novel combinations of abstract figures and ornamental lettering.

Carolingian and Ottonian scriptoria

The Palace school in Aachen formed the center of Carolingian culture. Its writing schools and scriptoria produced important manuscripts which contributed to the development of the mature Romanesque style. The flowering of the court school began around the year 800 and lasted until the death of Charlemagne in 814. It was Charlemagne himself who commissioned the Godescalc Gospel (around 780/83), the school's earliest recorded manuscript. It was usual to name manuscripts either after the place for which they were destined or the place where they were kept, or after the donor. Examples of such manuscripts produced at Aachen are the Gospels of St. Médard of Soissons (photo, p. 402) (which, incidentally, contains up to 600 different ornamental motifs) and the Ada Codex of Trier.

After the death of Charlemagne, the important task of communicating and spreading the style of the Palace school fell to the scriptorium of Fulda. The link between Aachen and Fulda was made possible thanks to one of Alcuin's pupils, Hrabanus Maurus, known as "Praeceptor Germaniae,", "the teacher of Germany", who was abbot of Fulda until 842. The Gospels of Würzburg were written there, a manuscript that took up the profusion of form and shapes displayed in the Gospels of St. Médard and varied and adapted them further.

Another workshop active during the Carolingian period was situated in Rheims and produced the Ebo Gospels and the Utrecht Psalter. Both manuscripts date from around 855. Following the example of Reims, there were founded further workshops and schools in Tours and in St. Denis which produced the Lothar Gospels (around 850) and the sacramentary of Charles the Bald (around 860). The artistic centers of Metz and Corbie should also be mentioned here.

The abovementioned places point to a whole network of artistic activity, so that there were a number of centers producing illustrated manuscripts, not just Aachen. In the wake of the Palace school founded by the Emperor Charlemagne, a number of other schools and workshops were established. They, too, all profited from the Hiberno-Saxon and Anglo-Saxon traditions and fused them with Byzantine elements, thus creating new compositions and a new language of form.

Carolingian book illumination retained its dominant position well into the tenth century, with the result that the Ottonian scriptoria at first followed in the tradition of the Carolingian ornamental and pictorial patterns. There is evidence that the first Ottonian manuscripts were mere copies of Carolingian codices, which might also be accounted for by, amongst other things, a drop in artistic production around the year 900. Artistic activity declined as a result of not only the Viking invasions and the threat posed by the Magyars, but also by the decline of domestic policy within parts of the Carolingian empire. The imperial tradition was not consolidated until the arrival of the Ottonian rulers during the tenth and eleventh centuries. There followed a cultural upswing which must also be seen in the context of the reform of the monasteries during this same period. The foundation of the monastery of Cluny in 910 served to promote the aesthetic ideals of Johannes Scotus who regarded pictorial representation as the highest form of perception. According to this Carolingian philosopher, beauty was the perfect expression of being. This meant that an art form had not only a symbolic significance but was also important to the salvation of the human soul. In this context, beauty is equated with light, and the "image-light" interpreted as a metaphor for heavenly, divine beings.

Such thinking might account for the intense coloring found in Ottonian miniatures. In the course of the tenth and eleventh centuries, these ideas gained momentum and led to the first formulation of a theory of art.

Book of Durrow, ornamental page. Iona.
Seventh century. Dublin, Trinity College.
Lib. Ms. 57, fol. 3v

From the Lindisfarne Gospels, Chi-Rho
initials. Around 698. London, British
Library. Cotton Ms. Nero D. IV, fol. 29r

PHOTO P. 402:
Soissons, Gospel of St. Médard.
Adoration of the Lamb. School of the
Palace of Aachen. Around 800. Paris,
Bibl. Nat. Ms. Lat. 8850 fol.1

PHOTO P. 403:
Trier (?), Codex Egberti. Dedicatory
picture "Egbertus." Around 980. Trier,
Stadtbibliothek. Cod. 24, fol. 2

EGB̄ TUS.
TREUERO RCHAR
CHI OPS

KERAL HARI
DUS. ETUS
AU GICAN
GES

403

Constantinople, Joshua scroll. Joshua
and the spies from Gibeon. Around 950.
Rome, Bibl. Apostolica Vaticana. V.
Palast. Graec. 431

For many years the island of Reichenau on Lake Constance was considered a place of prolific artistic production during the high Middle Ages. However, references to the "fluctuating nature of stylistic comparison and its unreliability" made about thirty years ago led to doubts as to whether the writing and illuminating school of Reichenau had ever even existed. Many codices originally attributed to the Reichenau school were now believed to have been produced in Trier, for example the Codex Egberti (which in this context will be discussed in more detail shortly). However, at the Congress of Art Historians in Constance in 1972 this theory was rejected, and thanks to studies relating to its liturgical history, the analysis of its form and shapes, and to its iconography, the school of Reichenau was "reestablished" as the artistic center of the Ottonian period.

A brief example to illustrate the nature of the controversy is the much-disputed Codex Egberti (photo, p. 403) which is constantly being reattributed to Trier or Reichenau. There are numerous indications that the manuscript was actually produced in Trier – not least the fact that it was commissioned by Egbert who was the archbishop of Trier. The "Reichenau" supporters counter this argument by pointing out that the dedicatory verses in the codex contain the information that the manuscript had been offered to the archbishop by the "augia fausta," the "happy meadow," that is, Reichenau.

The tendency today is again to defend the island of Reichenau as a center of artistic production. One of the main reasons for this is the Reichenau cleric Liuthar who has been connected with many of the codices attributed to Reichenau. They, in turn, show links with famous manuscripts, such as the gospel book of Otto III or the Bamberg Apocalypse. What everyone is agreed upon is that so far no conclusive evidence has been forthcoming to prove the actual existence of a writing and illuminating school at Reichenau. During the discussion no consideration was given, however, to the fact that between the eleventh and the twelfth centuries, regional monastic schools of art were of far less importance than they had been in the previous centuries, for example in the Carolingian empire. In the Ottonian period, many more laymen took part in the production of manuscripts. Apart from the king, there was a particularly large number of noblemen financing the production of precious manuscripts. Artistic production increased considerably during that period and was no longer confined to individual centers. The free exchange of artistic ideas was made possible by the royal court and its surroundings, particularly the bishops and the abbots and the aristocracy. Ottonian art was an art of the whole empire no longer confined to the limitations of regional art centers.

Whichever theory might be true, it is not possible to discuss the issue here. A question mark must therefore be added in the following pages whenever Trier is mentioned as the place of origin, if modern research suggests that a work was produced in Reichenau.

Many manuscripts of great diversity were produced in the Trier workshop between 980 and 1020, amongst them the Gospel Book of Otto III, the Registrum Gregorii, and the Bamberg Apocalypse. Echternach, an offshoot of the Trier writing school, created pictures of the Evangelists and the gospel book of Sainte Chapelle which are distinguished by their perfect and lavish design and presentation.

The Regensburg scriptorium tended to look towards Carolingian examples for inspiration, in particular those from the court school of Tours. The most important work produced in Regensburg includes the Uta Codex (late eleventh century) and the sacramentary of Henry II. The major work to emerge from the workshops in Cologne is without doubt the codex of the Abbess Hitda von Meschede, known as the Hitda Codex, which was produced in the first quarter of the eleventh century. The gospel book of St. Gereon, written at the end of the tenth century, could be regarded as a kind of preliminary stage to the Hitda Codex in terms of style and motifs.

There are a number of individual Austrian schools that deserve to be mentioned, although they did not necessarily belong to Ottonian art. One such school of high standing was at the monastery of Heiligenkreuz situated in the southern part of the Vienna woods and founded by the Margrave Leopold III in 1135. Around the year 1200, a number of very fine illustrators and scribes were working there. The manuscripts produced in the convent of Zwettl in the Lower Austrian woods are also distinguished by interesting pictorial patterns, as found, for instance, in the "Speculum Virginum". It is likely that artists from Heiligenkreuztal and Zwettl were active also in Reun in Styria. It is to them that we owe the "Reun pattern book" which was produced around the year 1200.

Finally, the Bohemian writing school should be considered. It includes the school of Vysehard where the Coronation Gospel Book was created (now kept in the Prague University Library). Although these works show close links with their Austrian models, they pale before the glories of Ottonian book production.

Italian and Spanish writing schools

Throughout the early and high Middle Ages, Italy was regarded as a "supplier of form and design" for the writing and court schools north of the Alps. After the Norman Conquest of England in 1066, Italian manuscripts also found their way to the island which until then had relied for formal and typological vocabulary largely on its own monasteries in Northumbria or Scotland.

In the eleventh century, the Abbot Desiderius of Montecassino had sent for artists and book illuminators from Constantinople who extended the Latin scriptorium in the monastery. From there, this "new style" soon spread throughout Italy. The fame of the Irish-trained book illuminators in the monastery of Bobbio in Lombardy began to fade. Particularly famous was the "Homiliary" and also the "Life of Saint Benedict." The "Homiliary" was a collection of sermons according to the order of the pericopes used for the gospel and epistle readings throughout the ecclesiastical year. With regard to the Codex of Saint Benedict, it has even been possible to trace the artist – the monk Leo.

Between the early tenth and the thirteenth centuries, a new pictorial genre came into existence. This was the "exultet roll" which took its name from the words which with it began: "Exultet iam angelica turba coelorum …" (Rejoice, ye heavenly hosts …). On Easter Saturday, these picture rolls, also called "rotuli," were lowered from the pulpit during the sermon. The text read out by the deacon was written on one side, while the congregation could see the pictures illustrating the text on the other side. The tradition of the rotuli can be traced back to ancient triumphal columns with sculpted pictorial friezes, such as the column of Trajan in Rome. The Joshua scroll (photo, p. 404) represents a variant of this type. It was produced in Constantinople, probably around the middle of the tenth century, and must soon have found its way to the countries north of the Alps where it exerted a decisive influence on the narrative style.

In a development similar to that found in the wall-paintings of Civate and Galliano near Cantù, a fusion of Byzantine form and Ottonian

traditions took place in many Umbrian and north-Italian workshops, one example being the scriptorium of Polirone, situated on the river Po southeast of Mantua.

Spain constitutes a special case, not least because of the Arab influence dominant there. The apocalypse manuscripts were a speciality of northern Spain. In order to understand them, it is necessary to look to the "Ashburnham Pentateuch" (photo, above), a codex probably produced in northern Africa in the seventh century. Its pictorial language, ornamental style, figure composition and coloring have prepared the way for the popular Mozarabic style. These apocalypse manuscripts are highly interesting both in iconographic and formal terms. One of the centers where they were created was the monastery of San Salvador de Tavara whose artistic production reached its peak in the second half of the tenth century.

With this brief reference to Spain, we have now completed a rough outline of the complex links that existed between the various countries and that resulted in the topographical as well as stylistic influences of Romanesque painting. The following sections will now look at how the various stylistic and iconographical variations developed.

Wall painting: stylistic development and composition
Byzantine pattern and Hohenstaufen form

The stylistic interconnections of Romanesque painting in Europe are many; they are also very difficult to categorize. This is partly because of the spread of medieval manuscripts, which occurred at a rate unusually fast for the time. By the eleventh century at the latest, all the relevant specialist artistic centers in Europe were acquainted with Carolingian, Ottonian and Byzantine codices. Lacking new stylistic ideas of its own, wall-painting often copied the composition and motifs of the manuscripts and adapted them for its own purposes. The high Middle Ages can be looked upon as a period of a truly international European style, since it was common practice for artists to work for different courts and dioceses. This exchange of artists contributed to the fact that distinct regional artistic styles only very rarely coincided with the regional boundaries.

Basically, four artistic movements can be distinguished:

1.) The Byzantine style which spread from Italy to continental Europe and reached as far as England. It affected both miniature and monumental painting.

2.) The Hiberno-Saxon and Anglo-Saxon style which advanced southwards across the continent as far as northern Italy. It was relevant mainly in the early phase of Romanesque painting and was used predominantly in book illumination.

3.) The art of the Carolingian and Ottonian empires which from its centers in Germany and France radiated in all directions. It manifested itself above all in work done in scriptoria that were active between the ninth and the eleventh centuries. There is evidence that the Carolingian codices exerted a direct and marked influence on the pictorial structure and subject matter of Ottonian painting.

4.) Finally there was Mozarabic art which, despite its strong regional limitations, had an immense impact. Between the eighth and the eleventh centuries, it gave rise to unusual and delightful variations in the Christian art of northern Spain.

The influence of the Italo-Byzantine style (which will be discussed in more detail shortly) meant that the intellectual heritage of antiquity came into direct contact with the Christian doctrine of salvation. It was, above all, the Carolingian court schools that valued the Byzantine spirit. After all, since the Emperor Justinian closed down the Platonic Academy of Athens in 529, Christian Europe had had only very sporadic access to the ancient sciences. The knowledge and beliefs of the ancients could reach Europe only in very small quantities and by a roundabout route via highly cultured Islamic Spain – if at all. The libraries of Constaninople, Rome and Venice, and later also those of Montecassino and Palermo, housed numerous volumes containing the thought and teachings of Classical antiquity but they were available only to enlightened Classical scholars. It

was really only during the Carolingian and the Hohenstaufen dynasties that Classical antiquity was idealized for its policies and highly valued for its culture. Today, there is a tendency to refer to such cases as a "Renaissance," a "Proto-Renaissance," or a "Renovatio," terms which will be dealt with at a later stage in this book. Our initial concern is to describe the Italo-Byzantine style in order to define Byzantine form and give an outline of the effect it had on the stylistic development of Romanesque wall painting.

The early Christian mosaics of Ravenna and Rome were a treasure-house of form and design for Carolingian monumental painting. Just how strong this influence was becomes impressively obvious in the little monastery church of Müstair in Graubünden. The walls of the aisles and the apses are decorated with numerous frescoes depicting subjects from the Old and New Testaments, with architectural shapes that decorate the background in an unobtrusive manner (photo, p. 407 on the left). The painted architectural elements such as arches, columns and pilasters help to articulate the groups of figures. Thus Christ is often placed beneath a semi-circular arch which allows for the harmonious integration of his halo. Columns and pilasters are useful devices to separate figures or groups of figures from the background. A certain spatial quality is suggested by the overlapping of figures and architectural elements, despite the fact that proper perspective has not yet been achieved. This "spatial plane" served as the stage, as it were, on which the figures stood or performed their actions. Similar compositional systems and treatment of figures can be found at Castelseprio south of Varese (probably dating back to the early eighth century). However, the characteristics described are also typical of the Byzantine mosaics in Ravenna and Rome. It is conceivable that there were even links to early Roman wall or catacomb painting. Important examples of this are Sta. Maria Antiqua (early eighth century) and the catacomb on the Via Nomentana (fourth century).

Such comparisons serve to illustrate in general terms how the Byzantine style was adopted. It does not however, account for the sheer wealth and joy of detail and narration that is so obvious in the apses of Müstair. The figures skipping past columns, ducking under arches, and hiding behind pilasters have a high-spirited but also traditional element about them which seems best suited to the faithful of a rural district. It is possible that pre-Carolingian book illumination also provided some inspiration, as is suggested by pages from the Ashburnham Pentateuch. It is worth remembering here that the latter codex, which was probably written in Spain or northern Africa in the seventh century, is representative of a number of early Byzantine manuscripts which use a comparable figurative and architectural pattern. A kind of model of this manner of representation so typical of Byzantine art can be seen in a folio showing scenes from the Old Testament story of Jacob and Esau (see photo, p. 405). Here, the structuring of figures and architectural elements works on a similar level to that of the Müstair paintings. Spatial depth is suggested by overlapping a figure with a column. Figures lined up side by side are articulated by round arches that seem to urge on the speed of the narrative. Here, too, the palace-like architecture has the overall function of a stage

Müstair, monastery church of St. John,
north wall: Christ healing the mute man.
Around 800

TOP RIGHT:
Aachen, Ada Gospel. St. Luke the
Evangelist. Around 800. Trier,
Stadtbibliothek. Cod. 22, fol. 85

BOTTOM RIGHT:
Müstair, monastery church of St. John.
Ornamental band near the apse window.
Around 800

set which defines the space in which the figures act, and divides it up into individual scenes.

Also of note are the window framings consisting of painted columns with a three-quarter circle profile, imitating classical forms (photo on the right, bottom). They clearly relate to ornamentation used in book illumination produced at around the same time (photo, top right). The colonnettes are decorated with stylized flowers and entwined by spiral ribbons. Such Byzantine ornamental motifs are typical of the illuminations produced by the Palace school of Charlemagne in Aachen. The folio with the Evangelist Luke from the Ada gospel book (around 800) depicts the Evangelist beneath a portal with columns. The arch is decorated with a delicate sawtooth frieze, while the slender colonnettes are ornamented with spiral ribbons and small cartouches. It is possible that the artist in this case wanted to indicate the existence of two levels – one in the secular world, represented by the architectural framing, and one in the hereafter, represented by the visionary appearance of the Evangelist who sits on his

heavenly throne and is accompanied by his apocalyptic symbol, the bull.

One can assume that the window framings in the church of Müstair are based on a similar concept of meaning. The ornamental features seen in context with the actual architecture of the window allows the "outsider" a glimpse onto and into the sacred space, and thus a symbolic glimpse of the Heavenly Jerusalem which is in turn represented by the actual church building. The references are therefore manifold and on many levels. The formal language of Byzantine art exerts its influence on both book illumination and monumental painting alike, and again and again we see how the two genres resemble each other in both style and motif.

What was already heralded by Müstair and the Ada Gospel Book – i.e. the artistic interplay between figure and architecture – is a characteristic feature of Byzantine decoration. Architecture, however, is not always restricted to the role of background articulation. Many Carolingian frescoes feature buildings and town districts which are not covered by figures. Although active figures are integrated into the overall architectural

Auxerre, Saint-Germain, crypt, St. Stephen's Chapel. The stoning of Saint Stephen

Montmorillon, Notre-Dame, Chapelle Sainte-Cathérine. The Virgin Mary and Child. Around 1200

unique at this early stage. Such compositions suggest the existence of a lively artistic center where experimentation with Byzantine compositional schemes had been going on for some time. Eventually they might have opened up new perspectives for the aesthetic design of wall spaces. What such examples also do is to underline the artistic potency and self-confidence of the Carolingian striving for artistic excellence. It is therefore a reasonable assumption that further instances of independent pictorial design would have come to light had more wall painting of the Carolingian period survived.

The artistic dialogue with Byzantium has still more variety to offer: form was interesting not only in its capacity for representing the political dignity of the ruler (see below). It also allowed the direct adoption of motifs which were transplanted, as it were, from their original Byzantine setting. Such a case can be seen in Notre-Dame in Montmorillon, near Poitiers (photo, below). The apse vault of the Chapelle Sainte-Cathérine is taken up by a representation of the enthroned Virgin Mary with the Christ child. His little arm stretches out beyond the confines of the mandorla in

design, the view remains unobstructed. Thus whole buildings or groups of buildings move into the foreground and become the pictorial subject.

In St. Stephen's Chapel in the crypt of St. Germain in Auxerre, the visitor is confronted by a surprising composition (photo, above): the stoning of St. Stephen is depicted in a tympanum. Nearly all of the left-hand half of the picture is taken up by the representation of a town which is scaled down in size in proportion to the figures. The towers, parts of buildings, and a spacious gateway adorned with a triangular pediment can all be looked upon as a reduced veduta. St. Stephen, it seems, has just been dragged through this city gate and onto the place of his execution by his judges. Towering behind the humble St. Stephen, his torturers are depicted with their arms raised up ready to throw the stones. The figure of Stephen himself projects into the right half of the picture which otherwise consists of an empty space, broken up to great effect by the appearance of the hand of God.

This unusual composition gives us two important pieces of information: the adoption of the Byzantine pictorial motif of the city, and the gradual development away from the Byzantine figure-architecture relationship. We are unlikely to come across a composition in Carolingian wall painting that can be compared with Auxerre; although ninth-century book illumination might offer some comparable examples.

There is another fresco in the Chapel of St. Stephen that breaks away from the Byzantine pattern usually employed at the time. Set within another tympanum, we are confronted by another unusual composition: depicted along the central axis is the upright figure of a saint around whom the other figures are grouped in such a way that they form a line rising up towards the center. This triangular composition is integrated harmoniously into the span of the tympanum. Nevertheless it seems unusual that not even smaller groupings of heads are shown in a staggered arrangement at the same height, as is the case with Byzantine models, and with sarcophagi from late antiquity in particular. The piling up of figures behind and next to St. Stephen creates an illusion of space that is almost

order to crown Ecclesia. Hovering above the scene are angels in various
elegant, mannered or acrobatically distorted poses.

Although the subject is typically Byzantine, the style is not. It is softer
and more animated and imparts to the divine couple a graceful
appearance. What this work dating from about 1200 makes clear is for
just how long Byzantine art served as a source of inspiration for many
artists in the most diverse manner, in terms of both formal style and
subject-matter. Typically, this kind of subject transfer with individual
stylistic design occurred in local schools. Having established a style of their
own, they nevertheless wanted to use a time-honored system of symbols
and types sanctioned by sacred tradition. In the first place this concerns, of
course, the main subject of Romanesque painting, the depiction of Christ
in Majesty. Three such Christs in Majesty provide examples: those in
Sant'Angelo in Formis (around 1080), San Clemente in Tahull (around
1123), and Berzé-la-Ville (around 1120). The starting point of this
typology is the church mentioned first, Sant'Angelo in Formis (photo,
right) which was founded by the Abbot Desiderius of Montecassino. It is
assumed that Desiderius summoned the Master of the Christ in Majesty
from a court school in Constantinople. He would therefore have been
familiar with the traditional east-Roman pictorial system. Nevertheless he
tried a novel approach. No depictions of a majesty with the Evangelists'
symbols are known in Constantinople. On the other hand, they have
occurred more frequently in the west since the Carolingian period. It is
also of interest that Christ does not appear within the mandorla, the
aureole of divine light – an unusual, albeit not a novel approach. Perhaps
the artist had seen the depictions of a Christ free from his mandorla which
had survived from the early Christian period in the apse mosaic of Old St.
Peter's and in St. Paul's in Rome. Everything else, however, follows Byzantine
traditions – the representation of detail, the strict linear parallelism of the
gowns, the sculptured quality of the bodies emphasized by dark shading.
The deep purple of the gowns with their connotation of preciousness can
also be traced back to eastern models, as can the magnificent golden throne.

What is remarkable is that the artist obviously integrated north
Carolingian and Roman/early Christian pictorial conceptions in order to
create his Christ in Majesty. It is quite likely that he occupies a special
position in the history of such Christ images, since the Christ in Majesty of
Sant'Angelo in Formis proved to be of interest to other artists in other
countries. This point will be discussed in more detail later.

The political configuration peculiar to the north of Spain resulted in
the dominance of Arab-derived designs, and it is difficult to find there
evidence of Byzantine art. In the course of the eleventh to the thirteenth
centuries, the reconquest of the peninsula from the Moors – the so-called
Reconquista – was gathering momentum. This meant, among other things,
that Christian and Byzantine shapes and designs gradually gained greater
significance. Like the one of Sant'Angelo in Formis, the Christ in Majesty
of Tahull (photo, p. 410) consists of two parts: God the Father is depicted
in the apsis calotte, while the plinth area shows Mary with the Apostles.
This is, however, where the similarity ends. Iconographical differences can
be seen in the presence of the mandorla, the segmental arches instead of

the throne, and the pictures of the Evangelists, some of which are framed
in medallions. What the two have in common are just matters of detail and
composition, such as the strict frontality and the axial symmetry of God
the Father, and the shading which emphasizes the hand muscles and parts
of the face. These are exactly the points at which one's attention becomes
focused: it seems that the Master of Tahull has made the Byzantine model
even more Byzantine, that he further stylized what was already stylized.
The facial contours, which in Italian examples had been indicated gently,
are now given great emphasis. The face of God in Sant'Angelo in Formis
turns into a mask in Tahull. Similar observations apply to the treatment of
folds in the garments and to the gestures: what in Italy is depicted in a
softer and more animated style appears harder and more rigid in Tahull.
This tendency can probably be explained by the arrival of the already
mentioned Mozarabic style, that fusion of Arab stylistic elements and
Christian western ideas of shape and form. And yet it is not sufficient
to characterize the Romanesque painting of northern Spain simply as
"Mozarabic," as the example just cited shows. Despite all the differences
described above, there is nevertheless a distinctive Byzantine factor which
contributed to the stylistic development.

The Christ in Majesty of Berzé-la-Ville (photo, p. 411) differs considerably from the examples just mentioned. In contrast to the strict and rigid

Fresco from Tahull (Santa Maria). Christ
in Majesty. Around 1123. Barcelona,
Museo de Arte de Cataluña

OPPOSITE PAGE:
Berzé-la-Ville, priory church. Christ in
Majesty (top), spandrel figure (bottom
left), martyrdom of Blasius (detail,
bottom right). Around 1120

plan found in Tahull, in Berzé-la-Ville we are faced with soft, flowing lines and a sublime use of color.

Apart from adopting a different iconographical layout (which will be dealt with in more detail in the appropriate chapter), the artist who worked in this Burgundian Cluniae daughter-church is also very likely to have worked from Byzantine models. And yet he must have interpreted them very differently. He seems to have examined the Byzantine style with regard to its finer structures, to its fine modeling of volume and its variety of design. This becomes particularly apparent in the way he shaped the gowns, the dense folds of which wind themselves along the various parts of the bodies like an elongated and elegant linear pattern, forming flat areas around the pelvis, the knees and the elbows. This treatment of the gown is apparent not only in the figure of Christ but also in the Apostles arranged around the sides. The frescoes on the side walls of the chancel were therefore presumably painted by the same master, even if the figures appear more rigid and clumsy (see, for instance, the figures in the

martyrdom of St. Lawrence). The figures nevertheless show the same characteristic arrangement of folds in the garments.

The indication of body shape through drapery was not a new idea and had already been employed in the Christ in Majesty of Sant'Angelo in Formis. As already mentioned, the Byzantine artist who worked for the monastery of Montecassino had drawn some of his inspiration with regard to style and subject-matter from Rome and probably also from Carolingian manuscripts. One might therefore assume that the artist active in Berzé-la-Ville had made use of the same or similar sources. Another comparison strengthens this observation: stylistic links can be established with the lower church of San Clemente in Rome. As far as the treatment of the garments is concerned (photo, left), the frescoes painted there around the year 1100 show surprising similarities to the paintings found in the Burgundy church. This applies in particular to the figures in San Clemente, those depicted in a slightly bent posture carrying the reliquary. The treatment of the garments there has been attributed, amongst other things, to the influence of Carolingian miniatures which, in turn, had been inspired by Byzantine art forms. Further evidence for this can be seen, for example, in the folios of the Gospels of Saint-Médard of Soissons which was produced around the year 800 in the court school of Aachen (photo, p. 402).

Around the year 1200, Germany saw the beginning of a new phase in the adoption of Byzantine or, to be more precise, proper Classical form elements. This phase found expression in a very different way. This period of Romanesque wall painting is generally defined by a strict formalism which was derived from the Byzantine monumental style. The examples of the mosaics in Palermo and of Cefalù on Sicily have been cited in this context. Indeed, many representations of Christ in Majesty might have served as comparison, as can be seen in the upper church of Schwarz-rheindorf near Bonn (around 1180, photo, p. 413, left): when compared with the Christ in Majesty in the Cappella Palatina in Palermo (around 1150, photo, p. 413, right) there clearly are some fundamental similarities in the posture and gestures of the figures, in the drapery and even in the form of the throne. Even such an unspectacular detail as the slightly billowing throne cushion has been included in both pictures. How a Romanesque church on the Rhine could have been connected to a distant chapel in Palermo on the island of Sicily might be explained as follows: the Cappella Palatina was built in the middle of the twelfth century by the Norman rulers, probably during the reign of Roger II. The decorative mosaics date from that period. At around the same time the chancellor of Konrad III of Hohenstaufen, Arnold von Wied, commissioned the construction of the palatine church of Schwarzrheindorf. The church was not painted until some years later, probably not until 1180. At that time, that is in the second half of the twelfth century, there already existed close links between the Hohenstaufen dynasty and the Normans who still resided at the court of Palermo. In the year 1186, Henry VI married Constance, a daughter of the Norman Roger II, and inherited the Norman empire. Via the house of Hohenstaufen, Germany thus found itself quite suddenly exposed to the Byzantine style, examples of which were to be found all over southern Italy and Sicily. Before long, the cultural heritage

Schwarzrheindorf, Ss. Maria and Klemens, apse of the upper church. Christ in Majesty. Around 1180

Palermo, Capella Palatina, apse. Christ in Majesty. Around 1150

of Byzantium had become very popular in the German countries north of the Alps. Schwarzrheindorf represents only one example of the new artistic style which soon became popular.

The imperial pretensions of the Hohenstaufen dynasty acquired even greater momentum with the arrival of Frederick II, and art became closely connected with his political ambitions. Frederick II entertained a vision of himself ruling over Europe like a Roman emperor from the Capitol in Rome, and creating a second "Pax Augustana." He therefore ensured an ample supply of works of art in the Classical Roman style for the regions and cities of his homeland north of the Alps. This so-called "Staufen Classicism" soon left its mark also on painting from around the year 1200 onwards. Unfortunately, the frescoes of Schwarzrheindorf have survived in a very incomplete and damaged state. Nevertheless, they serve as impressive illustrations of the change in aesthetic perception at that period.

As already observed in the figure of Christ in Majesty, there had been a noticeable change in the treatment of drapery and in the outlining of the physiognomy of the figures and the various parts of the body. Everything was softly undulating – a tendency which is even more pronounced in the figures in the lower church that are thought to have been painted a little earlier (around 1160). The so-called "jealousy picture" (named after

Ezekiel who mentions a picture which aroused the jealousy of God) in the western chapel has a clear resemblance to the figure of St. Matthew on the Angel Column in Strasbourg Cathedral. Incidentally, the sculptures of the Angel Column are often cited as perfect examples of the monumental style of "Staufen Classicism." What is even more astonishing is the similarity between the figure dressed in linen in the northern chapel, and the Roman statue of the emperor Augustus. Surely this must be interpreted as an example of the political nature of much of the art of Schwarzrheindorf.

With these comparisons we have completed our outline of the figurative style of "Staufen Classicism." By now the Byzantine elements had largely made way for a Classical Roman style, or had at least been modified by it. The drapery, with its emphasis on volume and long, flowing movement, derives from late Roman monumental sculpture, rather than from the ascetic figures found in Byzantine mosaics. The figurative style of "Staufen Classicism" manifested itself clearly in the frescoes of Schwarzrheindorf.

In France, the new and elegant formal vocabulary of the Gothic style had already emerged by the second half of the twelfth century. Compared with that, Germany's modern "Staufen" style appeared rather stolid and conservative. There were, indeed, hardly any stylistic possibilities and starting

413

Antependium from the monastery of
St. Walpurgis in Soest. Around 1170.
Oak-wood, 39 x 76 inches. Münster,
Westfälisches Landesmuseum

Altarpiece for the Wiesenkirche in Soest.
Holy Trinity, St. Mary, St. John. Around
1250. Berlin, Staatliche Museen
Preussischer Kulturbesitz

points which could have transformed such a compact and monumental figurative style into the graceful and mannered realm of Gothic form.

The "zigzag style"

In Germany, too, stylistic changes occurred, even if at a later date and in a manner different from that of of other European countries. The Walpurgis church in Soest was the original home to a majesty antependium painted around the year 1170, which, incidentally, is the only surviving Romanesque antependium in Germany (photo, top). What is noticeable about the voluminous treatment of the robes is the tapering folds of the red cloaks worn by Walpurgis, Mary, John, Augustine and Christ. They all end in an unusually sharp-edged jagged line. This provides a peculiar contrast to the forms otherwise employed in the garments and the bodies of the figures, which are undulating and gently rounded. Even at this very

early stage this is evidence of the beginning of the dissolution of the early Staufen form.

Of course, this example could be dismissed as merely an isolated case, occurring, as it did, at the end of the twelfth century. However, about eighty years later another Westphalian master painted an altarpiece (around 1250) probably intended for the Wiesenkirche in Soest. In this retable (photo, above) the jagged shapes are actually used as the main structural framework for the figures of the Holy Trinity, John, and Mary. The garments look as if they had been blown out and then frozen, as though the unexpected onset of a strong gust of wind just as suddenly subsided. The pointed folds project from the bodies in a rigid and unwieldy fashion. The shapes appear all the more bizarre as they are set in a framework of evenly rounded arches. The result of this combination is a heightening of artistic representation and of dramatic expression.

These two examples from Westphalia illustrate this exceptional form of Romanesque painting known as the German "zigzag style," or sometimes "jagged style." In the face of such atypical form and design, it remains open to question whether the "zigzag style" can really be categorized as Romanesque. At all events, it marks the transition to the Gothic style in that it began to change the figurative style of the Staufen period in a way that was very close to Mannerism.

There are other works that could be cited to document this strange and short-lived style. Amongst them are some panels painted on both sides that were probably destined for the Johanneskirche in Worms or for the cathedral. Today they are kept in the Hessisches Landesmuseum in Darmstadt. It is likely that the panels, painted around 1220, were part of a winged altarpiece. The jagged zigzag pattern is unmistakable, particularly in the ends of the folds of St. Peter's garment. Nevertheless, the composition of the figures as a whole appears more restrained than that of the Soest altarpiece. This might also indicate that the panels were painted at an earlier date.

Another remarkable example of this style are the vault frescoes in St. Maria Lyskirchen in Cologne (photos, right). They were the subject of an exemplary exercise in uncovering and restoration between 1972 and 1977. Dating from around 1250, the paintings are attributed to the Gothic style by some researchers, although they also show typical characteristics of the "zigzag style" in the treatment of the garments, where flowing folds are interrupted suddenly by sharp edges and end in nervous jagged points.

Where might the "zigzag style" have originated? Was it the eccentric invention of one master that was imitated by artists in other regions, or did it set a precedent and attract a proper following? No satisfactory answer can be given to these questions since very little evidence has survived. One can, however, speculate. A variation of this style appears on the west gallery of the cathedral in Gurk in Carinthia. Incidentally, it is set in the context of an interesting iconographical program. The throne of Solomon is depicted, along with the Transfiguration and the Birth of Christ. In the vault one can see the Earthly Paradise. The paintings were probably executed around the year 1260 and are not in a very good state of preservation. It is unclear whether one or several artists were involved in the work. What is clear is that there are differences between the figures depicted in Paradise and those depicted on the walls. With regard to our question as to the geographical spread of the "zigzag style," one figure is of particular interest: the figure of Mary on the tympanum above the apse portal. The garments worn both by her and by the secondary figures on both sides of the throne display the characteristic jagged features we have seen at Soest and at Worms. Interrupted by sharp and broken edges, most of the folds either end in a horizontal line or project in a kind of star shape, a formal variation of the Westphalian zigzag style. Such an artistic link between Soest and Carinthia could suggest a geographical spread of the style. This would further extend the possibility of the start of an independent stylistic development running parallel to the Gothic style.

It is fairly certain that the "zigzag style" was inspired by Byzantine examples in the wake of the cultural development under the Hohenstaufen dynasty. Therefore it was not only Classical form as adopted by the aforementioned

"Staufen Classicism" that was affected by the confrontation with Byzantium.

The transformation of the monumental draped figure of the Staufen style into a "figured garment" meant that the garment's movement and structure were freed from the body of the person depicted and had entered into an aesthetic life of its own. This development can indeed be said to mark the final stages of Romanesque and the beginning of Gothic painting in Germany.

It was not only the knowledge of Byzantine art, made accessible by the European policies of the Hohenstaufen dynasty, that provided a stimulus for the "zigzag style." Inspiration came from the west, too, although this had nothing to do with Hohenstaufen politics. It has already been mentioned that the Ottonian painting of Lower Saxony had links with artistic development in England. During the period from the tenth to the twelfth century, only Canterbury, Winchester and Bury St. Edmunds can be considered as the dominant English schools. The Holy Sepulchre chapel of Winchester Cathedral was decorated towards the end of the twelfth century. A noticeable feature of both the Deposition and the Entombment of Christ is the frequently employed device of interrupting flowing drapery by an horizontal arrangement of groups of folds. The result are sharp-edged corners not dissimilar to the shapes discussed earlier with regard to the majesty antependium at Soest. At the time, there was a strong link between the monumental paintings of Winchester and the scriptoria which were also housed there. The sacramentary of Robert of Jumièges (beginning of the eleventh century), with its similar treatment of drapery, might have served as an example. The variation in style can then be traced back to the artistic circle of the Carolingian period, such as the court school in Rheims, for instance. In the figures of both the Ebo Gospel Book and the Utrecht Psalter, we find the unmistakable characteristics of these schools in the nervous treatment of the drapery (photo, p. 422, left).

Seen in retrospect, the relationship between Carolingian scriptoria, English book illumination and wall painting, and German panel and monumental painting is a complicated one. It is also typical of the stylistic interaction of Romanesque painting in Europe. During the ninth century, the influence of Hiberno-Saxon and Anglo-Saxon book production on artists on the continent ceased, and the Carolingian court schools became increasingly dominant. It was not until towards the end of the tenth century that England once again opened its doors to the cultural developments on the continent. This was also the time when Ottonian book illuminators drew inspiration from the artistic tradition of the Carolingians, as was discussed earlier.

It is interesting that this connection can be established between English painting of the eleventh century and the final stages of Romanesque painting in Germany. Seen in the context of English and "concealed Carolingian" as well as Byzantine and Staufen influences, the German "zigzag style" can be regarded as a stylistic variant of the Romanesque, but certainly not as a "stylistic interlude."

Group compositions
The principal subjects of Romanesque painting are the Christ in Majesty and Virgin Enthroned. The stylistic conception and composition are simple and leave little room for variation owing to the fixed theological meanings. Both these types are discussed in more detail in the chapter on iconography (pp. 428 ff.). With regard to groups of people, the situation is different. The design and compositional possibilities are far greater and more variable than with a single figure.

Two basic types can be distinguished: the additive and the integrative principle. In the additive principle, the figures are placed next to one another without significant overlapping. In the integrative principle, on the other hand, the figures are arranged both side by side and behind one another. The resulting overlaps are very conspicuous and are supposed to suggest a feeling of spatial depth. But such group compositions often appear like a flat piling-up of bodies without conveying any spatial connection whatsoever. Romanesque painting had not yet succeeded in creating a space for the figure as Giotto later did, transforming the spot where a figure was positioned into an active space.

Group composition as defined by isocephaly, that is the arrangement of heads all at the same level, is a specific characteristic of Ancient and Byzantine art. The frescoes in Sant'Angelo in Formis which date from around 1080 represent a kind of stylistic and iconographical point of intersection between Byzantine tradition and the Christian teaching of form that had just been newly formulated at that time. The various principles of formal design and constellations of motifs that found expression in Sant'Angelo in Formis can at least make an important contribution to the definition of Romanesque monumental painting. The group compositions of the Last Judgement on the western wall of the church (photos, p. 417, top) are painted very much in the Byzantine tradition and refer back mainly to the formal ideal of Classical antiquity. Clergy and faithful are depicted standing side by side and the same size, raising their hands in prayer. Behind them, in the second row, only heads are to be seen. All that is visible of the faithful and the saints in the rows behind is their hair. The additive principle meant that here a large number of people had to be accommodated within a pictorial space of uniform definition that was "meant" to function as space. Given the Apocalyptic subject, this was fully intentional. The order and the static equilibrium of the picture also fit into the framework of meaning that the subject commands. The counterparts to the faithful, namely the damned, have been conceived in a dynamic, diagonally ascending composition. The wretched are rendered in a great variety of movement as they are pushed mercilessly into the mouth of Hell by blood-red devils. The bent and falling bodies overlap each other, are huddled together or drift apart. The turmoil of Hell has been captured in a quite masterly way in this scene. This serves as proof that the integrative principle is also dependent on the subject-matter. The additive principle cannot therefore be seen as conservative, nor the integrative principle be regarded as a progressive variation of Romanesque group composition, despite the fact that the latter principle naturally achieves a far greater "three-dimensional" effect.

Static equilibrium and dynamism, surface design and the urge to achieve the illusion of space; these pairs of opposites define the different stages of development of Romanesque painting and at the same time aptly

Sant'Angelo in Formis. The Last
Judgement, complete view and detail
(top), the Betrayal of Christ (bottom,
left), the Last Supper (bottom, right).
Around 1080

Schwarzrheindorf, Ss. Maria and
Klemens, upper church. Scene from the
Last Judgement: divine punishment.
Around 1180

describe the peculiarities inherent in both the additive and integrative principles of group composition.

The rich variety encompassed by these two groups is now so great and distributed so extensively over the individual centuries, that it is virtually impossible to trace their development. One should, however, bear in mind that the integrative principle, with its exploration of the spatial depth of pictorial space, has become the agreed standard type of the post-Romanesque era. The impressive evidence for this claim is to be seen in the group compositions of Schwarzrheindorf: the Divine Judgement depicted in the spandrel of the northern chapel in the lower church could almost be taken for a group composition of the early Renaissance period (photo, left). The figures are involved in dramatic movement and do not only overlap, but their staggered arrangement creates the illusion of depth to

such a degree that the whole spandrel seems to undergo a sudden transformation into an illusionistic spherical triangle. The ingenuity of the composition is further heightened by the fact that the scene is divided into smaller sub-groups, each of which is involved in one action. The tormentors, for example, are depicted in a staggered arrangement, one behind the other in an almost fan-like conception; equipped with spears and swords, their right hands are shown hitting and stabbing at the bodies of the damned. The group of the tormentors is faced by an equivalent but smaller group opposite, while below them there is a loose collection of the recumbent or falling bodies of the helpless and dying, still receiving mortal blows.

Within the context of the development of Romanesque painting, two levels must be distinguished within both principles of composition. On the one hand, both the additive and the integrative principle are restricted by the appropriate subject matter available. On the other hand, it appears fairly clear that the latter type does represent an element of progress away from the strict and diagrammatic Byzantine system. There is no doubt that even in the Carolingian era artists have always endeavored to find a way of creating the illusion of spatial depth on a flat pictorial space. A very good example of this desire is St. Stephen's Chapel in St. Germain in Auxerre (photo, p. 408). The integrative principle is also illustrated by the group compositions of the legend of Clement as depicted in the lower church of San Clemente in Rome, well known for its use of Byzantine expressive form (photo, p. 398). This applies above all to the group on the right next to the saint in front of the altar, from which bent figures emerge and break up the unity of the group. This group therefore suggests a greater degree of spatial depth than the painted architectural elements behind it, which look like mere wall decoration.

Now we come to the unique composition of Mary enthroned in the vaulted ceiling of the apse of St. Maria zur Höhe in Soest (known as the Hohnekirche, mid thirteenth century). Indebted more to the Staufen style in its formal conception, the majesty definitely used the additive principle. Mary's throne is surrounded by St. John the Baptist and St. John the Evangelist, who both have smaller "secondary angels" assigned to them, and by sixteen angels arranged in an arc formation (photo, p. 432). The division of the angelic gathering into groups of two or three is determined by the vault segments. A comparable composition can be found in the western chancel of the former collegiate church of Lambach (shortly before 1089). Instead of angels, we find magicians kneeling in adoration before the Mother of God seated on her throne in the vault of the central bay.

Perhaps the group depicted at Soest should not even be regarded as a homogeneous group, since the spherical shape of the vault makes the lined-up angels appear like a decorative pattern. Whichever way one looks at this ceiling painting – be it as a group composition or as a "figurative ornamental pattern" – one thing has become clear: group composition in Romanesque painting is determined primarily by the subject-matter. In other words, the formal structure is always used to convey the iconographical structure. The angels surrounding the throne of Mary in such a novel fashion represent, therefore, an unusual variation of Mary Enthroned.

Yet another composition of even greater iconographical ingenuity was created by the Master of Berzé-la-Ville (photo, p. 411, top). The arm of the

Reichenau, Niederzell, St. Peter and Paul,
apse. Christ in Majesty. Around 1120

Cologne, St. Gereon, baptistery. St.
Gereon (left) and St. Martin (right).
Around 1240/50

Lord is seen to project on the right-hand side beyond the shining boundary of his sphaira or mandorla in order to hand to St. Peter the scroll containing the statutes.

St. Peter is accompanied by five other Apostles and, like them, lowers his head in humility. The Apostles are seen crowding next to and behind one another, lined up in typical Byzantine additive style within the spherical spandrel that extends between the curve of the mandorla and the outer edge of the apse. Artistically speaking, this is a very clever composition, because the area showing the mandorla dominates the apse and separates off the spheres of the Apostles, at least as far as the viewpoint of the observer is concerned: on approaching the chancel along the central axis of the nave, all that is visible is the Christ in Majesty, the godly cosmos. Almost excluded, in terms of perspective anyway, by the spherical architecture of the apse, the figures of the Apostles are distorted into irregular line-work and blocks of color. But if one takes up a position underneath and to the side of the apsis calotte, the Apostles can be seen in their proper proportions, whilst the mandorla now seems to contract: the cosmos of God is omnipresent even if it is invisible from our human world.

The combination of Majesty depictions and group compositions takes on different forms. The examples of Soest and Berzé-la-Ville undoubtedly constitute special cases. A typical and widely used system is the Byzantine

one which we know from the church of Sant'Angelo in Formis (photo, p. 409). In a modified form, it applies to the apse paintings of Cefalù (1148), the upper church of Schwarzrheindorf (around 1180, photo, p. 413), the Church of St. Gereon in Cologne, or the Reichenau Church of St. Peter and Paul in Niederzell (around 1120, photo, top left). It is doubtful, however, whether the above examples represent real group compositions; although the figures are lined up in accordance with the additive principle, they are at the same time represented in strict isolation. This sense of isolation is further enhanced by the architecture of the windows and sometimes, as in the Reichenau example, also by painted arcading. Perhaps this problem can also be solved by taking into account the viewing position of the observers, i.e. the faithful. Standing in the circle of the chancel apse, the architectural conception meant that they could not help being surrounded by apostles, angels or other biblical figures. Aided by the framework of painted arcading such as in Niederzell, or by articulating windows such as in St. Gereon in Cologne, these figures can then be experienced as a real group.

The term "group composition" is therefore a flexible one when applied to Romanesque painting, since so far no definite typology has been established for medieval monumental painting. This term is useful merely as an explanatory model in order to make a distinction between the various stylistic developments possible.

Irish codex. Origin unknown. St. Mark.
Eighth century. St. Gallen,
Stiftsbibliothek. Cod. 51, Pag. 78

Evangelistary of Godescalc. Aachen,
Palace School. Christ in Majesty. 783
Paris, Bibl. Nat. Nouv. Acq. Lat. 1203,
fol. 3a

Book illumination
Spiral ornament and interlace. The Hiberno-Saxon influence

It has already been pointed out that the influence of Hiberno-Saxon and Anglo-Saxon book illumination on the continent was unusually strong even before the Carolingian period. When the Irish monks traveled to the countries both north and south of the Alps, they brought with them the learned writings which now found their way into the newly founded monasteries. There, the teachings were examined and the traditional concepts adapted. In this way, a cultural foundation was established upon which the newly founded court schools could develop and flourish towards the end of the eighth and throughout the ninth century.

In terms of artistic development, three aspects of style were of importance: firstly, the spiral-shaped and uniform ornamental designs swirling over and covering the surface like a carpet (hence the term "carpet page"); secondly, the intricately designed initial; and thirdly, the framing of the figure by means of extremely skilfully arranged architectural elements.

Early indications of the important features characterizing Irish book production can be seen in the ornamental page of the "Book of Durrow" pictured on page 401 (left; seventh century) and the St. Mark folio from a later Irish manuscript (photo, p. 420 left). In the second example, the dense spiral patterns from Iona (Book of Durrow) become "disentangled" and reorganize themselves into the figure of the Evangelist. The Evangelists' symbols placed in the corners of the page are hardly distinguishable from the dense vine scroll decoration in the other parts of the side margin. Another folio allows us to follow the metamorphosis from ornamental framing to architectural pictorial element as it almost unfolds before our very eyes: this is the Arrest of Christ in the "Book of

Book of Kells. The Arrest of Christ.
End of eighth century. Dublin, Trinity
College. Lib. Ms. 58, AI6, fol. 114r

Kells" dating from around the year 800 (photo, right). The scene takes place beneath an ornamental arch constructed of abstract decorative patterns that assume an architectural shape.

Such ornamental architectural elements were employed as clichés, as it were, for the pictorial construction of Carolingian illuminations. For the framing of the blessing Christ of the Godescalc Evangelistary produced in Charlemagne's Palace School in Aachen (781–83, photo, p. 420, right) the artist reverts back to the Irish interlace motifs as found in the Book of Kells. An attempt is made to use architectural elements as means of ornamentation, similar to the St. Mark folio and the folio showing the Arrest of Christ: the wall running along under the Christ in Majesty symbolizes a piece of the Heavenly Jerusalem, and alternates in its artistic expression between constructed architecture and decorative band.

During the course of the ninth century, a clear distinction was made in the miniatures of the Carolingian scriptoria between architectural pattern and interlace. The sublime outline drawing found in Irish ornamental architecture was avoided. Instead, a clear commitment was made to the combination of initial and ornament. Long after the Carolingian period, such works from Ireland were exemplary and unsurpassed in their artistic variety. They were appreciated in any monastery on the Continent, an aspect that is easily comprehended even today. One Irish codex dating from the eight century contains the initial "Chi", a reference to the first words of Matthew, 18: "Christus autem generatio sic erat" ("Now the birth of Jesus Christ was on this wise"). The initials combine interlace, spiral-shaped patterns, and stylized animal motifs. From the interaction of these pictorial elements, the initial develops into the framework which embraces the words quoted from the Evangelist. This initial "Chi," incidentally, occurs again and again and in ever-varying form in a number of other Hiberno-Saxon manuscripts and in miniatures from Carolingian and even Ottonian scriptoria. It must be understood as a kind of "signature" of Christ. This intimate combination of animal motif, interlace and spiral-shape, the artifical loops and knots, soon all formed part of the standard repertoire of all European book production. Growing from an axial symmetrical base, the interlacing often branches out into vegetative structures, capturing, as it were, the letters. Even in Ottonian manuscripts there is still evidence of the popular experimentation combining letter and ornamental forms with the framework of the illumination. In fact, there is evidence of this keen aesthetic experimentation in virtually every codex. This applies not only to the artistic design of text illustrations but also to the texts themselves. An Irish form of poetry known as "Hisperica Famina" abandons the meaning of a word in favor of the effect produced by words. It is concerned with the effect of sound which is created by means of imaginative word-play and which attempts to captivate the reader or listener by its use of truly labyrinthine syntax. One can indeed refer to this poetry as an "interlace of words" or a "spiral of words." In the same way as the search for meaning in the poetry of "Hisperica Famina" is pointless and unproductive, the spiral shapes and interlace in the book illustrations must also be regarded largely as a decorative pattern. It would be necessary to examine individual examples of the depiction of demonic animal motifs in order to establish to what extent an apotropaic function (i.e. designed to avert evil) was intended.

Irish art was allowed to develop independently from late Classical and Byzantine influences. This, at any rate, applies to the rich variety of ornamental shapes which still recall traditional Celtic patterns. To see them fundamentally devoid of any trace of the Classical cultural heritage would, however, amount to a misconception regarding the teaching program of the Irish and Northumbrian monastery schools. It is known that the abbot of Jarrow and Wearmouth was a keen collector. It is likely that he even had access to Byzantine codices and was able to study their pictures and their contents. As we know, there had been a "Byzantine link" to the island ever since the sixth century, if not before, when Pope Gregory the Great sent the Benedictine monk Augustine to England. King Ethelbert made the latter bishop of Canterbury in the year 597. Augustine must not be confused, by the way, with his namesake, the great theologian and philosopher who lived in Africa around 150 years before. The Italian Benedictine Augustine is reported to have taken with him a large collection of significant manuscripts. This would explain the obvious references to forms and shapes of Classical antiquity found in the treatment of both garments and figures, as well as in the depiction of gesture and movement. Since the artistic influence of the Irish on the continent goes hand in hand with their missionary activity, it is not even unreasonable to assume that Anglo-Saxon book illumination was responsible for the first impulses towards the great interest in Classical antiquity that later marked the "Carolingian Renaissance."

RIGHT
Gospel Book of Ebo. Rheims. St. Luke
the Evangelist. Before 835. Epernay, Bibl.
Municipal. Ms. 1, fol. 90v

FAR RIGHT
Vienna Coronation Gospel Book.
Aachen, Palace School. St. Mark the
Evangelist. Around 800. Vienna,
Schatzkammer, fol. 76b

The Carolingian Renaissance

The adoption and modification of Classical artistic forms by Carolingian artists has already been referred to. The first phase of adapting the art of Classical antiquity in the Middle Ages was at the service of ruling-class propaganda and scientific teaching. The political system of Charlemagne was in need of representative media to communicate aesthetic expression, and also of a well-functioning teaching program. His aim was to promote and stabilize the structures of the state – such as administration and the military – by raising the general level of education. A letter written in the year 790 by Alcuin of York, the "first scholar" at the court of Charlemagne, contains the following remarkable passage:

"If many were to follow the industry and enthusiasm of the King, a new Athens would be created in Aachen in the Frankish Empire, which in its service to the Lord Jesus Christ would surpass all academic wisdom. This old Athens shone merely through the teaching of Plato and the Seven Liberal Arts; but the new Athens, enriched by the abundance of the Holy Ghost, will surpass all the merits of wordly wisdom."

It is interesting that reference is made to a "new Athens" rather than a "new Rome." This is likely to apply to the Italian policy of Charlemagne who at that time was already trying to get Rome or, more precisely, the Vatican, to sanction his empire, then in the process of becoming a universal Christian empire. Of course it was paramount for Charlemagne to avoid any conflict with the Eternal City and the pope. There is also an unmistakable allusion to the former Platonic Academy of Athens and its broad spectrum of scientific teaching. Charlemagne, moreover, was not the only one to profit from the favor of the pope who had made him emperor. The pope himself had the opportunity to play an important trump card in terms of church policy: the imperial coronation allowed him to present an emperor who was "sanctified" by the Seat of St. Peter; he was an emperor for all Christians and all the faithful in eastern Rome alike. In the Treaty of Aix-la-Chapelle (i.e. Aachen) of 812, soon after his coronation in Rome, and two years before his death, Charlemagne was finally recognized as the Emperor of all Christians by the Byzantine Emperor Michael I. The handing over of Venice, Istria and Dalmatia was the high price Charlemagne had to pay for this recognition.

The Byzantine elements therefore played an important role in the universal thinking of Charlemagne.

Seen in this context, the "Carolingian Renaissance" at first presents itself as the result of political calculation between Aachen, Rome and Constantinople. Charlemagne's imperial claim to power was to find expression in a new "Pax Augustana." This was a utopian dream. In pragmatic terms, however, the sciences and arts from antiquity were presented as a means of strengthening social structures and as a sign of sovereignty.

How did these political connections find their expression in artistic production? Classical illusionism and Byzantine form were the principle characteristics of design. In the so-called Vienna Coronation Gospel Book of Charlemagne, produced by the Palace School of Aachen around 800, we find classically derived figures set against impressionistically shaped landscapes, according to the Byzantine tradition. The voluminous shape of Mark the Evangelist in flowing robes (photo, top right) is set against a terraced landscape. Spatial depth is suggested by overlapping shapes, so that elements that are on top of one another are made to appear behind one another. This device is typical of Classical antiquity and is used as a means of design in early Byzantine manuscripts. Any Irish influence is out of the question. Instead, this way of combining figure and landscape is a characteristic of the "Vienna Genesis" that was produced around the middle of the sixth century, probably in Constaninople or in Antioch. Indeed, so astonishing are the similarities with other Byzantine codices, such as the Codex Rossanensis dating back to the second half of the sixth century, that one cannot help but think of "Byzantine hands," i.e. artists who were summoned from Byzantium to the court of Charlemagne specifically for this purpose.

The gospel book of the Archbishop Ebo of Rheims was produced in the first quarter of the ninth century. The miniatures contained in its pages continue the tradition of the Vienna manuscript, although they move away from the Byzantine example and develop a style of their own. This style is best appreciated in the nervous and shimmering drapery and in the painterly, almost tachist treatment of the landscape in the background (photo, p. 422, left).

The Utrecht Psalter, too, is a product of the school of Rheims, where the artists achieved an unmistakable style thanks to their figurative design and the light painterly touch of their landscape formations.

That first phase of the development of the Carolingian scriptoria was marked by the important role played by the forms of Classical antiquity, or, to be more precise, the forms of Classical antiquity as handed down through Byzantine codices. There is evidence of an aesthetic program which takes into account the political significance of science, art, and education. It has been the achievement of the artists of the writing and illumination schools of Aachen, Rheims and Fulda, to combine the western and eastern art forms of Hiberno-Saxon and Byzantine book illumination, whilst at the same time creating a new style of their own.

Pictorial architecture and architectural pictures

It is relatively simple to distinguish between pictorial architecture and architectural pictures, using as an example the St. John folio in the Gospel Book of St. Médard of Soissons. This was produced in the Palace School of Charlemagne at Aachen around the year 800 (photo, right). Two areas, two kinds of architecture come to the viewer's notice: one that fulfills a framing function, and one that has an illustrative role. The first type includes the architectural elements such as columns and arches which are integrated into the painted framework presenting the Evangelist. In such a case the term pictorial architecture is appropriate since the painted architectural elements have the function of a presentation framework. The city wall, on the other hand, set at an angle and projecting into the picture in an almost three-dimensional fashion, with its front section representing the throne of the Evangelist, is meant as a reference to constructed architecture and also to the Heavenly Jerusalem. This is, therefore, a pictorial representation of architecture, and seen in isolation, such a detail would be an architectural picture. The architectural relationship into which the figure is set is a device used in many pictures of the Evangelists produced in the Carolingian scriptoria.

Just how dominant a position is played by the architectural picture becomes apparent in the subject of the fountain of life, or fountain of paradise. The Gospel Book of St. Médard which we have just mentioned, contains another folio which depicts the ascending columns and the dome of the fountain set against an imposing exedra (photo, p. 425, left). The architectural design of the fountain is without doubt derived from the canon tables which usually precede a manuscript (see special page on canon tables and text initials, p. 427). Often a direct connection between the fountain of life, or fountain of paradise, and canon table is deliberately included in the iconographical design, for example in the tympanum of the canon table of the last-mentioned gospel book. Here, a small fountain of life was placed alongside the Evangelists Mark and Matthew. The identity of the fountain as a "heavenly object" is established by the attributes of paradise which are distributed around the fountain, such as exotic plants and animals. The iconographical surroundings of the aforementioned folio depicting the fountain of paradise are very similar. The architecture of the exedra, which rises up like a palace in the background, is therefore probably an attribute of the Heavenly Jerusalem. The four columns, which

have been emphasized by their coloration, are in this context a reference to the four Evangelists, who, incidentally, are also included in the canon table. The four columns furthermore refer to the four rivers of paradise and the four corners of the world. Thus the gospel book represents, in pictures and words, a means of access to God's cosmos.

The combination of architecture and figure, and the distinction between pictorial architecture and architectural pictures, were matters of prime importance for the artists of the Ottonian period. This, of course, also throws some light on their special fondness for Carolingian miniatures. Towards the end of the tenth century, the "Codex Wittikundeus" was produced in Fulda. The folio showing the Evangelist Matthew (photo p. 425, right) can be regarded as a variation of the picture of the Evangelist painted in the Ada Gospel Book of Aachen (photo, p. 407), executed almost 200 years previously. The columns and arches framing the picture, and the meaningful construction (Heavenly Jerusalem) rising up behind

Trier (?), Gospel Book of Otto III. The Washing of the Feet of Peter. Around 1000. Munich, Bayerische Staatsbibliothek. Clm 4453, fol. 237r

The subject of the city is often used as a means of framing and structuring pictorial action: the central axis divides the city and intersects the head of Christ.

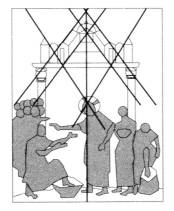

the throne are so close to the Carolingian model that one can assume with some certainly that the artist in Fulda based his composition and design of detail on such earlier codices.

This assumption is also natural because a Carolingian writing school had been active in Fulda. The Ottonian illuminators and scribes were therefore unlikely to be short of appropriate models.

The example just cited is an extreme one and must not be applied to the development of Ottonian book illumination in general. Apart from copies and modifications of the Carolingian models, there were also artists that explored novel and individual ways. Famous examples of this development are the manuscripts produced in Trier and in its subsidiary monastery in Echternach. Amongst the most magnificent and artistically refined codices of the Ottonian period is the Gospel Book of Otto III which was produced around the year 1000. As mentioned before, there is a dispute between Reichenau and Trier as to the place of its creation. The folio depicting the "Washing of the Feet of Peter" must be mentioned here, since its combination of figure and architecture is so surprising and the result so astonishing that it deserves a closer look (photo, on the left). What one notices first is that the separation of pictorial architecture and architectural picture has been largely abandoned. There are no architectural elements framing the picture. And yet the green columns with the architrave (which is developed into a "palace city") form the boundary of an area of gold leaf in front of which appear Christ, the arms of Peter, and the secondary figure of a water-carrier. In conceiving such a constellation, the artist might have intended to create "a picture within the picture" in order to show Christ clearly belonging to the sphere of God. In such a context, the columns may be understood as elements of pictorial architecture. Operating on the principle of reversed perspective, the building sections, towering up over the area of gold, form themselves into a "palace city," another reference to the Heavenly Jerusalem. The diagram shows that if a central axis is applied to the picture, it divides the city and intersects the head of Christ. If the lines of the outer sections are extended, they run parallel into the center of the picture and also intersect at the head of Christ. Whilst not opening up three-dimensional space, the system of perspective applied here brings out the link between the works of Christ on earth, and the promise of the Heavenly Jerusalem.

The use of pictorial architecture in other pages of this codex is sparing but effective. Columns, arches and architraves are defined as architectural components, and assume framing and symbolic functions at the same time. The architectural elements are frequently employed as means of articulation and combined with depictions of the city. The boundaries between architectural picture and pictorial architecture become blurred, with the former transforming itself into the latter in order to mark out the godly sphere. Alternatively, pictorial architecture may turn into architectural picture, when, for instance, figures are placed in front of columns. As they overlap, a distance is created between architecture and figure, in other words, spatial depth.

The different treatment of pictorial architecture and architectural picture in terms of overall design and composition is a typical charac-

Soissons, Gospel Book of St. Médard. Aachen, Palace School. The fountain of life. Around 800. Paris, Bibl. Nat. Ms. Lat. 8850, fol. 6

Fulda, Codex Wittekundeus. St. Matthew the Evangelist. End of the tenth century. Berlin, Staatsbibliothek zu Berlin, Preussischer Kulturbesitz, Ms.Theol.Lat.fol.1

teristic of Ottonian codices. It helps to create tension in a pictorial structure that otherwise tends to be quiet and monotonous.

It indeed remained a characteristic feature in the development of book illumination until the end of the Romanesque period. The subject of the city is frequently used as a means of framing and structuring the picture, while at the same time functioning as a representation of architecture. This, moreover, was already evident in a very early codex, the Ashburnham Pentateuch (photo, p. 405).

The range of artistic work touched upon here developed over the course of 500 years, from early Christian illustration up to the codices of the Ottonian period. It brings home to the observer the variety of ways in which architecture was used within the picture space: sometimes the principal subject is framed by architectural elements such as entablatures, pilasters or columns; sometimes stretches of wall, crenellations or arcades articulate the subject-matter. In many cases, pictorial architecture is also an important means of communicating, expression and meaning. In almost all cases, this takes the form of symbols of God's promise of salvation, such as the motif of the fountain of paradise, or the Heavenly Jerusalem. Sometimes a pillar, an architrave, or part of a building are enough to stand for a symbol of the whole of the heavenly sphere. It goes without saying that these architectural components are borrowed from church building, as the latter, the House of God on earth, was also worshipped as a symbol of God's heavenly city.

Gospel book, northern France. Around
860–80, Erzbischöfliche Diözesan- und
Dombibliothek, Dom Hs. 14

Canon table and text initial
The construction of a codex

The term "codex" (book) refers to the whole range of illuminated manuscripts which are classified according to different types; apart from the Bible, there are also the following: the evangeliar or gospel book with the complete gospel texts; the evangelistary or pericope book with excerpts (pericopes) from the Gospel; the sacramentary, a liturgical book with prayers for Mass; the lectionary, also a liturgical book containing passages from the Bible; and the psalter, the Book of Psalms.

Using a gospel book (evangeliar) as an example, a codex usually has the following structure: it begins with the canon table which is either preceded or followed by a Christ in Majesty. The canon table is intended to facilitate the finding of identical or similar text passages in the gospel book (concordance).

The canon table is often followed by the

Canon table
Soissons, Gospel Book of St. Médard. Aachen, Palace School. Around 800

1

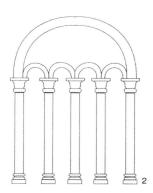

2

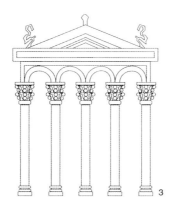

3

"titulus" as an introduction or preface to the gospel. The "titulus" is usually in verse form and pays homage to the Evangelist concerned. In some manuscripts the depictions of the Majesty are also accompanied by a "titulus."

Next follows the image of the Evangelist, after which there is an "initium" or "incipit." This term refers to the opening words of the manuscript which begin with an enlarged decorated letter, the initial. This initial page represents the opening of the gospel text with its accompanying illuminations.

The division into "titulus" – image of the Evangelist – "incipit" or gospel initial takes a different form in every manuscript and even varies in the gospel

books. There are no explanations as to the structural variations of these opening sections. They are obviously the result of certain preferences of individual scriptoria editors. In the Hitda Codex from Cologne, for example, the pattern outlined above was adopted for the Evangelists Mark and Luke, while a different system was applied to the other two. The editor responsible for the "first Evangelist," Matthew, omitted the "titulus" and replaced it with an incipit. The "titulus" or title page contains only text; and we are already familiar with the depiction of the Evangelist, of which many examples have been cited. It is therefore appropriate here to take a closer look at the canon table and the initial.

The canon table (see diagram):
Two types of canon table have been handed down from the Middle Ages: the arched type, and the entablature type. The latter is found mainly in the Carolingian writing school of Reims (diagram 1 – type: Ebo Gospel Book, around 800). The arched type which can be traced back to the sixth century is often used in Ottonian book illumination (diagram 2 – type: Gospel Book from St. Gereon, Cologne, around 1050). There is also a hybrid form consisting of entablature with pediment, another characteristic feature of the school of Cologne (diagram 3 – type: Gospel Book from Trier, around 1000).

The initial
A distinction is made between the body or outline, and the "filling" or contents of an initial. The body or outline of a letter often consists of two parallel gold lines that intersect and may take the shape of various ornamental formations. These are "filled" with interior details usually in the shape of vine scroll decoration. The design possibilities are, however, so great that it is virtually impossible to establish fixed categories. The following three examples are chosen to convey some idea of the rich vocabulary used in the decoration of text initials:
1. Gospel Book from Trier: text initial "N" (photo, top, right)
The initial "N" is decorated with interlace knots both within its main sections and endings. Foliage scrolls, symmetric along their axis, project from the center bar of the letter.
2. Gospel Book from Cologne: text initial "N" (figure, centre, right)
This initial appears more enclosed, almost as a square. The diagonal bar of the "N"

forms two triangles which are filled by the climbing and entwined forms of spiral-shaped sepals.
3. Gospel Book from the Court School of Charles the Bald: text initial "H" (figure, bottom, right)
This initial "H" (*Hic est Johannes*) from the Carolingian Palace School is still

dominated by the lavish chiseled shapes of Corinthian tendrils and sepals imitating Classical antiquity.
The initial begins the text of the gospel and sets the scene of the Life of Christ.

Often the scenes "jump" from Evangelist to Evangelist, depending on the narrative sequence chosen.

Iconography

Wall painting

The subject matter of sacred Romanesque wall painting is determined by its very location within a church building: the walls of the nave between the arcades and the clerestory windows, as well as the church ceiling (either barrel vault or flat wooden ceiling) were often intended to be decorated with narrative cycles from both the Old and New Testament. The Last Judgement with the mouth of Hell is sometimes depicted on the interior western wall. The east is the direction associated with Resurrection and Redemption and therefore equates with the position of the chancel in a church. The apse wall in this section almost always contains an image of Christ in Majesty, while the plinth area is filled with angels or Apostles, or is dedicated to particular saints.

The side walls of the chancel occasionally depict legends of the saints, usually in connection with a specifically local context.

The pictorial subject matter of Romanesque art therefore corresponds fairly closely to the respective significance of the particular section of the sacred building it decorates. Its iconography is therefore pre-determined. And yet it was this very fact that often led to attempts at undermining the general principle by including a greater variety of motifs. The aim was to break through the influence of Christology and balance the theme of the doctrine of salvation by introducing more profane subject-matter. It was also a means of expressing the belief that a life devoted to God could certainly be reconciled with a zest for life. And it is even possible that there was also a deliberate intention of overstepping the mark, as it were, by employing little-used marginal areas of the church for small exaltations and drolleries, which found expression in grotesque ornamentation and figurations, or in the shape of monsters and fabulous creatures.

The profane subjects created in the Christological context are among the most fascinating examples of Romanesque painting. Of course, they were repeatedly denounced as blasphemous and damnable since it was impossible to integrate them into the sacred context. In the year 1124, the strict Bernard of Clairvaux was moved by a visit to the monastery of Cluny to deliver this now well-known, passionate speech against the excessively luxurious nature of the building:

"Moreover, in the cloister, before the reading brethren – what is the purpose there of such a blasphemous monstrosity, such deformed shape-liness, and such shapely deformity? What is the purpose there of unclean monkeys? Of wild lions? Of monstrous centaurs? Of hunters blowing their horns? There you can see many bodies attached to one head, and many heads attached to one body. Here you see a quadruped with the tail of a serpent, and there a fish with the head of a quadruped. There you have a beast which has the front part of a horse and the hindquarters of a goat; there an animal with horns at the front but the shape of a horse at the back. In short, every space is filled up with such a manifold variety of astonishing creatures that one prefers to read the blocks of marble rather than the codices, and to spend the whole day in bewildering wonderment at such a display rather than contemplate the law of God. God forbid! If there is no shame about such foolishness, at least one should consider the expense!"

Bernard obviously enjoyed busying himself with such "foolishness," otherwise he would not have studied and described them in such detail. After all, his speech amounted to a kind of instruction manual for the production of constructed devils and the creation of a bestiary – even if this was completely unintentional on his part.

Strict in nature and not very receptive to the arts, it was Bernard's express wish to ban all non-Christian subject matter from the House of God. More than that: he was even in favor of removing any decoration from the churches, so that they could be redesigned as sober places without any "external" trappings of beauty, in accordance with the newly formulated Benedictine ideal. Such a decidedly hostile attitude towards the arts was in strong contrast to the attitude of St. Augustine. It was he who several hundred years previously had formulated the Classical Platonic artistic theory in order to make it available to the church. The early Christian sacred interior allowed the arts to enhance life and give some pleasure to mankind. St. Augustine believed that this would contribute to a fuller understanding of all the magnificence and greatness of God's creation.

Romanesque painting therefore had an inherent tension developed in an environment that ranged from a euphoric enthusiasm for art on the one hand, to an ascetic rejection of all art on the other. Within this context, Romanesque painting flourished and produced the most splendid and absurd results, even if they were only secondary imagery accompanying Biblical subject-matter.

The principal subjects of Romanesque painting are, without doubt, the depictions of Christ in Majesty and the Virgin Enthroned. They are usually seen in the apse, the most important and significant place for imagery in the Christian church. It is therefore all the more surprising that in the Oratory of Theodulf of Orleans at Germigny-des-Prés, a church that had a great significance for Carolingian culture, there was no Christ in Majesty in the apse, but a subject which was later almost completely disregarded: that of two angels hovering above the Ark of the Covenant (photo, p. 384). The question arises as to why such a strange subject was chosen for a place of such symbolic significance. The answer is quickly found: as already discussed in the first chapter of this book, Theodulf was the most important scholar at the court of Charlemagne after Alcuin of York. As the author of the Libri Carolini, the "cultural manifesto of the Carolingian Empire," Theodulf was greatly concerned towards the end of the eighth century with the Byzantine ban on images. He chose to follow a middle course between the resolute rejection of pictures with a divine content, and idolatry, the excessive worship of images. According to the bishop, the image was an important medium of communicating Biblical messages and therefore served an educational purpose. His range of images did, however, not include Christ or the saints since they were under "suspicion of idolatry." Before the year 825, it was therefore not yet possible to depict Christ in Majesty in Germigny-des-Prés. 825 was also the year of the Synod of Paris, at which a change of position occurred with regard to pictorial subject-matter. Subsequently, it was no longer an act of sacrilege to depict Christ, God, or the Virgin Mary. Now the figures of Christ in

Gospel Book of Henry the Lion. Christ in
Majesty. 1188. Wolfenbüttel, Herzog
August-Bibliothek, Cod. Guelf. 105
Noviss. 2°, fol. 172r
The Gospel Book of Henry the Lion is the
joint property of the State of Lower
Saxony, the Free State of Bavaria, the
Federal Republic of Germany, and the
Stiftung Preussischer Kulturbesitz.

Regensburg, Gospel Book of Henry II.
Portrait of a ruler. Around 1020. Rom.
Bibl. Vat. Ottobon. Lat. 74

Majesty and the Virgin Enthroned were assigned their proper place in the
most important part of the church – the apse of the east sanctuary.

Christ in Majesty and the Virgin Enthroned

The clearest way of breaking down the iconographical constellations of
these two types of Majesty in monumental painting, is by means of examples
from book illumination. If we compare the apse fresco in Sant'Angelo in
Formis (photo, p. 409) with a miniature from the gospel book commissioned
by Henry II around 1020 (that is, about fifty years previously; photo, above,
right), the similarity between them in terms of subject-matter and lay-out
are immediately obvious, and mark them out as Majesty depictions. There
is, however, one difference which at the time was quite revolutionary:
whilst in typological and formal iconographical terms we are confronted
with a Majesty, it is the image of Henry II that sits enthroned in the
mandorla instead of Christ or God the Father. The dove of the Holy Ghost
is seen hovering above his head, and the three-quarter medallions at the
sides and the rectangular spaces in the margin show the Virtues, alluded to
by means of human gestures. A scene of judgement is seen taking place

beneath the image of the emperor. There can be no doubt as to the message of
this miniature: as he passes judgement, the emperor "Dei gratia," inspired
by God (the dove), is represented as a personification of the Virtues.

Before an attempt is made to clarify what appears to be an act of
sacrilege, it is worth considering the motif of the circle. Here there is an
allusion to the earth, the globe, and therefore to the worldly empire
granted by the grace of God. The figure of Christ as the Ruler of the World
is familiar from other compositions. Christ in Majesty is often depicted
within a circular mandorla that identifies itself as sphaira of stars. This
motif can be traced back to Classical antiquity where it was used to depict
Zeus or Jupiter as ruler of the cosmos in the midst of the signs of the
zodiac. The transfer of meaning is obvious and compelling: the
interconnection of a claim to power derived from antiquity and divine
right allows for a dialogue between ancient and Christian motifs and
demonstrates a new self-assurance on the part of the medieval ruler. This
image of the "Ruler of the World" appears in many variations: in the Liber
Floridus (Flanders, around 1180), for example, Christ is represented
between the four elements (photo, p. 429).

to their belief that they could receive the imperial crown directly from God. When depicted in miniatures, they therefore used symbols that would magnify them, such as the dove of the Holy Ghost, or the hand of God. This amounted to a declaration of the absolute power of the God-given Empire, and was achieved in a way that was almost offensive to Rome, since the message was that it was not the pope who dominated the world, but the emperor chosen by God.

Whether before, during, or after the Investiture Contest, the tension between emperor and pope lasted until well into the twelfth century. It expressed itself sporadically in the form of severe conflicts culminating in the "Staufen confrontation," when Frederick II raised an army against the pope. At the Council of Lyons in 1245, Frederick was banished by the pope, declared a heretic, and deposed.

In the crypt vault of the cathedral of Auxerre there is an extremely rare but highly remarkable variation of the majesty image. Set at the point of intersection of a cross, Christ is depicted on horseback, holding a sceptre in his right hand and raising his left hand in a gesture of blessing (photo, left). The four marginal areas outside the cross show angel medallions. The paintings were probably painted around the year 1150. According to the words of the Prophet Malachi, "Ecce advenit dominator dominus ..." (Behold, the ruler and Lord is coming ...), we might here indeed be faced with a majesty variation which follows, however, along the lines of the Classical ruler typology. The significance of the so-called "Adventus Imperator" could possibly be explained further by passages from the Apocalypse which also justify the white horse: "And I saw heaven opened, and behold a white horse; and he that sat upon him was called Faithful and True, and in righteousness he doth judge and make war ...". This then establishes the link to the fragment of the Gospel of Lorsch, in which the symbolism of the ruler was derived from the adoption of the majesty image in its Classical context.

Apart from the example above, the typology of the Majesty offers little variety. This applies above all to the range of motifs and to a lesser degree to its formal design. Christ is surrounded by the four Evangelists, angels and saints. The universal claim of faith, the overcoming of evil, and redemption linked to the entry into paradise, are all different aspects of the message of salvation.

The standard attributes of the Majesty are the four Evangelists, often represented by the beasts of the Apocalypse: the angel for Matthew, the lion for Mark, the bull for Luke, and the eagle for John. Within the Majesty, the winged beasts and the winged man or angel play a double role: they inspire their "partners" to write down the Gospels, while at the same time embodying the basic characteristics of their Lord. The man refers to the incarnation of Christ, and the lion to the kingdom of the Lord. The bull symbolizes strength of faith, and the eagle soars skywards as a symbol of the Ascension of Christ. The Evangelists are frequently depicted gathered around the Throne of the Lord in the order just mentioned. Usually this subject-matter is represented in the chancel apse, virtually above the altar, proclaiming its message of salvation and redemption from the liturgical center of the House of God.

This "presumptuousness of pictorial subject" of course already contains the seeds of the fierce conflict between the emperor and the pope which was to break out openly a few decades later and culminate in the "Investiture Contest." There was nothing novel about this "profaned" Majesty. As the successor to the Roman Emperors, the emperor of Byzantium had already laid claim to this title, which the rulers of western Rome conceded to God alone. During the reign of Charlemagne, however, the attribute "Majesty" began again to be applied to the ruler in the context of the return to the culture of Classical antiquity. And Henry II saw the title not only as a reflection of his position but also regarded himself as the secular equivalent of Christ. It seemed therefore natural for him to be worshipped as the subject of a "Christ in Majesty."

The confrontation between profane and sacred majesty depictions is baffling. The only likely explanation for it might have been the rapidly increasing power of the Ottonian rulers. They wanted to give expression

Civate, San Pietro al Monte, eastern wall
of entrance hall. Fight with the dragon.
Around 1090

In the west, too, the combination of Christ and the Evangelists' symbols can be found, usually accompanied by angels with trumpets and by Mary and John. The Archangel Michael is also amongst them: the angels with the trumpets have just announced the coming of the Last Judgement; Mary and John are taking up their places by the Throne of God in order to plead for those souls who are tortured but not completely beyond salvation. In both cases, the majesty appears in the context of the divine promise of redemption. In the case of the Last Judgement this can also mean damnation.

A majesty of unusual constellation in both iconographical and formal terms can be seen in San Pietro on the Monte Pedale near Civate. The wall section under the formeret on the eastern wall of the entrance porch features the figure of Christ set in a dynamic compositional design. Painted around the year 1090, the fresco is regarded as one of the most important Italian contributions to Romanesque painting (photo, above). It illustrates chapter 12 of the Apocalypse: beneath the mandorla containing Christ in Majesty we see the writhing body of a dragon of gigantic proportions. Fighting the monster is the heavenly host, led by the Archangel Michael. The woman of the Apocalypse – chosen to crush the dragon underfoot – is shown crouching in the bottom left-hand corner of the picture. A wetnurse next to her offers up to the dragon a newborn child who is holding up his hands in defence against the beast. In this way, the child reaches the divine sphere above, from where he is handed to the Lord through the mandorla by an angel. The Apocalypse of John reads as follows: "And she brought forth a man child, who was to rule all nations with a rod of iron: and her child was caught up unto God, and to his throne." The boy is Christ, and the woman is his mother Mary who is introduced here in her role as the "woman of the Apocalypse."

A strange yet obvious interpretation of the Apocalypse: the sacrifice of Christ's life becomes a metaphor for the battle against evil, reflected in

OPPOSITE
St. Chef, abbey church, Chapelle
Conventuelle, ceiling. Christ in Majesty
and the Heavenly Jerusalem. Around
1080

Soest, Maria zur Höhe, dome. The Virgin
Enthroned. Around 1120

visual terms by combining the woman of the Apocalypse with the fight against the dragon. It epitomizes the message of salvation and the certain knowledge that eternal life may be gained through the sacrifice of Christ. In this Majesty, the ideas of redemption and paradise are expressed amidst a scene of battle and sacrifice.

The image of Christ in Majesty surrounded by the heavenly host appears in yet another iconographical context in the abbey church of St. Chef in Dauphiné, east of Lyons (around 1080). The picture in the vault of the Chapelle Conventuelle shows the mandorla depicting Christ enthroned on a bench covered with cushions and with his arms raised in blessing (photo, p. 433). Above the crown on Christ's head the Holy Lamb is placed rather awkwardly upside down as it belongs to another section of the vault, namely the narrow, spherically sloping part. On turning around, the viewer will thus find that the Lamb of God now represents the top of the heavenly castle which rests on the lower rim of the vault. The Virgin Mary and the host of angels are arranged to the side of the Heavenly Jerusalem and around the mandorla in such a way that the heavenly castle with the Lamb of God, the majesty, and Mary are aligned along the central axis. If this axis is continued as far as into the apse of the chapel, it leads to a second Lamb of God and another majesty in the calotte of the apse. It is perfectly natural and in no way unusual to find two majesty images relating to one and the same iconographical context, and distributed over various parts of the church.

There is no doubt that the vault at St. Chef is defined as the divine cosmos. The arch of the mandorla contains bands of clouds shaped like a curved sawtooth frieze, and can be interpreted as a cosmic reference. Continuing these iconographical observations within our dialogue with the church building, one realizes that the heavenly vault rests on the earth – in other words, the illusionistic presence of God is conveyed by means of the paintings on the walls. There we find the Evangelists, the Prophets and

the Apostles assembled, together with the twenty-four Elders of the Revelation engaged in dialogue, and the four Fathers of the Church. The word of God is taken up and "carried" along by the heavenly host, its message communicated by the Evangelists, and interpreted and taught by the Fathers of the Church. Incidentally, the central axis runs through the Book of Life which lies open in Christ's lap. The iconographical design is legible and relates directly to the faithful who would have circulated around the chapel with their heads held up high learning the Christian teachings. The notions of "above" and "below" have been suspended. Earthly standards and perspectives are no longer valid. What appears to be standing on its head is integrated into the divine order and opens up the connections through which the doctrine of salvation is communicated. The architecture of the chapel now has the sole function of conveying the pictorial narrative, and is thus defined as "heavenly architecture." The Chapelle Conventuelle in St. Chef is one of the few examples of fresco cycles from the Romanesque period which have survived in such a complete state.

The composition of the vault painting of St. Chef is strangely similar to the dome fresco of Maria zur Höhe in Soest, which has been described earlier (photo above). In both churches, a definite connection between architecture and image gives visual expression to the link between heaven and earth. The common strand within the iconographical program is illustrated by the position held by Mary both within the fresco and, at the same time, within the church interior. In Soest, Mary is not given a central position in the dome, but merely a place along the lower segment of the circle, effectively placing her above the altar. She could therefore be characterized as a kind of devotional image of the altar while at the same time belonging to the heavenly sphere: it is through the figure of Mary that the congregation learns of the direct connection between the altar in this world, and the divine cosmos in the hereafter.

433

Mary establishes this link in her capacity as the Mother of God and her role as intercessor. The image of the Virgin Enthroned is therefore much more strongly related to this world than that of Christ in Majesty. The absence of a mandorla and the lower positioning of the Virgin at the "cosmic margin" of the "Ordo Angelicus," that is the edge of the dome, should therefore not be interpreted as denoting a lesser value in the iconographical system compared to that of the Christ in Majesty.

The sole purpose of this interpretation is to establish their place within the sacred sphere of meaning. A similar constellation was noted in St. Chef: surrounded by angels, Mary is depicted standing at the edge of the dome above the triumphal arch of the apse. This establishes a visual connection with the altar below her, placing her firmly in the liturgical context.

Another variation in the positioning of Mary relative to Christ in Majesty had been noted in Civate. There she was represented as the woman of the Apocalypse, and therefore as a symbol of the conquest of evil, sacrifice, and redemption. In sacred terms, Mary and Christ/God the Father were put on the same level. Expressed in a theological and ecclesiastical context, Mary is given increasing significance in her function as a fighter for the cause and intercessor by the side of Christ and God the Father. Her position within the divine cosmos as heavenly queen is thus complete: the uncrowned Christ places the crown on the head of his mother, as depicted by Jacopo Torriti in his apse mosaic in Santa Maria Maggiore, Rome, in 1295. Mary's coronation in heaven can be regarded as the synthesis or result of the intellectual links between the images of Christ in Majesty and the Virgin Enthroned.

Mention has already been made of the host of angels surrounding the Mother of God, a constantly recurring motif in the depictions of the Virgin Enthroned. The compositions in Soest and also in St. Chef are particularly impressive. The angels are an allusion to the divine cosmos. It is, however, unlikely that the choir of angels might represent the equivalent of the majesty mandorla. Mary is too firmly connected to this world to be depicted within a mandorla when shown in majesty. In her role as the physical Mother of God and as intercessor, she is a figure that the faithful can directly relate to. The angelic choir is more concrete and much "closer" to mankind than the sphaira or mandorla, suffused with the light that surrounds God the Father.

The combination of the Virgin Mary and the choir of angels constitutes a clearly defined subject in the panel painting of the Italian 13th and 14th centuries, where it was stylized into a highly significant pictorial system. In the work of Duccio, Cimabue and Giotto, this type was referred to as "Maestà". There are clear differences both in terms of motif and style when compared to the Maestàs of the Virgin examined here. At the time, the new majesty contributed greatly to the popularization of a new generation of painters. Using the majesty as a vehicle, Duccio and Giotto developed the concept of the figure in space, and were therefore heralding the arrival of modern painting.

The Heavenly Jerusalem

At St. Chef, the dominant features of the heavenly castle, Christ in Majesty, and the Virgin Enthroned, are all arranged along the main iconographical axis. They can therefore be interpreted as a model for the spectrum of meaning inherent in the Heavenly Jerusalem depicted in Romanesque painting. The distant promise of redemption which finds its concrete form in the city of God can only be reached through the sacrifice of Christ's death and through Mary's intercessions at the throne of God. The center of the divine cosmos is occupied by "New Jerusalem" which therefore had to undergo a fusion with the figure of the majesty within the mandorla. In St. Chef, this combination of "heavenly identity" of the City of God, the Son of God, and the Mother of Christ is conveyed by its position above the central main axis of the vault.

"And there came unto me one of the seven angels … and he carried me away in the spirit to a great and high mountain, and shewed me that great city, the holy Jerusalem, descending out of heaven from God … and had a wall great and high, and had twelve gates, and at the gates twelve angels … and the city lieth foursquare, and the length is as large as the breadth … and the foundations of the wall of the city were garnished with all manner of precious stones … and the twelve gates were twelve pearls; every several gate was of one pearl: and the street of the city was pure gold, as it were transparent glass …"

There is a wealth of detail in the description of the heavenly city in chapter 21 of the Revelation of St. John the Divine. Indeed, the detail is often meticulously precise. The artists, however, took little notice of this lavish listing of the most precious building materials. For them, the New Jerusalem represented an allegory of the place of God. And it therefore made more sense to them to depict the city of God in the shape of a church, particularly since it was stated in Augustine's ever-present text *De Civitate Dei* (written between 412 and 426) that the realm of God is made manifest on earth in the shape of the church. In this way, the Heavenly City became a part of everyday experience for the faithful in the Middle Ages.

The depiction of the Heavenly Jerusalem in the genre of wall painting cannot be fully understood without taking into account its liturgical milieu and the resulting artistic motifs. The heavenly castle is integrated within a frame of reference whose allusions are the key to the whole range of meaning contained within them. The faithful are called upon to seek out and take up their respective positions. New Jerusalem is accessible only through the word of God (represented by the Majesty), the sacrifice of Christ's life (represented by the Lamb of God), and through intercession (represented by Mary). Humankind can receive the word of God in many ways, through either the Gospels or the Fathers of the Church. The believer is protected by the army of the king which is prefigured in the heavenly and fortified host depicted in Civate. The battle against evil to protect and redeem the faithful is therefore another reference to the Heavenly Jerusalem. According to the Apocalypse, the Heavenly Jerusalem was not revealed to John until after the Images of Wrath and the Judgement.

It is this very scene of the "apocalyptic confrontation" between Judgement and Revelation that has been chosen to illustrate the Heavenly Jerusalem at Civate. It is depicted in the eastern section of the vault, following the fresco of the formeret on the east wall (photo, p. 436).

God the Father is shown seated on his throne, with the Book of Life in his lap and the holy Lamb by his feet. He is set within a garden reminiscent of paradise and surrounded by walls fortified with towers. Here, the painter has followed the text of the Apocalypse fairly closely: in his right hand, the Lord holds the "golden reed" with which he has measured the city. Twelve faces look out of the twelve gates and "behold his countenance." Using the iconographical image of the garden to represent the Heavenly Jerusalem is not only a deviation from the text; it is also relatively unusual to find it rendered in such a quasi-impressionistic manner reminiscent of late antiquity. Landscape structures of this kind are known only from early Christian miniatures along the lines of the Genesis of Vienna. The combination of heavenly castle and garden of paradise signifies that the Judgement has already been passed and that the faithful and the blessed may be redeemed. Again, an iconographical connection can be made with the fresco in the wall section under the formeret, showing the fight against the dragon. For the faithful of the Middle Ages, this subtle link was immediately obvious: entry into paradise was gained only after completing the earthly sacrifice and overcoming evil, only gained at the end of time when the face of God would be revealed.

Schwarzrheindorf impressively illustrates just how important it is to combine and link meaning over several sacred rooms or sections. A kind of key image for both the upper and the lower church is placed in a central location in the lower church, in the eastern vault section of the crossing (photo, p. 437, top). It shows the buildings of a city with a disproportionately enlarged portal. In the opening, a figure can be seen which appears to be stepping out through the gate. This picture refers to a saying of the prophet Ezekiel, who is depicted with his scroll in the lower part of the picture: "Afterward He [the hand of God] brought me to the gate, even the gate that looketh toward the east: and, behold, the glory of the God of Israel came from the way of the east." Ezekiel is led through the city of God to the temple and before the altar. The medieval Fathers of the Church interpreted this image as the promise of the birth of Christ to the Virgin Mary. In relation to the passage in Ezekiel cited above, we find these words in the Revelation: "Come hither, I will shew thee the bride, the Lamb's wife. And he [the angel] carried me away in the spirit to a great and high mountain, and shewed me that great city, the holy Jerusalem, descending out of heaven from God …". The Annunciation of Mary, the Bride of God and the Mother of Christ, must therefore be seen as closely related to the Heavenly Jerusalem.

Views of city landscapes are also encountered in all the other vault segments of the crossing – with one exception: in the northern segment there is a representation of the table of the Lord. The western segment depicts the counterpart to the city gate just described, namely the heavenly city defined by God. These four areas are framed by an empty octagonal space in the ceiling which allows the viewer to look up into the apse of the upper church. The believer can thus establish his own "axis of heaven or redemption." Standing before the "gate of the Lord," that is, in the west beneath the heavenly city, he can look up towards the east – through the "gate of Ezekiel", as it were. He now finds himself looking up to the image of Christ in Majesty in the apse of the upper church. The image is framed by the octagon and the surrounding representations of the Heavenly Jerusalem (see also diagram on p. 437).

The depiction of the Heavenly Jerusalem and the presentation of architecture featuring the birth or miracles of Christ are popular themes of Romanesque painting. On the one hand, they provide a means of structuring both pictorial cycle and narrative, whilst at the same time containing references to the heavenly city. Seen in its biblical context, on the other hand, the New Jerusalem alludes to the possibility of redemption. It is also possible that the theme of the city was so popular because it reflected the increasing urbanization taking place in the twelfth century. The founding of new cities always went hand in hand with an increase in population and an upswing in the economy. Naturally, it also affected the power structures between the city population and their bishop. In the former Carolingian regions the lower aristocracy frequently formed alliances with the city people against the sovereignty of the church in order to take away power from the bishop. Such conflicts were encouraged by the controversies that raged on a higher level between the church and the empire. For the king, the situation was very useful, as it enabled him to win allies against the clergy as well as to gain taxes from the empire's economy. For this reason there was also an ambivalent element in the depiction of the city within the sacred place: according to Augustine, the heavenly city is presented as the better alternative to the wordly city, particularly as the latter adopted an anticlerical attitude. On the other hand, the king or emperor liked the idea of being represented through an urban environment within the sacred surroundings of the church especially since the ruler often acted as donor for the church.

Produced around the year 1220 in a Bohemian scriptorium, the Codex Gigas contains two full-page miniatures which, amidst a wealth of allusions, compare the Heavenly Jerusalem and the devil cowering in Hell (photos, p. 437, bottom). As is well known, in medieval times the opposition of Heaven and Hell referred to the whole of the cosmic system. Man was inextricably bound up within that system and had to prove himself, by looking both upwards and downwards. Man's contradictory position within the universe is the subject of the Codex Gigas and its encyclopedically extended Bible. The depiction of the city as a towering, monstrous construction is reminiscent of a medieval Manhattan. Presumably a reference to the political, social and religious development of the city in the twelfth and thirteenth centuries, such an image must be seen as the antithesis to Hell.

Civate, San Pietro al Monte, entrance
hall, the Heavenly Jerusalem. Around
1090

Schwarzrheindorf, St. Maria und
Klemens. View from the lower into the
upper church. The Heavenly Jerusalem
and Christ in Majesty. Around 1180

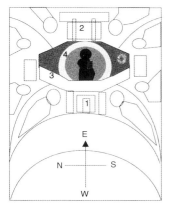

1 Ezekiel's vision
2 The Heavenly Jerusalem
3 Octagonal opening in the lower church
4 Christ in Majesty in the upper church

Codex Gigas. Bohemian. Heavenly
city and Hell. Around 1200.
Stockholm, Kungliga Biblioteket. Ms.
A 148

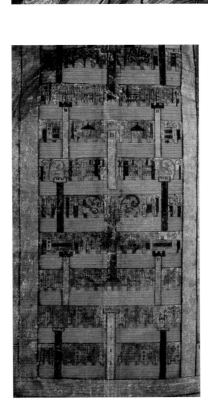

Mirabilia: themes of fantasy and animals

The castle in which a battle rages between mice and cats (photo, above) is certainly not a reference to the Heavenly Jerusalem, but rather to Hell. We know this as the picture was painted on the southern nave wall near the western wall, where the Last Judgement is depicted. Painted around the year 1180, the fresco in the Johannes Chapel in Pürgg is part of an extensive "Romanesque Bestiary" whose images are distributed amongst numerous medieval churches and codices. Even though Bernard of Clairvaux used harsh words to condemn such motifs within sacred surroundings, there are plinth areas, painted wall tapestries, and decorative surfaces and frameworks swarming and crawling with such creatures. The animals featured often have a basis in zoological reality; but there are just as many cases where they are based on unreliable sources and are depicted as monstrous, bizarre and fantastic creatures.

In the above fresco, cats and mice attack each other with bows and arrows and swords. One cat is seen with a shield on its shoulders and a sword strapped around its body. In this rather comical outfit, the cat comes creeping up towards a group of mice. Such a subject is far removed from the Christian message of salvation. The imagination of the artist, once released from such constraints, must have worked in a peculiar way in order to arrive at this image.

It has to be conceded, however, that Christian themes have never wholly excluded animal grotesques, strange hybrid creatures, or winged monsters. In their antithetical role as a personification of evil, they form part of God's grand scheme of salvation. This becomes particularly apparent in the areas framing the apse of St. Jakob in Kastellaz near Tramin in the southern Tyrol. The malicious creatures, dating back to around 1220, include centaurs, harpies, fish-like creatures, and dog-headed monsters devouring serpents. Armed with bow and arrow, serpent slings and clumsy bone tools, these grotesque creatures are also engaged in battle with one another (photos, p. 439, top).

It is unlikely that such creatures were merely a product of the artist's imagination, or always based on fantastic reports from dubious travelers. In accordance with medieval aesthetics, as first set out by John Scotus Erigena, demons and monsters can also be regarded as expressions of beauty. Even if their deformity means that they are not perfect, demons may nevertheless be considered "relatively perfect" creatures. They, too, share in "being," and are therefore equally God's creatures: "Everything which is takes its part in both good and evil." The idea of beauty is a relative one, since there is an imperfect as well as a perfect beauty. It is this very fact that makes the monsters so attractive: their aesthetic deformities encourage the believer to seek absolute beauty in God and the saints. These thoughts were written down by the aforementioned Irish philosopher John Scotus in his treatise *De divinis nominibus*. They soon gained popularity in church culture and were therefore worth depicting.

In addition, the so-called "Mirabilia" boast a literary tradition which can be traced back as far as the middle of the fifth century B.C. and the Indian reports of Herodotus. Such reports from the east of miraculous beings were received not only from non-Christian authors. Christian scholars, too, continued the tradition, amongst them the encyclopedist Isidore of Seville, whose *Etymologiae* from around the year 600 tells of fabulous creatures. He might well have referred to the *Naturalia historia* by Pliny the Elder which dates from the first century A.D. and was known in the medieval period. Pliny had included about fifty fabulous creatures in his encyclopedia and had provided detailed descriptions. His treatise was certainly known to the Frenchman Hugo of Fouilloy who was active in the middle of the twelfth century. In his own bestiary, he created a series of images depicting monstrous creatures half man, half beast: there are headless creatures with eyes set in their shoulders and faces growing out of their chests, followed by creatures with gigantic tusks protruding from their bodies (photos, p. 440). Pliny had established a typology of the eastern people based on the fantastic reports supplied by travelers through India. He called the creatures with the eyes set in their shoulders "Epiphagi" and those with faces on their chests "Blemmyes". The dog-headed creatures were categorized as the "Cynocephali" and the cannibals as "Anthropophagi."

Religious circles regarded the "Mirabilia" as perfectly realistic, despite the admonitions voiced by Bernard of Clairvaux. The monasteries still had a high respect for the "knowledge of the ancients", that is the vast store of knowledge handed down from antiquity. For this reason it states in the Acta Sanctorum, for example, that the Saints Christopher and Mercury came from the Cynocephali people of the Indian mountains.

LEFT AND RIGHT
Kastellaz, St. Jakob. Apse, plinth area.
Fabulous creatures. Around 1220

BELOW
De Arte Venandi cum Avibus. Southern
Italy. Falconry book of Frederick II
(Manfred edition). Animals and birds.
Rome, Bibl. Apost. Vat. Pal. Lat. 1071,
fol. 42v

In some respects, such "Mirabilia" can be seen as approaching the subject of the life and Passion of Christ via a "metaphorical bridge." The best example of this claim is the "Physiologus," the best-known and best-loved bestiary of the Middle Ages, which goes back to authors from late Antiquity.

The grey areas between scholarliness and imagination are dealt with in the encyclopedias of the Middle Ages. This was necessary in order to distinguish the world of the credible and empirically verifiable from the realm of pure fantasy. One of the first empirical works which can be said to approximate to serious zoology is the book of hawks *De Arte venandi cum avibus* (On the art of hunting with the hawk) by the Emperor Frederick II (photos, right). In the introduction, the author "Frederick II, Emperor of Rome, King of Jerusalem and Sicily" states that he spent thirty years collecting material for his work, so that he could show "the things which are, as they really are." In the year 1248, soon after the completion of the six-volume work, it was destroyed during armed conflict. Not long after its destruction, Manfred, Frederick's son, produced a facsimile of the codex which is housed today in the Vatican Library in Rome. Everything worth knowing about hawks, kestrels, sparrow-hawks and other birds is contained in this manuscript, along with information concerning the breeding and training of dogs. Everything is illustrated in detailed, colored drawings. After the decline of the Staufen dynasty, the codex was offered to Charles of Anjou. The vendor, a tradesman from Milan, praised the manuscript as "... a noble work about hawks and dogs ... whose admirable beauty and significance it is impossible to express in words."

LEFT AND RIGHT
Bird book of Hugo of Fouilloy. North-
western France. Bestiary according to
Pliny. Two folios with fantastic creatures.
Around 1280.
Malibu, The J. Paul Getty Museum,
Ludwig Ms. XV4, fol. 117r and v

OPPOSITE
Bestiary. About whales. End of the 12th
century. Oxford, Bodleian Library, Ms.
Ashmole 1511, fol. 86v

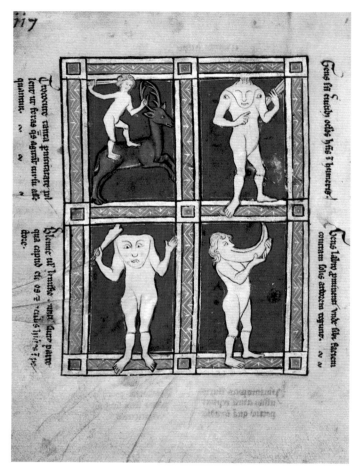

officium habeant. Amphi enim grece. utrumuq; dr. i.
op maquis i interis uiuunt. ut foce. cocodrilli ypota
mi. h. est equi fluctuales. ✠ De balena.

St belua inmari q grece aspido delone dr. latine ū
aspido testudo. Lete i dicta. ob immanitatem cor
poris. ē. enim sic ille qui excepit ionam. cuius altuis
tante magnitudinis fuit ut putaret infernus dicen

Byzantine psalter. Hannah's prayer.
Around 900.
Paris, Bibl. Nat. Graec. 139, fol. 428v

Book illumination
The Life of Christ

The Life of Christ, his miracles and his Passion constitute the main subject illustrated in medieval codices. First, there are the gospel books or evangelistaries which contain lists, either in complete form or in sections, of the writings of the Evanglists. It may be asked, however, what principles governed the distribution of the scenes from the Life of Christ, since it was important to avoid repetition of either narrative or pictorial content. An exemplary model of the successful organization of text sequence and illustrative picture is the codex of the Abbess Hitda of Meschede, known as the Hitda Codex. It was produced around the year 1020 in an Ottonian scriptorium in Cologne (photos, p. 443).

In the Hitda Codex, the Life of Christ is not arranged in a cycle, but is distributed between the four Evangelists and, importantly, is independent of the gospel texts. The Gospel according to St. Matthew, therefore, begins with the Tree of Jesse, but makes no mention at all of the Annunciation and the Presentation and contains only a passing reference to the Nativity. Nevertheless, the artist painted these scenes according to the respective passages in St. Luke. Only the scene of the Adoration is taken from St. Matthew. Such an arrangement of pictures and texts from different gospels is made possible by the fixed sequence of the Gospels and the very similar story told about Christ by the Evangelists. The Life of Christ therefore has

to be told in scenes reflecting an equal use of all four gospel stories. This means not only that omissions are necessary, but also that combinations of image and text have to be created which are independent of the story told by the Evangelist in question.

The Hitda Codex is marked out by another peculiar iconographical feature: the Passion of Christ appears only as a footnote in the scene of the Crucifixion, and the events after his death are not illustrated at all. It is possible that the artist was following the typically Ottonian tradition which placed great value on the representation of Christ's miracles. For political reasons the miracles certainly provided a more effective scenario than the Passion of our Lord. The choice of scenes also suggests that it was the artist's intention to produce a complete illustration of Christ's entire life. The patrons who commissioned the work were above all concerned that there should be an effective presentation of positive scenes from the Life of Christ. This view is further supported by the layout of the codex, which in terms of formal design and typology follows the topoi of forms and themes popular in Carolingian and Byzantine art. Scholars have, for example, discovered that the folio depicting the raising of the young man of Nain can be traced back to a scene of identical design in the Carolingian Arnulf Ciborium from the Court School of Charles the Bald (around 870). Incidentally, the same scene is executed in a very similar manner in the church of St. Georg, Oberzell, on the island of Reichenau (around 1000).

Obviously, the scene is represented according to a single iconographical standard, and is proof of the close artistic relationship between Carolingian and Ottonian book illumination. Such a standard can also be regarded as symptomatic of the "aesthetic commercial exploitation" of the Christian message of salvation. It is in turn a reminder of the Church's strong interest in the effective operation of what is now called public relations.

At that time, Carolingian and Ottonian codices were regarded as reliable sources of popular formal patterns and motifs. Certain parts of pictures showing, for instance, landscape formations, are quite clearly derived from east Roman miniatures of the late classical and early Christian period. The smooth walls of earth with their little furrows, and the hills rising up like dough, are typical features of the Byzantine landscape. Both can be seen in the Annunciation scene of the Hitda Codex (photo, p. 443, right). Standing in patient humility, Mary is approached by an angel whose foot and wing project beyond the left border of the picture. On the wall of earth rising up above the angel we see a city, probably a reference to the earthly realm of the chosen one. This stylization is derived from the pictorial idiom of the Byzantine period. A similar landscape formation provides the setting for the depiction of "Hannah's Prayer" (photo, left), found in a Greek psalter dating from around 900.

The artistic output of the Ottonian scriptoria was aimed at a limited audience. The above examples show how popular motifs and design elements were used to ensure that the sacred message contained in the images was expressed in an unambiguous manner. Because Byzantine style and form were the aesthetically accepted standard, the links to Byzantine art made a decisive contribution to the increasing popularity of contemporary scriptoria and the codices they produced.

442

Hitda Codex. Cologne. Annunciation. Around 1020. Darmstadt, Hessische Landesbibliothek. Cod. 1640, fol. 20r

Hitda Codex. Cologne. The raising of the young man of Nain. Around 1020. Darmstadt, Hessische Landesbibliothek, Cod. 1640, fol. 115r

Spanish Apocalypse manuscripts

The Apocalypse manuscripts produced in Spain are a special feature of Romanesque book illumination. A whole series of different and conflicting assumptions try to explain just why this exclusive subject-matter should have experienced such an incomparable flowering at that period and in the narrow strip of Christianity situated between Moorish Spain and the Pyrenees, as well as in northern Spain. Perhaps it was exactly the remote nature of Christian Spain, so isolated from the rest of Europe, that provided the cultural breeding-ground necessary for such a development. Another reason for choosing to give pictorial expression to these eccentric Biblical scenes may have been the perceived threat to the Christian faith and the need to defend it.

These are, however, mere speculations. There is no evidence that Spanish Christians were restricted in the practise of their faith under Moorish rule. If the issue of religious intolerance is in any way relevant, then it is the atttitude of the Christians towards the enlightened Arabs that must be examined. The Moors were, moreover, far superior to the Christians in terms of culture and scientific knowledge. It also seems unlikely that the much-cited phenomenon of "apocalyptic fear" of the imminent turn of the millennium could have been a serious source of inspiration for such subject-matter.

The isolated position of northern Spain at the time was also reflected in the extreme paucity of contacts to the humanistically inspired courts of the Carolingian rulers or to the scriptoria of the Ottonians. The Spanish therefore concentrated on the limited amount of scholarly knowledge that had been achieved in their own country. This manifested itself mainly in the form of the *Etymologiae* by Isidore of Seville written around the year

600. This was supplemented by the commentary on the Apocalypse, written in the second half of the eighth century, by the Asturian monk Beatus of Liébana.

This compendium is better known as the *Beatus Commentary*. After the Bible it was regarded as the most important source used in Spanish scriptoria. In this commentary on the Apocalypse, the exegetic writings of the Fathers of the Church are bound up with details from the cosmic speculations of Isidore of Seville.

The well-known Apocalypse manuscript "Codex Burgo de Osma" (photo, p. 445 top, right) is full of illustrations vibrant with color. The depiction from the year 1086 of the "woman of the Apocalypse" takes up the subject matter at Civate (photo. p. 431) which has already been discussed. But whereas the scene at Civate represents the fight against the dragon, the Spanish manuscript shows how the angels throw the damned into the mouth of Hell. The serpent is seen threatening the woman whose baby can be clearly seen inside her body. This illustration is unusually faithful to another passage from Revelation (12, 1–5):

"And there appeared a great wonder in heaven; a woman clothed with the sun, and the moon under her feet, and upon her head a crown of twelve stars:

And she being with child cried, travailing in birth, and pained to be delivered.

And there appeared another wonder in heaven; and behold a great red dragon, having seven heads and ten horns, and seven crowns upon his heads.

And his tail drew the third part of the stars of heaven, and did cast them to the earth: and the dragon stood before the woman which was ready to be delivered, for to devour her child as soon as it was born.

And she brought forth a man child, who was to rule all nations with a rod of iron: and her child was caught up unto God, and to his throne."

The "woman of the Apocalypse" is identified as Mary, and the male child as Christ. This point has already been made in connection with Civate. In the *Beatus Commentary*, the woman of the Apocalypse is interpreted as Ecclesia and the boy as "ecclesiae filius," the son of the Christian Church. Using this version of assignment, Beatus wanted to make clear that handing over the boy to God constituted a metaphorical act of penance:

"Each man who turns to God with the full ardour of his heart, and rises from the dead, as it were, through penance, will be drawn into the contemplative life once he has risen from the active life."

It is very revealing to compare these lines with an Ottonian miniature dealing with the same subject. Produced around the year 1020 in Trier or on the island of Reichenau, the so-called Bamberg Apocalypse contains a folio that also depicts the woman of the Apocalypse with the dragon (figure, p. 445, bottom, right). The painter refrained from illustrating every detail of the text, almost as if he took for granted an educated audience which would concentrate more on the religious idea rather than its narrative development. Both the woman and the dragon are represented as stylized symbols. The obligatory architecture at the top right lacks any thematic link to the subject of the picture. The building appears more like a padding, something to fill a void in the pictorial space and ensure a balanced composition. The *Beatus Commentary* was widely read and must presumably have been known to both scribe and artist alike. Nevertheless, there appears to be a lack of interest in translating the admittedly complicated situation described in the text into iconographical form. Far from being inspired by a mere naive pleasure in narration, the Spanish artists and scholars who worked on the Apocalypse manuscript also aimed at communicating a particular theological perspective by means of the picture.

These manuscripts relating to the commentary on the Apocalypse are often referred to as "Mozarabic," a term denoting the Moorish influence quite obvious in this illustration. Although, as is well known, the Christian Spaniards concerned themselves very little with the culture of the Moors, stylistic influences did nevertheless seep through. The influence of Moorish models can be seen in the pages full of rich color and contrast, and in the basic colors of a golden yellow, a deep and glowing red, and an earthy dark brown. Some details such as the saddles of the horses, some building formations, and some robes are also borrowed from the cultural milieu of the neighboring Moors.

The Arabic saddles and gowns are very obvious in a picture of the four riders of the Apocalypse from an early manuscript (around 980, figure, p. 445, left). The rich bands of color were laid down by the artist with great skill in order to indicate the spatial depth of the riders arranged behind and above one another. Just like his colleague from Burgo de Osma did later, he remained entirely faithful to the text of the Apocalypse (6, 2–8) and even followed the instructions given on color. The fourth rider (below right), "and his name that sat on him was Death, and Hell followed with him," is shown sitting on a "pale horse" exactly as described in Revelation. The first rider is described as sitting on a white horse, and "… had a bow; and a crown was given unto him …". Fitted neatly into the corner of the picture at the top left, an angel with blood-red feathers peeps out and "crowns" the rider. The inclusion of such realistic detail adds vividness and drama to the story of the four riders who come tearing out through the first four broken seals of the book with seven seals, in order to destroy the world. It is quite possible that such a colorful and vivid style of narration was actually encouraged by the "learned ignorance" of the artists and their isolation from the cultural centers of Europe.

Finally, Moorish influences can also be detected in the painted architectural elements and in the design of fauna and flora. Some Apocalypse manuscripts include Moorish ornamentation as well as stylized ornamental birds and plants. There are also a larger number of churches built in typically Moorish style that can be recognized by the restricted semicircular arches.

Both the artists and the scribes working in the Spanish scriptoria were probably far more interested in Arab culture than their Christian religion allowed. The rich variety of form and the iconographical quality of the folios make the Spanish manuscripts appear superior to comparable works produced in Ottonian scriptoria.

The four horsemen of the Apocalypse.
Around 980. Valladolid. Cathedral
library. Manuscript of the Apocalypse,
fol. 93

PAGE 446/447
Apocalypse of St. Sever. Mid-eleventh
century. Paris, Bibl. Nat., Mx. 8878, fol.
108v–109

TOP
Burgo de Osma, Museum of the
Cathedral, Codex No. 1, fol. 131v

BOTTOM
Bamberg Apocalypse. Trier (?). The
woman of the Apocalypse. Around 1020.
Bamberg, Staatsbibliothek. Cod. 140,
fol. 29v

Bible moralisée. God the Father measures the world. Around 1250. Vienna, Österreichische Nationalbibliothek. Cod. 2554, fol. 1r

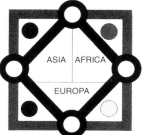

World graph, Salzburg. After an astronomical manuscript. Around 818

BOTTOM
The phases of the moon and the four elements. Astronomical-computist collection. Cologne. Around 805. Cologne, Erzbisch. Diözesan- u. Dombibliothek. Hs. 8311, fol. 83v. u. 84r

Artes Liberales. It is, therefore, likely to be a reference to the scientific aspect which forms part of the Creator's work. But what is most important about this concept of creation is its reconstruction: if God designed a plan for the world before he created it, then Man should be in a position to fathom out the design and construction of this plan. Thanks to the increasingly intensive development and progress of scientific activity it had become possible for both scholars and craftsmen to acquire skills and produce equipment and tools that enabled them at least to construct a model of the world. All this happened during the first half of the thirteenth century, at a time when the universities were reaching a position of monopoly within the state which granted them absolute freedom and, in some case, even their own jurisdiction.

The idea of creating a model of God's work of creation in the form of a pictorial allegory can be traced back to the Carolingian period. Such a "graph of the world" has been handed down to us in an astronomical manuscript from Salzburg (figure, above). Painted in around 818, the folio depicts a world scheme laid out according to the "T" shape generally used at that time: Europe, Asia and Africa are shown, together with the four parts of the world, or points of the compass in the corner tondi of the graph. The medallions placed in the spandrels represent the four elements. The meaning of the depiction could be interpreted as follows: "Terra" represents the center of the world and is surrounded by "cosmic matter", the elements. The number four is the key to "Terra". The underlying meaning is obvious: it is a reference to the four Evangelists who explain in their writings, the gospel books, the nature of God's creation and its message of salvation through his son Jesus Christ. It was popular practice to transfer this world scheme to representations of Christ in Majesty. The world graph is then replaced by a sphaira of stars and a mandorla with Christ sitting on his throne in the center. He is surrounded by the four beasts of the Apocalypse which represent the "elements", the four Evangelists who are filled with the word of God.

Carolingian ambitions to figure the cosmos were not only of an allegorical but also of a mathematically scientific nature.

Models of the world

A French manuscript from the thirteenth century, the *Bible moralisée*, shows on its first page God the Father bending down to measure the world with a pair of compasses (photo, above). Holding the cosmic orb in his left hand, he uses his other hand to place one arm of the instrument into the orb's center in order to draw a circle. One can already recognize the sun and the moon, and there is also a band of irregular and broken cloud. It is interesting that the artist who created this picture very deliberately painted the type of compasses used in the building trade at that time. That type was, incidentally, replaced in the second half of the thirteenth century by dividers.

The precise characterization and representation of the tool is a tribute to God the Father the designer, the brilliant craftsman who did not simply "create" the world but calculated and planned it carefully. The compasses are an attribute of *geometria*, one of the representatives of the *Septem*

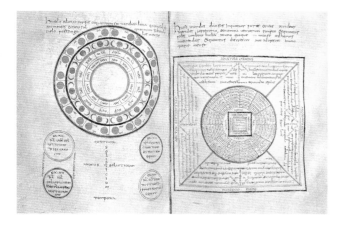

Isidore of Seville, Etymologiae. Benediktinerstift Göttweig. Second half of the twelfth century. Vienna, Österreichische Nationalbibliothek. Cod. 67

Glossarium Salomonis. Monastery of Prüfening. Representation of man as reflection of the world. 1158/65. Munich, Bayerische Staatsbibliothek. Clm 13002

An astronomical-computist collective work produced in Cologne in 805 contains eight diagrams and texts relating to the writings of Isidore of Seville and those of the Venerable Bede (photo, p. 448, bottom). The latter is concerned with the calculation of the phases of the moon and the four seasons and also contains speculations about the construction of the world which is held together by the four elements.

This speculative interpretation of the world as an event relating to the doctrine of salvation and the attempt to represent it in the form of allegories or diagrams, underwent a decisive change in the treatment of Isidore of Sevilla's *Etymologiae*. Compiled around the year 600 or soon after, and produced at the suggestion of one of Isidore's friends, the Bishop Braulio of Zaragoza, the "most important handbook of the Middle Ages," contained the whole wealth of contemporary knowledge in collected and classified form. For the Spanish scholar Isidore it also provided an opportunity to gain access to the knowledge of Classical antiquity in the midst of the busy cultural scene of the Moors. Braulio edited the work and published it in twenty volumes.

This very extensive work was written and illustrated by monks in a scriptorium in Prüfening between 1160 and 1165. Of the original twenty volumes only the first nine have survived. Another "Isidore manuscript" (Benediktinerstift Göttweig, around 1180) contains a sketch showing the Spanish universal scholar, balancing a sphaira model on his raised hand (figure, above). In the top circle there appears a small cross, representing Terra, with the world revolving around it. According to medieval thought, the planets, including the moon (Luna) and the sun (Sol), revolved around the earth. The divine cosmology of the firmament and its planetary movements found concentrated expression in the simple shapes of the circle and the sphere. Man felt himself to be part of this system since he was able to observe the movements in the sky. He therefore regarded himself as an integral part of the system, of the plan of creation, and therefore as a creature of God.

The correspondence between man and the universe has its origins in Pythagoras. It is thanks to Isidore of Seville that this idea also became known in the high Middle Ages. The interplay of world and man, of macrocosm and microcosm, is illustrated in the system of the so-called "macrocosm man" (photo, right). The model is based on the following idea: Man who carries God's creation within him must be identifiable as a kind of reflection of the world. Growing out of the tree of life, he receives his physical form from God, or one could say he receives his elementary existence via hands, shoulders and legs from the four elements: fire, air, water and earth. These correspond to the four temperaments of man, namely the choleric, the sanguine, the phlegmatic, and the melancholic temperaments. His head is surrounded by the heavenly sphere in which the planets revolve and relate to his senses: Luna and Sol originate from his eyes, Jupiter and Mercury from his ears, Mars and Venus from his nose, and Saturn from his mouth. Tracing the senses back to the characteristics of the planets would be to go too far, although it is absolutely possible, as the seven planets do represent the seven ages of man. In that capacity they are linked to the four elements as well as to the twelve signs of the Zodiac.

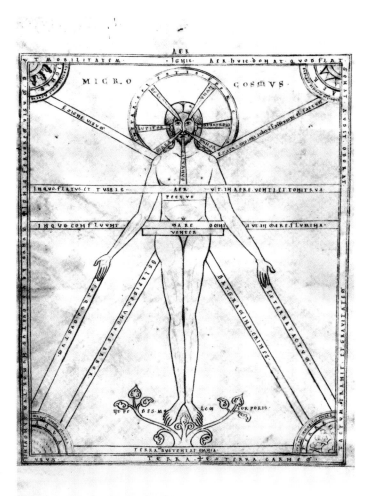

The complexity of the medieval conception of the world is truly astounding. One of the central themes of the humanist philosophy of the Renaissance, namely the harmony between microcosm and macrocosm, was already being explored in great detail in the Romanesque period. The direction of thought is clearly this: it might never be possible to look into the workshop of God in order to understand the mathematics behind his creation. Nevertheless, God has given us many signs enabling us to create a symbolic or allegorical model of his universe.

Reichenau/Oberzell, St. Georg. Wall
painting, around 980

TOP
The Gerasene demoniac (1)

CENTRE
The Healing of the Sick (2)

BOTTOM
The Storm on the lake (3)

Wall painting: the narrative style

The successive narrative style in St. Georg, Oberzell/Reichenau

The church of St. Georg in Oberzell on Reichenau is the home of one of
the few narrative picture cycles on the subject of Christ's miracles to have
survived as a complete set (photos, on the left, and also p. 451). It belongs
to the Ottonian period and is thought to have been created before the turn
of the millennium. It was certainly painted by Byzantine-trained artists
who continued their travels after completing their work in Oberzell. So far,
no other contemporary wall paintings even approaching the quality of
those in St. Georg have been discovered in the immediate or broader
environs of Reichenau. This fact supports the doubts about the previously
mentioned assumption of a school of painting at Reichenau which has
been asserted again and again but probably did not exist.

It is more than likely that a continuous painted cycle running around
the walls of the nave was designed from the very beginning as a narrative
cycle. With one single exception (the "Storm on the Sea of Galilee"), Jesus
enters each scene from the left, thus establishing the direction of reading:
from left to right. The viewer entering the space will also start on the left
side, the north wall. There we have first the Gerasene demoniac, followed
by the Healing of the Sick, the Storm on the Sea of Galilee, and the Healing
of the Man who was Born Blind.

The south wall contains the following scenes: the Healing of the Leper,
the Raising of the Young Man of Nain, the Healing of the Woman of her
Issue of Blood, the Raising of the Daughter of Jairus, and the Raising of
Lazarus from the Dead.

The sequence of reading gives us some first clues about the
dramaturgical construction of the narrative. The first few scenes deal
merely with the casting out of devils, the taming of nature, and the healing
of the sick. Gradually the diseases become more serious and finally appear
incurable. Eventually, Christ conquers death itself. The miracles of Christ
have become an allegory for man's path through life, defying evil, overcoming sin, and taking part in life eternal through the sacrifice of Christ.

The active champion of this scheme for salvation is the dragon fighter
and patron saint of the church, Saint George, who defeats evil in
exemplary fashion. The narrative can be reconstructed on two levels. The
first and most important level is represented by the performers of the
action. The second level, a kind of meta-level, is found in the architecture
which runs as a continuous band "behind" the frame into which the
picture has been set by the actual, constructed architecture. In this way, the
self-contained scenes are linked with one another, and interesting
associations and breaks occur. The second fresco on the north wall,
showing the Healing of the Sick (photo, left, centre), includes a building on
the right with a white wall made of ashlars. The same wall can be seen on
the left-hand side of the adjoining picture (photo, left, bottom) and then
suddenly stops. This is where the Sea of Galilee begins. Also visible is the
boat which is soon to find itself in a storm and at the mercy of high waves.
The white ashlar walls described above must therefore form part of the
fortification of the city which reaches down to the harbor.

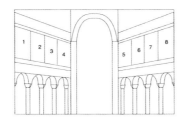

Reichenan/Oberzell
St. George, Wallpainting around 980.
The Healing of the Woman of her Bloody
Issue (7)

Thus the actions of Christ and his disciples take place in different spots, although all in the same general area. Accompanied by the observer, Christ proceeds to perform his miraculous healings.

A scene on the south wall shows the Healing of the Leper (photo, p. 450, middle). At the right-hand edge of the picture, one notices a slender little tower which might possibly be a bell tower or a tower in the town. The same tower, albeit somewhat shortened, appears on the left-hand side of the picture with the Sea of Galilee. This is presumably a way of marking chapters as regards subject matter: the "storm," the "man born blind," and the "leper" are allusions to faith, original sin, and the forgiveness of sin, respectively. On the boat, Christ causes his disciples to be ashamed ("Why are ye fearful, O ye of little faith?"). With the "man that was born blind" Christ makes a statement about the concept of original sin by exonerating all blind people from sin, since they will have their sight restored on the day of the Judgement. However, he reminds the doubting Pharisees of their own sins. In the scene of the leper, a man whom the laws of the time declared fatally ill and forced to remain outside the city walls is healed by Christ through the utterance of the words: "Be thou clean!"

The two towers divide the whole cycle into three parts. The first part consists of the two pictures dealing with the "casting-out of the demons" and "dropsy." These of course represent suffering in both body and soul. The second part is concerned with the issue of original sin, as described above. The third part represents the scenes where Christ is raising various people from the dead.

It now becomes apparent that the painted architectural elements fulfill an important function within the narrative. They structure the overall scenario according to aspects of the salvation story. At the same time they transcend, as it were, the boundaries of the actual church architecture bringing the scenes together as a homogeneous chapter in the Life of Christ.

Architecture also serves as an important means of articulation with regard to the detailed narrative structure. Christ is almost always shown emerging from a baldachin-like construction, followed by his disciples. The baldachin with its turned-up curtains provides a suitably dignified framework for Christ and his followers. Then he would meet one or sometimes several people who are positioned in front of a city backdrop. In this way two places which are planned in a chronological sequence, are brought into a chronological relationship with each other. The picture illustrating the story of the "man who was born blind" provides a particularly good example of this kind of "architecture of succession." The young man appears to emerge from a building, allows Christ to put clay on his eyes, and follows his instructions to go to Siloah in order to wash his eyes and gain his sight. Immediately to the right of this partial scene, the same young man is depicted a second time. Not only does he seem to have turned around, but the building, too. It is now placed perpendicular to the adjoining building and thus separates two chronological periods. The same narrative scheme can be observed in the penultimate fresco (photo, above). Here it is the artist's concern to put two scenes which are mixed up with one another, even in Matthew's gospel,

into the same sphere of action: while Jesus is called to the supposedly dead daughter of Jairus, a woman suffering from bloody issue is reaching out for his garment: "And Jesus turned around" and healed her, and immediately went on to dedicate himself to the little daughter of the worried Jairus. This "turning maneuver," represented by a change of figures, is staged in a very dramatic way, with the building sections emphasizing the two spheres of action.

The calculated interplay of figure and architecture achieved perfection at Reichenau and was never equalled in Ottonian painting. Even book illustrations dealing with comparable subject matter exhibit neither the narrative drama nor the sophisticated interplay between figure and architecture present in these frescoes. This, moreover, is another reason why it is hard to believe that works such as the Gospel Book of Otto III, for example, or the Egbert Codex were produced on the island of Reichenau: their narrative construction uses simultaneous images, narrative sequences set in uniformly constructed spaces, and falls far behind the mastery of the Oberzell frescoes. Indeed, there are only two sources which could be cited as models for such a narrative style: the Carolingian wall paintings of St. Johannes in Müstair (photo, p. 407), and the Byzantine mosaics of Ravenna or Rome. Since at Müstair, too, the Byzantine influence is very obvious, one must conclude that the Byzantine codices were the true artistic source of the pictorial narrative. This will be discussed further in the following pages.

The Old Testament picture cycles in St. Savin

The fresco cycle in the vault of the monastery church of St.-Savin-sur-Gartempe was painted 100 years after that of Oberzell. There is hardly anything in common between the two cycles. In St. Savin the use of architecture as a structural element for the pictorial and narrative sequences is largely non-existent. The situation, on the other hand, is formulated in a more vivid and figurative manner. The figures are more dynamic and are harmoniously integrated into the group compositions. This may well be a result of the lack of pictorial architecture, and also of the fact that the artists chose to depict the actions within a landscape setting.

The first reaction of a visitor to this church is one of confusion, as he or she scans the ceiling in vain for a unified and logical sequence of scenes. The vault is divided into two northern and two southern sections or strips (see diagram on p. 453). The reading direction is from west to east, but is interrupted by erratic jumps and about-turns from one strip of scenes to the other. The diagram on page 453 not only shows the sequence of the scenes but also indicates the reason for the intricate nature of the narrative order. One is struck by the fact that, with the exception of the first three bays in the northern section which depict the story of Creation, the scenes shown in the highest-placed northern strip are arranged from west to east and then switch over to the adjoining highest southern strip where they run from east to west. There they continue with the story of Abraham in the southern arcade strip which reads from west to east. After that the observer has to return to the fourth northern bay in order to follow the story of Moses as far as "Mount Sinai" which is represented in the northern arcade strip and has to be read in an eastern direction. With one single exception – that of the southern arcade strip – all scenes are laid out to be read from left to right.

The reason for such a "snail-like" narrative layout is a pragmatic one. It is known from documents that the decoration of the ceiling was supposed to be completed in time for the consecration of the church. During the last construction stage, the painters already began on the church and climbed onto the scaffolding where the bricklayers were still plastering the vault. While the latter were still working on the arcaded sections of the ceiling, the artists began painting onto the already plastered apex area of the vault. After the masons' work was completed, the painters could then continue their cycle in the arcade section.

Only one scene can be regarded as a simultaneous picture, i.e. a picture which contains events that unfold in chronological succession but are represented in a unified pictorial space. The scene depicts the creation of the first human couple (photo, p. 454, top): God the Father is seen bending over the reclining Adam and removing one of his ribs. Then Adam is depicted standing upright next to his creator, listening to his admonitions and winking at Eve. Eve, who has her back turned to the tree of knowledge, turns round and together with her husband leaves the Garden of Eden after the Fall of Man. Twice the change or turn of figure occurs which causes the breaks between the scenes within the unified space: the figure of Adam is depicted twice, once reclining and once standing up

behind his own reclining image, and Eve moves in a semi-circle around the tree of knowledge. This is a typically Byzantine system of narration. It appears in this specific form probably for the first time in the so-called Vienna Genesis (photo p. 456, bottom), a Byzantine manuscript dating from the last third of the sixth century.

With regard to the construction of the narrative sequences, Byzantine and Ottonian style are very similar. Nevertheless, an individual "western" style of narration developed which was illustrated, for example, in the Ottonian frescoes on the island of Reichenau. At St. Savin similarities with Ottonian frescoes and miniatures are observable in terms of the combination of architecture and figure. In the cycle of Joseph which extends along the major part of the southern arcade strip, for example, the action of the figures is linked to the accompanying architectural elements in a similar fashion to St. Georg in Oberzell. The narrative begins with Jacob who sends Joseph to visit his brothers, and ends with the triumph of Joseph. Parts of the frescoes are so badly damaged that the accompanying architectural strip cannot always be followed. The story of Joseph and the wife of Potiphar is framed by the great vaults and arches and the little turrets of the architectural setting. Potiphar's wife is shown making advances to Joseph and holding on to his garment as he is trying to escape. A little further to the left, again standing beneath an arch, we see her handing Joseph's gown over to her husband and accusing the young man. The narrative situation is full of piquancy: with her left hand, the woman points to Joseph as he flees from her in the preceding scene, whilst her other hand points to the gown already lying on Potiphar's lap. Thus the lie is made directly visible for the viewer, but not, however, for Potiphar who with his right hand points towards the prison.

As in Ottonian wall painting, the role of architecture here is also designed to give structure to the successive scenes – either by separating connecting elements, such as Joseph and Potiphar's wife, or by connecting separating elements, such as the woman who appears twice, and the Joseph of the first scene. Since the narrative sequence does not follow the reading direction of the cycle, the continuous succession of action is broken up. The architectural features can therefore be regarded as mere representative attributes of individual events.

The scene of "Joseph interpreting the dreams of Pharaoh" includes a magnificent example of city architecture which is developed into an exedra similar to the ones already seen in Carolingian miniatures (photos, pp. 423–25). In front of the exedra, we see Pharaoh sitting on his throne, leaning on his scepter and, head slightly inclined, listening to Joseph's reports. Bent forwards and full of reverence, the latter stands outside the architectural frame. One of the guards takes hold of Joseph's tied hands and points to the Pharaoh in a grand gesture. The following scene, "Joseph's Advancement," takes place in front of a similar city scenario. Here, Joseph enters the scene from the left and turns his back on the other image of himself, which had just been seen bending over and interpreting the Pharaoh's dreams.

As stated before, the narrative situation is a complex one. The general sequence of the narration, the advance from one picture space to the next,

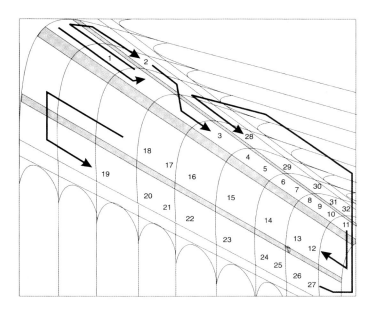

runs from left to right, that is in exact opposition to the direction of reading.

However, the individual scenes depicted within each pictorial space are arranged according to the normal reading direction. In most cases, the same applies to the direction in which the figures are moving. In order to give at least some compositional security to this recursive narrative situation, the painter constructed a continuous architectural strip which served at least to indicate the continuity of the action and to balance the interrupted flow of the narration.

The vault frescoes of St. Savin should certainly not then be judged merely by their formal or narrative qualities. The artist's concern was a different one: he had the task of representing the story of Moses, from the creation of the world until his death, and it had to be told by means of selected and exegetically representative scenes which were to be distributed all over the vaulted ceiling. When establishing the narrative composition, priority was therefore given to the arrangement of narrative events rather than to the continuous narrative flow. Thus, popular subjects such as the building of the Tower of Babel, or Noah's Ark, were made to stand out in spectacular fashion (photos, p. 454, centre and bottom). The scene showing the building of the Tower of Babel even turns into a kind of visual instruction in the state the of medieval building trade: the rough-hewn ashlar blocks are carried along on men's shoulders. Holding an angle-iron in his right hand, we see an architect standing on the tower, about to take up a stone which somebody is handing to him. A mason in the foreground is taking mortar out of a bucket. Next to the bucket there is a cable winch used to pull up the container. Then, suddenly, God the Father makes his appearance in order to punish the workers' actions with the confusion of tongues.

Set in a central place within the vault, this fresco is in distinct contrast to the other frescoes, thanks to its light and spacious composition which helps to relieve the often tightly constructed scenario. It is of iconographical interest that the picture opposite, its thematic "counterpart," as it were, shows the curse of Cain who has just murdered his brother. Thus we have two representations of the curse of God: the first referring to an individual, and the second to a whole nation. It is perfectly plausible that this link was consciously sought and executed.

Another popular pictorial subject was Noah's Ark. As was common practice in the Middle Ages, the artist who created this picture showed the ark as a lateral elevation. Judging by its hull, the ark is a Viking ship with a stem fortified by monsters, and a three-storey superstructure and small wheel-house just as described in the Bible. It takes up the entire picture space. Animals look out through the round-arched windows, and Noah's family crouch above. Corpses float in the water below, while in the sky above we see the dove hover, announcing the imminent end of the journey and of the storm. All this implies that the ark has been at sea for some time. Its passengers might even be about to look for a place to drop anchor, for Noah's sons can be spotted going astern and climbing about on the stem.

While the Tower of Babel formally relaxes the overall design of the vault paintings, the picture of "Noah's Ark" represents a kind of "narrative turning-point." It is a pleasure to spend time before the image and take in the details. It is possible to identify the animals and to check the ship as to its seaworthiness. Some observers might like to establish the exact moment in time depicted in this biblical sea journey, and look for the dove's message. The man of medieval northern Europe was not very "spoilt" as far as pictures were concerned. Biblical events apart, he knew very little about the world, although he had probably heard a lot about strange and foreign things. Seeing a picture of Noah's Ark was probably his first introduction to such exotic animals as tigers, lions, or tropical birds.

The artists of the vault paintings set great store on accompanying attributes. This applies not only to the cityscape described in the Joseph cycle, but equally to portrayals of medieval building practices or the grape harvest in the scenes relating to Noah. Moreover, again and again the viewer comes across plants and animals inserted into and between the scenes and functioning as attributes. At St. Savin, the story of the Bible turns into a concise account of the history of civilization of the medieval world.

OPPOSITE PAGE
St. Savin-sur-Gartempe. Fresco cycle in
the vault of the monastery church

LEFT
The creation of Adam and Eve

CENTRE
The Tower of Babel

BOTTOM
Noah's Ark

Moutier-Grandval Bible.Tours. Scenes
from the Book of Genesis. Around 840.
London, British Museum. Add. Ms.
10546, fol. 5 b

Vienna Genesis. Constantinople (?).
Scenes from the life of Jacob. Around
570. Vienna, Österreichische
Nationalbibliothek. Cod. Theol. Graec.
pag. 14

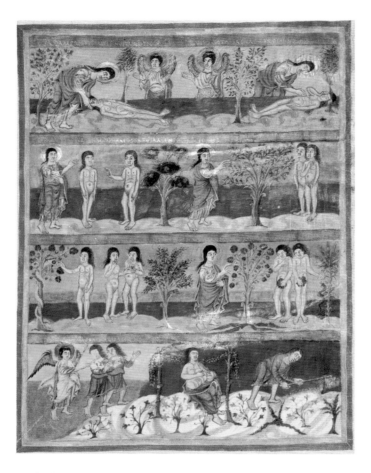

top, on the left, Eve is shown standing next to the tree and reaching for the apple. She turns around and hands it to Adam. This figure turn, this succession of scenes, is one of the standard themes of Byzantine pictorial narrative. A particularly clear example of this can be found in the Jacob cycle of the "Vienna Genesis." In a folio containing the scene of "Jacob and the Angel," the same angel figure is depicted back to back with himself in order to bring out more clearly the drama of the fight in such a brief sequence of scenes.

The same narrative theme is also found in Ottonian book illumination where it occurs in many variations. Only one example will be referred to here, the Gospel Book of Otto III. One folio depicts Christ turning to his disciples (figure, p. 457), and then turning round and kneeling down to pray at the Mount of Olives. The abrupt change in scene and time of the action is marked by a small, delicate tree. In this miniature, simultaneity and chronological succession are connected with one another in the most ingenious manner: Christ sets out on his way to the Mount of Olives. He is followed by his disciples who take a rest by the mountain while Christ "is sweating blood and water." The artist wanted to capture the moment in which Christ, just before climbing the mountain, encourages Peter to pray so that he would not be led into temptation. Peter looks up at his Lord while the disciples are already sleeping, an action that is supposed to take place later in time.

The bringing forward of chronological events and dramatic sequences brings out the message of the story, namely Christ's admonition and his fear of death, a fear that remained unnoticed by his disciples. This use of time-lapse within the dramatic structure of a narrative sequence is a typical feature of medieval pictorial narrative.

As we have seen, time-lapse and figure change belong to the most dominant narrative techniques used in Ottonian book illumination. Usually they are employed when it is rendered necessary by the biblical story, for example in the scene showing the storm on the Sea of Galilee. Apart from the miniature in the Hitda Codex, there is probably no other

Book illumination
Simultaneous images in Carolingian and Ottonian miniatures

Reference has already been made to the important role played by Byzantine codices in the development of the narrative style found in Carolingian and Ottonian book illumination. Without the illustrations in the "Vienna Genesis," the scenes from Genesis in the Grandval Bible from Tours (around 840, figure. above) would not have been possible. In the cycle of "Jacob and Rachel," the narrative sequence is structured by means of strips of earth, groups of trees, and sections of buildings shown in elevation. The differences are, of course, obvious: the dramatic and impressionistic style that characterizes the Byzantine model, was translated in the Tours manuscript into an incremental narrative sequence thanks to the clear layout of the pictorial structure. The strips are arranged like lines of text making the "picture text" more easily legible. The use of trees and figure changes as a means of structuring the individual scenes is, on the other hand, a typically Byzantine device. In the third strip from the

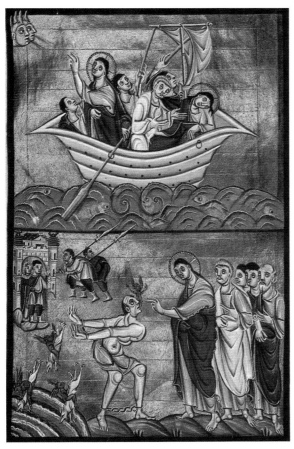

Gospel Book of Otto III.
Trier (?). Around 1000.
Munich, Staatsbibliothek.
Clm 4453

LEFT
The Sea of Galilee. fol. 103v

RIGHT
Gethsemane. fol. 244v

depiction of the Sea of Galilee which does not make use of these principles.

We have already looked at the picture in the church of St. Georg in Oberzell in which this subject is interpreted in a masterly style (figure, p. 450, center). In the miniature from the Gospel Book of Otto (figure, above), the same sequence of events was designed accordingly: Christ is seen resting in the stern of the boat. Above him we see the billowing sail hinting at the imminent storm. Now Peter bends down to him to waken him. Next to Peter, on his right-hand side, we see the awakened Christ as he calms the pale, horned gods of the wind.

It is the boat which ensures such a clear simultaneity: simultaneous actions depicted visually can only be be made to appear consecutive by repeatedly depicting individuals or groups of people. The "Storm on the Sea of Galilee" therefore constitutes a special case. Simultaneous space always requires the depiction of a homogeneous landscape, which in most cases is articulated by hills, trees, or architectural elements.

In addition to its function as a stage setting, the combination of landscape and architecture also plays a narrative role. Not only can it separate two successive scenes in order to indicate different points in time, but it also stretches the narrative flow emphasizing the sequence of actions. This means that one scene can be divided in such a way that the progress of the action is illustrated quite clearly as an event happening in time. The Golden Gospel Book of Henry III, produced around the year 1045, contains a depiction of the "Raising of the Daughter of Jairus from the dead". Christ and his disciples approach the house of Jairus who is standing outside the door. He points inside, allowing Christ to enter.

Christ is already engaged in raising up the girl laid out on her deathbed, her eyes already open. The 180-degree figure change executed by Jairus is marked by the door jamb. Christ keeps up the direction of both his walk and his gaze, as if he were already contemplating his next miracle. The inside and outside, or, the before and after, become tangible by means of the figure turn, by Jairus's rotation in the center of the composition. Both architecture and landscape are mere aids for the representation of periods in time.

Any event is defined by a temporal situation and a related spatial situation. In this sense, the biblical alpha and omega must be understood as the combination of space and time: at the end of all days, when time has literally run out, the space is folded up. This is indeed how the last days of the world are revealed to John in his famous vision on Patmos.

The many variations and possibilities of representing biblical events as successive action might, indeed, be seen as allusions to this space-time continuum of salvation. Each event within the space-time continuum brings man closer to the throne of God. Perhaps it should not be regarded as a mere accident that the time factor within pictorial representation gained such significance just around the turn of the millennium.

457

The Bayeux Tapestry

Tapisserie de Bayeux. By special permission of the City of Bayeux

"... the rather restless Norman people ..." is how the Bishop Otto of Freising referred, in a charming understatement, to the descendants of the Vikings in the middle of the twelfth century. In the eleventh century, they abandoned most of their bases in Scandinavia and concentrated their efforts on southern Italy and Sicily, and Normandy, today part of north-western France. The year 1066 saw the death of the Anglo-Saxon king Edward the Confessor. The crown was refused to William, Duke of Normandy, who, as a relative of Edward, had been recognised by the latter as his rightful heir. Instead, the crown was given to Harold, representative of the Anglo-Saxon national groups. There was no fear of attack on the island, which was, after all, only reachable by a wide stretch of water, the English Channel, which served as a barrier from far-off Normandy. The Anglo-Saxons obviously underestimated the tradition of the Normans, who, in the very same year, 1066, armed themselves and set off for England using the well-tried "Viking method."

Today we are familiar with almost every detail of the Norman campaign against those Anglo-Saxons who had broken their word. In 1077, either Queen Matilda or Bishop Odo of Bayeux commissioned a tapestry to be made which today measures 220 feet by about 20 inches. This unusual work of art features fifty-eight embroidered scenes telling the story of the military campaign, and is now kept at the Musée de la Reine Mathilde, an eighteenth-century building on the southern side of the cathedral of Bayeux.

The key scene (figure, p. 218, bottom) appears near the end of the first third of the tapestry: Harold, the favourite of the Anglo-Saxon faction, is depicted swearing an oath before William that he would recognize him as the rightful king after Edward's death. His right hand is resting on a reliquary, and his left on the altar. Sitting on the throne, sword in hand, in a ruler's pose, William is receiving the oath. The accompanying inscription above the scene reads: "Harold sacramentum fecit Willelmo duci." Set above this ceremonial scene is the royal beast, the lion, indicating the future kingdom of William. A few scenes later Edward is seen dying, with dull and tired eyes (1). Shortly afterwards Harold was himself crowned King of England by Archbishop Stigand in the presence of the Anglo-Saxon nobility. Astrologers announce the appearance of a comet

1

2

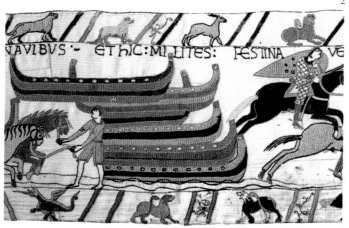

3

which is placed above Harold's palace like an arrow of fire. A messenger of bad tidings, the comet is a reference to the counter-action of William, who immediately begins to prepare for his invasion. He orders trees to be felled and Viking ships to be built along the coast of Normandy (2). In the top and bottom margins of the Tapestry, uneasy looking animals accompany the action. The viewer can see how felled trees are stripped of their bark, split, and made into planks for the ships. Then, with billowing sails, William's fleet crosses the Channel and lands on the coast of England (3). The animals in the accompanying margins have also formed themselves into troops and march in the same direction as the conquerors. William has barely moored and sent the first troops to secure the hinterland, when we see him making enquiries as to the actual whereabouts of Harold and his army. The soldiers, meanwhile, set fire to a house from which a woman flees, her arm held up in a defensive gesture, and holding a boy by the hand. (4). A messenger comes charging up with lowered lance, advising William of the approach of his enemy. The conqueror has already changed from his "traveling outfit" into a magnificent suit of armour complete with a coat of chain mail, helmet, and spurred boots. On horseback and accompanied by the nervously jumping lions in the tapestry borders, William rides towards the site of the battle (5) which is already unfolding in the following scenes. Now the animals, too, become active: the fox snatches some poultry, while the wolf stands growling at a goat. At the climax of the battle, the animals disappear from the lower margin and make room for the approaching archers. Hand-to-hand fighting breaks out, with swords being raised and lances stabbing at bodies (6). We see the first dead amongst the enemy, their mutilated and headless bodies tumbling towards the bottom margin of the tapestry. The battle is won, and "Harold rex interfectus est." An arrow strikes the eye of the English king. He stumbles. A Norman horseman comes charging up and butchers Harold with his sword. The lower margin of the tapestry shows the defeated putting their weapons on the ground. Some are stripped of their coats of chain mail.

The narrative style of this unique work of art follows the model of Byzantine codices.

The individual sequences of the succeeding events are separated by means

4

5

6

of stylized landscape formations and architectural elements. Far from interrupting the narrative flow, this device helps to keep it going, since the shapes of buildings, trees or hills are effective caesurae and point to the following scene. One example of this is the scene where we see the ship of Harold returning to England. It is steering towards a palace-like building with a balustrade on which an Anglo-Saxon man in typical look-out pose announces the arrival of Harold. The formal layout of the whole of the tapestry is ingeniously used to provide both the compositional principle and narrative structure.

The use of secondary narration in the top and bottom margins of the tapestry is also remarkable. Taken from an Anglo-Saxon collection of fables, the depictions of the animals may be interpreted as the symbolic representation of the principal action. When the battle reaches its dramatic climax the animals disappear to make room for the turmoil of the battlefield, a device which undoubtedly underlines the significance of the conflict. Finally the formal design of the tapestry should be considered. To our eyes the figures appear ungainly in their elongation, while to contemporary viewers they would have been understood as a stylistic device denoting elegance and nobility. The elongation allowed a high degree of movement and variety of gesture. Moreover there is a tendency towards depicting individual features – this is particularly apparent in the drawing of the physiognomy of the main characters, Edward, Harold, and William. Many individual scenes, such as a banquet or the depiction of a ruler, for example, follow the then customary motifs familiar from book illumination. The forward-facing ruler accompanied by both secondary secular and religious figures under an architectural baldachin may be understood as a well-known formal-iconographical topos. The banquet is nearly always a variation of the obligatory "Wedding of Cana."

The tapestry may be interpreted as a political manifesto. Its design was clearly established from a Norman perspective. The victory at the Battle of Hastings on October 14, 1066 is glorified, and with it the principal character, William the Conqueror, Duke of Normandy and King of England.

The story of the tapestry narrates not only the course of historic events or details of cultural history, such as the coronation ceremony. It also includes everyday events in charming subsidiary scenes which are skilfully interwoven with the main subject. The viewer witnesses, for example, the preparation and serving up of chickens roasted on the spit – a good opportunity to have a look at the interior and implements of a medieval kitchen. Another "interlude" shows how the camp of Hastings was built. Two of the workmen are engaged in an argument while the others stand about doing nothing. They only begin to work when William appears on the scene.

Stained glass windows of the Monastery of Alpirsbach. Samson with the city gates of Gaza. 1180–1200. Stuttgart, Württembergisches Landesmuseum

Stained glass windows

One of the developments that mark the end of Romanesque art is the rise of stained glass. The diaphanous structure of Gothic architecture resulted in the virtual elimination of the continuous wall space, and thus the main vehicle of pictorial representation used in Romanesque painting. The compact wall space of the Romanesque period was transformed into a lucid system of pillars and windows.

The new principles of composition can be observed in the stained glass window of the Abbey of Alpirsbach (photo, right, top). Stained glass window technology required a strict structure of both overall picture and detail. This, in turn, demanded clear articulation of both space and figures, and an exact linear delimitation of detail. The pictorial space of Romanesque art is broken up into colored shapes reminiscent of a mosaic. As it loses its spatial depth it turns into a mere ornamental pattern in relation to the action. The principle of the ornamental design of the figure space, and the emphasis of the figure within the decorative structure, becomes the central theme of the Gothic stained glass window and the Gothic miniature.

The first Gothic stained glass windows (photo, right, bottom) were created in Paris, Saint-Denis, almost 100 years before the end of the Romanesque period in Germany, and about forty years prior to the work in Alpirsbach. The differences between the two examples are considerable: while Samson acts in a space defined by means of architectural elements and walls of earth, the figures in Saint-Denis are integrated into an ornamental pattern which simultaneously acts as a decoration and as a vehicle to convey meaning.

Saint-Denis, Monastery church, ambulatory. Signum Tau from the lost Passion window. 1140–44

Appendix

Political map of Europe during the Romanesque period

Maps p. 463–65: Romanesque centres of art for
architecture, sculpture and mosaics

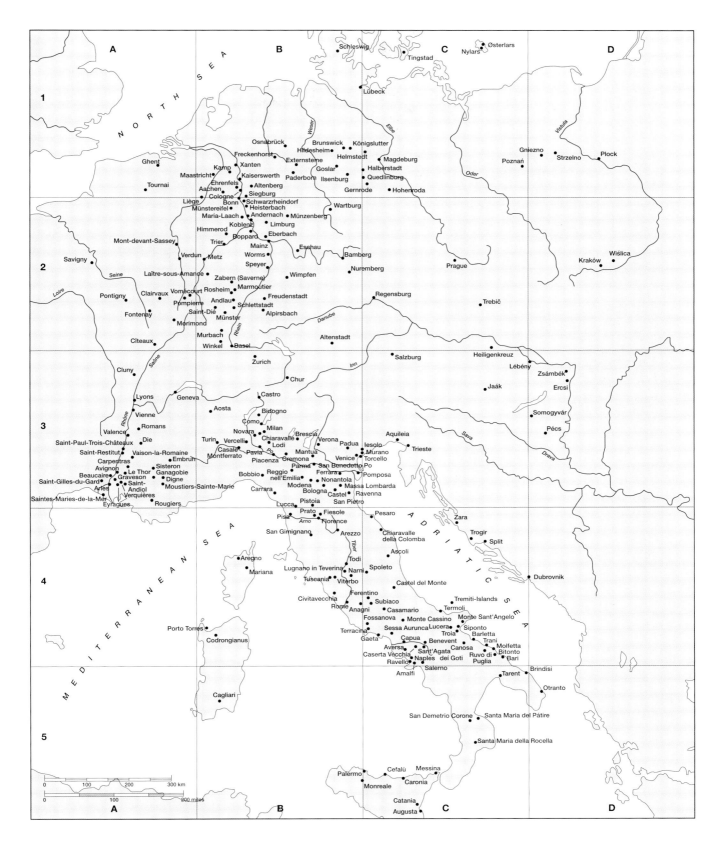

A

B

C

D

NORTH SEA

1

Schleswig
Nylars • • Østerlars
Tingstad

Lübeck

Gniezno • • Plock
Poznań • • Strzelno

Osnabrück
Brunswick • Königslutter
Freckenhorst Hildesheim Helmstedt
Externsteine Goslar Magdeburg
Ghent Kamp Xanten Paderborn Ilsenburg Halberstadt
Maastricht Kaiserswerth Quedlinburg
Ehrenfels Altenberg Gernrode • Hohenroda
Tournai Aachen Cologne Siegburg
Liège Bonn Schwarzrheindorf
Münstereifel Heisterbach Wartburg
Maria-Laach Andernach Münzenberg
Himmerod Koblenz Limburg
Mont-devant-Sassey Trier Boppard Eberbach
Verdun Mainz Eschau
Metz Worms Bamberg
Savigny Speyer Nuremberg
Laître-sous-Amance Wimpfen Prague
Vomécourt Rosheim Marmoutier
Pontigny Clairvaux Andlau Freudenstadt Regensburg Trebič
Pompierre Schlettstadt
Saint-Dié Münster Alpirsbach
Fontenay Mérimond Danube
Murbach Altenstadt
Cîteaux Winkel • Basel
Zurich

2 Seine
Loire
Rhein
Kraków • Wiślica

3

Cluny Chur Inn Salzburg
Lyons Geneva Castro Heiligenkreuz
Saône Vienne Aosta Bidogno Lébény
Romans Como Milan Brescia Zsámbék
Valence Novara Verona Aquileia Jaák
Saint-Paul-Trois-Châteaux Die Turin Vercelli Lodi Padua Iesolo Somogyvár
Saint-Restitut Vaison-la-Romaine Casale Chiaravalle Mantua Murano Trieste Pécs
Carpentras Embrun Montferrato Pavia Piacenza Cremona Venice Torcello
Avignon Sisteron Parma San Benedetto Po
Beaucaire Le Thor Ganagobie Bobbio Reggio Ferrara Pomposa
Graveson Digne nell'Emilia Nonantola
Saint-Gilles-du-Gard Saint-Andiol Moustiers-Sainte-Marie Modena Massa Lombarda
Arles Verquières Carrara Bologna Ravenna
Saintes-Maries-de-la-Mer Rougiers Castel
Eyragues Lucca San Pietro
Prato Pistoia Pesaro Zara
Pisa Fiesole Trogir
Arno Florence Chiaravalle Split
San Gimignano Arezzo della Colomba

Rhône
ADRIATIC SEA

MEDITERRANEAN SEA
Tiber
Aregno Todi Ascoli
Mariana Lugnano in Teverina Narni Spoleto Dubrovnik
Tuscania Viterbo Castel del Monte

4 Civitavecchia Ferentino Tremiti-Islands
Rome Subiaco Termoli
Anagni Casamario Monte Sant'Angelo
Porto Torres Fossanova Monte Cassino
Terracina Sessa Aurunca Lucera Siponto
Codrongianus Gaeta Troia Barletta
Capua Canosa Trani Molfetta
Aversa Benevent Bitonto
Caserta Vecchia Sant'Agata Ruvo di Bari
Naples deï Goti Puglia
Ravello Brindisi
Amalfi Salerno

Cagliari Tarent
Otranto

San Demetrio Corone • Santa Maria del Pátire

5

Santa Maria della Rocella

Cefalù Messina
Palermo Caronia
Monreale
Catania
Augusta

0   100   200   300 km
0   100   200 miles

A B C D

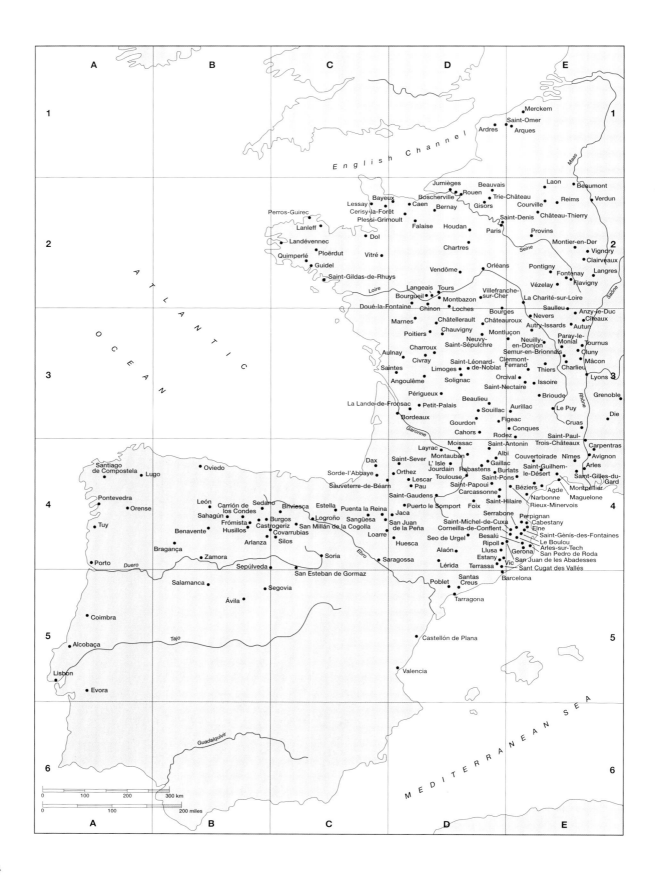

Map labels:

Row 1 / top region:
Merckem
Saint-Omer
Ardres
Arques

English Channel

Maas

Row 2:
Jumièges
Beauvais
Laon
Beaumont
Boscherville
Rouen
Trie-Château
Reims
Verdun
Bayeux
Caen
Bernay
Gisors
Courville
Lessay
Cerisy-la-Forêt
Château-Thierry
Plessi-Grimoult
Saint-Denis
Perros-Guirec
Falaise
Houdan
Paris
Provins
Lanleff
Montier-en-Der
Landévennec
Dol
Vignory
Quimperlé
Ploërdut
Vitré
Chartres
Seine
Clairveaux
Guidel
Vendôme
Orléans
Pontigny
Langres
Saint-Gildas-de-Rhuys
Fontenay
Flavigny
Vézelay
Saône

ATLANTIC OCEAN

Row 3:
Langeais
Tours
Villefranche-sur-Cher
Bourgueil
Montbazon
La Charité-sur-Loire
Saulieu
Anzy-le-Duc
Loire
Doué-la-Fontaine
Chinon
Loches
Bourges
Nevers
Cîteaux
Marnes
Châtellerault
Châteauroux
Autry-Issards
Autun
Poitiers
Chauvigny
Montluçon
Neuilly-en-Donjon
Paray-le-Monial
Tournus
Neuvy-Saint-Sépulchre
Semur-en-Brionnais
Cluny
Aulnay
Charroux
Saint-Léonard-de-Noblat
Thiers
Charlieu
Mâcon
Civray
Clermont-Ferrand
Limoges
Orcival
Lyons
Saintes
Solignac
Issoire
Angoulême
Saint-Nectaire
Brioude
Grenoble
Périgueux
Beaulieu
Rhône
La Lande-de-Fronsac
Petit-Palais
Souillac
Aurillac
Le Puy
Die
Bordeaux
Gourdon
Figeac
Cruas
Garonne
Cahors
Conques
Rodez
Saint-Paul-Trois-Châteaux
Carpentras

Row 4:
Layrac
Moissac
Saint-Antonin
Avignon
Dax
Saint-Sever
Montauban
Albi
Couvertoirade
Nîmes
Sorde-l'Abbaye
L'Isle
Jourdain
Rabastens
Gaillac
Saint-Guilhem-le-Désert
Arles
Orthez
Lescar
Toulouse
Saint-Pons
Burlats
Saint-Gilles-du-Gard
Sauveterre-de-Béarn
Pau
Saint-Papoul
Carcassonne
Béziers
Agde
Montpellier
Saint-Gaudens
Narbonne
Maguelone
Santiago de Compostela
Lugo
Oviedo
Puerto le Somport
Foix
Saint-Hilaire
Rieux-Minervois
Pontevedra
Orense
León
Carrión de los Condes
Sedano
Briviesca
Estella
Puenta la Reina
Jaca
Serrabone
Perpignan
Tuy
Sahagún
Frómista
Burgos
Logroño
Sangüesa
San Juan de la Peña
Saint-Michel-de-Cuxa
Cabestany
Benavente
Husillos
Castrogeriz
San Millán de la Cogolla
Corneilla-de-Conflent
Eline
Saint-Gènis-des-Fontaines
Covarrubias
Loarre
Besalú
Le Boulou
Arlanza
Silos
Huesca
Ripoll
Arles-sur-Tech
Bragança
Seo de Urgel
Gerona
San Pedro de Roda
Zamora
Soria
Alaón
Llusa
San Juan de les Abadesses
Porto
Duero
Sepúlveda
Estany
Vic
Sant Cugat des Vallés
San Esteban de Gormaz
Lérida
Terrassa
Barcelona

Row 5:
Salamanca
Segovia
Poblet
Santas Creus
Ávila
Tarragona
Coimbra
Tajo
Castellón de Plana
Alcobaça
Lisbon
Valencia
Evora

Row 6:
Guadalquivir

MEDITERRANEAN SEA

Scale:
0 100 200 300 km
0 100 200 miles

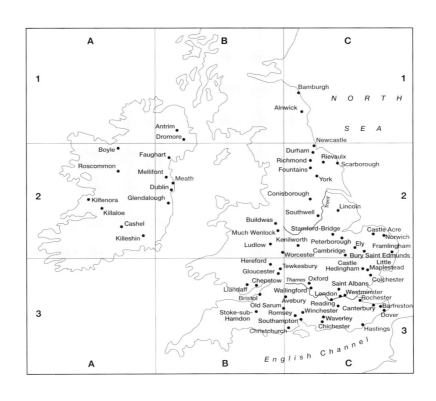

	A	B	C	
1			Bamburgh Alnwick Newcastle	**1**
2	Boyle Roscommon Kilfenora Killaloe Cashel Killeshin	Antrim Dromore Faughart Mellifont Meath Dublin Glendalough	*NORTH* *SEA* Durham Richmond Rievaulx Fountains Scarborough York Conisborough Lincoln Southwell Buildwas Stamford-Bridge Castle Acre Much Wenlock Kenilworth Norwich Ludlow Peterborough Ely Framlingham Cambridge Worcester Bury Saint Edmunds	**2**
3			Hereford Tewkesbury Castle Little Gloucester Hedingham Maplestead Chepstow Saint Albans Colchester Llandaff *Thames* Oxford Bristol Wallingford London Westminster Old Sarum Avebury Reading Rochester Stoke-sub- Romsey Winchester Canterbury Barfreston Hamdon Southampton Waverley Dover Christchurch Chichester Hastings *English Channel*	**3**
	A	B	C	

Glossary

Abacus, usually square uppermost part of a capital.

Acanthus, a thistle-like Mediterranean plant whose serrated leaves were the model for Corinthian capitals, and is often modified and used as a decorative motif on Romanesque capitals.

Aisle, the side of a nave (q.v.) separated from the nave proper by a colonnade; by extension, a similar feature in the transept (q.v.) or choir (q.v.).

Ambulatory, passageway around the choir, often a continuation of the side aisles of the nave. Cf. Radiating chapels.

Antependium, or altar frontal, ornamental covering for the front of an altar, originally made of fabric; later produced in stone, wood, precious metals or enamel; often contains figurative or symbolic pictures.

Apotropaic, object, picture or symbol used primarily in folk art to ward off evil; important feature of representations of animals and demons in Romanesque art.

Apse, a semi-circular or polygonal vaulted space behind the altar in a church.

Apsidiole, small apse-like chapel.

Arcade, a series of arches carried on piers or columns.

Archivolt, molding around the face of an arch, often ornamental.

Ashlar, hewn or squared stone, or stone facing.

Atrium, the colonnaded forecourt on the west side of an Early Christian church, originally the open central forecourt of a Roman house; cf. Galilee.

Barrel vault, semi-cylindrical vault with parallel abutments and of constant cross-section.

Basilica, in the architectural sense used in this book, a rectangular building with a definite orientation (i.e. symmetrical about the longitudinal axis only), consisting of a central nave (q.v.) and side aisles (q.v) separated by colonnades, with or without a transept (q.v.). Cf. Central-plan.

Bay, a vaulted division of a nave, aisle, choir or transept (qq.v) along its longitudinal axis.

Biforium, window divided into two arched areas by a central column.

Blind (arch, arcade), an arch or arcade with no opening, usually as decoration on a wall.

Calotte, the interior of a small dome or domical vault.

Capital, the head of a column.

Central-plan building, building symmetrical about its central point; a Central-plan building may be round, square, polygonal or cross-shaped. Cf. Basilica.

Chancel, interchangeable with Choir (q.v); sometimes, the area in front of the altar.

Chevet, an apse (q.v.), typically with ambulatory (q.v.) and radiating chapels (q.v.).

Choir, term borrowed from Classical Greek theater, used in Christian architecture to refer to the area at the end of the nave which is reserved for the clergy or monks, and which contains the altar and choir stalls.

Choir stalls, the rows of stepped seats on either side of the choir, facing inwards, for the use of the clergy.

Clerestory, the exterior wall of a nave (q.v.), above the level of the aisles (q.v.), with windows.

Cloister, quadrilateral enclosure surrounded by covered walkways, the centre of activity for the inhabitants of a monastery.

Concha, semi-circular niche with a semi-dome, usually called an apse.

Console, ornamental bracket that projects from the wall; also called a corbel.

Corbel, see Console.

Crossing, the area of a church where the nave is intersected by the transept.

Crypt, underground chamber beneath the altar in a church, usually containing a saint's relics. Though the chamber is underneath the choir, it can some times extend as far as the crossing. It is not always completely underground, so that the choir and altar are sometimes considerably higher than the nave and aisles; as a result, very impressive flights of steps were some times built to connect nave and choir.

Dendrochronology, tree-ring dating, method of dating the age of trees by the number of rings. The varying tree growth in dry and wet years causes uneven yearly rings; because of this, it is possible to use trees grown over a period of time in the same climate to produce a sequence of tree-rings . This in turn makes it possible to date the wood used in buildings precisely.

Domical vault, a dome-like vault with diagonal and transverse ridge ribs, used mainly in the Late Romanesque architecture of south-west France and Westphalia.

Donjon, central tall, strong tower in French castles which, unlike the keep, was designed for permanent habitation.

Dormitory, the room where monks slept in monasteries, and later, when individual cells were introduced, the term was applied to the building or floor which contained the cells.

Dwarf gallery, a low exterior passage lit by an equally low arcade, just below the roof of a building and usually in the apse of a church.

Engaged column, a column embedded in a wall, not free-standing.

Evangeliary, or gospel book, a liturgical book (handwritten in the Middle Ages, printed later) containing the complete text of the Gospels. Evangeliaries are among the most impressive examples of medieval book illumination.

Fresco, wall painting done with pigments suspended in water, which are painted onto wet plaster; the pigments are united permanently with the plaster as they dry.

Galilee, a chapel or porch at the entrance to a church.

Gallery, an upper storey, similar to a tribune, running along the side of a building and open on one side to the interior; in a church (basilica) above the side aisles, over the ambulatory (central-plan building) and also over the west end. The gallery was used to keep certain groups of worshippers apart (women, noblemen).

Great Hall, main living quarters of a castle or imperial palace.

Groin vault, type of vaulting caused by two equally large barrel vaults (q.v.) crossing at right angles; the angle formed by the intersecting vaults is the groin, hence the term.

Hall church, church whose nave (q,v.) and aisles (q.v.) are of equal height; a similar form has a raised nave but no clerestory (q.v.). Loosely, an aisle-less church.

Iconography, originally the discipline concerned with determining Classical portraits. In art history, the researching and interpretation of the content and symbolism of depicted objects, and in particular, Christian picture themes; an important feature is the consideration and researching of literary sources in philosophy and theology, which influenced the various motifs and the way they were depicted.

Impost, in church architecture, the course of stone at the top of a column or pilaster from which the arch or vault springs, and which transfers its weight to the columns or brickwork. Also: Voussoir.

Intrados, the inner face of an arch or vault.

Jamb, the part of a wall (cf. Reveal) lying at an angle to the sides of windows or portals, frequently containing columns or statuary within each stepped area. Cf. Portal.

Keep, tall, strong tower in medieval castles, used as an observation post and last refuge for those living in the castle, and, unlike the donjon (see p. 446), not designed for permanent habitation.

Lean-to roof, a one-sided pitched roof normally attached to a higher wall or building.

Lesene, or pilaster strip, a vertical strip designed to strengthen a wall; it has no base or capital, and in Romanesque architecture lesenes were often connected to each other by means of blind arches or round arch friezes.

Lintel, horizontal stone or timber at the top of a door or window.

Lunette, semi-circular space above doors and windows, sometimes framed and decorated.

Mandorla, almond-shaped stylized glory of light enclosing sacred figures such as the enthroned Christ or Madonna.

Meander pattern, or Greek key pattern, a continuous ornament consisting of lines turning at right angles to one another.

Narthex, the single-storey porch of an Early Christian church.

Nave, the area of a church between the façade and crossing or choir, specifically, the central area between the aisles (q.v.).

Nimbus, the disc or halo, usually golden, behind the head of a saint; the halo sometimes contains a cross, hence cruciform nimbus.

Octagon, eight-sided central plan building, or any building with eight sides; occurred frequently in the Middle Ages, not just in architecture but also in the design of crowns, as eight was considered to be a perfect number.

Oculus, a small circular opening admitting light at the top of a dome.

Pediment, a gable supported actually or apparently on columns.

Pendentive, curving triangular area linking a round dome or its supporting drum to the square space below.

Pilaster, a rectangular or polygonal pier used between doors or windows, which, like a column, has a base and capital.

Plate frieze, frieze composed of a number of plates arranged horizontally.

Portal, a doorway. A portal recessed in several steps was frequently used in Romanesque architecture; this meant that the often relatively small entrance was given considerable emphasis on the façade.

Profile, section of a building element such as a rib, jamb or cornice.

Psalter, a book containing the text of the 150 Old Testament psalms; it is an important prayer book in monasteries and frequently contains additions such as litanies and interpretations of the Old Testament. Occasionally commentaries or interpretations of the New Testament are added. Romanesque psalters and their illustrations are particularly important sources of information for understanding the symbolic content of medieval architectural sculpture.

Radiating chapels, chapels leading off from the ambulatory, and arranged in a semi-circular fashion.

Refectory, dining hall in a monastery, normally in the section of the cloister opposite the church.

Relic, mortal remains, or belongings, of a saint.

Respond, long narrow column or engaged column, mainly in Gothic architecture, which supports the arches and ribs of groin vaults or the profiles of arcade arches.

Retable, altarpiece, an artistically decorated back panel that is permanently attached to the altar.

Reveal, the part of a door, arch or window jamb which lies at an angle to the wall.

Rib, a structural moulding of a vault, not always visible because it is occasionally situated out of sight on the upper side of the vault.

Ridge turret, small narrow tower on the roof ridge, frequently used as a bellcote over the crossing of a church; particularly important feature of the churches of Cistercians and mendicant orders, as these do not have towers.

Rood screen, the screen dividing the choir (q.v.) from the nave (q.v.)

Rustication, rusticated ashlar, masonry with a rough surface finish; the front section projects and the stone block's edges are given a narrow straight edge to make it easier to move into position.

Sacramentary, the liturgical book used by the celebrant at Mass, and containing his part of the service. Pope Gregory the Great had already undertaken a reform of the mass, and under Charlemagne the various texts were collected and standardized; the emphasis of the illustrations in the book is on stressing particular initial letters. The pictorial program includes the Crucifixion, Christ in Majesty, scenes from the Life of Christ, and pictures of the Evangelists and saints.

Sanctuary, the part of a church or temple containing the shrine; in Christian churches the choir and high altar.

Scriptorium, the room in a medieval monastery where manuscripts were copied; also applied to particular schools of writing or painting that can be identified by stylistic characteristics.

Spolia, parts of a building, such as columns, capitals, friezes and cornices, that were originally in older, often Classical buildings, and were then reused when medieval buildings such as churches were built.

Spandrel, the approximately triangular space between the curve of an arch and the (usually rectangular) enclosing moldings.

Squinch, a series of arches placed diagonally at each corner of a square area to link it and the round dome above.

Strainer arch, an arch inserted into an internal space, such as a nave or between two buildings, to prevent the walls being pushed inwards.

Tetramorph, a composite figure combining the symbols of the four Evangelists derived from Revelation and Ezekiel; St. Jerome and Gregory the Great were the first to attribute the angel or man to Matthew, the lion to Mark, the ox (or bull) to Luke and the eagle to John.

Transept, section of a church at right-angles to the nave and in front of the choir.

Triforium, space above the nave (q.v.) arcade (q.v), below the clerestory (q.v.) The Triforium became general in the Romanesque period.

Triptych, picture, such as a winged altarpiece, made up of three panels, the outer ones being hinged so that they can be moved.

Triumphal arch, in ancient Rome an arch constructed for the entrance of a victorious general and his army. In the Christian basilica, the arch which forms the border between the choir and crossing, and the nave.

Trulli, conical, stone-roofed buildings used as dwellings in south-eastern Italy that date back to the Stone Age.

Trumeau, the central pier supporting the lintel of a monumental doorway or window.

Tympanum, in Classical times, the triangular area enclosed by a pediment, frequently decorated with sculptures; in medieval churches, the area above a portal enclosed by an arch, and the most important site for sculptures on the exterior of the church.

Voussoir, see Impost.

Westwork, a structure with towers to the west of the nave of an episcopal or monastery church; its lower storey often contains the portal, or the passageway from the portal to the nave, and the upper storey consists of galleries opening into the nave.

Acknowledgements

The great majority of photographs not listed here have been specially taken for this book by **Achim Bednorz**. He was commissioned by the publishers to photograph Romanesque architecture throughout Germany, France, Italy and Spain. **Klaus Frahm** took the new photographs in England (see below).

The publishers would like to thank all the museums, archives and photographers that have assisted in the preparation of this book and have given kind permission for their photographs to be reproduced:

Adam, Helmut: 438
Anders, Jörg P. (BPK, Berlin): 353 right, 414 bottom
Böhm, Osvaldo: 77 bottom, 396
Boreham Wood, Herts, Aerofilm Ltd. 119
Calveras, Jordi; Sangristà, Joan: 346, 348, 353 left, 388, 410
Charpy, Jean-Jacques: 422 left
Domkapital Aachen (Foto Münchow): © illus. 374 bottom left and right

Frahm, Klaus: 221, 222, 223 left, right, 225, 227 top right, bottom, 228 top, bottom, 229, 230, 231, 232 left, right, 234, 236 top, bottom, 237, 238 left, center, right, 239 bottom, 240, 241 left, center, right, 242, 243, 244, 245 top left, top right, bottom left, bottom right, 246 top, bottom left, bottom right, 247 top, bottom, 251, 320 top, center, bottom, 321 left, right, 322, 323 top, bottom left, bottom right, 390, 391 top
© Gallimard – Dessin Jacques Person (maps): 146, 462, 463, 464, 465
© Gallimard – Photo Pierre Belzeaux/Rapho: 372
© Gallimard – Photo Jean Bernaud: 460 bottom
© Gallimard – Photo Robert Emmet Bright/Rapho: 362 right
Grammes (BPK, Berlin): 364 bottom
Hunting Aerofilms Ltd.: 119
John Gibbons Studios: 8 left, center
Kersting, A. F.: 224, 239, 249, 250
Kirtz, Bernd: 378
Landesbildstelle Baden: 68 top

Landesbildstelle Rheinland-Pfalz: 51 top right
Liepe, Jürgen (BPK, Berlin): 365
McLean, Alick: 92 top right, 99
Monheim, Florian: 69 top
Mues-Funke: 361 left
National Monuments Record: 227 top left
© Photo R. M. N.: 373 top
© Photo R. M. N. – Arnaudet: 367 bottom left
Psille (BPK, Berlin): 364 top
Rheinisches Bildarchiv: 369, 375, 376, 377 top
© Photo Scala, Florence: 75 top right, 76, 90 top, 103 left, 110 left, right, 111 top right, bottom right, 112 top left, top right, bottom, 113, 280 top right, 305, 351 right, 398, 431, 436
Zodiaque: 78, 82, 85 bottom, 88, 98 left, 140, 141 center, right, 142 left, right, 199, 208 right, 339 top, 370, 413 right

Bibliography

The bibliography follows the sequence of essays in this volume. It is a combination of the secondary literature used by each author, and suggestions for further reading. This means that occasional repetitions of titles are unavoidable. Readers should bear in mind that each section is only a selection of the available literature.

ROLF TOMAN
Introduction

Ariès, Philippe, Bilder zur Geschichte des Todes, Munich/Vienna 1984
Bandmann, Günter, Mittelalterliche Architektur als Bedeutungsträger. Berlin 1994 (10th edition)
Barral I. Altet, Xavier; Avril, François; Gaborit-Chopin, D., Romanische Kunst. First volume: Mittel- und Südeuropa. Munich 1983; second volume: Nord- und Westeuropa. Munich 1984
Beck, Rainer (ed.), Der Tod. Ein Lesebuch von den letzten Dingen. Munich 1995
Beumann, Helmut (ed.), Kaisergestalten des Mittelalters. Munich 1985
Boockmann, Horst, Einführung in die Geschichte des Mittelalters. Munich 1985
Borst, Arno, Lebensformen im Mittelalter. Frankfurt/Berlin/Vienna 1979
Dinzelbacher, Peter (ed.), Europäische Mentalitätsgeschichte. Stuttgart 1993
Droste, Thorsten, Romanische Kunst in Frankreich. Cologne 1992
Duby, Georges, Die Zeit der Kathedralen. Frankfurt 1980
Duby, Georges, Die drei Ordnungen. Frankfurt 1981
Duby, Georges, Die Kunst der Zisterzienser. Stuttgart 1993
Durliat, Marcel, Romanische Kunst. Freiburg 1983
Durliat, Marcel, Die Kunst des frühen Mittelalters. Freiburg 1987
Durliat, Marcel, Romanisches Spanien. Würzburg 1995
Fischer, Hugo, Die Geburt der westlichen Zivilisation aus dem Geist des romanischen Mönchtums. Munich 1969
Franz, H. Gerhard, Spätromanik und Frühgotik (Kunst der Welt). Baden-Baden 1969
Fuhrmann, Horst, Deutsche Geschichte im hohen Mittelalter. Göttingen 1978
Fuhrmann, Horst, Einladung ins Mittelalter. Munich 1987
Geese, Uwe, Reliquienverehrung und Herrschaftsvermittlung. Die mediale Beschaffenheit der Reliquien im frühen Elisabethkult. Darmstadt and Marburg 1984
Goetz, Hans-Werner, Leben im Mittelalter. Munich 1986

Gurjewitsch, Aaron J., Das Weltbild des mittelalterlichen Menschen. Munich 1986
Hell, Vera and Hellmut, Die große Wallfahrt des Mittelalters. Tübingen 1964
Hennemann, Jürgen, Formenschatz der Romanik. Würzburg 1993
Herrmann, Bernd (ed.), Mensch und Umwelt im Mittelalter. Stuttgart 1986
Kubach, Erich; Bloch, Peter, Früh-und Hochromanik (Kunst der Welt). Baden-Baden 1964
Lambert, Malcolm, Ketzerei im Mittelalter. Munich 1981
Legner, Anton (ed.), Ornamenta Ecclesiae. Kunst und Künstler der Romanik. Vols. 1–3 (catalogue), Cologne 1985
Legner, Anton; Hirmer, Albert and Irmgard, Deutsche Kunst der Romanik. Munich 1982
Le Goff, Jacques, Die Geburt des Fegefeuers. Stuttgart 1986
Le Goff, Jacques, Die Intellektuellen im Mittelalter. Stuttgart 1986
Leriche-Andrieu, Françoise, Einführung in die romanische Kunst. Würzburg 1985
Luckhardt, Jochen; Nichoff, Franz (eds.), Heinrich der Löwe und seine Zeit. Vols. 1–3 (catalogue, essays), Munich 1995
Mirgeler, Albert, Revision der europäischen Geschichte. Freiburg/Munich 1971
Mrusek, Hans-Joachim, Romanik. Leipzig 1972
Oursel, Raymond; Stierlin, Henri, Architektur der Welt: Romanik. Berlin (undated)
Oursel, Raymond, Romanisches Frankreich. 11. Jahrhundert. Würzburg 1991
Oursel, Raymond, Romanisches Frankreich. 12. Jahrhundert. Würzburg 1991
Pernoud, Régine, Die Heiligen im Mittelalter. Munich 1994
Petzold, Andreas, Romanische Kunst. Cologne 1995
Schwaiger, Georg (ed.) Mönchtum, Orden, Klöster. Ein Lexikon. Munich 1993
Simson, O. v., Das Mittelalter II. Das hohe Mittelalter (Propyläen Kunstgeschichte, vol. 6). Berlin 1972
Toman, Rolf (ed.), Das hohe Mittelalter. Besichtigung einer fernen Zeit. Cologne 1988
Warnke, Martin, Bau und Überbau. Soziologie der mittelalterlichen Architektur nach den Schriftquellen. Frankfurt 1984
Wolf, A., Deutsche Kultur im Hochmittelalter. 1150–1250. Essen 1986
Wollasch, J., Mönchtum des Mittelalters zwischen Kirche und Welt. Munich 1973
Wollschläger, Hans, Die bewaffneten Wallfahrten gen Jerusalem. Geschichte der Kreuzzüge. Zurich 1973

WOLFGANG KAISER
Romanesque architecture in Germany

Adam, Ernst, Baukunst des Mittelalters I and II. Frankfurt 1968
Adam, Ernst, Baukunst der Stauferzeit in Baden-Württemberg und im Elsaß. Stuttgart 1977
Badstübner, Ernst, Klosterkirchen im Mittelalter. Munich 1985
Bandmann, Günter, Mittelalterliche Architektur als Bedeutungsträger. Berlin 1951
Binding Günter; Untermann, Matthias, Kleine Kunstgeschichte der mittelalterlichen Ordensbaukunst in Deutschland. Darmstadt 1985
Braunfels, Wolfgang, Die Welt der Karolinger und ihre Kunst. Munich 1968
Braunfels, Wolfgang, Karl der Große. Hamburg 1972
Dehio, Georg, Handbuch der deutschen Kunstdenkmäler, Baden-Württenberg I. Munich 1993
Eckstein, Hans, Die romanische Architektur. Cologne 1975
Einhard, Vita Caroli Magni. Stuttgart 1971
Fillitz, Hermann, Das Mittelalter I, Propyläen Kunstgeschichte vol. 5. Berlin 1969
Franz, H. Gerhard, Spätromanik und Frühgotik. Baden-Baden 1969
Haas, Walter, Romanik in Bayern. Stuttgart 1985
Hahn, Hanno, Die frühe Kirchenbaukunst der Zisterzienser. Berlin 1957
Heinrich der Löwe und seine Zeit, vols. 1–4, exhibition Brunswick 1995. Munich 1995
Hotz, Walter, Handbuch der Kunstdenkmäler in Elsaß und in Lothringen. Darmstadt 1970
Jantzen, Hans, Ottonische Kunst. Hamburg 1959
Kaiserin, Theophanu, vols. 1 and 2, exhibition Schnütgen Museum. Cologne 1991
Kiesow, Gottfried, Romanik in Hessen. Stuttgart 1984
Kubach, Hans-Erich; Bloch, Peter, Früh- und Hochromanik. Baden-Baden 1964
Kubach, Hans-Erich; Elbern, Victor H., Das frühmittelalterliche Imperium. Baden-Baden 1968
Kubach, Hans-Erich; Verbeek, Albert Romanische Baukunst an Rhein und Maas, 3 vols. Berlin 1976
Legner, Anton (ed.), Ornamenta Ecclesiae. Kunst und Künstler der Romanik. Vols. 1–3 (catalogue), Cologne 1985
Messerer, Wilhelm, Karolingische Kunst. Cologne 1973
Ecclesiae, Ornamenta, Kunst und Künstler der Romanik, vols. 1–3, exhibition Schnütgen Museum. Cologne 1985
Das Reich der Salier, exhibition of the Römisch-Germanisches

Zentralmuseum in Mainz. Sigmaringen 1992
Rhein und Maas, Kunst und Kultur 800–1400, vols. 1 and 2, exhibition Schnütgen Museum. Cologne 1972
Schütz, Bernhard; Müller, Wolfgang, Deutsche Romanik. Die Kirchenbauten der Kaiser, Bischöfe und Klöster. Freiburg 1989
Stadtluft, Hirsebrei und Bettelmönch, Die Stadt um 1300, exhibition Landesdenkmalamt Baden-Württemberg and Zurich. Stuttgart 1992
Thümmler, Hans, Romanik in Westfalen. Recklingshausen 1964
Wischermann, Heinfried, Romanik in Baden-Württemberg. Stuttgart 1987
Wischermann, Heinfried, Speyer I – Überlegungen zum Dombau Konrads II. und Heinrichs III., Berichte und Forschungen zur Kunstgeschichte vol. 11. Freiburg 1993
Die Zeit der Staufer, vols. 1–5, exhibition Württembergisches Landesmuseum. Stuttgart 1977

ALICK MCLEAN
Romanesque architecture in Italy

General:

Anthony, E. W., Early Florentine Architecture and Decoration. Cambridge, MA 1927
Bandmann, G., Mittelalterliche Architektur als Bedeutungsträger. Berlin 1994
Bandmann, G., Zur Bedeutung der romanischen Apsis, in: Wallraf-Richartz-Jahrbuch XV (1953), 28–46
Belli D'Elia, P., La Puglia. Milan 1987
Braunfels, W., Mittelalterliche Stadtbaukunst in der Toskana. Berlin 1988 (6th edition)
Busignani, A.; Bencini, R., Le chiese di Firenze: il Battistero di San Giovanni. Florence 1988
Cadei, F., L'Umbria. Milan 1994
Chierici, S., La Lombardia. Milan 1991
Ciccarelli, D., La Sicilia. Milan 1986
Conant, K. J., Carolingian and Romanesque Architecture 800–1200. Harmondsworth, New York 1959
Coroneo, R., Architettura Romanica dalla metà del mille al primo '300. Nuoro 1993
Cowdrey, H. E. J., The Age of Abbot Desiderius: Montecassino, the Papacy, and the Normans in the Eleventh and Early Twelfth Centuries. Oxford 1986 (2nd edition)
D'Onifrio, M.; Pace, V., La Campania. Milan 1981
Delgou, R., L'architettura di medioevo in Sardegna. Rome 1953
Demus, O., The Church of San Marco in Venice. Washington DC 1960
Fanucci, Q., La Basilica di San Miniato al Monte sopra Firenze, in: Italia Sacra II (1933) 1137–1207

Friedman, D., Florentine New Towns. Cambridge, MA 1988
Guyer, S., Der Dom in Pisa und das Rätsel seiner Entstehung, in: Münchner Jahrbuch der bildenden Kunst 1932, 351–376
Il Romanico Pistoiese nei suoi rapporti con l'arte romanica dell'occidente. Atti del I convegno internazionale di studi medioevali di storia e d'arte. Pistoia 1965
Jones, P., Economia e società nell'Italia medievale: la legenda della borghesia, in Storia d'Italia: Dal feudalismo al capitalismo. Annali I, ed. R. Romano and C. Vivanti, Turin 1978, 187–372
Kling, M., Romanische Zentralbauten in Oberitalien: Vorläufer und Anverwandte. Hildesheim, Zurich, New York 1995
Krautheimer, R., Introduction to an "Iconography of Mediaeval Architecture", in: Studies in Early Christian, Medieval and Renaissance Art, New York 1969, 115–150
Leccisotti, T., Le vicende della Basilica di Montecassino attraverso la documentazione archeologica, Miscellanea Cassinese, 36, 1973
Little, L. K., Religious Poverty and the Profit Economy in Medieval Europe. Ithaca 1978
McLean, A., Sacred Space & Public Policy: The Origins, Decline and Revival of Prato's Piazza della Pieve. Princeton University, Diss. 1993
Moretti, I.; Stopani, R., La Toscana. Milan 1991
Parlato, E.; Romano, S., Roma e il Lazio. Milan 1992
Porter, A. K., Lombard Architecture. New Haven 1917
Prandi, A.; Chierici, S.; Tamanti, G.; Reggiori, F., La basilica di Sant'Ambrogio a Milano. Florence 1945
Rill, B., Sizilien im Mittelalter: Das Reich der Araber, Normannen und Staufer. Stuttgart, Zurich 1995
Rivoira, G. T.; Rushforth, G. M. (trans.) Lombardic Architecture: Its Origin, Development and Derivations, 2 vols. Oxford 1933
Romanini, A. M. and others, L'arte medievale in Italia. Florence 1988
Romano, C. G., La Basilicata, La Calabria. Milan 1988
Salmi, M., Decorazione Romanica in Toscana, in: Spazio 2:4 (1951), 1–4
Salmi, M., L'architettura romanica in Toscana. Milan, Rome 1927
Salmi, M., Chiese romaniche della Toscana. Milan 1961
Sanpaolesi, P., Il Duomo di Pisa e l'architettura romanica toscana delle origine. Pisa 1975
Santoro, R.; Cassata, G.; Costantino, G.; Schaffran, E., Die Kunst der Langobarden in Italien. Jena 1941
Schulz, H. W., Denkmäler der Kunst des Mittelalters in Unteritalien. 4 vols. Dresden 1860

Seidel, M., Dombau, Kreuzzugsidee und Expansionspolitik. Zur Ikonographie der Pisaner Kathedralbauten, in: Frühmittelalterliche Studien 11 (1977), 348–350
Serra, R., La Sardegna. Milan 1989
Shearer, C., The Renaissance of Architecture in Southern Italy. Cambridge 1935
Silva, R., Architettura del socolo XI nel tempo della riforma pregregoriana in Toscana, in: Critica d'Arte XLIV, 163–165, 1979, 66–96
Stocchi, S., L'Emilia-Romagna. Milan 1988
Suitner, G., Le Venezie. Milan 1991
Tabacco, G., Power and Struggle for Hegemony in Medieval Italy. Cambridge 1992
Thummler, H., Die Baukunst des 11. Jahrhunderts in Italien, in: Römisches Jahrbuch für Kunstgeschichte 3, 1939, 141–226
Toesca, P., Storia dell'arte italiana dalle origini alla fine del secolo XIII. Turin 1927
Trachtenberg, M., Gothic/Italian Gothic: Towards a Redefinition, in: JSAH 50:1 (March 1991), 22–37
Venturi, A., Storia dell'arte italiana III. Milan 1904
Verzár Bornstein, C., Portals and Politics in the Early Italian City State: The Sculpture of Nicholaus in Context. Parma 1988
Verzone, P., L'architettura religiosa dell'alto medioevo nell'Italia settentrionale. Milan 1942
Waley, D. P., The Italian City Republics. London, New York 1988

Monasteries and the Ideal City:
Braunfels, W., Monasteries of Western Europe, The Architecture of the Orders. Princeton 1972
Dynes, W., The Medieval Cloister as Pritco of Salomon, in: Gesta: The Cloister Symposium XII (1973), 62–69
Horn, W., On the Origins of the Medieval Cloister, in: Gesta: The Cloister Symposium XII (1973), 13–52
Horn, W., The Plan of St. Gall. A Study of the Architecture and Economy of, and Life in a Paradigmatic Carolingian Monastery. Berkeley 1979
Rosenau, H., The Ideal City: Its Architectural Evolution in Europe. Cambridge 1983

BERNHARD AND ULRIKE LAULE
Romanesque architecture in France

General:

Conant, Kenneth John, Carolingian and Romanesque Architecture, 800–1200, Pelican History of Art, 1959

Congrès Archéologique de France, ed. Société française d'archéologie. Paris 1834 ff.
G. Dehio and G. v. Bezold, Die kirchliche Baukunst des Abendlandes. Stuttgart 1884–1901
Le dictionnaire des églises de France, 5 vols., Paris 1966–1969
Enlart, Camille, Manuel d'archéologie française, 3 vols., 3rd edition. Paris 1927
Frankl, Paul, Die frühmittelalterliche und romanische Baukunst (Handbuch der Kunstwissenschaft). Wildpark-Potsdam 1926, 151ff.
Lavedan, Pierre, Histoire de l'art. Moyen Age et Temps modernes. Paris 1944
de Lasteyrie, Robert, L'architecture religieuse en France à l'époque romane, 2nd edition. Paris 1929

Burgundy and territories belonging to it (Nivernais and western Switzerland):

Anfray, Marcel, L'architecture religieuse du Nivernais au moyen-âge. Paris 1951
Armi, Clement Edson, Saint-Philibert at Tournus and the wall systems of first Romanesque architecture. Diss. Columbia University, USA 1973
Conant, Kenneth John, Cluny. Les églises et la maison du chef d'ordre. Mâcon 1968
Erlande-Brandenburg, Alain, Iconographie de Cluny III, in: Bulletin Monumental 126 (1968), 293–332
Gall, Ernst, Die Abteikirche Saint-Philibert in Tournus, in: Der Cicerone 4 (1912), 624–636
Gall, Ernst, Studien zur Geschichte des Chorumgangs, in: Monatshefte für Kunstwissenschaft 5 (1912), 134–149, 358–376, 508–519
Gall, Ernst, Saint-Philibert in Tournus, in: Zeitschrift für Kunstgeschichte 17 (1954), 179–182
Hahn, H., Die frühe Kirchenbaukunst der Zisterzienser. Berlin 1957
Hubert, Jean, L'architecture religieuse du haut moyen-âge en France. Paris 1952
Marino Malone, Carolyn, Les fouilles de Saint-Bénigne de Dijon (1976–1978) et le problème de l'église de l'an mil, in: Bulletin Monumental 138 (1980), 253ff.
Oursel, Raymond and Anne-Marie, Les églises romanes de L'Autonois et du Brionnais. Mâcon 1956
Salet, Francis, Cluny III, in: Bulletin Monumental 126 (1968), 235–292
Salet, P., La Madeleine de Vézelay. Melun 1948
Schlink, Wilhelm, Saint-Bénigne in Dijon. Untersuchungen zur Abteikirche Wilhelms von Volpiano (962–1031). Berlin 1978
Sennhauser, Hans Rudolf, Romainmôtier und Payerne. Studien

zur Cluniazenserarchitektur des 11. Jahrhunderts in der Westschweiz. Basel 1970

Stratford, N., Les bâtiments de l'abbaye de Cluny à l'époque médiévale. Etat des questions, in: Bulletin Monumental 150 (1992), 383–411

Vallery-Radot, Jean, Saint-Philibert de Tournus. Paris 1955

Virey, Jean, Paray-le-Monial et les églises du Brionnais. Paris 1926

Wischermann, Heinfried and others, Saint-Philibert in Tournus. Baugeschichte und architekturgeschichtliche Stellung. Berichte und Forschungen zur Kunstgeschichte 10. Freiburg 1988

Wollasch, Joachim, Cluny – Licht der Welt. Aufstieg und Niedergang der klösterlichen Gemeinschaft. Zurich, Düsseldorf 1996

Northern France (Champagne, Normandy, Belgium):

Anfray, Marcel, L'architecture normande. Paris 193?

Baum, Julius, Romanische Baukunst in Frankreich. Stuttgart 2nd edition 1928, V

Baylé, Maylis, La Trinité de Caen. Sa place dans l'histoire de l'architecture et du décor romans. Paris 1979

Bellmann, F., Zur Bau- und Kunstgeschichte der Stiftskirche von Nivelles. Munich 1941

Bony, Jean, La technique normande du mur épais à l'époque romane, in: Bulletin Monumental 98 (1939), 153ff.

Carlson, Eric G., The abbey church of Saint-Etienne at Caen in the 11th and early 12th centuries. Diss. Yale 1968

Carlson, Eric G., Excavations at Saint-Etienne, Caen (1969), in: Gesta 10 (1971), 223ff.

Chanteux, Henri, L'abbé Thierry et les églises de Jumièges, du Mont-Saint-Michel et de Bernay, in: Bulletin Monumental 98 (1939), 67ff.

Froidevaux, Yves-Marie, L'église abbatiale de Cerisy-la-Forêt, in Les Monuments Historiques 103 (1979), 33ff.

Guérin, Jean, Les abbayes de Caen, in: Les Monuments Historiques 103 (1979), 43ff.

Liess, Reinhard, Der frühromanische Kirchenbau des 11. Jahrhunderts in der Normandie. Analysen und Monographien der Hauptbauten. Munich 1967

Merlet, Jean, L'église Saint-Etienne de Caen, in: Les Monuments Historiques 14 (1968), 62ff.

Mottart, A., La Collégiale Sainte-Gertrude de Nivelles. Nivelles 1962

Rave, Paul Ortwin, Der Emporenbau in romanischer und frühgotischer Zeit. Bonn, Leipzig 1924

Vallery-Radot, Jean, Le Mont-Saint-Michel. Travaux et découvertes, in: Congrès Archéologique (1966), 413ff.

Wischermann Heinfried and others, Die romanische Kirchenbaukunst der Normandie – ein entwicklungsgeschichtlicher Versuch. Berichte und Forschungen zur Kunstgeschichte 6. Freiburg 1982

Pilgrimage churches/Auvergne:

Deyres, Marcel, Sainte-Foy de Conques, in: Bulletin Monumental 123 (1965), 7ff.

Durliat, Marcel, La basilique St. Sernin de Toulouse, in: Bulletin Monumental 121 (1963), 149ff.

Herbers, Klaus, Der Jakobsweg. Wiesbaden 1986

Kubach, Hans Erich; Bloch, P., Früh- und Hochromanik (Kunst der Welt). Baden-Baden 1964, 84ff.

Lesueur, Frédérique, Sainte-Foy de Conques, in: Bulletin Monumental 124 (1966), 259ff.

du Ranquet, H. and E., L'église Saint-Paul d'Issoire, in: Bulletin Monumental 94 (1935), 277ff.

Western France (Aquitaine, Poitou, Maine):

Crozet, René, L'art roman en Poitou. Paris 1948

Crozet, René, Fontevrault, in: Congrès Archéologique (1964), 426–481

Darans, Ch., La Cathédrale Saint-Pierre d'Angoulême, in: Bulletin Monumental 120 (1962), 231ff.

Erlande-Brandenburg, Alain, Le "Cimetière des Rois" à Fontevrault, in: Congrès Archéologique (1964), 482–492

Roux, J., La basilique Saint-Front de Périgueux. Périgueux 1920

Salet, Francis, Notre-Dame de Cunault. Les campagnes de construction, in: Congrès Archéologique (1964), 636–676

Tonnelier, P. M. A., La Cathédrale d'Angoulême, in: Mélanges offerts à René Crozet, vol. 1. Poitiers 1966, 507ff.

Southern France (Provence and Languedoc):

Aubert, Marcel, L'architecture cistercienne en France, 2nd edition. Paris 1947

Laule, B. and U.; Wischermann, H., Kunstdenkmäler in Südfrankreich. Darmstadt 1989

Puig i Cadafalch, J., La géographie et les origines du premier art roman. Paris 1935

Secular buildings:

Babelon, Jean Pierre (ed.), Le Château en France. Paris 1986

Deyres, Marcel, Le Donjon de Langeais, in: Bulletin Monumental 128 (1970), 179–193

Deyres, Marcel, Les Châteaux de Foulques Nerra, in: Bulletin Monumental 132 (1974), 7–28

Enaud, François, Châteaux forts en France. Paris 1958

Harmand, Louis, Houdan et l'évolution des donjons au XIIième siècle, in: Bulletin Monumental 127 (1969), 188–207

Harmand, Louis, Le Donjon de Houdan, études complémentaires, in: Bulletin Monumental 130 (1972), 191–212

Héliot, Pierre, L'Age du donjon d'Etampes et de Provins, in: Mémoires de la Société nationale des antiquaires de France (1967), 289–308

Héliot, Pierre, La Genèse des châteaux de plan rectangulaire en France et en Angleterre, in: Bulletin de la Société nationale des antiquaires de France (1965), 238–257

Ritter, Raymond, Châteaux, donjons et places fortes. L'architecture militaire française. Paris 1953

Salch, Charles-Laurent, Dictionnaire des châteaux et des fortifications du Moyen Age en France. Strasbourg 1979

BRUNO KLEIN
Romanesque architecture in Spain and Portugal

General:

Durliat, M., Hispania romanica. Die hohe Kunst der romanischen Epoche in Spanien. Vienna, Munich 1962

Gòmey Moreno, M., El arte románico español. Madrid 1934

Gudiol, Ricard, J.; Nuño, Gaya J. A., Arquitectura y escultura románicas (Ars Hispaniae V). Madrid 1948

Whitehill, Muir W., Spanish Romanesque Architecture of the Eleventh Century. Oxford 1941, reprint 1968

de Palol, P.; Hirmer, M., Spanien: Kunst des frühen Mittelalters vom Westgotenreich bis zum Ende der Romanik. New edition Munich 1991

Spanische Kunstgeschichte, Eine Einführung. Vol 1: Von der Spätantike bis zur frühen Neuzeit. Ed. Sylvaine Hänsel and Henrik Karge. Berlin 1992

Vinayo Gonzalez, A., L'ancien royaume des Leon roman. La Pierre-qui-vivre 1972

Yarza, J., Arte y arquitectura en España 500-1250. Madrid 1987

Pre-Romanesque architecture:

Arenas, J. F., La arquitectura mozárabe. Barcelona 1972

Fontaine, J., L'Art préroman hispanique, I. La Pierre-qui-vivre 1973

Noack-Haley, S.; Arbeiter, A., Asturische Königsbauten des 9. Jahrhunderts. (Madrider Beiträge 22). Mainz 1994

Schlunk, H., Arte visigodo, arte asturiano (Ars Hispaniae II). Madrid 1947

Early and High Romanesque in Catalonia, Aragon and Navarra:

Crozet, R., L'art roman en Navarre et Aragon. Conditions historiques. In: Cahiers de la civilisation médiévale 5 (1962), 35–61

Durliat, M., L'art roman en Navarre et en Aragon. In: Centre international d'études romanes 1973, I, 5–18

Durliat, M., La Catalogne et le "premier art roman". In: Bulletin Monumental 147 (1989), 209–238

Junyent, E., Catalogne romane. La Pierre-qui-vivre 1960–61

Krüger, K., Die katalanische Kapitellskulptur des elften Jahrhunderts. In: Mitteilungen der Carl Justi-Vereinigung 5 (1993), 26–42

de Lojendio, L.-M., Navarre romane. La Pierre-qui-vivre 1967

Lorente, E.; Francisco, J.; Galtier Martí, F.; García Guatas, M., El nacimiento del arte románico en Aragón. Arquitectura. Zaragoza 1982

Puig i Cadafalch, J., Le premier art roman. Paris 1938

Puig i Cadafalch, J.; de. Falguera, A.; Goday i Casals, J., L'arquitectura romànica a Catalunya. Barcelona 1908–18

Architecture along the pilgrim route:

Bottineau, Y., Les chemins de Saint-Jacques. Paris 1964

Conant, K. J., The Early Architectural History of Santiago de Compostela. Cambridge 1926

D'Emilio, J., The Building and the Pilgrims' Guide. In: J. Williams, A. Stone (eds.) The Codex Calixtinus and the Shrine of St. James. Tübingen 1992, 185–206

Herbers, K., Mit einem mittelalterlichen Pilgerführer unterwegs nach Santiago. 2nd edition, Tübingen 1986

Iñiguez Almech, F., Las empresas constructivas de Sancho el Mayor. Es castillo de Loarre. In: Archivo Español de Arte 43 (1970), 363–373

Lambert, E., Le pèlerinage de Compostelle. Etudes d'histoire médiévale. Paris, Toulouse 1959

Moralejo-Alvarez, S., The Codex Calixtinus as an Art-Historical Source. In: J. Williams, A. Stone (eds.) The Codex Calixtinus and the Shrine of St. James. Tübingen 1992, 207–227

Viellard, J., Le guide du pèlerin de Saint-Jacques de Compostelle. 5th

edition, Paris 1984
Williams, J., La arquitectural del Camino de Santiago. In: Co mostelanum 29 (1984), 267–290
Williams, J., San Isidoro in León: Evidence for a New History. In: Art Bulletin 55 (1973), 170–184

Regionalisms in the middle of the twelfth century:

Rincón García, W., Arte medieval. In: Summa Artis. Historia general del Arte vol. XXX, "Arte portugués." Madrid 1986, 11–238
Hesey, C. K., The Salmantine Laterns: Their Origin and Development. Cambridge 1937
Gaya Nuño, J. A., El románico en la provincia de Soria. Madrid 1946

New tendencies towards Internationalisation and regional traditions:

Moralejo-Alvarez, S., Le porche de Gloire de la Cathédrale de Compostelle – Problèmes de sources et d'interprétation. In: Les Cahiers de Saint-Michel de Cuxa 16 (1985), 92–116
Lambert, E., Les chapelles octogonales d'Eunate et de Torres del Río. Paris 1928
Lambert, E., L'art gothique en Espagne. Paris 1931
Dathe, S., Die Kirche La Vera Cruz in Segovia. Untersuchungen zur Bedeutung des romanischen Zentralbaus. In: Mitteilungen der Carl Justi-Vereinigung 5 (1993), 92–121
Martinell, C., Les monastères cisterciens de Poblet et de Santes Creus. In: Congrès archéologique 117 (1959), 98–128
Lambert, E., La cathédrale de Lérida. In: Congrès archéologique 117 (1959), 136–143
Lara Peinado, F., Lerida. La Seo antigua. Lerida 1977

HEINFRIED WISCHERMANN
Romanesque architecture in Great Britain

Andrew, Martin, Chichester Cathedral, The Problem of the Romanesque Choir Vault, in: Journal of the British Archaeological Association 135 (1982), 11ff.
Aylmer, G. E. and Reginald Cant, A History of York Minster. Oxford 1977
BAACT (British Archaeological Association Conference Transactions) I, 1975 Worcester (1978), II, 1976 Ely (1979), III, 1977 Durham, IV, 1978 Wells and Glastonbury (1981), V, 1979 Canterbury (1982), VI, 1980 Winchester (1983), VII, 1981

Gloucester/Tewkesbury (1985), VIII, 1982 Lincoln (1986), X, 1984 London (1990)
Bandmann, Günter, Die Bischofskapelle in Hereford, in: Festschrift H. von Einem. Bonn 1964, 2ff.
Barlow, Frank, The English Church 1000–1066. London 1979
Barlow, Frank, William Rufus. London 1983
Barlow, Frank, The Norman Conquest and Beyond. London 1983
Barlow, Frank, Thomas Becket. London 1986
Bennett, Paul and others, Excavations at Canterbury Castle. Canterbury 1982
Biddle, Martin, Excavations near Winchester Cathedral 1961–1969. 1970
Bony, Jean, Tewkesbury et Pershore – deux élévations à quatre étages de la fin du IIe s., in: Bull. Mon. 96 (1937), 281ff., 503ff.
Bony, Jean, Le technique normande du mur épais, in: Bull. Mon. 98 (1939), 153ff.
Bony, Jean, Durham et la traditionne saxonne, in: Festschrift Louis Grodecki. Paris 1981, 72ff.
Brett, Martin, The English Church under Henry I. Oxford 1975
Brown, Reginald Allen, The Norman Conquest and the Genesis of English castles, in: Château-Gaillard 1966 (1969) 1ff.
Bussby, Frederick, Winchester Cathedral 1079–1979. Ringwood 1979
Chambers, James, The Norman Kings. London 1981
Cherry, Bridget, Romanesque Architecture in Eastern England, in: Journal of the British Archaeological Association 131 (1978), 1ff.
Clapham, Alfred, English Romanesque Architecture before the Conquest. Oxford 1930
Clapham, Alfred, English Romanesque Architecture after the Conquest. Oxford 1934
Colvin, Howard, The History of the King's Works, I. London 1963
Cronne, Henry Alfred, The Reign of Stephen. London 1970
Crook, John and others, Winchester Cathedral. Chichester 1993
Douglas, David C., William the Conqueror. London 1977
Draper, Peter, Recherches récentes sur l'architecture dans les îles britanniques à la fin de l'époque romane et au début du gothique, in: Bull. Mon. 144 (1986), 305ff.
English Romanesque Art, 1066–1200. London 1984
Fawcett, Richard, Scottish Abbeys and Priories. London 1994
Fergusson, Peter, Architecture of Solitude: Cistercian Abbeys in 12th-century England. Princeton 1984
Fernie, Eric, Enclosed Apses and Edward's church at Westminster, in:

Archaeologia 104 (1973), 235ff.
Fernie, Eric, The Architecture of the Anglo Saxons. London 1983
Gem, Richard, The Romanesque Rebuilding of Westminster Abbey, in: Proceedings of the Battle Conference 3 (1980), 33ff.
Gem, Richard, Chichester Cathedral: When was the Romanesque Church Begun? in: Proceedings of the Battle Conference 3 (1980), 61ff.
Gibson, Margaret T., Lanfranc of Bec. Oxford 1978
Goege, Thomas, Theorie und Praxis der Restaurierung im Gothic Revival: Die Restaurierungsbewegung der "Ecclesiologists." Diss. Freiburg 1981
Guillaume le Conquérant et son temps, Rouen 1987/88
Hearn, Millard F., The Rectangular Ambulatory in English Medieval Architecture, in: Journal of Social Archaeological History 30 (1971), 187ff.
Hearn, Millard F., Romsey Abbey, in: Gesta 14 (1975), 27ff.
Hobbs, Mary and others, Chichester Cathedral. Chichester 1994
Kahn, Deborah, Canterbury Cathedral and its Romanesque Sculpture. London 1991
Kenyon, John R., Medieval Fortifications (The Archaeology of Medieval Britain). Leicester, London 1990
Kidson, Peter and others, A History of English Architecture. Harmondsworth 1965
Knowles, David, The Monastic Order in England, 940–1216. Cambridge 1940
Knowles, David, The Monastic Constitutions of Lanfranc. Cambridge 1949
Knowles, David and others, The Heads of Religious Houses: England and Wales 940–1216. Cambridge 1972
Lehmann-Brockhaus, Otto, Lateinische Schriftquellen zur Kunst in England, 4 vols. Munich 1955–1960
Little, Bryan, Architecture in Norman Britain. London 1985
McAleer, Philip, The Romanesque Church Façade in Britain. Diss. London 1985
Musset, Lucien, Angleterre Romane, 2 vols. La Pierre-qui-vivre 1984–88
Norton, Christopher; David Park, Cistercian Art and Architecture in the British Isles. Cambridge 1986
Phillips, Derek, Excavations at York Minster II: The Cathedral of Archbishop Thomas of Bayeux. London 1985
Platt, Colin, Medieval England: A Social History and Archaeology from the Conquest to AD 1600. London, New York 1978
Renn, Derek, Norman Castles in Britain. London 1968, 1973
Rowley, Trevor, The Norman Heritage. London 1983
Schünke, Susanne, Entwicklungen in

den Chorformen englischer Kirchen vom 11. bis ins 13. Jh. Diss. Cologne 1987
Service, Alastair, The Buildings of Britain: Anglo-Saxon and Norman. London 1982
Stoll, Robert Th.; Roubier, Jean, Britannia Romanica – Die hohe Kunst der romanischen Epoche in England, Schottland und Irland. Vienna, Munich 1966
Warren, Wilfred L., Henry II. London 1977
Watkin, David, English Architecture, A Concise History. London 1979
Webb, Geoffrey, Architecture in England: The Middle Ages. Harmondsworth 1954
Wilson, David M., The Bayeux Tapestry. London 1966
Wilson, David M., Die Schlacht von Hastings und das Ende der angelsächsischen Herrschaft, in: Sachsen und Angelsachsen. Hamburg 1978, 117ff.
Wischermann, Heinfried and others, Der romanische Kirchenbau der Normandie – ein entwicklungsgeschichtlicher Versuch (BuF 6). Freiburg 1982
Wischermann, Heinfried and others, Die romanische Kathedrale von Worcester – Baugeschichte und architekturgeschichtliche Stellung (BuF 9). Freiburg 1985
Wischermann, Heinfried, Die Rippengewölbe der Kathedrale von Durham – Überlegungen zur Frühzeit der Gotik in England (BuF 12). Freiburg 1996
Wood, Margaret, Norman Domestic Architecture. London 1974
Zarnecki, George, English Romanesque Sculpture, 1066–1140. London 1951
Zarnecki, George, Later English Romanesque Sculpture, 1140–1210. London 1953
Zarnecki, George, Romanesque Lincoln, The Sculpture of the Cathedral. Lincoln 1988

Architecture in Scandinavia:

Anker, Peter; Andersson, Aron, L'art scandinave. La Pierre-qui-Vire 1968/69
Bugge, Gunnar, Stabkirchen – Mittelalterliche Baukunst in Norwegen. Regensburg 1994
Donnelly, Marian C., Architecture in the Scandinavian Countries. Cambridge, MA 1992
Phleps, Hermann, Die norwegischen Stabkirchen. Sprache und Deutung der Gefüge. Karlsruhe 1958
Ringbom, Sixten and others, Konsten i Finland. Helsingfors 1978
Tuulse, Armin, Scandinavia Romanica. Die hohe Kunst der romanischen Epoche in Dänemark, Norwegen und Schweden. Vienna, Munich 1968

Romanesque art in central Europe:

Kampis, Antal, Kunst in Ungarn. Budapest 1966
Merhantová, Anezka, Romanische Kunst in Polen, der Tschechoslowakei, Ungarn, Rumänien, Jugoslawien. Prague 1974
Dercsényi, Dezsö, Der königliche Palast von Esztergom. Budapest 1974
Dercsényi, Dezsö, Romanische Baukunst in Ungarn. Budapest 1975
Genthon, István, Kunstdenkmäler in Ungarn. Munich, Berlin 1974
Zachwatowicz, Jan, Polnische Architektur bis zur Mitte des 19. Jhs. Warsaw 1956
Knox, Brian, The Architecture of Poland. London 1971
Swiechowski, Zygmunt, Romanesque Art in Poland. Warsaw 1983
Lozinski, Jerzy Z., Kunstdenkmäler in Polen: Südpolen. Warsaw, Leipzig 1984
Bachmann, Erich and others, Romanik in Böhmen. Munich 1977
Kuthan, Jirí, Die mittelalterliche Baukunst der Zisterzienser in Böhmen und Mähren. Munich, Berlin 1982
Poche, Emanuel, Kunstdenkmäler in der Tschechoslowakei: Böhmen und Mähren. Darmstadt 1986

UWE GEESE
Romanesque sculpture

Ariès, P., Geschichte des Todes. Munich 1982
Bandmann, G., Mittelalterliche Architektur als Bedeutungsträger. Berlin 1951
Barral, I.; Altet, X.; Avril, F.; Gaborit-Chopin, D. (eds.) Romanische Kunst. First volume: Mittel- und Südeuropa 1060-1220. Munich 1983; second volume: Nord- und Westeuropa 1060–1220. Munich 1984
Borella, M., Modena e provincia. Guida artistica e monumentale. Bologna, undated
Borst, O., Alltagsleben im Mittelalter. Frankfurt 1983
Bredekamp, H., Die nordspanische Hofskulptur und die Freiheit der Bildhauer, in: H. Beck, K. Hengevoss-Dürkop (eds.), Studien zur Geschichte der europäischen Skulptur im 12./13. Jahrhundert. Vol. 1 Text, Frankfurt 1994
Bredekamp, H., Romanische Skulptur als Experimentierfeld. In: Hänsel/Karge (eds.), Spanische Kunstgeschichte: Eine Einführung. Vol. 1: Von der Spätantike bis zur frühen Neuzeit. Berlin 1991
Bredekamp, H., Wallfahrt als Versuchung. San Martin in Frómista. In: Kunstgeschichte – Aber wie? Berlin 1991
Budde, R., Deutsche Romanische Skulptur 1050–1250. Photographs by

Albert Hirmer and Irmgard Ernstmeier-Hirmer. Munich 1979
Bußmann, K., Burgund. Kunst, Geschichte, Landschaft. Cologne 1977, 1987
Chierici, S., Romanische Lombardei. Würzburg 1978
Chierichetti, S., Verona. Illustrated artistic guide. Milan, undated
Claussen, P. C., Künstlerinschriften, in: Ornamenta Ecclesiae. Exhibition catalogue, Cologne 1985, vol. 1, 263ff.
Dietel, A., Künstlerinschriften als Quelle für Status und Selbstverständnis von Bildhauern, in: H. Beck, K. Hengevoss-Dürkop (eds.), Studien zur Geschichte der europäischen Skulptur im 12./13. Jahrhundert. Vol. 1 Text, Frankfurt 1994
Dinzelbacher, P., Europäische Mentalitätsgeschichte. Stuttgart 1993
Droste, T., Romanische Kunst in Frankreich. Cologne 1989, 1992
Duby, G., Sculpture. The Great Art of the Middle Ages from the Fifth to Fifteenth Century. New York 1990
Durliat, M., La sculpture romane en Roussillon. Vols. I-IV, Perpignan 1952–54
Durliat, M., Romanisches Spanien. Würzburg 1995
Eco, U., Kunst und Schönheit im Mittelalter. Munich 1991, 1993
Eliade, M., Die Religionen und das Heilige. Darmstadt 1976
Fegers, H., Provence, Côte d'Azur, Dauphiné, Rhône-Tal. Reclams Kunstführer Frankreich. Vol. IV, Stuttgart 1967, 1975
Fillitz, H., Das Mittelalter I. Propyläen Kunstgeschichte. Special edition, Frankfurt, Berlin 1990
Fischer, Pace and others, Kunstdenkmäler in Rom. Vol. 2, Darmstadt 1988
Fischer, H. J., Rom. Zweieinhalb Jahrtausende Kunst und Kultur in der Ewigen Stadt. Ein Reisebegleiter. Cologne 1986
Forster, K. W., Benedetto Antelami. Der große romanische Bildhauer Italiens. Munich 1961
Grimme, E. G., Goldschmiedekunst im Mittelalter. Form und Bedeutung des Reliquiars von 800 bis 1500. Cologne 1972
Gurjewitsch, A. J., Das Individuum im Mittelalter. Munich 1994
Heinrich der Löwe und seine Zeit. Herrschaft und Repräsentation der Welfen 1125-1235. Vol. 1-3, ed. by J. Luckhardt and F. Niehoff. Exhibition catalogue Brunswick 1995, Munich 1995
Huizinga, J., Herbst des Mittelalters. Stuttgart 1969
Kauffmann, G.; Andreae, B., Toskana (ohne Florenz). Kunstdenkmäler und Museen. Reclams Kunstführer Italien. Vol. III, 2, Stuttgart 1984
Kauffmann, G., Emilia-Romagna,

Marken, Umbrien. Baudenkmäler und Museen. Reclams Kunstführer Italien. Vol. IV, Stuttgart 1971, 1987
Kerscher, G., Benedictus Antelami oder das Baptisterium von Parma. Kunst und kommunales Selbstverständnis. Diss. Munich 1986
Krüger, R., Kleine Welt in Elfenbein. Dresden 1967
Legler, R., Apulien (DuMont Kunst-Reiseführer). Cologne 1987
Legler, R., Languedoc – Roussillon. Von der Rhône bis zu den Pyrenäen. Cologne 1981, 1985
Legler, A.; Hirmer, A. and I., Deutsche Kunst der Romanik. Munich 1982
Lyman, Th., Heresy and the History of Monumental Sculpture in Romanesque Europe, in: H. Beck, K. Hengevoss-Dürkop (eds.), Studien zur Geschichte der europäischen Skulptur im 12./13. Jahrhundert. Vol. 1 Text, Frankfurt 1994
Mende, U.; Hirmer, A. and others, Die Bronzetüren des Mittelalters 800–1200. Munich 1994
Meyer, Schapiro, Romanische Kunst. Cologne 1987
Michel, P., Tiere als Symbol und Ornament. Möglichkeiten und Grenzen der ikonographischen Deutung, gezeigt am Beispiel des Zürcher Großmünsterkreuzgangs. Wiesbaden 1979
Minne-Séve, V., Romanische Kathedralen und Kunstschätze in Frankreich. Eltville 1991
Moretti, I.; Stopani, R., Romanische Toskana. Würzburg 1983
Pace, V., Kunstdenkmäler in Süditalien. Darmstadt 1994
Palol, P. de, Spanien. Kunst des frühen Mittelalters vom Westgotenreich bis zum Ende der Romanik. Photographs by Max, Albert and Irmgard Hirmer. Munich 1991
Peroni, A., Wiligelmo von Modena: Erörterung zum Kontext, in: H. Beck, K. Hengevoss-Dürkop (eds.), Studien zur Geschichte der europäischen Skulptur im 12./13. Jahrhundert. Vol. 1 Text, Frankfurt 1994
Petzold, A., Romanesque Kunst. Art in Context. London, Cologne 1995
Pevsner, N., Berkshire. The Buildings of England. Harmondsworth 1966
Pevsner, N., Wiltshire. The Buildings of England. Harmondsworth 1963
Philippovich, E. von, Elfenbein. Munich 1961, 1982
Romanik in Mitteldeutschland. Wernigerode 1994
Rupprecht, B., Romanische Skulptur in Frankreich. Munich 1975, 1984
Schomann, H., Kunstdenkmäler in der Toskana. Darmstadt 1990
Schomann, H., Lombardei. Kunstdenkmäler und Museen. Reclams Kunstführer Italien. Vol. I, 1, Stuttgart 1981
Stocchi, S., Romanische Emilia-Romagna. Würzburg 1986
Tetzlaff, I., Romanische Kapitele in

Frankreich. Löwe und Schlange, Sirene und Engel. Cologne 1976, 1992
Willemsen, R., Abruzzen (DuMont Kunst-Reiseführer). Cologne 1990
Zimmermann, K., Umbrien (DuMont Kunst-Reiseführer). Cologne 1987

BARBARA DEIMLING
Medieval church portals and their importance in the history of law

Effmann, W., Die karolingisch-ottonischen Bauten zu Werden, vol. I, Straßburg 1899; vol II, Berlin 1922
Evers, H. G., Tod, Macht und Raum als Bereich der Architektur. Munich 1939; 2nd edition 1970
Erler, A., Das Straßburger Münster im Rechtsleben des Mittelalters. Frankfurt 1954
Hahnloser, H. R., "Urkunden zur Bedeutung des Türrings," in Festschrift für Erich Meyer zum sechzigsten Geburtstag 29. Oktober 1957: Studien zu Werken in den Sammlungen des Museums für Kunst und Gewerbe Hamburg. Hamburg 1959, 125–146
Werckmeister, O. K., "The Lintel Fragment Representing Eve from Saint-Lazare, Autun," Journal of the Warburg and Courtauld Institutes, 35 (1972), 1–30
Claussen, P. C., Chartres-Studien: Zur Vorgeschichte, Funktion und Skulptur der Vorhallen. Wiesbaden 1975
Verzár Bornstein, C., Portals and Politics in the Early Italian City State: The Sculpture of Nicholaus in Context. Parma 1988
Bandmann, G., Mittelalterliche Architektur als Bedeutungsträger. Berlin 1994

EHRENFRIED KLUCKERT
Romanesque painting

Assunto, R., Die Theorie des Schönen im Mittelalter. Cologne 1963
Bauer, G., Corvey oder Hildesheim. Zur ottonischen Buchmalerei in Norddeutschland. Hamburg 1977
Bauer, G., Abendländische Grundlagen und byzant. Einflüsse in den Zentren der westlichen Buchmalerei, in: Kunst im Zeitalter der Kaiserin Theophanu. Cologne 1993, 155–176
Beckwith, J., Die Kunst des frühen Mittelalters. Darmstadt 1967
Beer, E. J., Zur Buchmalerei der Zisterzienser im oberdeutschen Gebiet des 12. und 13. Jahrhunderts: Baukunst und Bildkunst im Spiegel internationaler Forschung. Festschrift für E. Lehmann. Berlin 1989, 72–87
Bertemes, P., Bild- und Textstruktur. Eine Analyse der Beziehungen von Illustrationszyklus und Text im Rolandslied des Pfaffen Konrad.

Frankfurt 1984

Bloch, P.; Schnitzler, H., Die ottonische Kölner Buchmalerei. 2 vols., Düsseldorf 1970

Blume, D., Wandmalerei als Ordnungspropaganda. Bildprogramme im Chorbereich franziskanischer Konvente Italiens bis zur Mitte des 14. Jahrhunderts. Worms 1983

Borinski, K., Die Antike in Poetik und Kunsttheorie. 2 vols., Darmstadt 1965

Bornheim; Schilling, W., Bemalte und gemalte karolingische Architektur, in: Deutsche Kunst und Denkmalpflege 36 (1978), 7–20

Burger, L., Die Himmelskönigin der Apokalypse in der Kunst des Mittelalters. 1937

Demus, O., Romanische Wandmalerei. Munich 1968

Dodwell, C. R.; Turner, D. H., Reichenau Reconsidered. 1965

Frodl, W., Austria. Medieval Wall Paintings. New York 1964

Glats. J., Mittelalterliche Wandmalerei in der Pfalz und in Rheinhessen, in: Ges. f. mittelrheinische Kirchengeschichte. 1981

Harnischfeger, E., Die Bamberger Apokalypse. Stuttgart 1981

The Golden Age of the Anglo-Saxon Art 966-1066, exhibition catalogue British Museum. London 1984

Hauck, K., Karolingische Taufpfalzen im Spiegel hofnaher Dichtung. Göttingen 1985

Hecht, J. K., Die frühmittelalterliche Wandmalerei des Bodenseegebiets. Sigmaringen 1979

Heinrich der Löwe und seine Zeit, Catalogue for the Ausstellung Brunswick (eds. I. Luckhardt and Fr. Niehoff). Munich 1995

Hinkle, W. M., The Iconography of the apsidal Fresco of Montmorillon, in: Münsteraner Jahrbuch der Bildenden Kunst 3, no. 23, 1972, 37–62

Hoffmann, K., Buchkunst und Königtum im ottonischen und salischen Reich. 2 vols., Stuttgart 1986

Hoffmann, K., Die Evangelistenbilder des Münchner Otto-Evangeliars (Clm 4453), in: Zeitschrift des Deutschen Vereins für Kunstwissenschaft, bk. 1/2, XX, 1966

Holländer, H., Die Kunst des Frühen Mittelalters. Stuttgart 1978

Hucklenbroich, J., Text und Illustration in der Berliner Handschrift der "Eneide" des Heinrich von Veldeke. Würzburg 1985

Hunger, Stegmüller and others, Die Textüberlieferung der antiken Literatur und der Bibel. Munich 1975

Imdahl, M., Sprache und Bild. Bild und Sprache. Zur Miniatur der Gefangennahme im Codex Egberti, in: Festschrift für G. Bott zum 60. Geburtstag. Darmstadt 1987, 15–22

Klein, M., Schöpfungsdarstellungen mittelalterlicher Wandmalereien in Baden-Württemberg und in der Nordschweiz. Freiburg 1982

Klemm, E., Das sogenannte Gebetbuch der Hildegard von Bingen, in: Jahrbuch der Kunsthistorischen Sammlungen in Wien (Vienna) 74 (1978), 29–78

Köhler, W.; Mütherich, F., Die karolingischen Miniaturen V. Berlin 1982

Kühnel, E., Drachenportale, in: Zeitschrift für Kunstwissenschaft vol. 4 (1950), 1–18

Kuder, U., Der Teppich von Bayeux. Frankfurt 1994

Kupfer, M., Romanesque Wall Painting in Central France. The Politics of Narrative. New Haven 1993

Langosch, K., Profile des lateinischen Mittelalters. Darmstadt 1965

Martin, K., Die ottonischen Wandfresken der St. Georgskirche, Reichenau-Oberzell. Sigmaringen 1975

Mayr-Harting, H., Ottonische Buchmalerei. Darmstadt 1991

Masal, O., Buchkunst der Romanik. Granz 1978

Mütherich, F., Studien zur mittelalterlichen Kunst. 800–1250. Festschrift für F. Mütherich. Munich 1985

Murbach, E., Zillis, Zürich. Freiburg i. Br. 1967

Nitschke, A., Die Wege der Toten. Beobachtungen zur irischen Ornamentik, in: Festschrift M. Gosebruch. Munich 1984, 49–60

Legner, A. (ed.), Ornamenta Ecclesiae. Kunst und Künstler der Romanik. Exhibition catalogue Schnütgen Museum. Cologne 1985

Nordenhagen, P. J., Studies in Byzantine and Early Medieval Painting. London 1990

Pächt, O., The pre-Carolingian Roots of early Romanesque Art, in: Studies in Western Art 1 (1963), 67–75

Plotzek, J. M., Anfänge der ottonischen Trier-Echternacher Buchmalerei, in: Wallraf-Richartz-Jahrbuch 32 (1970), 7–36

Plotzek. J. M., Darstellungsprinzipien in der ottonischen Echternacher Buchmalerei, in: Aachener Kunstblätter 41 (1971), 181–189

Prins. F. (ed.), Mönchtum und Gesellschaft im Frühmittelalter. Darmstadt 1976

Rudloff, D., Kosmische Bildwelt der Romanik. Stuttgart 1989

Schrade, H., Die romanische Malerei. Cologne 1963

Stein, H., Die romanischen Wandmalereien in der Klosterkirche Prüfening. Stuttgart 1987

Weilandt, G., Geistliche und Kunst. Ein Beitrag zur Kultur der ottonisch-salischen Reichskirche und zur Veränderung künstlerischer Tradition im späten 11. Jahrhundert. Cologne, Weimar 1992

Werkmeister, O. K., Irisch-northumbrische Buchmalerei des 8. Jahrhunderts und monastische Spiritualität. 1967

Weitzmann, K., Studies in Classical and Byzantine Manuscript Illumination (ed. H. Kessler). Chicago 1971

Wischermann, H., Romanik in Baden-Württemberg. Stuttgart 1987

Index of artists' names

Index of place names